INVENTING AMERICA

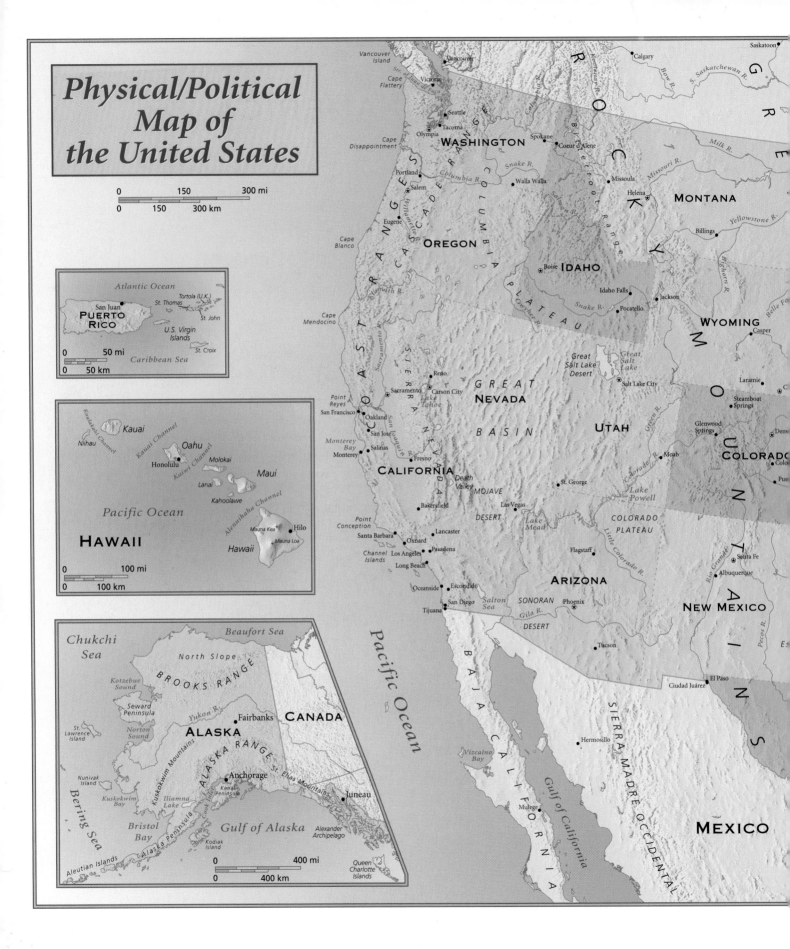

Physical/Political Map of the United States

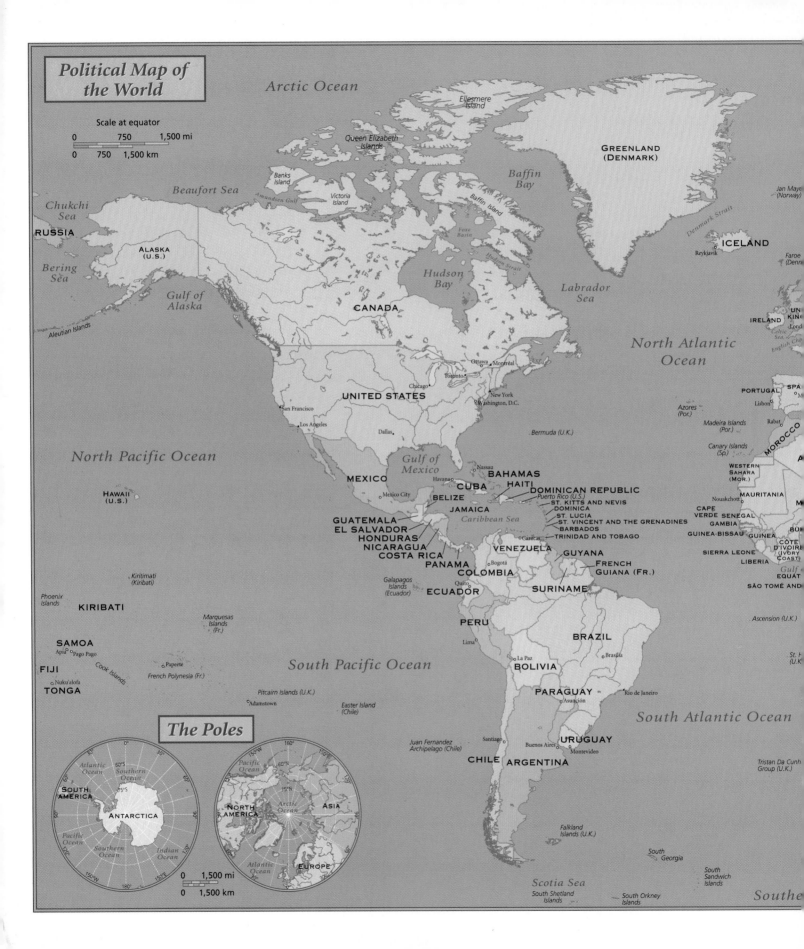

Political Map of the World

Scale at equator

0   750   1,500 mi
0   750   1,500 km

The Poles

Arctic Ocean

Chukchi Sea

RUSSIA

Bering Sea

ALASKA (U.S.)

Aleutian Islands

Gulf of Alaska

Beaufort Sea

Amundsen Gulf

Banks Island

Victoria Island

Queen Elizabeth Islands

Ellesmere Island

Baffin Bay

Foxe Basin

Baffin Island

Hudson Strait

GREENLAND (DENMARK)

Denmark Strait

Jan Mayen (Norway)

ICELAND

Reykjavik

Faroe (Denm

North Pacific Ocean

HAWAII (U.S.)

Kiritimati (Kiribati)

Phoenix Islands

KIRIBATI

Marquesas Islands (Fr.)

SAMOA
Apia Pago Pago

FIJI

Nuku'alofa

TONGA

Cook Islands

Papeete
French Polynesia (Fr.)

South Pacific Ocean

Pitcairn Islands (U.K.)

Adamstown

Easter Island (Chile)

Juan Fernandez Archipelago (Chile)

CANADA

Hudson Bay

Labrador Sea

Ottawa Montréal

Toronto

Chicago

UNITED STATES

New York
Washington, D.C.

San Francisco

Los Angeles

Dallas

MEXICO

Gulf of Mexico

Mexico City

Bermuda (U.K.)

Nassau

BAHAMAS

Havana

CUBA

BELIZE

JAMAICA

GUATEMALA
EL SALVADOR
HONDURAS
NICARAGUA
COSTA RICA
PANAMA

HAITI

DOMINICAN REPUBLIC
Puerto Rico (U.S.)
ST. KITTS AND NEVIS
DOMINICA
ST. LUCIA
ST. VINCENT AND THE GRENADINES
BARBADOS
TRINIDAD AND TOBAGO

Caribbean Sea

Caracas

VENEZUELA

GUYANA

FRENCH GUIANA (FR.)

SURINAME

COLOMBIA

Bogotá

Galapagos Islands (Ecuador)

Quito

ECUADOR

PERU

Lima

La Paz

BOLIVIA

Brasília

BRAZIL

PARAGUAY

Asunción

Rio de Janeiro

Santiago

Buenos Aires

URUGUAY

Montevideo

CHILE ARGENTINA

North Atlantic Ocean

IRELAND

UNI
KIN
Lond

Celtic Sea

English Cha

PORTUGAL

SPA

Lisbon

Azores (Por.)

Madeira Islands (Por.)

Rabat

MOROCCO

Canary Islands (Sp.)

WESTERN SAHARA (MOR.)

MAURITANIA

Nouakchott

CAPE VERDE SENEGAL

GAMBIA

GUINEA-BISSAU GUINEA

SIERRA LEONE

LIBERIA

CÔTE D'IVOIRE (IVORY COAST)

EQUAT

SÃO TOMÉ AND

Gulf

South Atlantic Ocean

Ascension (U.K.)

St. H
(U.K

Tristan Da Cunh
Group (U.K.)

Falkland Islands (U.K.)

South Georgia

South Sandwich Islands

Scotia Sea

South Shetland Islands

South Orkney Islands

Souther

SOUTH AMERICA

Atlantic Ocean

Southern Ocean

ANTARCTICA

Pacific Ocean

Indian Ocean

NORTH AMERICA

Arctic Ocean

ASIA

EUROPE

Pacific Ocean

Atlantic Ocean

0   1,500 mi
0   1,500 km

Inventing America

A HISTORY OF THE UNITED STATES

VOLUME 1: TO 1877

PAULINE MAIER

MERRITT ROE SMITH

ALEXANDER KEYSSAR

DANIEL J. KEVLES

W. W. NORTON & COMPANY
NEW YORK LONDON

The text of this book is composed in Minion, with the display set in Frutiger,
    Copperplate 31, and Texas Hero.
Composition by UG / GGS Information Services, Inc.
Cartography by maps.com
Manufacturing by the Courier Companies, Inc.
Book design by Joan Greenfield
Cover designer: Brenda McManus/Skouras Design
Page layout: Alice Bennett Dates
Editor: Steve Forman
Manuscript editor: Susan Gaustad
Production manager/project editor: JoAnn Simony
Photo researchers: Sara Hadley, Neil Hoos, Nathan Odell, Ede Rothaus
Editorial assistants: Lory Frenkel, Julia Paolitto

The Library of Congress has cataloged the one-volume edition as follows:

Inventing America: a history of the United States/Pauline Maier . . . [et al.].
        p. cm.
    Includes bibliographical references and index.
    ISBN 0-393-97434-0
    1. United States—History. I. Maier, Pauline, 1938–

E178.1.I58 2002
973—dc21
                                                                2001044648

ISBN 0-393-97435-9 (pbk.)
W. W. Norton & Company, Inc., 500 Fifth Avenue, New York, NY 10110
                        www.wwnorton.com

W. W. Norton & Company Ltd., Castle House, 75/76 Wells Street, London,
    W1T 3QT
2 3 4 5 6 7 8 9 0

For Eleanor Smith Fox (1908–2001), mother, guiding light, friend. —Merritt Roe Smith

For Anne Kevles, who so much wanted to cast her vote in the next election;
Eric F. Goldman, who shepherded a young physicist into American history;
Bettyann, partner in all things; and Jonathan, Beth, David, and their children
here and to come, shapers of the new century. —Daniel J. Kevles

To the memory of my parents, Alexander and Grace Atkinson Keyssar, who
made many things possible. —Alexander Keyssar

For my parents, Irvin L. and Charlotte Rose Rubbelke; my children, Andrea,
Nicholas, and Jessica, and also Corinne Maier (b. 2000), who will help make
American history in the twenty-first century. —Pauline Maier

Contents

CONTENTS

CONTENTS

Maps

Inventing America is a new history of the United States whose unifying theme is innovation. It aims to integrate into a compelling narrative the persistent inventiveness of Americans in devising new political institutions and practices, economic arrangements, social relations and cultural motifs, adaptations to the natural environment, and exploitations of science and technology.

Americans have repeatedly resorted to experiment in the face of changing circumstances, drawing on ideas and practices from abroad or from native soil. They have long considered this penchant for innovation a distinguishing feature of their culture and history. The willingness of Americans to remake their world has run from the adaptations the colonists made to survive in an unfamiliar environment to the New Deal's try-anything response to the Depression; from the adoption of a radically redesigned corporation as a distinctive and powerful economic institution to the establishment of regulations intended to bind industry to the public interest; from the forging of an African American culture by slaves to the resourceful efforts of women to find ways of combining family and career. And since the late nineteenth century, Americans have sought to remake their position in the world, mixing pragmatism with evangelism, drawing from the experience of failure as well as success.

Our text is concerned throughout with the bold experiment in popular self-government that characterized the birth of the United States and continues in our politics and society. While writing a national narrative, we weave together numerous stories on the ground, tales of regions, institutions, businesses, social groups, and individual men and women. We place renewed emphasis on national and state governments; both have often acted as powerful agents of social and economic change, and the states have provided laboratories of political innovation. We also recount the transforming dynamism of business enterprise and its effects throughout society.

We are acutely aware that a good deal of the American story does not merit celebration. It has entailed retreat as well as advance, conflict as well as consensus, and the use of government to block change as well as to advance it. We probe the gap—originally wide and, in many respects, ongoing—between the promise of the United States and the reality of its practices, including slavery, the brutal treatment of Native Americans, the discrimination against women, immigrants and minorities, political and economic inequities, and the degradation of the environment. Yet we are also concerned with how Americans have narrowed that gap by enlarging the scope and meaning of the nation's founding ideas and ideals.

The most original aim of this text is the treatment of science and technology as integral elements of American history. Technical innovation has been important from earliest times, when, in a remarkable feat of plant breeding, pre-Columbian peoples cultivated primitive grains into maize. With the arrival of Europeans, Americans began importing knowledge, technology, plants, and animals from abroad, a process that mirrored the import of capital, people, and culture, and they established themselves as members of a global exchange. They adapted the imports to their own needs while developing an indigenous capacity for innovation that produced its own, increasingly transforming effects. The activities of naturalists and scientific societies in eighteenth-century America contributed to the creation of an American identity. The technological and organizational innovations of the nineteenth century changed the ways Americans worked, lived, and spent their leisure. And at least since the nation's centennial, in 1876, science and technology have been crucial to its security, economy, health, and quality of life.

Despite the enormous importance of technology and science in American history, most texts do not come to grips with it. Our book seeks to remedy that neglect, while refraining from giving technological change undue weight in the overall narrative. We have introduced science and technology as parts of mainstream history, recounting their broad social and economic consequences—how electricity lit up the urban night, for example, or how domestic innovations changed the daily lives of women. At the opening of the twenty-first century, the enormous impact of science and technology on the world is beyond dispute. Our text seeks to explain to students how they came to exercise so much influence and power in the United States, emphasizing that both are the products of human agency rather than of forces beyond human control. We have found that such a focus provides students in survey courses with a recognizable bridge to periods in the past when science and technology were also transforming the world. Students respond to accounts of these changes and readily acknowledge their importance.

Readers will find that the integration of science and technology into the story enriches and, in certain respects, reconfigures our understanding of familiar events. For example, antebellum reform movements take on new meaning when seen as intersecting with the technological changes that were helping to spread their messages. In the late nineteenth century, inventors, entrepreneurs, and then corporations began drawing on the boundless frontier of scientific laboratory knowledge to supplement the resources of the closing physical frontier. In the nineteenth and twentieth centuries, technologies such as moving conveyor belts and electrically driven cutting tools made industrial production more efficient but also fostered unrest among workers. And advances in communications such as radio contributed to the emergence of the United States as a world power, as did the new understanding of yellow fever, which protected the crews building the Panama Canal.

Our attention to science and technology sheds new light on the impact of war on U.S. history. War and preparedness have incubated or accelerated social, economic, and technological change. The War of 1812, for example, emerges as a watershed in American economic history. It created the conditions in which entrepreneurs were able to establish the first successful integrated textile factory—at Waltham, Massachusetts. Moreover, as a direct result of the war, the U.S. Army collaborated with arms manufacturers to pioneer the development of interchangeable parts. Both developments were critical to the nation's early industrialization.

Before World War I, the armed services encouraged the new technologies of radio and aircraft, and their development was whirled ahead by mobilization for the conflict. World War I also opened new opportunities for women and blacks and other minorities, and so even more dramatically did World War II, which also stimulated vast migrations across regions and fueled economic recovery and expansion around the country. Further, World War II established the federal government as the dominant patron of scientific research and produced the atomic bomb, microwave radar, electronic computers, jet aircraft, and antibiotics. Under the goad of the Cold War, federal patronage stimulated compara-

ble innovations and provided industry with the knowledge that, in the last quarter of the twentieth century, made possible the creation of biotechnology, personal computers, and the information economy.

Each of the coauthors took responsibility for drafting different sections of the text: Maier, Chapters 1–8; Smith, Chapters 9–16; Keyssar, Chapters 17–22 and 24; Kevles, Chapters 25–33; and Kevles, Maier, and Smith, Chapter 23. However, all of us fully collaborated from the beginning of the project, jointly developing its themes and an outline of the book, and then reading and critiquing each other's chapters with the aim of achieving consistency in approach throughout.

We have made every effort to produce a history that is fully accessible to students, including those who are new to American history. We consider it essential to guide students through the discussions, taking care to facilitate their understanding of the material. We use anecdote and vignette to bring the narrative to life. We also include boxed inserts of primary source materials throughout. Called "American Journal," this feature is intended to illustrate commonplace life as it was shaped by science and technology. Under titles such as "What's for Dinner?" and "What if You Get Sick?," the Journal entries speak directly to the broader themes of the text, and, perhaps more important, are fun to read.

The design and pedagogy of the text are also meant to support student readers throughout. Each chapter opens with a Chapter Outline and a set of Focus Questions on the key subjects that students need to address. The Focus Questions then reappear in the running heads of the chapter to help students keep sight of the main issues in play. The chapters end with Chronologies and brief lists of further readings. (More extensive lists of the sources on which the book rests are provided in the Bibliography on the Norton website for the text.)

With innovation as our main theme, we saw an opportunity to introduce a new dimension to the traditional survey book. Even the most vital prose falls short of conveying, say, the din of the weave room at the Lowell mills when the machinery was operating at full speed, but a palpable, sensory experience of history can be gained from archival audio and visual materials. Digital technology has for some time promised the integration of audio and video materials with print text, and with the support of the Alfred P. Sloan Foundation, *Inventing America* attempts to achieve that goal. Packaged with each new copy of the print text is a CD-ROM (two with the hardcover edition) that contains archival and original multimedia materials designed to enhance the discussion in the text itself. (Icons in the print text signal the corresponding multimedia materials on the CD.) Students reading about the Lewis and Clark expedition, for instance, will be able to listen to audio readings from their journals recorded by studio professionals. The CD includes a wealth of materials ranging from readings from the court records of the Salem witch trials through recordings of slave spirituals to a video of Franklin Roosevelt's "Day of Infamy" speech. It also contains multimedia teaching/research units on the following subjects:

slavery and Washington's Mount Vernon, the Lowell mills, Ellis Island, and the Hanford Nuclear Reservation on the Columbia River. The CD was researched and composed by Robert Martello, of Olin College. We hope that the combination of CD and print text makes *Inventing America* a valuable innovation in the survey course.

DJK
AK
PM
MRS
April 2002

Acknowledgments

The authors of this text have accrued many debts in writing it, and they take pleasure in thanking those who helped. Daniel J. Kevles is grateful to John L. Heilbron for helping to point the way to this book; to Ellen Chesler and James Hershberg for early advice; to William Deverell and Peter Westwick for comments on chapters; to Michelle Brattain and Richard Kim for research reports on particular subjects; and to Frederick M. Hodges for aid with the proofs. He is greatly indebted to Wendy Wall for her research during the project's start-up phase and for her insights in a jointly taught course on recent America. His debt is immeasurable to Karen Dunn-Haley, who lived with this project almost as long as he did, unflaggingly providing material and analyses, historiographical assessments, critical commentary, and encouragement. He is also grateful for the assistance of the Division of the Humanities and Social Sciences at the California Institute of Technology, especially John Ledyard, Susan Davis, Marion Lawrence, and Michelle Reinschmidt; and of the Department of History of Yale University, particularly Jon Butler, Jean Cherniavsky, Carolyn Fitzgerald, and Michael Margonis. And he wishes to thank the Andrew W. Mellon Foundation, whose support enabled him to spend more time on the writing.

Alexander Keyssar would like to thank D'arcy Brissman, Elisa Slattery, Eve Sterne, Nicole Perrygo, Andrew Neather, Noeleen McIlvenna, Daniel Levison Wilk, and especially Paul Husbands for their labors in gathering materials for this book. He is also grateful to the many undergraduates in his introductory U.S. history courses on whom he first tried out much of the material in his chapters. He would like to acknowledge the valuable and cheerful support of the History Department staff at Duke University, especially Vivian Jackson, Andrea Long, and Caroline Keeton.

Merritt Roe Smith is grateful for help with research from Karin Ellison, Greg Galer, Rebecca Herzig, Hannah Landecker, David Mindell, Jennifer Mnookin, Russell Olwell, and Tim Wolters. He also thanks Charles Dew, who undertook some of the revisions of Chapters 14–16 at a crucial stage. Pauline Maier is indebted to Meg Jacobs, Karen Ordahl Kupperman, Mary Beth Norton, and Harriet Ritvo for their generous, expert help on parts of her chapters. Both Maier and Smith are happy to express their gratitude to Greg Clancey and Rob Martello for the research assistance they provided; Victor McElheny for the excellent substantive and stylistic comments that arose from his reading of their chapters; and the students in their team-taught course on American history to 1865, whose responses to their draft chapters led to several improvements. Both greatly appreciate the support of the staff in the MIT Department of Science, Technology, and Society, especially Judy Spitzer, Debbie Meinbresse, and Christine Bates.

The coauthors collectively are grateful for the critical comments provided by the readers of their manuscript:

Robert Angevine, George Mason University
James Axtell, College of William and Mary
Michael Barnhart, State University of New York
    at Stony Brook
Mark V. Barrow Jr., Virginia Tech
Amy Bix, Iowa State University
Angela Boswell, Henderson State University
Albert S. Broussard, Texas A & M University
Anthony Carey, Auburn University
Paul G. E. Clemens, Rutgers University
Charles B. Dew, Williams College
Glen Gendzel, Tulane University
A. W. Giebelhaus, Georgia Institute of Technology
Larry Gragg, University of Missouri at Rolla
Michael G. Hall, University of Texas at Austin
Dwight Henderson, University of Texas at San Antonio
Richard R. John, University of Illinois at Chicago
Frank Lambert, Purdue University
Daniel Lewis, California Polytechnic State University,
    Pomona
Eric T. L. Love, University of Colorado, Boulder
David S. Lux, Bryant College
William M. McBride, United States Naval Academy
Robert M. S. McDonald, United States Military Academy
James Mohr, University of Oregon
Jerald E. Podair, Lawrence University
Chris Rasmussen, University of Nevada at Las Vegas
Jan Reiff, University of California at Los Angeles
Susan Rugh, Brigham Young University
Andrew Schocket, Bowling Green State University

Ron Schultz, University of Wyoming
Bryant Simon, University of Georgia
Robert Stoddard, University of British Columbia
David Tanenhaus, University of Nevada at Las Vegas
Stanley J. Underdal, San Jose State University
Helen M. Wall, Pomona College
Wendy Wall, Colgate University
Jessica Wang, University of California at Los Angeles
Kenneth Winkle, University of Nebraska

The authors are deeply indebted for generous support of the project to the Alfred P. Sloan Foundation, especially to Arthur Singer for his decisive early interest, and Doron Weber for his ongoing enthusiasm. They are very grateful to W. W. Norton for the care it has taken in producing the book—in particular, to Steve Forman, their editor, for his patience, advice, and critical readings; and to Susan Gaustad for her skilled copyediting of the manuscript. At Norton they owe many thanks also to JoAnn Simony, Lory Frenkel, Julia Paolitto, Sarah Hadley, Neil Hoos, Nathan Odell, Ede Rothaus, and Alice Bennett Dates for keeping this big project on the rails. Rob Martello conceived, researched, and drew together the digital materials on the CD. The efforts of Steve Hoge at Norton were critical in bringing the digital history component to fruition. Finally, the authors wish to thank Karen Dunn-Haley for digging up the materials for the "American Journal" entries and parts of the CD.

About the Authors

PAULINE MAIER is William R. Kenan Jr. Professor of American History at the Massachusetts Institute of Technology. Her specialty is the period of the American Revolution, on which she has published extensively, including *From Resistance to Revolution: Colonial Radicals and the Development of American Opposition to Britain, 1765–1776* and *The Old Revolutionaries: Political Lives in the Age of Samuel Adams*. Her most recent book is *American Scripture: Making the Declaration of Independence*.

MERRITT ROE SMITH is Leverett and William Cutten Professor of the History of Technology at the Massachusetts Institute of Technology. Roe's research focuses on the history of technological innovation and social change. His publications include *Harpers Ferry Armory and the New Technology* and *Military Enterprise and Technological Change*. He is a fellow of the American Academy of Arts and Sciences.

ALEXANDER KEYSSAR is Matthew W. Stirling Jr. Professor of History and Social Policy, John F. Kennedy School of Government, Harvard University. His specialty is the social and political history of the late nineteenth and early twentieth centuries. Alex's first book was *Out of Work: The First Century of Unemployment in Massachusetts*. His most recent book is *The Right to Vote: The Contested History of Democracy in the United States*.

DANIEL J. KEVLES is Stanley Woodward Professor of History at Yale University. Dan has published extensively on the history of science and the intersections of politics, science, and technology in the twentieth century. His works include *The Physicists: The History of a Scientific Community in Modern America* and *In the Name of Eugenics: Genetics and the Uses of Human Heredity*. His most recent book is *The Baltimore Case: A Trial of Politics, Science, and Character*.

INVENTING AMERICA

Chapter 1

"MEN PRONE TO WONDER":

AMERICA BEFORE 1600

Sailors navigating by the stars with a sea full of monsters, from a woodcut of 1575.

■ **Who were the peoples of ancient America, and how did they live?**

■ **What was the process that first brought Europeans to America?**

■ **How did Spain establish an empire in America?**

■ **What was the global significance of the Columbian exchange?**

It was a strange sight—"a very lion to our seeming, in shape, hair, and colour," swimming in the sea not by moving its feet like other beasts, "but rather sliding upon the water with his whole body (excepting the legs) in sight," not diving and then rising above the water like whales or porpoises, but "confidently shewing himselfe above water without hiding." As the creature passed between the ship of watching Englishmen and the shore, "turning his head to and fro, yawning and gaping wide, with ougly demonstration of long teeth, and glaring eies," he "sent forth a horrible voyce, roaring or bellowing as doeth a lion, which spectacle wee all beheld . . . as men prone to wonder at every strange thing, as this doubtlesse was, to see a lion in the Ocean sea, or fish in the shape of a lion."

The story appeared in an account of English navigator Sir Humphrey Gilbert's return voyage from America in 1583. What the sailors saw in the cold waters of the North Atlantic was not a lion, but something altogether new and unknown to them. How full of strange things, this "America," this place so long unknown to Europeans and so full of unfamiliar creatures that could only be described with language from another place that did not quite fit what stood before the observers' eyes ("a very lion to our seeming"). How could European readers distinguish truth from myth, reality from the fables of popular books such as *The Travels of Sir John Mandeville, Knight* (1356), which told of "men . . . without heads" who had "eyes in either shoulder" and mouths that were "round shaped like a horseshoe, y-midst their breasts"? In 1557, a French visitor to Brazil confessed "that since I have been in this land of America, . . . everything to be seen—the way of life of its inhabitants, the form of the animals, what the earth produces—is so unlike what we have in Europe, Asia, and Africa that it may very well be called a 'New World' with respect to us."

Were the people who lived in this "New World" equally struck by the peculiarities of Europeans? One of the first accounts of a meeting between the two cultures, in the logbook of the explorer Christopher Columbus for December 18, 1492, reports the reactions of a native "king" and his "councilors" (more European words of approximation) on the island of Tortuga when Columbus described Spain's king and queen, who "commanded and ruled over all the best part of the world," and displayed colorful banners with the royal arms or the holy cross emblazoned upon them. "I saw well," Columbus wrote, "that they took everything as a great wonder." But did the Tortugans wonder at the Spanish king and queen and their banners or at Columbus's babbling in a language they could not understand? For both sides in the scene, surely there was cause enough for wonder in every sense—provoking amazement and awe, as well as inspiring reflections on the disparity between the known and the newly encountered.

Those first confrontations of Europeans and Indians remain a cause of wonder today because of the epic stories that lay behind them, and also because of their consequences. The meetings of strangers in the northern reaches of the western Atlantic or on beaches in the West Indies brought the descendants of migrants from Asia who had moved south and east over the American continents through thousands of years face-to-face with men who heralded a new migration to America, this time westward from Europe. There were no human occupants of these "new" lands when the first migrants arrived, so all Americans without exception were, are, and always will be immigrants or the children of immigrants from every part of the earth. And however inauspicious the first encounters of Indians and Europeans might have seemed, with their handful of scruffy participants, the effects—on the lives of the first Americans and those who joined them; on power relationships; on the cultures and economies of both America and Europe; on the movements of plants, animals, people, and diseases across space; on European understandings of humans and the natural world—were monumental. Some of the most horrific consequences showed themselves with remarkable speed. Others came more slowly, but in time penetrated all parts of the globe, provoking or sustaining changes that everywhere deepened the chasm between the Old World of the past and the New World of the future.

The Peoples of Ancient America

The stories of the "Indians" (a word based on the mistaken belief of Columbus, who first encountered them, that he had reached the East Indian islands of Asia) and those of Europeans are different in character and content for a reason of enduring importance. The Indians, who had mastered techniques for surviving in America that Europeans would only painfully acquire, never learned the technology of writing. (There are exceptions to that rule: the Mayan people of central America, or "Mesoamerica," for example, did have a system of writing.) All the nations of Europe, by contrast, knew how to read and write their languages; and by the time Europeans arrived in America, the printing press had also become part of their lives (mid–fifteenth century). As a result, the first extant descriptions of the earliest Americans were written by Europeans, whose accounts often tell as much or more about the writers than they do about the peoples observed.

Those sources of information have since been supplemented by the work of modern anthropologists, archaeologists, and demographers, who analyze the physical remains of the ancient peoples of America, quantifiable data (population size, for example), and other forms of evidence to reconstruct lost worlds. Even geneticists and linguists contribute to the debate over the earliest occupants of the Americas. What they can tell about the past is often different from what contemporary written sources reveal. The questions they ask are, however, often the same that fifteenth-century Europeans asked. Who, to begin, were these Indian peoples, and where did they come from?

CREATION AND MIGRATION

Christians and Jews knew where they came from. The Bible told of the first human being, Adam, and how God formed a woman, Eve, from Adam's rib so that Adam would not be lonely. They lived in a paradise until God drove them out because, after being tempted by a serpent, they ate the fruit of a forbidden tree. From that first human couple all living persons were descended. The Bible also told how God, angered by the sins of humankind, once destroyed the world with a great flood, saving only one good man, Noah, his family, and the animals he gathered together, two by two, on a great ark. Were the peoples of America, then, the scattered children of Noah? Or were they perhaps the lost tribes of Israel, of which the Bible also spoke?

Sea monsters depicted on the Carta Marina, a map from 1539.

5

Indians had their own **creation stories,** passed on not through books but orally, told and retold from generation to generation. Sometimes, as with the Arapaho people of North America's Great Plains, priests related a story to a few chosen elders for fear that errors would creep in with uncontrolled retellings. Although the stories differ from one Indian people to another, they frequently describe an earlier life unlike the present, and a benevolent Great Spirit or god who set rules for the people. Sometimes they tell of early ancestors who were driven from underworlds as a punishment for disobeying their god or gods; sometimes they describe the emergence of earth from a watery world. Some tales include "trickster" figures in the shape of animals—a coyote, for example, or a raven—whose influence, like the Bible's serpent, accounts for pain and illness, strife and death. These stories gave the people who related them a sense of common origin and common purpose, accounted for evil, provided a basis for rules that sustained order, and sometimes promised a return of harmony in an afterlife.

Modern scientific accounts of the Indians' origins are less colorful, though also wonderful in their way. Today's humans (*Homo sapiens sapiens*), they say, evolved from apelike ancestors in Africa and appeared (as Cro-Magnon Man) in Europe some 40,000 years ago. From the first, human beings showed a marked penchant for travel: indeed, it seems that before they appeared in Europe, some early humans managed to make their way from Africa to Australia, which means they had already learned to build and operate boats. Others pushed overland into Asia. And eventually human beings began to migrate from Asia to America. Many experts think these migrations began about 15,000–20,000 years ago. Or perhaps they came earlier: archaeological evidence from a site in Canada's northern Yukon Territory indicates that people lived in Arctic regions of America as early as 27,000 or 29,000 years ago. Some archaeologists, on the other hand, question all evidence that humans lived in the Americas before about 10,000 years ago. The issue remains unsettled.

The earliest migrants, hunters in search of prey, may have traveled over a subcontinent, now known as Beringia, that linked today's Siberia and Alaska at the site of the Bering Strait and extended as much as a thousand miles north to south.

"There were no human occupants of these 'new' lands when the first migrants arrived, so all Americans without exception were, are, and always will be immigrants or the children of immigrants from every part of the earth."

That soggy, treeless landmass existed because great glaciers had sucked up so much water that the world's oceans sank some 300 feet. The Ice Age that produced these glaciers, known as the Pleistocene, began some 2.5 million years ago, but its frigid climate waxed and waned, with periods of intense cold giving way at times to temperatures like those of today. One particularly severe stretch lasted from about 80,000 to 9,000 or 10,000 years ago, time enough for migratory hunters to make their moves. Then the ice began to melt, once again submerging lands and whatever physical evidence they held of their human inhabitants deep below the ocean's surface. Even then, the distance between Asia and America at the Bering Straits—about fifty-six miles, with islands breaking the gap—was not so great as to prevent people with wooden dugout or skin boats from crossing to the other side.

Not all early migrants, however, crossed there. Skeletal remains suggest that a people distinct from modern American Indians, Caucasoid people whose biological features indicate that they might have come from southern parts of Asia or perhaps even Europe, once lived on the North American continent. They could have traveled east from Asia over the Aleutian Islands, or west from Europe through the North Atlantic, which offered a long but feasible route over ice and land during the Ice Age. There could thus have been several distinct migrations at different times from different places.

Once the migrants had arrived in North America, they found wonderful prey for hunting: giant, elephant-like mastodons; mammoths, some of which are the largest elephants ever known (a full fourteen feet tall), and others with thick, woolly coats and long, upward-turning tusks; and enormous, shaggy bison, saber-toothed tigers, and a variety of game birds. There were also native horses and camel-like creatures, fearsome wolves, and giant, slow-moving ground sloths. Much of the land, however, was anything but hospitable: a thick sheet of ice extended from western Alaska and the Yukon River drainage area in central Alaska, which remained unglaciated, eastward across the North American continent to Long Island (New York) and down to where the Ohio and Mississippi Rivers now join. Tundra, great treeless plains like those in northern Arctic regions today, stretched below the ice from the Great Plains eastward into Pennsylva-

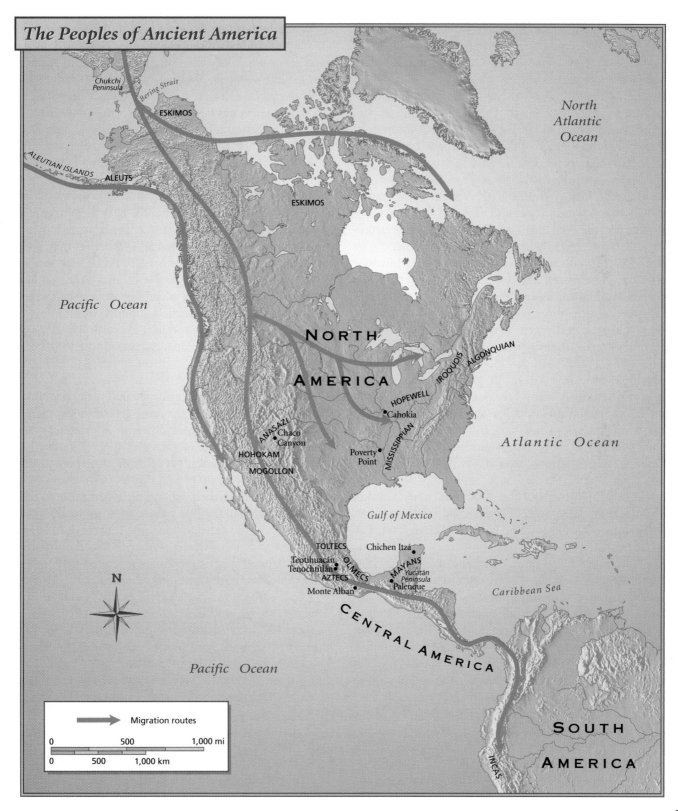

The Peoples of Ancient America

Chukchi Peninsula

Bering Strait

ESKIMOS

ALEUTIAN ISLANDS

ALEUTS

ESKIMOS

North Atlantic Ocean

Pacific Ocean

NORTH

AMERICA

IROQUOIS

ALGONQUIAN

HOPEWELL

Cahokia

ANASAZI

Chaco Canyon

HOHOKAM

MOGOLLON

Poverty Point

MISSISSIPPIAN

Atlantic Ocean

Gulf of Mexico

TOLTECS

Chichen Itzá

Teotihuacán

Tenochtitlán

OLMECS

MAYANS

AZTECS

Yucatán Peninsula

Monte Alban

Palenque

Caribbean Sea

CENTRAL AMERICA

Pacific Ocean

SOUTH AMERICA

INCAS

N

Migration routes

0   500   1,000 mi

0   500   1,000 km

nia and New Jersey; farther south, forests like those of modern Labrador covered places such as Virginia, while the lower elevations of what is now the western United States and Mexico were filled with grasslands.

The end of the Ice Age (9,000 or 10,000 years ago) transformed the land and its climate. The melting of the glaciers not only caused the sea to rise but probably brought massive flooding throughout the world—which might explain why many Indian folktales tell, like the Old Testament, of a great deluge deep in the past. As the glaciers receded, they left deposits of topsoil scraped from the north in the Missouri and Ohio Valleys and mixed stones and big rocks with the soil of what later became New England. Everywhere temperatures moderated; wet places gradually became dry; deciduous forests appeared and spread across North America but later gave way in some places, like the Great Plains, to perennial grasslands with only occasional stands of trees in streambeds and wherever else their roots could find water.

These changes challenged both animals and humans. Many of the largest animals probably found adaptation impossible and gradually died out. (Some scholars argue, alternatively, that they were wiped out by Indian hunters, who reduced their numbers beyond the point of recovery.) Again, Indian tales sometimes associate great floods with the end of a time when monsters ruled the earth. Maybe three dozen categories (or genera) of mammals disappeared, among them mammoths and mastodons, the massive sloths, camels, and horses. Those animals fed on plants. Later, many meat-eating animals, including American cheetahs, lions, tigers, the dire wolf, and a short-faced bear, followed them into extinction. Smaller creatures like birds found it easier to survive, often by changing habitat.

Humans did the same thing. The penchant of early peoples for migration seems to have continued almost nonstop once they arrived in America. Some moved across the northern edge of the North American continent to Greenland in the North Atlantic—or did they get there by some route from the east? Others fanned out over North America or pushed farther south, into Mexico and beyond. Charcoal samples found in Brazil indicate that humans lived there long before the end of the Ice Age. By 10,000 B.C., these irrepressible travelers appear to have walked or sailed along the coast all the way to the southernmost tip of South America.

People came to occupy all the unglaciated parts of both continents with remarkable rapidity. They had probably always lived by gathering seeds, nuts, berries, and other foods as well as by hunting the great prey of the Ice Age. Now, as the largest animals disappeared, they continued to gather food from the wild while replacing the flesh of mammoths and the like with fish, poultry, and relatively small mammals such as rabbits and deer or, on the plains, bison. They also developed ingenious devices to help them survive in environments of an astounding variety. For example, hunters used spears with chiseled stone points to kill their prey, and invented the atlatl (spear-thrower), essentially a long stick from which spears were thrown to increase their thrust. Even so, it wasn't easy to penetrate the tough hide of a bison, so hunters stampeded herds of bison over cliffs. They then butchered the carcasses and dried strips of meat or made pemmican, a mixture of dried meat with animal fat and berries that, properly stored in containers made of hide, could be kept as a winter food source. In dry areas, people created basins or wells to collect rainwater, and took advantage of the cactus's capacity to store liquid. Acorns became a common dietary staple. The Miwok, who lived in the foothills of North America's Sierra Nevada Mountains, developed ways not only to store, shell, and grind acorns, but to leach the bitter-tasting tannin out from acorn meal.

Although there is some evidence that many people of ancient America came from the same genetic stock, there were probably also persons from different cultures who arrived over a sustained period of time and spoke a variety of languages. Once in America, cut off from their homelands and faced with the necessity of adapting to a variety of new environments, the differences among them became even greater. Without writing to stabilize speech, base languages splintered into hundreds of related tongues that became mutually unintelligible. And as people spread over the land, particular groups claimed specific territories separated from others by what were often imprecise, porous borders.

These early American peoples traded goods with each other across great distances. Sometimes, as the palisades (stake fences) that often surrounded their villages suggest, they went to war. Perhaps they even wondered at other groups' languages, customs, and accomplishments. And in time, there developed in central Mexico a great cultural homeland for many inhabitants of Central and North America.

MEXICO

About 9,000 years ago, people in the Tehuacán Valley, on a high plateau in the south-central part of today's Mexico, about 160 miles southeast of Mexico City, began to cultivate a wild grass called teosinte. They carefully selected mutant forms of that primitive grain—which had only two rows of small seeds (or kernels) and no cob or husks—that displayed more desirable characteristics, planted them, again used the best plants as seed stock, and continued the process season after season, generation after generation. The result was maize, which Americans call corn, a cultivated food so unlike its wild ancestor, and so adaptable to different growing conditions, that its creation was perhaps the most important plant-breeding achievement of all time. By the time they developed corn, these early agriculturists had probably begun growing crops such as avocados, chili peppers, grain amaranth, and squash. Different people to their north and east were growing pumpkins and gourds. Soon these budding farmers—probably women, since among Indians women tended the fields—added beans and cotton to the list of what became staples of Indian agriculture. These New World developments took place perhaps 1,000 years after people in Southeast Asia began growing wheat and barley. It is likely that both areas developed agriculture independently as a means of survival in the unfamiliar circumstances of a post–Ice Age world.

An Indian cultivating corn with a digging stick.

The invention of agriculture had similar effects wherever it occurred. It made people less dependent on nature's chance bounty, facilitated the gathering of plant foods, and made possible the survival of larger and more concentrated human populations with more complex social structures than where hunting and the seasonal gathering of noncultivated foods were the only means of sustenance. At first, it seems, people grew food to supplement the hunt. Then, as growing populations pushed hunters toward the territory of other peoples, agriculture became a way of slowing or stopping physical expansion, of providing food without invading neighbors' lands and incurring the risk of war. As agricultural people found

ways to dry and store crops such as corn, they became sedentary—a change that often coincided with the making of pottery, which is too fragile to keep hauling from place to place. None of these changes happened overnight: the first pottery seems to have appeared in the Valley of Mexico about 2300 B.C., several millennia after the beginnings of agriculture. In the meantime, the population continued to grow. And some of the greatest concentrations of people and the most complex cultures in the Americas were found in areas of Mesoamerica, where the climate allowed the cultivation of crops year-round, and agriculture became an established way of supporting life.

Villages appeared in the Tehuacán Valley about 5,000 years ago. At first, their populations grew more slowly than that of the neighboring Olmecs ("people of the land of the gum tree"), who lived on lowlands along the Gulf of Mexico near the modern city of Vera Cruz. The Olmecs supported themselves in part by commerce, trading jade and obsidian, a form of hard volcanic glass that could be made into tools with extraordinarily sharp edges. They also produced great sculptures and buildings, the first of note in the region's history. After a time, however, the Tehuacán highlanders outpaced their coastal rivals; they extended their cultivated lands, compensating for a lack of regular rainfall by systems of terracing and irrigation. Perhaps they also learned to create chinampas, incredibly fertile—only the wet-rice culture of east Asia compares with that of early Mexico—raised beds of land formed by cutting canals in swampy areas along Lake Texcoco, fertilized with pond weeds and mud.

There, in the high mountain plateau of central Mexico, the great city of Teotihuacán, the most powerful of pre-Columbian America, emerged some 2,000 years ago. The city was a religious as well as a trading center, with massive pyramidal temples along a broad central street, all built by human labor—by slaves who had to move great slabs of stone without the help of either large work animals or wheeled vehicles. The elite lived in stone apartment buildings where windowless private rooms, some with elaborately painted walls, opened onto courts or patios, while artisans huddled in warrens of tiny rooms along the city's back streets. Teotihuacán was the home of workshops where specialized craftsmen made knives, spearheads (spear points), scrapers for cleaning animal hides, and other tools from obsidian; and it was a mecca for merchants from other parts of Mesoamerica, who brought their goods to exchange for other exotic items. Estimates of the city's population vary. Some say it reached

The Pyramid of the Sun at Teotihuacán, near today's Mexico City.

45,000 in the second century A.D., others that it was that large much earlier. At its height, in about A.D. 650, it numbered at least 125,000 people, and might have been twice that size. No city of contemporary Europe could compare.

Elsewhere, too, urban centers appeared, with great temples and also ball courts of stone with tiered bleachers from which spectators could watch ball games. These contests seem to have been as much religious or civic ritual as sport, since at their end one set of players was put to death. Monte Alban, a city in the mountains near the trading town of Oaxaco, resembled Teotihuacán in its design, in its practice of an intensive agriculture supported by terracing and irrigation, and in the presence of both massive religious structures and housing for its people. On the Yucatán peninsula, in the midst of jungle-like forests, and sweeping south and west through parts of modern-day southern Mexico and into Guatemala, the Mayan people also created impressive ceremonial centers—over a hundred of them after about A.D. 300, many of which remain hidden today beneath tangled tropical growth, unexcavated.

The Mayans possessed an advanced knowledge of astronomy and mathematics, a complex calendar more accurate than the Julian calendar of contemporary Europe, and a written language composed of both ideographs (pictures that represent ideas) and phonetic components. They used this language to make illustrated manuscripts or books of bark paper, long inscriptions on funerary vases, and stone engravings. The Mayan written language proved difficult for modern scholars to decipher, although the inscriptions seem to pro-

vide dynastic histories of the Mayan rulers. The lands the Mayans occupied were often unsuited for intensive agriculture, particularly at a time when people farmed with "digging sticks," not plows, and without oxen or work horses. Perhaps for that reason, they lived in scattered clusters. Their greatest cities, such as Chichen Itza in the Yucatán or Palenque in Chiapas, boasted massive temples, public buildings, and great plazas that remain stunning testaments to the engineering capacities and ability of their creators to command massive human labor. Still, the Mayan cities never approached the population of Teotihuacán.

The great centers of Mesoamerica in its classic period, a time that saw the creation of massive architectural monuments, came to a mysterious end. Teotihuacán was abandoned

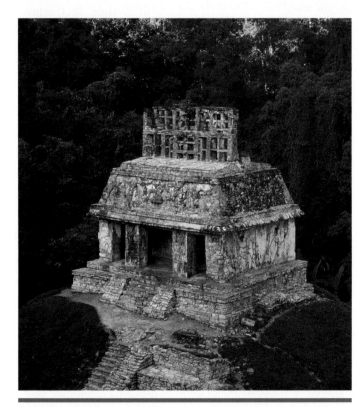

A temple at Palenque, a Mayan town in today's southern Mexico.

and burned sometime around 700. The Mayans left one cere-monial center after another in the decades before and after 800, and Monte Alban suffered the same fate a century later. The catastrophe was like the fall of the Roman Empire (ex-cept that there's little evidence of imperial rule on a similar scale in this period of Mesoamerican history), and yet, since there are virtually no written records, its cause or causes re-main unknown. Did natural calamities precipitate the decline of the great cities? Did the ancient cities outgrow their capac-ity to sustain themselves? Did peasants, pushed to despera-tion by the demands of their urban and theocratic masters, revolt? Or did attacks from outside, perhaps by the Toltec people from the north, lead to the abandonment of these cities and religious centers?

Hundreds of years later, beginning in the thirteenth cen-tury, the Mexica, or Aztecs, a people from the north who claimed descent from the Toltecs, would sweep down into the Valley of Mexico, found a new great city, Tenochtitlán (the "place of the prickly-pear cactus"), on an island in Lake Tex-coco, and conquer the neighboring people. But the arrival of the Aztecs, whose empire was in place by the mid–fifteenth century, cannot explain the earlier disappearance of Teoti-huacán and other centers of classic Mesoamerica.

The results of that disappearance are only slightly easier to trace. Some lesser population centers managed to survive and even grow, particularly in the high valley of central Mexico, but overall the period after the abandonment of Teotihuacán seems to have been one of war, instability, and population decline in one part of the region after another. The highly de-veloped architectural and engineering feats, commerce, and agriculture of classic Mesoamerica nonetheless continued to influence faraway places, including the colder lands to the north of Mexico.

NORTH AMERICA

North America, which Europeans would later sometimes de-scribe as an "empty" continent, was in fact occupied by human beings from at least the end of the Ice Age. Some if not all of the first settlers of what became the continent's temper-ate regions swept south from Alaska to the east side of the Sierra Nevadas, then spread east and south over the continent. Certain Indians today, including the Cherokees, Choctaws, and Chickasaws, recall old stories of long marches from west to east. The Creeks say that their ancestors traveled in search of the land of the rising sun until they arrived at a great

ocean; then they stopped, making a home in what is today the southeast section of the United States. The Delawares tell a similar migration story, but with a twist: they say that the first Algonquian-speaking peo-ples stopped to settle the middle of the continent before some moved on to the east coast.

According to many of these often-told tales, the In-dian peoples did not choose their homelands by chance or simply because they had arrived at the land's end. They received some sign of where they should stop: for example, a sacred pole that pointed in the direction the migrants should go became still when they had arrived at their destination. Their lands, then, had been chosen for them by the Great Spirit. In the West, simi-larly, many Indians understood certain places as particularly sa-cred. Land provided subsistence, but it was also closely bound up

An oversize human hand, made of mica by Hopewell Indians; excavated from an Indian gravesite in Ohio.

with many Indians' sense of themselves, their bonds with an-cestors, children, and the gods, and so had spiritual as well as practical meaning. And yet many Indian peoples moved to new parts of the continent because of war, climatic changes, or some other compelling reason. Their history is one of migra-tions long and short, contacts with other peoples, the sharing of ways and goods, and sometimes deadly conflicts that fol-lowed after groups crossed the zigzagged frontier zones that divided the lands and cultures of North America's peoples and transformed the continent into a oversized jigsaw puzzle.

WAYS OF LIFE

Although some coastal Indians subsisted on fish, most of the earliest Americans were hunters. Large, fluted, Clovis stone spear points (so named after a site near the town of Clovis in New Mexico where they were first found), which were mounted on wooden staves and used to hunt the huge animals of the Ice Age, have been discovered in every part of the mainland United States. Their use seems to have ended about 9200 B.C., and their successor, the artfully fluted Folsom spear points (which were again first discovered in New Mexico), were smaller and better suited for the smaller prey of the post–Ice Age hunt. The bow and arrow was a far more accurate and powerful weapon, but, like much American technology of later times, it first appeared in Europe or Asia: wooden arrow shafts dating back to 9000 B.C. have been found in northern Germany. The bow and arrow moved via Asia to the Arctic region of North America by 3000 B.C., which suggests that some contact between the continents continued after the Ice Age had ended. The weapon spread eastward, then slowly to the south, reaching the Great Plains about A.D. 200 and other parts of what is now the United States several centuries later. The proud peoples of Mesoamerica, however, refused to adopt it. Did they consider the bow and arrow a weapon of the "barbarians" to their north?

The peoples of ancient North America were capable of amazing creations. At Poverty Point, in today's Arkansas, they built, sometime between 1800 and 500 B.C., a peculiar set of earthworks—three mounds, one large and two small, and six concentric groups of parallel ridges formed in a semicircle, like an amphitheater, which extended over two-thirds of a mile. How they moved so much earth remains unknown, except that it had to be by the labor of people with only modest tools. The site also held materials from far-flung places—copper from the Great Lakes region, lead from Missouri, stone from Kentucky, Indiana, and Ohio. Trade networks, it seems, were already in place. And the community at Poverty Point included craftsmen who made jewelry, polished stone figurines, tools, and clay objects that were probably heated in a fire, then thrown into water-holding baskets to make the water boil. Nor was Poverty Point an isolated phenomenon: its influence can be seen at another hundred sites as far away as Florida and Missouri.

Farther north, in the Ohio Valley, other peoples of a later time (500–100 B.C.) built more earthworks, sometimes in the shapes of animals; one 1,254-foot slithering snake was raised four or five feet from the ground. The tradition of mound building continued among the Hopewell people, named after a site in southern Ohio (100 B.C.–A.D. 400), who built enormous burial mounds in geometric shapes. Beneath the mounds lay extraordinarily beautiful artifacts: the profile in mica of a long-fingered human hand; pipes, sometimes inlaid with pearls and bone, in the form of animals; a falcon made of cold-hammered copper. The materials used, again, came from places hundreds of miles away in all directions. The Hopewell grew some of their food, including squash, pumpkins, and sunflowers, and they made pottery. Did agriculture in the Ohio Valley begin independently, rather than through contact with the by-then experienced farmers of Mesoamerica? It's possible, since the Hopewell do not seem to have grown corn.

The peoples of the far north, Eskimos and Aleuts, adapted to the conditions of their lives with great ingenuity, building homes and fishing shelters of ice, creating clothes of fur and feathers to ward off the cold, developing fish traps, kayaks, and harpoons for hunting seals and whales. Others who lived along the Pacific Northwest and the

Aerial photograph of the great serpent mound created by American Indians hundreds of years before the birth of Christ.

California coast exploited the bounty of the sea so successfully that they became relatively sedentary even without inventing or adopting agriculture. But perhaps the most distinctive cultures of subarctic North America were in the Southwest, adjacent to Mesoamerica. There, in a region that included parts of modern-day Utah, Colorado, Arizona, New Mexico, and northern Mexico, people were growing corn and other food some 3,500 years ago, long before agriculture appeared elsewhere in North America.

By A.D. 500 the Southwest contained three distinct but similar cultures, each with its own language or languages. The Hohokam people probably migrated from the south and took up lands in today's Arizona, where they demonstrated their Mexican heritage by building hundreds of miles of canals to irrigate their crops and constructing ball courts reminiscent of those found throughout Mesoamerica. Like their neighbors, the Hohokam were traders and craftsmen whose products included graceful ceramic jars with red geometric designs painted on a buff background. Farther east and south, the Mogollon people, ancestors of the Zuni, set-

Ruins of Anasazi cliff dwellings at Mesa Verde, Colorado.

tled in forests and upland meadows in Arizona and northern Mexico. There they lived year-round in houses dug into the earth and grouped in villages near their farmlands. They also created ceramic pottery, some of which dates back as early as A.D. 750–1000, which they painted in intricate black and white patterns.

To the north of the Hohokam and Mogollon, the Anasazi, ancestors of the Pueblos, also lived in pit houses and produced handsome ceramics painted in gray or black on white. But between A.D. 700 and 1000, they began building apartment complexes above ground. Chaco Canyon in northwestern New Mexico, which the Anasazi developed around 900, included nine towns, whose buildings often formed a semicircle that opened to the south to maximize solar heat. Some structures were huge: Pueblo Bonito ("beautiful town" in Spanish) was four or five stories high and could house 800–1,000 people—more than any other American apartment building before the late nineteenth century. Chaco Canyon also had a highway system, built in the eleventh or

twelfth century, with hundreds of miles of unpaved roads, some thirty feet wide—which is strange for a people with no draft animals or wheeled vehicles. A farming people who lived in an arid region, the Anasazi developed elaborate water systems with terraces, dams, reservoirs, and irrigation ditches. All of these North American accomplishments resembled similar developments in the great Mesoamerican cultural centers, yet each was different; each achievement—whether in architecture, town planning, or ceramic design—carried the distinctive mark of the culture that created it.

The most direct influence of Mesoamerica was probably felt far to the east, along the Mississippi River, where invaders or colonizers, possibly fleeing the turmoil in Mexico that caused or followed the abandonment of Teotihuacán, arrived around A.D. 850–900 and quickly dominated earlier inhabitants. Part of the evidence is at Cahokia, an enormous site four miles east of the Mississippi River and across from modern St. Louis. A trading center with perhaps 20,000 people at its height, Cahokia was the largest city in North Amer-

A ceramic vase or urn, one of a very few artifacts found at the Cahokia site (in today's Missouri).

ica. It covered some 200 acres divided into plazas and gardens, all surrounded by a palisade that required 20,000 logs. Its most prominent landmark was a massive pyramid, 100 feet tall, made of earth, not stone, but otherwise reminiscent of Mexican structures. The Mississippian people of Cahokia also began to grow maize, or corn, with large cobs, like those painstakingly developed over several centuries by Mesoamericans. Corn culture soon spread between the Mississippi River and the Atlantic, where Cahokia's influence was strongest.

Corn cultivation also spread up the Mississippi and to lands north of the Ohio River, then east to the Atlantic. There Algonquian and Iroquoian people adopted the easily grown plant. Not all of these incipient farmers became sedentary; many cultivated crops only as a supplement to the hunt. Nuts, berries, and other products of the wild also remained important food sources for the Indians of the East and North, many of whom burned the forests' underbrush every year to encourage the growth of strawberries and other natural food crops, reduce the population of pests such as rodents and mosquitoes, and encourage deer and other game to move nearer the forests' edge. But agricultural products, particularly corn, became a continuing part of the Indian diet because they could be stored for winter consumption—or, as the Iroquian-speaking Hurons of the Great Lakes area would discover, used as trade goods with other peoples who lived too far north to grow corn.

Then, around 1140, some disaster or disasters struck. The Anasazi abandoned Chaco Canyon at this time, and the Hohokam left many of their population centers. Even Cahokia's population began to drop around 1300, and by 1500 the city was in ruins. Elsewhere, too, there were signs of trouble: in about 1450, for example, large villages on the Queen Charlotte Islands of the Pacific Northwest were abandoned. Why? In the Southwest, drought perhaps explains the crisis. But the answer

is nowhere certain. It seems likely, however, that the population of pre-Columbian North America—a disputed figure, with estimates ranging from 1 million to 18 million—peaked at about 1200, then began to decline.

At almost every point, uncertainty surrounds the Indians' earliest history. Their story is told in terms of spear points and pottery fragments, of what they made, not what they said. It's a story in which millennia pass like months in the histories of cultures with written records, a story for the most part without heroes or villains. Even the names of Indian peoples and places are often inventions of a later time: "Anasazi" means "enemy ancestors" in the language of the Navajo people who arrived in the Southwest after 1700; "Cahokia" is the name given the city by Indians who arrived after it had been abandoned. The original names have been lost.

We know enough, however, to recognize that the earliest peoples of America were tough pioneers who survived one calamity after another, produced rich and varied cultures, created extensive trading networks, and accomplished impressive feats of engineering. Mobility, diversity, and inventiveness were American characteristics long before the first Europeans arrived.

European Discovery and Conquest

Like their Indian predecessors, the earliest European arrivals seem to have stumbled on America. Beginning in the eighth century, Norsemen, or Vikings, who had been pushed from their homes in Scandinavia by wars and population growth, settled the Faeroe, Shetland, and Orkney Islands in the eastern North Atlantic. Then they moved farther west, first to Iceland in about 874 and later, under the leadership of Erik the Red, to Greenland. In about 986, a ship blown off course on its way to Greenland sighted the North American coast, which Leif Erikson, the son of Erik the Red, and other members of his family explored. The Norse founded at least one camp there at L'Anse aux Meadows in northern Newfoundland, where in the 1960s archaeologists discovered remains that date back to about A.D. 1000. Aside from that evidence, the tale of the Viking explorations is known mainly through Norse sagas written down long after the events they describe. In any case, the Newfoundland settlement failed, perhaps in part because of encounters with hostile Indians whom the sagas call "skraelings." By the thirteenth century, Iceland and

Greenland had also entered a period of decline, so little came of that beginning, knowledge of which remained confined to Scandinavia.

The results were different in 1492, when Christopher Columbus set eyes on lands in the western Atlantic. News of his discovery spread and led to further explorations, and then to efforts at conquering and controlling the newly discovered lands and their peoples. The European discovery of America (whose existence was, of course, nothing new for the Indians) has long been considered a central event of the Renaissance, a period roughly from the mid–fourteenth through mid–sixteenth century in which Europe saw a "rebirth" of learning that was increasingly focused on humans and the world. In truth, Europeans who ventured out to discover new lands generally did so for economic as well as intellectual reasons. The religious mindset of Europe's medieval past also shaped those people of the Renaissance who enlarged Europe's understanding of the world, leading them to try to serve the cause of God while enriching themselves and advancing their own places in the world.

"The process that ultimately brought Europeans to America began with expeditions that headed not west but east."

FROM THE MEDITERRANEAN TO THE ATLANTIC

The process that ultimately brought Europeans to America began with expeditions that headed not west but east. Beginning in the late eleventh century, European Christians undertook a series of Crusades to win control of the Holy Land from its Islamic rulers. After a first flush of success, the Crusaders failed in the face of powerful resurgent Muslim forces, and by the late thirteenth century they had been forced back to Europe. But militant Western Christianity persisted, above all in Spain, where Christians spent hundreds of years attempting to rid the land of Muslims who had arrived there in 711, an effort known as the *reconquista* (reconquest). By the fifteenth century, the Muslims, or Moors, were confined to the kingdom of Granada, which bordered the Mediterranean Sea in the southern side of the Iberian peninsula. Granada finally fell to Spanish Christians in 1492, ending the *reconquista*; but there were other places where crusading Christians could exercise their zeal on people who might be more open to conversion than the Islamic followers of the prophet Mohammed. The Spanish carried to America both institutions and attitudes that had been formed over the centuries of the *reconquista*.

Although Western Christians' efforts to conquer the Holy Land failed, that experience increased their knowledge of the Mediterranean, a region whose technology in one area after another was at the time superior to that of western Europe. There, too, Europeans encountered writings of the ancient world that had been lost in Europe, and acquired a taste for new foods and flavors. In the fifteenth century, the Mediterranean was a vigorous trading area. That great water highway carried to Europe items produced along its shore, such as grain and salt for preserving fish, as well as a vast array of luxury goods from Asia. Among imports from the East were Chinese silks, Indian cotton, precious stones, and, above all, spices, a category that included drugs, cosmetics, dyes, perfumes, even glue and sugar. Pepper, cinnamon, cloves, and other condiments, used for flavoring and preserving food, proved a welcome addition to the bland diets of Europe. Certain Italian city-states, particularly Genoa and Venice, controlled the trade between the Mediterranean and western Europe. They used their monopoly to raise the prices of goods, which would have been high in any case since the items were often brought overland from Asia to ports on the eastern Mediterranean. The high prices, in turn, increased the desire of purchasers to find other suppliers, and of potential suppliers to find new routes to Asia.

Portugal led the way. Situated on the far western side of the Iberian peninsula, with a long Atlantic coast, the country was well positioned to extend its influence into the Atlantic and down, south and east, to Africa. Old histories sing the praises of Dom Henrique, the son of Portugal's King John I (r. 1385–1433), who became known among English scholars as Prince Henry the Navigator. Prince Henry was supposedly driven by a curiosity about things "which were hidden from other men, and secret" and maintained a center for the study of navigation at Sagres, in southwest Portugal. It now seems that he was more of a latter-day Crusader against Muslim "infidels" than a man possessed by curiosity about the unknown, and more driven by the need to support his dependents and style of life than by a desire or capacity to patronize navigational studies. Prince Henry nonetheless supported Portugal's capture of Ceuta in Muslim North Africa (1415) and sponsored voyages that, through the early fifteenth century, pushed ever farther down the West African coast, through waters once thought impenetrable, to destinations previously unknown to Europeans. By the time of Prince Henry's death in 1460, Portuguese sailors had traveled as far south as Sierra Leone, well below the point where, according to legend, a Sea of Darkness consumed those foolhardy enough to venture into its waters. Then, after a pause, Portugal's King John II, who ruled from 1481 to 1495, resumed explorations of the African coast. Under John II, Bartholomeu Dias finally sailed all the way to the southernmost point of Africa and around the Cape of Good Hope, in 1487–88. From there, the Portuguese could sail up the east coast of Africa to India, which Vasco da Gama did in 1497–99.

This portrait of the Portuguese royal family includes Prince Henry (often called "the Navigator"), the mustached man standing above the kneeling central figure, King Afonso V (r. 1438–81). Prince Henry encouraged Portuguese exploration of the African coast.

Explorations of Africa had not one but several profitable by-products. Portuguese ships blown off course first discovered Madeira, an island in the Atlantic that the Portuguese claimed (1418–19), colonized, and made into a profitable source of sugar (an ascending commercial product) and wine. They developed the Cape Verde Islands (1445) and attempted unsuccessfully to take the Canary Islands, which became instead a possession of Spain. The Portuguese also acquired the Azores (1431–54), which stretched a thousand miles into the Atlantic from western Portugal, about a third of the way to America, and islands along the African coast farther south, including São Tomé. West Africa, aside from providing a route to Asia, produced a number of valuable trade products, including ivory, fur and oil from seals, black pepper, some gold dust, and a supply of "black gold"—dark-skinned slaves who were first used as domestic servants, artisans, and market or transportation workers in Lisbon or Seville, and later as laborers on sugar plantations in the Atlantic islands.

To reach West African or island locations and return home raised challenges beyond any faced by European sailors at the time of the First Crusade. As a result, the Portuguese (and other Europeans) began using and developing navigational devices, many of which were of Arab origin, and building better ships for the needs of explorers and traders who sailed not the Mediterranean, an inland sea, but the open ocean.

FIFTEENTH-CENTURY NAVIGATION

The Norse had sailed the North Atlantic on small, single-decked and single-masted ships with one square sail. Their route to Greenland included a stretch on the open sea of over 1,000 nautical miles; otherwise, most of their voyages involved piloting ships along coasts or crossing less formidable stretches of water while remaining within sight of land. The Greenland crossing was, however, daunting, and the Vikings made it regularly over several centuries without the benefit of any known charts or instruments, except perhaps for a lead that could be dropped to determine depth and the nature of the sea's floor. The Vikings gauged the distance they had traveled mainly by dead reckoning, estimating their speed and so their distance from their point of departure. Like other sailors of early times, they took into account sounds and smells, the presence of birds or other animals, of ice or fog, or the color of the sea to determine their location. It could even be that

A fourteenth-century English quadrant, used to determine latitude at sea. Mariners aligned sights on the right with the polestar, then noted where the plumb line hit the scale on the rounded edge. Accurate readings were difficult on a turbulent sea.

the Mediterranean, the compass was the standard instrument for keeping ships on course. But the deviation of magnetic from true north made the compass of only limited use for navigation (the term for bringing ships from one location to another without sight of land) over substantial distances across several degrees of latitude. Out on the open ocean, European seamen instead followed the technique of "running down the latitude": once they knew the latitude of their destination, they would sail north or south to that degree of latitude, then turn east or west until they caught sight of land. At first, they determined latitude by observing celestial bodies, as the Vikings might have done, but by the late fifteenth century two instruments existed to make that job easier: the quadrant and the astrolabe.

The quadrant was an instrument in the shape of a quarter circle with 90 degrees marked off on the outer, circular edge, and with a plumb line (a line with a weight at one end) that hung down from the apex (the circle's center) toward the edge. Pinhole sights along one of the straight sides were aligned with the polestar. Then, by noting where the plumb line hit the scale, mariners could determine their latitudes with reasonable accuracy—provided the readings were taken when two other stars (the "Guards," the outer stars of the "Little Bear") were in the same position. Accuracy also required a relatively calm sea or the plumb line would bob around, making useful readings impossible.

As a result, seamen came to prefer other devices, such as the mariners' astrolabe, which was a simplified version of a

when Norse seamen were beyond sight of land, they studied the height of the sun at midday or, at night, the polestar (or North Star), by which they could figure at least roughly on which latitude they were. Exactly how they made those measurements remains unknown, but by knowing their latitude and the latitude of their destination, the Vikings could keep on course in the open sea. Unfortunately, clouds or fog often prevented celestial observations. Norse sagas testify that the seamen often lost all sense of direction or landed at the wrong place.

Most fifteenth-century European sailors were not much better off. Dead reckoning was still the usual way of determining location. Seamen did have the use, though, of the compass, an instrument of Chinese origin that arrived in Europe from the Mediterranean. It consisted of a magnetized iron wire or needle mounted on a pin so it could move freely, which was itself mounted on a base, or "card," that marked off directions. The needle pointed to the north, but not exactly, and the extent to which magnetic north deviated from true north at different points on the globe (as a result of mineral deposits in the earth) was understood and charted only in the sixteenth century. Within confined sea spaces, such as

The mariner's astrolabe, also used to determine latitude at sea, was usually hung in some central part of the ship because it needed to be perpendicular when a reading was taken. That was a problem at sea, where the ship often bounced around and false readings were common.

A sailor "shooting a star" with a cross staff, a late sixteenth-century device used, like the astrolabe and quadrant, to determine latitude.

complex instrument used by astronomers since the Middle Ages. It consisted of a disk, usually six to ten inches wide, with degrees marked along the outer edge, and an alidade, or indicator, mounted across the center and pointing outward toward the edge. The astrolabe was usually hung at a place onboard convenient for taking readings, since it needed to be perpendicular (again a problem on a heaving deck); then a seaman moved the alidade until it pointed to the polestar. Later, in the sixteenth century, a cheaper, wooden handheld device, the cross staff, emerged to measure latitude. A seaman aimed the instrument at a star, much as a crossbowman took aim (thus "shooting" the star), then adjusted a sliding crosspiece so that it indicated the distance between the horizon and the star. He could then read the star's altitude from a scale marked along the central rod. Accurate readings, however required great skill, and mistakes were common.

The quadrant and astrolabe depended on readings based on the polestar—which gradually disappeared from sight as ships, such those of Portugal exploring the African coast, slipped below the equator. As a result, Portugal's King John II commissioned a set of mathematicians to work out a method of determining latitude by observing the sun. From their work emerged the first European navigation manual, which was published in 1509 but probably circulated in manuscript before then. The book included a list of latitudes for locations from Lisbon to the equator, a table of the sun's declinations, and instructions on figuring latitude with reference to either the sun or the North Star. The manual was the most advanced statement of fifteenth-century navigation. It became the basis for navigators' training in Portugal and Spain after 1500, and these navigators spread its influence beyond the

Iberian peninsula. To decide how far a ship had traveled, however, sailors remained dependent on dead reckoning, because the determination of longitude was much more complex than that of latitude. No practical means of finding longitude at sea emerged until the late eighteenth century.

The Portuguese also developed ships that were exceptionally maneuverable and well suited for open-ocean sailing. Most European ships at the beginning of the fifteenth century had been designed for carrying cargoes along coasts over relatively short distances. They were short and broad, and powered by a single main sail that worked well when the wind was behind it. On other occasions, they depended on galleys of oarsmen to keep the boat moving, which was possible only for trips of short duration. Soon designers in Portugal and southern Spain began building ships longer and narrower than the usual merchant ships—the caravels, which became the main vessels of the explorers—and equipped them with triangular lateen sails, borrowed from Arab predecessors, that allowed a ship to sail with winds blowing not just from behind but from either side. Ships gradually became still longer and also larger, higher in the water with more

Caravels, the ships developed by the Portuguese for overseas exploration, had long, narrow hulls, and carried triangular lateen sails, which allowed them to maneuver and "catch the wind" even when the wind was to their side.

decks and more space for cargoes and crews (necessary on voyages that could last several months), and equipped with a complex combination of sails. By late in the fifteenth century, ships with two large square sails and a lateen auxiliary sail, allowing both speed and maneuverability, became common on oceangoing vessels.

Mapping, too, underwent substantial development. The Renaissance brought new means of conveying proportions and distance in drawings and paintings, and a similar effort to make maps that accurately portrayed the earth's geography. First, expert mapmakers in Venice, Genoa, and Majorca (or, later, Barcelona and Lisbon) expanded the "portolan," or sea chart, which existed mainly for the Mediterranean in the late Middle Ages, to incorporate islands in the Atlantic and the West African coast. These navigation charts, which showed distances and bearings according to the compass between given locations, included remarkably accurate sketches of coastlines on single large sheets of vellum, with the names of ports written perpendicular to the coasts. They specified offshore hazards such as rocks or shoals, but gave no information on currents, tides, or sea depths. Later marine charts included the western Atlantic and sometimes indicated the degree of latitude at which ports were located and the deviation between true and magnetic north.

World maps were different. Created in the Middle Ages for devotional purposes or to express cosmological beliefs, not as aids to navigation, they characteristically showed a single large landmass surrounded by water with Jerusalem at or near the center. In the fifteenth century, they, too, changed—in response first to the rediscovery of ancient learning, including the *Geography* of Claudius Ptolemy (long known to the Arabs but first translated into Latin in 1406), and later to firsthand information brought back by explorers and traders. Ptolemy, an Egyptian who lived in the second century A.D., attempted to summarize all the geographical knowledge of his time. He not only understood that the earth was round (as did others before him and most knowledgeable Europeans of the fifteenth century), but proposed a system of dividing the sphere into 360 degrees of latitude and longitude. Although the use of such coordinates to locate places on the globe was not entirely unknown in medieval Europe, Ptolemy's use of them seemed revolutionary when his *Geography* reappeared there in the fifteenth century. The system he used as a basis for constructing maps had the effect of reducing a world filled with mystery to a predictable geometric order. However, Ptolemy underestimated the size of the earth by about a quarter, and his depiction of lands and bodies of water outside the Mediterranean world was more imaginative than accurate. He nonetheless became the leading source of geographical information for Renaissance scholars. His errors would be corrected by the observations of sailors who often understood the utility of sailing by latitude without knowing the term or understanding the mathematics behind the use of celestial observations.

Maps were not simply artistically presented records of known facts. They also had a political function: they designated those parts of the world that specific European countries claimed as their own, erasing in the process the claims of native peoples and ignoring the boundaries of indigenous political geography. Moreover, printing, which allowed maps to be replicated and widely distributed, increased their imperial influence.

And yet the very incompleteness of the information maps conveyed provoked curiosity and inspired further explorations. What exactly lay in the waters west of Europe and east of Asia? One theory proposed the existence of antipodes, countervailing masses of land on opposite sides of the earth, which implied that there was another vast continent or continents somewhere out in the "Ocean Sea," as Europeans called the water to their west, to balance Eurasia and Africa. Another theory said that there was nothing much unknown out there, that the world's surface was mainly covered by land,

A portolan, a map for navigators, characteristically on vellum, which was made from a sheep's skin and often retained some echoes of the animal's shape (see the neck on the left). This portolan, drawn by mapmaker Graziosa Benincasa in 1469, includes not only the Mediterranean but the coast of western Europe.

This Byzantine reconstruction of the lost map that accompanied Ptolemy's *Geography* shows a world divided, according to Ptolemy's system, into lines of latitude and longitude. There is no America, and parts of the world that were, for the ancients, relatively remote, such as southern Africa and the Indian Ocean, are represented inaccurately. However, much of Europe, western Asia, and North Africa are shown with remarkable precision.

most of which was known, and that the Ocean Sea was not as wide as many people thought. One prominent cosmographer estimated the distance from the Canary Islands to Cathay, or China, as 5,000 miles. That was not quite navigable in the fifteenth century, but the journey could be broken at Japan and other islands that were known or hypothesized. In fact, fifteenth-century world-map makers included in the waters west of Europe not only newly discovered or rediscovered islands such as the Azores and Canaries, but others as yet unseen with names such as Antillia or Isle of Brasil. Were they real, like the "lion in the Ocean sea" that Sir Humphrey Gilbert's crew would observe in 1583, or a figment of someone's imagination? The only way to know for sure was to go and have a look.

CHRISTOPHER COLUMBUS

The man who most wanted to go was Christopher Columbus, the red-haired, ruddy-faced son of a Genoese weaver and textile merchant. Columbus, born in 1451, became a merchant seaman and made several voyages in the Mediterranean and along the eastern Atlantic coast. In 1476, he is said to have joined a Genoese fleet bound for England that the French attacked off the Portuguese coast. He was rescued from the wreckage and went to Lisbon, where his brother Bartholomew was a map and chart maker. At some point in the mid-1470s, still working as a merchant seaman, he probably sailed to England, Iceland, and Ireland, which would have increased his knowledge of the Atlantic. Columbus eventually rose to become the captain of his own ship. In 1479, he married a Portuguese woman whose father collected maps and writings on the Atlantic, and they spent a few years in the Madeira Islands. After his wife's death in 1484, he returned to Lisbon with a son, Diego, and in 1485 moved again, this time to the Spanish city of Seville, another lively maritime center.

By then, Columbus was convinced that it was possible to reach Asia by sailing west from Europe. He had little formal education but was fluent in several languages, including Portuguese, and kept up with contemporary cartography, geography, and cosmology as best he could. He was also a devout Christian who somehow decided that the Garden of Eden was on the side of the earth exactly opposite Jerusalem, such that each provided the center for different, antipodal hemispheres.

 His idea of sailing westward to Asia was, however, based more firmly on a set of mutually reinforcing **geographical and mathematical errors**. Columbus owned a copy of Cardinal Pierre d'Ailly's *Imago Mundi,* written about 1410. He read and reread the book, filling its margins with handwritten comments, and seems to have accepted virtually everything d'Ailly said, including his estimate of the width of Asia—which was far too large. Columbus also knew Ptolemy's estimate of the circumference of the globe, which was incorrect, making the earth much smaller than it is. Together, these two mistakes had the effect of moving the eastern edge of Asia farther toward Europe (and, of course, took no account of the fact that America lay between them). How great was the gap between Europe and Asia? Florentine cosmographer Paolo Toscanelli argued that some 5,000 miles separated the Canary Islands and the Chinese city of Quinsay (Hangzhou), whose riches the thirteenth-century traveler Marco Polo had described. But from the readings he had taken, Columbus figured the voyage was only about 3,500 miles. The distance to Japan was even less—maybe by as much as 1,500 miles if Japan was that far from the Asian coast, as Marco Polo claimed (incorrectly)—and so technically possible.

When Columbus presented his proposal to Portugal's King John II, the king was uninterested. Not only did his expert advisers question Columbus's reasoning, but after Dias had rounded the Cape of Good Hope in 1487–88, Portugal had no need for another route to Asia. Columbus then tried unsuccessfully to interest England, France, and Spain in his scheme. Finally, in 1492, Queen Isabel of Castile agreed to sponsor his voyage. Expansion within the Iberian peninsula had been a prerequisite for external expansion, and in that year Spain finally succeeded in defeating the Moors in Granada. Isabel then promptly expelled the Jews from Spain, the name for the kingdoms joined as a result of her marriage, in 1469, to Ferdinand of Aragon. With the Spanish Crown's

Christopher Columbus as painted by Sebastiano del Piombo in 1519, after Columbus's death. There is no known portrait of Columbus made from life.

power at home reasonably secure, it could use its experience in conquering internal enemies to facilitate conquest elsewhere. In 1492, Spain—or, more exactly, Isabel—was ready to turn outward.

In April, the contract was signed: Columbus would be admiral and become governor of whatever land or lands he discovered, with a claim to one-tenth of all the trade or treasure from those newly discovered territories. The promises made to Columbus were in the tradition of the *adelantados,* men licensed by the Crown to win territory from the Moors and so to extend the frontiers of Christianity. In return, they were given governing powers and a share in the spoils. The *adelantados* were normally self-financed, but the Crown ordered the port of Palos to supply the newly appointed "**Admiral of the Ocean Sea**" with three ships. Those chosen included two 60-ton caravels, the *Niña* and the *Pinta,* and, as the flagship, a cumbersome, 120-ton merchant vessel, probably built to carry wine and not particularly well suited for Columbus's purpose, which he renamed the *Santa María.*

The small fleet sailed first to the Canaries and then, on September 6, 1492, set to sea, heading first south to the 28th parallel, then due west, "riding the latitude" with a good wind. A little over a month later, on October 12, a crew member on the *Pinta* caught sight of land, perhaps Watling Island in the Bahamas, where the Spaniards first landed. Columbus renamed the island San Salvador ("holy savior"), then went on to explore the Bahamas as well as Cuba and what he called Hispaniola ("Spanish island," now Haiti and the Dominican Republic). There, after the *Santa María* was wrecked on Christmas, he founded a post called La Navidad ("the Nativity"), the first European settlement in the Americas since the time of the Vikings. He left thirty-five men on Hispaniola when he set sail for Spain in January 1493. With him he brought a few Arawak Indians, parrots, and some gold jewelry bartered from the natives, but no news of gold mines despite his prayer, "Our Lord in his pity guide me that I may find gold." The inhabitants of the islands, Columbus assured Queen Isabel, were friendly and generous, and would make fit converts to Christianity. As for the land and the animals and plants of this island world, they were sometimes much like those of Spain but at other times strange. The fish were a particular surprise, "so *different* from ours," with such beautiful colors "that everyone marvels . . . and takes great delight in them," and the birds, too, were "of so many sorts and so different from ours, that one is left marveling." Even the foods were different: Cuba grew vegetables that were "like carrots" but tasted "like chestnuts" (probably potatoes) and beans *very different from ours.*"

The news of Columbus's discoveries preceded his return: a letter he sent a supporter of the expedition on February 15, 1493, while still off the Canaries on the return trip was printed at Barcelona, then reprinted another eight times that year. As the news spread, questions necessarily rose over possession of the lands Columbus had found, and also over just what it was he had "discovered." The pope confirmed Spain's claim in two bulls (official papal pronouncements) entitled *Inter Caetera* (1493) that also said that all future discoveries west of a north-south line 100 leagues west of the Azores and Cape Verde Islands would belong to Spain. Portugal's John II protested; and by the Treaty of Tordesillas (1494), Portugal and Spain agreed to move the dividing line to 370 leagues west of the Cape Verde Islands, with Portugal holding title to lands discovered to the east. In that way, Portugal won what became Brazil on the eastward bulge of South America, which Pedro Álvares Cabral discovered in 1500.

Columbus lived to make three more voyages to America. The second (1493–96) was the greatest: he set off from Cadiz with seventeen ships and some 1,200 men. After claiming

The earliest depiction of Columbus's landing in the New World, from Giuliano Dati's *Narrative of Columbus,* 1493.

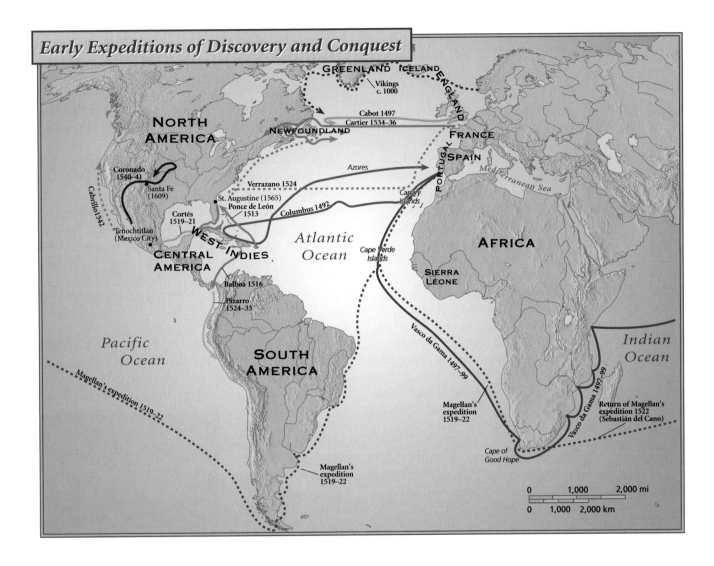

Early Expeditions of Discovery and Conquest

Dominica, Antigua, Guadeloupe, and Puerto Rico for Spain, the expedition arrived at Hispaniola to discover that La Navidad had been totally destroyed. That led to brutal reprisals against the natives, whom the Spanish enslaved and used to seek gold and to work the land. Columbus left his brothers in charge of a new settlement called Isabela, but—in a pattern that would be repeated again and again—the settlers broke into bitter factions, food supplies failed, and disease wasted away the weakened population. Columbus's third voyage (1498–1500) was smaller, and ended disastrously when the new Spanish governor of Hispaniola charged the admiral and his brothers with having grievously misgoverned the colony and sent them home in chains. His fourth and final voyage (1502–04) was no more successful. Although Columbus ex-

plored the coast of Central America, which he came to think was a new part of Asia that no one had previously mapped, all four ships of the expedition were lost, and he returned to Spain only after being rescued from Jamaica, where he had been marooned for a year.

Columbus's death in 1506 went almost unnoticed, and his reputation since has experienced ups and downs as extreme as those of his lifetime. He clearly was no administrator, and he proved perfectly willing to take the lands and enslave the Arawak people of the West Indies, who, like the native people of the Canary Islands, were wiped out by imported diseases within a century of the Spaniards' arrival. His own inclination, however, was toward establishing trading factories in the lands he discovered, like those of Portugal on the

23

west coast of Africa, rather than colonies that displaced older inhabitants. His vision was more mystical than scientific—especially by the time of his third voyage, when he thought of himself as chosen by God for some great Christian mission—and he never knew exactly what he had found.

But it was Columbus who announced to Europe the existence of lands in the western Atlantic that were previously unknown to them. And he was without dispute a superb navigator, one of the greatest of all time, a man who was not just remarkably lucky (after all, the Caribbean islands lay about where he expected to find Japan, and the American mainland where China should have been), but who quickly found the best and shortest routes in the middle latitudes to and from America. In 1492, he set out west from the Canaries near the 28th parallel with the northeast trade winds behind him, and on his return struck north looking for a westerly wind, which he quickly found on the latitude of Bermuda. He improved the route slightly on his second voyage and—although he failed to take advantage of the Gulf Stream, which remained unknown to Europeans for another twenty years—thus established the routes that became standard for later Spanish voyages. For a man who lived in an age of navigation, that alone was a claim to distinction.

FURTHER EXPLORATIONS

Not everyone agreed with Columbus that the lands he discovered were parts of Asia. Peter Martyr, another Italian who, like Columbus, settled in Spain, author of the popular *De Orbe Novo*, remarked in 1494 that "when treating of this country one must speak of a new world, so distant is it and so devoid of civilization and religion." In the next century, more and more observers came to share Martyr's conclusion. The truth, however, could only be established by further observations, and in Columbus's wake one voyage after another set out to survey the "New World" and discover what opportunities it offered.

Two years after Peter Martyr made his observation, King Henry VII of England commissioned John Cabot to explore the North Atlantic for a passage to the Orient. Cabot was an Italian (Giovanni Cabato), probably from Genoa like Columbus, but he became a citizen of Venice. After studying navigation in Spain, he made his home in Bristol, an English port on the Atlantic that traded regularly with Portugal and Spain (including the Madeira and Canary Islands), as well as Iceland, and so was well acquainted with the Atlantic. Already in 1480 and perhaps earlier, Bristol ships had sailed "to serche & fynde a certain Isle called the Isle of Brasil," which supposedly lay west of Ireland, in the hope of locating new and rich fishing grounds. There is some evidence that the Bristol explorers found land in the western Atlantic in the 1480s or even earlier, although, again, that discovery was not widely publicized.

In 1497, Cabot went to sea in a small ship, the *Matthew*, with a crew of only eighteen or twenty men. The ship swung out beyond Ireland, turned north, and then west, riding the latitude without, it seems, benefit of either astrolabe or quadrant (some seasoned seamen disdained the use of those tools). They made a landfall in what the English would later call "New Found Land," or Newfoundland, which Cabot claimed for England. Members of the Cabot expedition saw no people on these lands, though they observed signs of human habitation. The coastal waters, they noted, were so alive with fish that they could be caught with baskets.

Cabot became a hero after reporting his findings, and English merchants eager to find a northwest passage to China helped finance a second and larger expedition in 1498. It ended badly: all four of Cabot's ships were lost, and he with them. Later, in 1504 and 1508–09, Sebastian Cabot, John's son, made additional voyages into northern waters, perhaps reaching the Hudson Bay, but failed to find a northwest passage. By then, fishermen had brought cargoes of fish, especially cod, to Bristol from the North Atlantic fisheries. English ships soon began sailing every spring to Newfoundland, returning with their catch in the fall. The Cabot voyage of 1497 gave England a claim to North America, and the annual pilgrimages of fishermen added to the country's knowledge of the North Atlantic. Portuguese, French, and, from the 1520s, Spanish fishermen also visited Newfoundland, making the town of St. John's an international meeting place where fishermen from many countries gathered and swapped nav-

John Cabot (Giovanni Cabato).

The famous Waldseemüller map of the world, first published in 1507, gave America its name. Note the figures of Ptolemy and Amerigo Vespucci at the top.

igational information. It was from Newfoundland that Sir Humphrey Gilbert sailed in 1583, when his men sighted the curious "lion" swimming in the sea.

Other voyages added to people's knowledge of North America. In 1524, King Francis I of France sent Giovanni de Verrazano, a Florentine, to find a route through North America to Asia. He failed, but in the course of his search Verrazano explored the Atlantic coast from the Carolinas up as far as Nova Scotia, observing along the way the harbor at New York and Narragansett Bay. And between 1534 and 1536, Jacques Cartier, who came from Normandy in northern France, explored the waters west of Newfoundland for Francis I. Cartier sailed up the St. Lawrence River to Quebec and then, in smaller boats, to Montreal. True to form, he claimed the land for France, although the climate proved dishearteningly cold and gave little real evidence of the gold and other riches Cartier sought.

Spain and Portugal—or Italians sailing under those flags— explored the lands farther south. Amerigo Vespucci, a wealthy

and well-connected Florentine businessman who took an interest in geography and navigation, participated in three or four of these voyages—first from Spain between 1497 and 1499, and then two more after he moved to Portugal. Vespucci commanded neither these expeditions nor any others that explored the Caribbean and the mainland coasts. He traveled, as one source said, as a person "who knew cosmography and matters pertaining to the sea." Later he wrote accounts of his voyages—or, more likely, someone else fabricated reports based on a handful of letters by Vespucci himself—that proved very popular. Vespucci, it seems, doubted from the first that the lands Columbus found were part of Asia. After seeing Brazil, he concluded like Peter Martyr before him that the explorers had discovered a "new land," a continent that was, in effect, a barrier between Europe and Asia.

At about the time Vespucci's travel account was published, a set of scholars assembled at the Cathedral of St. Die in today's Alsace-Lorraine to create a new edition of Ptolemy's world atlas that would include the discoveries of Portugal and

25

Spain. In 1507, they published an *Introduction to Cosmography . . . to which are added The Four Voyages of Amerigo Vespucci. . . .* The atlas proposed that the "fourth part of the earth"—beyond Europe, Asia, and Africa—that "Amerigo discovered" should be called "Amerige, the land of Amerigo . . . or America." Accordingly, a set of maps by Martin Waldseemüller that were published with the book labeled the western landmass "America," and even included decorative portraits of Ptolemy and Vespucci. Other cartographers copied the map, so the name "America" caught on—although Spain continued to refer to its discoveries as "Las Indias" or "the Indies."

On Waldseemüller's map, America appears as a long, thin strip of land with no geographical features marked on its western side. Thereafter, explorers gradually accumulated more information on the geography of America and what lay beyond it. In 1513, Juan Ponce de León explored the coast of Florida; three years later, Vasco Nuñez de Balboa arrived at Panama and caught sight of another great body of water, the Pacific Ocean, on the other side. The ocean's dimensions, however, remained unknown until Fernando Magellan, a Portuguese navigator sailing for Spain, circumnavigated the globe (1519–22) on a voyage that was perhaps the age's most spectacular navigational achievement. Magellan did not live to see the trip completed, though; he and several crew members were killed in the Philippine Islands in 1521. Juan Sebastián del Cano, who assumed command, continued on to the Spice Islands (now the Molucca Islands of Indonesia), down around the east coast of Africa, and up the Atlantic to Spain. The voyage disproved Ptolemy's estimate of the world's size: the distance west from Europe to Asia was enormous, and two continents, North and South America, blocked the route. Vast regions remained to be explored and mapped, and the search for a passage through or over the Americas continued. But in less than a century, knowledge of world geography had been transformed.

THE CONQUEST OF MEXICO

For a quarter century after Columbus's first voyage, Spain concentrated its attention on the islands in the western Atlantic. In 1496 the Spanish began building the city of Santo Domingo, their first governmental center in the Americas on Hispaniola. Then they began the conquest of Puerto Rico, Jamaica, the Bahamas, and, in 1511, Cuba. The settlers clustered in cities, as they had in Spain, forcing the natives to supply

Cortés arriving at the Aztec capital, Tenochtitlán (later Mexico City), by an unknown Aztec artist, 1519–22.

gold and food and to work on sugar plantations founded on the model of Madeira. In the late 1490s, royal officials formally granted groups of Indians to specific settlers in reward for service. Those grants were known as *encomiendas.* The recipient of an *encomienda,* an *encomendero,* formally assumed responsibility for the protection and Christianization of the Indians entrusted to him, and in return received from them tribute in the form of goods and labor. In fact, however, the *encomienda* led to the virtual enslavement of the Indians.

Some clergymen questioned the Spaniards' right to rule and exploit native peoples, but defenders of the system insisted that in 1493 the pope had granted Spaniards dominion over "pagans" whom they were to convert. On encountering new groups of native peoples, the Spanish formally read a *requerimiento,* or notice, written in Spanish, demanding that the natives accept Spanish rule and Christianity or their lands would be seized and they would be killed or enslaved. Soon, however, the Indian population began to decline: the native people of Hispaniola, who numbered as many as a million in 1492, all but disappeared by the middle of the next century as a result of imported illnesses as well as Spanish cruelty and exploitation. The supply of gold also began to run out. So the Spaniards looked for other places to supply the wealth and labor that the Caribbean islands lacked.

In 1517, an expedition that explored Yucatán and the Gulf of Mexico reported the existence of civilizations on the mainland that were richer and more populous than any in the Caribbean. Two years later, the Spanish governor in Havana commissioned the thirty-four-year-old Hernando Cortés, a headstrong and ambitious *encomendero* who had helped conquer Cuba, to make contact with the Indian empire in Mexico. The governor soon thought better of that appointment, but before he could do anything, Cortés set sail with eleven ships and over 500 men, including Bernal Días del Castillo, who later wrote a detailed history of the conquest of Mexico.

The invaders landed near the modern town of Vera Cruz on the Gulf of Mexico. Upon learning that the center of power and wealth lay inland, they began a march to the Valley of Mexico, collecting thousands of Indian allies along the way. The Aztec rulers of Mexico had established their power only within the previous century, and their yoke was not light. They collected heavy tribute, or taxes, and enslaved and seized the lands of defeated people. They also herded thousands of them to Aztec temples; there, executioners cut their hearts from their bodies and offered the still-throbbing organs to a god who, the Aztecs believed, demanded human sacrifices to make the sun rise and the world continue. Re-

A depiction of the battle for Tenochtitlán by an unknown Indian artist. The Spaniards have muskets, a cannon, and a type of bow for shooting arrows. The Indians fight back with spears.

sentment served the conquerors' cause: Cortés had little difficulty winning support from Indian peoples anxious to break loose from the Aztecs' hold. After thousands of the powerful Tlaxcalans joined the Spanish forces, the Aztec ruler, Montezuma II, decided to invite Cortés to enter his capital, Tenochtitlán, peacefully.

The Spaniards were amazed as they wound through the mountains at the southern end of the Valley of Mexico and looked down at the cities and villages below, some on dry land, another in the midst of a great lake and connected to the land by causeways, with temples and other stone buildings "arising from the water . . . like an enchanted vision." Indeed, Bernal Días recalled, "some of our soldiers asked whether it was not all a dream. . . . It was all so wonderful that I do not know how to describe this first glimpse of things never heard of, seen or dreamed before." Tenochtitlán, the island city, which the Spaniards entered on November 8, 1519, held some 300,000 people, far more than any city in Spain. The market to its north at Tlatelolco, where a vast array of goods including foods, jewelry, feathers, birds, utensils, building materials, and slaves were bought and sold daily by tens of thousands of people, was again like nothing they had ever seen. And the Spaniards found Tenochtitlán's blood-stained temples and, even more, the Aztecs' consumption of human flesh both surprising and profoundly repugnant. To be sure, the Spanish were themselves capable of vicious cruelty and had witnessed extensive bloodletting during the *reconquista,* but cannibalism was not in their repertoire. The wonders of this New World were of all sorts, exciting both desire and disgust, both personal avarice and a god-given mission to replace the natives' "satanic" religious practices with the more kindly ritual of the Catholic mass.

Montezuma fed the Spaniards' greed with gold and other gifts. But, distrusting his intentions, they seized and held him captive until he was killed in the midst of a massive uprising against the invaders. Then, on the night of June 30–July 1, 1520—"La Noche Triste" (sorrowful night)—Aztec insurgents forced the Spaniards to flee the city, losing the riches they had collected as well as a third of their men. But over the next year, Cortés reorganized his followers, mobilized his Indian allies, and built thirteen brigantines—twin-masted, square-rigged vessels—that he equipped with firearms and used to control the causeways and block supplies from entering the island city. Finally, on August 21, 1521, the Spanish retook Tenochtitlán, destroying many of its buildings and people in the process.

There, on the ruins of Tenochtitlán, Cortés began to build Mexico City, a center of Spanish colonial power over what became New Spain. The metropolis would be, Cortés decided, a New World creation more beautiful than even the city of Venice, with which it was frequently compared. The building of Mexico City exceeded any European project of the Renaissance. In the spring of 1523, according to contemporary reports, some 400,000 Mexican Indians were working "with such fervor that the labourers sang, and the songs and voices scarcely ceased at night." Forced labor was nothing new to the common people of Mesoamerica, but under the Spanish, unlike under all previous rulers, workers had access to an array of European building tools such as nails, screws, pulleys, wheelbarrows, and wheeled carts with, equally astonishing, mules to pull them. The Mexicans, Spanish observers commented, were "friends of novelties." And why not? For once, European imports served not to increase the Indians' burdens, but to lighten them.

THE SPREAD OF SPANISH POWER

With the defeat of the Aztecs, the *conquistadores,* or conquerors—tough, avaricious Spaniards, generally of low birth or the younger sons of noble families, eager to improve their place in life—set out in search of other peoples to subdue and despoil. Between 1524 and 1533, Spaniards under Francisco Pizarro defeated the Inca peoples of Peru's Andean highlands, accumulating in the process thousands of pounds of gold and silver. Like Cortés, Pizarro used divisions among the Incas to his advantage. The hierarchical structure of Incan society, like that of the Aztecs, also made conquest easier; by putting themselves at the apex of power in place of the old Incan rulers, the Spanish assumed command of the whole—although factional disputes among the Spaniards delayed final consolidation of their power until the 1570s. The conquest of the Mayan people of the Yucatán peninsula and Guatemala, who lacked a central government, was more difficult. The campaign against the Mayans began in 1527, but it took eighteen years for the Spanish to establish control.

From Peru, expeditions of discovery and conquest extended out to Chile and Colombia. Other Spaniards from Mexico City journeyed to parts of Central America unclaimed by Europeans and then to the north. Francisco Vásquez de Coronado marched into New Mexico and ventured as far north as Kansas in 1540 and 1541, and Juan Rodriguez Cabrillo

Francisco Pizarro.

sailed up the California coast and took possession of that land for Spain in 1542. When neither these explorers nor their successors found new empires rich in gold and silver, interest in North America declined. In 1565, the Spanish founded a post at St. Augustine in Florida—the first permanent European settlement in North America—mainly to protect the route of the treasure ships that carried vast cargoes of precious metals from Peru and Mexico to Spain. That outpost was originally part of an elaborate scheme by the *adelantado* Pedro Menéndez de Avilés to establish a settlement in Florida from which the Spanish could control the east coast of North America. By 1600, only St. Augustine remained as a monument to Menéndez's failed dreams. A military outpost with some 500 people, mostly men who lived on government salaries, St. Augustine was sufficiently costly and its continued strategic value so questionable that the Crown decided to abandon it in 1606. Only the pleas of Franciscan missionaries that converted Indians needed access to the sacraments and that the missions needed military protection changed the mind of Spain's "most Christian King." As a result, that isolated Spanish base survived and then slowly grew, so that by 1700 St. Augustine held perhaps 1,500 people, including black slaves and Hispanized Indians.

The story of New Mexico was much the same. The *adelantado* there was Juan de Oñate, a wealthy, Mexican-born man from a high-ranking family, who formally took possession of New Mexico in 1598. He had promised the Spanish king, who gave Oñate permission to settle the area at his own expense, "a new world, greater than New Spain." Oñate dreamed of rich mines, abundant Indian laborers, and an easy passageway to the Atlantic or the Pacific, both of which he believed were so near that New Mexico could be supplied by sea. But within a year, his dreams began to go sour: hungry soldiers threatened mutiny; Spanish abuse provoked a revolt by the pueblo of Acoma, which Oñate's soldiers brutally repressed; and many colonists, fearing starvation, fled to Mexico. Bankrupt and charged with mismanagement, Oñate lost his commission in 1606, and the settlement of what a Spanish official called that "worthless land," hundreds of miles beyond the nearest settlements in northern Mexico, was nearly abandoned. Again the pleas of Franciscan missionaries secured the colony's survival. Through most of the seventeenth century, the Villa Real de Santa Fe (1610) was New Mexico's only municipality, though another community grew up after 1659 at El Paso del Norte (today Ciudad Juárez). Meanwhile, Hispanic settlers, who never numbered more than 3,000 before 1700, spread out along the Rio Grande to take advantage of Indian labor. The Spanish waited until late in the eighteenth century to establish frontier garrisons (*presidios*) and missions in California at San Diego (1769), Monterey (1770), and San Francisco (1776).

Charles V (r. 1516–56) was the embodiment of Spanish power in this period.

In short, the Spanish found what they sought in Central and South America: sources of wealth greater even than what Portugal gained from trade with Asia. The Crown would have trouble enough establishing its authority over that mainland empire given the independent, ambitious men who had taken possession of the Indians and their lands. As for the relatively barren territory to Mexico's north that Spain also claimed, there was no reason to pay the cost of consolidating her hold on it. In effect, most of North America was left to the Indian peoples who already lived there. In time, that terrain would provide bases for European nations who joined the contest for America relatively late and had to take whatever lands they could get.

IMPERIAL GOVERNMENT

The Spanish Crown actively asserted and protected its authority over the territories it claimed in the Americas. The fate of Columbus was symptomatic: in 1492, Queen Isabel not only gave him permission to explore, but made him "Viceroy and Governor" of whatever islands in the ocean he might discover. But once the Crown received reports of misgovernment in Hispaniola, it quickly removed Columbus from that position and replaced him. Later, in the sixteenth century, the Crown instituted an imperial governing structure in which ultimate power, in theory and often in fact, rested in its hands.

The Crown exercised its authority over the Spanish American empire through the Council of the Indies, an institution created in 1524 out of the Council of Castile, the queen's closest advisers. The Council of the Indies, which remained in Spain, drafted and issued laws for Spain's American territories and served as an appellate judicial court for civil cases that arose in the colonies. It also nominated both religious and secular officers and actively monitored their conduct in America, replacing those who were inept, corrupt, or in any way disloyal to the Crown.

Viceroys were the highest Spanish imperial officials in America. The viceroy of New Spain (first appointed in 1535) presided over the territories north of the Isthmus of Panama; that of New Castile (1544) governed Peru. Later, the Crown established other viceroyalties. The men appointed as viceroys were almost always born in Spain—*peninsulares,* not Creoles, or persons of Spanish blood born in America—and held office at the queen's or king's pleasure. They had responsibility for executing the Council of the Indies' edicts, maintaining civil and military order, and overseeing the collection of revenues, the administration of justice, and Indian welfare—in short, for all aspects of Spanish rule in the colonies.

Audiencias, advisory and judicial bodies that could also do some provisional legislating for the territory under their supervision, were a step lower on the imperial hierarchy. There were more of them in America than there were viceroyalties, which they often predated: *audiencias* were founded for Santo Domingo in 1511, Mexico City in 1528, Panama in 1538. They answered directly to the Council of the Indies. The system of rule also included a variety of local governments whose officers were at first appointed by the viceroys or *audiencias,* but later became Crown appointees. Municipal councils that once involved popular participation also gradually became closed bodies controlled by the Crown. By 1700, little remained of municipal autonomy.

The pattern was consistent: the Crown and its advisers worked to undercut the development of contrary interests and competing sources of power. Local governments remained royal agencies, or the province of powerful families who acted as adjuncts of the Crown. Even regional assemblies that once advised imperial officials failed to develop into autonomous bodies with bonds to the local population; they were dominated by royal agents and met only when called by Crown officials. The exclusion of "heretics" from the colonies had a similar effect. No religious cleavages would divide the Spanish population of the New World, nor would there be communities of colonists at odds with the Crown's militant Catholicism.

The Spanish Crown selected as colonial officials only persons highly likely to remain its loyal servants; that was the point of appointing viceroys who were Spanish-born. In the entire history of the Spanish empire, up into the nineteenth century, only four viceroys were American-born. Creoles were generally considered only for lower positions—and not in the regions where they were born, to which they might feel an affiliation that compromised their complete loyalty to the Crown. Viceroys' conduct in office was also monitored through *visitas,* special commissions that visited incumbents to examine their enforcement of critical laws, or *residencias,* formal hearings held at the end of their commission. Retired viceroys could be punished severely for deviations from strict loyalty to the Crown when they were in office.

To be sure, the system was more perfect on paper than in reality. The communications system of the sixteenth and seventeenth centuries, which required months if not years for reports of problems to arrive in Spain and the appropriate orders conveyed back to America, limited the Crown's capacity to control its empire. Official inaction frequently greeted unpopular laws or edicts, and little could be done to make the system more responsive. "If death came from Madrid," one Spanish official commented, "we should all live to be very old men." The greatest threat to Crown dominance came, however, in the persons of the *encomenderos,* local strongmen who had received grants of rights over groups of Indians. Not only was their exploitation of the natives at odds with the Crown's religious sense of responsibility for the Indians' well-being, but the *encomenderos* became a locus of power potentially at odds with the Crown.

In one way after another, Spain attempted to stem the power of the *encomenderos.* It forbade the granting of more *encomiendas,* then declared that those in existence could not be passed on to *encomenderos'* heirs. When that edict proved unenforceable, the Crown attempted to limit the number of generations that could receive an *encomienda* by right of inheritance. These edicts more than any others tested the effectiveness of the Crown in maintaining its dominance. In the end, it won out over the *encomenderos*—not so much because of its power to force compliance, but because of a development that it by no means desired. A massive decline in the Indian population gradually undercut the power of the *encomenderos.* And so the pyramidal structure of Spanish imperial governance remained in place, providing both a model and a point of contrast for subsequent European regimes in the Americas.

The Columbian Exchange

What allowed Cortés and a few hundred Spaniards to defeat the Aztecs, who vastly outnumbered them? For one thing, his recruitment of allies among Indians discontented with Aztec rule redressed the imbalance of numbers. And Cortés, like Columbus, was lucky: he arrived in the first year of a fifty-two-year cycle in the Aztec calendar, just when, according to prophecy, the god Quetzalcoatl ("feathered serpent") would return from the East. It is possible that Montezuma thought Cortés was the returning god, which would help explain why he welcomed the Spaniard to Tenochtitlán.

Or did European technology explain the Spanish conquest? Cortés and other *conquistadores* carried gunpowder, which Europe had received from China. And the Spaniards' cannons and primitive, slow-loading muskets, or *harquebuses*, which were less accurate than the traditional crossbow, still provoked terror and panic among the Indians, who had no previous acquaintance with firearms. The Indians were also terrified by the horses the Spaniards rode, and by their mastiffs, huge dogs that could rip men apart, so different from the small dogs Mexicans knew. Nevertheless, the Aztecs recovered sufficiently to force the Spaniards from Tenochtitlán, raising the very real prospect that their conquest would be short-lived. Then Spanish technical advantages really came into play as they built, in effect, a navy, which, with their horsemen, Indian allies, and a ferocity born from desperation, allowed them to seize what remained of the city.

Spaniards on horses as depicted in a wall painting at Canyon de Chelly, in Arizona.

The Spanish also possessed a deadly, unseen ally that tipped the balance in their favor: smallpox. After Cortés and his men had been driven from the city, according to an Indian account, "there came amongst us a great sickness. . . . It raged amongst us, killing vast numbers of people. It covered many all over with sores: on the face, on the head, on the chest, everywhere." Many died of the disease and others of starvation because "there was no one left alive to care for them." The pestilence lasted for "sixty days of horror," then diminished. "And when this had happened, the Spaniards returned." Smallpox seems also to have claimed the ruler of the Incas, which led to a division between claimants for his office that Pizarro used to great effect.

Diseases brought from Europe devastated the populations of the Americas. They were, however, only part of the "Columbian exchange"—a vast, complex intercontinental transfer of goods, plants, animals, and diseases that occurred in the wake of 1492. The results were more far-reaching than anyone anticipated.

DISEASE AND DEMOGRAPHY

When Columbus arrived, most and perhaps all the peoples of the Americas had been isolated from other parts of the world for thousands of years. They were also descended from peculiarly healthy ancestors. The weak and the sick were unlikely to join those parties of long-distance hunters who made their way across Beringia or the islands to its south, and any who died in the cold lands of the north were left there, with whatever infectious agents had caused their illnesses. Later, after Europeans had arrived, Indians could look back on earlier times with longing. "There was then no sickness," recalled a Mayan from Mexico's Yucatán peninsula, "they had no aching bones; they had then no high fever; . . . they had no burning chest" or "abdominal pain" or "consumption" or "headache," and "the course of humanity was orderly. The foreigners made it otherwise when they arrived here." In truth, however, the pre-Columbian peoples of America were far from disease-free. Ancient skeletons and deposits of human waste yield evidence that Indians suffered from dietary deficiencies, intestinal parasites of one sort or another, tuberculosis, and syphilis. The earliest Americans probably also suffered from various bacterial or viral infections whose presence defies detection after so long a passage of time.

But the Indians had had no exposure and so developed no resistance to many illnesses of fifteenth-century Europe. Those diseases, which were often contracted from airborne bacteria or viruses, proved to be even more deadly in the New World than they were in the Old. Smallpox appeared on Hispaniola in 1519, then spread to the mainland, wiping out large numbers of native people. Individuals who survived smallpox might then succumb to measles, influenza, mumps, typhus,

This Aztec drawing shows some victims of a smallpox epidemic in shrouds (center), while two others, covered with pox, are dying at the right.

diphtheria, or plague, which swept through the islands and then the mainland's population in waves after 1493.

What percentage of the native population died in the immediate aftermath of the European arrival? To answer requires knowing what the American population was in 1492, and on that there is no consensus. Estimates range from just over 8 million to 100 million. (By contrast, the population of the kingdoms of Castile and Aragon—contemporary Spain—was under 7 million in 1492, and in 1500 the population of all Europe, east as well as west, was about 70 million.) One study of the Valley of Mexico estimates the population there at about 25 million in 1519, when Cortés arrived, and 1 million in 1600—a decline of 96 percent. Even if the original population was substantially lower, say 10 million, then dropped to 2 million, the decline was still on the order of 80 percent. No doubt acts of Spanish brutality, which **Fray Bartolomé de Las Casas** carefully described in his *Brief Account of the Destruction of the Indies*, a report submitted to the Hapsburg emperor Charles V in 1540, contributed to the problem. If Las Casas and other observers were correct, the Indians not only

suffered from overwork, but were so demoralized that they frequently chose not to bear children. But steep population declines occurred even among the scattered peoples of North America who remained free of subjection to the Spanish or any other European power. Disease and depopulation, in fact, often preceded the arrival of Europeans. That was true, for example, in sixteenth-century Peru, and again in seventeenth-century New England, where Indians "died in heaps" during a severe epidemic before the English colonists arrived. It did not require a European to transmit European diseases: that could be done very effectively by contagious Indians who traveled from place to place infecting others, after even brief contacts with European explorers or fishermen.

Nor were Europeans untouched by illness: the influenza that arrived in Hispaniola with Columbus's second voyage in late 1493 struck down settlers as well as Indians. By 1495, the combined effects of hunger and illness had reduced the newly arrived Spanish population by two-thirds. Columbus himself became deadly sick on several voyages, and in 1500 a missionary reported that all his fellow friars were in bad health and that "here one finds oneself always somewhat ill." Over the next centuries, one group of Europeans after another went through a trying period of seasoning before their bodies adjusted to American conditions. But Spaniards and other Europeans who had contracted diseases such as smallpox, measles, or mumps as children were immune for life, which meant they could sometimes sleep in the same cabin with dying Indians without suffering any ill effects. Europeans were, however, vulnerable to syphilis, a disease that appeared in a new and severe form in Europe soon after Columbus first returned, and so probably (though not certainly) came from America. Syphilis has devastating effects, particularly when it first appears in a population, but it spreads more slowly than diseases like smallpox since it is transmitted sexually. Its impact on the European population was thus nowhere near that of European diseases on America.

Whatever the percentage decline in the Indian population, the results were catastrophic, and hardly pleasing to the Spanish, who were counting on the Indians to be their labor force. In the Caribbean, where the native population disappeared altogether, the Spanish soon began importing African slaves to take their places. On the mainland, where the base populations were greater, the decline stopped short of extinction, and eventually the Indian population began to recover. By then, however, European hegemony was firmly established. Complete cultural recovery was impossible. Massive death broke the lines of transmission by which the old told the stories they had heard as children to the young and enjoined them to carry on the ways of their ancestors. Not even cultures whose past was recorded escaped: afraid that the written books of the Mayas perpetuated idolatry and superstition, the Spanish destroyed as many of them as they could. The presence of the Spaniards and the plants, animals, religious practices, and ways of doing things they brought with them altered the Indians' world in such far-reaching ways that survival itself required that they adapt to circumstances different from anything their ancestors had known.

PLANTS AND ANIMALS

While the human populations of the Americas declined, their animal populations—or, more exactly, that of animals imported from Europe—multiplied. The Spaniards wanted meat and imported pigs—not the docile, slothful animals of modern farms, nor wild boars, but lean, mean animals that could survive on their own in the wild. And more than survive: one account claimed that two dozen hogs shipped to Cuba in 1498 had grown to 30,000 within some sixteen years. Explorers customarily left sets of pigs on uninhabited islands as a ready source of food in the future. They also brought sheep, goats, and, above all, cattle, which again quickly multiplied—and caused immense distress by invading Indians' unfenced fields and consuming their crops. In the short run, the importation of European animals contributed to the Indians' malnutrition and susceptibility to disease; in the long run, however, it added to the food supply because cattle transformed grass into meat. Cattle also provided hides for leather, which itself became a major export as well as an important new product for domestic consumption, and tallow for making candles—one of the most important devices the Spanish added to Indian life, a relatively safe way to banish the dark of night.

Chickens (and so eggs, another welcome addition to the Indians' diets), rats, and cats were also imports, as were mules and oxen, the first draft animals many Indians saw. Horses, too, came on Spanish ships back to America, where their ancestors began. Horses were critical to Spanish rule, since they allowed the rapid movement of orders, information, and, most important, soldiers across great distances. In effect, the horse served as one of the first American communications systems. Moreover, once horses escaped into great grasslands like those in northern Mexico and the North American plains, they formed enormous herds with mounts for any person

who could capture them. Only then did formerly settled, agricultural Indians such as the Sioux or Comanches of the North American West become hunters and horsemen whose riding and shooting skills would slow down European invasions of their lands.

The Spanish also imported plants such as olive trees for oil and grapevines for wine, but these crops did not thrive everywhere in America. Spaniards preferred wheat to corn, and by the mid–sixteenth century Mexico was producing enough wheat that it could export grain to the Caribbean. And rice (originally from Southeast Asia) and bananas (from Africa) did well in wet lowlands where not much else would grow. The Spanish imported some other plants inadvertently. Grass and weed seeds, hidden in dirt or dung or in the cuffs of clothing, soon spread on fields overgrazed by the prolific new livestock, gradually replacing native ground cover. Kentucky bluegrass, daisies, and dandelions are among these imports.

The most portentous imported plant was, however, sugarcane. Spain's Muslim population originally taught Spanish Christians how to grind sugarcanes to extract their juice, then boil the juice down to produce sugar. Northern Europeans developed a taste for the sweet stuff at the time of the Crusades, when they came into contact with Mediterranean Muslims. By the fifteenth century, the European demand for sugar was strong and on the rise. Portugal began growing sugar profitably on Madeira and Spain in the Canaries and then, beginning in 1493, in the Caribbean, where it thrived. From there, the crop spread to those extensive parts of the Ameri-

Arawak hunters carrying a wild hog to the village. The Arawaks apparently considered pork, the meat of hogs introduced into the Americas by the Spaniards, particularly nourishing.

can mainland with adequate sun and rain. The Spanish cultivated sugar from the Gulf of Mexico down into South America, but within a century Portuguese Brazil became an even greater producer, with hundreds of mills turning out thousands of tons of sugar for European markets. High profits from sugar sales allowed planters to continue purchasing African slaves wherever Indian sources of labor declined or disappeared. Indeed, sugar production was a major reason for the importation of some 9.5 million African slaves to the Americas between 1505 and the late nineteenth century. That development, too, altered the demography of the New World: in the Caribbean, above all, blacks soon outnumbered all other peoples.

Animals and plants moved not just from east to west, but also in the reverse direction. And although American animals rarely became more than curiosities in Europe, American plants were something else again. Explorers quickly noted the unfamiliarity of many American trees and other plants and brought seeds or specimens home, where they were absorbed into newly founded botanical gardens so quickly and thoroughly that even experts lost track of what came from where. Agricultural plants produced the greatest impact. America, for example, gave Italy the tomato, France the string bean, and Ireland the potato, to say nothing of chocolate and raspberries, its gifts to mankind. Tobacco also traveled from America to Europe, where it was welcomed as a means of preventing or curing illnesses, though before long critics of the addictive stuff, including England's King James I, made their voices heard.

More important, the spread of American crops increased the earth's capacity to feed ever larger numbers of people by allowing a more efficient and productive use of the land. Maize (corn) is the best example: it prospers in soils too dry for rice and too wet for wheat, requires a relatively short growing season, and can feed both humans and cattle. Its caloric yield per unit of land is double that of wheat. The potato grows, like wheat, in temperate climates, but produces more food per unit of land than wheat, and farmers can cultivate it productively on small plots, even at high elevations (as did the Incas in Peru). The sweet potato, again a crop native to America, produces high yields even in bad soils and is resistant to drought. And the thick roots of manioc, or tapioca, a shrub grown in frost-free climates, can be processed into a flour widely used in tropical parts of the world where wheat cannot grow.

People outside the Americas adopted these new crops only slowly, so it took time before the impact of American crops became observable. After 1650, the world's population began to grow dramatically, more than quadrupling in the next 300 years, with that of Europe (including Russia) increasing more than fivefold. The reasons it rose so rapidly are open to debate, but the introduction of American crops surely allowed the earth to sustain the population growth in Europe, Asia, and even Africa. Many people from those continents would later migrate to America, voluntarily or involuntarily, filling the places of those who had died from the diseases Europeans had carried there.

WAYS OF THOUGHT

From the beginning, Columbus and other explorers noted that they were discovering facts about the world "unknown to the ancients," whose learning Renaissance Europe had rediscovered. In fact, Europeans of the fifteenth and sixteenth centuries identified error after error in ancient writings about the world. Finally, in the 1570s, the Antwerp geographer Gerhardus Mercator declared that Ptolemy's *Geography* was no longer useful and that henceforth geographical information should be conveyed in new ways, as did the atlases of his time, great books of maps that presented modern knowledge of the world both artistically and accurately, area by area. To be sure, Mercator's famous "projection"—the mathematically derived lines that governed his depictions of the earth's surface—was built on Ptolemy's own system for defining locations on the earth. But the *Geography*, Mercator maintained, had become so out-of-date that it remained only of historic interest.

The accumulation of new information was by no means confined to geography. Take botany: in the mid–sixteenth century, German and English herbalists, who studied plants and their uses, particularly those of medicinal significance, listed about 500 different plants. That was roughly the number known to the

> *"The introduction of American crops surely allowed the earth to sustain the population growth in Europe, Asia, and even Africa. Many people from those continents would later migrate to America, voluntarily or involuntarily, filling the places of those who had died from the diseases Europeans had carried there."*

ancient world. In the early seventeenth century, a Swiss professor of anatomy and botany described some 6,000 distinct plants; and at the end of that century, an English botanist could catalogue almost 12,000—a twenty-four-fold increase in a century and a half. Many of the new listings came from the Middle East, Africa, and Asia, but soon American specimens added to the total. How could naturalists make sense of their sprawling subject matter? At first, they tried to reconcile new observations with inherited works, suggesting that some new plant might be the same as another known to the ancients, but that was a losing game. The proliferation of known plants strained traditional ways of cataloguing them and led ultimately to the creation of a new unit of taxonomy, the genus, by which the plant world was organized into a more manageable 600 groups.

Beyond these specific developments lay a more basic one: gradually Europeans were becoming less dependent on inherited authority and more inclined to base their knowledge of the world on empirical observations, defining general principles on the basis of known facts. This transformation led in time to what the world would call "science." The conventional event marking the birth of modern science is the publication of Sir Francis Bacon's *Instauratio Magna* (Great Instauration, or restoration) at London in 1620. The cover of that work showed a great ship, with square and lateen sails, moving from the Mediterranean past the pillars of Hercules into the Atlantic Ocean. The voyages of discovery, by which European explorers found the Americas, had become a metaphor for all of mankind's quests for new knowledge.

None of these changes happened quickly. The great age of botanical and biological classification, for example, came some 250–300 years after Columbus first commented on the novelty of American plants and animals. Ancient texts did not immediately loosen their grip on people's minds; indeed, the authority of the Bible retained its power long after the rise of modern science. Moreover, older ways of making sense of experience persisted, particularly that which explained events not as the results of natural forces but as specific, conscious interventions of God in human affairs. From that perspective, the massive deaths of Indians was itself a "wonder" in a now-archaic sense—an extraordinary event that revealed God's will for the world. As one seventeenth-century Protestant clergyman concluded, God sent epidemics to clear New England of "those pernicious creatures," the Indians, "to make room for better growth." At times, the Spanish exhibited a similar way of thought: in the battle for Tenochtitlán, when

The cover of Sir Francis Bacon's *Instauratio Magna* (London, 1620), whose publication is often taken as the starting point of modern science. Here, a great ship of exploration sails from the Mediterranean past the Pillars of Hercules, the western entrance to the Strait of Gibraltar, into the Atlantic Ocean. By 1620, the voyages of exploration had become a metaphor for all of mankind's search for new knowledge.

"the Christians were exhausted from war," a follower of Cortés recalled, "God saw fit to send the Indians smallpox."

Could there be any greater testimony to the Europeans' superiority—and that of the Christian God over Indian gods—than their survival and, indeed, the multiplication of the European population as the Indians' numbers declined? How could Europeans explain the marvelous events that left them in control of so many parts of the New World except as an act of God's providence, and perhaps as a reward for their efforts to repress heathenism in America?

People, like the plants and beasts that populated the earth, were different from one another and so subject to classification, and the categories commonly used once again reflected European assumptions of superiority. By their nakedness,

Chronology		
986	Norse settlement at L'Anse aux Meadows in Newfoundland.
1487–88	Bartholomeu Días sails around Cape of Good Hope.
1492	Christopher Columbus lands in the Bahamas.
1497	John Cabot claims Newfoundland for England.
1497–99	Vasco da Gama sails to India.
1513	Juan Ponce de León explores the Florida coast.
1519–22	Fernando Magellan sails around the world.
1521	Cortés takes Tenochtitlán from the Aztecs.
1534–36	Jacques Cartier explores the St. Lawrence River.
1565	The Spanish found St. Augustine in Florida.

their "idolatrous" religions, their lack of critical skills such as writing, the Indians—particularly those who lived, as observers put it, "without magistrates or republic," were nomadic, or lived in caves like wild beasts—were "barbarians" or "savages" and distinctly backward compared with the "civilized" people of contemporary Europe. The arrival of Europeans did not therefore simply add to an American mosaic of peoples that had been thousands of years in the making. There could be no middle way between idolatry and Christianity, barbarism and civilization, no celebration of diversity. A tolerance of differences seemed to imply that every way of life was equally worthy of respect. Europeans knew that their ways and beliefs were superior and would triumph over all rivals'.

Vast numbers of Indians remained, assisting or resisting the newcomers. In remote parts of America, some continued traditional patterns of life as if little had changed. But Indians who rode on horseback or cooked their meals in iron pots already lived in a world different from that of their ancestors, a world in many ways as new to the Americas' oldest residents as it was for its most recent immigrants. That strange new world would put the Indians' historic skill at adaptation to its most severe test.

Suggested Reading

James Axtell, *Beyond 1492: Encounters in Colonial North America* (1992)

Michael Coe, Michael Dean Snow, and Elizabeth Benson, *Atlas of Ancient America* (1986)

Alfred W. Crosby, *The Columbian Exchange: Biological and Cultural Consequences of 1941* (1972)

Felipe Fernández-Armesto, *Before Columbus: Exploration and Colonisation from the Mediterranean to the Atlantic, 1229–1492* (1991)

Charles Gibson, *Spain in America* (1966)

Stephen Greenblatt, *Marvelous Possessions: The Wonder of the New World* (1991)

Frederick E. Hoxie, *Encyclopedia of North American Indians* (1996)

Karen Ordahl Kupperman, ed., *America in European Consciousness, 1493–1750* (1995)

J. H. Parry, *The Age of Reconnaissance* (1964)

David J. Weber, *The Spanish Frontier in North America* (1992)

■ **What developments in Europe propelled early French and English explorations of North America?**

■ **What were the characteristics of the early French, Dutch, and Swedish colonies?**

■ **How did the British establish their colonies in the Chesapeake?**

■ **What was distinctive about the British colonies in New England?**

In 1600, the Spanish had established only two bases in the lands north of Mexico: a two-year-old settlement in the Southwest, where Juan de Oñate's dream of a New Mexico more glorious than the old was already going bad, and the small, shabby community of soldiers and settlers at St. Augustine, whose future remained far from secure. Aside from the seasonal visits of fishermen to Newfoundland, those fledgling settlements constituted the European presence in North America, tenuous beachheads on a continent still securely possessed by Indians who had lived there since time immemorial.

Spain, however, could no longer depend on an exclusive title to North America based on a papal grant. The pope's jurisdiction, France's King Francis I told the Spanish ambassador in 1540, was spiritual and did not extend to dividing the world's lands among kings. Title to territory in America, as the king saw it, depended on exploration, conquest, and, above all, colonization.

That was easier said than done. Both France and England had tried but failed to establish settlements in North America before 1600. Success demanded sending groups of people to the New World who could survive while performing or getting others to perform activities that enriched the parent state. On that standard, Spain had been conspicuously successful in Mexico and lands farther south, but her example was not of much use—and could be positively misleading—in North America, which had a colder climate, different resources, and fewer native people.

In the first half of the seventeenth century, several northern European nations did found lasting settlements along the St. Lawrence River and on the eastern shore of North America. And those colonies discovered a variety of ways to live in the New World: they differed from one another in their economies, religious traditions, cultures, even their relationships with Indians. Some of the distinctions faded away with time; more often, however, they set patterns whose influence, for better or worse, were felt far into the future.

False Starts

Two dreams first attracted France and England to North America: finding a water route to Asia and discovering kingdoms rich in silver and gold, as the Spanish had done in Mexico and Peru. Those aspirations continued long after their fulfillment seemed highly doubtful. Europeans were also propelled into North America by rivalries that developed during the sixteenth century.

EARLY FRENCH INITIATIVES

Verrazano's voyage of 1524 demonstrated that there was no "northwest passage" below Nova Scotia. As a result, a decade later the French explorer Jacques Cartier headed farther north and sailed up the St. Lawrence. That river, he learned, drained a great landmass, and, moreover, rapids barred all but skilled canoemen from proceeding beyond the Indian village that later became Montreal. In short, the St. Lawrence provided no passageway to China.

After spending the winter of 1535 at Quebec, Cartier and what remained of his crew (twenty-five men failed to survive the season) returned to France. They took along a set of kidnapped Indians who told vague stories of a fantastically rich kingdom just a little farther west of where Cartier had gone. And so the French returned in 1541, but found no more gold-rich nations than did an expedition by the Spaniard Francisco de Coronado in the Southwest during the same year. A second taste of a Canadian winter, moreover, snuffed out for the rest of the century France's desire to found a settlement in that "savage" north country, "uninhabitable" through half the year.

If the French couldn't find gold and silver, perhaps they could seize it—which was one reason they founded Fort Caroline on the Florida coast, near the homeward route of the Spanish treasure ships. Spain had sat back while the French pushed up the St. Lawrence, but this it could not tolerate. Pedro Menéndez de Aviles brutally massacred Fort Caroline's men in 1565, when France and Spain were at peace. The attack provoked France's protests, but not much more. One reason was that Fort Caroline, like a short-lived French settlement on the Carolina coast, was a project of Huguenots, French Protestants who had broken away from the Catholic Church. The French Crown, however, remained Catholic.

LEFT: Martin Luther, whose criticisms of church practices led to a splintering of the Christian community.

RIGHT: John Calvin, who developed the doctrine of predestination, which called into question the efficacy of good works.

On August 24, 1572, a powerful faction of France's Catholic nobility attempted to suppress religious divisions within France by slaughtering Huguenot leaders who had gathered in Paris. That event, the St. Bartholomew's Day Massacre, triggered two decades of civil wars, which prevented further French activity in North America. Many of France's most knowledgeable and ardent proponents of overseas expansion were Huguenots, and those who survived the massacre shared their rich knowledge of the New World with explorers and colonizers from Protestant countries. In that way, and in many others, the great sixteenth-century split in Western Christianity known as the Reformation had a powerful impact on America's future.

THE REFORMATION

In 1492, when Columbus first sailed west, all Christian Europeans acknowledged the spiritual leadership of the pope in Rome. Then, in 1517, Martin Luther, a German monk, nailed a list of ninety-five theses, or propositions for public debate, on the door of a church in the town of Wittenberg. Luther raised the issue of the church's sale of indulgences, credits against time in purgatory that could be bought and stored up by the faithful. He also questioned whether good

works could earn salvation. Some of his arguments had been raised by earlier reformers who also wanted to rid the church of corruption and return to the simpler piety of early Christianity, but Luther went further. He founded his own church. His standard of truth was the Bible and the Bible alone. He rejected saints, fast days, a celibate clergy, transubstantiation (the belief that in the mass, bread and wine are literally transformed into the body and blood of Christ), and all but two sacraments, baptism and holy communion, because he could find no scriptural basis for them. Luther had the Bible translated from Latin into German and encouraged his followers to read it. He also made sermons, presented in the vernacular, and the singing of hymns (some of which he composed) by the congregation important parts of religious services.

The splintering of the Christian community did not end with the founding of Lutheranism. In Germany, a variety of Protestant sects emerged whose beliefs were still more radical than those of Luther's followers. They included pacifists and radical egalitarians who wore plain clothes, refused to respect worldly rank or to take oaths, and rejected infant baptism. Elsewhere, reformers sometimes went in the other direction and established theocratic regimes whose rigid control of both church and state rested on a particular understanding of

God's will. In Geneva, Switzerland, for example, John Calvin—an exiled French Lutheran (the term for French Protestants until the mid–sixteenth century, when they began to be called Huguenots)—founded a tightly governed community under God's "saints," that is, those He knew would be saved and so were predestined for salvation. The Calvinists, as determined believers in predestination, denied that people could in any way earn salvation by acts of will. Their fates were wholly in the hands of God, who could give or withhold saving grace for reasons beyond human understanding or control. In general, however, all Protestants shared Luther's emphasis on the Bible; his belief that faith (belief and trust in God), not works, merited salvation; and his rejection of saints, indulgences, most sacraments, transubstantiation, and many other practices of the Catholic Church, including its insistence on a celibate clergy and submission to the pope's authority. Soon

Europeans divided into two camps, Catholic and Protestant, whose convictions seemed to dictate that they fight each other to the death.

England at first remained on the Catholic side. King Henry VIII (r. 1509–47) denounced Luther's teachings by writing a tract in *Defense of the Seven Sacraments,* for which the pope bestowed on him the title "Defender of the Faith" (which British monarchs still claim today). Then, in 1533, after a twenty-year marriage that produced only one daughter, Henry decided to divorce his Spanish wife, Catherine of Aragon, and marry Anne Boleyn. When the pope refused to give his permission, Henry cut the link between England and Rome. He also dissolved England's monasteries and seized church lands, but changed little else, essentially putting himself in the pope's place as head of the Church of England and leaving the rest in place.

Under the brief reign of Henry's son Edward VI (r. 1547–53), reformers pushed for greater changes in the Church of England. But on Edward's death, his older sister Mary, the Catholic daughter of Henry and Catherine of Aragon and wife of the man who became Philip II of Spain, inherited the throne. She returned England to the pope and tried to purge her realm of Protestants, burning hundreds of them at the stake for their "heretical" beliefs. Many others fled to the Continent, including Calvin's Geneva. After Mary's death in 1558, those "Marian exiles" returned home, anxious to bring English Protestantism nearer in line with the more extensive reforms of continental Europe.

The new queen, Elizabeth I, was securely Protestant; as the daughter of Anne Boleyn, her birth and claim to the throne were illegitimate in the eyes of the Catholic Church. Elizabeth's reign was long, from 1558 to 1603. During that time, England laid the foundations for subsequent overseas expansion.

THE FOUNDATIONS OF ENGLISH EXPANSION

At the time Portugal and Spain were first establishing their American empires, England faced an array of obstacles—diplomatic, reli-

LEFT: Queen Elizabeth I gained the throne at age twenty-five and proved an intelligent, able administrator.

RIGHT: Sir Francis Drake, whose actions it was said were "like a cord laced and knotted round the throat of the Spanish monarchy."

gious, economic, and political—to overseas expansion. During the sixteenth century, however, these constraints disappeared or shifted in ways that encouraged England to claim territory outside the British Isles.

Diplomatic Change. Until the mid–sixteenth century, deference to her ally Spain helped keep England from claiming land in America. After Elizabeth I became queen, however, England and Spain inevitably became enemies. Spain supported the claim to the English throne of Mary, Queen of Scots, a Catholic, over that of Elizabeth, which did not please the woman who was one of England's all-time toughest monarchs. Hostility between the two countries increased after 1566–67, when Spain's King Philip II decided to put down a revolt in the Spanish Netherlands and so began an eighty-year war with Dutch Protestants. Finally, in 1585, England and Spain also went to war.

The Spanish Armada, 130 ships and 30,000 men strong, was devastated by storms and English forces in the summer of 1588.

Religious Change. The conflict between Protestants and Catholics within Europe naturally expanded into a contest in the New World for souls as well as territory, as each side aspired to teach the Indians "true religion" and save them from Catholic or Protestant "heresy." Moreover, Henry VIII's dissolution of England's monasteries freed for overseas expansion young gentlemen who in earlier times might have spent their days cloistered from the world.

Economic Development. The English Reformation (which began with Henry VIII's split from the Catholic Church) coincided with a major transformation in England's economy. In the early sixteenth century, England's commerce focused on selling woolen cloth at a great international market in Antwerp (in Belgium), where English traders received in exchange a wide range of imported merchandise. But after the Antwerp market collapsed in the mid–sixteenth century, the English had to find new ways of selling their exports. For that

purpose, they founded great trading companies such as the Muscovy Company (1555), the Levant Company (1581), and the East India Company (1600), which developed trade routes to Russia, the eastern Mediterranean, and India.

Individual entrepreneurs also joined the search for new sources of profit. In 1562, Sir John Hawkins began a series of voyages to sell slaves from West Africa to colonists in the Caribbean, where Spanish traders had a monopoly. In 1568, the viceroy of Mexico mounted a devastating attack on his fleet, during which Hawkins managed to save only 100 of his 400 men and two of his six ships. After that "outrage," English seamen, like their Huguenot mentors, took to plundering Spanish ships and territory. Sir Francis Drake, who was with Hawkins on the 1568 expedition, became one of the greatest English raiders, a man who was for all practical purposes a pirate, except that, as he noted later in life, the word "pirate" applied only to those who undertook risk "for small things," not for "millions." In 1572, Drake seized Spanish treasure being carried across the Isthmus of Panama; in 1585–86, he plundered Spanish settlements at Santo Domingo and Cartagena; then, for good measure, he burned the Spanish garrison at St. Augustine, Florida, on his way home.

In the course of these events, England became a seafaring nation—a prerequisite for colonizing North America. Despite her island location, England had been a nation of landlubbers in Columbus's day. Even her sixteenth-century trade with Antwerp depended on foreign ships to carry goods across the English Channel. But then King Henry VIII began the task of building a royal navy, and in 1577 Queen Elizabeth I appointed Sir John Hawkins as treasurer of the navy and asked him to restore and expand her father's fleet. Eleven years later, England boasted some twenty-five large or mid-sized ships and eighteen oceangoing pinnaces (ships with both oars and sails), a formidable force for the time. Trading companies and free-wheelers like Drake, who circumnavigated the globe in 1580, also added to England's stock of ships and skilled seamen. These developments explain why English expeditions to find a northwest passage to Asia or to search for gold in North America during Elizabeth's reign were led not by Italians like John Cabot but by natural-born Englishmen such as Martin Frobisher (three voyages, 1576–78) and John Davis (another three, 1585–87). England's historic defeat of the Spanish fleet, the Armada, in 1588 finally announced her arrival among the maritime powers of the world.

The sixteenth century also saw major changes in English mining and metal processing. In 1540, the English introduced use of the blast furnace, in which iron ore was melted down to liquid with a fluxing agent that separated iron from other elements in the ore. The country's annual output of iron rose almost five times in the next century, but still failed to satisfy the demand for utilitarian items such as skillets, trivets, nails, andirons, locks, and keys. Similar advances in glassmaking and textile production added to the list of newly available consumer items that were quickly absorbed into the middle-class's standard of living.

England's ready supplies of coal, lead, and iron ore sustained this early industrial development. But iron mills and glass producers absorbed prodigious amounts of timber. So did shipbuilding (it took over 2,000 large oak trees to build a warship) and the concurrent "great rebuilding" of rural England, as increasingly prosperous landowners built, expanded, and refurnished their homes. By the early seventeenth century, England was in the midst of a timber crisis, with the price of firewood doubling and tripling. That predicament turned English eyes westward, to the densely wooded lands of North America.

Political Consolidation. Overseas expansion required internal territorial and political integrity. But during the fifteenth century, as Portugal began to move into the Atlantic, the British Isles contained several kingdoms whose people spoke a variety of languages. Gradually, they fell under English rule—Wales, to England's west, when Elizabeth's grandfather became King Henry VII, in 1485; Cornwall and Devon in the island's southwest after the Crown crushed uprisings there in the sixteenth century. Scotland remained outside the realm until the accession of James I, the son of Mary, Queen of Scots, in 1603. By then, much of Ireland was also under English control. In this process of expansion, England became Britain, a nation consisting of what once had been separate peoples, and a nation ready to continue extending its dominion outside the British Isles. The English conquest of Ireland, moreover, shaped England's colonization of America, much as Spain's campaign against the Moors produced institutions and attitudes that the Spanish carried to the New World.

> *"The English conquest of Ireland shaped England's colonization of America, much as Spain's campaign against the Moors produced institutions and attitudes that the Spanish carried to the New World."*

THE ENGLISH AND IRELAND

Early seventeenth-century Englishmen spoke not of colonizing America but of "planting," or founding plantations, there. A plantation was a segment of England "transplanted" abroad so it could take root, grow, and mature into a place much like England itself. The English had developed the concept of planting in Ireland, which during the sixteenth century became England's first (to use the more modern word) colony.

England's claims to Ireland went back to when Anglo-Norman conquerors invaded Ireland during the twelfth century. But by 1485, when Henry VII became king, English control of Ireland was limited to the English Pale, a narrow strip on the island's east coast that extended from a few miles south of the English capital at Dublin north to Dundalk. The rest of Ireland ("beyond the Pale") consisted of fifty or sixty little kingdoms ruled by chiefs who were either of native Irish descent or "Old English"—that is, the descendants of Normans who had become in name, manners, even language almost indistinguishable from the native Irish.

Ireland was important to England because it lay sufficiently near England's west coast to serve as a center of intrigue for factions within England and for her enemies on the European Continent. Its location also made Ireland a potential threat to England's expanding trade. In the early sixteenth century, the English Crown tried to secure greater control over Ireland by negotiating agreements with Irish chieftains. When that failed, the English concluded that they could not work with the natives and so attempted to pacify and Anglicize Ireland by repopulating it with people from England.

The first plantations were located in the Midlands, an area from which the "wild Irish" could mount raids on the Pale, and the next in Munster, in the southwest of Ireland. In the early seventeenth century, the English founded still another plantation to the north in Ulster, where the native Irish were deeply entrenched. After suppressing an insurrection there, the English declared the land forfeit, expelled the old owners, and made plans for resettling Ulster with emigrants from England and now also Scotland. As in earlier plantations, many Irish actually stayed on their old lands as tenants. Others fled into the woods and made occasional plundering expeditions on the plantations while waiting for a chance to overthrow them altogether. The plantations necessarily became military outposts; and "planters" concluded that there could be no living with the native Irish unless they somehow consented to adopt English "civilitie."

The English carried that conclusion to America, where the Indians seemed to them much like the Irish. The English told, for example, of Indians wearing "large mantels of deare skins not much differing in fashion from the Irish mantels," and compared Indians' leggings with "Irish trousers." The Indians' way of building houses also seemed "much like the wild Irish." And both people fought in similarly "savage" ways, letting out "horrible shouts and screeches" at the start of battles like "infernall hellhounds." Moreover, many of the people involved in planting Ireland later helped plant America. They included Sir Francis Drake and Sir Humphrey Gilbert (who was knighted for service in Ireland) as well as Gilbert's half-brother Sir Walter Raleigh, who made the first efforts to found English settlements in North America.

HAKLUYT AND ENGLAND'S VISION OF AMERICA

The story of Gilbert and Raleigh begins with their supporter, Richard Hakluyt the younger, an English geographer and historian who never visited America but strenuously encouraged English overseas expansion. In 1587, Hakluyt published his great work, *The Principall Navigations, Voyages, and Traffics of the English Nation,* which he then enlarged into a massive, three-volume documentary record of previous English voyages (1598– 1600) meant to inspire further explorations. He is also known for his *Discourse of Western Planting,* a treatise written in 1584 to persuade Queen Elizabeth to support English efforts to found plantations in America. In the end, the queen decided that private enterprise would have to foot the bill. Hakluyt's *Discourse* remains nonetheless a splendid summary of the most advanced English thinking on the benefits American colonies would bring.

A depiction by John Speed of a "wild Irish" man (left) and woman (1616).

"Broad Quay," full of ships, in Bristol, a port in England's West Country, during the early eighteenth century.

English plantations, Hakluyt believed, would "inlarge the glory of the gospell and from England plante sincere [that is, Protestant] religion," and if the English would "seate and plante there in time," they would keep "the spanishe kinge from flowinge over all the face of . . . America." The Indians, Hakluyt said, would remain quiet and contented, since the English would treat them with "humanitie, curtesie, and freedome," unlike the Spanish. Indeed, when word of England's kindly rule spread, the Spanish king's Indian subjects would "revolte cleane from the Spaniarde" and "yelde themselves" to Elizabeth's government. North America would also provide a fine market for English wool and a source of goods that England had otherwise to buy from other European nations. Further, America could supply the Royal Navy with masts, pitch, tar, and hemp. Since merchants would not venture across the Atlantic except with ships of "greate burden," trade with America would serve to increase England's overall naval strength.

England's American plantations, Hakluyt assumed, would provide a refuge for Protestants "from all partes of the worlde." But most immigrants to British America would be English, and foreigners would, of course, adopt English ways and rule. Just which Englishmen would migrate? Sol-diers too unruly to be absorbed at home once wars ended, young men ruined by debt or who "by some folly of youthe . . . are not able to live in England," the children of wandering beggars, unemployed seamen, indeed the unemployed of all types "hurtfull and burdensome to this Realme." Such troublesome folk could be "unladen" in America, where they would magically become a productive people serving England and "their own more happy state."

Hakluyt's vision of migration and personal transformation reflected a sense of social crisis that pervaded England in the 1580s. The population of England and Wales was expanding rapidly: between 1500 and 1650, it grew from less than 3 million to over 5 million people. When Hakluyt wrote, moreover, landlords were enclosing their lands—fencing off open fields, which were then used for intensive agriculture or, more often, for pasture—and evicting tenants. An extraordinary rise in the price of rents as well as of other basic goods, including cereals, meat, and wood and other building materials, made survival in the countryside increasingly difficult for those who did not own or hold secure leases on land. Some took up marginal plots on the outer edges of England's settled areas. More often, people migrated to towns and ports such as York, Bristol, Newcastle, or Norwich, whose populations doubled and tripled in the century between 1550 and 1650, or to London, which grew almost tenfold, from a city of 60,000 in 1500 to one of 550,000 people in 1700. There, in the urban centers, England's "excess," unsettled people were highly visible: they were not scattered and hidden in obscure rural enclaves, but gathered together where they were hard to ignore.

But would the people England wanted to get rid of make good colonists? Hakluyt did not ask that question. For him and his countrymen, interest in America rested not only on a pull, a desire to reap predictable gains, but a powerful push, to relieve the home country of a real and growing burden. "If Englande crie oute and affirme that there is so many in all trades that one cannot live for another as in all places they do," Hakluyt said, then a colony in North America "offreth the remedie."

SIR HUMPHREY GILBERT

Gilbert, a soldier and courtier from the southwest part of England ("the West Country"), seems to have first picked up the idea of colonizing North America from Huguenots who had tried to establish bases in Carolina and Florida during the 1560s. But first he went off to the plantation in Munster, where he was known for his severity against the native Irish. Then, in 1578, the queen gave him license to found a settlement in an uninhabited part of North America within the next six years. In 1583, after making plans for his new colony and selling some lands there to finance the venture, Gilbert set out to have a look at the place. He claimed Newfoundland for the English Crown as John Cabot had once done, studied the coast for possible sources of precious metals, then decided to return home and gather support for further expeditions. But his ship went down in a storm off the Azores. Gilbert was last seen, the story goes, with a book in his hands, shouting out, "We are as near heaven by sea as by land."

SIR WALTER RALEIGH

A year after Gilbert's death, Queen Elizabeth granted Gilbert's half-brother Walter Raleigh an extension of Gilbert's patent. Raleigh's attention shifted from the northern regions to the coastlands south of the Chesapeake Bay, which, as a tribute to his "virgin Queen," he named Virginia. In April 1585, Raleigh sent Sir Richard Grenville (a buddy from Ireland) to Roanoke Island off North Carolina with seven vessels carrying 108 settlers. Early reports said the place was a paradise with a pleasing climate and fertile soil, and that the local "savages" were "most corteous, and very desirous to have clothes." But the English proved unwilling and perhaps incapable of

doing anything to feed themselves except demand food from the native people, who had no great excess to give away. And when the Indians tried to get rid of their rapacious, uninvited guests, the English governor, Ralph Lane (who again had been involved in planting Ireland), killed the chief and his advisers. Then the hungry settlers hitched a ride to England with Sir Francis Drake, who had stopped at Roanoke after torching St. Augustine.

Grenville, who had sailed back to England for supplies, returned to find the Roanoke colony deserted. When he left again, fifteen men remained on the island. Indians killed some; the rest tried to sail away, then disappeared altogether. Not content to leave bad enough alone, Raleigh sent another 117 men, women, and children to America in 1587 under the leadership of John White, an artist who had joined the earlier expedition to sketch the plants, animals, and people of the New World. Although Raleigh wanted this new expedition to

These watercolors by John White portray an Indian woman and child and an Indian town called Secoton. Note the neatly arranged tobacco and corn fields (and an enclosure, upper right, for a "watcherman" who scared birds and "beasts" away from the corn with "continual cryes and noyse"), scattered buildings, and a religious ritual being performed (lower right). White's subjects lived in coastal North Carolina in the late sixteenth century.

The 1590 edition of Thomas Hariot's *A Briefe and True Report of the New Found Land of Virginia* included a series of engravings by Theodore De Bry based on John White's paintings and drawings of the Indians. This example shows the Indians' "verye wonderfull" way of making boats by burning out the center of a log and scraping away the destroyed wood with shells.

settle farther north in the Chesapeake Bay area, it ended up on Roanoke again, with predictable results. White went back to England; when he returned to Roanoke in 1590, he found the settlement deserted, his books in ruins, the armor he had carefully brought to America turning to rust. "Croatoan," the name of a nearby island, had been carved on a post. But no trace of the settlers was ever found.

England remained without a base on the North American continent. Raleigh's expeditions produced, however, one enduring document: *A Briefe and True Report of the New Found Land of Virginia* (1588), by Thomas Hariot, a mathematician who joined the first expedition to observe the country's natural resources. Hariot, who tried to learn the Indians' language before going to America, gave a detailed and essentially sympathetic account of the native people. A 1690 edition of Hariot's book included **engravings by Theodore De Bry** based on John White's drawings of the Indians. These pictorial images introduced Europeans to a dignified Indian people who lived in ordered villages surrounded by carefully cultivated fields and who exercised considerable ingenuity, for example, by burning away parts of logs to help shape them into boats. De Bry's Indians even looked remarkably like the "barbarian" ancestors of contemporary Englishmen, whom the book also

portrayed. Apparently no intrinsic inferiority distinguished "savage" Americans from "civilized" Europeans, and so, with time, the former could become like the latter. Indeed, a people so inventive in building communities and boats or creating ingenious devices for fishing, as another engraving indicated, were already partway there. Hariot's text and De Bry's prints suggested that North America might not replay the history of Ireland.

Hariot was all for trying to found another settlement. The problem at Roanoke, he said, was with settlers who missed their soft English beds and did nothing but complain. Nonetheless, the fate of Raleigh's colony along with England's war with Spain, which continued until 1604, put an end to English colonizing efforts through the rest of the sixteenth century.

True Beginnings

By the time the English began planting again, they had neighbors. France, and later the Netherlands and Sweden, also established settlements along the Atlantic coast in the early seventeenth century.

NEW FRANCE

Cartier's sixteenth-century explorations did not find rich and populous empires to conquer like those of the Aztecs and Incas, but the French eventually discovered a more modest reason for maintaining a presence in North America. Beaver pelts, bought from the Indians, found a profitable market in Europe, where they were made into fashionable felt hats. French fishermen along the northern coast began that trade. They processed their catch for shipment home by cleaning, salting down, and packing large fish, which could not be dried successfully. Smaller fish, which they filleted and dried on racks, brought a better price, and the drying process required that fishermen dawdle on shore, which in turn gave them a chance to know and trade with the local Indians. Fish paid for the voyages, and pelts obtained from the Indians added profits that eventually became an attraction in themselves.

In 1606, a company of merchants to whom the French Crown granted a monopoly of trade established a year-round base at Port Royal on the Bay of Fundy. Two years later, the company began another at Quebec under the leadership of Samuel de Champlain. The St. Lawrence narrowed at Quebec,

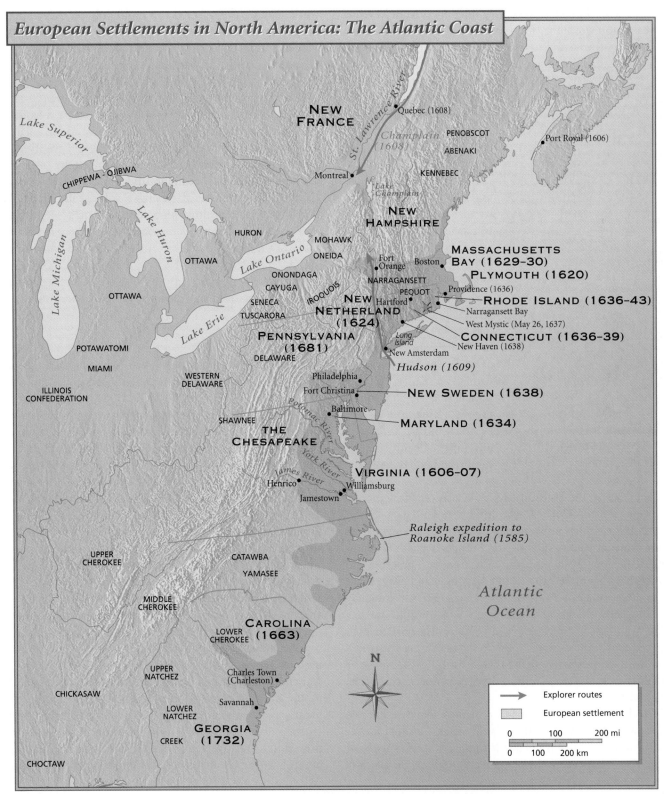

European Settlements in North America: The Atlantic Coast

Lake Superior

NEW FRANCE

Quebec (1608)

St. Lawrence River

Champlain 1608

PENOBSCOT

Port Royal (1606)

ABENAKI

CHIPPEWA - OJIBWA

Montreal

Lake Champlain

KENNEBEC

NEW HAMPSHIRE

Lake Michigan

Lake Huron

HURON

MOHAWK

Lake Ontario

ONEIDA

Fort Orange

Boston

MASSACHUSETTS BAY (1629–30)

OTTAWA

ONONDAGA

PLYMOUTH (1620)

NARRAGANSETT

OTTAWA

CAYUGA

IROQUOIS

PEQUOT

Providence (1636)

RHODE ISLAND (1636–43)

SENECA

NEW NETHERLAND (1624)

Hartford

Narragansett Bay

West Mystic (May 26, 1637)

TUSCARORA

Lake Erie

CONNECTICUT (1636–39)

POTAWATOMI

PENNSYLVANIA (1681)

Long Island

New Haven (1638)

New Amsterdam

MIAMI

DELAWARE

Hudson (1609)

WESTERN DELAWARE

Philadelphia

ILLINOIS CONFEDERATION

Fort Christina

NEW SWEDEN (1638)

Potomac River

Baltimore

MARYLAND (1634)

SHAWNEE

THE CHESAPEAKE

York River

James River

VIRGINIA (1606–07)

Henrico

Williamsburg

Jamestown

Raleigh expedition to Roanoke Island (1585)

UPPER CHEROKEE

CATAWBA

YAMASEE

Atlantic Ocean

MIDDLE CHEROKEE

CAROLINA (1663)

LOWER CHEROKEE

N

UPPER NATCHEZ

Charles Town (Charleston)

CHICKASAW

Savannah

LOWER NATCHEZ

GEORGIA (1732)

CREEK

CHOCTAW

Explorer routes

European settlement

0   100   200 mi

0   100   200 km

so it was an ideal site for preventing interlopers from traveling further inland. Since the Iroquois who had once occupied that area near Quebec had died or left, the new settlers could begin growing food, ending their dependence on unreliable supply ships from Europe, without displacing Indians from the land.

This watercolor sketch by a Jesuit in New France shows native fishing techniques.

The Quebec settlement existed, however, not to grow crops for export, but to trade furs. That demanded good relations with the Indians in surrounding areas, as did the other great activity that brought the French to Canada: the harvesting of souls. Franciscan missionaries first performed that work; then, after 1625, Jesuits took over. The Jesuits were willing to go to the Indians and share their ways of life, risking their own lives in the process, and without insisting that the Indians entirely conform to French "civilization."

After joining an Indian war party, Champlain became acquainted with the water route that linked the St. Lawrence to the Hudson River. He also established trade relations with the Hurons, who lived between Lakes Huron and Ontario and became trading middlemen, exchanging furs from more northern Indians for European goods. Indians taught the French to make birchbark canoes, graceful and wonderfully light boats that could carry men and heavy loads of trading goods over inland rivers. The French gradually came to know the Great Lakes region, which would one day be part of France's North American empire. They had, in fact, claimed the foremost water route to the interior of the continent. In 1642, they strengthened their control of that route by establishing a post at the falls of the St. Lawrence, which they called Montréal.

The French hold on Canada remained weak in the late 1620s, when King Louis XIII's first minister, Cardinal Richelieu, oversaw the creation of a new company, the Company of New France, to develop the settlements and foster missionary work. The Crown granted it a monopoly on everything but fishing. In return, the company had to settle at least 4,000 French Catholics in North America within fifteen years. No Huguenots could go: religious dissension would divide the colony and compromise its Catholic missionary work.

The first contingent of 400 new immigrants arrived in 1628, when Quebec had only 60–80 colonists, a handful of buildings, and maybe twenty acres of farmland. To encourage migration, the Company of New France tried granting long, narrow plots of land along the St. Lawrence to "seigneurs," who then imported more settlers at their own cost. The church also bought land and prepared it for settlement. Support came from wealthy, pious Catholics who were perhaps inspired by the *Jesuit Relations*, an account of Jesuit activities that was published annually from 1632 to 1673 and circulated among educated people. Despite these efforts, however, the colony grew very slowly. By 1650, New France's population stood at about 2,000, and its future remained uncertain.

NEW NETHERLAND

The story was much the same to the south along the Hudson River, where the Dutch West India Company established a colony, New Netherland, on lands Henry Hudson described after sailing the ship *Half Moon* (in 1609) up the river that now carries his name. Fifteen years later, the first major contingent of settlers, mainly French-speaking Walloons from what today is Belgium, arrived in New Netherland and established bases on the Delaware and Connecticut Rivers and at the site of an older trading post, which became Fort Orange, on the Hudson River where Albany now stands. Since large ships could navigate the Hudson for some 150 miles inland, the river provided a splendid route to the interior of the continent and the Indians who traded furs there. In 1626, however, the Dutch abandoned their dispersed, hard-to-defend settlements—only temporarily in the case of Fort Orange—and brought settlers together at the southern tip of Manhattan Island. There they built the city of New Amsterdam.

Like New France, the Dutch colony was primarily a trading post, not a plantation. Still, the Dutch West India Company needed to found a stable settlement to establish its claim to the land. It supplied early settlers with farming tools, plants, and livestock so they could, like their trade rivals at Quebec, feed themselves. New Netherland, however, soon proved to be relatively unprofitable and remained far less important to the company than its possessions in Africa, the

NIEUW AMSTERDAM
op t Eylant Manhattans.

New Amsterdam, the main settlement of the New Netherland colony.

West Indies, South America, and Batavia (Indonesia). Indeed, after first capturing Bahia in Brazil in 1624, the Dutch West India Company concentrated its resources and attention there and in the development of sugar plantations to supply the expanding European market. But rather than abandon New Netherland, the company found ways to pass the cost of settlement on to others. In 1629, it offered patroonships, substantial grants of land for a manorial estate, to persons who brought sixty other settlers to New Netherland (thirty if they went to New Amsterdam) at their own expense within a three-year period. The company also offered land grants to individuals willing to settle in New Netherland at their own expense. These grants led to the development of Rensselaerwyck on the Hudson near Fort Orange, which became not just a private estate but a thriving community that engaged in the fur trade and also sustained such varied activities as a brickyard, tanneries, and even sawmills to process trees into marketable wooden planks.

Despite these attractions, few Dutch people saw reason to leave the Netherlands for America. Perhaps as much as half of the colony's population consisted of Swedes, Germans, Frenchmen, Danes, even Englishmen, some of whom had made homes in the Netherlands, whose religious tolerance attracted refugees from all over Europe. The Dutch West India Company began importing African slaves to remedy its chronic labor shortage in the 1620s; forty years later, persons of African descent constituted between 7 and 9 percent of the colony's population. By then, some had become free and were themselves holders of property, including slaves. A colony so diverse in its peoples, and with relatively few Dutch settlers, was no "New Netherland" in anything but name. The colony's

ethnic diversity resulted from necessity, not desire: the strong-willed Peter Stuyvesant, the colony's most able director, saw New Netherland's population, created as it was from "the scrapings of all sorts of nationalities," as a potential cause of disunity and so a serious disadvantage to a colony surrounded by European rivals and Indians who were often hostile.

Since the company existed primarily to trade, its relationship with the Indians should have been amicable, like that of the French. The company also respected Indian titles and bought the lands it wanted, occasionally for bargain prices. Its purchase of Manhattan for sixty guilders of trade goods, a mere trifle, might well be the world's greatest real estate coup. New Netherland nonetheless experienced serious and persistent conflicts with the Indians. Between 1641 and 1645, it suffered a devastating war caused in part by the belligerent policies of the colony's director at the time. A spurt in the colony's growth probably also excited the Indians' hostility. After 1639, the company increased the amount of land offered to immigrants and allowed settlers to engage in trade. The population doubled within five years, which meant colonists were moving onto still more territory that had once belonged to Indians. Close contact between Euro-

Peter Stuyvesant, the director-general of New Netherland from 1647 until 1664.

51

peans and Indians itself caused friction: Indians' dogs (which were still much like wolves) ate Europeans' cattle and chickens; Europeans' livestock trampled Indians' fields, and so on. In 1655, an apparently trivial conflict in an orchard led to an Indian attack on Manhattan that spread to distant settlements. Fifty colonists and sixty Indians died, twenty-eight houses burned, and large numbers of farm animals died or disappeared before the so-called Peach War ended.

The colony's main settlement, New Amsterdam, developed slowly, like the colony itself. In the 1620s, it consisted of a fort, some thirty primitive houses, a market, a two-story mill, and a few canals and streets. The company maintained farms, or "bouweries," north of the settled area. An appointed director and council, whose members were given to quarreling with each other and with the director, ruled through most of New Netherland's life with no input from the settlers. A minister who arrived in 1628 described the colonists as oppressed, often hungry, and not much inclined to work. When Stuyvesant became director in 1647, he found the place dilapidated and the occupants notable mainly for their persistent drunkenness, which was facilitated by the presence of no less than seventeen tap houses. Stuyvesant limited tavern hours, repaired New Amsterdam's streets and buildings, completed a church on which work had languished, and started a school. He also gave the city a government. At first its officers were appointed, but after 1653, when the Dutch States General granted New Amsterdam a charter, they were elected. The officials met together as a court once a week in the Stat Huis, or State House, a converted tavern, and exercised both civil and criminal jurisdiction.

NEW SWEDEN

Peter Stuyvesant also eventually took over New Sweden, a colony on the Delaware founded by the Swedish West India Company in 1638. That first and only Swedish colony in the Americas claimed territory by right of Indian purchase from what is today Trenton, New Jersey, south to Cape Henlopen at the mouth of the Delaware Bay. Its major base lay on a small river (Christina Kill) that flowed into the Delaware Bay, where the city of Wilmington stands today. There, the New Sweden Company built Fort Christina, named after the Swedish queen, and later established a village, Christinahamn, beside it. The colony monopolized the fur trade in the Delaware Valley. It could not sell furs in Sweden, which had enough already; but having been all but abandoned by the parent company once it proved unprofitable, New Sweden exchanged furs for supplies from other colonies. This trade was sufficiently important that New Sweden rigidly excluded interlopers from its trading area, establishing subsidiary forts at several locations to reinforce its control. Then in 1654, the Swedish governor seized a fort the Dutch had built at New Castle, Delaware. The Dutch West India Company promptly sent New Netherland's Stuyvesant and 300 men to recapture the fort, which they did the following year. Stuyvesant went on to capture Fort Christina and, with it, New Sweden.

The Swedish colony's impact persisted, however, thanks to some Savo-Karelian Finnish settlers who were already experienced frontiersmen when they arrived in America. Descended from ancestors who lived near Lake Ladoga in today's Finland, they had made their way by 1600 from Savolaks and Karelen near the Russian border to interior Sweden. In the course of their migrations through the woodlands of northern Europe, they developed skills and techniques appropriate to other forested frontiers: they became expert axemen who could build crude structures with readily available materials, hunters who also raised hogs and cattle, and farmers who cut and burned brush and other growth to prepare fields for planting. Their ways of life were so well suited to the American frontier that subsequent generations of American frontiersmen carried them on. Of particular importance were the Finns' way of making log cabins with a distinctive V notch at

A "snake," or "worm," fence, made by arranging sets of split or small logs at an angle to each other. This still-used technique of fencing in fields came to America with the Finnish settlers of New Sweden, who probably learned it from the Laplanders of Europe's extreme north.

corners, where the logs locked into each other; their three-sided hunter's shanty, built with the open side toward the fire, whose heat the shanty's pitched roof reflected downward in a remarkably efficient way, and their way of making worm, or snake, fences consisting of whole or split logs placed at an angle to each other in panels six or seven rails high. Each of these structures seems to have appeared at an early time among the Savo-Karelian Finns of northern Europe (or, in the case of the worm fence, the neighboring Laplanders). New Sweden's Finnish settlers introduced them to the Delaware Valley, and they persisted in a similar form on later North American frontiers.

In 1655, New Netherland absorbed New Sweden's roughly 700 people, of whom 40–50 percent were Finns. In the next decade, a healthy flow of immigrants further increased the Dutch colony's population, which reached 8,000–9,000 in the mid-1660s. By then, however, the British colonies of North America held about 90,000 settlers. It was, in fact, primarily the British who "peopled" European North America. They established thriving plantations first along the Chesapeake Bay, then in New England. Two more different places are difficult to imagine.

The Chesapeake

The Virginia colony, founded in 1607, and its northern neighbor Maryland, begun a quarter-century later, had so much in common that they are often together referred to as "the Chesapeake." It was in Virginia, though, that the British discovered by trial and error, mostly error, what it took to succeed at planting the New World. The first problem they confronted was basic. How would they pay the costs?

THE COMPANY AS COLONIZER

The failed colonial efforts of Gilbert and Raleigh made clear that planting a colony cost more than any one private person could afford. And since the Crown was unwilling to foot the bills, private investors would have to pool their capital to finance overseas expansion. The English, like the French, Dutch, and Swedes, did this through companies formed primarily to carry on trade. The demands of trade and colonization, however, were different, and company sponsorship was not necessarily well fitted for setting up anything but modest and reliably profitable trading posts.

A similar need to finance costly operations had inspired the creation of Britain's great trading companies, such as the East India Company. Those that were formally incorporated received a charter from the Crown that defined their governing structure and, to make the start-up costs worthwhile, gave them an exclusive right to carry on trade with a stated market, such as with Russia. Sometimes companies financed ventures from a "joint stock," a fund collected from many investors who later divided any profits in proportion to the amount they had invested or, which was the same thing, the number of shares they had purchased. The joint stock device allowed not only merchants to invest, but others, including large landholders, whose wealth increased substantially as England's population and rents swung upward. Merchants characteristically favored companies that paid solid profits. Members of the gentry were often also attracted by projects that could enhance the power and glory of England or serve a religious purpose. They were therefore good investors for colonial projects, which seldom provided quick returns and often produced none at all. In the course of Virginia's troubled history, the balance of investors shifted from merchants to gentry.

A ceramic jug excavated at the site of the Jamestown settlement in Virginia. It was made during the early seventeenth century in Frechen, Germany, which exported a great quantity of stoneware to England before England established its own stoneware manufactories in the 1680s.

FOUNDING VIRGINIA

In 1606, the British Crown granted a charter to two separate groups of investors for the settlement of Virginia, which then included all of North America along the Atlantic Ocean between the 34th and 45th degrees of north latitude (that is, between a point in Maine just north of modern Bangor and North Carolina's Cape Fear River). The Virginia Company of

Painting of an Indian chief, probably from the area near Roanoke in the late sixteenth century, by John White. John Smith made note of the bows and arrows the Indians used to hunt and fish.

Indian women found him irresistible; and his guns never missed their mark. With just one shot, he could make Virginia's "naked devils" tumble "one over another," and the Indians hated fighting with him, he wrote, "almost as ill as hanging, such fear they had of bad success."

Smith also had a keen eye for the plants and peculiar animals that thrived in Virginia, which he knew were of interest in England, and made careful observations of the Indians and the way they lived. He saw himself as a Cortés-like figure, and thought the Indians (or "savages," as he and most Englishmen called them) should work for the English, much as the peoples of Mexico worked for the Spanish. But he admired the natives' agricultural skills and praised Indian corn as more productive per seed planted than European wheat. Smith noted how the Indians built their warm, snug houses (with young trees, which were "bowed and tied," then covered with mats or the bark of trees, leaving a hole at the top to allow smoke from their fires to escape), and how they made the boats, nets, hooks, and bows and arrows with which they fished and hunted. At certain times of the year, he observed, the Indians left their "habitations" and divided their people into "companies" that traveled inland to the heads of rivers, where there was "plenty of game." Despite the sense of superiority he shared with other Englishmen, Smith was thus able to learn from the Indians.

Once in charge of the colony, he divided settlers into groups and forced them to work, declaring, "He that will not worke, shall not eate (except by sicknesse he be disabled)." He also moved men out of Jamestown, where they had become sick, especially in July and August; in those months, the spring discharge of water from the mountains ceased, the river's level dropped, its salt level rose, and the water the settlers drank became contaminated with sediment and sewage (or, as a contemporary account had it, with "slime and filth"). The colonists probably suffered from dysentery, typhoid, and also salt poisoning, which explains in part their "swellings," lassitude, and irritability as well as their tendency to die. By scattering colonists in the countryside, like the Indians, moving them toward freshwater springs and away from the James estuary, Smith lowered the death rate substantially. Between the fall of 1608 and summer of 1609, at most 21 of 130 persons died, and 11 of those drowned.

THE CHARTERS OF 1609 AND 1612

With a "first seat" that seemed, at last, firmly set in the New World, the Virginia Company of London decided to build on acquired experience and develop a proper plantation. In 1609, it received a new charter from the Crown that extended the Virginia colony's boundaries two hundred miles north and south from Old Point Comfort at the base of the Chesapeake Bay and "from sea to sea, north and northwest"—an enormous grant, far greater than anyone actually understood, since Europeans, who still could not measure longitude, had no idea just how far the Pacific lay from the eastern coast of North America. The charter of 1609 also made the London company a joint-stock company, able to sell shares to the public, and gave it greater control over the colony. Effective power rested in the company's treasurer, Sir Thomas Smith, whose rule was as autocratic as John Smith's had been in Virginia. Still, the change was significant. The British Crown did not centralize colonial power in its hands, as the Spanish

Crown had done, but, like some other European nations, granted major responsibility for its first North American colony to a private concern.

In 1612, the Crown granted the company another charter that extended the colony's boundaries far enough out to sea to include Bermuda, or Somers Island, which had been discovered in 1609 when a ship was wrecked there. It also gave the company a seven-year exemption from paying English customs duties and allowed it to run national lotteries to raise money for Virginia. The Crown revised the company's government in a way that ended all remnants of the old royal council and gave responsibility for company affairs to its stockholders. All members of the company would meet as a "great court" four times a year to decide matters of general policy. "Ordinary courts," which only twenty members had to attend, would met weekly with the treasurer to discuss more immediate issues. Perhaps investors would prove more willing to support a company over whose affairs it had greater influence. Of course, profits were the greatest inducement to investment—and of those, the company had seen precious little. But hope springs eternal.

DEVELOPING VIRGINIA

In 1609, with its new charter in hand, the London company mounted a national campaign to recruit investors and settlers. It offered shares in the company not just for money (from "adventurers," or investors) but as a reward for migration (by "planters"). All the company's assets would remain pooled for seven years. During that time, settlers would be company employees, drawing food and supplies from a common storehouse. Then, in 1616, shareholders would divide the company's wealth, and each of them, planters and adventurers alike, would receive at least 100 acres of land. The response was encouraging: by the spring of 1609, some 600 men, women, and children climbed on board the nine ships of a "great fleet" that the London company sent to Virginia.

The company also revised the colony's government in Virginia. Henceforth, a governor would have "full power and authority" over both military and civil affairs. In the next few years, the colony's strong governors imposed a quasi-military regime under a set of harsh laws remembered as the "Laws Divine, Moral and Martial." Those laws organized settlers into work gangs, as Smith had done, and they required "everie man and woman" to attend religious services twice a day or face severe punishments. They prescribed the death penalty for a wide range of crimes—sodomy, rape, adultery; stealing from the general store or from other colonists, even taking grapes or "any ears of corne" from public or private gardens; and, what seemed to evoke the most extreme concern, attempting to leave the colony, whether by sea or by fleeing to the Indians. Even under these laws, however, colonists worked only five to eight hours a day in summer, three to six in winter.

The worst times for the colony occurred when there was no governor or deputy governor. One particularly hard period, Virginia's "starving time," came in the winter of 1609–10, after Smith suffered a gunshot wound and set sail for England but before the new governor or deputy had arrived. One contemporary account said that of 500 colonists alive when Smith left, many recently recruited by the London company, there remained six months later "not past sixtie men, women, and children," all "miserable and poore creatures" who had survived by consuming "roots, herbes, acornes, walnuts, berries, now and then a little fish." A modern study argues that slightly fewer than 200 colonists actually spent the winter of 1609–10 in Virginia, and of them 100 survived, 15 were killed by Indians, and 80 died of other causes. That was bad enough. By spring, the survivors decided to abandon Virginia, and were sailing down the James when the new governor arrived and convinced them to turn back. Again in 1611, two months after one governor left and before his replacement arrived, the people could be found "at their daily and usual work bowling in the streets."

Still, Virginia survived and even expanded geographically as many people left sickly Jamestown to live in fortified set-

The cover of a brochure advertising the splendors of living in Virginia. Published in London during 1609, its aim was to lure settlers to the struggling colony.

tlements between the mouth of the James River and the new town of Henrico (now Richmond) at the fall line, where water drops from the mountains in falls or rapids that block upriver navigation. A modest allocation of land to some settlers in 1614 made the colony something more than a company camp. These new landowners assumed responsibility for feeding themselves and for contributing corn to the company store, which newcomers drew upon. The colonists remained dependent on the Indians for much of their food, but that didn't keep them from treating the Indians with contempt. In fact, they had a nasty but persistent habit of murdering Indians

Pocahontas, the daughter of Powhatan and wife of Virginia colonist John Rolfe.

with a nonchalant brutality and then, stranger still, destroying their fields of corn.

The colony also found, finally, something it could sell profitably. John Rolfe, a settler who had married Powhatan's daughter Pocahontas, began experimenting with tobacco seed from the West Indies in about 1612. That seed produced a plant whose leaves were milder and more pleasant for Europeans to smoke than the variety of tobacco grown by Virginia's Indians, and in 1617 Virginia sent a cargo of this tobacco to England. It sold for three shillings a pound—less than tobacco from the West Indies, but more than anything else the Virginians produced.

But could you found a colony on **tobacco**? Europeans first welcomed tobacco for its supposed medical benefits, but soon smoked it simply for pleasure. Sure, it was addictive, and smoking rapidly became less than entirely respectable. Tobacco provided, however, a beginning, a way of making the colony solvent. Then perhaps it could produce other goods of more basic importance to England.

THE GREAT CHARTER

Something about Virginia fostered dreams despite its way of making them go sour. The dream that took over the Virginia Company of London in 1619 belonged to Sir Edwin Sandys,

leader of a contingent of stockholders who elected him treasurer. Sandys proposed to develop and invigorate the colony by an ambitious plan. He would, to begin with, build up the population by offering land to immigrants. Anyone who paid his own way to Virginia or the passageway of others would receive a "headright" of fifty acres. Sandys encouraged groups to migrate by offering them adjacent grants of land in separate communities known as "particular plantations." And he offered to bring impoverished people to the colony at the company's expense if they would then work company lands for seven years on a sharecropping basis, keeping half their earnings; then, after their term of indenture (the contract by which they agreed to work a set number of years) was over, they, too, would receive a grant of fifty acres. Undeveloped land in Virginia was of little value to the company; it might as well give land away, then charge landowners a modest quitrent (tax on land) of a shilling a year per fifty acres held.

Sandys saw no reason Englishmen would travel to a place where they had far less freedom than at home, so he ended the old "Laws Divine, Moral and Martial." From now on, the colony's government would include an assembly consisting of an appointed governor's council and an elected House of Burgesses. The assembly could make laws for the colony, although the laws required the company's approval before going into effect. Colonists welcomed the instructions Sandys gave Virginia's new governor, which included these changes, as their "great charter" because they established "English liberty" in Virginia, much as the Magna Carta (1215) had done for England itself. The new assembly met on June 30, 1619. It was the first representative assembly in British America—but not the last.

As if to gild the lily, Sandys promised to "ease all the Inhabitants of Virginia forever of all taxes and public burthens" to the extent possible, and so to remove "all occasion of oppression and corruption." In lieu of salaries paid by public levies, officeholders would be paid from the proceeds of lands worked by company tenants. Sandys also tried to develop new exports. He sent Germans to build sawmills that would cut timber into boards for sale abroad; skilled Italians to create a glassworks; and an English gentleman, John Berkeley, an experienced iron maker, to oversee the construction of a well-equipped ironworks at a place called Fallen Creek. Sandys proposed to Anglicize the local Indians so Anglo-Virginians could live with them in peace. Some Indian families would reside within the English settlements; others would be educated at a new Indian College built at Henrico and supported by a grant of 10,000 acres of land that would be worked by company tenants. The colonists could only conclude that they were destined to become "the most happy people in the world."

FAILURE

It didn't work. Over a three-year period, Sandys recruited over 3,500 people to join the 700 already in Virginia. Most of them died, some quickly of disease, especially when, weakened by long, ill-supplied voyages at sea, they arrived to find no shelter and little if any food provided for them. By March 22, 1622, the colony's population stood at only 1,240; about 3,000 people had already disappeared. Then another 347 died in a massive Indian attack mounted by Opechancanough, Powhatan's warlike brother and successor, in an all-out effort to stop, once and for all, the colonists' expansion onto Indian lands.

The attack took the colonists by complete surprise. Indians had moved easily through the settlements, trading, eating, and even sleeping at homes of colonists who, it seems, felt no sense of danger. On the morning of the massacre, Smith reported, some Indians "sat downe at breakfast with our people, whom immediately with their owne tools they slew most barbarously, not sparing either age or sex, man woman or childe." Indians familiar with colonists' work patterns also found it easy to kill men in the fields, often again with their own weapons. Among the casualties were the man appointed to develop the Indian college and the ironmaster, John Berkeley. The Indians burned the buildings at Fallen Creek and tossed the workmen's expensive imported tools into the water. The English then decided that "wee must drive them, or they us out of the country," but that was no easy thing given the colony's reduced manpower and the Indians' preference for surprise attacks (a "skulking kind of war") over open battles.

The Indians actually killed far fewer Virginians than those company officials who shipped large numbers of settlers without making sufficient provision for their needs on arrival, or the greedy men who held power in the colony, including some Sandys had appointed, and ruthlessly exploited newcomers to produce tobacco for their own personal profit. After a brief dip, tobacco prices rose back to three shillings a pound, enough to make a man rich if he could produce the

"The Indians actually killed far fewer Virginians than those company officials who shipped large numbers of settlers without making sufficient provision for their needs on arrival."

leaf in quantity. But tobacco was a labor-intensive crop: seedlings had to be planted in a sheltered place in early spring and transplanted to prepared fields sometime in April, and then, during the growing season, the top growth bud had to be carefully picked off so the plants branched out, producing more leaves. Plants also needed to be inspected regularly and insects picked off and destroyed. Once harvested, tobacco was hung to dry in shaded places or, later, sheds. Then, after about six weeks, leaves could be removed from the branches and packed in barrels for shipment abroad. To produce a lot of tobacco, and so to make a fortune during the "boom" of the 1620s, required therefore not just land, which was still relatively easy to come by, but a lot of workers. Labor, which in England seemed to be in excess supply, was the key to wealth in Virginia.

Who would fill the demand for workers? Not the handful of African slaves brought to Virginia by a Dutch ship in 1619. There were not enough of them; they were too expensive, and there was not much incentive to buy a lifetime of slave labor when life was short. Nor could Indians fill the need. Before the massacre of 1622, they sometimes did odd jobs around the colony for pay. But Indians considered agriculture women's work, and Indian women were busy growing their own crops. To capture Indians and force them to work for the colonists would, in any case, only have increased resentments and sparked reprisals. Better to ship captured Indians to places where they could cause fewer problems and from which they would find it more difficult to escape and go home. That left Englishmen, who were not great workers, but they would have to do.

So the avaricious henchmen of early Virginia—no longer the gentlemen of the colony's opening years, who had long since died or returned home, but men of humbler birth who fought to better themselves in this new land and who maneuvered themselves onto the governor's council or into other colonial offices—took control of the colony's new immigrants. First they purchased the labor of some indentured servants. Then they stole others, tricking freemen into becoming tenants or making company servants work on their private lands. Often they treated white indentured servants more like things than fellow men. "I thought no head . . . able to hold so much water as hath and doth dailie flow from my eyes," a young English servant, Richard Freethorne, wrote his "love-

A tobacco plant, drawn by an unknown artist in the sixteenth century. Tobacco was the main export product of the colonial Chesapeake.

ing and kind" parents in 1623. He was cold, having few clothes, and hungry. Since arriving, he'd consumed nothing but peas, "loblollie" (a thin mixture of cereal and water), a bit of beef, and a few mouthfuls of bread. "I have eaten more in a day at home" than in an entire week in Virginia, he said. Day and night, he claimed, the people cried out, "Oh that they were in England," even if they had to sacrifice an arm or leg to get back and were required to spend the rest of their lives begging from door to door. Such boys rarely lived long enough to realize the dreams that had brought them to Virginia.

A ROYAL COLONY

In 1624, after a special investigative commission confirmed rumors of extreme mismanagement, the Crown vacated Virginia's charter. The next year, Charles I became king and announced that the colony's government would henceforth "depend upon ourself, and not be committed to any company or corporation." So Virginia became a royal colony. The down-

ward trajectory of power was, it seems, reversed; now the English Crown, like its Spanish counterpart, would rule its overseas possessions.

But royal governors soon found that to govern Virginia, they needed the help of large planters who knew the colony well and had established positions of power within its developing society. Governors appointed such men to their council—but at times it wasn't altogether clear who governed whom. In 1635, when councillors disagreed with Governor John Harvey over Indian policy and the colony's stand toward the new colony of Maryland, they "thrust him out." That is, the councillors seized Harvey, put him under armed guard, sent him back to England, and chose one of their number to serve as governor in his place. The king reappointed Harvey, but later replaced him with a governor more acceptable to the Virginians.

When the new governor arrived in 1639, he announced that the colony's assembly would be reinstated. In fact, the elected House of Burgesses, which was dear to the Virginians, had never completely disappeared. It met on scattered occasions after 1624, and in 1634 took the monumental step of organizing local governments in the form of county courts. By then, the colony's population had spread along both sides of the James River up to the falls that divided the tidewater from the hill country, or piedmont, farther inland. Virginians had also moved north, claiming land between the James and York Rivers, settled the York's northern shore, and crossed the Chesapeake to take up lands on the Eastern Shore (the large peninsula that separates the Chesapeake Bay from the Atlantic).

As the population spread out, trips to the capital, Jamestown, to register land titles and wills or perform similar tasks became increasingly inconvenient. Officials in Jamestown also found executing those routine jobs for the entire colony more onerous as Virginia's population grew, which it did in great jumps after the mid-1630s. Under the new system, each of eight large counties (whose number later increased) established courts made up of justices of the peace who heard minor criminal and civil cases and executed various administrative tasks. Each county also had a sheriff, a clerk, and a variety of other officers. Over time, the assembly gave them responsibility for one job after another until the counties became the colony's most important administrative centers.

The governor appointed county officials in the name of the Crown. But it soon became customary in Virginia for governors to appoint county officeholders from residents nominated by the county courts. Local officials in the British colonies were not exclusively dependent on the Crown like their counterparts in Spanish America. They had local interests, local loyalties. Although the political system centered in the Crown, it incorporated colonists in the making of laws, and in many cases depended on them to execute these laws. This was an empire with a difference.

MARYLAND

In 1632, Charles I granted the new colony of Maryland to his friend George Calvert, Lord Baltimore, a Catholic who wanted to found a refuge for English Catholics. The original charter gave Calvert land west from the Delaware Bay along the 40th parallel down to the south bank of the Potomac River and west to the Potomac's "first fountain" (waterfall). The Potomac turned more sharply to the northwest than anyone suspected, but what Calvert lost in land he gained in power. He was the absolute owner and lord of Maryland. He held the land in his own name and could establish and conduct its government by himself, although the colonists had to give their advice and consent to laws. And Calvert could pass the colony to his heirs. Since he died before the charter was sealed, Maryland became the possession of his son Cecelius Calvert, who shared his father's ambition.

Maryland thus became a "proprietary" colony under the Calverts, who were its proprietors. The colonies Britain founded in the West Indies at about the same time—St. Christopher (1624), Barbados (1627), Nevis (1628), Montserrat and Antigua (about 1632)—were also begun as proprietary colonies. By then, the Virginia Company of London's lamentable record had brought the use of commercial companies for founding colonies into some disrepute. However, by giving land to settlers who paid their own way to America and provided their own supplies, the old London company had hit upon a way to pass many of the costs of founding settlements on to the colonists themselves. Later colonies followed suit. Calvert, for example, offered settlers liberal land grants. Most of those who went to Maryland (beginning in 1634), though, were Protestants, and that led to

> *"'I thought no head . . . able to hold so much water as hath and doth dailie flow from my eyes,' a young English servant, Richard Freethorne, wrote his 'loveing and kind' parents in 1623. 'I have eaten more in a day at home' than in an entire week in Virginia."*

persistent conflicts between the proprietor and colonists, who used the elected assembly to oppose Calvert, his governor, laws, and religion.

Although different issues arose in the politics of Maryland and Virginia, their systems of government were similar. In Maryland, the proprietor appointed the governor, which the Crown did in Virginia; but both colonies elected assemblies, and as its population spread, Maryland established a county court system much like Virginia's. The two colonies experienced much the same climate, and both of their economies depended on tobacco. In part for those reasons, the Chesapeake colonies developed societies that distinguished them not only from other parts of British North America, but from England itself.

A PLACE LIKE ENGLAND?

The idea of overseas plantations implied that colonies would replicate their mother country. And in some ways, Virginia and Maryland did so. Their language, values, and habits all reflected their English origin. The settlers' devotion to elected assemblies and to local government also had roots in England, as did their sense of what kinds of work were appropriate for men and for women.

But there were differences, too. For one thing, in any settled society such as England, there is a roughly equal number of men and women. The first settlers of Virginia, however, were usually single men in their twenties, although some (like Richard Freethorne) were younger. They had traveled alone or in pairs from hundreds of places in the west and south of England to ports such as Bristol or London and, finding no work or perhaps hoping for adventure and opportunity, signed on for America. Since only a handful of women migrated, men vastly outnumbered women. In Virginia's second decade, there were about four or five men for every woman, so it was impossible for the population to grow substantially by natural increase. The colony's labor system only made the problem worse. Young women who arrived as indentured servants—virtually all of them—could not marry until their terms of service were over, which chopped from four to seven years off their prime childbearing time. If a girl bore a "bastard" child before her indenture had expired, she had to work an additional year or two to repay her master for labor lost and the "trouble of his house." Probably few immigrant women married before age twenty-five, which meant that, assuming they nursed infants, which affected birth intervals, they bore at most four or five babies. In Maryland, at least a quarter of all children died within their first year and 40–55 percent before age twenty. And so through most of the seventeenth century, Virginia's and Maryland's populations grew less from births than from immigration.

Life was short in the early Chesapeake. In one Virginia county, which was much like many others, women generally died in their late thirties. Probably many suffered from malaria, a mosquito-borne disease especially dangerous to the young, the old, and pregnant women. If they made it past their childbearing years, women could expect to live longer than men of the same age. But most men died in their forties, about a decade earlier than Englishmen "at home." Since women typically married older men, they frequently survived their husbands—and then remarried quickly. Women of virtually all sorts were in demand since there were so few of them, but in Virginia, at least, widows with inherited wealth became the prize catches. They brought with them at least their "dower right" to a third of their dead husband's estate, and frequently served as executors of their children's inherited property—a role their new husband generally took over. And wives were useful: they raised vegetables, milked cows, made cheese and butter, cooked, washed, and took care of children. Sometimes in the seventeenth century, especially if a family lacked servants, they even worked in the fields. That was not customary women's work, and, it seems, women shed fieldwork when better times arrived. The records suggest that these women of early Virginia were a tough bunch. They had more power than their English sisters, and felt no compunction about expressing their convictions and desires in what some might have considered unbecoming ways.

With so many adults dying in their childbearing years, Virginia produced crop after crop of orphans. Almost a quarter of all children had lost one or both parents by the time they were five, and over half by the time they turned thirty. Some-

times orphans found themselves in families with no natural parent—living, for example, in the household of their dead mother's second (or later) husband and his "now wife," as the phrase went. Such children had to grow up fast, if only to protect their inheritances from dishonest stepfathers. Here, the government helped. In Virginia, guardians had to present their accounts for auditing every year at special "orphans' courts." Children could request a new guardian when they reached their fourteenth year, still pretty young by modern standards. Under the circumstances, with death lurking at the door, communities of people formed to take care of each other: networks of blood relatives and quasi-kin—godparents, relatives by marriage, or just caring neighbors—stepped in to protect stranded children.

The early Virginians' tendency toward laziness had some roots in England, where laws attempted to pass work around so that everyone had a little and discouraged go-getters who selfishly tried to hold two jobs at once. New Netherland's colonists weren't all that inclined to work, either. Maybe these early Americans were more sensible than their modern descendants, who find it perfectly natural to work all the time. Some people in the Chesapeake were able to live the easy life because they forced others to work for them. The Virginia gentry's early treatment of servants, whom they bought, sold, and even gambled away like pieces of property, established patterns for the future—as one servant suggested when he complained that his master treated him like a "slave." It also reinforced an old English dislike of working for others in any capacity, even for wages. Independence was highly esteemed in Virginia, where men aspired to work for themselves so they didn't have to take orders and could do as they chose. Dependence was for women, children, and servants of one sort or another. A commitment to individualism in that sense was a value Virginia contributed to American culture.

Virginia and Maryland were similar in some ways to British West Indian colonies such as Barbados, which in the 1620s and 1630s grew tobacco on farms with white indentured servants, and had high mortality rates and few women. But even more, the Chesapeake resembled what later generations knew as the American West. In 1607, Jamestown was Europe's Far West. The resemblance was clearest in Virginia's

> *"The records suggest that these women of early Virginia were a tough bunch. They had more power than their English sisters, and felt no compunction about expressing their convictions and desires in what some might have considered unbecoming ways."*

early years, when its rivers were full of floating taverns where lonely men gathered to gamble and drink their misery away. Death was a constant presence on the western frontiers of European settlement, and women rare—but unusually strong. And what frontiersman showed respect for Indians or absentee owners or anyone else who interfered with their ambitions?

By the 1630s, however, a more settled life had begun to emerge in Virginia. Tobacco prices fell; then planters began growing more corn, and they found ways to protect their hogs from wolves and wandering Indians. Feeding themselves ceased to be a problem. Virginians still lived in small wooden, hut-like houses that looked remarkably ephemeral compared with the stone houses of England. Their farms were not clustered together in towns or villages, but spread out along rivers and navigable streams, the highways of their time, so tobacco could be more easily loaded onto boats and shipped to markets far away. Still, the increased incidence of families and of communities in which people traveled fair distances to visit each other, talk, dance, play games, and help each other in times of trouble marked the emergence of something more than a frontier outpost. So did the establishment of county governments. Virginia and soon also Maryland were becoming societies of a type that remained unique on the North American mainland. The Chesapeake's distinctiveness becomes all the more clear when it is compared with its sister colonies in the North.

New England

About 100 Englishmen crossed the Atlantic in 1620 on the *Mayflower* and founded a colony at Plymouth in New England. Soon thereafter, others made homes or started fishing posts at scattered places along the northern Atlantic coast. But what posterity remembered as the **"Great Migration" to New England** began in 1630 when a fleet of eleven ships carried some 700 men, women, and children as well as livestock and other supplies to a new colony in the Massachusetts Bay, north of Plymouth. By the time the Great Migration ended, twelve years later, some 20,000 English people had gone to New England. That region would eventually include several colonies—Massachusetts, Connecticut, Rhode Island, and New Hampshire, as well as Plymouth and New Haven, which remained separate colonies in the early seventeenth century.

New England was dramatically different from the Chesapeake in many ways. For one thing, Englishmen began to settle it several decades after Virginia had been founded, and their leaders tried to avoid Virginia's mistakes. Since New England could not grow a single staple crop such as tobacco for sale in Britain, it developed a more varied economy than the Chesapeake. Most early New England settlers came, moreover, not from the south and west of England, which sent many settlers to the Chesapeake, but from the east ("East Anglia"). They traveled not alone but in groups that included entire families, and then made their homes in towns, not isolated plantations. Immigration to Virginia continued throughout the seventeenth century, but that to New England slowed to a trickle after 1642, when the outbreak of civil war in England prompted potential settlers to stay home. New England's population nonetheless grew rapidly by natural increase, since sex ratios there were relatively even, couples bore many children, infant mortality was low, and adults lived long lives.

Portrait of Elizabeth Freake and her baby, Mary, painted in New England during the 1670s.

Some of these distinctions can be explained by the accidents of place and time. Others, however, stemmed from the fact that most of those who settled New England were Puritans, members of a particular radical strain in English Protestantism whose beliefs shaped the region's society and culture.

PURITANISM

"Puritan" began as a term of denigration for English Calvinists of the sixteenth and seventeenth centuries who wanted to purify the Church of England by eliminating still more remnants of the pre-Reformation Catholic past. Puritans compiled long lists of "unscriptural" practices that the Church of England retained—various liturgies and set prayers (they described the Book of Common Prayer, for example, as "culled and picked out of that popish dung-hill, the mass book," and thus "full of abominations"); the rituals in baptism, communion, marriages, and burials; clerical vestments; tithes, canon law, bishops' courts, and on and on. These reformers wanted a simpler church with no central bureaucracy, a church that would emphasize the essence of religion—piety and Bible reading—over outward show.

At the core of Puritanism, however, lay a concept of the church not as a building, or a vast structure of clergymen and believers, but as a community of covenanted "saints." Like other Calvinists, the Puritans believed in predestination: God knew who was destined to spend eternity with Him (His saints) and who was damned even before those people were born. The Puritans believed that God's church on earth (the church visible) should approximate the church destined to exist in heaven (the church invisible) by consisting, to the extent possible, only of the saved. These saints had to form voluntary agreements—covenants—by which they agreed to help each other live according to God's will. That belief rested on a passage from the Book of Psalms (50:5) in the Old Testament: "Gather my saints together unto me; those that have made a covenant with me by sacrifice."

John Winthrop, the first governor of the Massachusetts Bay Colony.

The main problem with the Church of England, Puritans said, was that it was formed not by covenant but by the state. Moreover, it excluded nobody—everyone born in England was automatically a member—and lacked "discipline," a capacity to admonish and ultimately expel serious sinners. Some Puritans, known as Separatists, thought that those failures so corrupted the established church that God's people had no choice but to leave it and form their own separate churches. One group of such Separatists went into exile in Leyden, Holland. Later, some members of that congregation, fearing that their children were becoming Dutch, moved on to America, and they founded the Plymouth Colony in 1620. Other Puritans saw within the Church of England a core of saints sufficient to legitimize it in God's eyes; the founders of the Massachusetts Bay Colony (1630) were of that sort. The first governor of Massachusetts, John Winthrop, even condemned the Separatists for the "spiritual pride" that led them to abandon those "weak Christians" within the Church of England who were in need of "tender care." Once in New England, however, the Massachusetts Bay colonists organized their own covenanted churches, and gradually became much like their Separatist brethren.

Puritanism's appeal lay precisely in traits that most modern people find distasteful: its tight communities of "mutually watchful" people who were always prying into each other's affairs, noting moral lapses, admonishing sinners, and encouraging them to live according to God's word. Individual privacy had no place in Puritanism. But in an England where old bonds were disappearing—where tenant families were being forced off the land, young people moving about in search of work, and new forms of commerce and manufacturing pulling workers to places far from their ancestral homes—the involvement of individuals with each other was appealing. Puritanism offered a way of belonging, of connecting with others, in a lonely world. The Puritan assurance of salvation to God's chosen "saints" and of His "providence" (special care) for His people was also comforting at a time when death was always near and little in life could be called secure. The doctrines and group orientation of Puritanism also made it extraordinarily well suited to master the challenges of colonization.

THE CROWN AND THE COLONY

Why did the Puritans leave England? Most of those who went to Massachusetts were people with some property who expected to maintain certain basic comforts in America, and they were more than ready to exploit what opportunities for profits America offered. But considering that their Great Migration occurred in a relatively short period of time, it seems likely that most left England not for economic opportunity so much as to flee oppression and for a chance to practice their religious beliefs freely.

Under James I (r. 1603–25), who was no friend of Puritanism, many Puritans found ways of making do within the Church of England. They might, for example, subsidize ministries and so win the right to appoint a sympathetic clergyman, or pay special lecturers who preached to Puritan-minded worshipers after regular Anglican church services. But began to function well only in the 1640s, when its president, Henry Dunster, established a four-year program—which was taught entirely by Dunster until a few capable graduates came to his aid. He modeled the curriculum on that of English universities, and especially on Emanuel College of Cambridge University, from which he and several other Puritans had graduated. Students studied the natural sciences as well as staples such as rhetoric, logic, philosophy, Latin, and Greek.

Puritans established Harvard because they wanted educated clergymen; but only about half the men it graduated in its first half century went into the ministry. As a result, the ripple effects of the college, and indeed of the colony's general willingness to invest resources in developing human capacities, reached far beyond the church. The migrants came from a sophisticated culture; in America, they continued to read not just the Bible but the works of men like the English Puritan poet John Milton or the beloved *Pilgrim's Progress* by John Bunyan. And they themselves kept journals to trace the workings of God in their lives. New England established the first press in North America, and the great majority of titles published in the British colonies came from New England, which continued thereafter to exert an influence on American thought and letters out of all proportion to the number of people who first settled that area.

Here again, the Chesapeake was different. "I thank God, there are no free schools nor printing" in Virginia, wrote that colony's royal governor, William Berkeley, in 1671; "and I hope we shall not have these hundred years; for learning has brought disobedience, and heresy, and sects into the world, and printing has divulged them, and libels against the best government. God keep us from both!"

WORK, WORK, WORK

If people in the Chesapeake knew how to relax, the New Englanders knew how to work. The difference was clear from the very beginning. Soon after Governor Winthrop landed in Massachusetts in 1630, according to one account, he perceived "what misery was like[ly] to ensue through idleness," and so "fell to work with his own hands and thereby so encouraged the rest . . . that there was not an idle person to be found in the whole plantation." Within a decade, the settlers prepared 12,000 acres for planting crops.

The Puritans celebrated industriousness as a godly virtue, and understood work as a religious obligation. God, they believed, gave everyone a "calling" in life, and all callings—

An English cartoon of 1653 that shows a Puritan, on the left, telling Father Christmas to "keep out." The cartoon ridiculed the Puritans' hostility toward Christmas as a "popish" holiday.

whether to the ministry or the farm, the shop or the countinghouse—were honorable in His eyes. Although He expected His people to work hard at their callings, they were not to work for profit alone. What wealth they collected was held "in trust" from God, who expected them to use it, as Governor Winthrop explained in his speech on the *Arbella*, "for the glory of his Creator and the good of the Creature, Man."

If some people lost their way and became greedy, both the church and the state were there to set them right. In the 1630s, when the rapid increase in population caused runaway inflation, Massachusetts tried to force merchants to ask no more for an item than a "just price," which was the price people would normally pay for it, and to prevent money lenders from charging "usurious," or exorbitant, rates. Before long, however, the government essentially abandoned its effort to regulate the market. Puritans nonetheless continued to stress people's Christian obligation to help neighbors in need, not profit from their distress. As Winthrop said, a righteous man had a duty to give to a needy neighbor "according to his necessity," even if the neighbor's capacity to repay his benefactor was in doubt. Persons who honored their obligations in that way and still prospered could interpret their wealth as a sign of God's blessing—which was itself a powerful reason to work hard.

Puritans had another stimulus to work: they did not recognize a large number of "popish" holidays like Christmas that, in England, were occasions for closing up shop. Once sabbaths and holy days were deducted from the total, England was left with about 220 workdays per year, while New England had over 300.

DISSENSION

Did the Puritan's way of life make New England a peaceful haven? Maybe at first, and in some places for a generation or more. But soon enough, the colony was wracked by controversy over what they cared about most: religion.

As the Dedham town covenant indicated, Massachusetts was not designed to accommodate persons of different religious views. Puritans tolerated only adherents of their own beliefs. Others had, as one writer put it, complete freedom to go somewhere else. After 1631, the colony declared that only church members could be freemen (voters in colony-wide elections). Clergymen could not participate in the government (the settlers had had enough of that with Archbishop Laud), but the state supported and sustained the church, which in theory performed a civic function by teaching morals. But how wide a range of views were acceptably orthodox? That question emerged quickly because the flood of committed, contentious Puritans who arrived in the colony during the 1630s included both trained theologians and articulate laypersons whose views were not always compatible with each other or with those of the colony's rulers.

Take Roger Williams, a likable enough fellow who had studied at Cambridge University before coming to Massachusetts in 1631. His views proved more Separatist than those of the colony: he refused an invitation to serve the Boston church as its minister unless it repudiated all ties with the Church of England. When the Boston church held firm, he went off to Plymouth—but even Plymouth's Separatism wasn't up to Williams's standards. Soon he began raising one "dangerous" argument after another. Williams didn't like the way Massachusetts ministers met to consult each other,

"That a woman led the Antinomians only made things worse. Women were supposed to be meek and submissive; public controversies and intellectual argument were outside their proper sphere."

which looked to him like the beginning of a disgusting church hierarchy; he questioned the legitimacy of the colony's charter because, he said, the king had no right to give away lands that belonged to the Indians; and he wanted the state to have nothing whatsoever to do with religion. He argued that officials should not administer oaths to "unregenerate," or unsaved, people, and that regenerate people should not pray with the unregenerate even if they were family members. Williams's extreme form of Puritanism threatened the colony's civil and social structure. After his fellow ministers failed to persuade him that his views were in error, the General Court expelled him from Massachusetts. Rather than return to Archbishop Laud's England, Williams fled south in early 1636 to what became Rhode Island, a new colony that provided a home for those whose views were too far out for the Bay Colony.

The controversy around Anne Hutchinson was even more divisive. Hutchinson and her family followed her minister in England, the Reverend John Cotton, to Massachusetts. Cotton, who became minister at the Boston church, emphasized that grace alone, not good behavior, identified God's saints, and he instituted a change in the requirements for church membership. Living a moral life was enough to qualify for membership in English Puritan churches, but in Boston, and then elsewhere in the colony, prospective church members had to explain how and when they first experienced God's grace. That reduced the number of people who became church members. Hutchinson then took Cotton's teachings to even greater extremes.

Sometime in 1635, she began holding meetings of women in her home, where she commented on recent sermons. Soon men began attending. Before long, Hutchinson criticized local ministers for teaching that, by living a good life, people could prepare themselves for God's grace. People could do nothing to affect God, she insisted; He was omnipotent and inscrutable to humans, bestowed His grace freely, and could save even the most wicked human devil if He so chose. Opponents characterized Hutchinson and her followers as Antinomians—literally, people "against law"—because their teachings undermined all attempts to live according to God's laws. Hutchinson also attacked the colony's ministers, all of whom except Cotton and her brother-in-law John Wheelwright were "without grace" in her opinion and so unqualified to preach God's word. She and her followers soon started heckling the "unregenerate" ministers or marching from meetinghouses when they began to speak. The controversy ripped apart a community that was supposed to be "knitt together"—but so what? Christ came, Wheelwright proclaimed, to send fire upon the earth. Others disagreed. That a woman led the Antinomians only made things worse. Women were supposed to be meek and submissive; public controversies and intellectual argument were outside their proper sphere.

After a public fast day failed to restore peace, leading ministers attempted but failed to convince the Hutchinsonians of their errors. Finally, the General Court tried and banished the sectaries—first the men, including Wheelwright, whom it convicted of "contempt and sedition" for kindling bitterness in the colony. Then the court tried Hutchinson, who did a fine job of parrying questions put to her by Governor Winthrop until, finally, she announced that God revealed Himself to her directly. That was heretical: orthodox Puritans believed that God revealed Himself only through the Bible. As a result, the General Court banished Hutchinson from the colony, and even the Boston congregation, which was once full of her supporters, excommunicated her. She went, of course, to Rhode Island—although Wheelwright and about twenty families of his own followers moved instead to New Hampshire, where they founded the town of Exeter. Before long, Winthrop recorded, the divisions within Boston declined, "all breaches were made up, and the church was saved from ruin."

NEW COLONIES

Except for Plymouth, the various colonies of New England were settled primarily by migrants from Massachusetts. In 1636, a group from Watertown, Dorchester, and Newtown (later Cambridge), with the grudging permission of the General Court, moved to the Connecticut Valley, where they founded the towns of Wethersfield, Windsor, and Hartford. These settlers of Connecticut ostensibly sought more and better lands than were available near the Massachusetts Bay, but theological considerations probably also prompted their move. Their leader, the Reverand Thomas Hooker, favored less demanding standards for church membership than John Cotton, whose views dominated Massachusetts Bay churches.

The seal of the Connecticut colony. Seals, made by pressing a metal impression into hot wax, were an important way of authenticating documents. The Connecticut seal shows a hand coming from a cloud and carrying a banner with the Latin phrase for "He who has transplanted us sustains us." Below are several vines. The imagery was probably inspired by the psalm "Thou hast brought a vine out of Egypt. Thou hast cast out the heathen and planted it." The Puritans of New England saw themselves as God's chosen people, like the Jews of the Old Testament. In America, the "heathen" were Indians.

Rhode Island, which was settled by religious refugees from Massachusetts, was still less restrictive; there, tolerance extended to almost any form of religion. But the people of New Haven, a separate colony founded by a group of London Puritans who left Boston in March 1638, were conservative Puritans. New Haven's churches closely regulated the lives of their members, and were quick to censure or even excommunicate those who did not conform. In time, the New Haven Colony absorbed several other towns, including Milford, Guilford, and later Stamford and Greenwich, as well as several towns on Long Island (in today's New York). It also established a settlement on the Delaware River, which brought it into conflict with the Dutch. Similarly, Plymouth became the center of settlements that stretched from Cape Cod west to the Narragansett Bay.

In all of these colonies, the town became the basic unit of government. The Massachusetts General Court delegated one task after another to the towns, which became responsible for

71

defense, education, collecting taxes, and a host of other public activities. And after 1634, delegates to the Massachusetts general assembly were elected by town meetings. The Fundamental Orders of Connecticut (1639), the basic instrument of government in Connecticut, brought the separate towns of Hartford, Windsor, and Wethersfield together in a federation. Rhode Island presented an even more extreme example of town power. That colony's legal existence depended on a patent that Roger Williams successfully acquired in 1643 from England's Parliament, which authorized the union of "Providence Plantation" with settlements on Aquidneck Island. As such, the colony of "Rhode Island and Providence Plantations" confederated the towns of Providence, Portsmouth, Newport, and Warwick. The colony's assembly, which met four times a year, moved from town to town, with no home base.

The importance of town government in New England was much like that of counties in the Chesapeake. Indeed, the vitality of local government became a distinction of the English colonies—and provided a grounding in self-government lacking in most other colonial empires.

THE COST OF EXPANSION

Puritans' first encounters with Indians near their settlements were relatively peaceful simply because there were very few native people there. An epidemic between 1616 and 1619 had left much of the area near Plymouth and the Massachusetts Bay unpopulated. To the colonies' south, however, the Pequots, who lived in what would become eastern Connecticut, and the Narragansetts, whose territory ringed the Narragansett Bay in what became Rhode Island, had avoided the epidemic's ravages. Those two tribes were rivals for the fur trade down the Connecticut River, which the Pequots dominated. The establishment of trading posts on the river by the Plymouth colonists and the Dutch and later the founding of settlements there threatened the Pequots' hegemony and led to violent clashes. At first, those incidents were between traders and Indians, but they spread. And after Indians attacked Wethersfield, Connecticut, the colonies of Massachusetts Bay and Connecticut undertook "an offensive warr ag't the Pequoitt."

"The violence at West Mystic shocked even the Narragansetts, whose mode of warfare, like that of most other Indians, was more ceremonial than deadly, and who never sought so total a devastation of noncombatants."

The decisive action took place at an Indian fort in what is now West Mystic, Connecticut, in the early morning of May 26, 1637. With their Narragansett and Mohegan allies encircling the fort, the English forced their way inside, where they discovered a large number of wigwams—which they decided to burn, using gunpowder to build a fire that "blazed most terribly." Those who tried to flee the conflagration were cut down by Indians or English soldiers outside. In about half an hour, some 400 Pequots died, most of them old men, women, and children. In the following weeks, the English and their allies chased the terrified Pequots into the woods, slaughtering many and selling others into slavery. Within two months, about 700 Pequots had died or been captured, although the English lost fewer than 100. In 1638, the Treaty of Hartford put an end to the Pequots as a people, taking away their name as well as their lands.

The violence at West Mystic shocked even the Narragansetts, whose mode of warfare, like that of most other Indians, was more ceremonial than deadly, and who never sought so total a devastation of noncombatants. Once the massacre ended, an English officer reported, the Narragansetts cried, "*Mach it, mach it*; that is, it is naught, it is naught, because it is too furious, and slaies too many men." The English brought such a deadly way of war with them from their experience with wars in the Netherlands and from Ireland. But Indians, too, could learn to burn homes and massacre enemies' families.

The English took pride in their weaponry. In an earlier maneuver on nearby Block Island, one Englishman rejoiced that only a single volley showed the Indians that "our bullets . . . out-reach their arrows." But volleys were about all the English could shoot. They used old-fashioned matchlock muskets that were fine for formal battles in good weather on open fields, where, as in Europe, each side began by shooting volleys at the other side. Those muskets couldn't be aimed; in fact, they had no sights. They were so heavy that a brace was necessary to support the barrel, and unless the match—a rope of combustible material—could be kept lit, a gunman had no way of detonating his gunpowder and making the gun fire. Such weapons were unsuited for forest warfare, or for so wet a climate as New England's. Nor were they hunting weapons—but then, New England's settlers were no more hunters than those who founded Virginia. Hunting in England was a sport

A seventeenth-century engraving depicting the battle at what is now West Mystic, Connecticut, on May 26, 1637. At the center is the Pequot village, with its burning houses inside a palisade fence with two openings where, the engraving indicates, the colonists entered. Settlers are shown firing guns at Indians armed with bows and arrows. Outside the palisade fence are more colonial soldiers and, behind them, their Mohegan and Narragansett allies.

One colony after another tried to prevent the sale of guns to Indians, but there was always some trader somewhere, often from New Netherland, who was willing to give the Indians what they wanted in return for the furs that they alone could supply. Indians, moreover, spent enough time working in the settlements that they soon learned to repair their weapons and even cast bullets. They proved, in fact, to be a technologically adaptable people who, for example, melted down swords (which are pretty useless in a forest) and kettles to make metal arrowheads, fitting European materials to their own needs and culture.

In short, the Indians learned from the Europeans a more devastating form of warfare than they had known and acquired firearms that allowed them to practice war with a vengeance. Before long, the English settlers had reason to regret being such good teachers. Their only recourse was to become students themselves: to obtain better guns, learn to aim them, and pick up Indian ways of war—ambushes and surprise attacks, which settlers had first condemned as an unmanly "skulking kind of war" compared with the formal battlefield encounters they somehow considered more civilized. The results would be deadly.

A PLACE LIKE ENGLAND?

New England was in many ways true to its name: the region meant to become a new and better version of the mother country, not its replication. Certainly its narrow religious character distinguished it even from the England of the 1650s, which was also ruled by Puritans. There, the need for civil peace in a nation filled with persons of different religious convictions prompted Oliver Cromwell and the English Puritans to adopt a system of religious toleration, which most New Englanders considered a sinful concession to error. Righteous and proud of their church establishment and laws requiring religious uniformity, Massachusetts Bay and the colonies closest to it pulled away from England; only Roger Williams was at home with Oliver Cromwell. New England's economy, however, had much more in common with the mother country than that of the tobacco colonies. It developed a genuine mixed economy, one that was primarily agricultural but included a commercial sector and even some manufacturing.

The middle-class immigrants to Massachusetts did not expect to reduce their standard of living substantially by com-

for the upper class. Sometimes the colonists could shoot at a thick flock of birds and hit something, anything, but that was about it. Most of the meat colonists ate came from farm animals. Occasionally they feasted on deer or waterfowl, but they usually bought those foods from Indians, who knew how to hunt.

Indians were from the first interested in acquiring guns, but not the matchlock muskets that most colonists owned. The Indians insisted on the more modern and expensive flintlock muskets, which dispensed with the match and used flint to create a spark that detonated gunpowder more reliably. Flintlock muskets were also lighter, and the Indians preferred relatively short barrels because they were more convenient for hunting in the woods. Accustomed to hitting targets with bows and arrows, they quickly became expert marksmen. They probably also shot several small balls ("swan shot") rather than the customary European musket balls, which increased their chances of hitting their prey.

ing to America. That standard required textiles, metal tools and utensils, and other items that were generally imported from England. During the 1630s, paying for these imported items was no problem. The masses of arriving immigrants brought money with them, since they had sold their homes and businesses in England. On arrival, they bought what they needed to get settled—homes or the materials to build them, food, and livestock. Merchants then used the money they received to pay for imports. But when the flood of arrivals stopped, the New England economy went into crisis: the price of cattle, for example, fell as much as 75–80 percent in a year. How to pay for imports became a real problem.

A flintlock musket from 1640. Flintlock muskets were lighter than their predecessors, the matchlock muskets. They also dispensed with the "match," a string of combustible material used to ignite gunpowder, and used instead a flint, which worked much better, especially in damp conditions.

What could New England trade for the goods it needed? The region's climate was so much like England's that it could produce few products that England lacked. The greater part of New England's people were farmers who set out to grow the grains they knew in England, particularly wheat, barley, and

A soldier with an old matchlock musket, which required the use of a brace before firing. Although in Europe the weapon was commonly used on the battlefield, it was ill-suited to frontier uses, such as hunting.

also rye for making beer, using traditional farming techniques and tools. Unlike Plymouth in its opening years, the Massachusetts Bay Colony had plows—thirty-seven of them by 1637, each of which served many farms—and also oxen to pull the plows. But familiar grains did not always do well in American soil. Indian corn (maize) did much better, and soon became a popular crop. But it was even less likely to find a market in Europe than grains that the English were growing in sufficient quantities for themselves. Similarly, the colony's expanding stock of cattle, pigs, and poultry allowed it to feed its people but did not provide an easy way to pay for manufactured imports. And although New Englanders did collect beaver pelts from the Connecticut Valley and northeastern New England for shipment abroad, the supply of pelts from those areas soon dried up, and the Dutch controlled trade with Indians west of the Hudson.

One way to deal with the problem was to reduce imports, which the Massachusetts General Court tried to do by encouraging domestic cloth production. The colony's sheep herds grew, promising a good supply of wool, and merchants began importing cotton from Barbados. But except in remote areas where there was no alternative to homespun, New Englanders continued to use imported cloth. Their need for iron, however, led to one of the most technologically advanced industrial projects in seventeenth-century America: the Hammersmith Iron Works on the Saugus River in Lynn, Massachusetts.

John Winthrop Jr., the gregarious, enterprising son of Massachusetts's grave first governor, put together the set of English investors who funded the enterprise. He then surveyed possible locations and, after one bad choice, settled on the Saugus site, which had a good supply of bog iron. After the

General Court agreed to give the enterprise free land, tax exemption, freedom from militia duty for employees, and a twenty-one-year monopoly on iron making, the organizers brought in skilled ironmasters and constructed an ironworks that was large and technologically advanced even by English standards.

The Hammersmith Iron Works included an enormous blast furnace, some twenty-five feet tall, whose fire was fed by a huge leather bellows opened with power from a waterwheel and closed by counterweights. Iron ore was melted down in the furnace with charcoal and gabbro rock, a fluxing agent (that is, a material that combined chemically with waste products to separate them from iron) readily available in the area. Then skilled workmen drained off the waste (or slag) and ran the molten iron into a sand mold that resembled a sow nursing piglets. The resulting product, called "pig iron," could be cast in clay forms to make pots and similar iron products. But it still contained too many impurities to stand stress. So the Hammersmith Works also maintained a three-hearth forge. There, skilled ironworkers reheated the pig iron, stirring it to burn off excess carbon, let it solidify, and then, to remove more impurities, worked the red-hot iron with an enormous hammer powered by one of the forge's four waterwheels. The result was wrought iron, which local blacksmiths formed into horseshoes or tools such as axes, hoes, spades, and mattocks to peel back sod and open fields for planting. Hammersmith even had a water-powered rolling and slitting mill, where iron was formed into long sheets, then cut into strips that could easily be made into nails. To construct so sophisticated a plant in seventeenth-century Massachusetts was, according to historian Stephen Innes, "akin to building a nuclear accelerator in the Amazonian wilderness today."

Hammersmith generated a great amount of iron—but no profits. The investors cried mismanagement and dismissed one director after another. A more certain reason was the high cost of wages and supplies. Then, too, in return for its concessions, the General Court had insisted that the company export no iron until domestic needs had been supplied. But people in Massachusetts had no money. By

the 1650s, the investors refused to throw more good resources after bad, creditors panicked, and the company collapsed amid a flurry of lawsuits. Although a group of local merchants tried to start it up again, high costs finally forced Hammersmith to close in 1676. A number of less ambitious furnaces, or "bloomeries," continued, however, at several other sites. At a bloomery, a single operator melted a small quantity of iron over a charcoal fire on a stone hearth, fanning the fire with bellows to reach high temperatures; that separated out most of the slag. The ironmaster then hammered the iron as it cooled to break up remaining lumps of waste products. The resulting bar iron could be heated and hammered into various shapes, and thus answered most colonial needs. Some of these bloomeries lasted into the nineteenth century.

A local supply of iron was invaluable, but it remained relatively expensive and left unanswered the big question of how New England would pay for its imports. Selling fish was one possibility. When troubles in Britain kept English fishermen from American waters in the 1640s, the colonists moved right in. At first, they supplied fish to local consumers; then New England fish merchants paired up with London merchants in an arrangement that brought American fish—often dried

A modern reconstruction of the seventeenth-century Hammersmith Iron Works in Massachusetts, showing an "undershot" waterwheel, with which the water hit the wheel at its bottom.

cod—to Spain or the Wine Islands (the Azores, Madeira, the Canaries) for credits that paid for shipments of manufactured goods from Britain.

After a while, New Englanders were able to make voyages to southern Europe on their own. And they discovered a new market in the Caribbean Islands, where, after growing tobacco and then briefly cotton with limited success, planters began in the 1640s, with the encouragement and instruction of Dutch traders, to produce sugar instead. On Barbados, planters were so busy making sugar, a correspondent wrote Governor John Winthrop in 1647, that they would "rather buy foode at very deare rates than produce it by labour, so infinite is the profitt of sugar workes after once accomplished." In the Caribbean, New Englanders could sell "refuse" fish—dried cod that was broken, oversalted, or damaged and so could not be sold in southern Europe—to feed the slaves that sugar planters bought in place of indentured servants. Caribbean planters also needed horses and livestock, grain and timber. And they wanted more slaves. One New England voyage of 1644 brought fish to the Canary Islands and picked up slaves, which the crew then sold in Barbados. That opened an entirely new line of trade. Soon New England became a major source of supplies for the West Indies, where again it received credits from British merchant houses with which to pay for imports.

MILLS

A key device in New Englanders' changing ways of life was the mill, an ancient machine that harnessed some source of power to turn a wheel, which could be used to perform tasks otherwise done by human labor. In the West Indies, treadmills often ground sugarcane, a step in the refinement of sugar. There, the power often came from horses that trod in endless circles—which helps explain why New England shipped so many horses to the Caribbean. Barbados also built windmills, as did New Amsterdam (which used them to grind grain) and some Massachusetts towns including Boston and Charlestown. Watermills were, however, the most advanced form of mechanical power in the early seventeenth century, and New Englanders built them almost everywhere they could. Although English workers were known to burn down mills that replaced human labor, in America the scarcity of workers made labor-saving devices like watermills popular. New England could also count on a wealth of rivers, streams,

A sugar mill, using horses to turn a "treadmill" and so to grind sugarcane.

and waterfalls to turn the wheels. And the region's long coast allowed the construction of tide mills, which captured water in a special pond or cove at high tide, then slowly released it through a sluice, where it nicely turned a wheel while making its way back into the sea.

Sometimes the mechanisms were simple. Horizontal mills, for example, consisted of a wheel, often of wood, attached to a horizontal millstone by means of a central rod. The wheel was so positioned that a stream of water turned it, rotating the millstone above. Millers ground grain between that top stone and another just beneath it. These devices were cheap and popular: people would walk miles to have their grain ground in a gristmill rather than eat the coarse bread produced by grinding grain in a mortar or a hand-worked set of grinding stones known as a quern.

Other New England mills, like those at Hammersmith, were more elaborate. They had great wheels immersed perpendicular to moving water, which either ran below them (undershot wheels), dropped down from above (overshot), or hit them at some point midway ("pitchback," or "breastshot"). Then by a series of cranks and gears, usually fashioned of wood, the power could be used to perform a large number of tasks such as opening bellows, working trip-hammers—or sawing wood.

Without a sawmill, timber had to be sawed into planks by hand, often by pit sawing, where one man worked down in a hole or pit and another man worked above, pulling or pushing a long saw blade up and down through a log held in a frame. That was hard work and especially nasty for the guy on the bottom. How much better to have waterpower work the blade or blades up and down (circular saws remained two centuries away) and, sometimes, move a log against the blade. By the end of the seventeenth century, virtually every Massachusetts township had at least one sawmill, which produced boards mainly for local consumption. Sawmills also made possible large-scale commercial production for export—which was the primary purpose of a string of sawmills first built in the 1630s along the Piscataqua River in New Hampshire. In the 1640s, Boston merchants who recognized the mills' commercial possibilities began to take them over, and then built more there and in Maine (which remained part of Massachusetts). The first patent to be issued in Massachusetts—and perhaps anywhere in the mainland colonies—went in 1646 to an ironmaster, Joseph Jencks, "for the

making of Engines for mills to goe with water for the more speedy dispatch of worke . . . with a new Invented Saw-Mill, that things may be afforded cheaper than formerly." By contrast, as late as 1649, Virginia, with its rich supplies of timber and iron, had no sawmills whatsoever. Later, however, it, too, would possess abundant grist and sawmills, though mainly to supply local demand.

The demand for boards and other timber products was almost unremitting in a country being built anew. And nothing made of wood was forever: Boston, for example, suffered devastating fires no less than nine times in its first 130 years, so it had to be rebuilt again and again. A good part of the homes and plantation structures in the British West Indies were made of wood that generally came, like Boston's, from northern New England. The ready availability of sawn boards also opened other opportunities. They could be used, for example, to build furniture—or at least to provide the crude backs and drawer bottoms for pieces otherwise made of hand-processed wood.

More important, relatively cheap sawn boards made the work of constructing houses easier. House frames were usually made of oak logs shaped into a square with a broadaxe. If the shaped logs were visible, their sides were evened out with an adze, a hoe-like tool whose blade was curved and sharp, but which nonetheless left the telltale clefts still observable today on the exposed beams of historic houses. Wooden pegs (tenons) inserted through holes (mortices) held together the carefully shaped parts of "mortise and tenon" joints in the frame, but colonists tried to keep the need for such "joinery" to a minimum. It helped a lot when colonists could enclose their houses by nailing mill-sawn pine boards to vertical posts or fastening them on beams to make floors. Roofs, which were at first covered with bundles of rush or straw, were later sheathed with boards and then covered with shingles—which colonists split from a log, then shaped by hand with a drawknife, a two-handled tool for shaving wood.

Sawn boards also allowed the development of shipbuilding. As New England's commerce grew, merchants needed ships, and it made sense to build them in America. England lacked the wood; indeed, she became a major purchaser of ships made in shipyards at Salem, Boston, and other points along the New England coast. Ships also required iron for bolts, braces, and anchors, and those needs provided more incentive to develop a domestic iron industry. To build a ship was a complex task that, in a major shipyard, involved many

An "Iron back" probably made at the Hammersmith Iron Works in 1660. Iron backs, which are today called "firebacks," were put at the rear of fireplaces to protect the bricks and reflect heat into the room. They were made by pressing a carved wooden pattern into sand, and then filling the depression with molten iron.

Chronology		
	1517	Martin Luther's 95 theses usher in the Protestant Reformation.
	1585–87	Sir Walter Raleigh sends settlers to Roanoke Island.
	1606–07	The Virginia colony founded at Jamestown.
	1608	Samuel de Champlain founds Quebec.
	1620	Pilgrims found colony at Plymouth.
	1624	The Dutch found New Netherland.
	1629–30	Puritan settlers found the Massachusetts Bay Colony.
	1632	Charles I grants proprietary colony of Maryland to George Calvert, Lord Baltimore.
	1636	Roger Williams founds Rhode Island.
		Harvard College established.

skilled workers: shipwrights to oversee the work, ship smiths to do ironwork, sawyers to produce irregular structural pieces of wood that could not be milled, carpenters, joiners, and caulkers. And some products, particularly cordage and sailcloth, had to be imported.

Shipyards, like mercantile voyages, sawmills, forges, and wharves and docks, were usually financed by sets of investors who pooled their capital and divided the profits—another example of New England's penchant for group efforts. Creative finance and mercantile initiative contributed to New England's early economic growth, but the most important factor was the capacity of one activity to inspire other "linkages"— fishing and trade, for example, brought a need for ships, which increased the demand for sawn boards and iron fittings, and so for building more sawmills and forges. The high cost of labor as well as the widespread demand for iron tools and utensils and for high-quality milled grain encouraged the development of water-driven technology. And literacy equipped people to recognize opportunities and figure out how to implement them. Enterprises sometimes failed, mainly because of high labor costs, but not for lack of effort. New Englanders' godly industriousness saw to that.

SUCCESS OR FAILURE?

By 1660, New England was a bustling, prosperous place. Most of its people were farmers who worked their own land or that of their fathers, but even inland towns produced some livestock and food for export. Boston had become the preeminent colonial port, leaving behind New Haven and other would-be rivals along the Atlantic coast. It was a very different town from the Boston of Anne Hutchinson, and its changes paralleled those throughout the region. Young John Winthrop Jr. seemed to typify his generation. Less obsessed with theology than science, especially chemistry and metallurgy, Winthrop became the first American member of the Royal Society, England's premier scientific organization. He was also an entrepreneur who moved easily between England and America and was welcome in both crazy Rhode Island and rigid New Haven. The Puritans' work ethic, group orientation, and attention to the education of the young had helped produce a people far more prosperous than anyone familiar with the rocky, thin soil of cold New England would have predicted, and more worldly than the founders had hoped.

Had New England lost its way, giving in to those "carnall intencions" of which Winthrop's father had warned on the *Arbella* thirty years earlier? Surely it had to make compromises along the way. The fishermen who worked the waters off the Massachusetts and Maine coasts were seldom Puritans: most had arrived after 1640, when the Great Migration was over, and were often west-country fishermen who wandered down from Newfoundland when the fishing season ended. Like the first Virginians, they were young, single, poor, and had a penchant for drink and brawling. The imported ironworkers were much the same: when not engaged in the intense labor of their craft, they were given to beating their wives and raising Cain. These were not the kind of folk John Winthrop Sr. had expected to people his "City upon a Hill."

Had the colony given up too much of its original vision in pursuing economic success? Or did its prosperity witness God's pleasure in His New World chosen people? Whatever the answer, there could be no doubt that by 1660 the New England and Chesapeake colonies were firmly planted on a land where no stable European settlements had existed only sixty years earlier. In only a few decades, settlers established cultural, economic, and political patterns whose influence would last for centuries.

Before long, the prosperity of these colonies attracted the attention of England's newly restored Crown. Then their independence would pass, and they would be become, happy or not, part of an empire.

Suggested Reading

Virginia DeJohn Anderson, *New England's Generation: The Great Migration and the Formation of Society and Culture in the Seventeenth Century* (1991)

James Axtell, *Natives and Newcomers: The Cultural Origins of North America* (2001)

Carol E. Hoffecker et al., eds., *New Sweden in America* (1995)

Stephen Innes, *Creating the Commonwealth: The Economic Culture of Puritan New England* (1995)

Peter C. Mancall, *Envisioning America: English Plans for the Colonization of North America, 1580–1640* (1995)

Edmund S. Morgan, *American Slavery, American Freedom: The Ordeal of Colonial Virginia* (1975)

David Quinn, *The Elizabethans and the Irish* (1966)

Oliver A. Rink, *Holland on the Hudson: An Economic and Social History of Dutch New York* (1986)

Thad W. Tate and David Ammerman, eds., *The Chesapeake in the Seventeenth Century: Essays on Anglo-American Society* (1979)

Daniel Vickers, *Farmers & Fishermen: Two Centuries of Work in Essex County, Massachusetts, 1630–1850* (1994)

Focus QUESTIONS

■ How did England's colonies in America become part of a British empire?

■ How did New France expand as part of the French empire?

■ How did the Iroquois respond to European imperial conflicts in this period?

■ What was the significance of the Pueblo uprising against Spanish rule in 1680?

■ What were the connections between the Salem witchcraft experience and the Indian wars on the New England frontier?

Rebecca Nurse did not seem like a witch. The wife of a prosperous farmer in Salem Village, Massachusetts, a covenanted member of the church in Salem Town, a beloved mother and grandmother, she was to all appearances a model Christian. But in late March of 1692, she stood accused of mysteriously torturing another villager, Ann Putnam, who suffered a "grievous fit" during the public hearings for all to see, as well as her daughter, also named Ann, and a young neighbor, Abigail Williams. Then another Salem Villager, Henry Kenny, testified "that since this Nurse came into his house he was seizd twise with an amazd condition."

"What do you say" to these accusers? the magistrates asked. "Oh Lord help me," the old woman cried, "& spread out her hands"—at which the accusers seemed "grievously vexed." How could she explain the extraordinary sufferings of those who charged her? Rebecca agreed they were "bewitcht," but not by her. That they saw a ghostly "apparition" of her proved nothing, since "the Devil may appear in my shape." And if Rebecca Nurse said so, who could doubt that Satan was on the loose in Massachusetts, urging people to "sign his book" and join his empire in its epic struggle against the rule of God?

Satan was apparently one of several powers trying to enlarge their dominion in North America during the late 1600s. Great Britain, France, Spain, and nearby Indians engaged more tangibly in an all-out effort to extend or reestablish their hold on the continent; and the French, Spanish, and Indians often seemed like the devil incarnate to the British settlers. Those imperial struggles had an impact not only on the famous Salem witchcraft crisis, but on all American colonists through much of the next century.

Great Britain

Oliver Cromwell, England's Protector and leader of the Puritan forces that had executed King Charles I, died in 1658. His son and heir, Richard Cromwell, could not control the army or the territory his father had governed. Exhausted by disorder, the English Parliament finally called the son of Charles I back from exile. The new king, Charles II, was an easygoing chap interested above all in his mistresses and the gay pastimes of court life. By the time of his death in 1685, he had produced no legitimate heir. As a result, the crown passed to his brother James, the Duke of York, who spent most of his short reign alienating his subjects.

King James II saw no reason why he, unlike the French king, should have to work with Parliament. He tried to rule autocratically, without Parliament but with the help of the army, and made no effort to conceal his Catholicism. When his Catholic wife gave birth to a son who would be raised Catholic, and became first in line to inherit the throne, his Protestant subjects had had enough. They rallied behind the king's Protestant son-in-law William of Orange, who invaded in November 1688 and forced James II and his son into exile. In 1689, the English called to the throne William and his wife, Mary, James's Protestant daughter by an earlier marriage.

At first glance, that story seems as filled with stops and starts as the complex history of earlier seventeenth-century England, with its civil wars and wild swings from monarchy to Commonwealth to Protectorate. During that earlier time of troubles, the British colonies in the Chesapeake and New England had become virtually independent. But not now: Britain's hold over North America increased in a more or less continuous way between the Restoration of Charles II in 1660 and 1702, when Anne, a second Protestant daughter of James II, inherited the throne from the childless William and Mary.

FILLING IN THE COAST

During the reigns of Charles II and James II, the British claimed or seized lands that linked and extended their previous holdings on the eastern coast of North America. Upon those lands, they established six new British mainland colonies.

Carolina. In 1663, Charles II rewarded eight of his supporters by giving them a proprietary title to all the land between Florida and the southern border of Virginia and westward "sea to sea," from the Atlantic to the Pacific. He also granted them considerable power over this new colony of Carolina: like the proprietors of Maryland, they received all "Rights, Jurisdictions, Privileges, Prerogatives . . . and Franchises of what kind soever . . . in as ample manner as any Bishop of Durham, in our Kingdom of England" had ever exercised. Like the lands of the bishops of Durham, which lay on England's border with Scotland, Maryland and Carolina were frontier regions whose proprietors would need, it seemed, substantial authority to defend their territory against hostile neighbors.

By the 1660s, the sense that England contained a surplus of people, once so powerfully expressed by the younger Richard Hakluyt, had disappeared. The mother country had work enough for her people and was anxious to keep them at home. New colonies would have to be peopled from older ones or from other sources. Barbados was one promising source of settlers. Over the previous two decades, wealthy planters there had expanded their landholdings so they could produce more sugar, an extremely profitable commodity. Those ex-planters who were squeezed out would surely go to Carolina in return for generous grants of land as "headrights" for themselves and the servants and slaves they brought with them. Virginia's Governor William Berkeley was sure that

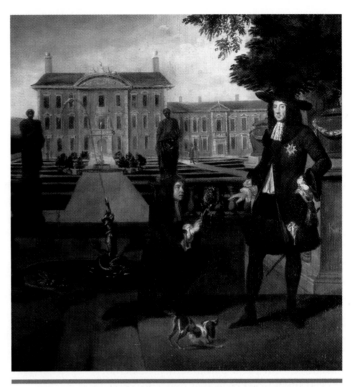

Charles II, here receiving a pineapple from the colony of Barbados.

some Virginians would also move to Carolina, since all the land in Virginia's Tidewater section was already claimed. Migrants from New England and Bermuda, both of which were well populated, might also settle in Carolina. Then, without incurring the loss of much except the empty territory they used to lure settlers, the proprietors could make good money by charging annual quitrents on land.

Virginians did cross their southern border and settle the more northerly regions of the Carolina grant along Albemarle Sound. And settlers from Barbados went farther south, bringing their slaves along. As a result, what later became South Carolina was the first British mainland colony that began with a labor system based on black chattel slavery. Under this system, persons of African origin or descent were bound to work not for a set number of years, like white indentured servants, but for life; their children were also born into a life of perpetual servitude, and they stood in law as the property, or chattel, of their masters. (On the development of slave labor in America, see Chapter 4.)

Plans for the colony took the form of a written document, the Fundamental Constitutions of Carolina of 1669, which was prepared by one of the proprietors, Sir Anthony Ashley Cooper (later the Earl of Shaftesbury), and John Locke, who would become an English political theorist of considerable significance but for the moment served as secretary to Cooper and the proprietors. The document provided for the progressive division of the land into squares of 12,000 acres each, which would be organized into units called provinces, counties, seigniories, baronies, and still-smaller colonies. Two-thirds of the land would be held by hereditary nobles with exotic titles like "landgrave" and "cacique," the rest by manorial lords and ordinary landowners. The Fundamental Constitutions decreed that no one could "disturbe, molest or persecute another for his . . . opinions in Religion or his way of Worship," which made Carolina attractive to dissenters, but at the same time allowed state support for the established church and so avoided alienating potential Anglican settlers. It also gave masters absolute control over their slaves. The document provided for a governor and a Grand Council, which would serve as both a court and a plural executive, and for a parliament, or assembly, elected by men who needed only fifty acres to qualify for the vote and would have the benefit of a secret ballot, which was far ahead of the time.

The Fundamental Constitutions of Carolina, in short, was a curious blend of provisions inspired by an older European feudal world that were ill suited to a thinly settled frontier territory and more advanced policies adopted to attract immigrants such as religious toleration and broad political participation. The document never went entirely into effect, but it made a lasting impact on the colony both for what it did and what it neglected to do. It did not, for example, provide for local government, which failed to develop in Carolina as it had in the Chesapeake and New England.

Carolina grew slowly at first because of internal divisions and conflicts with Indians and the Spanish. The proprietors' dream of easy riches never materialized: they were forced to contribute heavily to the colony and to forgo quitrents during its first decades. For those sacrifices they received little in return.

In 1680, settlers founded the city of Charles Town (which became Charleston a century later) on land adjoining a harbor with good ocean access at the confluence of the Cooper and Ashley Rivers. Carefully laid out with streets at right angles to each other, it was the first planned city of British North Amer-

"Carefully laid out with streets at right angles to each other, Charles Town was the first planned city of British North America."

ica. In the next two years, the colony's population doubled, reaching 2,200 in 1682. It continued to grow with new influxes of French Huguenots, English dissenters, and Scots. After experimenting with a variety of warm-climate crops including cotton and indigo, the colonists developed a profitable trade in timber products, livestock, and, by the end of the century, rice. Both the open-range cattle farming practiced in South Carolina and the rice culture depended heavily on the skills of African slaves. By 1708, a majority of South Carolina's 9,000–10,000 people were black.

A very different society emerged in the Albemarle province, or North Carolina, as it was called after 1691. Although there, too, livestock and timber products provided good sources of income, planters also grew substantial amounts of tobacco, which, having no good port of their own, they sold through Virginia. Dense forests and unpassable swamps separated the Albemarle settlers from Virginia, and yet they shared many characteristics with people in the Chesapeake region. Slaves, for example, represented a far smaller percentage of the 4,000–5,000 North Carolinians in 1700 than they did of the more prosperous Carolinians to their south. The two Carolinas maintained little contact with each other and had separate governments, although they were formally split only in 1729, when England's Parliament bought out the proprietors. At that time, the Crown, to the colonists' delight, assumed responsibility for governing the two colonies.

New York and New Jersey. A year after the Carolina grant, Charles II gave his brother James, the Duke of York, the territory between the Connecticut and Delaware Rivers, including the Hudson Valley and Long Island. That stretch of land later became the states of New Jersey and New York. It also included a good chunk of Connecticut. In fact, the duke's grant took in lands in Maine, the islands of Nantucket and Martha's Vineyard, and the entire Dutch colony of New Netherland. Negotiations might settle conflicts of title between the Duke of York and other Englishmen, but James sent commissioners and a fleet to establish his power over the Dutch colony, which he proposed to reduce to "an entyre submission and obedience." The fleet arrived at New Amsterdam in August 1664. A few days after its arrival, Governor Peter Stuyvesant, who commanded too few soldiers and supplies to hold out against the invaders, surrendered. Before long, Dutch outposts on the Hudson and the Delaware followed suit, and New Netherland—including what had been New Sweden—fell under the English Crown and the proprietorship of the Duke of York. The Dutch managed to reconquer the area in 1673, but lost it again for good a year later.

James's charter from the Crown did not require him to call an elected assembly to help govern the province, and he was not inclined to do so on his own. As he wrote one of his governors, assemblies showed an "aptness . . . to assume to themselves many priviledges w[hi]ch prove destructive to . . . the peace of the governm[en]t." Nevertheless, his need for money and the resistance of many colonists to paying taxes imposed without their consent convinced the duke to call an assembly in 1683, although it came to an end four years later, when James had become king.

Within months of first receiving his proprietary grant, James gave the area between the Hudson and Delaware Rivers, which became New Jersey, to a couple of followers, Sir George Carteret and John, Lord Berkeley (brother of the Virginia governor, William Berkeley). Unfortunately, James neglected to inform his governor in New York that he had done so, and the governor meanwhile also gave out land in New Jersey, some to groups of testy New England Puritans, on generous terms different in critical details from those of Carteret and Berkeley. Then, in a complicated set of maneuvers during the mid-1670s, Berkeley sold his portion of the colony, which became West New Jersey, to a group of Quakers, and Carteret became sole proprietor of the more heavily populated East New Jersey. After Carteret's death in 1680, his heirs sold his claims to a group of men who in turn sold off the lands, which were often poorly surveyed, in rather haphazard ways. Is it any wonder that much of New Jersey's colonial history consists of fights over land claims and what political rights they conferred?

Pennsylvania. By 1681, when the Crown granted William Penn title to the last of Britain's seventeenth-century North American colonies, it had reason to question the wisdom of creating more private jurisdictions. But Penn was a friend of the Duke of York, and his father, Admiral William Penn, held a claim on the royal treasury of some £16,000 for loans and service in the Royal Navy at the time of his death.

After briefly attending Oxford University, studying law, and managing his father's Irish estates, the younger Penn, to his father's dismay, joined the ranks of Quakers, a not-yet-respectable religious movement. The Quakers (a derogatory term, like "Puritan," that somehow stuck), or Friends (because they were members of the Society of Friends), believed that God's spirit was in all people equally and without exception, which made it hard to say one person was better than another by virtue of birth or any other distinction. They saw no need of priests or ministers—people could discover God simply by attending to their "Inner Light"—or of ceremonies or religious artifacts. They despised rank and outward show, dressed in plain clothes, and addressed each other as "thee" and "thou." Quakers refused to kneel or bow to anyone, even to tip their hats to men of what the world considered high rank, to take oaths, or to fight war or engage in any acts of violence, all of which violated God's rule of love. To many in Restoration England, the Quakers were ridiculous fanatics—and, it should be said, some early Quakers had acted in pretty outrageous ways, disrupting church services, for example, or appearing naked in public places to show how God would strip men down to essentials. They were also considered threats to the standing order and safest locked up in jail. Penn, who was himself imprisoned four times for publicly professing his beliefs, dreamed of founding a refuge for Quakers and other persecuted religious dissenters. In return for a colonial grant to lands west of the Delaware between New York and Maryland, where he hoped to set up that refuge, Penn was willing to forget the Crown's debt to his father.

A Quaker meeting, in which women participated equally with men.

In 1681, after nine months of bureaucratic scrutiny, Charles II granted Penn's petition for the colony. The king liked Penn personally, and having the lands west of the Delaware between New York and Maryland settled with Englishmen would be very much to Britian's advantage. It's possible that Charles II also looked with pleasure on the prospect of shipping a fair number of annoying Quakers off to a part of the world far from England. Penn's patent to what became Pennsylvania took effect in March, when it received the "great seal" from England's lord chancellor. At the time, William Penn was thirty-six years old. He would live another thirty-seven, dying in 1718.

Penn's lands were extensive: they stretched from New York to Maryland, and west through five degrees of longitude. His charter described some of the province's borders, particularly that to the south, only vaguely or in ways that made no sense given the geography of the area. As a result, Penn spent a considerable part of his life trying to settle Pennsylvania's border with Maryland—a feat that was not finally accomplished until the 1760s, long after his death, when Charles Mason and Jeremiah Dixon surveyed what became known as the Mason-Dixon line.

Penn became the absolute proprietor over the new colony with not only a claim to specified lands but great powers of governance. These, however, were restricted in several ways. In the ordinary course of affairs, he needed the advice and consent of an elected assembly in promulgating laws. Penn had to honor and respect the laws of Parliament regulating trade, and to keep an agent in England to answer charges of dereliction in that regard. And the Crown explicitly required him to allow customs officials within his province, permit appeals to the Crown from the decisions of Pennsylvania courts, and send to England for review transcripts of all laws within five years of their enactment. No earlier proprietary charter included that last provision, which was a sign of changing times. Penn's charter also protected the place of

William Penn, the founder of Pennsylvania.

Anglicans within the colony. But it did nothing to bar his intention of opening the colony to people of dissenting views.

And so Penn set out to found a "holy experiment," a colony that would serve God's "truth and people" and provide "an example . . . to the nations." But unlike the example to others that John Winthrop had once hoped Massachusetts would become, Penn's experiment would show how people of different religious convictions, Quakers and non-Quakers alike, could live together with **complete freedom to worship God as they chose.** To advertise his colony, Penn wrote two pamphlets that circulated widely within England, Wales, and Ireland, and, once translated into Dutch and German, through northern Europe. From the beginning, Pennsylvania's population included Swedes and Finns, Dutchmen and Germans, along with English, Welsh, and Irish settlers. They came for the liberty Penn offered and for land: "fifty acres shall be allowed," he said, "to the Master for every Head [brought into the colony], and Fifty Acres to every Servant when their time is expired." Penn also purchased from the Duke of York an additional three counties farther south on the Delaware River (later the separate colony of Delaware) to assure that the new port of Philadelphia would have secure access to the sea. Pennsylvania would indeed be a land of opportunity for, as Penn put it, "a sober and industrious people."

Penn assured prospective settlers that they "would be allowed to make their own laws." The Frame of Government he designed for the colony in 1682 provided for an elected council and assembly. As proprietor, he or, in his absence, a deputy governor would act with the council to propose laws (which the assembly could approve or reject), create courts and appoint judges, manage the treasury, and in general see that the colony was well governed. To the Frame of Government he attached forty laws. The first—which the colony's first assembly confirmed on December 4, 1682—provided freedom of religion for all who believed in God.

Even the port city of Philadelphia, located at the confluence of the Delaware and Schuylkill Rivers, attracted Penn's careful attention. He wanted it to be "a green country town, which will never be burnt" as London had been in a horrible fire during 1666, "and always be wholesome." After late October 1682, Penn worked with Thomas Holme, an Irish Quaker whom Penn had appointed the province's surveyor general, to create a plan by which the city's streets formed a rectangular grid whose longest sides ran east and west between the rivers. Five square, symmetrically arranged open areas broke the pat-

This painting by Peter Cooper shows Philadelphia some forty years after its founding, when it had become a prosperous port.

tern's monotony. Four were meant for recreation, but the plan dedicated the largest, a central area of ten acres, to "Houses for Public Affairs." None of the public buildings built there were so designed that they dominated the city, which remained spread out, decentralized. Streets were at first named after people, but within a few years that form of human vanity yielded to simple numbers, descriptive names like "Front," "High," and "Broad" Street, and other nonpersonal designations such as "Walnut," "Chestnut," and "Mulberry" Street. Penn allowed rich purchasers choice river locations, particularly along the Delaware. Still, the city plan, with its grid of identically sized blocks formed by cross-cutting streets, shared a certain consonance with Quaker ideals. It was simple and orderly, and suggested a society where people were free and equal, not tucked under the superior authority of some dominant family or institution.

These provisions failed to make everyone happy. Some settlers, including large investors whom Penn had favored, resented the locations assigned them and the fact that Penn's and Holme's plans were foisted on people without consultation. The settlers expressed their dissatisfaction in a "Humble Remonstrance & address" they presented to the proprietor. But their grievances were neither the beginning nor the end of Pennsylvania's discontents. Members of the assembly complained about their inability to initiate laws, and the mutterings grew louder after Penn—who, unlike most proprietors, actually lived for a time in his colony—returned to England to defend his land titles in 1684 and ended up staying there until 1701. Colonists bickered with a deputy governor named John Blackwell so persistently that Penn confessed deep personal sorrow over their fighting and urged them by mail "for the love of God, me and the poor country be not so governmen-

tish, so noisy, and open in your dissatisfaction." Blackwell rejoiced when, finally, Penn revoked his appointment. Of the Pennsylvania Quakers, Blackwell observed that "each prays for his neighbor on First Days and then preys upon him the other six."

That was not what Penn had envisioned. His experiment was hardly the first and surely not the last effort by Europeans to create in America a model society that would fulfill God's will and improve the state of mankind. None, if any, worked out as their projectors dreamed. But considered against those other experiments, Pennsylvania's actually turned out pretty well. In a time when people were still being killed for their religious beliefs, the colony established a system of religious toleration that remained a monument to freedom on into a later, more enlightened time.

WAR AND REBELLION

So dramatic an expansion of English settlement caused a new wave of conflicts with Indians. Englishmen often considered their cultivation of what were once Indian lands as a sign of civilization's victory over barbarism and savagery. Roger Williams—who disagreed with other Puritans on this as on so many other issues—recalled New Englanders' calling Indians "Heathen Dogges" who should be "all cut off" so the colonists would be "no more troubled with them" and the land opened for settlement by Christians. The colonists' successful displacement of Indians seemed to them a sign of God's providence for His chosen people, much as He had provided for the Jews when He settled them in Israel. The Indians and a handful of New Englanders such as Williams saw things differently.

William Penn's 1681 plan of Philadelphia. Penn wanted an open city, with streets arranged on a grid plan like that of other late seventeenth-century American cities, but with parks that broke the checkerboard pattern.

So did William Penn. Indians, the Quakers believed, were entitled to respect like all other people. Perhaps, as Penn said, they remained "under a dark Night" with regard to Christian truth, "yet they believe in a God and Immortality, without the help of Metaphysicks." Penn even suspected that the Indians descended from the Old Testament Jews—a nice switch on New Englanders' self-serving use of the Bible. He insisted on purchasing from the natives those lands the king had granted him. He also wrote the Indians that they and the settlers were alike dependent on "one Great God" who had "been pleased to make me concerned in your part of the world," which he hoped to enjoy with their "love and consent" and to avoid "the unkindness and injustice that hath been too much exercised toward you by the people of these parts of the world." In realizing that ambition, it helped that earlier Swedish and Dutch inhabitants of the Delaware valley had also purchased the lands they took and had maintained amicable relations with the local Indians, and that only the southeastern and western reaches of Pennsylvania were still home to substantial Indian populations. Even there, however,

the Quakers' pacifism kept Pennsylvania's early history free of those egregious acts of violence against Indians that marked Virginia's and New England's early history.

At the time of Pennsylvania's settlement, moreover, the wisdom of maintaining peaceful relations with the Indians was undeniable. New England had just suffered an Indian war that came close to totally destroying the settlements there. At almost the same time, a conflict with Indians in the backcountry of Virginia sparked a devastating civil war between two groups of Englishmen that left the colony's capital in ruins.

King Philip's War. New England's troubles began in Plymouth Colony. There, in 1621, the first settlers had negotiated a peace treaty with Massasoit, the chief, or sachem, of the nearby Wampanoag Indians. The peace lasted through Massasoit's lifetime and that of his son and successor, Wamsutta (or Alexander), who died in 1662. Then the new sachem, Wamsutta's brother Metacom, or King Philip, as he was also called, accepted a new agreement that formally acknowledged his people's subjection to the English Crown. But thirteen years later, Philip turned against the English settlements. Was he angered by fines that were levied on him by Plymouth courts? by the colonists' seemingly unending quest for land on which to pasture their cattle? by their cultural and political imperialism, which threatened to extinguish the Indians' identity altogether? Or was he pushed into hostilities by younger warriors, who in turn were angered by the colonists' hanging three Indians convicted of murder? Rumors that King Philip was planning war circulated long before an English settler shot and killed an Indian who was looting abandoned homes in the Plymouth Colony town of Swansea. In retaliation, Indians attacked the town on June 20, 1675—and the war was on.

It did not remain confined to Plymouth Colony. The litany of towns attacked or destroyed by Indians hopped across the map of New England, utterly oblivious of the lines that separated colony from colony. Terrified for their lives, colonists flocked toward the coast until, by April 1676, the town of Sudbury, only seventeen miles west of Boston, had become a frontier town. Some twenty-five New England towns, over half the total, were severely damaged or destroyed. Estimates of deaths among the colonists vary, but perhaps a tenth of the region's men were killed along with another 1,500 women and children. And the war's cost must also include the cattle taken off or killed and the hay, corn, and other crops destroyed.

Southern New England's Indians were no longer fighting the quasi-ceremonial wars of times past, nor were they sparing noncombatants. They had learned the English style of war at places like West Mystic, Connecticut, nearly forty years earlier. They used torches and special "fire arrows" (arrows wrapped with rags sometimes containing brimstone) to set colonists' houses in flames, and at one point even employed a wheel-born device carrying burning materials to attack a colonial garrison under siege. Rather than adopt the traditional English preference for open-field battles, though, the Indians continued to mount ambushes and surprise attacks on towns and militia companies—with extraordinary success. Their skillful marksmanship with flintlock muskets, acquired at first for hunting, added to the death tolls. Distinctively clothed colonial officers seem to have been a favored target.

The war was not, however, a simple fight of Indians against Europeans. The Wampanoags found allies among the Narragansetts, who also lived near the Narragansett Bay, and the more northerly inland Nipmuc and Pocumtuck Indians. But some Indians remained neutral, and others, including those along the Massachusetts coast, the Nausets on Cape Cod, the Mohegans, and what remained of the Pequots, as well as certain tribes along the Connecticut River, sided with the colonists. The English could also draw on resident communities of "praying" Indians, who had been converted to Christianity by devoted missionaries such as the Reverend John Eliot, the famous "apostle to the Indians." There were probably over 2,000 of them on the eve of the war, but in Massachusetts they—and other friendly Indians—attracted so much suspicion that the Bay Colony sent its Christian Indians to Deer Island in Boston Harbor, where many died during their internment.

After the colonists had suffered extensive losses, however, some militia officers began enlisting Indians as scouts (a job at which colonists seemed particularly inept) and then as soldiers. Connecticut had used loyal Indian scouts and units "part English and part Indians" early on, and suffered far less devastation than its eastern neighbors. Now, with the help of Indian allies, companies of Massachusetts and Plymouth soldiers began pushing back the Indian offensive. A change in tactics also helped. Prejudices in favor of European-style warfare continued, but gradually colonists stopped condemning what they had once called the Indians' "skulking kind of war" and came to appreciate the military value of stealth, sudden raids, and good marksmanship. At long last, they even abandoned matchlock for flintlock muskets, as had the Indians long before. The man who finally shot King Philip on August 12, 1676, was an Indian who fought in a unit of both Indians and Englishmen under Plymouth's Captain Benjamin Church, who advocated the colonists' adoption of Indian raiding tactics and practiced what he preached. A century later, those tactics would not be Indian, but American.

The colonists' victory—indeed, their survival—depended, in short, on divisions among the region's Indians and on the settlers' adoption of Indian tactics. But for New England's Indians, friend and foe alike, King Philip's War was a massive defeat. In the six months before Philip's death, the colonial forces killed or captured thousands of enemy Indians. The victors executed some prisoners and sent others, including Philip's wife and child, to the West Indies, where they were sold as slaves. Indian losses represented a greater part of their shrunken population than did those of the settlers against their own increasing numbers. Surviving Indians sometimes fled to New York or Canada and were absorbed into other tribes. Indian allies also suffered, since close contact with col-

King Philip, or Metacom, sachem of New England's Wampanoag Indians, who turned against the settlers and so helped begin the bloody conflict remembered as King Philip's War, 1675–76.

onists, John Eliot testified, taught many "to love strong drink," which "proved a horrible snare." Thereafter, New England's Indian population—ally and enemy, Christian and "heathen"—continued to decline from disease until, by the middle of the next century, only a few thousand remained.

Colonists welcomed news of King Philip's death as if it meant the war had ended. But fighting soon began on the Maine frontier, where the Abenaki Indians continued to attack English settlements. An incident at the seaport town of Marblehead, Massachusetts, in July 1677 suggests the extraordinary hatred these wars provoked: there, a crowd of women attacked and killed two captured Indians, leaving the bodies "with their heads off and gone, and their flesh in a manner pulled from the bones." Elsewhere the enormous task of rebuilding began, absorbing New England's energy and resources and reducing its capacity to defend its independence against further threats.

Bacon's Rebellion. The situation in Virginia was different. After mounting a deadly but unsuccessful uprising in 1644 (in which some 500 colonists died), the descendants of Powhatan moved inland. Under a treaty negotiated in 1646, they could not even enter sections of coastal Virginia without the colony's permission. By 1660, however, most lands along the Tidewater had been claimed by a relatively small number of land-speculating Virginians. As a result, new immigrants—about 1,000 of whom were arriving every year—and ex-servants whose indentures expired after mid-century had either to become tenants, leave Virginia altogether, or, the alternative many preferred, go farther upriver in search of land. But as they pushed toward the interior, they once again came in contact with Indians, some of whom were bound by the 1646 treaty and others who were not. The situation was ripe for trouble, and in July 1675 an Indian raid on a frontier plantation set off a series of bloody raids and counter-raids. News of King Philip's War increased the frontiersmen's fear: they decided that Indians all along the Atlantic coast had joined a "Generall Combinacion" to exterminate white settlers. By March 1676, 300 Virginians and uncounted numbers of Indians were dead.

Violence also occurred between two groups of white Virginians who differed, among other things, on how to respond to the frontier crisis. On one side was Governor William Berkeley, an Englishman of wit and sophistication, then in his seventies, who had been reappointed as Virginia's governor (a job he first held in the 1640s) by Charles II, but who had made

some serious enemies in Virginia. For one thing, he bestowed many lucrative privileges on a handful of followers known as the Greenspring faction because they gathered at "Greenspring," Berkeley's handsome home outside Jamestown. He had also refused to call a new assembly election since 1661, and in 1670 the pliant assemblymen he kept in office restricted the vote to landholders. As Berkeley and his faction centralized authority, the power of local governments declined. That left discontented frontiersmen few peaceful, legal ways to defend themselves and their interests.

Sir William Berkeley, longtime governor of Virginia.

In early 1676, Berkeley decided not to march against the Indians, but, with the assembly's consent, to build a series of forts along the heads of rivers and station there hundreds of generously paid soldiers recruited from the Tidewater counties along with some friendly Indians. The frontiersmen protested that hostile Indians would sneak through the forest between Berkeley's forts, whose costs would in any case come from their taxes and go to the same people whose pockets Berkeley always lined. To people of the frontier, moreover, all Indians were bad: even if they weren't cutting settlers' throats, they were holding lands Englishmen could put to better use. So the frontiersmen decided to take matters into their own hands. They recruited as their leader Nathaniel Bacon, the twenty-nine-year-old son of a good English family. Bacon's overseer had been killed by Indians, and Bacon himself had some private grievances against Berkeley.

Then the story got truly complicated. Berkeley declared Bacon and his followers rebels and sent 300 men to stop them from attacking the Indians. He also announced the election of a new assembly and, despite the law of 1670, let all freemen, whether or not they owned land, cast ballots. Bacon was among the elected delegates, but when he went to Jamestown to take his seat, Berkeley arrested him. Then, after Bacon apologized, Berkeley pardoned him and promised to give him a commission to march against the Indians. Was the governor trying to avoid alienating an assembly sympathetic to

Bacon's cause? Probably, since Berkeley again declared Bacon and his followers rebels against the king after the assembly dissolved. At that point, Bacon moved his troops—he had raised some 1,300 volunteers—not west, against the Indians, but east, against Berkeley, who promptly fled Jamestown for Virginia's eastern shore.

Bacon's Rebellion was not a simple war of the have-nots against the haves. To be sure, the "Declaration of the People" Bacon issued on July 30, 1676, condemned raising taxes "for the advancement of private Favourites and other sinister ends" and promised "to ruine and exterpate all Indians in general" as well as the trade with them that had enriched the fortunes of Berkeley's "favourites." Moreover, Bacon's followers on the frontier had little love for the land-rich, selfish planters of the Tidewater. But Bacon had no objection to elite rule in principle; he just thought Berkeley's followers were unqualified for the power and privileges they enjoyed. Let us examine their origins, Bacon once proposed, and see whether their "extractions and Education" were not "vile." For three months, while Bacon fought the Indians, some of his followers and Berkeley's went about pillaging the estates of men on one side or the other, carrying off whatever "fine goods" they fancied. The result was a redistribution of property not so much from rich to poor, in the manner of Robin Hood, as from one group of rich people to others who figured they should be richer. Little property was destroyed until late September 1676, when, after Berkeley had briefly reoccupied Jamestown, Bacon burned the town to the ground so the governor could not return. Bacon remained in control another month, but after October 26, when he died suddenly, the rebellion collapsed like a pricked balloon.

Charles II sent a fleet of ships and 1,000 men to put down Bacon's Rebellion. He also appointed a three-man commission to investigate the settlers' grievances and assure that insurgents were treated fairly. One of the commissioners was supposed to replace Berkeley as governor, but the old governor would have none of it. He proceeded to execute rebels right and left and to confiscate their property. Then he set out for England, where he died before he had a chance to justify his actions.

Is Bacon's Rebellion a story worthy of Shakespeare's art, or a slapstick comedy? Surely it included moments of high the-

> *"Before long, the descendants of Bacon's and Berkeley's rather indelicate followers began to intermarry and produce what magically became, by the middle of the next century, the very classy 'first families of Virginia' (or FFVs)."*

ater. Consider the governor's speech to one of Bacon's fallen followers: "Mr. Drummond, you are welcome. I am more glad to see you than any man in Virginia. Mr. Drummond, you shall be hanged in half an hour." Like King Philip's War in New England, Bacon's Rebellion augured the end of the game for nearby Indians, whom settlers soon pushed beyond the mountains. The nastiness between groups of white Virginians during 1675–76, however, soon faded away. Before long, the descendants of Bacon's and Berkeley's rather indelicate followers began to intermarry and produce what magically became, by the middle of the next century, the very classy "first families of Virginia" (or FFVs).

Charles II's forceful response signaled another portentous change. Virginia would no longer be left to do more or less what it wanted; the colony had become too valuable to the Crown. The reason lay in England's new laws regulating trade and taxing imports, including tobacco.

DEFINING THE EMPIRE: TRADE

Mid-seventeenth-century Englishmen knew that trade was the route to wealth and power. The most powerful trading country of the time was the Netherlands: Dutch ships sailed everywhere—to the Baltic and the North Sea, to Asia and the South Pacific, to other European ports, and west to North and South America. Their ships and navigational equipment were superior to those of their competitors; their cargoes were more capacious, their pricing and credit policies more advantageous. During those years when England remained preoccupied with domestic affairs and unable to protect her commercial interests abroad, the Dutch moved in, trading freely with both royalist Virginia and Puritan New England.

Parliament tried to stop the Dutch from reaping the economic benefits of Britain's empire. A Navigation Act passed in 1651 stipulated that only British ships could bring goods from America, Asia, or Africa into British territory. Goods from Europe had to be carried in British ships or those of the country that produced them, which hurt Holland since it produced few of the items her merchants sold. Four years later, Oliver Cromwell sent a fleet to seize territories in the Spanish Caribbean and on the mainland of South America, and so to help extend the markets of British merchants. The

An engraving of the harbor at Amsterdam from the seventeenth century, when Dutch commercial power was near its height. Note that ships are shown moored outside the city because the regular docks were filled.

fleet seized Jamaica, but that was about it. And the Navigation Act was equally unsuccessful, since the government in London had no effective means of enforcing it. Then, in 1660, when Charles II regained the throne, the Navigation Act expired along with all the other laws Parliament had passed since the execution of his father, Charles I.

The idea of squeezing the Dutch out of Anglo-American trade nonetheless persisted, since the king and his advisers were anxious to encourage British merchants. Soon Parliament passed a series of new trade laws that were far more successful than their predecessors. These laws defined the economic relationship of Britain with her American colonies for the next century.

The Navigation Acts. The basic Navigation Act of 1660 required that all goods shipped into or out of British territory (which included Ireland and the American colonies) had to be carried in ships of British manufacture with British masters and crews that were 75 percent British. It also required that certain "enumerated commodities" (goods that were explicitly mentioned in the act) be sent only to British territory. Most of the enumerated commodities, such as sugar, cotton, ginger, indigo, and various other dyewoods, came from the West Indies; the only major item from the North American mainland was tobacco. Colonial governors had to take oaths that they would enforce the act within their provinces, and shippers carrying enumerated goods had to post a bond at

their part of departure guaranteeing that they would carry those goods to another British port. Enumerated goods were also subject to a duty when imported to Britain but not if they were shipped to another colony.

Subsequent laws extended the system and tightened its enforcement. Where the Navigation Act of 1660 concerned exports from British territories, the Staple Act of 1663 regulated imports. Any goods sent from Europe to the British colonies, it said, had first to go through Britain, where they would be unloaded (and any duties on them collected), then reloaded for reshipment on British ships. There were some exceptions: salt for the New England fisheries (though not for the Southern colonies), wine from the Azores, and horses as well as servants and various provisions from Ireland could be shipped to the colonies directly. The Staple Act gave British merchants a monopoly on the export trade and, since British import taxes often raised the price of goods from foreign countries, provided British manufactures of similar goods with a competitive advantage in colonial markets.

Massachusetts got off easily. She had no products on the 1660 enumerated list and benefited greatly from the provision that allowed her to import salt directly from places such as Portugal's Cape Verde Islands. But where the laws interfered with their interests, Massachusetts shippers found ways of getting around them. They (and some shippers from other colonies) would take on goods, including enumerated products such as sugar and tobacco, go to another colonial port where they'd get their bond refunded, then dart off to Amsterdam or another European port where they could often get a far higher price for their cargoes than in Britain. Moreover, the goods they smuggled home could often be sold for less than British imports.

The Plantation Duty Act of 1663 tried to end such illegal trade by making shippers pay duties on enumerated goods *at the port of embarkation*, not on arrival in Britain. That required establishing customs agents to collect duties within the colonies. The agents whom the Crown appointed and stationed in America were everywhere a physical manifestation of the king's power—and in many places the first and only personal representatives of the Crown colonists had ever seen. And they served under a new, permanent Board of Customs Commissioners in London.

The Lords of Trade and the Board of Trade. In 1674, King Charles II appointed certain members of his Privy Council to serve as a standing Committee for Trade and Plantations. That body, known as the Lords of Trade, remained responsible for encouraging England's trade and oversaw the administration of her plantations until 1696, when King William III replaced it with another, similar committee known as the Board of Trade. Those advisory committees received reports on the colonies and any complaints lodged against them, and sometimes appointed special boards to obtain information they wanted. They also recommended persons for appointment as royal officials, oversaw their performance, and played a central role in setting colonial policy. Other departments of the king's government bore responsibility for administering policies that the Board of Trade defined and the Privy Council approved. Nonetheless, with the establishment of the Lords and then the Board of Trade, Britain finally had an agency responsible for overseeing its empire.

Later Legislation. In 1696, Parliament passed a new Navigation Act that regularized the procedures of colonial customs agents throughout the king's dominions and, most important, established special courts of admiralty in the colonies. Before then, customs cases were tried in ordinary courts, where colonial juries had a way of acquitting fellow colonists accused of wrongdoing. In admiralty courts, there were no juries. Instead, judges trained in the specialized law of the seas decided cases. Those judges would be more likely than local juries to crack down on colonial scofflaws.

The commercial structure of England's empire was then more or less complete. Its development had continued, almost seamlessly, despite changes in regime. Later modifications of the system added new products to the enumerated list such as rice and naval stores (masts, pitch, tar, and other products, usually produced from pine trees in places such as North Carolina or northern New England). Other acts restricted specific colonial manufactures: the Wool Act of 1699 outlawed the exportation of wool textiles from Ireland and the colonies, the Hat Act of 1732 prevented colonists from exporting hats, and the Iron Act of 1750 made illegal the construction of new iron mills to make finished iron

goods (although it also allowed colonial pig and bar iron to enter England tax-free). Finally, the Molasses Act of 1733 placed a high duty on molasses imported into the colonies from the non-British West Indies. All these measures were designed to make sure that each colony contributed to the growth and prosperity of England and the other English colonies, not to that of the Dutch or other commercial rivals of Britain.

Effects of the Trade Laws. At first, Britain's navigation regulations devastated the economy of the Chesapeake. Planters could no longer sell their tobacco to whatever shipper offered the best price. They had to send tobacco on British ships to Britain, where it was either consumed or reexported to purchasers elsewhere by British merchants. But since in the early 1660s British merchants could not handle all the tobacco from the Chesapeake, supply exceeded demand, and tobacco prices fell precipitously. The Royal Treasury, however, came out fine. It received 2 pence (or cents) on every pound of tobacco imported, which was more, and often a lot more, than the planters who grew the tobacco got for their trouble. Tobacco prices dropped to .5 pence a pound in 1666, and rarely rose

A Virginia planter smokes a pipe while a slave cultivates tobacco and another moves a cask (for shipping tobacco). The illustration comes from an English tobacco label of about 1730.

above 1.2 pence before 1700. But duties on tobacco from Virginia and Maryland produced a quarter of all England's customs revenue during the 1660s and made up perhaps a twentieth of the government's total income. That amount exceeded returns from duties on sugar or any other import. As the fleet sent to put down Bacon's Rebellion demonstrated, Charles II was not about to tolerate any threat to the well-being of that golden egg.

New England's economy was affected far less by the regulations. Not only did the Navigation Acts rest more lightly on New England than on the Chesapeake, but in 1662 and 1663 the king granted Connecticut and Rhode Island new charters that allowed them powers of self-government like those of Massachusetts and left their religious establishments virtually untouched. He also offered to renew the Massachusetts charter so its people could "enjoy all their privileges and liberties." The king did demand that oaths of allegiance be taken and justice dispensed in his name, that Anglicans enjoy freedom of worship, and that qualifications for the vote depend on property rather than church membership. But considering what he might have demanded from colonists who had been so disloyal to his father, that wasn't much.

Massachusetts was not grateful. The colony refused Charles's offer, denied the authority of a commission the king sent there in 1664 (indeed, it issued a public proclamation urging people not to cooperate), and insisted that its charter of 1629

> *"Duties on tobacco from Virginia and Maryland produced a quarter of all England's customs revenue during the 1660s. As the fleet sent to put down Bacon's Rebellion demonstrated, Charles II was not about to tolerate any threat to the well-being of that golden egg."*

gave the colony's government complete and exclusive authority over its internal affairs. Meanwhile, local merchants and shippers did what they could to circumvent those provisions of the Navigation Acts that did cause them trouble, such as the 1673 provision making certain goods sold to other colonies subject to British duties. Edward Randolph, whom the Lords of Trade sent on a mission to the Bay Colony and who later became Boston's collector of customs, complained about the colonists' disregard for royal authority almost from the moment he arrived in 1676.

Randolph was a splendid example of the royal bureaucrats who were suddenly appearing throughout King Charles's dominions. Ambitious, hungry for the fees and other material benefits they expected their offices in America to bring, they interpreted all resistance to them as opposition to the Crown and sent letter after letter to England urging their superiors to show the colonists who was boss. Randolph, who came from a wealthy English family that had fallen on hard times, looked down on the government of Massachusetts as run by "inconsiderable Mechanicks." He claimed that the colony's disregard for the laws of trade cost the Crown £100,000 a year—a vast exaggeration—and urged the king to send out the navy to force Massachusetts into line. Royal authority could be established easily, he said, because King Philip's War had reduced the colonists' capacity to resist.

This detail, taken from a map of the West Indies dated 1700, shows traders packing merchandise in chests, which are then loaded on ships.

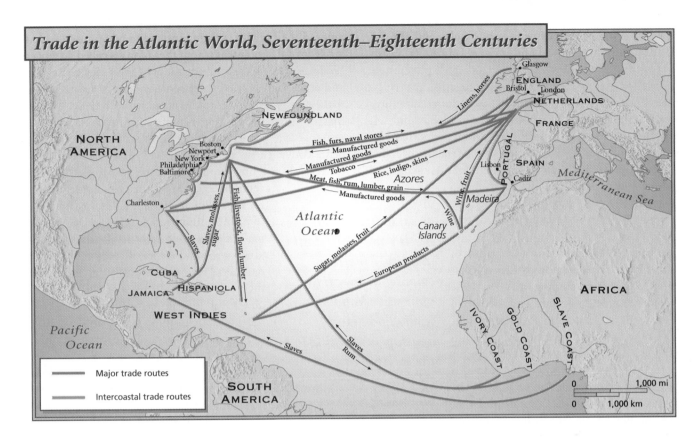

Trade in the Atlantic World, Seventeenth–Eighteenth Centuries

Massachusetts was not the only colony that tried to get around the new trade laws. In Maryland, for example, Lord Baltimore's deputy governor actually killed a royal customs collector. But Massachusetts's strident opposition to any infringements of its independence finally convinced the Crown that enforcement of the trade laws required more than sending customs agents to America. It required taking control of the colonies' internal governments.

TIGHTENING THE CROWN'S HOLD

At the time of the Restoration (1660), Virginia was the only colony in North America ruled directly by the Crown. In 1679, New Hampshire became the second. The patent given William Penn in 1681 placed restrictions on his government that had not been imposed on earlier proprietors, but such restrictions soon seemed insufficient. In 1683, the king's government formally decided against granting any new private jurisdictions, and then started canceling old ones. The Crown filed charges against Massachusetts for exercising a long list of unlawful powers, and in 1684 revoked the Bay Colony's old

charter. Next the Crown turned against Rhode Island and Connecticut; then the proprietary government of New Jersey came on the block.

With the accession of James II to the throne in 1685, this centralizing trend took a new turn. James and his ministers decided to group colonies in administrative units similar to the viceroyalties of the Spanish empire. First they combined New Hampshire, Massachusetts, Plymouth, Rhode Island, and Connecticut into a new government called the Dominion of New England, with a governor and council appointed by the Crown but no elected assembly. Sir Edmund Andros, a former military man who had served as governor of New York, became governor of the dominion and took up residence in Boston late in 1686. Two years later, the Crown added New York and New Jersey to the dominion, which then stretched all the way from Maine to the Delaware River.

THE "GLORIOUS REVOLUTION"

King James's policies in America were of a piece with those in England, where he tried to rule without Parliament, canceled the charters of independent towns or boroughs, and also appointed Catholics to political and military offices. To justify those appointments, James proclaimed a policy of toleration, which implied that he could, by royal prerogative, overrule a 1673 act of Parliament, the Test Act, that required all office-holders to take communion in the Church of England. He thereby alienated both the liberal Whigs, who supported Parliament, and the conservative Tories, who normally defended the Crown but were deeply committed to the established Church of England. In fact, James II found that he had so little support in November 1688, when William of Orange invaded, that he fled to France.

In February 1689, members of the House of Lords and House of Commons issued a Declaration of Rights proclaiming that "the late King James the Second" had endeavored to "Subvert and Extirpate the Protestant Religion, and the Laws and Liberties of this Kingdom." It listed the acts by which he did so (for example, by "Dispensing with, and Suspending of Laws and the Execution of Laws, without Consent of Parliament"), and noted that he had "Abdicated the Government," leaving the throne "vacant." The Declaration of Rights then stated in positive terms the rights that James had violated (for example, it said "That levying . . . Money for . . . the Use of the Crown . . . without Grant of Parliament . . . is illegal"). Finally, it offered the Crown to James's daughter Mary and her husband, William of Orange, with "intire Confidence" that they would preserve the people "from the violation of their Rights, which they have here asserted, and from all other Attempts upon their Religion, Rights, and Liberties." In later times, the British would call this series of events and the constitutional changes they brought their "Glorious Revolution."

As if to prove their British and Protestant identity, the American colonies followed suit, throwing off the oppressive hand of James and his henchmen—and adding to the internal disorder that was a way of life in late seventeenth-century America.

Massachusetts. Massachusetts led the way. There, Governor Andros had managed to alienate virtually all the colonists, including those Anglican merchants who initially rallied to his support. He at first appointed such men to his council but

> *"As if to prove their British and Protestant identity, American colonies threw off the oppressive hand of James and his henchmen—adding to the internal disorder that was a way of life in late seventeenth-century America."*

ignored their advice, turning instead to a handful of recently arrived royal appointees whom the colonists called "strangers." Many people still resented the loss of their elected assembly, and after Andros tried to raise taxes, several towns declared that Englishmen could not be taxed without their consent or that of their elected representatives. Andros promptly arrested several protesters, some of whom were punished after being convicted by juries said to be "packt." He also forbade towns from meeting more than once a year to elect local officers and demanded that landholders petition for royal patents to their lands. Petitioners had to pay fees to the king's officials for "regularizing" titles to their inherited lands (indeed, the king's men had a way of charging "extraordinary fees" for one "service" after another) and then pay annual quitrents to the Crown. The new royal government also tried to take over the ungranted lands, fields, and woods that the towns used for timber or pasture or as reserves for future generations.

Religious concerns added to the colonists' discontent. Andros ended public support for the Congregationalist (Puritan) Church and seized part of a public burying ground on which to build King's Chapel, Boston's first Anglican church (indeed, its first non-Puritan church of any sort). Were old-time Puritans going to be forced to attend Anglican services? Worse yet, was Andros perhaps not Anglican but, like his king, Catholic? Did he plan to turn the province over to Catholic France? When Indians friendly to the French attacked frontier settlements in Maine, the governor marched against them with both royal and provincial troops. In doing so, his critics charged, he left Boston vulnerable to French attack.

Early in the morning of April 18, 1689, armed mobs gathered in Boston's streets, where they were soon joined by militia companies. Around noon, a group of prominent local leaders—Puritans, merchants, even a few who had been on Andros's council—took charge of the insurrection. Soon armed countrymen began flooding into Boston and nearby Charlestown. By nightfall on April 19, British soldiers stationed on Fort Hill and a royal ship in the harbor had surrendered, and royal officials including Andros and Edward Randolph were under arrest. Massachusetts once again lay in the hands of men who were mostly of Puritan descent. They justified the overthrow of the Dominion of New England as an effort like that of William of Orange to save Great Britain from "Popery and Slavery." In fact, Boston would not receive confirmation of the Glorious Revolution in England until more than a month had passed. In the meantime, the province resumed government under its old charter in May, although many people questioned the charter's authority. Until a clearly legitimate government emerged, order and stability in Massachusetts would remain a dream.

New York: Leisler's Rebellion. Elsewhere, events mirrored those in Massachusetts, though with differences that reflected local circumstances. In New York, where Andros's lieutenant governor, Francis Nicholson, and a set of local councillors exercised authority under the Dominion of New England, some colonists (especially old New Englanders on Long Island) resented the elimination of an elected assembly. And almost everyone hated the fees exacted by the new royal officials and the monopolies and other privileges the officials granted to a few favorites, including themselves. The presence of Catholics among local royal officials provoked fear of a plot to deliver the colony to France, and those fears increased when Nicholson (a "pretended Protestant," some said) failed to announce the fall of James II and proclaim the new king and queen.

Finally, on May 31, 1689, local militias in New York City seized the city's fort. After a few days, a leader emerged among the militiamen, Captain Jacob Leisler, a German immigrant and New York merchant who, like Virginia's Nathaniel Bacon, gave the rebellion a name although he didn't begin it. An elected Committee of Safety confirmed Leisler's leadership in early June, and a few days later Nicholson fled to England. In an Address to William and Mary, the New York militiamen expressed "exceeding joy" at England's "deliverance from popery tyranny and slavery" and explained they had risen up against "bitter papists" to keep New York from being "betrayed to any forraigne Ennemy." The insurgents proclaimed the new king and queen on June 22, and insisted that their "taking & securing of the fort" was "singely & Solely for their ma[jes]ties service."

Regaining control of the colony was, however, no easy matter. Parts of the countryside and the city of Albany on the Hudson were ready to accept William and Mary, but not Leisler's leadership. Nor were remaining members of Nicholson's council willing to agree that they were traitorous papists. The Leislerians, two old councillors charged, were "all men of meane birth sordid Education and desperate For-

William and Mary, joint rulers of England from 1689 (Mary died in 1694, William in 1702).

tunes" and therefore unqualified to govern. And so New York, like Massachusetts, remained in an uncertain state as it awaited news from England of William and Mary's "disposing of our government," as the militiamen put it.

Maryland. Maryland wasn't even part of the Dominion of New England. Nonetheless, like colonists elsewhere, Marylanders suffered from low tobacco prices, rising taxes, and oppressive fees, and they resented the doling out of lucrative privileges to a few favored insiders. Maryland Protestants also suffered fears of a Catholic plot much like Protestants in Massachusetts and New York. The Calvert family had founded Maryland as a refuge for Catholics, but by the 1680s some 95 percent of Maryland's 25,000 people were Protestant. Antiproprietary insurrections occurred there in 1659, 1676, and 1681; indeed, Maryland was in such persistent "torment," one observer informed the Lords of Trade, that it was "in very great danger of falling in pieces."

These discontents came to a head after the messenger to whom Lord Baltimore entrusted orders for the proclamation of William and Mary died before boarding ship in England. By June of 1689, when the new king and queen had been proclaimed almost everywhere except Maryland, colonists began organizing "An Association in arms for the defense of the Protestant religion and for asserting the right of King William and Queen Mary to the Province of Maryland and all the English dominions." The association rose up in July, overpowered Lord Baltimore's supporters, and called a convention of county delegates to form an interim government and investigate charges of a Catholic conspiracy. Turmoil continued after September, when Maryland's revolutionary government declared William and Mary king and queen with enormous fanfare. Soon explanations and declarations, memorials and antimemorials with long lists of signatures arrived in England from Maryland. Whether the colony would be Baltimore's again was an issue for the new king and queen to decide.

THE REVOLUTIONARY SETTLEMENT

In England, the Glorious Revolution firmly established the power of the House of Commons. No king could henceforth set aside laws that Parliament had approved, or raise taxes or maintain an army ("the purse and the sword") without the consent of the House of Commons. A new Triennial Act required the Crown to call a new election every three years. That interval was later changed to seven years, but the point remained the same: no members of the House of Commons could remain in office without regular reaffirmation of support from the country. Sovereign power in Britain lay not in the Crown alone, but also in Parliament, that is, in the king, House of Lords, and House of Commons acting together.

"In America, too, the Glorious Revolution established elected assemblies as an essential part of colonial government."

The power of Parliament was even more firmly established in the next century. After 1707, the Crown in effect lost its right to veto acts the Lords and Commons had approved. In that sharing of power by King, Lords, and Commons, each part of the government supposedly checked the others, preventing abuses of power. There lay the glory of what eighteenth-century writers described as the "British constitution," which was not a written document but a system of government. The British constitution, its admirers said, was so constructed that it protected the liberty of the people more reliably than the constitution of any other nation.

In America, too, the Glorious Revolution established elected assemblies as an essential part of colonial government. It also ended once and for all efforts to combine colonies into units like the Dominion of New England. Henceforth the colonies returned to their separate, historic identities. King

William was not, however, far different from James II in his desire to centralize the government of Britain's colonies and establish Britain's power over its dominions—as the Navigation Act of 1696 and the establishment of the Board of Trade suggests. He also, like James II, tended to appoint military men as royal governors. The administration of the colonies remained first and foremost a Crown responsibility, and evidence suggests that by the beginning of the eighteenth century, the colonists had reconciled themselves to that situation. Not one colony tried to reestablish an independent status after the insurrections of 1689; instead, the colonies looked to London for a reestablishment of legitimate government.

The immediate outcome of the 1689 insurrections differed, however, from place to place. The postrevolutionary "settlement" was least settling in New York. Leisler, still afraid of a Catholic plot, hesitated to accept the credentials of the emissary sent by the colony's new royal governor. Once in power, that governor restored many of Nicholson's old councillors to power and had Leisler and his son-in-law tried and convicted of treason. They were condemned to be "hanged by the Neck and being Alive their bodys be Cutt Down to the Earth that their Bowells be taken out and they being Alive burnt before their faces that their heads shall be struck off and their Bodys Cutt in four parts." For the next quarter century, the colony remained torn by bitter factionalism between Leislerians, who deeply resented the injustice done to men profoundly loyal to the Protestant cause, and anti-Leislerians, who thought no punishment too harsh for upstart revolutionaries.

Maryland and Massachusetts avoided that fate. Maryland became a royal colony in which onetime insurgents became part of the ruling order (although a subsequent Lord Baltimore, who was raised a Protestant, regained title to the province, but with less extensive powers than under the original grant). Massachusetts received a new charter in 1691 that gave the Crown more power over internal government than it had exercised under the colony's original charter of 1629. Under its terms, Massachusetts would have a governor appointed by the Crown and an elected assembly (though property, not membership in the established church, determined who could vote). Its council, which advised the governor and also served as an upper house of the legislature, was not appointed by the Crown, as in other royal colonies, but elected by the assembly, although the royal governor could veto the assembly's choices. Under the Massachusetts charter of 1691, Plymouth lost its separate existence and became part of the Bay Colony, as did Maine to the north. But Rhode Island and Connecticut (which absorbed the New Haven colony) succeeded in getting their old charters back.

Despite such variety, the power of England over its colonies was clearly on a continuing ascent. If in 1660 there had been only one royal colony, Virginia, by 1730 New Hampshire, New York, New Jersey, North Carolina, and South Carolina—altogether a full half of the colonies at the time—fell into that category. Of the others, three were charter colonies: the essentially self-governing Connecticut and Rhode Island, as well as Massachusetts, whose government was more exactly a hybrid with aspects of both a charter and a royal colony. By 1730, Maryland had again become a proprietary colony, as had Pennsylvania and also Delaware, which consisted of the three "lower colonies" on the Delaware River that Penn had acquired to assure Philadelphia's access to the sea. Delaware elected its own assembly but shared a governor with Pennsylvania. Except for Pennsylvania, all of the colonies had bicameral legislatures; and their governors, whether elected or appointed by either the Crown or a proprietor, were answerable to the Crown. The British imperial system was perhaps imperfect, including as it did various administrative inconsistencies. But by the early eighteenth century, the colonies were undeniably part of a British empire.

Competitors for a Continent

In the background of each 1689 colonial insurrection lay the rumble of frontier wars with Indians who acted, the settlers feared, as agents of Catholic France. Soon those conflicts expanded as European and native American powers mounted major campaigns for trade, land, people, and political dominion, adding to the astonishing instability of late seventeenth-century North America.

FRANCE

The small northern colony of New France had all it could do to survive in the mid–seventeenth century. It existed to trade furs and convert Indians to Catholicism, and the Huron na-

tion of the Georgian Bay area, north and west of Lake Ontario, was critical to both of those activities. The Hurons, who had been a trading people since long before Europeans arrived in America, collected furs from Algonquian tribes to their north and west, then exchanged them for goods from the French. Jesuits had established several missions among them but found it difficult to convert the Hurons to Christianity—until 1635–40, when baptisms rose dramatically just as a lethal disease swept through the Huron villages, reducing the population (estimated at about 18,000) by half. Then the Iroquois, relatives of the Hurons with whom they had long been estranged, began a devastating attack on the weakened Huron nation, initiating the deadly "Beaver Wars."

The Beaver Wars. The Iroquois Five Nations—the Mohawks to the east, the Senecas to the west, and the Oneidas, Onondagas, and Cayugas between them—lived south of what is now Lake Ontario in the area between the Mohawk and Genesee River valleys. Until the 1630s, their inland location apparently shielded them from European germs, but once the Dutch, English, and French moved onto the margins of their homelands, the Iroquois suffered one epidemic after another. By tradition, the Iroquois adopted war captives to replace lost warriors; now, with population losses on an unprecedented scale, they again embarked on what was in part a "mourning war" to replace their dead.

The Iroquois also needed furs to trade for European goods, on which they had become dependent. Since beavers were no longer to be had on their lands, they highjacked canoes loaded with pelts gathered farther north and west at the junction of rivers. Now they went even further, turning viciously against the Hurons, trying at once to seize captives and to put themselves in the Hurons' place as middlemen between northern hunters and European purchasers. The Iroquois traded, however, not with the French but with their Dutch (and later English) rivals at Fort Orange (or Albany). By 1649, the Iroquois had massacred hundreds of Hurons, martyred French missionaries, and burned their missions. They adopted some of the survivors and forced others to flee their old homes and seek refuge with other Indian groups— whom the Iroquois then also attacked and destroyed.

Based on nonmilitary criteria, the Iroquois' victories were not entirely successful. Without the Hurons to block them, resourceful French fur traders themselves pushed west from Montreal, a new settlement on an island at the confluence of the Ottawa and St. Lawrence Rivers, into the interior. There they secured furs directly from the Ottawas who lived on the shores of Lake Superior, and later French *coureurs de bois* ("runners of the woods," a term for inland traders and adventurers) ventured all the way north to the Hudson Bay, establishing trade with Indians there. In that way, the French prevented the Iroquois from replacing the Hurons as middlemen and kept the northern and western fur trade for France.

Still, the continual threat of Iroquois attack wore away the colony of New France, whose future required that the Iroquois threat be somehow stopped. The old Company of New France was nearly bankrupt and so unable to defend the colony. An effort by the colonists to take over also proved unequal to the challenge. Finally, a savior appeared in the form of the French Crown.

Colbert's Reforms. In 1663, King Louis XIV took direct control of New France, making it a royal province and delegating its direction to Jean-Baptiste Colbert, his imaginative and energetic minister. Colbert wanted the colony to serve the prosperity of its mother country, supplying materials to France and her island colonies that they would otherwise have to buy from non-French sources. Like the British, he worked to end the colony's trade with the Dutch, and by the mid-1670s succeeded in giving French merchants a monopoly of trade with both the French West Indies and New France. He encouraged the colonists to become self-sufficient in all essentials and to export foodstuffs and timber to the West Indies. For a

Jean-Baptiste Colbert.

time, the Crown subsidized the transportation of immigrants and livestock to New France. Colbert wanted to establish in Canada a diversified economy, one that would exploit mineral deposits and develop forest industries. His vision was not altogether unrealistic: the economy he projected for New France closely resembled that of neighboring New England.

The government Colbert provided was, however, strikingly different from New England's. The internal administration of New France, as of the French West Indies, was divided between a governor-general and an intendant. The governor-general was always a professional soldier who held responsibility for maintaining law and order, defense, and Indian relations. The intendant, often a lawyer, was responsible for everything else—in effect, for civil government, including the administration of justice and finance. The Crown appointed both officials, and both oversaw subordinate officers within the colony. There were no elected assembly, but high-ranking officials developed other ways of receiving information from the colonists—through militia companies, for example, or ad hoc assemblies of the people that the governor-general and intendant occasionally gathered to advise them on

The city of Quebec, as shown in an engraving of 1722. The city looked down on the St. Lawrence River, protected from water-borne enemies by high bluffs and from others by the walls that encircled it. Quebec's riverfront is shown as more neat and developed than it probably was at the time.

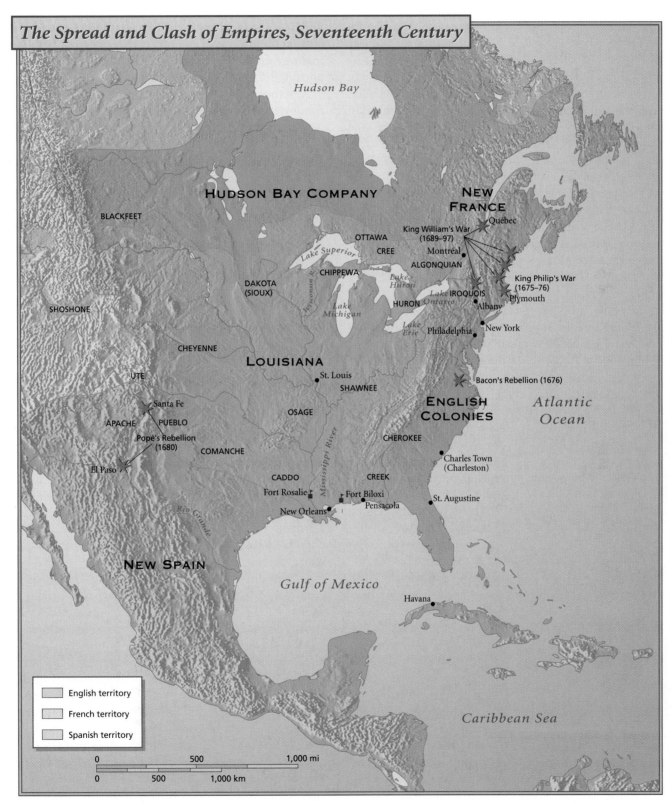

The Spread and Clash of Empires, Seventeenth Century

Hudson Bay

HUDSON BAY COMPANY

NEW FRANCE

BLACKFEET

OTTAWA

CREE

Lake Superior

CHIPPEWA

Wisconsin R.

DAKOTA (SIOUX)

ALGONQUIAN

Lake Huron

Lake Michigan

Lake Ontario

IROQUOIS

HURON

Lake Erie

SHOSHONE

Québec

King William's War (1689–97)

Montréal

King Philip's War (1675–76)

Albany

Plymouth

Philadelphia

New York

CHEYENNE

LOUISIANA

St. Louis

UTE

SHAWNEE

Santa Fe

APACHE

PUEBLO

Popé's Rebellion (1680)

OSAGE

COMANCHE

El Paso

Bacon's Rebellion (1676)

Atlantic Ocean

ENGLISH COLONIES

CHEROKEE

Charles Town (Charleston)

CADDO

CREEK

Mississippi River

Fort Rosalie

Fort Biloxi

Pensacola

New Orleans

St. Augustine

Rio Grande

NEW SPAIN

Gulf of Mexico

Havana

Caribbean Sea

English territory

French territory

Spanish territory

0	500	1,000 mi

0	500	1,000 km

101

specific issues or problems. The government of New France was centralized and autocratic, but not arbitrary. Colonists rarely complained about the system, although they did occasionally express discontent with particular officeholders.

Most important of all, the Crown took on the colony's defense, and dispatched a regiment of some 1,500 men to Canada. After the French mounted two campaigns against the Mohawks, the Five Nations negotiated a peace at Quebec. It lasted until the 1680s, some twenty years, which gave Colbert time to get his policies in place. During these years, the colony began to expand. Immigration increased while royal subsidies lasted; and soldiers sent to the colony were encouraged to remain when their military campaigns were over. Then the population continued to grow by natural increase. Canadian women married on average at twenty-two, two or three years younger than in France, and Canadian families had five to six children, compared with four to five in France—not all that much of a difference. However, the survival rate of children was so much higher in America that the Canadian population doubled every generation while that of France grew hardly at all. By the time of Colbert's death in 1683, the population of New France, thanks to both immigration and births, had grown to over 10,000—a fourfold increase since 1650.

Louis de Buade de Frontenac, governor-general of New France from 1672 to 1682.

The colony's economy also grew, stimulated in part by supplies bought by the Crown to support the king's regiment. Colonists gradually cleared and settled the forested lands along the St. Lawrence between Quebec and Montreal, and the production of wheat increased substantially. But no extensive trade in timber or masts emerged. The cost of preparing and shipping them to France proved too high, and ships built in New France cost twice those built in the mother country. Nor did trade with the French West Indies thrive, despite a great increase in sugar production and therefore the islands' capacity to purchase goods. In truth, the Canadians were not very interested in these forms of enterprise; they preferred farming and trading furs for quick profits. If the economy of Canada did not fulfill Colbert's ambitions, it nonetheless allowed ordinary settlers—the *habitants*—lives that were notably more comfortable than those of their counterparts in rural Europe, which was apparently good enough for them.

French Expansion. Colbert wanted the French to build a strong, defensible trading base along the St. Lawrence, not to spread through the vast interior. But he could not control the *coureurs de bois*, nor, for that matter, contain the expansionism of the colony's intendant, Jean Talon, or the powerful governor-general, Louis de Buade de Frontenac, an egotistical, strong-willed man who arrived in 1672 and governed New France for the next decade as if it were his feudal domain. Frontenac did not find sharing power easy, and Talon left soon after he arrived. In spite of Colbert's directions, the governor-general established Fort Frontenac on Lake Ontario in 1673, then additional trading posts at Niagara (between Lakes Erie and Ontario) and at Michilimackinac (between Lakes Huron and Michigan), all of which stamped the Great Lakes as French trading territory. Tightening France's hold had become increasingly important after the British Hudson Bay Company (1670) established posts along the bay and took over much of the French trade with the nearby Cree Indians. Henceforth, the French and British were in competition for trade in the far north and the Great Lakes region.

The greatest expansion of France lay, however, in the Mississippi Valley. After hearing Indian reports of a great river that flowed to the Gulf of Mexico or perhaps to California, providing the long-sought passageway to the Pacific, Frontenac dispatched two men to explore the Mississippi—Louis Joliet, a priest turned fur trader, and Jacques Marquette, a Jesuit who knew several Indian languages. Setting out in May of 1673 from Green Bay on Lake Michigan, they paddled down the Wisconsin River to the Mississippi and into a world that filled them with wonder. They saw vast prairies, animals like none they'd seen before (catfish that could overturn a canoe, huge cougars), and the rough waters of the Missouri River ("I have seen none more dreadful," Marquette reported). The two men made it to the Arkansas River before local Indians convinced them that the river did not flow into the Pacific and that particularly fierce Indians lived farther south.

"New Biloxi" was still a primitive camp in 1720, when it served as a stopping point for settlers waiting for small boats to take them up the Mississippi. It had only one permanent structure, a large warehouse.

War in Europe kept the French from following up on Joliet and Marquette's discoveries, but the project caught the attention of René-Robert Cavelier, the Sieur de La Salle, who had settled in Canada in the 1660s and, as a fur trader, became familiar with the continent's northern interior. La Salle returned to France in 1677 and convinced Colbert that he should secure the Mississippi Valley for France. After building a series of posts in the north, La Salle began moving down the Mississippi accompanied by a fellow explorer, Henri de Tonty. They arrived at the river's mouth in 1682, and there La Salle claimed "all the nations, peoples, provinces, cities, towns, villages, mines, minerals, fisheries, streams and rivers" that fed into the Mississippi for France. He named that vast territory Louisiana, after his king.

The claim was brazen, and in the short run nothing came of it. After reporting his discovery in France, La Salle sailed back in 1685, but was unable to locate the mouth of the Mississippi from the Gulf of Mexico. He had, like so many others, made an erroneous reading with his astrolabe, and, looking for a landfall at the wrong degree of latitude, ended up in Texas. There, in circumstances that remain clouded in mystery, he died at the hands of his own men.

Another decade passed before France began to make good on La Salle's claims. It established a base at Fort Biloxi on the Gulf of Mexico in 1699, then at Mobile and at Fort Rosalie (Natchez), and finally founded New Orleans as the administrative center of Louisiana in 1722. Peopling the colony was a challenge, even after the Crown abandoned its restrictions on the migration of non-Catholics and of French vagrants, prisoners, and other social undesirables to Louisiana. It also recruited German and Swiss settlers, even though many of them were Lutherans. But the migrants, who remained predominantly male, often died en route or soon after arriving, much as in early Virginia, which made recruiting voluntary settlers still more difficult. In the end, Louisiana, unlike New France, came to depend on the labor of African slaves.

The purpose of Louisiana was imperial: France claimed it first and foremost to edge out the Spanish and, even more, the British, whose traders were already moving west from the Carolinas. By claiming a great arc of land from the mouth of the St. Lawrence west and south all the way to the Gulf of Mexico, a stretch of territory so vast that its hold was necessarily loose, France seemed to invite conflict with other powers. Its claims to the Illinois Country provoked the first such conflict—with the Seneca Indians, part of the Iroquois Five Nations, who considered that territory theirs.

THE "IMPERIAL IROQUOIS"

The people known to us as the Iroquois were, in fact, only called that by the French in the seventeenth century. The Dutch and British referred to them as the Five Nations (or, in the early 1700s, when the Tuscaroras migrated from the Carolinas and joined up, the Six Nations). Sometimes they used the name "Seneca" or "Mohawk" for all members of the Iroquois league. The Iroquois identified themselves with words that meant "extended house," or "longhouse," the dwelling that characterized them and their culture. Through most of the colonial period, they probably included fewer than 10,000 people, but they have long been described as an imperial power virtually without parallel among the Indian peoples of eastern North America, "the Romans of the Western World."

LEFT: An Iroquois cradle board, used to carry a baby on the back.

RIGHT: An Iroquois longhouse, showing smoke emerging from the roof. Most longhouses were about 120 feet long, but some could be as much as 400 feet in length. Several families occupied a longhouse, and groups of them shared meals cooked over fires built at intervals along a central corridor.

It now seems, however, that the notion of the "imperial Iroquois" is a good example of the errors that come from seeing the Indians through European eyes. Although the Iroquois did not found a state, much less aspire to an empire, on a European model, they were nonetheless a force to be reckoned with, one that commanded both respect and fear. They played a critical role in the struggle among Europeans for economic and political control of North America.

The Iroquois were an agricultural people whose women, like other Indian women, grew corn, beans, and squash while the men hunted and fished. They spoke a language distinct from that of neighboring Algonquian peoples to their east and southeast. And they were communal: the Iroquois characteristically lived in towns or adjacent hamlets whose population density of 200 per acre was greater than any other part of the northeast, European or Indian. They built palisades around their towns, and within them constructed, in parallel rows, longhouses some 20 feet wide and up to 400 feet long. First the Iroquois dug saplings into the ground, side by side in long lines, then bent them over to form a rounded roof that they later covered with bark, leaving holes roughly every 20 feet to let out smoke from fires spaced along a central corridor. The interior walls held compartments with sleeping and storage space for individual families, who shared a fire and the food cooked over it—generally a soup of vegetables with meat or fish—with those on the opposite side. Reciprocity was, in fact, at the center of life in the longhouses, where people huddled together through the cold winters, eating from one kettle. Families did have property of their own, but it was distributed according to need and use rather than abstract title. And property was valuable, aside from its immediate practical uses, mainly because it could be given away, forming bonds of obligation that extended and reinforced the ties that made up Iroquoian societies.

Women held substantial authority among the Iroquois. There is some evidence that Iroquoian customs were "matrilocal," that is, that men generally went to live in their wives' villages, and that lineages were traced through the female line. The elder women chose and advised the men who headed their villages, and it was the women who called for mourning wars to replace dead family members and so to replenish the family's strength. They also decided whether to adopt or execute the captives warriors brought home. The Iroquois adopted so many people taken from other groups that eventually those among them who could claim pure Iroquois blood became a minority. Rejected prisoners, however, were tied to a stake and burned from feet to head with firebrands or similar instruments held by villagers (including women and children), then were scalped, had hot sand thrown on their bare skulls, and were finally killed with a knife or hatchet, disemboweled, and chopped into pieces, which were then tossed into the soup pots, cooked, and consumed.

The Great League of Peace and the Iroquois Confederation. Since they valued the lives of family members so highly, the Iroquois tried to fight in ways that avoided fatalities among their men. They favored surprise raids and ambushes over the open-field confrontations that Europeans staged, and fled when clearly outnumbered. They also worked hard to maintain peace among themselves. Sometime in the fifteenth and sixteenth centuries, after a period of incessant wars, the Iroquois peoples negotiated a series of alliances and established a Great League of Peace. Each year thereafter, a Grand Council of some fifty headmen, or sachems, from the various towns of the Five Nations met, registered complaints, and exchanged gifts, reinforcing the bonds that preserved peace. When one of the sachems died, he was ceremonially "requickened," or reincarnated, in a kinsman chosen by the older women of his clan, so the league continued over time. But the Great League of Peace was not a state, much less an empire. It provided a means of maintaining peace, not of setting policy. It had no governing authority.

An Iroquois confederation of village leaders with something akin to political authority emerged only in the 1600s as a result of the first Beaver Wars. Its members were diplomats, men who negotiated peace with the French between 1665 and

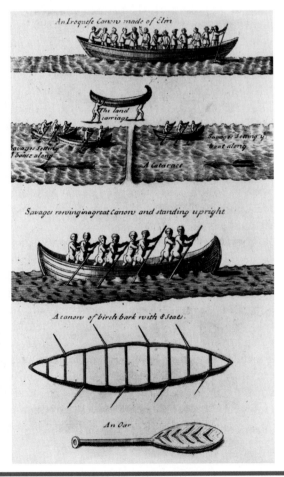

The Iroquois were masters at canoe transport. This early English illustration shows, from the top, an Iroquois canoe made of elm, the process of portage (carrying) and navigation in rough waters, Indians paddling while standing upright, and, at bottom, the scheme of a birchbark canoe with eight seats and an Iroquois oar.

1667. One such leader was the Onondaga Garakontié, a skilled orator with a peculiar capacity to understand Europeans. The leaders adapted the internal peacekeeping rituals of the Great League of Peace, including protracted speeches and extended gift-giving, to a new purpose: negotiating the Iroquois' relationships with European powers. By the 1660s, it seems, leaders from the four western Iroquois nations—the Mohawks came in only later—met occasionally to discuss issues of common concern, forming a loose confederation separate and distinct from the Great League of Peace. The confederation was emphatically not a single nation like those of Europe, but instead an alliance whose members retained autonomous power. At times, whether for convenience or from misunderstanding, the British and French regarded the confederation as if it could speak and negotiate with authority for its member nations. In the 1660s, however, each group made peace with the French separately.

That peace opened the way for Jesuit missionaries to enter Iroquoian villages, which in turn provoked conflicts among three factions of Iroquois—Catholics sympathetic to the French, others more attracted to the British (who had by then taken control of New York and the formerly Dutch trading post at Albany), and those Iroquois who saw wisdom in staying clear of European conflicts altogether. In the 1670s, those who sided with the British won out. The governor of New York negotiated an alliance, or "Covenant Chain," with the Five Nations, whose headmen joined the British in elaborate rituals at Albany that echoed those of the Iroquois' Great League of Peace. Gradually, the Iroquois forced the Jesuits out of their villages, and Catholic Indians moved to New France.

With the stabilization of their relationship with the British, the Iroquois began once again to lash out against French "intruders" and other enemies in the West. In 1687, after treacherously seizing Iroquois ambassadors who had gone to Fort Frontenac to negotiate peace at the French governor-general's invitation, the French sent a force of some 800 men against the Senecas, destroying their villages and food supplies. The Iroquois retaliated with a series of devastating raids on New France. And so the Beaver Wars reopened, but with a twist. Now they were tangled in European politics.

King William's War. After the Glorious Revolution, King William brought Britain into a war with France. As a result, the early battles between the Iroquois and New France became absorbed into a larger imperial confrontation known in Europe as the War of the League of Augsburg (1689–97) and in British America as King William's War. In this conflict, the Iroquois fought as allies of the British, and their attacks on towns and isolated farms along the St. Lawrence soon left New France near to collapse. The French king then recalled the seventy-year-old Count Frontenac for a second term as governor-general. He quickly rallied the militias of New France and their Indian allies and in 1690 organized a three-pronged attack to the south. The first sought nothing less than to capture New York, which would give France an ice-free route to the Atlantic via Lake Champlain and the Hudson River. Frontenac also hoped that his show of force would rupture the Iroquois-English alliance. His expedition chose to attack the small palisaded village of Schenectady some thirteen miles to the north and west of Albany. It was an easy target: the sleeping villagers had left the town's gates open, guarded only by a couple of snowmen, and they paid dearly for their negligence. The attackers killed about sixty people and took another twenty-seven captives, leaving only women and children to watch the village burn. But then the soldiers returned to Canada.

Frontenac's other targets were in northern New England. There, the Abenaki peoples of the area had formed a confederation to drive the English out of the north country. British

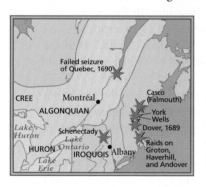

settlements in Maine were mostly small, poor, desolate frontier outposts, dedicated to fishing and subsistence farming or, farther south, particularly along the Piscataqua River where the colonists had built dozens of sawmills, to producing timber products for export. Homes were not clustered as in the early Massachusetts towns, but scattered across the landscape, which made them particularly vulnerable to attack. Defense strategy rested on a series of garrison houses made of thick, squared logs and built specifically to withstand Indian attacks, where neighboring settlers gathered in times of trouble. However, carelessness at the garrison house in Dover, New Hampshire, led to a devastating attack in June 1689. Visiting "friendly" squaws who were allowed to spend the night inside waited until the others were asleep, then opened the doors to warriors. The Indians killed, tortured, and captured settlers, and left their homes and mills plundered and burned. Additional

attacks on Pemaquid and New Harbor in August prompted the British to abandon all their settlements north of Casco (Falmouth), Maine.

In the late winter of 1689–90, Frontenac's armies joined the attack on New England—first at Salmon Falls, a small milling village near the ill-fated Dover, which a company of French and Indians destroyed on March 18, 1690. Two months later, a larger Franco-Indian force took Casco, Maine, and Fort Loyal at nearby Portland. There, Indians slaughtered or took captive colonists who had surrendered after being promised safe passage to another English settlement. The Indians also killed livestock and burned and sacked what remained of the settlements in what was becoming a painfully repetitive story. A New England army under Sir William Phips tried to end the attacks in 1690 by seizing Quebec, but the attempt failed. In fact, the war in northern New England continued until 1699, two years after the European war ended with the Peace of Ryswick (1697). Among the casualties were the towns of York, Maine, so thoroughly destroyed in 1692 that it seemed unlikely ever to be rebuilt, and Durham, New Hampshire, which the Indians destroyed in 1694. They also attacked Wells, Maine, and crossed the Merrimack River and to mount raids on the towns of Groton, Haverhill, and Andover, Massachusetts, all within thirty or forty miles of Boston. The wars were devastating as well to the Abenakis, whose numbers were seriously depleted by 1699, when, finally, they negotiated peace.

In the meantime, the French turned directly against the Five Nations: in 1696, they ruined Onondaga and Oneida villages, destroying their crops and opening a real prospect of famine. New York provided the Iroquois with some military supplies, but not as much as the Indians needed nor what they could reasonably expect from an ally. By the end of the war, the Five Nations had lost a quarter to a half of their fighting men, and perhaps 2,000 of their 8,600 people. There is little mystery why, in treaties negotiated at Montreal and Albany in 1701, the Iroquois agreed to remain neutral in European wars, or why over the next decades—in which the European powers again went to war—they became increasingly united on a policy of neutrality.

SPAIN

The Spanish carefully monitored the expansion of other European powers within North America. In 1685, they learned of La Salle's designs on the "Mischipipi," which would pose a threat to Spanish shipping on the Gulf of Mexico and perhaps to its mines in Mexico. They mounted several expeditions to find La Salle, and it was Spaniards who finally discovered the ruins of his camp in Texas and learned the story of his death from Indians and a few survivors of the French expedition. Spain still maintained its old post at St. Augustine on the Atlantic. In November 1698, it began building another small fort at Pensacola to strengthen its hold on the gulf, and just in time: two months later, a French expedition entered the bay, only to discover that it was already occupied. Thereafter, the Spanish let the French develop their Louisiana colony for a strange and unanticipated reason: in November 1700, the (Spanish) Hapsburg emperor Carlos II died after naming as his heir Phillipe d'Anjou, the grandson of France's King Louis XIV. Carlos's decision put the rivalry of France and Spain on hold.

New Mexico. Spain's greater efforts at the time were concentrated in New Mexico. The number of Spaniards there was, however, never large, and the settlement remained dependent on coerced Indian labor. Even the Franciscan missions in the area were built by Indians who worked the missions' fields, raised their livestock, and carried the surpluses to market, sometimes voluntarily and maybe even "with pleasure," as one friar insisted, but often unwillingly. The tributes exacted by local *encomenderos* increased Indian resentment. So did the Spaniards' patently illegal—because it violated a royal edict—practice of selling Indians into slavery.

The Indians of New Mexico rebelled on a fairly regular basis, destroying property and killing Spaniards, including missionaries. The insurgents had numbers on their side. There were about 17,000 Pueblos living in about two dozen separate towns, far fewer than the 60,000 in New Mexico earlier in the century but still more than the roughly 3,000 Spaniards there. However, the Pueblos were spread over several hundred miles and spoke a variety of often mutually unintelligible languages. As a result, their revolts tended to be local, limited, and so relatively easy for the Spanish to repress.

Pueblo discontent increased after a serious drought reduced their food crops. Then neighboring Navajo and Apache Indians made repeated raids on the Pueblos' fields and farms,

increasing the shortages. The distressed Pueblos could only wonder why, if the friars' God was real, He provided for them so poorly, and they turned back to their traditional gods. The Spaniards, however, could not tolerate such a retreat to paganism. In 1675, they hanged three Pueblo priests and whipped another forty-three Indian participants in the native religious revival, among whom was a man named Popé. Five years later, shortly after King Philip's War ended in New England, the Pueblos and some Apaches united behind Popé. Within a few weeks, they mounted the most successful Indian revolt in North American history, a massive uprising that destroyed the New Mexico colony.

Popé's Rebellion. On August 10, 1680, the revolt erupted with massive force against the scattered Spanish farms and ranches. Refugees flocked to a town that remained loyal to the Spaniards, from which they fled a month later down the Rio Grande to El Paso (now Ciudad Juárez), some 300 miles away, or to Santa Fe, which the Pueblo insurgents put under siege. On September 21, the rebels allowed the Spaniards to leave. Soon the refugees followed their predecessors to El Paso, leaving New Mexico to the Indians.

The toll was high: the Spanish governor estimated that over 400 colonists died, including 21 of the colony's 33 Franciscan missionaries. The insurgents also destroyed or ransacked the physical remains of Spanish occupation, including the churches. The revolt was, in fact, against the Christian religion as well as exploitation and other injuries, and against Spanish culture, including Spanish language and crops. Popé, according to one account, ordered followers to "break up and burn the images of the holy Christ, the Virgin Mary and the other saints," even to throw the holy water and oils into the river and then plunge in and wash themselves of the "holy sacraments," including baptism.

The revolt didn't stop there. All along the northern edge of New Spain, or Mexico, an array of Indian peoples shed Spanish rule and destroyed missions and settlements. For the next fourteen years, New Mexico remained in Indian hands. When the Spanish returned in the 1690s, under the leadership of Diego de Vargas, who by diplomacy and force secured the allegiance of several Pueblo communities, their hold on

107

the territory remained insecure. Vargas retook Santa Fe in 1694, then subdued other Pueblos—who, however, mounted another massive uprising two years later. With the help of Indian allies, Vargas suppressed the rebellion, but failed to win the total subordination of the region's Indian peoples. For them, the struggle for autonomy was costly, reducing the population from 17,000 to 14,000, which itself caused a reshuffling of people and places. But there were some positive results. The Spanish were henceforth less intolerant of native religions, less exploitative, less oblivious of royal edicts issued for the protection of Indians.

Not that the Spanish took responsibility for provoking the revolt. They explained the event as a form of divine punishment for otherwise unacknowledged sins. If not the work of God, they added, the Indian uprising was surely the work of the devil. That way of thinking was by no means confined to the Catholic Spanish. It was shared, in fact, with the most anti-Catholic European settlers in America: the Puritans of New England.

Satan Joins the Fight

How could New Englanders make sense of the calamities that hit their New World promised land? Troubles had rained down on the region like the trials of Job. First customsmen and other royal emissaries threatened New England's autonomy; then Massachusetts lost the charter it had proudly held for over a half century; and before long, Governor Andros and other servants of James II invented new ways to harass the colonists. Moreover, a plague of Indians almost destroyed the settlements in the 1670s and, in 1690, seemed to be at it again, this time with the help of the Catholic French.

Long before, on board the *Arbella* as it sailed westward across the Atlantic, John Winthrop had told the first settlers that their covenant with God required them to be "knitt together" with an unselfish "bond of love." He also warned that if the colonists' commitment to each other failed and they embraced "carnall intencions, seeking great things" for themselves and their posterity, the Lord would "break out in wrathe against us." Were the colonists now feeling God's wrath?

So it seemed to the acting governor and General Court of the Massachusetts Bay Colony. They issued a proclamation in

March 1690 stating that New England's "long Series of Afflictions and Calamities" showed "the anger of the righteous God." The edict called for a rigorous campaign against "*Provoking Evils*" such as blasphemy, Sabbath-breaking, idleness, drunkenness, and "Uncleanness." Only by reform could the colonists ward off the "imminent danger of perishing."

The Reverend Cotton Mather agreed. In a 1689 sermon entitled *The Present State of New England Considered*, written, as its published title revealed, *Upon the News of an Invasion by bloody Indians & French-men begun upon Us*, Mather said that New England was in danger of being delivered to its "old Land-Lord, *Satan*," who ruled the region before Christians arrived, when it remained in the possession of Indians. The reason lay in that "most *Bewitching* thing," a love of the world, whose enchantment "should be Dissolved by the other *Devils*, that are coming to take *This* away." Mather, one of the colony's most erudite clergymen, knew that "the Divils have a great

The Reverend Cotton Mather.

hand in Exciting and Supporting" New England's enemies, which he learned from "the mouth of a possessed child." The devil appeared, however, not only on the northern frontier in the guise of Frontenac's armies, but in Salem, Massachusetts, where he seemed to take possession of more than a single child.

SALEM WITCHCRAFT

Even now, after more than three centuries and despite shelves of books on the subject, it remains hard to know precisely what happened at **Salem in 1692**. The records are incomplete, and the guesses of earlier historians have taken their place in standard histories as if they were established facts. What does seem clear is that the event began not in Salem Town, a prosperous seaport, but in Salem Village, a poorer, inland agricultural community that remained legally part of Salem Town but had its own church. There in the early months of 1692, Betty Parris, the young daughter of the Reverend Samuel Parris, contracted a strange illness, and a physician suggested her ailment was of supernatural origin. Soon a group of Betty's friends accused three women of causing her illness. The accused were older women whose morals or personal circumstances made them obvious suspects—Sarah Good, a poor, pipe-smoking, contentious hag given to begging; Sarah Osborne, who had lived with a man before marrying him, and Tituba, an Indian slave in the Parris household. In late February, the state issued warrants for their arrest, and two members of the provincial council held a public examination of the accused witches in the Salem Village meetinghouse. The event could have ended there, but Tituba confessed, implicating Good and Osborne at the same time. The villagers' worst fears were confirmed. The devil was at work in Salem.

Soon the number of accused people began to multiply, taking in women and men who would ordinarily have seemed above criticism, such as Rebecca Nurse. The number of accusers also grew as women like the elder Ann Putnam joined in, and others, male and female, readily offered testimony against one or another of the accused. The examinations became public spectacles where the "victims" screamed out as their bodies twisted into hideous contortions whenever the accused witches came in sight—but then they were cured when touched by the "witches," supposedly because the demons possessing them returned to the oppressors' bodies. Within weeks, the jails—nasty, unhealthy places—became packed with would-be witches. Under Massachusetts law witchcraft was a capital offense, but the accused were not tried until May, when the new Massachusetts charter arrived along with the colony's new royal governor, William Phips.

Within a few days of his arrival, Phips created a special Court of Oyer and Terminer—a type of court meant for instances where a short-term incident produced many cases to be heard—to pass judgment on the accused witches. The first session was held on June 2, and on the 10th the first convicted witch, Bridget Bishop, was hanged. The court clearly sought, and won, convictions: when a jury declared Rebecca Nurse innocent, Lieutenant Governor William Stoughton, the presiding chief justice, sent it back to deliberate further. That was a violation of the established practice in England, where no judge could interfere with a jury's decision to acquit. By early October, twenty-six people had been convicted of witchcraft, and nineteen of them were already executed. At least another two of the accused had died in jail, and a twenty-second victim, Giles Cory, was pressed to death with heavy stones in an effort to make him enter a plea and so recognize the authority of the court, which he refused to do. Another fifty of the accused had confessed, and the jails were still full of people awaiting trial.

There were many reasons to question the proceedings, but the most troubling concerned the evidence admitted in court. Confessions were considered particularly convincing. Those who confessed were not executed—perhaps because their testimony against other accused witches was so useful. After all, dead witches could tell no tales. The court also looked for evidence of peculiar growths on witches' bodies, which could serve as "tits" for nursing "familiars" (little demons); of instances where people suffered some misfortune after provoking the accused person's anger, and of superhuman capacities of one sort or another. In case after case, however, the court also admitted "spectral evidence," that is, evidence in the form of testimony by accusers that they had seen ghostly images of the accused afflicting them. Following the advice of Cotton Mather, the judges concluded that Satan could not assume a person's shape without the person's permission. If so, the appearance of a specter was proof that the accused had made a pact with the devil. But what if, as Rebecca Nurse asserted, the devil could take the shape of an innocent person? Even the Bible told of his doing that on occasion.

On October 3, 1692, the Reverend Increase Mather, Cotton Mather's father, preached a sermon to a meeting of ministers in Cambridge that contested the validity of spectral evidence. It was better, he said, that ten witches escape than that one innocent person be condemned. His sermon was published

An English print published with a 1589 pamphlet that told the story of three women who were convicted of practicing witchcraft and hanged. On the lower right, an animal seems to suckle from a woman's face. At Salem in 1692, authorities again sought evidence of strange growths on an accused witch's body, assuming that "familiars," strange beasts that were in fact devils, would suck there.

later in the month as *Cases of Conscience Concerning Evil Spirits Personating Men* with the endorsement of several noted clergymen. That helped break the bubble. By then, too, the accusers had begun implicating persons whose rank or status put them beyond suspicion—high members of the provincial government, the wife of a minister who had supported the trials, maybe even Lady Mary Spencer Phips, the governor's wife. Soon Governor Phips, who had recently returned from a military campaign in Maine, announced that there would be no further imprisonments or trials for witchcraft and, supported by a vote of 33–29 in the General Court, dissolved the Court of Oyer and Terminer. In early 1693, the state's new Superior Court of Judicature tried the remaining cases. Although Stoughton remained that court's presiding judge, it acquitted forty-nine people and convicted only three, whom Phips immediately reprieved. In April, the governor dismissed all remaining prisoners and issued a general pardon.

The witchcraft crisis defies all simple explanations. Deep factional conflicts within Salem Village and between Salem Village and Salem Town contributed to the crisis, at least in its early stages. Those who accused others of being witches tended to be supporters of the church in Salem Village and of its minister, the Reverend Mr. Parris, and also members of the local Putnam family. The accused were often Salem Villagers who were not members of the village church and opposed Parris; often, too, they lived in or had some close association with Salem Town and its thriving commercial economy and with the town's prominent Proctor family. But in the end, accusations extended well beyond the borders of Salem Village and Salem Town.

The Indian wars help explain why the crisis spread. The witchcraft proceedings began about the time news arrived of the Indian massacre at York, Maine. Essex County, which includes Salem and borders the coast of northeast Massachusetts, had received many refugees from New Hampshire and Maine during 1677–78, and maintained close ties with the communities that were attacked and often destroyed during King William's War. Some of the accusers were themselves refugees who had lost parents and other family members to Indian violence and now supported themselves as servants in

---

American Journal

What if You Get Sick?

The first step in any treatment program is diagnosis, and in the seventeenth century explanations for illness included supernatural as well as natural considerations. Note that this passage from the Reverend Cotton Mather's diary was written in 1693, when the Salem witchcraft crisis was over, and Mather apparently participated in a dissection to discover the cause of his child's death. "Scientific" investigations of the body clearly existed side by side with what would today be regarded as superstition.

"On March 28[, 1693]. Tuesday, between 4 and 5 A.M. God gave to my Wife, a safe Deliverance of a Son. It was a child of a most comely and hearty Look, and all my Friends entertained his Birth, with very singular Expressions of Satisfaction. But the Child was attended with a very strange Disaster; for it had such an obstruction in the Bowels, as utterly hindred the Passage of its Ordure from it. Wee used all the Methods that could bee devised for its Ease; but nothing wee did, could save the Child from Death. . . .

"When the Body of the Child was opened, wee found, that the lower End of the Rectum Intestinum, instead of being Musculous, as it should have been, was Membranous, and altogether closed up. I had great Reason to suspect a Witchcraft, in this praeternatural Accident; because my Wife, a few weeks before her Deliverance, was affrighted with an horrible Spectre, in our Porch, which Fright caused her Bowels to turn within her; and the Spectres which both before and after, tormented a young Woman in our Neighbourhood, brag'd of their giving my Wife that Fright, in hopes, they said, of doing Mischief unto her Infant at least, if not unto the Mother; and besides all this, the Child was no sooner born, but a suspected Woman sent unto my Father, a Letter full of railing against myself, wherein shee told him, Hee little knew, what might quickly befall some of his Posterity."

From the *Diary of Cotton Mather, 1681–1708*

Salem Village households. What mixture of resentments and desperate fears fed into their conduct is hard to assess, but young people who had witnessed inhuman violence on the frontier knew evil firsthand and were no doubt ready to war against the devil themselves. As the frontier pushed down toward Essex County, the notion that the devil stalked the land and had, as witnesses often said, "tawny" skin like the Indians, became all too believable. In 1692, an accused witch in the town of Billerica—which would suffer an Indian attack three years later—confessed that she had made a pact with the devil while "under great discontentedness & troubled w[ith] feare" in return for a promise that "if she would serve him she would be safe from the Indians."

If the executed Salem witches were in some measure war casualties, the number of victims was modest: far fewer died in Salem than in those obscure, vicious, forgotten Indian attacks on Salmon Falls, Maine, and Dover, New Hampshire. Salem lives on in memory because its victims were cut down not by wartime enemies but by neighbors, persons who set in place a classic witch hunt in which the accused could save their lives only by confessing and implicating others and so extending the net of accusations until, finally, they crossed the line of credibility. The fascination of the Salem episode also lies in the vivid example it provides of people's capacity to turn against fellow humans, however innocent, in an effort to save themselves. That so extreme an example of cruelty occurred in a community that first set out to realize Christian charity is somehow especially disheartening. Observers can still argue over whether or not a personal Satan exists and was at work in Salem. But that evil walked the town's dusty roads is beyond controversy.

WITCHCRAFT AND THE RISE OF MODERN SCIENCE

In Europe, witchcraft crises had often coincided with major wars. They reached a peak there between 1450 and 1650, and were particularly severe in areas torn by chaos during the Thirty Years' War (1618–48). In America, too, accusations of witchcraft tended to coincide with wars or war scares. Today, however, charges of witchcraft seem archaic, an expression of superstitions utterly out of keeping with modern scientific thought.

"The heritage of the seventeenth century in North America lay in a hardening of imperial systems and territorial claims that continued to produce armed conflicts thereafter."

The seventeenth century saw the birth of a modern science based on objective experimentation and observation. In England, it was the age of Sir Isaac Newton, whose *Mathematical Principles of Natural Philosophy* (1687) demonstrated that all motion conformed to mathematical laws; of Sir Robert Boyle, a founder of modern chemistry; and of William Harvey, who on the basis of observations first described the circulation of blood, and whose revolutionary studies of anatomy and physiology eventually gave rise to scientific medicine. The discovery of mechanical rules of motion were particularly significant since they suggested a world that went on without the *ad hoc* interventions of God (or Satan). But in America as in Europe, some enthusiasts for the new science such as Cotton Mather were also ready to defend the existence of witchcraft. If God governed the world by discoverable laws, the study of those laws was a way to know God; but who could doubt that an all-powerful God could, on occasion, act outside the laws He had enacted? Even those who came to regret their roles in Salem sometimes affirmed the existence of occult forces and divine intervention in human life. Samuel Sewall, for example, publicly apologized for his role as a judge in the witchcraft trials after his family suffered several afflictions, which he saw as punishments for some horrible sin. After 1700, however, skepticism about the irregular intervention of supernatural forces in human affairs increased among educated people in both Europe and America, and witchcraft prosecutions gradually disappeared.

War, however, did not. The heritage of the seventeenth century in North America lay in a hardening of imperial systems and territorial claims that continued to produce armed conflicts thereafter. The primary European contenders remained France, whose claims in 1700 included lands from the mouth of the St. Lawrence west to the lake country and south along the Mississippi Valley; Spain, whose empire centered in Mexico, but which also held territory in Florida and New Mexico; and Great Britain, whose major mainland colonies stood between the Appalachians and the Atlantic coast in a long but now continuous strip from Maine to the Carolinas.

Indian peoples lived in scattered communities throughout these territories. On occasion, as in New Mexico or New England, they tried with considerable success to push European

Chronology		
1618–48	The Thirty Years' War in Europe.	
1660	Parliament passes the first Navigation Act.	
1675–76	King Philip's War (Indians vs. New England settlers).	
	Bacon's Rebellion in Virginia.	
1680	Popé's Rebellion against Spanish rule in New Mexico.	
1681	William Penn founds Pennsylvania.	
1682	The Sieur de La Salle claims Louisiana for France.	
1689	Glorious Revolution in England.	
1689–97	King William's War (in Europe, War of the League of Augsburg).	
1692	Witchcraft trials begin in Salem, Massachusetts.	

clothing or to abandon various crops or livestock introduced by the Spanish. For their part, the Europeans had become Indianized in their cultivation of corn and, above all, in their ways of war.

The outcome of all these changes was unlikely to depend exclusively on alliances and wealth, or on political and technical competence. The future also turned on those peculiar and somewhat mysterious forces that allowed one people to multiply while others watched their children die, or had none to watch. And was God's will irrelevant? For European contenders, the contest for America represented in good measure a war of religion between the Protestant British and the "Catholic Powers." Both sides thought God was on their side, and only time could tell if either was right.

Suggested Reading

Charles McLean Andrews, *The Colonial Period of American History*, vol. 3: *The Settlements* (1937)

Paul Boyer and Stephen Nissenbaum, *Salem Possessed: The Social Origins of Witchcraft* (1974)

W. J. Eccles, *France in America* (1972)

Jill Lepore, *The Name of War: King Philip's War and the Origins of American Identity* (1998)

Patrick Malone, *The Skulking Way of War: Technology and Tactics Among the New England Indians* (1991)

Daniel K. Richter, *The Ordeal of the Longhouse: The Peoples of the Iroquois League in the Era of European Colonization* (1992)

Carl Ubbelohde, *The American Colonies and the British Empire, 1607–1763* (1975)

Richard White, *The Middle Ground: Indians, Empires, and Republics in the Great Lakes Region, 1650–1815* (1991)

settlers from their ancestral lands. The Indians, though, were not one people but many who were often at odds with each other and as anxious to win European support in those rivalries as the Europeans were for Indian support in their own. And the Indians, who had become dependent on imported trade goods, were often more interested in establishing stable relationships with Europeans than in reclaiming the continent for themselves alone. Both sets of peoples had been changed by the other. The Indians had become Europeanized in their use of foreign textiles, metals, and foods, and sometimes in their religions. Even Popé's Rebellion in New Mexico, the century's greatest effort to reclaim Indian culture, failed to convince the Pueblos to give up the comfort of wool

QUESTIONS

■ **What were the sources of population growth in the British North American colonies in this period?**

■ **What were the major characteristics of slavery in British North America?**

■ **In what ways did American society and culture grow more refined in the eighteenth century?**

■ **How did the colonists forge a stronger common identity as Britons and as Americans in the eighteenth century?**

"Your kind present of an electrical tube, with directions for using it, has put several of us on making electrical experiments, in which we have observed some particular phaenomena that we look on to be new." So a little-known Philadelphia printer named Benjamin Franklin wrote Peter Collinson, a London merchant who had sent scientific apparatus to the Library Company of Philadelphia for the use of its patrons. The year was 1747, and Philadelphians knew full well that they did not live at the center of civilization. What we've discovered, Franklin said apologetically, "may not be new to you, as among the numbers daily employed in those experiments, on your side the water, 'tis probable some one or other has hit on the same observations." At least Collinson would know that his electrical tube and the accompanying information on its applications were not lying around unused.

Collinson was a member of the preeminent institution for the promotion of experimental science of its day, the Royal Society of London. First formed in 1660, the society won a charter from King Charles II in 1662, and turned its attention to a stunning range of subjects. It drew no line between the investigation of nature's basic principles (science in the modern sense) and their practical applications (technology); indeed, its charter committed the society to promote "by the authority of experiments" both "the sciences of natural things" and "of useful arts." The structure of plants and animals was of as much interest to members as astronomy, the nature of electricity, medicine, or "Mechanical Inventions" like the "Engin fit to strike the Whales with more ease and surnesse, and at a greater distance," whose possible development the society discussed in 1663.

The Royal Society harbored no illusion that all the information it needed could be had in England. Even before receiving its royal charter, it appointed a Committee for Foreign Correspondence to establish contact with like-minded people in distant parts of the world, including the American colonies. Moreover, the society—or individual members, like Collinson—requested information from its correspondents, and sometimes supplied data-gathering instruments such as thermometers (first devised in 1606 by Galileo), barometers, telescopes, and even, it seems, an occasional electrical tube. The information gathered was often read to the society and sometimes later published in its *Philosophical Transactions*, which by the mid–eighteenth century had become the world's foremost scientific publication.

From the first, moreover, the Royal Society included colonists as members. John Winthrop Jr., the promoter of the Hammersmith Iron Works and governor of Connecticut, was one of the original members. Between 1663 and 1783, the society elected another sixteen American colonists as a result of their interest in and contributions to science. Their presence on the membership list indicates how far the colonies had come since their opening years. At first, as Winthrop wrote in 1668, settlers had "work enough" and "difficulties sufficient to settle a comfortable way of subsistence" by breaking ground, clearing land, planting orchards, and constructing buildings, fences, and fortifications "as in beginning of the world." But by the eighteenth century, the physically absorbing job of planting colonies had, for the most part, been done, and there was time for study and reflection. With a little help from the Royal Society, men of science within America found each other, exchanged letters and papers across colonial borders, and bound them together in what the society itself once referred to as an international "Republic" of men attempting "to Promote & advance Science and usefull knowledge."

The British North American colonies grew spectacularly in population and prosperity during the early eighteenth century. This growth allowed a new refinement of life in one area after another. Colonists rebuilt their homes in ways inspired by English models and filled them with new "comforts"—consumer goods, many of which were imported from the mother country. Such improvements, like the colonists' connections with the Royal Society, reinforced their identity as Britons, as did their provincial politics and their participation in Britain's recurrent wars against France and Spain. By the 1760s, the colonists were self-consciously British to an extent unequaled at any earlier period. At the same time, the old sectarian hostilities that separated them from one another started to give way, and the colonists also began to assume a common identity as Americans.

"The British North American colonies grew spectacularly in population and prosperity during the early eighteenth century. This growth allowed a new refinement of life in one area after another."

Population Growth

Benjamin Franklin was a dabbler in science, as were many people of his time; it was for them a pastime, not a profession. Born at Boston in 1706, the youngest son in a large family (he remembered thirteen children sitting at dinner) of a Boston candle and soap maker, Franklin received only a few years of formal education. His father removed him from grammar school at age ten to assist him in his business, Franklin later recalled in his autobiography. When young Benjamin didn't take to making candles, his father sought an alternative trade that would better suit the boy, and ended up apprenticing him to Benjamin's brother James, a printer. Under the terms of his indenture, Benjamin—then twelve years old—"put himself apprentice to his brother to learn his art, and with him, after the manner of an apprentice, to serve" until he was twenty-one.

It was a fortunate choice. James soon began publishing his own newspaper, *The New England Courant,* which, with Boston's two other newspapers, heralded a new era. Newspapers were the first mass medium, and print would remain the only way of reaching a broad public for another two centuries. Benjamin Franklin was in at the beginning, setting type and, like other printers at the time, writing some of the texts he printed. He had always been a reader; he later claimed that he could not remember a time he could not read. He began with works of divinity in his father's library (and later regretted the time he "wasted" with them), then turned to more secular writings. Now, as he worked at perfecting his prose style, he took as models contemporary English publications, such as the stylish *Spectator.* The fruit of his efforts was a series of letters to the editor of the *New England Courant* from one "Silence Dogood"; the fourth letter alone—a satire on Harvard College published in May 1722, when Franklin was sixteen—would do credit to an essayist many times his age.

"Prose writing," Franklin later pronounced, "has been of great use to me . . . and was a principal means of my advancement." His ability to describe his electrical work clearly and logically, in language accessible to any intelligent reader, certainly contributed to his reputation as a scientist. In the short run, however, his celebrity as an author created a strained relationship with his brother. At age seventeen, Franklin ran away to Philadelphia, leaving his apprenticeship behind. There, he eventually published his own newspaper and, in time, became an investor in several papers. That allowed him to retire from active printing in the 1740s and devote his time to electrical experiments, as well as a variety of other activities. One of the subjects that attracted his attention was demography.

OBSERVATIONS CONCERNING THE INCREASE OF MANKIND

Franklin took up the subject of demography in an essay attacking the Iron Act of 1750, by which Parliament prohibited the establishment of new mills and forges for processing iron in the American colonies. There was no real danger of competition with British manufactures, Franklin asserted; the American demand for British goods was increasing so rapidly that it would soon be "beyond her Power of supplying." As a result, Britain should not restrain colonial manufactures. "A wise and good Mother will not do it. To distress, is to weaken, and weakening the Children, weakens the whole Family."

A register for the family of Massachusetts resident Samuel Colton. His first wife, Flavia, died childless at the age of twenty-two. Samuel remarried two and a half years later. He and his second wife, Lucy, had seven children, four of whom survived to adulthood. Note the number of children and their lifespans, and also the lifespans of the parents.

Clearly he thought of the Americans as part and parcel of the British family. But his argument depended in good part on his analysis of population dynamics distinct to America. Population theories based on "fully settled old Countries," Franklin wrote in his *Observations Concerning the Increase of Mankind* (1754), do not suit "new Countries, as America." A population increases, he argued, in proportion to the number of marriages, and marriages grow in proportion "to the ease and Convenience of supporting a Family." Where families are easily supported, "more Persons marry, and earlier in Life."

In crowded cities and in "Countries full settled," people delay marriages until late in life or avoid marrying altogether, and that, he suggested, was generally true in Europe—but not America. Here, land was plentiful, and laboring men who understood "Husbandry" could "in a short Time save Money enough to purchase a Piece of new Land" sufficient to support a family. As a result, "marriages in America are more general, and more generally early, than in Europe":

> If it is reckoned there, that there is but one Marriage per Annum among 100 Persons, perhaps we may here reckon two; and if in Europe they have but 4 Births to a Marriage (many of their Marriages being late) we may here reckon 8, of which if one half grow up, and our Marriages are made, reckoning one with another at 20 Years of Age, our People must at least be doubled every 20 Years.

The situation, moreover, was destined to continue, since the vast territory of North America "will require many Ages to settle . . . fully." In the interim, colonial labor would remain expensive, since men agreed to work for others only temporarily and for high rates of pay; then they went off to work for themselves on their own land, have children, and send the population spiraling. The original 80,000 English immigrants to America, Franklin said, had multiplied until by the mid–eighteenth century the American population stood at about a million. If in the next century that population doubled "but once in 25 years," its progeny would constitute "more than the People of England, and the greatest Number of Englishmen will be on this Side the Water. What an Accession of Power to the British Empire," he exclaimed, "by Sea as well as Land!"

Although Franklin's figures were estimates, not measurements, no generalization about the colonies was repeated more often by Americans after mid-century than his claims on demographic growth. Every colonist seemed to know that the population of British North America was doubling every twenty years, which was taken as a sign of vitality and a source of enormous pride.

Was Franklin's estimate correct? Not for all colonies in all periods. The Chesapeake, for example, got off to a rocky start. By 1700, however, sex ratios among white Virginians and Marylanders approached balance, indentured servitude (which delayed marriage) declined, native-born women married at relatively young ages (twenty-two or twenty-three by the mid–eighteenth century), and longevity increased. A marriage produced on average seven or eight children in the eighteenth century, and five or six were likely to reach adulthood. As a result, the population began to grow by natural increase, as it had in New England long before. Modern efforts to define population levels (which were not directly measured by the decennial censuses until 1790) indicate that Franklin's estimates were close to the mark. The total population of the mainland British colonies stood at about 250,000 in 1700; by 1775, it had reached 2.5 million That was already over a third the population of England and Wales combined, and the rate of growth in America was substantially higher than that "at home." At some point in the future, more English people would live in America than in Britain itself—as Franklin predicted.

SOURCES OF GROWTH

Why was the British North American population growing so fast? The base cause was, again as Franklin surmised, a high birth rate. By the eighteenth century, colonial women married from four to five years earlier than their counterparts in Europe, which in a precontraceptive society translated into more births. The colonial population was also healthier, probably because it had more reliable access to food, particularly meat. Better nutrition not only led to higher survival rates among infants and longer lives, but explains why by the 1770s men from the continental North American colonies averaged 3 to 3.5 inches taller than their British counterparts.

If births accounted for 80 percent of the new population, immigration made up the other 20 percent. And it was particularly important in the middle colonies, including Franklin's Pennsylvania, where in the eighteenth century immigration helped push the annual population growth rate to about 3.4 percent, substantially higher than New England's 2.4 percent or the Chesapeake's 2.7 percent.

Franklin didn't talk about immigration, particularly that from non-British sources, perhaps because he didn't like it. There was no need for foreign emigrants, he argued; left alone, the British would readily fill the land by "natural generation." He drew an analogy with plants, any type of which ("for Instance, . . . Fennel") would take over vacant lands where they had no need to compete with other plants for the "Means of Subsistence." So, too, a land "empty of other Inhabitants . . . might in a few Ages be replenish'd from one Nation only . . . for Instance, with Englishmen," whom he preferred especially over the "Spaniards, Italians, French, Russians and Swedes," all of whom he described as having a "swarthy Complexion." So did the Germans, as Franklin saw

it, except for the Saxons, ancestors of the English, whom he was willing to include among "White People."

Immigration nonetheless constituted an important component of colonial population growth. It also transformed the character of colonial life, which, although still dominated by persons of British origin, was becoming more ethnically diverse—despite Franklin's preferences.

IMMIGRATION

In the late seventeenth century, the British government began restricting emigration, particularly of craftsmen (although many made their way to America despite these restrictions). The one exception was criminals, who after 1718 could accept "transportation" to the colonies as an alternative to punishment in England. Most of the estimated 50,000 convicted felons Britain sent to North America went as servants to the Chesapeake. Franklin, as usual, had something to say on the subject. In a newspaper essay of 1751 (roughly the time he

Eighteenth-century artist Lewis Miller's watercolors and sketches depict scenes of everyday life in York, Pennsylvania. Here we see a Lutheran christening of a baby boy.

was conducting electrical experiments and writing on demography), he noted that the British government had decided to prevent colonial assemblies from barring the immigration of felons because "such Laws . . . tend to prevent the IMPROVEMENT and WELL PEOPLING of the Colonies." So kind a concern, he said, deserved a return favor. He proposed sending to England American rattlesnakes, which were as likely as felons to change their nature with a change of climate. The snakes, he proposed, should be *"transported"* to Britain and released in "Places of Pleasure about London; in the Gardens of all the Nobility and Gentry . . . but particularly in the Gardens of the *Prime Ministers*, the *Lords of Trade* and *Members of Parliament*," to whom the colonists were *"most particularly* obliged."

French Huguenots—Protestants from a Catholic country—were a more respectable and welcome set of immigrants. Between 2,500 and 5,000 of them, a relatively modest number, arrived in America sometime after 1685, when Louis XIV revoked the Edict of Nantes, which since 1592 had granted freedom of worship to French Protestants. Most went to New England, the rest to New York or South Carolina. The Huguenots were, for the most part, an enterprising, middle-class people who fit readily into colonial society. A small component of Jews, mostly of Portuguese or Spanish origin who came from refugee communities in the Caribbean, also appeared in Newport, New York City, Philadelphia, and Charleston. There were altogether only about 250 Jewish families in the mainland colonies by the 1770s. The Jews were generally merchants or tradesmen. They had their own synagogues, charitable organizations, and schools, and, unlike the Huguenots, remained for the most part a people apart.

There were also Scottish immigrants—often Jacobite supporters of the exiled James II and his son, Bonnie Prince Charlie, who came from the highlands of Scotland. Catholic, clannish, and given to speaking Gaelic rather than English, they settled in isolated places such as the Mohawk Valley of New York or the western reaches of North Carolina, and were again less integrated into the old population than the Huguenots. The first contingents arrived after a failed Scottish uprising of 1715, but another migration including perhaps 40,000 Scots arrived between 1763 and 1775, when Parliament outlawed further emigration from Scotland. Smaller numbers of more cosmopolitan Scots from cities like Glasgow also went to the Chesapeake as "factors," or agents, to manage the tobacco trade.

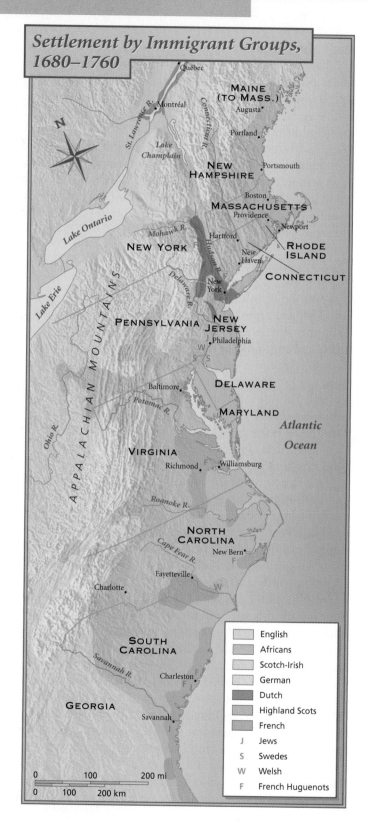

Settlement by Immigrant Groups, 1680–1760

Legend:
- English
- Africans
- Scotch-Irish
- German
- Dutch
- Highland Scots
- French
- J Jews
- S Swedes
- W Welsh
- F French Huguenots

A Conestoga wagon, or covered wagon, which was first made in western Pennsylvania during the mid–eighteenth century. The wagon, set over broad wheels and pulled by a team of horses, was designed to carry heavy loads over rugged terrain. Its ends were higher than the middle to keep goods from spilling out on inclines. The name comes from Pennsylvania's Conestoga Valley.

Some Catholics from the south of Ireland also came. By the 1760s, there were about 6,000 in Pennsylvania and 10,000 in Maryland. Catholics found little welcome in the militantly Protestant American colonies of the eighteenth century. In Maryland, provincial statutes forced "Papists" to worship in private (1704), and then, in 1715 and 1718, excluded them from office and denied them the vote, even in local elections, unless they took oaths that proclaimed their allegiance to the British king and denied the doctrine of transubstantiation (that bread and wine were turned into the body and blood of Christ at consecration in a Catholic mass). And in 1756, Maryland's provincial assembly, which had to raise revenue for Britain's war with Catholic France, taxed their land at double the rate of that paid by Protestant neighbors. Even so, Maryland Catholics were probably better off than their counterparts in England or Ireland, where the law restricted their purchase, lease, and inheritance of property.

A far larger flow of immigrants came from the north of Ireland—the old seventeenth-century plantation of Ulster—and were Protestant dissenters from the Church of England, usually Presbyterians. In the American context, these people were identified as Scotch-Irish, although their ancestors might have come from England as well as the lowlands of Scotland before crossing the Irish Sea to help plant Ireland. After 1715, they left Ireland in droves, moving westward like their predecessors, this time across the Atlantic to establish new homes in North America; by 1770, there were perhaps 200,000 of them in the colonies. As dissenters from the Anglican Church, the Scotch-Irish suffered legal discrimination in Ireland, but by 1717–18, when the first great waves of migration from Ulster began, their reasons for leaving were probably economic. They suffered from a series of bad harvests and a wave of "rent racking": as the long-term leases on their land expired, English landlords racked up the rents by two or three times to levels the Scotch-Irish settlers could not pay and still maintain what was to them an acceptable standard of living. A depression in the linen industry led to another immigration spurt later in the eighteenth century.

The Scotch-Irish first tried settling in northern New England, but, finding a less than cordial welcome there, in the mid-1720s began going to western Pennsylvania. From there, they moved into the Great Valley of the Appalachians, then steadily south until they made up a conspicuous part of the population in the western reaches of Maryland, Virginia, the Carolinas, and also the new state of Georgia. The Scotch-Irish were quintessential frontiersmen, carving farms from the wilderness, ignoring the land claims of both Indians and eastern speculators, and so, from the perspective of some older colonists, causing more than their share of trouble.

Another substantial addition to the colonial population came from German-speaking parts of northern Europe and,

A beautifully decorated chest from Pennsylvania, used for storing clothes and other articles. The design is characteristic of German craftsmen.

121

again, was Protestant. The Germans were an enormously diverse group both in their place of origin (they came from parts of what is today Germany, Luxembourg, and Switzerland) and, more dramatically, in their religious convictions. Many were members of Protestant pacifist sects—Mennonites, Amish, Dunkers, Schwenkfelders, and the like—who wanted to live simple lives in isolated communities where they could worship God as they chose without interference. Another sizable group of Moravians, or United Brethren, espoused a similar life-style except that they were less committed to isolation and were not pacifists. Most of the German immigrants, however, were mainline Lutherans and Reformed Protestants, whose reasons for migration were more economic than religious.

A relatively small number of Germans began emigrating during the 1720s; by the 1770s, perhaps 125,000 Germans had arrived. Many paid their own way; others contracted to work for periods of time, usually three or four years, as "redemptioners," a variety of indentured servitude. (Redemptioners borrowed money for their passage and provisions from shippers, then, once in America, indentured themselves to farmers or merchants who then redeemed the loans.) There were German settlers all along the colonies' western frontier, but the greater part of them settled in Pennsylvania, where they made up a third of the population by the 1770s. These were the Pennsylvania Dutch, or, more accurately, the Pennsylvania Deutsch (*Deutsch* is the German word for "German")—that is, Germans, not Hollanders. The settlers' tendency to "Germanize" his beloved Pennsylvania distressed Franklin, who exchanged letters with Collinson on how to induce the Germans to abandon their native tongue and speak English.

All of these immigrants came as the result of both a push—religious oppression or economic misfortunes—and a pull, the prospect of religious freedom and economic opportunity, which lay for most in the availability of freehold land. They came, too, with the encouragement of the British government, which from the late seventeenth century lured immigrants from rival nations to its colonies with promises of liberty, economic advancement, land, and the "rights of Englishmen." And so America became a land of opportunity. However, the largest group of eighteenth-century immigrants—one that included some 250,000 people, more than all the other post-1680 immigrant groups combined—did not cross the Atlantic voluntarily or in pursuit of a better life. They were African slaves. Their arrival exerted an impact not just on the colonies' labor system and economy but on their society and politics—on attitudes toward race and toward freedom—that was nothing less than revolutionary.

The Development of American Slavery

The Spanish had long since brought African slaves to their colonies, and English seamen tried to break into the slave trade even before their countrymen began planting the New World. But since the English did not own slaves, English law did not recognize the institution. It did, however, recognize other forms of unfreedom. Men and women who indentured themselves as apprentices to learn a craft or to work as servants in the colonies for a period of time in return for passage to America and certain "freedom dues" at the end of their servitude were not free during the term of their indenture. When slaves first arrived in the mainland British colonies early in the seventeenth century, they were treated much like other unfree persons.

The conditions of their lives changed dramatically, however, in the late seventeenth and early eighteenth centuries. It was only then that great numbers of slaves arrived in North America and many colonies passed from being, as the historian Ira Berlin put it, "societies with slaves" to "slave societies."

SEVENTEENTH-CENTURY BEGINNINGS

The first slaves arrived at Jamestown on a Dutch ship—not a "slaver" but a "man-o'-war" that happened to stop there—in 1619. "Twenty Negars" were sold on that occasion to John Rolfe, a large number for the time. Most slaves arrived in small lots of ten or less brought in by privateers or pirates, or as the leftover portion of cargoes that went unsold in the prime slave markets of the West Indies, where by the mid–seventeenth century sugar plantations seemed to consume an unending stream of slaves. Rarely did whole ships of

> *"The largest group of eighteenth-century immigrants—one that included some 250,000 people—did not cross the Atlantic voluntarily or in pursuit of a better life. They were African slaves."*

slaves sail to the mainland, and rarely did the slaves that arrived come directly from Africa. These "Atlantic Creole" people, as Berlin calls them, were part of a polyglot society that had emerged on the coast of Africa, in Europe, and in the West Indies. There, along the wide rim of the Atlantic Ocean, Africans, Europeans, and sometimes native Americans met each other, interbred, learned each other's languages, became acquainted with and sometimes adopted new religions, and acquired skills necessary in their peculiar world at the interstices of several older cultures. Those black Creoles who survived their initial contact with other peoples had or perhaps developed a resistance or even an immunity to the diseases that produced high death rates at slave factories on the African coast.

Once in North America, slaves often worked side by side with indentured servants and free whites, even on occasion with their owners. They were usually expected to support themselves and received in return the right to any excess food or livestock they produced and the profits from its sale—which eventually allowed some enterprising slaves to purchase their freedom. Some ex-slaves even acquired servants and slaves of their own.

Since Chesapeake planters had to make do with slaves that could not be sold in the West Indies, where planters strongly preferred male slaves, the slaves sold on the mainland included women. Consequently, the ratio of men to women among the Chesapeake's black population was probably more equal than the ratio among whites through most of the seventeenth century. That made marriages and thus children more frequent. Since the blacks were also relatively healthy, their numbers grew by natural increase long before the white population could even replace itself. Those who were free founded communities, most notably on the eastern shore of Virginia and Maryland, where members of leading black families sometimes took white spouses, without, it seems, imposing any stigma on the white partner. Like other colonists, these freedmen wanted to own land, and they took care to register land titles and debts and have their wills notarized in the county courthouse. They could sue and be sued in the courts like other colonists. To be sure, free blacks were a minority: most blacks remained slaves. But in the early seventeenth-century Chesapeake, where personal freedom, property holding, and family conferred status and blacks shared in all those blessings, and where the overall population included only a tiny percentage of black people, race was neither an automatic sign of inferiority nor an obstacle to membership in the larger society.

Nor was slavery confined to the southern colonies. Some of the largest concentrations of slaves were in New York, since the Dutch had drawn on Africa as well as European sources to people New Netherland. About 30 percent of New Amsterdam's population was slave in 1638, and 20 percent in 1664, when the English took over. By then, slaves constituted about 5 percent of New York's overall population—about the same as in the contemporary Chesapeake. Although the Dutch

CHARLESTOWN, *April 27, 1769.*

TO BE SOLD,

On WEDNESDAY the Tenth Day of MAY next,

A CHOICE CARGO OF

Two Hundred & Fifty

NEGROES:

ARRIVED in the Ship COUNTESS of SUSSEX, THOMAS DAVIES, Mafter, directly from GAMBIA, by

JOHN CHAPMAN, & Co.

*** THIS is the Veffel that had the Small-Pox on Board at the Time of her Arrival the 31ft of March laft: Every neceffary Precaution hath fince been taken to cleanfe both Ship and Cargo thoroughly, fo that thofe who may be inclined to purchafe need not be under the leaft Apprehenfion of Danger from Infection.

The NEGROES are allowed to be the likelieft Parcel that have been imported this Seafon.

Advertisement for the sale of 250 slaves, probably by auction, at Charlestown (Charleston, South Carolina) on May 10, 1769. Note the statement at the bottom. Smallpox was a deadly disease, and colonists took great precautions to prevent its spread. The ship *Countess of Sussex* arrived on March 31, and was probably kept in isolation away from the community until it and its slaves could be safely brought into the town.

Slave women working as field hands under the supervision of a white overseer. This watercolor dates from the eighteenth century.

made manumission (emancipation) difficult, one in five slaves had become free. As in the Chesapeake, blacks owned land, could sue in Dutch courts, sometimes married and baptized their children in the Dutch Reformed Church, and even participated in the Dutch militia. Rhode Island also had a substantial number of slaves; and they were present in smaller concentrations throughout New England and the middle colonies. Slaves, in short, were few but ubiquitous.

Like other colonists, most slaves worked on farms, or else in rural tanneries, mines, or iron furnaces. Slaves in the cities could be found on the docks or in homes, where they served as domestic servants. Those slaves or their ancestors had generally arrived singly or in small groups from the West Indies and almost never directly from Africa. They were familiar citizens of the Atlantic world who might or might not be of mixed blood, spoke English and perhaps a few other languages as well, and adjusted readily to the routines of provincial life. Such slaves fit right in to a society that wove various forms of unfreedom into the fabric of life. But as their numbers rose, they increasingly became a people apart.

"In the early seventeenth-century Chesapeake, race was neither an automatic sign of inferiority nor an obstacle to membership in the larger society."

TOWARD A SLAVE SOCIETY

In the late seventeenth and early eighteenth centuries, slaves began arriving in North America by the shipload, not odd lots, and they increasingly came straight from Africa. At the same time, colonial legislators adopted statutes that defined the **American institution of black chattel slavery**. Slavery, those laws declared, meant servitude for life; it was a condition confined to blacks (and sometimes Indians); and the children of slave mothers were also slaves. New laws, like one adopted by the Virginia General Assembly in 1691, also outlawed interracial marriages. In the next half century, Chesapeake lawmakers prohibited free blacks from employing white servants, voting or holding office, serving on juries, or bearing arms. Blacks were also forbidden or discouraged from practicing various crafts or engaging in trade. The details of such laws and the extent to which they were enforced varied from colony to colony, but everywhere the ambiguities of the past gave way, and slavery became a distinct, racially defined, established institution.

Why the change? It coincided with a decline in the supply of English indentured servants, who originally came to Amer-

ica because they could not find work in England. By the last decades of the seventeenth century, as the English population stabilized, more jobs opened up and real wages increased in England, so noncriminals who had a choice often chose to stay home. Parliament also began to discourage English migration to America. The opening of new colonies on the Hudson and Delaware rivers, moreover, gave all white immigrants, whether from Britain or continental Europe, alternative destinations that offered greater opportunities to the poor than the southern colonies, which would absorb the greater part of the new slave population.

In any case, indentured servitude had disadvantages that were fresh in the minds of Virginia's leading planters in the late 1670s: servants not only eventually became free, forcing their masters to find new workers, but discontented ex-servants could be very dangerous, as Bacon's Rebellion proved. As life expectancy increased in the Chesapeake, it began to make economic sense to pay the extra money to buy a lifetime of labor and the labor of slaves' children rather than a few years of work from a servant. The turning point probably came around 1660, when Virginia adopted its first slave laws, but low tobacco prices caused by the Navigation Acts prevented planters from buying slaves in quantity at that time.

Slaves packed together in the hold of a Spanish ship seized by a British warship as it sailed from Africa to the West Indies.

By the end of the century, however, the supply of available slaves increased. Dutch traders who dominated the slave trade at mid-century had rarely ventured to North America: there was business enough in Brazil and other markets nearer Africa. Similarly, the Royal African Company, which displaced the Dutch as supplier of slaves to the British colonies, did most of its business in the West Indies and seldom sailed as far west as the North American mainland. But the company could neither fill the colonies' demand for slaves nor protect its lawful monopoly, which it lost altogether in 1698. So private traders moved in, happily supplying slaves to Chesapeake purchasers who by 1700 were able to pay prices that more than compensated for the longer voyage. By then, in fact, the profitability of tobacco compared well with that of the West Indies' sugar, the price of which had dropped substantially over the previous decades.

Slave huts made of brick with thatched roofs on a Tidewater plantation.

As Virginia and Maryland planters bought more and more slaves, the Chesapeake passed from being a society with slaves to a slave society where slaves were not incidental but fundamental, a basic component of the social fabric that transformed all other parts. That transformation occurred, however, in different ways in different parts of the colonies.

"As Virginia and Maryland planters bought more and more slaves, the Chesapeake passed from being a society with slaves into a slave society."

The Chesapeake. The change to a slave society took place rapidly in the Chesapeake. In 1668, there were more than five white servants for every slave in one Virginia county, which was much like the rest of the Chesapeake. But by 1700, black slaves outnumbered white servants. During the intervening decades, slave imports began to soar: planters bought more slaves between 1695 and 1700 than in the previous twenty years. One Virginian out of twenty was a slave in the mid-1660s; by 1720, slaves constituted one out of four. Twenty years later, 40 percent of all Virginians were slaves.

The change was in character as well as quantity. The new slaves came increasingly not from communities along the West African coast, as had earlier slaves, but from the interior of the continent, where marauding bands of African slave traders captured people for sale. Slaves from coastal regions had come from distinct communities: those from the north, for example, might be Ashantis and Yorubas, and those from the south Ibos or Mbundus. Slaves from the interior of Africa similarly belonged to hundreds of different "nations," some small, others extending over great distances, each distinguished from the others by language, religion, and leadership. These people knew themselves not as "Africans" but as Akan, Igbo, Mande, or some other specific association. And for them, no process of cultural homogenization, such as distinguished the Atlantic Creoles of the early seventeenth century, had occurred. They rarely spoke a European language or a "pidgin," or creole, language that would allow communication, and they had no acquaintance with European religions, work routines, or culture. To govern such a people seemed to require force; and provincial laws allowed owners far greater leeway in disciplining slaves than they had with white servants. Slavery became more brutal than it had been, and also more demeaning. In the seventeenth century, Chesapeake slaves generally had names that suggested their rich cultural history and a certain dignity, such as Antonio (or Anthony) Johnson, Domingo Mathews, or John Francisco. Thereafter, owners gave slaves, like animals, single names like Joe or mocked them with names like Julius Caesar or Cato.

The slaves arrived in a weakened condition, having spent some six months from capture marching toward the coast or confined in dungeons or herded into open pens at the slave

The survival of African culture among American slaves is evident in this late eighteenth-century painting of a South Carolina plantation. The musical instruments, pottery, and clothing are of African origin, probably Yoruba.

made them peculiarly attractive to planters in the malaria-prone southern lowlands. Resistance to malaria became all the more valuable after 1680, when a common, mild form of the disease gave way to a far more virulent and lethal type of malaria.

Survivors of those dangers faced a life different from the ones their seventeenth-century slave predecessors had known. Opportunities for earning an independent income and using it to buy freedom were virtually gone. Indeed, the Chesapeake's old communities of free blacks disappeared as their members fled, managed to pass as white, or, in some cases, were re-enslaved. The social and working relationships with whites that characterized the lives of the Atlantic Creoles also disappeared. Even ties with other blacks, particularly family ties, were difficult to establish in the Chesapeake, where much of the slave population lived on scattered, remote plantations. Owners eventually grasped

"factories," where they were sold to slave merchants from Europe. Perhaps half of all slave deaths occurred in Africa, although the mortality rate varied from place to place. On the ships, slaves were crammed into tight spaces with sick and dying people for an additional two months, with little food or sanitation facilities. On average, 10–20 percent of the slaves (and many white crewmen as well) died on the "Middle Passage"—the middle leg of the slavers' transit from England to Africa to America and back to England. Not all slaves submitted passively: one out of ten slave voyages experienced rebellions, and it seems that insurrections were most likely on ships carrying a relatively high number of female slaves. More slaves expired soon after their arrival when exposed to European childhood diseases such as measles and whooping cough, which could be fatal to people who had never encountered them before. On the other hand, because they came from places where yellow fever was endemic, slaves had often acquired an immunity to that disease. The high incidence among Africans of the sickle-cell trait, a malformation in blood cells that provides some resistance to malaria, also

the economic advantage in possessing "breeding negroes": "a woman who brings a child every two years [is] more profitable than the best man on the farm," the Virginia planter Thomas Jefferson wrote in his *Farm Book*, since "what she produces is an addition to the capital, while his labor disappears in mere consumption." But it took time before owners came to that understanding, purchased women as well as men, and were willing to reduce the workloads of pregnant female slaves. Meanwhile, planters bought young males—and the black population's sex ratios became unbalanced as those of whites became balanced. Decades passed before a small, native-born black population emerged and, approaching the mid–eighteenth century, began to grow.

These blacks produced a culture unlike that of the relatively assimilated Atlantic Creoles. Theirs was a separate African-American culture that carried forward elements of the African past and borrowed only selectively from the cultures of whites. The gradual acceptance of an African identity by people who had thought of themselves as Mande, Bambara, Igbo, or Akan was a phenomenon not unlike that of the

Wurtembergers, Alsatians, Palatines, and Swiss who found themselves grouped together as Germans, an identity they had never known in Europe.

At the same time, the relationships among the Chesapeake's white people changed. In earlier days, slaves and servants readily associated with each other; in fact, their liaisons, not those of masters and slaves, were probably responsible for the greatest number of mulatto children born in the colonies during the early parts of the seventeenth century. But as slavery became an increasingly demeaning status reserved for blacks, even the whites lowest on the social scale pulled away, making skin color a powerful social distinction. In the past, rich planters and poor freemen stood against each other, as during Bacon's Rebellion; now they bonded together. The great planters expected a certain deference from those not of their status. But they also welcomed smaller landowners to their homes, helped them get their tobacco to market, and cultivated a common identity among free white Virginians.

Was Virginia's ruling class consciously using the color line to divide onetime servants and black slaves, who in 1676 had joined Bacon's army in roughly equal numbers? Whatever they meant to do, that was the effect: divisions in Virginia became more of race than of class; or, more exactly, the classifications that defined Virginians' identity became racial. And white Virginians shared, above all, a profound pride in the freedom they enjoyed whatever the extent of their wealth. They knew the value of liberty because they witnessed on a daily basis the degradation of people who lacked it. The strength with which Virginians espoused the cause of freedom would shape their future and that of colonists throughout the North American mainland.

South Carolina. The story elsewhere resembled the situation in the Chesapeake, with some variations. Many of South Carolina's first settlers were slaves brought by their masters from Barbados. In the early pioneer years of the colony, slave and master could be found working together side by side, and slaves received a certain amount of autonomy (and respect) as guides, cattle herders, even militiamen. But the extent and character of the colony's slave system shifted with the development of rice culture in the 1790s and the production of indigo (a blue dye) a half century later.

The presence of black laborers probably contributed to the development of rice culture. The English had no experience growing that crop, and apparently failed at one earlier attempt. Rice had, however, been grown for centuries in West Africa, and the methods adopted in South Carolina showed a striking similarity to those used in Africa. Gangs of barefoot black workers planted the crop, pressing seeds into the ground with their heels, as in Africa. Then they flooded the fields until the seeds sprouted, drained and hoed the fields, and repeated the whole process, working in muddy soil under a scorching sun with swarms of insects adding to their discomfort. After the harvest, slaves (often women) beat the rice in a mortar, then winnowed it, using woven instruments, like those used in Africa, to separate grain and chaff. And particularly after rice production moved from uplands to the coastal plain in the mid–eighteenth century, the massive earthworks that directed water to the fields needed constant repair. Growing rice was backbreaking, unpleasant work that whites saw as "only fit for slaves."

Processing indigo was no better. South Carolinians turned to producing the dye in the 1740s, when King George's War (1739–48) led to a dramatic drop in rice prices. The teenaged Eliza Lucas (later Eliza Lucas Pinckney) began experimenting with indigo production as manager of her father's plantations near Charleston. She sold her first crop in 1744. From the planters' perspective, indigo held great advantages: it grew on soil too dry for rice, required attention when rice did not (allowing a more efficient use of slave laborers), and could still be sold profitably when the market for rice fell. Slaves cultivated the crop and then, after the plants leafed out in July (and again in August and maybe also September), carefully pruned them and placed the leaves in great tubs. There, as the leaves fermented, they gave off what became an increasingly disgusting smell and attracted clouds of flies. Finally, slaves picked out the leaves, drained the liquid into other vats, and beat it with paddles until the brew was ready to be set with lime. This process produced a mud-like blue sediment, which, after the liquid was again drained off, could be dried and cut into

> *"These blacks produced a culture unlike that of the relatively assimilated Atlantic Creoles. Theirs was a separate African American culture that carried forward elements of the African past and borrowed only selectively from that of whites."*

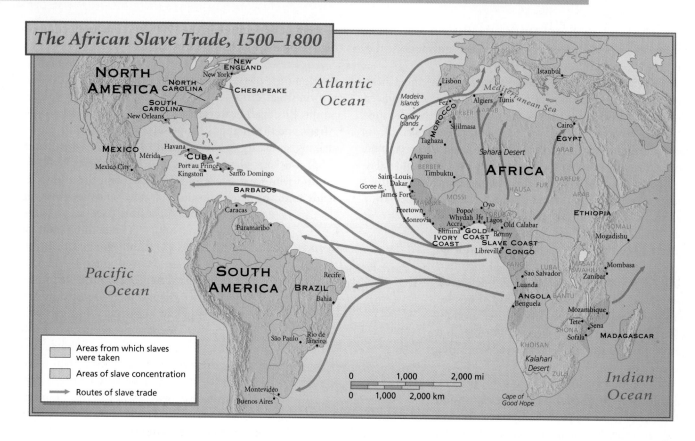

The African Slave Trade, 1500–1800

Areas from which slaves were taken

Areas of slave concentration

Routes of slave trade

blocks for sale to textile producers abroad. The work was arduous and often unpleasant. It required great skill to make indigo cakes of the right color and consistency, and also to construct the necessary vats and other equipment. All of that was done by slaves.

Rice and indigo made coastal Carolina home to the greatest concentration of wealth in North America. Planters used the profits from selling those slave products to purchase more slaves. Before 1710, about 300 slaves entered the colony each year; in the 1720s, the annual arrivals exceeded 2,000. Slave imports dropped after 1739, when an uprising by some 60 "Angolan" slaves at Stono, South Carolina, murdered about 20 whites. But soon planters overcame their fears, and the slave trade recovered. In the 1770s, about 4,000 slaves arrived in South Carolina each year. Some 40 percent of all slave immigrants to colonial British North America were brought to Charleston. Many were reshipped elsewhere, but many remained. Blacks constituted a majority of South Carolina's population by 1708, and they outnumbered whites two to

one by 1720. One visitor commented that the colony looked "like a negro country."

There was no similar concentration of slaves elsewhere on the mainland. The closest equivalent lay in the sugar islands of the West Indies, where the population was often 80 percent black. And, as on the islands, only continued importations kept the slave population from falling. South Carolina's black population began once again to grow from native births in the 1760s, several decades after that occurred in the Chesapeake.

Most of the slave population of South Carolina was clustered on large plantations. In 1720, three-quarters lived on plantations with at least ten slaves, and by 1750 about a third lived on large plantations with fifty or more slaves. Owners were often absent, spending seasons that were uncomfortable and unhealthy in more salubrious places like Charleston or Newport, Rhode Island. That gave slaves a certain autonomy. So did the colony's task system of labor. Slaves had to complete a set amount of work per day—for example, planting or weeding a quarter acre. Afterward, their time was their own to tend private gardens, raise livestock, weave baskets, or do anything else they chose. If slaves sold surpluses of their own production, the proceeds were theirs; as a result, slaves became big-time peddlers in South Carolina, even though buying freedom was no longer a likely outcome. The harder they worked at their task, the more quickly they could turn to their own thing. The task system provided an ingenious way to build incentive into a nonwage economy, and so to keep slaves at work without close supervision or persistent discipline.

In part because there were large numbers of Africans nearby, slaves on South Carolina's plantations sometimes found it possible to continue religious rituals and social traditions from their past. They even lived in quarters that they built using traditional African methods. To allow communication among people whose native tongues were often mutually unintelligible, they developed a new common language, Gullah, which contained elements drawn from both English and African languages. And once the unbalanced sex ratios and high mortality that afflicted the first generations of African immigrants subsided, the physical proximity of plantation slaves facilitated family life: South Carolina's slaves had less need to travel miles to visit a spouse than slaves scattered on the small farms and plantations of the Chesapeake.

When the slave system became particularly harsh, slaves resisted. They could feign ignorance and an incapacity to learn jobs assigned them, or break tools—which reduced demands for sustained hard work but reinforced stereotypes of

This detail from a 1773 map of a low-country county in South Carolina shows the process of preparing indigo. Note the slaves carrying leaves for processing, and the racks for drying blocks of indigo on the right.

blacks as fecklessly childlike "Sambos." Arson and poison, crimes whose perpetrators were difficult to trace, also held a place in the slaves' repertoire. And they could run away. After 1700, few places to hide remained in the Chesapeake, but "maroon societies" of runaways proliferated in the tangled, swampy lowlands of Carolina and on its upland frontier, where pioneer farmers often felt little sympathy for the wealthy, slaveholding planters near the coast. The governor of Spanish Florida provided another refuge when he founded a black settlement north of St. Augustine, Gracia Real de Santa Teresa de Mose, as a home for runaway slaves from the North. The slaves who participated in South Carolina's Stono Rebellion of 1739 planned to go to "Mose."

But not all of South Carolina's slaves lived on plantations, and those in Charleston or Beaufort led radically different lives and had far less reason to escape than their rural relatives. Through most of the eighteenth century, those city slaves lived in a world dominated by whites. They picked up English quickly and, like the earlier Atlantic Creoles, learned the ways and adopted the styles of the prevailing white culture. Many became artisans (or mechanics, in the language of the day), working as coopers (who made barrels for shipping products abroad), carpenters, blacksmiths, seamstresses, and the like. Sometimes they were allowed to hire themselves out, recompensing their owners from their earnings and renting their own independent quarters. Surrounded by planter wealth and a profusion of consumer goods, they frequently flaunted their own prosperity, riding about in fancy clothes on handsome horses—which raised eyebrows and provoked largely unsuccessful efforts to exclude blacks from various economic activities. A greater contrast with plantation slaves, planting rice seeds in steaming, fly-ridden mudflats, is hard to imagine.

The North. The northern colonies never became slave societies like the Chesapeake and South Carolina, but there, too, the slave population increased, and legislatures adopted new laws that defined the institution and established rules and procedures specially for slaves. New England was the least affected: there, farmers, still the vast majority of the population, remained true to their traditional system of family labor. But in Boston, as in Newport, New York, and Philadelphia, slaves became standard fixtures in the households of wealthy merchants and common even in the homes of middle-class people such as the Franklins. They also worked at the docks and often in trades that were connected with shipping such as rope making, sail making, and shipbuilding. Everywhere in the North, slave imports rose when conditions such as war kept white workers in Europe. When the supply of white immigrants increased, slave imports dropped. The flow was therefore uneven, but the net yield was significant. Newport's population was 10 percent slave in 1750, twice what it had been thirty years earlier. And New York City's population was 14 percent black—part new, part native born, and mostly slave—by the 1760s.

South of New England, moreover, slaves became increasingly prominent in the rural workforce. In fact, it was not altogether easy after the mid–eighteenth century to define a clear line between the economy of the Chesapeake and that of the middle colonies. Planters in Maryland and northern Virginia began switching from tobacco to grain, which found a profitable market in Europe, while Pennsylvania farmers, who had long grown grain, began buying slaves. Along the Hudson Valley and on Long Island in New York, or in parts of northern New Jersey, farmers switched to slave labor in even higher proportions.

Prosperity, built on slave labor, allowed a new, more refined style of life in the colonial South. This watercolor, from 1754, shows a lively party given by Peter Manigault, speaker of the South Carolina House of Assembly (one figure says, "Pray less noise, Gentlemen"). Note the men's fine clothes, the wood paneling on the wall in the background, and the large window with glass panes as well as the caged bird, all of which were signs of wealth.

Legislatures quickly regulated the new situation. To avoid having the white nonslaveholding population bear the burden of indigent former slaves (freed, for example, because of age), one legislature after another restricted manumissions or forced owners to support ex-slaves who became dependent on charity. Other laws restricted or prohibited blacks' voting, serving in militias, testifying in court, or holding property. In both North and South, legislatures periodically combined *ad hoc* regulations into comprehensive slave codes that bore strong similarities wherever they were passed.

From a modern perspective, the lack of opposition to slavery seems as striking as its rapid spread. In 1700, Samuel Sewall, the onetime judge in Salem's witch trials, wrote a tract entitled "The Selling of Joseph" that attacked slavery on religious grounds. "It is most certain," he said, "that all Men, as they are the Sons of Adam, are Coheirs; and have equal Right unto Liberty, and all other outward Comforts of Life." Some Quakers also publicly opposed slavery. But theirs were voices crying in the wilderness. Slavery, it seems, struck most seventeenth- and eighteenth-century white colonists as an alternative to indentured servitude, with one form of service no more immoral than the other. They also argued that slaves were "cut out for hard Labour and Fatigue" and that their situation was better in America than in Africa. It took another time, and a major change in principles and sensitivities, before Americans were ready to condemn the institution of slavery.

Expansion, Prosperity, and Refinement

The growth of the colonies and their increasing prosperity, which the expansion of slavery both reflected and enhanced, transformed American life. Population spread; life among many persons of European origin became less harsh, with more material comforts; and white colonists increasingly engaged in fashionable forms of study and reflection. Life became, in the language of the time, refined.

THE FOUNDING OF GEORGIA

In 1700, colonists remained clustered in separate settlements that were rarely far from the Atlantic or the major rivers that fed into it. A half century later, the British colonial population stretched almost continuously along the coast and perhaps 150 miles inland. In the North, settlers claimed lands in upstate New York (including what became Vermont), Maine, New Hampshire, and Nova Scotia; in the West, farmers moved into the Great Valley of the Appalachians, beginning often in Pennsylvania but arriving by the 1750s in the western regions of the Carolinas. And in the South, the eighteenth century saw the founding of Georgia, the last of the original thirteen colonies.

In a sense, Georgia was there waiting to be founded in the lands between Florida and South Carolina. To the British, that territory was part of Carolina; to the Spanish, it was Florida. The local Indians' sympathy for Spain made the British even more anxious to tighten their hold on the contested territory. South Carolinians, moreover, hoped that its settlement would plug the hole through which their slaves escaped to St. Augustine. The Board of Trade took up a suggestion by General James Oglethorpe, an old, militantly anti-Spanish soldier, that the land be settled by "the poor persons of London." As a member of Parliament, Oglethorpe had inspected London's prisons, and came away appalled at the treatment of persons who often had been jailed for crimes no worse than falling into debt. He put together an ingenious plan to hit two birds with one stone: he would stem the Spaniards' ambitions by settling Georgia—a colony he named after Britain's King George—with England's poor. Unfortunately, the scheme turned out to be literally too good to be true.

The Crown, more protective of its power than it had been a century earlier, granted a charter in 1732 to a set of twenty-one trustees who would hold Georgia in trust for twenty-one years, after which it would revert to the Crown. The new colony ran between the Savannah and Altamaha Rivers and, again, from "sea to sea." To believe the literature, Georgia was heaven on earth, a fertile field where exotic crops would thrive and the depressed of England would be magically transformed into productive subjects of the king. The trustees (a third of whom were fellows of the Royal Society) planned the new colony carefully. They would appoint a president and the members of a Common Council, who would govern the colony without, strangely, an elected assembly. Individuals could own no more than 500 acres, so the settlement would be more concentrated and easier to defend. Georgians could pass on their lands only to male heirs, who could shoulder a gun against enemies; if a planter had no sons, title to his land went back to the trustees when he died. Slavery was illegal, since slaves (whose loyalty to their masters remained suspect)

This engraving of Savannah, Georgia (c. 1735), was based on a drawing by Peter Gordon, the town's first bailiff. The engraving was shown in England to encourage emigration to Georgia.

would weaken the colony militarily. The trustees allowed no "rum, brandies, spirits or strong waters" in the colony, and would not let just any poor people migrate there. Only those who were "virtuous and industrious" could pass muster with the Georgia trustees and their agents.

Oglethorpe set out in the fall of 1732 with 32 families, and together they founded the city of Savannah. Before long, however, it became clear that the venture wasn't working. By 1740, about 3,000 people had journeyed there, but many had already left. The trustees had to make the place more attractive, which they did by destroying their vision, point by point. They allowed women to inherit land, lowered quitrents, and permitted settlers to own up to 2,000 acres. The ban on alcohol and slaves fell, along with restrictions on buying and selling land. Still the settlers objected: why didn't they have a voice in their government like other colonists? The trustees allowed them an assembly, but only to voice grievances, not to make laws. With such a forum and no more constructive role to perform, the colonists complained up a storm. Finally, sick of it all, the trustees turned control of the colony over to the Crown in June 1751, two years before the trusteeship expired.

"It is clear as light itself," a pamphlet of 1743 insisted, "that negroes are as essentially necessary to the cultivation of Georgia, as axes, hoes, or any other utensil of agriculture." As if to prove the point, once the trustees' restraining hand disap-

A watercolor of Yuchi Indians near Savannah, Georgia, in 1736. Note the guns hanging in the roofed enclosure (upper left), which the Indians could have obtained through trade—and the southeastern part of North America was a rich area for Indian-European trade—or from the colonists to help with military services that the Indians provided.

peared, Georgia quickly came to look like another South Carolina. The planters were "stark Mad after Negroes" and bought them in volume until coastal Georgia had a black majority whose members were busily growing rice, and Savannah sprouted planter mansions much like those of Charleston. Georgia became a slave society almost overnight. There was, it seemed, no other way the colony could prosper.

THE DISTRIBUTION OF WEALTH

With the growth of population and the expansion of settlement, the development of rice, indigo, and grain exports, and the establishment of a slave labor system, the British colonies prospered. The rewards went disproportionately to planters who possessed enough assets to purchase slaves and to merchants who could tap into the profits of overseas trade. There were also poor white people in the colonies, including victims of war, new immigrants, and young persons who had not yet inherited land or whose families' lands had been divided over so many generations that their own shares were meager. Compared with Europe, though, the American population included relatively few poor people, while the middle class—composed of individuals with sufficient means to support themselves with some independence—was extraordinarily large. The size of the middle class was, in fact, the most distinctive characteristic of British North American society by the 1760s and 1770s.

The rich were easy to find: they lived in the great plantation houses of the Chesapeake or the lower South, in fine urban mansions at Savannah or Charleston, or in the spacious homes of merchants in northern cities. Like their British ancestors and generations of later Americans, they used their new wealth to improve their living conditions. And the benefits of prosperity were not confined to the rich. Colonists of "middling" rank also remodeled their homes or built new ones and added new possessions that ameliorated their onetime hardscrabble lives. The growth of a consumer economy encouraged the growth of domestic manufactures, which remained, however, a relatively small part of the overall economy.

LIFE AT HOME

Forget the spanking clean, neat, freshly painted houses in "colonial villages" constructed for modern tourists. Most seventeenth- and eighteenth-century colonial homes looked nothing like them. For one thing, few were painted on the outside. Most were made of split or sawed boards that, like modern wooden garden benches, faded into a gray that blended into the landscape. And they were small affairs, often consisting of a single room measuring perhaps eighteen by twenty feet on the inside with a chimney at the end. Sometimes there were two rooms with a chimney at the center. Upstairs there might be a loft reached by a ladder or ladder-like stairway. New Englanders occasionally added a lean-to on the back of a house, giving it a characteristic saltbox shape. Some early "puncheon" houses were not carefully framed but consisted of crude exterior walls nailed to corner posts that were simply punched into the ground. Early colonial houses often lacked masonry foundations, although some contained cellars in which boards held back the earthen walls. And some, but by no means all, had whitewashed interior walls; otherwise, the interiors went unfinished. Easily built, most houses didn't last long, so historians need to reconstruct them imaginatively using information in wills, travelers' accounts, and archaeological evidence.

These modest houses were everywhere in the early years of settlement, and some persisted on into the early nineteenth century. They were not comfortable. Their air conditioning was of the natural, earth-friendly variety that works best in cold weather. Cracks between exterior boards might be filled with mud or some other material, but the walls were generally uninsulated. Windows consisted of small openings covered with oiled cloth or wooden shutters and only rarely with expensive glass. Heat came from vast fireplaces whose drafts pulled cold air into a house through cracks and other openings until a person was, as Franklin once noted, "scorch'd before while he's froze behind." Ink was known to freeze in inkwells, even in heated rooms. And since fireplaces were used for cooking as well as warmth, they continued to pump heat into houses in summer when outside temperatures soared.

Water for cooking or cleaning came from streams or had to be hoisted from wells with buckets and carried inside. There were no indoor bathrooms: the great outdoors was the place to go—most of the time. Even in the *late* eighteenth century, according to a French traveler, American men were given to urinating through the holes in broken windowpanes. The traveler followed their example, and when he encountered a place where the windows were too high, his host kindly provided a cooking pot to stand on! Add that practice to the presence of manure, a by-product of the preferred transportation system, horses, as well as of various other animals wandering around, and it's hard to avoid the conclusion that early America rarely smelled like a rose.

In the eighteenth century, colonists often divided single-room houses or added a second room, separating the old, all-purpose hall from a parlor used for entertaining guests. A new second story sometimes provided additional sleeping space with more privacy than was possible when an entire family (including servants) crowded into one room. Cooking, too, was gradually relegated to separate buildings in the southern colonies or the lean-to tacked onto New England

> *"The size of the middle class was, in fact, the most distinctive characteristic of the British North American society by the 1760s and 1770s."*

homes. This differentiation of space was a fundamental characteristic of home improvements, eighteenth-century style.

Most of the great colonial mansions of Virginia, as elsewhere, were built between 1720 and 1760. Until then, perhaps 80 percent of Virginia's wealthy planters still lived, like most of their neighbors, in one- or two-room houses that were one or one and a half stories high. In building their great houses, wealthy colonists imitated not the homes of English aristocrats, which remained well beyond reach, but those of middle-class Englishmen. Like their English prototypes, colonial America's Georgian mansions characteristically displayed balanced facades embellished with classical details such as pilasters beside doorways or at corners. Inside, a spectacular central staircase divided the house into sections that allowed abundant space for entertaining visitors. Many of the new houses were made of brick, which surely stood out from the mass of dull gray houses nearby. So did those clapboard houses that were increasingly painted after the middle of the eighteenth century—and, the evidence suggests, in strong

The late seventeenth-century house of John Ward in Salem, Massachusetts. The house was probably changed substantially before this modern photograph was taken (and it has since then been restored). However, we can clearly see the lean-to addition on the back, which added to the long rear sloped roof and so gave the house its characteristic saltbox shape. Note also the characteristic central chimney, which would have served fireplaces in several rooms.

LEFT: Large fireplaces such as this one, in the Paul Revere House, Boston, were used for cooking as well as heating. Note the chains and hooks for hanging pots and the oven to the right. Red coals would be shoveled into the oven to heat it, then pushed aside when baking bread, pies, and other foods. Large fireplaces were inefficient sources of heat for a house.

RIGHT: A new-style small fireplace, which was more successful than the large old fireplaces in heating a room. Such small fireplaces demanded that cooking be relegated to another part of the house. This fireplace, which dates from 1750, is in the Seth Wetmore House in Middletown, Connecticut. Note also the wood paneling and classical pilasters on either side of the fireplace, characteristic of eighteenth-century home improvements.

merchant Thomas Hancock built on Boston's Beacon Hill between 1737 and 1740 served as models that others could imitate. To build such houses required, of course, substantial wealth, but that was not enough. They also awaited the availability of carpenters, plasterers, and other craftsmen who had learned to execute fashionable designs in London, then moved to the English provinces or to America—where they arrived in substantial numbers during the early eighteenth century along with English guidebooks for realizing the new styles.

Before long, the aesthetic influence of the great houses trickled down to less affluent households. More than a few substantial farmhouses, for example, sprouted carved wooden pilasters beside their south-facing doors, and added staircases and rooms for specialized functions, including parlors for receiving visitors. Gradually, too, houses of both rich and middling colonists became more comfortable. Enclosing windows with glass brought more light into homes while making them more weather-tight—which meant more windows could be added, brightening interiors still more. The inefficient large fireplaces disappeared from major interior rooms once cooking moved elsewhere. Openings of two or three feet, it turned out, improved the draft and produced more heat.

Adding an iron stove was better yet, although the famous "Franklin stoves" are misnamed. The design Franklin proposed in a 1744 tract, *An Account of the New Invented Pennsylvanian Fire-Places*, employed contemporary scientific principles to increase heat while siphoning smoke down through a duct and then out through the chimney of an extant fireplace. Franklin hoped to see his "Pennsylvania Fire-Place" mass-produced and thus available at a price ordinary people could pay. But unfortunately, his stove didn't work: smoke would not siphon down through the masonry duct unless it was uniformly hot. Later, other inventors modified Franklin's design, usually adding a smoke outlet on the top like those on other stoves in use at the time. Franklin himself continued to experiment with heating devices on into the 1780s. His attempt to improve life for the common man as well as the rich was a sign of the time.

shades of red, brown, green, or blue, not soft pastels or pusillanimous white.

Ornamental gardens, too, came into style. The fashion began in England during the seventeenth century as travelers to Italy or France began attempting to replicate the gardens they had seen on the Continent. Most were formal, with straight paths, sometimes filled with gravel or sand, dividing square or rectangular beds that might include exotic plants collected from distant parts of the earth. Such gardens first began to appear in the North American colonies in the late 1600s, and were almost mandatory for elegant homes by the 1720s.

The new styles sometimes arrived in the colonies through fashion setters like Governor Francis Nicholson, who moved Virginia's capitol from Jamestown to Williamsburg, then built a governor's mansion there in the style of the English architect Christopher Wren that was unlike any other house in early eighteenth-century Virginia. Buildings such as the Virginia governor's mansion or, in New England, the house

Consumer "Comforts." The acquisitions of the colonial rich are familiar: graceful Chippendale furniture, sets of imported dishes and silver flatwear, "turkey" rugs, mirrors, the portraits of eighteenth-century colonists in velvet waistcoats or satin dresses. Unlike today, textiles were the premier article of conspicuous consumption: the rich displayed them draped over tables or beds, hanging over windows, or fashioned into the clothes they wore. These were the appurtenances of the genteel life that provided a standard for others to emulate.

The articles accumulated by less affluent people were less likely to survive. But accumulate them they did, beginning in the late seventeenth century and continuing in increased volume in the eighteenth. The middle classes added to the spare furnishings of earlier times, which generally consisted of stools, benches, an occasional chair, small chests for storage and sitting, and beds (mats or mattresses). Tables were often planks on trestles that, like the beds, could be moved aside when not used. Now even ordinary families began to acquire bedsteads (essentially frames, with or without headboards, that allowed them to lift bedding off the floor) and more chairs. No longer did people eat from shared cups and bowls that they passed around or trenchers (platters) from which they scooped up food with spoons or, sometimes, their hands. Individual knives and forks appeared along with individual ceramic dishes.

Franklin chronicled the first arrival of such "luxuries" into his household when he was still a working printer living with great frugality. For breakfast, he recalled, he usually ate "Bread & Milk (no Tea,) . . . out of a twopenny earthen Porringer with a Pewter Spoon." Then one morning, Franklin found his meal "in a China Bowl with a Spoon of Silver . . . bought for me without my Knowledge by my Wife" for the "enormous Sum of three and twenty Shillings," since "she thought her Husband deserv'd a Silver Spoon & China Bowl as well as any of the Neighbours." Later, he noted, "as our Wealth encreas'd," they added to their china and silver until it was worth "several Hundred Pounds."

What people ate and drank also changed. Sugar was one of Europe's first luxury goods, tobacco another. And tea, the favored drink of colonists as well as the English, soon joined the list. Early in the eighteenth century, the gentry adopted the drink along with elaborate devices for its ritual service—tea pots, cups, strainers, sugar tongs, and the like. By mid-century, everyone, including the inmates of Philadelphia's poorhouse, was drinking tea—not from china cups with silver spoons, but perhaps from ceramic cups made in the English midlands. The diet of the rich became more varied as English cookbooks began to appear in the eighteenth century, necessitating still more elaborate tableware and varied cooking utensils. How long would ordinary folk remain content with the once-standard yeoman's midday meal of boiled meat, beans or porridge, bread, cheese, and beer or milk?

The Family. Changes in houses and their furnishings signaled changes in family life among white colonists. The provision of separate sleeping quarters for adults and children allowed a privacy impossible in the crowded houses of the seventeenth

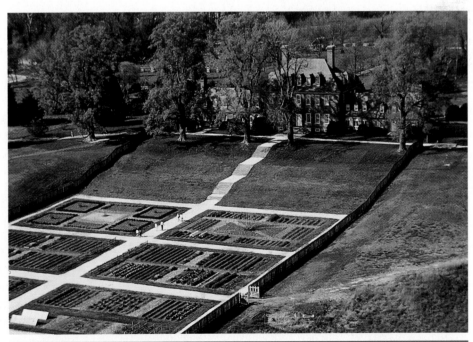

This large formal garden is at Carter's Grove, a plantation near Williamsburg, Virginia. Gardens of this type often included exotic plants. Guests were invited to walk through the gardens, so they in effect extended the spaces for entertaining within the house.

135

century. And as houses became more comfortable, they became places where family members might choose to linger, not just find shelter from the elements. Meals, once utilitarian events that interrupted labor, became occasions where people might break up their day with pleasure, and perhaps engage in discussions like those Franklin recalled from the family meals of his childhood. Tea provided another occasion for sociability.

Even marriage seemed to be changing. In seventeenth-century New England, marriages were in good part property arrangements negotiated by parents for their children. Couples needed to be emotionally compatible, but affection did not decide the bargain. In the eighteenth century, couples increasingly chose their own spouses, even without parental permission (as indicated by a surge in premarital pregnancies), and affection became an expected part of the relationship. (Of course, this kind of union sometimes failed, as a rise in Massachusetts divorce petitions after 1764 indicated; and court records confirm that domestic abuse is not a modern invention.) Children, whom seventeenth-century Puritans regarded as natural sinners whose will needed to be broken so they would be subject to their godly parents, came to be understood as needing nurture as much as discipline. In the Chesapeake, too, parents gave evidence aplenty that they took delight in their children. To some extent, these developments were heralded among Pennsylvania Quakers, who had long since seen children as innocent "tender plants" and allowed them, when older, to choose their own spouses. As houses

American Journal

What's for Dinner?

In the course of a trip during 1744, Alexander Hamilton, an Annapolis physician, encountered the keeper of a ferryboat on the Susquehanna River "att vittles" with his wife and family. They ate "a homely dish of fish without any kind of sauce. They desired me to eat, but I told them I had no stomach. They had no cloth upon the table, and their mess was in a dirty, deep, wooden dish which they evacuated with their hands, cramming down skins, scales, and all. They used neither knife, fork, spoon, plate, or napkin because, I suppose, they had none to use. I looked upon this as a picture of that primitive simplicity practiced by our forefathers long before the mechanic arts had supplied them with instruments for the luxury and elegance of life. I drank some of their syder, which was very good."

The family's meal seemed to Hamilton a throwback to an earlier, less refined time, when few people had knives or forks or napkins or tablecloths, and most people scooped up their meals from a common bowl with their hands (or, more often, spoons). In fact, many mid-eighteenth-century colonists of rural America probably ate much like the Susquehanna ferryman's family. Surely travelers could not expect elegant meals at every stop, and the foods provided and the way they were served could be surprising.

One day "att two a'clock," Dr. Hamilton "dined att one Corson's," an inn across "the Narrows" from New York's Long Island. "The landlady spoke both Dutch and English. I dined upon what I never had eat in my life before—a dish of fryed clams, of which shell fish there is abundance in these parts." The family said grace; then "we began to . . . stuff down the fryed clams with rye-bread and butter. They took such a deal of chawing that we were long at dinner, and the dish began to cool before we had eat enough. The landlady called for the bed pan. I could not guess what she intended to do with it unless it was to warm her bed to go to sleep after dinner, but I found that it was used by way of a chaffing dish to warm our dish of clams. I stared att the novelty for some time, and reaching over for a mug of beer that stood on the opposite side of the table, my bag sleeve catched hold of the handle of the bed pan and unfortunately overset the clams, at which the landlady . . . muttered a scrape of Dutch of which I understood not a word except mynheer, but I suppose she swore, for she uttered her speech with an emphasis."

From *Gentleman's Progress: The Itinerarium of Dr. Alexander Hamilton, 1744* became homes, families were increasingly defined by emotional bonds.

In a sense, the family lost many of its public functions, and so became more private. Above all in seventeenth-century New England, families had been primarily responsible for tasks such as housing nonrelatives who were poor or indigent and educating their children; now such responsibilities were sometimes delegated to institutions such as almshouses or schools. The family remained a unit of production in which men and women had defined roles. And women's roles—which emphasized indoor activities—in some ways increased in importance as the home became more of a haven, the meal more of an event, and the parlor a place where friends and neighbors gathered. Visiting and being visited was at the core of colonial social life, particularly in rural areas; and women, as mistresses of their houses, were essential to a process by which disparate people were woven into a new and largely voluntary community.

A family portrait of the eighteenth century that shows off not only the family members' fancy clothing but also their tea service.

DOMESTIC MANUFACTURES

The greater part of the goods colonists collected came from abroad. Some were supplied by colonial craftsmen, although high labor costs effectively prevented the development of extensive manufacturing. The gentry insisted on fine imported tableware, but their poorer neighbors made do with cruder pottery that was, as the eighteenth century proceeded, increasingly produced in the colonies. Where wood was the material of choice, as in furniture manufacturing, American craftsmen sometimes held an advantage over English competitors. By the late colonial period, major colonial cities boasted skilled artisans who created highly finished chests and chairs and tables, perhaps taking into account guidebooks like Thomas Chippendale's *Gentleman and Cabinet-Maker's Directory* (1754), but incorporating in their furniture distinctive design elements that are well-known to modern antique collectors. The mass of colonial-made furniture was, however, simpler, for a less elite domestic market or for export to the West Indies. Bulky items like sledges and sleighs, wagons and carts, and most of the coaches and carriages owned by colonists were made on this side of the Atlantic. Most of these were no doubt inelegant vehicles suitable

"In the eighteenth century, couples increasingly chose their own spouses, even without parental permission (as indicated by a surge in premarital pregnancies), and affection became an expected part of the relationship."

mainly for farm use—but not necessarily all of them. On the other hand, the colonies were the prime source for one luxury item, spermaceti candles—which were notably superior to tallow or wax candles—once whale hunting took off in the North Atlantic after about 1715.

It's also worth noting that some 26 colonial refineries satisfied a full three-quarters of the domestic demand for sugar by the late colonial period, and that mainland colonists consumed 60 percent of the 8.5 million gallons of rum distilled from imported molasses in British North American distilleries. The iron industry was even more impressive: by the mid-1770s, the colonies maintained 82 charcoal-fueled furnaces, 175 forges, and a large number of bloomeries whose total product was greater than that of England and Wales. Indeed, it amounted to about one-seventh of the world's iron production overall. Again, a good part of that iron was used to make items such as axes, hoes, and shovels—or stoves—for domestic consumption.

The extent of American manufacturing can easily be exaggerated. The colonies' primary products remained agricultural, and most were produced with traditional, even ancient,

137

maica as well as Virginia, and regularly sent carefully collected plant specimens to England. Finally, in 1720, Sir Francis Nicholson, now the newly appointed royal governor of South Carolina, granted Catesby an annual pension of £20 "to Observe the Rarities of that Country for the uses and purposes of the [Royal] Society." Soon other English patrons joined Nicholson, as did the planter elite once Catesby arrived in South Carolina. In return, the naturalist supplied them with specimens for their private gardens.

During the three years he remained in America, 1722–25, Catesby traveled to different regions, always taking extensive notes, making drawings and watercolors of the plants and animals he saw, and collecting specimens. After returning to England, he worked in nurseries that specialized in American plants while preparing his masterpiece, *The Natural History of Carolina, Florida, and the Bahama Islands.* The book, which included text in both French and English, was the first fully illustrated guide to American plants and animals. It became an important reference work both for naturalists in the field and for persons debating classification systems. Even in its time, the book was understood—like the great maps of the Renaissance—as a work both of science and of art.

People born in America also became caught up in the task of collecting and classifying American plants, which was international in character. Individuals with the same interests knew each other, corresponded, and exchanged writings, drawings, and specimens, whether they lived in Britain, the Netherlands, Sweden, or America. For colonists, however, the critical link to that small world was in England, and more specifically in the circle of people associated with the Royal Society of London. For example, Peter Collinson, Franklin's benefactor, not only encouraged Americans interested in science to make their work known to the Royal Society, he also introduced them to each other and to persons of note in Europe.

Take the case of John Bartram (1699–1777), a largely self-educated Quaker who started out with modest means but managed to buy a farm on the Schuylkill River about three miles outside Philadelphia, where he developed a five-acre botanic garden. His interest in botany recommended him to other Pennsylvanians who not only exchanged plants with him but lent him books and, best of all, put him in contact with Collinson. Bartram corresponded with Collinson, who was himself an avid gardener, from the 1730s until Collinson's death in 1768. In that period, Collinson sent Bartram supplies, seeds, plants, even clothes. He also recruited other patrons for Bartram's extensive collecting expeditions, told him whom to contact in other colonies, and introduced him to men of like interests abroad, including Catesby and Linnaeus, who once called Bartram "the

ABOVE: An ivory-billed woodpecker, a watercolor done by the artist and naturalist Mark Catesby in 1724, during a visit to America funded by several English patrons and Governor Francis Nicholson of South Carolina. Nicholson wanted Catesby to record Carolina plants and animals "for the uses and purposes of the [Royal] Society [of London]."

RIGHT: A charming buffalo painted by Mark Catesby. His *Natural History* was considered a great work of science and of art.

greatest natural botanist in the world." Collinson even got Bartram appointed royal botanist in 1765, an appointment that surprised Alexander Garden, a physician of Scottish birth and education who lived in Charleston. Garden (after whom the gardenia was named) was also a botanist and later a fellow of the Royal Society who sent specimens to Linnaeus and corrected some of his classifications. Bartram, Garden said, "knew nothing of the generic characters of plants" and could "neither class them nor describe them," and, indeed, could "scarcely spell," although he was "indefatigable in his pursuits, and will collect many rare specimens." And that was what his patrons wanted.

By modern standards, what a peculiar scientific community these men made up! Most participants were amateurs: the study of plants required little specialized knowledge. Field naturalists, persons caught up in the gardening craze, and men such as Linnaeus, who were attempting to define the taxonomic relationships within the realms of plants and animals, all found much to say to each other. The fact that building gardens with exotic plants was a genteel pastime, a way of marking off the members of a social elite, certainly drew wealthy patrons into the group. Nonetheless, the community's borders readily stepped over social boundaries: talented men of no particular social distinction such as John Bartram—or Benjamin Franklin—were warmly embraced. In fact, many tradesmen and other "common men" flocked to scientific lectures, which became vastly popular in America and Europe during the eighteenth century. Gender proved a more formidable obstacle to membership than class, although Cadwallader Colden, a New Yorker of wide-ranging scientific interests, trained his bookish daughter Jane in botany. She became an informed and creative naturalist; the discriminating Dr. Garden described her as "a great master of the Linnaean method," and both Collinson and Linnaeus were impressed by her drawings.

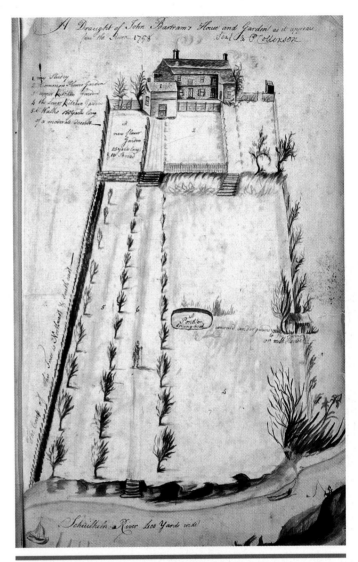

The house and garden of Pennsylvania naturalist John Bartram in 1758. Franklin and Washington were frequent visitors to the house and grounds of this great naturalist.

SCIENCE AND SUPERSTITION

If a fascination with plants and, to a lesser extent, animals bound together many eighteenth-century American men of science, their interests usually spilled over into other subjects. Take, for example, the Reverend Cotton Mather, an early colonial member of the Royal Society. Mather sent the society a vast collection of *Curiosa Americana,* "facts" and observations that touched on astronomy, botany, zoology, geology, mathematics, anthropology, and medicine. Some of his submissions—on the existence of monsters, for example—seem today, as they did to members of the Royal Society, unsubstantiated and of questionable relevance to experimental science.

In truth, the line between science and superstition was not always easy to draw. Mather's greatest achievement, for example, lay in his advocacy of inoculation to avoid smallpox, one of a handful of advances in eighteenth-century medicine, a form of science that lagged behind others. Inoculation, ac-

141

cording to one authority, was "the chief American contribution to medicine prior to the nineteenth century." Mather read about inoculation in the Royal Society's *Philosophical Transactions* and received confirmation of its efficacy from his slave Onesimus, who was familiar with its use in Africa. In short, liquid taken from a smallpox pustule on a stricken person's body was injected into slashes or with pinpricks on the arms of people undergoing the procedure. Inoculated people then came down with a mild form of smallpox (which, however, they could pass on in the natural way to others, who would get it in full force) and were henceforth immune.

When Mather and a local doctor began inoculating people after a smallpox epidemic hit Boston in 1721, they were greeted with outrage from, among others, the city's one university-trained medical doctor. It turned out, however, that while the mortality rate among noninoculated people who contracted the disease was 15 percent, the rate among the inoculated was about 2 percent (and those who died, Mather speculated, could have contracted smallpox or some other lethal disease before being inoculated). Those results were duly reported to the Royal Society. But before the results were in, it was not irrational to consider the injection of smallpox "juice" into healthy people an irresponsible act akin to the techniques used to identify witches.

A more compelling antidote to the mindset of times past lay in astronomy, a field in which, like botany, data from America was of compelling interest to Europeans. John Winthrop (1714–1779), a great-grandnephew of John Winthrop Jr., the first American fellow of the Royal Society, was for some forty years Harvard's Hollis Professor of Mathematics and Natural Philosophy (the contemporary term essentially for the physical sciences). One of the few professional scientists in the British colonies, Winthrop introduced several generations of Harvard students to modern science and mathematics, collected scientific instruments for the study of physical phenomena, submitted various papers based on his own celestial observations to the Royal Society, and also prepared lectures and articles of a scientific nature for the interested public. In 1755, he explained earthquakes, which were traditionally understood as manifestations of God's displeasure, in physical terms, noting their wave-like character. Although a prominent Boston minister insisted

> *"The scientific community's borders readily stepped over social boundaries. Many tradesmen and other 'common men' flocked to scientific lectures, which became vastly popular in America and Europe."*

that the famous Lisbon earthquake of 1755 (which killed more than 60,000 people) was a sign of God's anger, such interpretations no longer commanded the assent of learned society as they had in the previous century.

Winthrop wrote about meteors and comets, which again were once understood as wonders by which God sent special messages to humans. His most novel contribution to speculative astronomy suggested a way of calculating the quantity of matter in comets. Winthrop also participated in an extensive international effort to collect data on Venus's transit between sun and earth in 1761 and 1769, on the basis of which astronomers hoped to calculate the distances between the sun, earth, and other planets.

The most significant contributions to scientific understanding that emerged from the colonies were, however, Franklin's theories, confirmed by experiment, on the nature of electricity.

FLYING KITES

Even as a young man, **Benjamin Franklin** knew who was who in science: on a visit to London in 1725, when he was not yet twenty, he wanted to meet Sir Isaac Newton and Sir Hans Sloane, both of whom would become presidents of the Royal Society. Franklin lacked the mathematical preparation to read Newton's *Principia* (1687), but he carefully studied Newton's *Optics* (1704), which was written in plain English and included scientific propositions with a "proof by experiments" provided for each. Soon he set out to do some experimenting himself.

When Franklin and a handful of fellow Philadelphians began studying electricity in the mid-1740s, it was a relatively new subject. English and French observers had described electricity as a liquid that spread from areas of greater to lesser charge and noted that some materials conducted electricity and others did not. A French investigator had also observed the existence of two kinds of electricity, vitreous and resinous, which were created by rubbing different materials against each other, and noted that the same kinds of electricity repelled each other but different kinds were attracted. Franklin, who knew so little of European scientific writings that he had no idea how much of what he said was new, also argued that electricity (or "electric fire," in the language of the day) behaved like a fluid and, moreover, was a distinct natural element made up of minute particles that could penetrate the particles of other types of matter. Rubbing materials against each other did not create electrical fluid, Franklin said, but altered matter by removing fluid (making it negatively charged) or adding extra fluid (and so becoming positively charged). Negatively charged bodies attracted and were attracted by positively charged ones. Electrical discharges, moreover, brought together equal amounts of negative and positive electricity and so restored an equilibrium between them (this is now designated the principle of conservation of charge). Franklin's letters to Collinson described in detail experiments that suggested or confirmed his theories.

European experimenters of the time wondered at the workings of the Leyden jar, a device capable of storing electricity. Franklin believed that the jar's outside was positively charged, the inside negatively. He tried coating the sides of a plate of glass with metal foil, and found it worked as well as a jar. One could, he reasoned, link a series of glass plates into an "electrical-battery" and so increase the electricity stored. Franklin also observed that pointed objects were more effective in attracting electricity than blunt ones, and he hypothesized that lightning consisted of electrical discharges that neutralized positive and negative charges between clouds or between clouds and the earth. Lightning and electricity, he wrote, had many common characteristics: they gave off light of the same color, moved quickly, made cracks or noises, and could kill animals and melt metals. That suggested they were the same, but were they? "Let the experiment be made."

The experiment Franklin first proposed required the construction on some high tower or steeple of a sentry box large enough to hold a man and an electrical stand. An iron rod with a pointed top should extend out the door of the sentry box and upward another twenty or thirty feet. The experimenter, whom Franklin instructed to keep his feet on the dry floor or on an insulated stool, should hold a loop of wire by a wax handle (which would act as an insulator). If, as Franklin hypothesized, the rod pulled electricity down from the clouds, it would produce sparks when the wire came near it. The sentry box experiment was successfully performed in France during 1752, after a French translation appeared of Franklin's *Experiments and Observations on Electricity*.

Then Franklin had another idea. Forget the sentry box: send a kite up during a thunderstorm, and that could pull electricity down from the clouds just as well. The kite, he said,

should be made of silk and have a foot-long pointed wire attached to its upper end. At the other end of the twine, near the person flying the kite (who was to remain in a shelter, keeping the end of the string dry so it would not conduct electricity), a key should hang from a silk ribbon. When the kite and twine became wet by rain, they would "conduct the electric fire freely" and emit sparks when brought near the key. The electricity derived from that source could be used to "perform all the . . . Experiments which are usually done by rubbing a Glass Globe or Tube," which demonstrated "the Sameness of the Electric matter with that of Lightning." Franklin carried out the experiment in June 1752, but did not sent a report to Collinson until October, the same month a full account of his "Electrical Kite" experiment appeared in the *Pennsylvania Gazette*. By then, he had learned about the successful sentry box experiments in France.

Collinson published Franklin's *Experiments and Observations on Electricity, Made at Philadelphia in America* (first edition, 1751), a compendium of his letters on electricity, and

An eighteenth-century print depicting Franklin's kite experiment.

presented it to the Royal Society. Two years later, the society awarded Franklin—whom its members had never met, and first heard of only five years before—its prestigious Copley Medal, the highest distinction it could bestow, for his "Curious Experiments and Observations on Electricity." And in 1756, it elected him to membership, allowing him to add the prestigious letters F.R.S. (Fellow of the Royal Society) to his name.

Franklin's achievement was outstanding by any measure; his contributions to the basic understanding of electricity were of such significance that contemporaries compared him with Newton. Franklin did not, however, stop at the theoretical level, but probed the practical applications of his discoveries. In 1753, for example, he published instructions on "How to Secure Houses, etc., from Lightning" by use of pointed lightning rods, which could safely conduct strokes of lightning into the ground. Franklin regularly used scientific principles in inventing useful items—not just lightning rods but bifocals, the "Pennsylvania stove," and a musical instrument called the "armonica." Even his foray into demographic theory had, or so he argued, practical implications for British policymakers. Later in life, he conducted research on the Gulf Stream, an investigation into oceanography that he knew had important implications for navigation.

When Franklin began conducting experiments with his fellow Philadelphians, they in turn conferred with colonists elsewhere. By 1743, he appreciated the utility of these contacts sufficiently to propose forming an American Philosophical Society that would bring together "virtuosi or ingenious men residing in the several colonies." Members would "maintain a constant correspondence" on a long list of topics, from "new-discovered plants, herbs, trees, etc.," and their uses to new ways of treating diseases, "new and useful improvements in any branch of mathematics" or chemistry, and "new mechanical inventions for saving labor, of improving the breed of animals, in planting or gardening, etc." Franklin's Philosophical Society would, in short, foster inventiveness among Americans for their own advantage and that "of mankind in general." And it would keep up a correspondence with the Royal Society of London and a similar group in Dublin that was "already begun by some intended members."

The suggestion came too early. It took another generation before "The American Philosophical Society . . . for Promoting Useful Knowledge" was successfully launched in Philadelphia. By then, Franklin had left behind the most fertile period in his scientific work, from 1743 to 1752, and embarked on another career, in politics.

Being British, Becoming American

It was no accident that Franklin wrote about the "American" population, grouping the colonies together, or proposed an American Philosophical Society, not an organization for Pennsylvania alone. A sense of common identity was slowly developing among many people of British North America, one that involved an intense identification with the mother country and also an understanding that they were members of the British family with certain marked distinctions.

The imitation of British styles in all the colonies and the increased contact between colonists with an interest in science helped bind together what were once separate and distinctive communities. But the most powerful forces working to break down colonial particularisms and forge a common identity as British and American during the eighteenth century were politics, religion, and war.

KING AND COMMONS, COLONIAL STYLE

Each colony's politics possessed characteristics unique to itself, but the politics of all the colonies—with the possible exception of Connecticut and Rhode Island, where all officials were elected—had a lot in common. Colonists thought of their governments as versions of the much-praised British constitution, under which the king (or governor), Lords (or council), and Commons (or colonial assembly) shared power. In Britain, it was said, those powers were balanced after the Glorious Revolution, allowing a stability in government that also protected liberty by preventing any one power from oppressing the people. That was not, in fact, how government worked in Britain: the king usually found ways to influence members of the increasingly powerful Commons so they could work together. In America, however, governors and assemblies often squared off against each other. Such squabbles resembled English politics—but of the previous century, when Parliament, and particularly the House of Commons, grappled for power with formidable kings. The reason for the difference lay in the contrasting impacts of the Glorious Revolution in England and in America.

The post-1688 revolutionary settlement curtailed monarchical power in England but imposed no similar checks on the power of royal governors. As a result, royal governors wielded some powers that the king could not claim "at home." In England, for example, the king lost his right to veto acts of Parliament early in the eighteenth century. Royal governors could, however, veto acts of assembly and in fact were required by their instructions from the king to veto certain kinds of laws and to suspend the operation of others until the Crown could review them. A governor could also dissolve, or prorogue, an assembly: he could, that is, bring it to an end and call a new election, or else tell the representatives to go home until he felt like calling them back into session. While governors could keep particularly congenial assemblies in place indefinitely, the king had to call an election at least every three, and later every seven, years. Governors could appoint judges, who, beginning in the 1750s, held office at the king's pleasure, which meant they could be removed from office if the king (or his representative, the governor) didn't like the way they operated. English judges, by contrast, held office for life on good behavior. And where the king had to contend with a House of Lords made up in part of nobles who inherited their offices, governors worked with councils whose members were, like the governors, appointed by the king—which meant they should have been, and generally were, on the governor's side in any controversies. In all these ways, the governors were, within their colonies, even more powerful than the king.

Not that the royal governors (or, with some variations, the governors in the proprietary colonies of Pennsylvania, Delaware, and Maryland) had it easy. A governor was usually dependent on the assembly for his salary, which gave the assembly quite a bit of leverage over him. Governors were always instructed to secure a permanent salary, but the assemblies (with the exception of Virginia, which after Bacon's Rebellion levied a tax on tobacco to pay its governor) refused. Nor did governors enjoy the patronage power—the power to appoint people to various offices—that helped the king influence the House of Commons to support him and his policies. What patronage the governors once exercised was, in the course of the eighteenth century, whittled away by either the Crown or the assembly. Nor did they have much flexibility in establishing working relationships with the assemblies, since their instructions and also their com-

missions (formal public documents that laid out the government of a colony) constrained their freedom of action in one way after another. Finally, since governors were appointed through the British patronage system, they were vulnerable once they left for America: others could play the same game they had, and force them out of office. The average tenure of an eighteenth-century royal governor was only about five years—not enough time to build up much power.

The assemblies not only commanded greater stability than governors (some members might lose an election, but rarely if ever were all delegates replaced) but held a strong sense of their importance as the provincial equivalent of Britain's House of Commons. The assemblies demanded privileges enjoyed by the Commons, such as the exclusive right to initiate money bills. Then they claimed powers the Commons did not have: they insisted, for example, on extraordinary powers over the colonies' finances and on appointing the colonies' treasurers. The assemblies were usually the only organ of provincial government chosen by the people, which added to their sense of importance. The people, in turn, were represented by a relatively wide electorate for the time, consisting of white adult Christian males who could fulfill a property qualification such as fifty acres of land, which was often not difficult to acquire. Nonlandholding urban craftsmen could

The Boston State House, built in 1713. The colony's General Court (its legislature) met there.

also often vote. (It should be said, however, that large numbers of qualified colonists chose not to vote.)

As the elected assemblies rose in strength, the powers of appointed councils gradually declined. As a result, provincial politics often led to knock-down, drag-out, two-sided fights between the governors and assemblies, or more exactly between groups within the assembly that supported one side or the other. Conflict of that sort was not yet considered altogether legitimate: the day when struggles for power were "just politics" with no suggestion of sedition remained at least a century away. Contenders could justify their opposition to the king's governor by claiming that he was attempting to usurp authority beyond his allotted share and to violate the liberty of the people. That was what the opponents of Charles I and James II had argued in the seventeenth century. And so the colonists lapped up late seventeenth-century Whig writings such as Algernon Sidney's *Discourses Concerning Government* and John Locke's *Second Treatise of Government,* which were written to justify opposition to James II, or eighteenth-century writings that drew on those and similar sources, such as John Trenchard and Thomas Gordon's popular newspaper essays, "Cato's Letters." They also read French political writings, including Montesquieu's *Spirit of the Laws,* which discussed the British constitution.

In general, writers in the English revolutionary tradition saw political officials as trustees for the people, who had first set up government to protect their freedom. Should officials exercise powers the people had not given them or fail to protect popular freedom, the people could remove them from office and, if they chose, reconstitute government so it would better serve their interests. To be sure, revolution was not to be indulged in casually. Liberty required a stable rule of law; it could not thrive in the midst of anarchy, so writers articulated a series of conditions to be met before the people could resist or replace their rulers. Their grievances had to be so significant that "the body of the people" recognized their

The seventeenth-century political philosopher John Locke.

danger, and all the peaceful means of resistance had to be tried before force became acceptable.

Colonists did not need to read Sidney or Locke or Trenchard and Gordon to learn these "revolution principles": they encountered them in a score of other writers, in newspapers and sermons, even in a book like Sir William Blackstone's *Commentaries on the Laws of England,* first published in the 1760s, which treated Locke as an authority on the Glorious Revolution of 1689. The colonists had good reason, then, to assume that their political ideology was nothing less than orthodox English thought. "The people" were, moreover, an active force in eighteenth-century American communities. "The people" acted as militia or posse members to enforce the law and, sometimes, as mobs to defend the public interest extra-legally where the established government did not or could not act.

To the powers that governed Britain, however, the idea that the people had a real and practical power to judge their rulers was part of a past that had to be buried so Britain could enjoy its eighteenth-century stability. Parliament—king, Lords, and Commons acting together—was sovereign: that is, it exercised ultimate power that was over and beyond the people "out of doors." From that perspective, the truculence of colonial assemblies and other popular institutions (town meetings and juries, for example) constituted a violation of good order; and from mid-century, British officials proposed several different plans for reorganizing colonial governments to reinforce the power of the mother country and its appointed colonial officials. Once Britain tried to implement those plans, however, the results were predictable. The colonists would resist, citing perfectly fine, seventeenth-century English principles to justify their opposition.

THE RECONSTRUCTION OF AMERICAN RELIGION

Religion more than anything else made the first British colonists turn their backs on each other. Few who lived in seventeenth-century Massachusetts had anything good to say about Quakers, and Virginians were not altogether welcoming toward Puritans. By the 1760s, however, hostility between different Protestant groups had declined considerably. One reason was a wave of mid-eighteenth-century religious revivals remembered as the "**Great Awakening.**"

The revivals answered a decline in religious fervor that was apparent in a reduced incidence of "conversion experiences" among second- and third-generation New Englanders. The children of church members, these people had been baptized as infants, but, unless they later gave evidence of receiving grace, they could not become full members of their Congregational (or Puritan) churches. But then could their own children be baptized? Ministers, dismayed as they watched church membership decline precipitously, met in 1657 and came up with a makeshift solution known as the "Half-Way covenant": the children of church members who lived upright lives but had not experienced God's grace could become "halfway" members of the church, distinguished from full members only in that they could not take communion or vote on church matters. They could also have their children baptized. That was a big step back from the rigor of first-generation Puritanism, and the back-stepping continued thereafter. The difference between full and halfway church members gradually faded away, and membership came to turn not on the willingness of an inscrutable God to save depraved sinners, but on human reason and will. "Try whether you can't give . . . consent" to God's will, Cotton Mather urged his listeners; "if you *can,* 'tis done." Church membership, even so, continued to decline.

Much the same process had occurred outside New England by the eighteenth century—until the revivals instituted an about-face. They began among the Dutch Reformed congregations in New Jersey after the Reverend Theodore Frelinghuysen arrived from Holland in 1719, preached moving sermons that stressed piety over good works, and within a decade had waves of people "awakening" to religion. Soon the revivals spread to the nearby Presbyterian congregation of the Reverend Gilbert Tennent; then they began to appear farther north, in Connecticut. In 1734–35, the Reverend Jonathan Edwards set a revival going in Northampton, Massachusetts, that spread through the Connecticut Valley. Suddenly, Edwards recalled, "all the talk in companies . . . was upon the things of religion, and no other talk was anywhere relished," and "the spirit of God went on in His saving influences . . . in a truly wonderful and astonishing manner."

The flood tide of the revivals came, however, with the arrival of George Whitefield, a twenty-four-year-old English evangelist, in 1739 at Philadelphia. In only nine days, Whitefield effected a wonderful change in the ways of Philadelphians who had been "thoughtless or indifferent about religion."

Suddenly, Benjamin Franklin recalled, "one could not walk thro' town in an evening without hearing psalms sung in different families of every street." Whitefield traveled through New Jersey, New York, and New England, with similar results everywhere: the audience for his farewell sermon in Boston was estimated at over 23,000, more than the town's total population. Later he toured the South, then revisited the middle colonies and New England before returning to England in 1741. Waves of religious awakenings continued to break out here and there

The young Jonathan Edwards, New England's most famous eighteenth-century revivalist.

over the next few decades—among Virginia's Presbyterians in 1748, and later among Methodists—but they never reached the high pitch of 1739–41.

It's possible to dismiss the revivals' appeal as an exercise of theatricality in a society starved for entertainment. The preachers were nothing if not moving speakers: even Franklin, who remained untouched by Whitefield's message, admired his oratory (though he seems to have spent his time during one outdoor sermon conducting experiments to see how far the evangelist's voice carried). That cannot explain, however, why an ordinary farmer like Nathan Cole in Connecticut dropped everything when he heard Whitefield was going to preach at a nearby town, and found himself "in a trembling fear" even before the evangelist opened his mouth. Or why, after realizing that his "righteousness would not save" him, Cole became obsessed with "hell fire" and his own sinfulness until he was, like Puritans of old, reborn with the grace of God. Whitefield and other revivalist preachers, unlike most of their counterparts in Europe, were distinctly Calvinistic: they stressed the distance between man and God, and shouted out—like Tennent—that men were "damned, damned, damned." Did audiences perhaps sense that the pleasures eighteenth-century prosperity brought, and the efforts they invested in a struggle for material things, were

The Methodist evangelist George Whitefield, as painted by John Wollaston, soon after Whitefield's famous 1739–41 tour of colonies that sparked revivals everywhere.

deviations from God's way, and find some relief in confronting their sinfulness? Or is it best to explain the Great Awakening, as Jonathan Edwards did, simply as an amazing work of God?

The results were no less amazing. The Awakening led to the founding of a host of new colleges, including today's Brown, Princeton, Dartmouth, Rutgers, and the University of Pennsylvania. Revivalists were clearly not anti-intellectual; they founded educational institutions to train American-born ministers who could carry on their religious traditions.

More important, the revivals redrew the map of American religion. Not everyone was swept in by the Awakening: old-line conservatives who found the revivalists offensive or dangerous refused to let them preach in their churches, forcing itinerant ministers to preach to crowds in public halls or outdoors in open fields. But then the revivalists lashed back at the conser-vatives, condemning them as an "un-converted ministry," in Tennent's words, or a

body of "dead men" to God, in Whitefield's. Communities split between conservative "old lights" and revivalist "new lights" (or the "new side" among Presbyterians) who left their local parishes and joined congregations gathered by choice and conviction, not place of residence. The Presbyterian Church split into two synods, adding to the religious diversity that new immigrant groups brought to Pennsylvania and the southern backcountry. Even the orthodox Congregationalist colonies of New England were transformed. Some conservatives gravitated toward the Anglican Church, going all the way in their search for order and stability, while dissenters distributed themselves among hundreds of religious congregations, many of which eventually became Baptist. The dozen or so American Baptist churches in 1740 had increased to some 500 by 1775, and they were spread throughout the colonies, from New England into the South.

So dramatic a transformation necessarily brought pressure on the established churches—that is, churches that provincial governments endorsed and supported—that existed in all the colonies except Pennsylvania, Delaware, and Rhode Island. The Baptists in particular resented requirements that they contribute to another church or suffer civil disabilities as a result of their convictions. Eventually, Baptists opposed any interference whatsoever by civil government in people's religious beliefs and practices. Moreover, despite the bickering that the revivals first provoked, the

A baptism on the Schuylkill River in Pennsylvania. From an engraving of 1770.

multiplication of religious groups ultimately led to a new acceptance of religious differences. What once had been sects arrayed against each other became denominations, groups within American Protestantism distinguished by the convictions of their members, which others could respect even if they did not share those convictions.

Colonial Catholics were left out of that development. They remained, in the opinion of their Protestant neighbors, outsiders, advocates of a false religion. Despite the splintering of churches under the influence of the Awakening, most British colonists developed a common identity as militant Protestants in the course of the eighteenth century, as a result of the long series of wars that they and their mother country were fighting against the Catholic powers, France and Spain.

The British taking of the French fortress at Louisbourg in July 1758.

THE COLONIAL WARS

Most of America's eighteenth-century wars were spillovers from struggles that centered in Europe. The war known in America as King William's War (1689–97), and in Europe as the War of the League of Augsburg, had scarcely ended when Queen Anne's War (1702–13), known in Europe as the War of the Spanish Succession, began. After a generation of peace came King George's War (1739–48), also known as the War of Jenkins's Ear (after a smuggler who said he lost an ear to the Spanish in an encounter off Florida) and then as the War of the Austrian Succession once France entered the conflict.

The generation of peace was, it should be said, interrupted by events such as the Yamasee War of 1715, which pitted Yamasee and Creek Indians against European settlements on South Carolina's western frontier; but even that war might well have been provoked in part by the Spanish in Florida and perhaps also the French in Louisiana, who were delighted to do whatever possible to prevent British expansion into or toward territory they claimed. And in 1722, the French encouraged the Abenakis to attack the

Maine frontier once again—although the colonists struck back, driving the Abenakis inland and ending that particular threat for good.

These first colonial wars followed well-trod tracks over and over with few permanent effects. The British won Newfoundland and Nova Scotia from France in the Treaty of Utrecht (1713), which ended Queen Anne's War. The French then built a fort at Louisbourg to protect the entrance to the St. Lawrence River, and it became a place where privateers (private ships licensed to attack enemy ships) found harbor and so a thorn in the side of New England. Massachusetts mounted a major attack on the fort at enormous expense in 1745, and managed to take it. But the British returned it to France under the Treaty of Aix-la-Chapelle (1748). Expeditions against St. Augustine in the South had no more lasting results.

Military action brought some people—contractors, for example—enormous profits, but the most enduring results of the early colonial wars were death and instability. Mortality rates for soldiers were appalling, though more from disease than combat. Only about 600 of the 3,600 colonists who joined a 1741 campaign against Porto Bello and Cartagena nial delegates to meet at Albany in 1754. Seven delegations appeared, but neither the colonial legislatures nor the Crown showed much enthusiasm for a plan of union, largely drafted by Franklin, that the delegates proposed. It called for "one general government" with a governor-general and representative Grand Council to manage Indian affairs and defense and to raise taxes for those purposes. "Everyone cries, a union is necessary," Franklin wrote, "but when they come to the manner and form of the union, their weak noodles are perfectly distracted." Negotiations with the 150 Indian delegates who appeared were equally ineffectual. The Iroquois held tight to their neutrality.

The British nonetheless decided to answer the events of 1754 with a complex military campaign to check French advances. They sent General Edward Braddock to command the operation, but it came to no good end. Braddock set out in 1755 with an army of 2,500 men to take Fort Duquesne, which at the time held some 250 French regulars and Canadian militiamen with about 800 Indian allies nearby. In desperation, the French persuaded the Indians to ambush the advancing British column—which they did as it passed along a ravine beneath a forested hill that the British command had carelessly failed to secure. The lead soldiers retreated under fire, causing chaos among the troops behind them, which was made worse by the spray of Indian fire down from the woods. In the end, some 900 men died, including Braddock, who left this life in ignominious defeat.

The war didn't turn around until the great war minister William Pitt came into power in 1758 and decided not to concentrate on the war that had broken out in Europe two years earlier, but to put Britain's main effort into taking Canada. Pitt promised to compensate colonists for their expenses in the war, which produced a magical effect on the assemblies' willingness to cooperate, and sent Britain's best commanders to march against French strongholds. In 1758, the British suffered a serious defeat at a French fort at Ticonderoga, on Lake Champlain, but an army under General Jeffrey Amherst finally took Louisbourg. Then the French abandoned Fort Duquesne as British troops came near and their Indian allies defected. For the British, it was a good beginning.

The next year went even better. Pitt planned an ambitious campaign. First he would take Fort Niagara, between Lakes Ontario and Erie, and so cut the French off from access to the lakes to its west. Then a two-pronged attack would move against Quebec and Montreal. The first, under Amherst, would come up from New York along the water route from the Hudson River through Lakes George and Champlain to the Richelieu River and the St. Lawrence. The second, under General James Wolfe, would travel up the St. Lawrence from Louisbourg.

The scheme worked, but not exactly as planned. A combined British, American, and Indian force took Fort Niagara on July 25; and the expedition under Amherst captured Ticonderoga in 1759 but could get no farther than Lake Champlain before winter set in. The taking of Quebec was then left to Wolfe, who faced a ticking clock—he had to be out of the St. Lawrence be-

A romanticized painting of the death of General James Wolfe during the battle at Quebec in September 1759. The American painter Benjamin West created this, his most famous work, in 1770.

fore the water froze. Wolfe put Quebec under siege, but the French commander, the Marquis de Montcalm, refused to engage, waiting for winter to save his day. Finally, in September, Wolfe found a way to float ships down the river at night to a spot from which his troops could scurry up a hill to a flatland, the "Plains of Abraham," outside the city. When morning broke on September 13, Montcalm looked out on Wolfe's army in formation. He engaged; in the resulting battle, both Wolfe and Montcalm were killed, but when the shooting stopped, the British held Quebec. The next year, they easily took Montreal, and for all practical purposes the war was over in America although it lingered on abroad.

The Peace of Paris (1763), which finally ended the war, redrew the map of North America. All of Canada and Louisiana east of the Mississippi, with the exception of New Orleans, went to Britain. Spain, an ally of France, gave Florida to Britain—although by a secret protocol, France gave Spain those portions of Louisiana west of the Mississippi. Except for two islands in the Gulf of St. Lawrence, which were to be used by fishermen, and the sugar islands of Guadeloupe and Martinique, the French had lost their American empire.

TAKING PRIDE

The British victory was great, and the colonists, above all those who had fought in the war along with British regulars, shared in the glory. To be sure, they had been confined in separate units and consigned much of the slug work of war. New England soldiers in particular had looked on the regulars and their willingness to hold the field under fire with a kind of amazement: imagine, just standing there, when you could hide behind a tree. The neatly ordered British camps, with tents arranged according to rank and sanitary facilities removed from eating and sleeping areas, must also have awakened awe. The provincials' camps were so different, made up of a wild assortment of huts and shacks and sometimes framed houses arranged willy-nilly; and the farm-boy soldiers were hard to restrain from relieving themselves anywhere near at hand, much as they did at home. Their armies, too, were different, made up of like people commanded by local dignitaries who were often kinsmen, and who tried to persuade their men to do the right thing rather than order them around.

Benjamin Franklin printed this "Join, or Die" cartoon just before the Albany Congress convened in 1754. Franklin was a strong advocate of colonial unity then and in later times.

And what sense could colonists make of the cruel British discipline, the horrible floggings of soldiers with cats-o'-nine-tails, sometimes for hundreds of lashes until a man's back had no more skin? Or the executions for what sometimes seemed minor infractions of rules? The British soldiers' proclivity for "cussing" and lewd women, their disregard for the Sabbath, also seemed alien and morally repulsive. If the British found the New Englanders bad soldiers, the provincials found the redcoats sinful men.

How important were these differences? The colonists were not a people apart but a people among, a denominated group within the British family with certain distinctions, but no more than differentiated the Scots from the English or the Welsh. Americans' differences from fellow Britons "at home" were far less in the eighteenth century than they had been in the seventeenth, when poverty and the task of surviving kept them from imitating English ways and fashions. Colonists had no intention of following the morals of the king's armies, but in other ways they expected to be more, not less, like the British as time went on. What most colonists wanted was to approximate the ways of the mother country, their model of achievement and fashion.

Benjamin Franklin was no longer in America when the peace came. He had traveled to London to persuade the

153

Chronology

1619	First African slaves arrive at Jamestown.
1702–13	Queen Anne's War (in Europe, War of the Spanish Succession).
1704	The first colonial newspaper, the *Boston News Letter,* appears.
1722–25	Mark Catesby's travels result in the first guide to American plants and animals.
1732	Georgia founded.
1739	Stono Rebellion, slave uprising in South Carolina.
1739–41	High point of the Great Awakening.
1739–48	King George's War (in Europe, War of the Austrian Succession).
1745	Siege of Louisbourg, on the St. Lawrence River.
1752	Benjamin Franklin performs "Electrical Kite" experiment.
1754–63	The French and Indian War (in Europe, beginning 1756, the Seven Years' War).

How wonderful to have such esteemed intellectual colleagues close at hand, and to be able to talk and argue and speculate together almost at will. In that company, the American master of electricity commanded a certain respect: in 1760, Franklin became an elected member of the Royal Society's governing council; the next year, he helped select papers for the *Philosophical Transactions.* He was living the good life. Best of all, there was no reason it should ever end.

Suggested Reading

Fred Anderson, *A People's Army: Massachusetts Soldiers in the Seven Years' War* (1984), and *The Crucible of War: The Seven Years' War and the Fate of Empire in British North America, 1754–1766* (2000)

Bernard Bailyn, *The Origin of American Politics* (1967)

Bernard Bailyn and Philip D. Morgan, eds., *Strangers Within the Realm: Cultural Margins of the First British Empire* (1991)

Ira Berlin, *Many Thousands Gone: The First Two Centuries of Slavery in North America* (1998)

Richard L. Bushman, *The Refinement of America: Persons, Houses, Cities* (1992)

Cary Carson, Ronald Hoffman, and Peter J. Albert, eds., *Of Consuming Interests: The Style of Life in the Eighteenth Century* (1994)

I. Bernard Cohen, *Benjamin Franklin's Science* (1990)

Philip D. Morgan, *Slave Counterpoint: Black Culture in the Eighteenth-Century Chesapeake and Lowcountry* (1998)

Raymond Phineas Stearns, *Science in the British Colonies of America* (1970)

Crown to displace the proprietors and govern Pennsylvania directly. Once there, he formalized his membership in the Royal Society and attended meetings regularly, presenting letters and papers, joining in discussions, making it his "club."

Chapter 5

TOWARD INDEPENDENCE:
1764-1783

This engraving of the events at Lexington and Concord, by Amos Doolittle, shows British soldiers marching through "the South Part of Lexington" while being shot at by colonists on April 19, 1775. At the time, Doolittle was a twenty-one-year-old apprentice silversmith who learned to engrave copper plates. He was also a member of the New Haven militia, which arrived in Massachusetts soon after the battles were fought. Doolittle therefore did not witness the events he portrayed, but claimed to work "from original paintings taken on the spot," apparently by someone else. His engravings, which he sold to the public, present the American side of the story. They prominently display, for example, private homes set on fire by the king's soldiers.

■ **What were the main points of dispute between the American colonists and Britain in the 1760s and 1770s?**

■ **How did the Americans gradually assume authority over their own affairs in the period before independence?**

■ **How did the United States manage to defeat Britain in the War for Independence?**

Focus QUESTIONS

Never were the American colonists more proud of being British than at the end of the French and Indian War. Britain's heroes—above all the great war minister William Pitt and his generals, Sir Jeffrey Amherst and James Wolfe—were American heroes. In every colony, Americans expressed the deepest affection for King George III, who was only twenty-two in 1760 when he inherited the throne from his grandfather.

By all signs, Britain's victory and the Peace of Paris (1763) marked a watershed in American history. With all of French and Spanish North America east of the Mississippi except for the city of New Orleans under the British flag, the persistent wars that had dogged colonial life for a century and more were, it seemed, finally over. Moreover, once the free government of Protestant Britain replaced what the colonists described as the "absolutism" of Catholic France and Spain, an unparalleled era of growth and prosperity seemed sure to follow. Celebratory sermons by New England clergymen told the story: by bringing about "the downfall of New France, the North American Babylon," one preacher explained to his congregation, God had transplanted "British liberty to where till now it was unknown." With the colonists' "peaceful and undisturbed enjoyment of this good land, and the blessings of our gracious God with it," he foresaw "towns enlarged, settlements increased, and this howling wilderness become a fruitful field which the Lord hath blessed." Another Congregationalist pastor went so far as to predict that the population of America, now that it was thrown open to British colonization, would grow to 60 million in a century and a half—a figure that understated by over 30 million the population of the United States alone in 1910.

Nowhere in the victory celebrations of the early 1760s was there even a hint of the greater historical watershed to come, the event remembered as the American Revolution. Yet thirteen years after the Peace of Paris established Britain's hegemony on the North American continent, the people of the original thirteen British colonies declared their independence, threw off not just the rule of George III but of kings and all other hereditary rulers, and reinvented themselves as a new nation "separate and equal" among the "powers of the earth." Independence was not what either the Americans or the British wanted; each side, in its way, struggled to prevent it for over a decade. And yet it came. The question is why.

> *"Independence was not what either the Americans or the British wanted; each side, in its way, struggled to prevent it for over a decade. And yet it came. The question is why."*

"No Taxation Without Representation," 1764–1774

There was one problem with the colonists' expansive vision of their future at the end of the French and Indian War. The lands between the British settlements and the Mississippi River were already inhabited, and the Indians' presence was likely to interfere with British-Americans' "peaceful and undisturbed enjoyment of this good land."

In the past, the Indians, although divided into nations and villages, had been able to exploit European rivalries on behalf

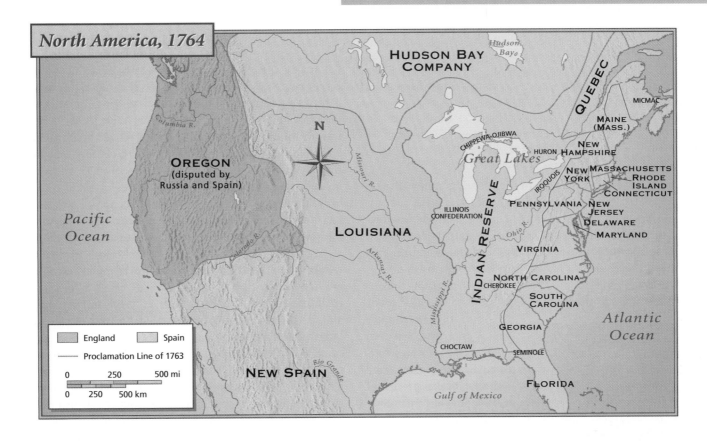

North America, 1764

OREGON (disputed by Russia and Spain)

LOUISIANA

NEW SPAIN

| England | Spain |
| Proclamation Line of 1763 |
0 250 500 mi
0 250 500 km

of common goals: to retain their lands and their freedom from enslavement, and to obtain ready access to the guns, cloth, knives, pots, and other trading goods on which they had become dependent. In 1763, the British tried to pacify the frontier by issuing a proclamation that forbade colonial settlements west of a line that ran through the Appalachians, an inland chain of mountains that extended from New England into the Carolinas. The proclamation dismayed Americans who dreamed of westward expansion.

It was, however, poorly enforced. Britain decided to retain French posts in the trans-Appalachian West, correctly raising Indian suspicions of their intentions. Now, as the only power in the field, the British felt no need to court the Indians' favor. General Jeffrey Amherst, the British commander in chief, abruptly ended the French practice of giving Indians substantial presents, which had sustained the chiefs' influence over more restive young warriors. Amherst arrogantly expected the Indians to obey the peremptory orders he issued. Instead, in the spring of 1763, the Ottawa leader Pontiac at-

tacked Detroit. Other Indians followed his example, bringing death and chaos to British forts and settlements from the Great Lakes to the western reaches of Pennsylvania. King George replaced Amherst with General Thomas Gage, who managed to undo much of the damage. Pontiac's Rebellion nonetheless suggested that, if only to retain the lands it had won in the West, Britain needed to keep an army in America.

Who would pay for it? The war left the British government with a debt of almost £130 million, an enormous sum by contemporary standards. Responsibility for the budget lay with a stern and rigid minister, George Grenville, who since April 1763 had been first lord of the treasury and chancellor of the exchequer. To him, it seemed obvious that the colonists, as major beneficiaries of the British victory, should help shoulder the burden not perhaps of paying off old debts, but at least of keeping a British army in postwar America. Estimates put that cost at about £250,000 a year, and other expenses added another £100,000 to the projected new annual expenditures stemming from Britain's enlarged North American empire.

159

And so the division between Britain and America began with an argument over taxes. From there, it grew into a larger conflict over authority and subjection not unlike that between Amherst and the western Indians—and with similar consequences.

ROUND ONE: THE SUGAR AND STAMP ACTS

Customs duties were one way to begin raising money. Britain had regulated American trade for a century, but the customs establishment in America brought in substantially less revenue than its cost to the Crown. That was not as strange as it might seem, since British trade laws were designed primarily to shape the course of trade. British officials used devices such as duties and bounties to encourage Americans to confine their trade to the British empire and to produce goods that the mother country would otherwise have to purchase from foreign suppliers. Britain's gains were indirect, in the profits of her shippers and manufacturers, or in the prosperity of colonists in the West Indies, which ultimately increased the tax revenues flowing into the king's treasury. But now, desperate for new sources of income, the king's government decided to make the colonial customs service a paying proposition.

George Grenville served as first lord of the British treasury and chancellor of the exchequer beginning in the spring of 1763. Determined to raise additional revenue for the Crown by taxing the colonists, he was responsible for the Sugar Act of 1764 and the Stamp Act of 1765.

On March 9, 1764, Grenville proposed that Parliament level new duties on a series of articles imported into the colonies. Among them was molasses, a by-product of sugar refining that the colonists used as a sweetener or, more often, distilled into rum, which they then exchanged for imports such as slaves or sold locally in enormous quantities. Parliament subsequently approved the Revenue Act of 1764, known as the Sugar Act. It imposed a duty of "3d" per gallon (three pennies, or pence, written "d" for the old Roman denarius coin) on molasses imported from the non-British West Indies, which was half the duty set by an earlier law, the Molasses Act of 1733. That older, heavier duty had not prevented colonists from importing molasses from the "foreign," particularly the French, West Indies, where it was plentifully available (the French preferred brandy to rum, and so had less use for molasses) and also cheaper than in the British islands. Colonial shippers did not always pay the duty: instead, they smuggled foreign molasses into the colonies, bribing customs agents to look the other way. There was, in fact, a set rate for bribing agents that varied from port to port, but was always substantially less than six pence per gallon.

Grenville assumed that colonists could easily pay the new, reduced duty. And now the king's government intended to enforce the law. It had, in fact, already begun reforming the customs service to make it more efficient and responsible; and in 1763, Parliament authorized the peacetime use of British naval vessels in American waters to enforce British trade laws. The Sugar Act itself included provisions to facilitate its enforcement, demanding elaborate procedures and paperwork of colonists trading with the West Indies to prove that the molasses they carried came from the British islands. The act also changed the rules for prosecuting persons accused of violating the law in ways that stacked the cards against them.

The Sugar Act looked superficially like earlier trade laws, but it was more than an effort to regulate commerce: "it is just and necessary," read the preamble, "that a revenue be raised . . . in America for defraying the expense of defending, protecting, and securing the same." In other words, it was meant to raise money from the colonists. The only problem from the government's point of view was that the act seemed unlikely to raise enough money: the ministry estimated that it would bring in £40,000–£50,000 per year, a small part of the Crown's projected postwar costs in America. As a result, the parliamentary resolutions that initiated the Sugar Act proposed another measure to help fill the budgetary gap, a direct excise tax, similar to a modern sales tax, in the form of a stamp duty—that is, tax stamps would be required on specified items sold in the colonies, like taxes on whiskey and some other alcoholic beverages today. Never before had Parliament imposed a direct tax on colonists. Implementation of that measure was, however, delayed a year so that the Americans could be consulted. Grenville suggested that the colonists might propose a better way of raising a revenue, and perhaps

*What were the main points of
dispute between the American colonists
and Britain in the 1760s and 1770s?*

assume responsibility for collecting it themselves. But he made no serious effort to let the colonists tax themselves, and never so much as answered inquiries about the amount they would need to raise. What he really wanted was the colonies' prior consent to a Stamp Act, and that he did not get.

The colonists' arguments against the Sugar Act were generally economic in character. A three-pence duty on a gallon of molasses was no less prohibitive than one of six pence, they said. If enforced, it would choke off trade, wiping out the income colonists used to purchase imports from the mother country, which had increased so substantially in recent years that they exceeded British exports to the British West Indies. As molasses imports into the American mainland fell, Britain would lose not only the expected revenue from the new duty, but the profits from selling those goods to the colonists. In short, *British* interests would suffer, not just those of the Americans.

Both the substance and tone of the American argument shifted dramatically once news of the proposed stamp tax crossed the Atlantic. Thereafter, colonists employed the language of rights. Parliament, they insisted, had no right to impose a stamp tax or, for that matter, to raise revenue from the colonists in any way whatsoever. Within the British system, taxes were a "free gift of the people" and so could be imposed only with the consent of the people or of their representatives, which protected their property from rulers' avarice. Freedom from taxation without consent was a basic right of Englishmen that the colonists in no way gave up by migrating to America: the original settlers and their descendants were "free-born subjects, justly and naturally entitled to all the rights and advantages of the British constitution." Since the colonists elected representatives to their provincial legislatures and not to the House of Commons, only their provincial legislatures could tax them.

Several colonies petitioned against passage of Grenville's Stamp Act. Parliament refused even to receive the petitions, because they denied its right to tax colonists; indeed, colonial opposition strengthened Parliament's support for the Stamp Act, which it finally approved in March 1765. That measure, which would take effect on the first of November following, laid direct taxes on a number of articles sold in the American colonies including pamphlets, almanacs, newspapers and newspaper advertisements, and playing cards and dice, as well as on a wide range of legal and commercial documents. The taxes would have to be paid in gold and silver, which were hard to come by in the colonies. Some of the taxes were

quite high: a tax of two shillings sterling on newspaper ads plus a half-penny tax on the newspaper itself were substantial compared with the basic price of the newspaper and, moreover, put pressure on printers, the colonies' leading opinion makers. By taxing legal documents, the Stamp Act also stepped on the toes of lawyers, who were among the most articulate and politically active Americans. Persons accused of violating the Stamp Act would be tried, furthermore, in admiralty courts, whose usual jurisdiction covered cases that arose on the high seas, and which had no juries. Parliament assumed that the colonists would simply obey its orders.

One of the stamps prepared for sale in the colonies under the Stamp Act of 1765.

Colonists condemned the provision for trying cases under the Stamp Act in admiralty courts as an effort to circumvent their right to trial by jury—which it was, since colonial juries had a way of acquitting fellow colonists. But the colonists' opposition to the Stamp Act remained firmly centered on the principle of "no taxation without representation." In response, British spokesmen insisted that Americans were "virtually" represented in Parliament. Members of the House of Commons, they explained, spoke for the interests not only of those who voted for them, but for the good of all the British people everywhere—those who had the right to vote and those who did not; those in the British Isles and those in distant British colonies.

The concept of virtual representation was an ingenious effort to make sense of what the House of Commons had become, a collection of some 558 members selected, for reasons buried deep in the past, by a peculiar set of constituencies that bore no relation to population levels or contemporary importance. The Universities of Oxford and Cambridge sent representatives to the House of Commons, as Scotland had done since 1707; but most members were chosen from English counties, which contained relatively broad electorates, or from English boroughs where the right to name a member of Parliament was sometimes attached to a few parcels of land.

Paul Revere helped prepare an obelisk for Boston's celebration of the Stamp Act's repeal. Made of oiled paper on a wooden frame and lit from inside by candles, the display caught fire and was destroyed. Revere, however, produced this engraving of its design and inscription, which celebrated the support colonists had received from British "patriots" such as William Pitt and affirmed the Americans' loyalty to Britain. "No disaffection stains these peaceful Climes," it read. "The foes of Britain only are our Foes."

local circumstances cannot be, represented in the House of Commons in Great Britain." Only provincial legislatures could tax the colonists. The Stamp Act Congress also affirmed the colonists' right to trial by jury, and condemned "the duties imposed by several late Acts of Parliament" as "extremely burthensome and grievous." Petitions including these resolutions were promptly sent to the king and both houses of Parliament in the hope of securing repeal of the Stamp Act and the objectionable restrictions on trade enacted in 1764.

 The town of Boston hit upon a more effective way **to fight the Stamp Act.** On the morning of August 14, 1765, an effigy of Andrew Oliver, who had been appointed stamp distributor for the Massachusetts Bay Colony, appeared hanging from a tree in Boston's South End. All day it remained on display, dutifully "stamping" goods brought into the town for sale. That evening, a crowd took down the effigy, which it paraded

through the streets and then down to the docks. There the crowd destroyed a small office Oliver had recently built, perhaps to carry out his duties as stamp officer, and finally burned the effigy in a great bonfire. A contingent of the crowd went on, against the orders of its leaders, and attacked Oliver's home. The next day, amid rumors of further violence, Oliver promised to give up the stamp distributorship. And if no one distributed the stamps, the Stamp Act could not go into effect. The Stamp Act had been nullified in Massachusetts, with no loss of blood and relatively little property damage.

The technique was so compelling that in one colony after another stamp officers resigned their offices either voluntarily, to avoid Oliver's fate, or under the immediate threat of mob violence. Only in the distant and thinly populated colony of Georgia did the stamp distributor avoid having to resign his office, and only there did the Stamp Act take effect for even a brief period. Elsewhere, on November 1, newspapers ceased to publish, and many courts and offices closed for lack of the required stamps. But gradually they reopened, often under pressure from people who argued that the Stamp Act was "unconstitutional" and need not be obeyed. By the late winter and early spring of 1766, colonists were going about their business much as if the Stamp Act had never been passed. For good measure, colonial merchants formed nonimportation agreements, arranging to cut off purchases of certain imports such as mourning clothes and the gloves customarily given out at funerals. They hoped to disrupt specific sectors of British manufacturing and so to provoke pressure for a repeal of the Stamp Act within England. As a result, colonial imports from Britain dropped by 13 or 14 percent between 1764 and 1765, and those Britons facing ruin because of the shrinking American market did not suffer in silence.

Parliament had little choice but to give in. That was relatively easy, since George Grenville had been forced from office in July 1765 by the king, who objected not to Grenville's policies but to the minister's way of lecturing him in a protracted and querulous manner. Grenville's successor, Charles Watson-Wentworth, the Marquis of Rockingham, had opposed the Stamp Act and was unwilling to enforce it. As a result, in March 1766, Parliament repealed the Stamp Act. But first it approved a Declaratory Act that affirmed the right of Parliament to make laws and statutes that bound the colonies and people of America "in all cases whatsoever." In short, it abandoned the Stamp Act, but not the principle of parliamentary supremacy.

ROUND TWO: THE TOWNSHEND CRISIS

Many colonists regarded the Declaratory Act as a face-saving device upon which Parliament would never act. However, a handful of Americans anticipated more trouble. "What could not be brought to pass by an undisguised and open attack upon our liberties," predicted a patriot in Providence, would be attempted again "by secret machinations, by artifice and cunning." Boston's Samuel Adams, who was emerging as a leading defender of colonial rights, privately suggested that Parliament's next attempt to raise revenue from the colonies would come in the form of a trade law—like the Sugar Act, which seemed superficially familiar and had attracted less opposition than the Stamp Act.

Rockingham fell from power after only fourteen months in office. Charles Townshend, the chancellor of the exchequer, dominated the new government and did exactly what Adams had predicted. In 1766, Parliament had reduced the duty on molasses from three to one pence per gallon and levied it on molasses from the British as well as the "foreign" West Indies. All pretense of using the duty to regulate trade—that is, to encourage mainland colonists to confine their trade to the British islands—was abandoned. The duty on molasses was designed simply to raise revenue for the Crown; it was therefore a tax. Nonetheless, Townshend noted, the colonists paid it. If the colonists preferred to enrich the royal treasury through levies on trade rather than direct taxes, he reasoned, why not let them have their way?

In 1767, the chancellor brought into Parliament a series of measures known as the Townshend Revenue Acts. The most significant of them imposed new duties on colonial imports of glass, lead, paint, paper, and tea. The colonists were already required to purchase those articles from Britain, so the law obviously was not meant to regulate trade in the interest of the British community as a whole. Indeed, the colonists could avoid the duties only by manufacturing the articles themselves, which was directly contrary to the mother country's economic interests. Not only did the Townshend duties undermine the provincial assemblies' exclusive right to tax colonists, but the funds raised would be used "for defraying the charge of administration of justice, and the support of civil government in such provinces where it shall be found necessary" as well as to meet the expenses of "defending, protecting, and securing the said dominions." At the time, colonial assemblies were responsible for paying the salaries of royal governors, judges, and other Crown appointees, and they had used their role as paymaster to make the king's officers more amenable to colonial interests.

Townshend was determined to end once and for all the colonial assemblies' self-proclaimed right to exercise powers like those of the House of Commons, as he made absolutely clear in his heavy-handed treatment of the New York legislature. The problem there began in 1765 when Grenville ushered a Quartering Act through Parliament. Under its terms, colonial assemblies were required to house British troops stationed within their territory in public barracks or uninhabited houses and to supply them with a specified list of items, including firewood, candles, bedding, vinegar, salt, cooking vessels, and a prescribed amount of beer, cider, or grog (rum mixed with water at a ratio of one to four). The New York assembly balked. The Quartering Act, it argued, was nothing but a tax law whose levies were collected in goods instead of money, and was therefore as objectionable as the Stamp Act. When, finally, the assembly agreed to supply British troops, it pretended to do so on its own initiative, without mentioning the Quartering Act or complying with its terms exactly, supplying firewood, candles, and cooking uten-

Samuel Adams, as painted by John Singleton Copley in 1770, when Adams was Boston's leading opponent of British infringements on American rights.

sils but not salt, vinegar, cider, beer, or grog, and so avoided any acknowledgment of Parliament's right to tax Americans. In retaliation, Townshend persuaded Parliament to pass the New York Suspending Act, restraining the New York assembly from passing any laws until it complied completely with the Quartering Act of 1765.

In the event that any colonists had failed to notice the drift of British policy, they were wakened in December 1767 by twelve newspaper essays that began to appear in the *Pennsylvania Chronicle.* The essays were quickly reprinted in other colonial newspapers and then, when the series was complete, as a pamphlet published not only in America but in London, Dublin, and (translated into French) Amsterdam. John Dickinson's **"Letters from a Farmer in Pennsylvania"** began by attacking the New York Suspending Act: if the New York assembly could be deprived of the "privilege of legislation" for refusing to submit to parliamentary taxation, "why may they not, with equal reason, be deprived of every other privilege?" And if Parliament could deprive New York of its rights, it could do the same to the other colonies. Nothing, the "Farmer" argued, would so encourage such attempts as the colonies' inattention to the interests of each other, "for the cause of *one* is the cause of *all.*"

The main target of the "Farmer's Letters," however, was the Townsend duties. A tax, Dickinson said, was "an imposition on the subject, for the sole purpose of levying money," and under that definition the Townshend duties were taxes that demanded opposition every bit as much as had the Stamp Act. Colonists should unite against them. But caution was necessary to avoid anger producing anger until the quarrel turned into "an incurable rage." Like virtually every other American, but perhaps more ardently than most, Dickinson wanted to avoid independence. If

An eighteenth-century engraving of John Dickinson, a Philadelphia lawyer who wrote the influential "Letters from a Farmer in Pennsylvania" and so rallied colonial opposition to the Townshend duties in 1767 and 1768.

once the colonies were separated from their mother country, he asked, "what new form of government shall we adopt, or where shall we find another Britain to supply our loss? Torn from the body, to which we are united by religion, liberty, laws, affections, relation, language and commerce, we must bleed at every vein." He recommended "the constitutional modes of obtaining relief," particularly petitions from colonial assemblies "to the powers that can afford us relief." He thought the chances were good that they would do the job. "We have an excellent prince, in whose good dispositions . . . we may confide," he wrote, and "a generous, sensible, and humane nation, to whom we may apply." But if petitions to king and Parliament proved ineffectual, he recommended "withholding from Great Britain all the advantages she has been used to receive from us"—that is, another boycott on imports.

Accordingly, once their petitions for repeal of the Townshend Revenue Acts failed, the colonists organized nonimportation associations. Specific provisions varied somewhat from colony to colony, but, overall, the associations led to dramatic reductions in imports: in New York and Philadelphia, imports fell to less than half of previous levels. The associations' impact on Britain was offset by an expanding European market. Nonetheless, by 1770, the king's new first minister, Frederick, Lord North, who would remain in office for twelve years and bring some welcome stability to the king's government, was ready to repeal the Townshend Acts. He abandoned all of Townshend's duties "on commercial principles," except for the tax on tea. That he kept to demonstrate Parliament's continuing right to tax Americans.

When news of the Townshend Acts' partial repeal arrived in America, first Newport, then New York, then one port after another abandoned their nonimportation agreements. Some colonists, however, continued to boycott tea—except for tea imported from Holland by "patriotic" smugglers.

A "QUIET PERIOD"?

On March 5, 1770, the day the House of Commons approved the partial repeal of the Townshend Revenue Acts, British troops shot into a hostile crowd in Boston, wounding eleven and killing five in what would soon be called the Boston Massacre. The troops had been sent to Boston in the fall of 1768 to strengthen the king's government and keep the peace. The Bostonians were not pleased. Like all Britons, they disliked peacetime armies and governments that depended on military force to buttress their authority. Free men, they said, were not governed at the point of a gun. The soldiers' fondness for whores and coarse language, their disregard for the Sabbath, and their willingness to work for wages below the norm also led to repeated clashes with local people. Now, with blood spilled on King Street, the town demanded that the soldiers be sent to Castle William, a fort on an island in Boston Harbor. The acting governor, Thomas Hutchinson, complied. But the trials of soldiers indicted for murder were put off until the fall, when the anger that greeted the massacre would have cooled. Then, finally, a welcome but uneasy peace arrived in Boston.

Elsewhere, too, the early years of the 1770s were a "quiet period" in which the struggles between colonists and mother country ceased. Still, the imperial relationship remained more troubled than a decade before: the conflict between Parliament's claim to an absolute and universal authority and the colonists' insistence that its powers were limited remained unresolved. Early in the dispute, colonists assumed that Parliament's effort to tax them was a mistake that would easily be corrected; but their optimism dimmed as king, Lords, and Commons violated American rights, as they saw it, with one measure after another. Moreover, the British government seemed to be following similar policies in England, Ireland, and elsewhere. Who was responsible? The king's ministers fell under suspicion and also the members of Parliament; by 1770, even King George, a dogged defender of parliamentary right, was occasionally accused of complicity in the sowing of grievances. Enthusiasm for the future of British North America, so high after the French and Indian War, was gone, and in place of their old British heroes Americans now had at least two of their own—Daniel Dulany, the brave Marylander who had refuted to his countrymen's satisfaction the ridiculous notion that colonists were virtually represented in Parliament, and the eloquent "Pennsylvania Farmer," John Dickinson.

What the Anglo-American world experienced in the early 1770s was, then, not so much peace as, in Samuel Adams's phrase, a "sullen silence" among contenders who lacked for the moment a pressing issue over which they could fight. The quiet could have persisted, allowing suspicions to dissipate and differences to be worked out over time. The Americans still wanted to remain under the British Crown as desperately as the Crown sought to preserve the empire. But the British government had not learned to let sleeping dogs lie.

Paul Revere's engraving of the Boston Massacre, March 5, 1770. Revere—who copied with only modest changes a painting by the Boston artist Henry Pelham—shows soldiers lined up, purposefully shooting civilians. In the background, gunsmoke comes from a window in the Customs House, which suggests that the hated British customsmen were involved in that doleful event. The engraving gives no indication that Bostonians had helped provoke violence by taunting the soldiers, throwing snowballs (some with rocks inside) at them, and even calling out "Fire! Fire!"

TEA AGAIN

The calm ended with Parliament's adoption of a Tea Act in May 1773, a measure meant to help the East India Company, then near bankruptcy, recover financially by selling in America the 17 million pounds of tea it had on hand. Under that act, Parliament agreed to refund all taxes levied within England on tea that the company later reexported to the colonies, a course of action that lowered the company's costs and so the price it had to charge colonial purchasers. Henceforth, moreover, the East India Company could sell tea in America through its own agents, or "consignees." Previously the company had had to sell its tea at public auction to middlemen who then sold it elsewhere after tacking their own profits onto the price. The company asked that the old Townshend duty on tea also be removed, but the government refused,

167

An engraving depicting "Indians" throwing tea into the harbor during the Boston Tea Party.

Philadelphia, and Charleston. In the last three of those ports, opponents of the Tea Act succeeded in persuading the consignees to resign. New York and Philadelphia also managed to persuade the captains of tea ships to turn around before they had formally entered the harbor and to return their cargoes to England. Charleston's tea ship entered the harbor and sat there, with its tea still on board, until a twenty-day waiting period expired. At that point, the king's customs agents seized the "noisome leaf" and stored it in the basement of the customs house, where it remained, with the duties unpaid.

In Boston, however, the tea ship slipped into the harbor. And there the consignees fled to the protection of British guns at Castle William and adamantly refused to resign their commissions. For a full twenty days, Bostonians tried to find a way for the tea ships to leave the harbor and take their cargoes back to England with the duties unpaid. However, the customs agents, and then Governor Hutchinson, refused to grant clearances so the ships could legally leave the harbor. Since the British navy was guarding the sea lanes, no uncleared vessel could make an escape. If the tea remained on board and the customs agents seized it (as the law allowed) twenty days after the arrival of the first tea ship, the *Dartmouth*, on November 28, there was little doubt that the consignees would pay the duty.

holding tight to that one remaining assertion of parliamentary supremacy. Even with the old duty in place, the ministry thought that East India Company tea, freed of English internal taxes and middlemen's profits, could undersell smuggled tea.

For the colonists, however, cheap East India Tea was a sugar-coated bitter pill: if they swallowed it, they admitted that Parliament could lay taxes on them. Other taxes would likely follow. Since the Tea Act gave the East India Company a monopoly on the sale of tea in the colonies, it also threatened the livelihoods of all independent American tea merchants, including those patriotic smugglers who had allowed colonists to drink tea without compromising their political principles. Then, to make a bad situation worse, the East India Company decided to appoint as consignees men whose politics were suspect from the American perspective, including two sons and a nephew of Thomas Hutchinson, who had become royal governor of Massachusetts. Governor Hutchinson publicly defended parliamentary supremacy. Moreover, a series of his letters to England, which Benjamin Franklin had sent to Massachusetts, seemed to prove that he had recommended policies that violated American liberty.

In September 1773, the East India Company decided to send a half million pounds of tea to Boston, New York,

Finally, on the evening of December 16, 1773, the night before the *Dartmouth*'s cargo became subject to seizure and after Hutchinson had refused a final appeal for clearances, Samuel Adams told a mass meeting that they could do nothing more to save their country. With a whoop, a crowd of men from Boston and surrounding towns, some disguised as Indians, swept down to the ships and threw into the sea some 90,000 pounds of tea from the *Dartmouth* and two other tea ships that had arrived more recently. Despite the noise with which it began, the Boston Tea Party was a carefully ordered event. Observers reported that the night was interrupted only by the sound of axes breaking open the tea chests and of tea being dumped into the water. A young lawyer from Braintree named John Adams, a country cousin of Boston's better-known Samuel Adams, found the event "magnificent." The destruction of the tea, he said, was "so bold, so daring, so firm, intrepid, & inflexible, and it must have so important Consequences and so lasting, that I cannot but consider it as an Epocha in History."

THE COERCIVE ACTS

The British government's reaction confirmed Adams's prophesy. It had had enough. Now, with the full cooperation of Parliament, the Crown set out to bring the colonists to heel, starting with those annoying Bostonians. On the government's initiative, Parliament passed a series of four Coercive Acts in the spring of 1774.

■ The *Boston Port Act* prohibited the loading or unloading of ships in the port of Boston after June 1 and until the town had paid the East India Company and the customs service for losses stemming from the Tea Party. All whose livelihoods depended on the port, from merchants through humble porters, were suddenly unemployed; even food and fuel could be brought into the town only under escort and with the permission of customs officers, who were relocated to Salem, a smaller port north of Boston.

■ The *Massachusetts Government Act* annulled Massachusetts's charter of 1691 and revised its government to cut back popular participation and enhance the power of the Crown. The colony's council, or upper house, which had been elected by the assembly (the lower house), would henceforth be appointed by the Crown and hold office at the king's pleasure. Juries were to be summoned by the sheriffs, who were royal appointees, not, as before, elected by the towns, and the colonists' beloved democratic town meetings could henceforth meet only once a year unless they received the prior consent of the governor.

■ The *Administration of Justice Act* allowed Crown officers in Massachusetts who were accused of committing a capital offense while putting down a riot or executing the revenue acts to be tried in Britain. The colonists, who called that law the "Murder Act," predicted that it would encourage royal officials to kill colonists, knowing they would be acquitted in England. The suggestion that officials could not receive a fair trial in Massachusetts was particularly resented since soldiers involved in the Boston Massacre had

been defended by two lawyers who were also ardent defenders of the American cause, John Adams and Josiah Quincy Jr. Four soldiers and their captain were acquitted, and two guardsmen were found guilty only of manslaughter, a remarkable outcome given the widespread anger that followed the event.

■ A final measure, a new *Quartering Act*, which permitted British troops to be quartered within towns, applied not just to Massachusetts but to all colonies. Its force, however, was first felt in Massachusetts, where a heavy contingent of troops were brought back into Boston, and

This British print of 1775 suggests that merchants were forced to sign the Continental Association—the nonimportation and nonconsumption agreement adopted by the First Continental Congress in response to the Coercive Acts—by the threat of being tarred and feathered if they refused.

Benjamin Franklin was portrayed as an unpretentious American in a simple fur hat and spectacles in this French print. The French idolized Franklin, who served as an American diplomat in Paris during the late 1770s and early 1780s.

it ought to lay," on Hutchinson. And that, he hoped, would open the way to reconciliation.

The plan misfired. The colonists became enraged at Hutchinson, but in the controversy that followed, Franklin—who felt compelled to acknowledge that he had sent the letters to America—found himself accused of fomenting sedition. On January 29, 1774, at a meeting of the king's Privy Council to consider a petition from Massachusetts that Hutchinson be removed from office, the solicitor general, Alexander Wedderburn, mounted an hour-long, bitter attack on him. Franklin had stolen the letters, Wedderburn charged; and he was the "true incendiary" behind colonial unrest. On the advice of his counsel, Franklin stood silent while Wedderburn spoke. The hall was crowded with dignitaries who came to see the spectacle. The humiliation was not something Franklin would forget.

He nonetheless remained in England, watching the government take ever harsher steps against the colonists, until, finally, he set sail in March 1775. Even then he thought he might return to England the next fall. But on May 6, the day after he landed in Philadelphia, Pennsylvania elected him a delegate to the Second Continental Congress, and he quickly became fully absorbed in American affairs. Reconciliation became for Franklin, as for other colonists, an impossible dream; and by June 1776, he was ready for independence. Alexander Wedderburn had done the Americans a great service; he had assured that in any imperial division, Franklin would be with the colonists. And Franklin's services were an enormous asset.

LOYALISM

Some colonists continued to hold back from independence. Loyalists—American opponents of independence—constituted,

by modern estimates, a fifth of the total population. They were a miscellaneous lot, including artisans and common farmers along with wealthy merchants whose income depended on trade with England and British officeholders who supported the Crown almost instinctively. Some were tenants whose landlords sided with the Revolution; others lived in the backcountry and opposed independence because of long-standing resentments toward the "patriots" who ruled in the East or because they had never heard about the events that gradually undermined other Americans' affection for Britain. The supporters of independence had devised methods of spreading news, such as the committees of correspondence Boston established in 1772 to inform and politicize particularly those colonists in remote towns. Still, the arrival of news on the distant frontier remained uneven at a time when newspapers and letters, carried from place to place on ships or horseback, were the major means of internal communications.

Many Loyalists, however, had good reason for opposing independence. Some came from ethnic or religious minorities, such as the Anglicans in Connecticut, who thought their liberty would be more secure under the Crown than in a system of majority rule. Slaves, too, could well see their greatest prospect of freedom in supporting the king. Still other Loyalists were recent British immigrants who could not take sides against the country in which they had been born and raised. And even informed, white, American-born colonists could decide against independence out of fear. Despite the assurances of *Common Sense*, they said, the colonists had no chance of holding out against the power of Great Britain, and a severe repression would surely follow military defeat. But by the summer of 1776, most colonists seem to have concluded that they could avoid destruction by the king and his German "mercenaries" only if they declared independence and sought outside help. Self-preservation made independence necessary; there really was no choice.

TOWARD INDEPENDENCE

Meanwhile, the war entered a crisis that seemed to support the predictions of doom. The Canadian campaign had begun slowly and then gone from bad to worse: American forces put Quebec under siege, then attacked the city on December 30, 1775. The result was disastrous. General Richard Montgomery was killed; the second-in-command, Colonel Benedict Arnold, was wounded; and the Americans suffered 60 casualties and lost another 400 men who were taken prisoner.

A lack of supplies and the ravages of smallpox weakened the remnants of the invading army until, with the arrival of British reinforcements in May 1776, the Continental army retreated in total chaos. A second offensive in June ended in similar disarray, leaving the northern frontier open to incursions by Canadians and their Indian allies.

The Continental army was more successful in Massachusetts. With cannons and other heavy supplies heroically floated down the Hudson, then dragged with sleds, wagons, and oxen some 300 miles from Ticonderoga by a company commanded by Henry Knox, a portly twenty-five-year-old former Boston bookseller, the Americans succeeded in fortifying Dorchester Heights to Boston's south. That made the British position untenable. General William Howe, who had replaced Thomas Gage as commander of the British North American army, evacuated the town on March 17, 1776, and sailed his

This painting by John Trumbull, often labeled *The Signing of the Declaration of Independence*, actually shows the drafting committee presenting its draft declaration to Congress on June 28, 1776. Trumbull painted the scene several decades after it occurred, and he exaggerated the number of men in attendance.

men to Halifax, Nova Scotia. There he gathered forces for a major offensive somewhere along the Atlantic coast. In late June, hundreds of British ships began to arrive, sails aloft, at the entrance to New York's harbor.

On July 1, the Second Continental Congress resolved itself once again into a Committee of the Whole. The debates on Richard Henry Lee's resolutions recapitulated earlier discussions, and culminated with a divided vote of 9–4 in favor of independence. The next day, with some abstentions from the Pennsylvania delegation, the arrival of Caesar Rodney, who swung the Delaware delegation into line, and a change of position by South Carolina, Congress approved independence with the support of twelve colonies. Only New York held out. A week later, it, too, finally instructed its delegates to consent, and independence became a unanimous decision of all the colonies, or, as they had become, states. The British government's decision to force the Americans into obedience had, in effect, brought the loss it most feared.

Once it had approved independence, Congress again resolved itself into a Committee of the Whole to consider the **Declaration of Independence** proposed by the committee it had appointed on June 11. The draft was, as Josiah Bartlett of New Hampshire commented, "a pretty good one," written by Thomas Jefferson under guidelines set by the drafting committee. Parts of the manuscript were musical, others overstated and in need of a good editing, which the delegates gave it, changing phrases, rewriting passages, and cutting out about a quarter of the proposed text. Finally, on July 4, 1776, Congress approved the Declaration and arranged for it to be "authenticated and printed" and sent to "the several assemblies, conventions and committees, or councils of safety, and to the several commanding officers of the continental troops" so it could be "proclaimed in each of the United States, and at the head of the army." As John Hancock, the president of Congress, explained, it was important "that the People may be universally informed" that they had, as the document stated, assumed a "separate station" among the "powers of the earth."

And so the Declaration of Independence wound through the country and was publicly read in both major port cities and small towns or villages, always with abundant "huzzahs." In place after place, crowds seized the occasion to tear down statues, paintings, or other symbols of the king and British monarchy, trampling them underfoot or burning them in great bonfires. It was not one "unfeeling" king, as Paine had called George III, that they rejected, but all kings. This was not a simple colonial rebellion, but a revolution, an effort to create a different form of government from Britain's, a republic in which the people would rule. But first they would have to establish the independence they proclaimed—on the battlefield.

A War for Independence

Only a gambler who liked betting against high odds would have put his money on the Americans. Britain had a long military tradition; its army was organized, trained, and equipped, and had just won a major world victory, as the Peace of Paris (1763) affirmed. Britain also boasted a powerful navy, with some eighty-two "ships of the line"—the largest naval vessels—at sea or ready to be armed in June 1776. Congress had no navy to speak of, and the Continental army was a motley collection of volunteers who shocked General Washington when he first laid eyes on them at Cambridge. The men were willing to fight, he said, but they lacked all discipline. When he tried to impose order, the men had a way of not reenlisting. And when the army left Massachusetts, many New Englanders were unwilling to go with it.

To win **the war,** Washington argued, the Americans needed regular soldiers who enlisted for three years or the duration of the war and officers paid well enough that "men of quality" would take on the job. That proposal ran smack into an old Anglo-American suspicion of "standing armies," that is, regular, paid, professional military forces, which were regarded as dangerous instruments with which ambitious rulers could enforce obedience and "enslave" the people. Congress therefore hesitated. Navies were more difficult to turn against the governed, and so less feared. Early in the war, Congress tried to build a Continental navy, and American shipbuilders—who had never before built a warship—managed by Herculean effort to produce thirteen frigates (medium-sized warships). By 1779, the British had captured or destroyed most of them. The navy was also crippled by sailors' preference for sailing on privateers, private ships that attacked British vessels with the permission of Congress for a share of

What's for Dinner?

American Journal

"As to provision of victuals, . . . When we [*soldiers in the Continental army*] engaged in the service we were promised the following articles for a ration: one pound of good and wholesome fresh or salt beef, or three fourths of a pound of good salt pork, a pound of good flour, soft or hard bread, a quart of salt to every hundred pounds of fresh beef, a quart of vinegar to a hundred rations, a gill of rum, brandy, or whiskey per day, some little soap and candles. . . . But we never received what was allowed us. Oftentimes have I gone one, two, three, and even four days without a morsel, unless the fields or forests might chance to afford enough to prevent absolutte starvation. . . .

"If we had got our full allowance regularly, what was it? . . . The beef that we got in the army was,

generally, not many degrees above carrion; it was much like the old Negro's rabbit, it had not much fat upon it and but a very little lean. When we drew flour, which was much of the time we were in the field or on marches, it was of small value, being eaten half-cooked besides a deal of it being unavoidably wasted in the cookery. . . .

"When General Washington told Congress, 'The soldiers eat every kind of horse fodder but hay,' he might have gone a little farther and told them that they eat considerable hog's fodder and not a trifle of dog's—when they could get it to eat."

Joseph Plumb Martin, *Private Yankee Doodle; Being a Narrative of Some of the Adventures, Dangers and Sufferings of a Revolutionary Soldier* the spoils. The ships Americans built for privateering (which could also serve the needs of pirates) were beautiful to behold. Exceptionally tall of mast, they could catch the wind and cut through the waves at far greater speed than more conventionally outfitted ships, but it took great skill to keep them from tipping over. The privateers performed a substantial service for the American cause, bringing the war even into British home waters. Theirs was, however, a rather scattershot operation, directed by private initiatives, not central command.

The British understood their advantages. They had also learned in 1775 that victory would be harder to gain than they originally thought. The police action they attempted to carry out in Massachusetts was insufficient: they could not simply capture a few leaders and expect the rebellion to collapse. The British had a war on their hands, and wars they knew how to win. And so, in the summer of 1776, they gathered outside New York City one of the strongest armies and fleets ever seen in North America to that time. By August, General William Howe and his brother, Admiral Lord Richard Howe, had under their command some 45,000 soldiers and sailors—against Washington's 28,000, of whom only 19,000 were at all fit for duty. Manhattan Island, surrounded by water, was an ideal place for the British: with their powerful fleet, they could easily move troops from place to place, outflanking the Continentals almost at will.

THE CAMPAIGN OF 1776

General Washington defended New York City only because Congress insisted upon it. His situation was impossible. First he divided his troops, sending some to defend Brooklyn Heights on Long Island, which he had to control in order to defend New York City. But when the British took the offensive there on August 27, 1776, the American lines collapsed, and Washington's forces suffered 1,500 casualties to the enemy's 400. Fortunately, General Howe did not advance after his victory, and on the night of the 29th, under cover of a heavy fog and with the help of some expert mariners from Marblehead, Massachusetts, Washington managed to transfer the rest of his battered troops across the East River—which the British navy had failed to secure—to Manhattan.

The retreat from Long Island was the first of many American retreats in the campaign of 1776. On September 12, Washington moved his troops to northern Manhattan; he built fortifications at Harlem Heights, then, after Howe sailed

up the East River and made a landing to the north, moved to White Plains in Westchester County on the mainland. There he fought a battle with Howe on October 28, then slipped away again while Howe waited for reinforcements. But on November 16, Howe took the American garrison Washington had left behind at Fort Washington on the western side of Manhattan, capturing its 2,800 men. Two days later, a contingent of redcoats under Charles, Lord Cornwallis, captured Fort Lee, on the opposite shore of the Hudson River, and with it a substantial store of military supplies. Washington then retreated down through New Jersey, whose people were busily signing oaths of loyalty to the Crown to avoid being punished as traitors after the imminent collapse of the American cause.

Even Washington was near despair. He managed to bring his troops across the Delaware River into Pennsylvania on December 11. The next day, Congress, fearing a British attack, fled Philadelphia for Baltimore. But then Washington broke the string of defeats on December 30–31, when he recrossed the Delaware and surprised a British garrison at Trenton, New Jersey, taking 918 prisoners and killing 30 of the king's soldiers, while the American troops suffered only 5 casualties. Three days later, he won another victory at Princeton. The battles of Trenton and Princeton were among the most important of the war. They restored morale and allowed Washington to take his troops into winter camp—war in the eighteenth century was a summer and fall sport, since the guns of the day fired poorly in cold weather—at Morristown, New Jersey. That meant the Continental army would be around to fight again in 1777.

The victories also secured Washington's leadership. With the fall of Forts Washington and Lee, dissatisfaction with the commander in chief had mounted, and some saw an alternative leader in General Charles Lee, an erratic Englishman who had joined the American forces and become the darling of several members of Congress. Lee differed from Washington in his concept of how the war should be fought: he proposed an "irregular" war fought by citizen soldiers on a variety of fronts. If the militia were trained and ready to engage whenever the British entered their territory, the king's troops, Lee reasoned, would find themselves simply overwhelmed and incapable of putting down the "rebellion." Washington preferred to fight a more conventional war, with trained troops under respectable officers. Lee's ambitions eventually got the better of him: he dawdled in following orders to join forces with Washington in late 1776, perhaps hoping that if Washington failed to reverse his pathetic record, Congress would

The Revolutionary War in the North, 1776–1777

American victory

British victory

American/French
troop movements

British troop
movements

0   50   100 mi

0   50   100 km

Québec

St. Lawrence River

Montréal

Lake
Huron

BRITISH NORTH
AMERICA

Burgoyne

Richelieu R.

Lake Ontario

Lake
Champlain

VERMONT

Crown Point
Fort Ticonderoga

*Lake
George*

NEW
HAMPSHIRE

Fort Oswego

Lake Erie

Saratoga
(Burgoyne surrenders
Oct. 17, 1777)

Arnold

Bennington
Aug. 16, 1777

NEW YORK

Freemans Farm,
Sept. 19, 1777

Albany

Boston

Kingston

MASSACHUSETTS

Hudson R.

CONNECTICUT   RHODE
ISLAND

Peekskill

Fort Lee   Fort Washington

PENNSYLVANIA

Morristown

New York

Newton

Valley Forge

Allentown

Brandywine,
Sept. 11, 1777

Philadelphia

NEW
JERSEY

Howe

Wilmington

MARYLAND

DELAWARE

*Atlantic
Ocean*

VIRGINIA

0   10 mi

0   10 km

NEW
JERSEY

Hudson R.

White
Plains

Ft. Washington

Hackensack

Ft. Lee

Howe

Morristown

Newark

Harlem
Heights

Manhattan

Long Island

Brooklyn
Heights

Washington

Cornwallis

Staten
Island

New Brunswick

Gen. Wm. Howe

Adm. Lord Howe

Princeton

*Atlantic
Ocean*

fire him and put Lee in command. But the British managed to capture Lee in a New Jersey tavern, which effectively removed him from contention for the army's top job.

In the dark days of late 1776, Congress finally agreed to expand the Continental army and to recruit men willing to sign up for at least three years in return for a bounty payment of $20 (which would later be increased), a yearly clothing issue, and the promise of 100 acres of land if they served until the end of the war. It became therefore ever more likely not only that Washington would remain as commander in chief, but that the war would be fought in his way. Indeed, the war henceforth was fought not by irregular troops like the militiamen who rallied after Lexington and Concord to take potshots at redcoats—although militiamen did play important supportive roles in many actions—but by a regular army. Its men, often drawn from the poorest and most marginal members of society, including blacks, joined in response to material incentives, and its officers also joined up to receive the concrete inducements Congress offered, not just from a selfless patriotism. In other words, the Americans relied on a standing army to win their independence, and, under Washington's leadership, defended their Revolution with a military strategy that was decidedly conservative.

ARMS

If Washington's strategy was traditional, so were the arms on which his army depended. In truth, Americans were more innovative in their use of weaponry at the beginning than at the end of the war. When he first took command of the Continental army, Washington expected great things from the "six companies of expert riflemen," soon increased to nine, that the Second Continental Congress had ordered raised in Pennsylvania, Maryland, and Virginia and sent to the front at Boston. "They are the finest marksmen in the world," claimed John Hancock, and could "do execution of their Rifle Guns at an amazing distance." That was possible because rifles, unlike the more common muskets, contained spiraled grooves in the interior of their barrels, and the grooves made bullets spin, facilitating their projection through the air. A capable rifleman could hit a target at least twice the distance possible for soldiers armed with smoothbore muskets, whose range of effectiveness was no more than 75–100 yards.

The rifle was first developed in central Europe during the fifteenth or sixteenth century and brought by German immigrants to Pennsylvania, where gunsmiths gradually adapted its

The "Pennsylvania rifle," an elegant gun with remarkable accuracy for the time, was actually manufactured in shops all along the American frontier from western New York south. Unfortunately, it took too long to load to be of much use in battlefields during the Revolutionary War.

design to American needs. The "Pennsylvania rifle," a strikingly handsome gun of brass, iron, and wood, was manufactured in shops from western New York down into Georgia by the time of the Revolution. Since each gun was custom-made for its purchaser, no two were exactly alike. In general, however, American rifles had a longer barrel than their European counterparts, which improved their balance and accuracy. They were also lighter, with a smaller caliber and narrower exterior dimensions, which fitted the needs of men who used rifles not for stationary sports, as in Europe, but on the move, for hunting and Indian warfare. No doubt riflemen could also help pick off redcoats. And so Washington welcomed the riflemen who arrived in 1775 with their distinctive frontier attire—buckskin breeches, hunting shirts, moccasins trimmed with porcupine quills, toting tomahawks and hunting knives—and gave them special quarters. Clearly he regarded them as an elite force.

But experience didn't match expectations. The independent-minded riflemen found little to do during the siege of Boston, and proved so unruly that even Washington came to regret their presence. In most battle situations, moreover, the riflemen turned out to be useless or worse. Their capacity for hitting distant targets was no help in the miserable street fighting at Quebec in December 1775, and they were essentially defenseless while reloading their weapons, which was a relatively slow process. Muskets, which could be loaded faster than rifles and, unlike rifles, had bayonets attached to their barrels, were preferable in close combat. They could also be fired with coarser powder than rifles, and during the Revolutionary War having any powder whatsoever was something of a triumph. Just getting enough muskets was a big problem. Not all militiamen owned guns at the war's beginning, and those they had were often obsolete or broken and so different from one another that, as the Pennsylvania Council of Safety reported in 1776, one militia company could need as many as seven different kinds of ammunition. To acquire large numbers of Pennsylvania rifles would have been an impossible task, since those rifles were crafted in American shops, required far more hand tooling, and were therefore significantly more expensive than muskets.

Congress did what it could to encourage the domestic production of armaments, calling on the states in 1775 to keep their gunsmiths at work and specifying standard dimensions (guns should have "a good bridle lock, ¾ of an inch bore," and be "of good substance in the breech," with a barrel 3 feet 8 inches long and an 18-inch bayonet). Congress also encouraged the establishment of gunpowder mills, and pamphlets like *Essays Upon the Making of Salt-Petre and Gunpowder*, published by Pennsylvania congressman Henry Wiser, provided directions. Many communities operated kilns to produce charcoal or created artificial niter (a mineral of potassium nitrate) beds to leach saltpeter (a salt-like mineral) from human urine or animal droppings, but sulfur,

> *"The way a nation fights reflects its state of economic and managerial development, and the United States in 1776 was a decidedly undeveloped nation."*

another critical ingredient in gunpowder, had to be laboriously distilled from the earth and water near sulfur springs. Gunpowder mills nonetheless appeared along streams in almost every colony, and by 1780 Americans had produced some 200,000 pounds of gunpowder—a small fraction of the amount needed, most of which came from abroad, but still an impressive achievement. The presence of German immigrants acquainted with the art of making gunpowder helped, as did the colonists' familiarity with watermills. Many gunpowder mills were converted gristmills—which resumed grinding grain when the war was over, assuming they hadn't blown up in the interim, as many did.

The colonies' impressive prerevolutionary production of iron was also a distinct asset. In the course of the war, American furnaces and forges, many of which were located in Maryland and western Pennsylvania, produced musket barrels, cannons, cannon and musket balls, and other military supplies. Among their products was an enormous iron chain, 500 yards long, with heavy links 2 to 3½ feet in length, that Americans stretched across a narrow point in the Hudson in April 1778 to keep enemy ships from sailing up the river. Most manufacturing of war supplies was done by hand, but in the largest gun manufactures waterwheels powered trip-hammers, grinding wheels, and boring machines. The Americans remained nonetheless dependent on European suppliers for most firearms as well as gunpowder and saltpeter for domestic gunpowder mills. The challenge of gathering an adequate volume of any weapons that required skilled craftsmanship was so great that at one point Benjamin Franklin, the very symbol of American inventiveness, suggested that pikes (pointed stakes) and bows and arrows should become the standard American weapons. The way a nation fights reflects its state of economic and managerial development, and the United States in 1776 was a decidedly undeveloped nation.

By late 1776, the high hopes that first greeted the riflemen at Cambridge had passed, and the army began phasing them out in favor of musketmen. To use musketmen most effectively required training so they could shoot volleys of fire in disciplined formation. But careful training made little sense unless men would remain in the army from one campaign to another. That was, of course, what Washington wanted—a trained, regular army.

A contemporary drawing that shows an American soldier from the frontier, carrying a rifle and dressed in buckskin with a tomahawk stuck in his belt. Note the black British soldier on the left; both he and the soldier beside him are carrying muskets with bayonets attached.

1777: A REVERSAL OF FORTUNE

The British planned a major military campaign again in 1777. Lord George Germain, who had become the king's American secretary in 1775, approved plans for an expedition from Canada down to the Hudson under General John Burgoyne, which would be met by an upriver campaign under Howe. Then, with control of the same western water route that Benedict Arnold and Ethan Allen had tried to secure for the Americans in 1775, the British could seal radical New England off from the rest of the country. Germain also approved a proposal by Howe that he take Philadelphia, which the secretary assumed could be done quickly, freeing Howe for his rally with Burgoyne.

In the campaign of 1777, the British learned that they, too, faced some powerful disadvantages. In earlier wars, they were able to depend on the colonists for food and vehicles such as carts and wagons. Now the army's supplies had to be shipped from England across the Atlantic, where vessels were frequently picked off by privateers or blown to the West Indies. Administrative inefficiency also took its toll: various snafus in England delayed the arrival of supplies for the 1777 campaign until late in the fighting season. Then Howe, suddenly wary of Washington's troops, decided that rather than risk attacks on a marching army, he would sail to Philadelphia. He set out from Manhattan on July 23 with 15,000 men (leaving another 7,300 there under the command of General Henry Clinton), sailed down the Atlantic past the Delaware Bay, then turned up the Chesapeake. He finally landed on August 25 some 50 miles southwest of Philadelphia, which was about 100 miles from where he began. Given prevailing winds, Howe had traveled the equivalent of 1,000 miles, losing precious time in the process. On September 11, however, he defeated the Continentals at Brandywine Creek, where Washington tried to block British access to Philadelphia. Once again the Second Continental Congress, which had returned to Philadelphia in March, fled its capital, this time to Lancaster and then York, Pennsylvania.

The British took Philadelphia on September 26 and put down an American counteroffensive at Germantown on October 4. They remained in Philadelphia through the winter of 1777–78, dancing, feasting, and enjoying a fine social season, since it was much too late to get back for their appointment with General Burgoyne on the Hudson. Howe, it seems, was never all that anxious to make the rendezvous, anyway. Did he fear enhancing the record of a potential rival within the British officer corps? Or was it just another example of his usual hesitation to move decisively against the Americans? After the Battle of Brooklyn Heights, and again later in 1776, when Washington was dragging his way down New Jersey, Howe failed to attack the vulnerable Continentals. The Crown had commissioned the Howe brothers as peace negotiators—a role Congress gave them little chance to exercise—as well as military commanders. Did they think that a vigorous execution of the war would make peace even less likely? Did they feel some lingering affection for the Americans, who had paid great honor to their elder brother, a British officer beloved by the colonists, who had died in the French and Indian War? Or was General Howe simply being prudent, refusing to risk his army since its men themselves and virtually all their supplies had to be supplied from England at enormous cost? Whatever the reason, Howe's inaction might well have cost the British victory in 1776 and 1777, when their chances of putting down the American "rebellion" were far better than in the years to come.

General John ("Gentleman Johnny") Burgoyne, as portrayed by Sir Joshua Reynolds eleven years before Burgoyne surrendered to the Americans at Saratoga, New York, in October 1777.

Meanwhile, poor John Burgoyne was learning the hard way that Britain's military advantages nosedived once they moved inland, away from the sea and other major water routes. In mid-June, the general set out from Canada with about 7,700 men, including Canadians and Indians as well as British and German troops. Burgoyne did not travel light: with his troops came some 2,000 women and children as well as 1,500 horses, many of which were needed to pull a large and cumbersome baggage train that included 30 wagons for the personal necessities of "Gentlemen Johnny"—silver service, various changes of uniform, cases of his preferred champagne. The contingent at first moved south by boat, taking Fort Ticonderoga with its large store of gunpowder and supplies in early July. Then, after fighting off a group of Americans at Hubbardston, Vermont, he took Skenesborough, where he settled in for three weeks, apparently feeling delight at his progress and little concern for the future. Burgoyne decided to advance not by returning north to Ticonderoga and sailing down Lake George, but by a land route that, it turned out, required hacking his way through thick woods, building bridges so his wagons could cross creeks, even constructing an extensive wooden causeway. The Americans countered by toppling trees across Burgoyne's path, slowing him to a snail's pace and complicating the arrival of supplies.

The general's Indian allies made things even worse. On July 27, 1777, they shot, stripped, and scalped young Jane McCrea, the fiancée of a Loyalist soldier. That news alarmed Americans, who feared for the safety of their own families, particularly after Burgoyne failed to punish the murderers. He had, in fact, rigidly forbidden the Indians to engage in atrocities, but feared that reprisals would alienate his Indian allies. Thereafter, local militiamen rushed to join the fight in defense of home and hearth, multiplying the number of men Burgoyne faced. As the balance of forces shifted, Burgoyne's Indians, who were no fools, gradually chose discretion over valor and slipped away from the British camp, turning the odds even more radically against the king's forces.

Burgoyne's first military setback came at Bennington, Vermont, where he sent a contingent of soldiers to capture some badly needed supplies. American troops, mostly militiamen under General John Stark, put an end to the attack on August 16, killing or taking prisoner all 700 men in the initial British detachment and a third of the additional 650 soldiers Burgoyne sent when he learned that things were not going well. Burgoyne then crossed to the western side of the Hudson and tried to move south toward Albany, but found his route blocked by American entrenchments at Bemis Heights, New York. He attempted to break through, but on September 19 Benedict Arnold and Daniel Morgan attacked the British line at Freeman's Farm. Burgoyne lost 556 men to the Americans' 280, then pulled back. Help from New York failed to reach him: General Clinton had started up the Hudson with 3,000 men on October 3, but rather than push on past Esopus (now Kingston, New York), he returned to Manhattan for reinforcements. Four days later, Burgoyne advanced on the Americans, but lost 600 more men and was thrown back toward Bemis Heights when Arnold, who had been relieved of his command by General Horatio Gates, his jealous superior officer, nonetheless rushed forward, leading an American charge that saved the day. At that moment, Arnold, who suffered a serious leg wound in the engagement, seemed destined to become one of the great military heroes of the American war.

Burgoyne retreated seven miles north to Saratoga, New York. But his cause had become hopeless: the Americans already outnumbered his men by 3 to 1, and day by day their forces grew while his dwindled. Finally, on October 17, Burgoyne surrendered. His remaining 5,700 men laid down their arms and, under the terms Burgoyne negotiated, would be sent back to England and take no further part in the war.

The American triumph at Saratoga transformed the war because it led directly to an American alliance with France. The French court, determined to weaken its traditional enemy, Great Britain, had sent secret aid to the Americans even before they declared their independence. However, France hesitated to conclude a formal alliance in 1776, when a succession of military defeats brought the survival of the American cause into question. But in December 1777, after news of Saratoga arrived, French officials told the American envoys in Paris that France had decided to recognize American independence. Negotiations began in January, and on February 6, 1778, French and American representatives in Paris signed three agreements. By the first, a treaty of amity and commerce, France recognized American independence, and in return, the Americans granted France certain trading privileges. By the second, a treaty of alliance, France agreed to fight with the Americans in "common cause" if and when war broke out between France and Britain and to continue engaged until American independence was assured. The United States was left free to conquer Canada and Bermuda. France could seize the British West Indies, but promised to take no territory on the North American mainland. Both countries agreed not to conclude peace with Britain without the other's consent, and the alliance would continue "forever." The third agreement, which was secret, allowed Spain to enter the alliance.

In April 1778, in a desperate effort to forestall American ratification of the treaties, the British ministry introduced into Parliament a series of measures designed to provide the basis for reconciliation, then appointed the Earl of Carlisle to head a peace commission authorized, as earlier efforts were not, to negotiate with Congress. The terms—repeal of the Tea and Coercive Acts, a parliamentary promise not to tax the Americans, the possibility of suspending all other objectionable laws passed since 1763—might have worked a few years earlier, but not then. On June 17, Congress replied to the Carlisle Commission's request for a conference by saying that it would consider only an agreement for the withdrawal of British troops from America and British recognition of American independence. A few days earlier, an engagement between French and British ships near Ushant, an island off the coast of Brittany, had led to war, so France joined with the Americans in their struggle for independence. Another year would pass before Spain entered the war; but Spain, anxious about her own colonial possessions, refused to recognize American independence. In fact, Spanish participation in the war was less significant than that of France, which made all the difference for the American cause.

General George Washington and his generals at Yorktown. The American artist Charles Willson Peale did the painting in 1781 soon after the decisive Battle of Yorktown.

The Franco-American alliance dramatically reduced British chances of victory in America. No longer could the British concentrate their forces there, as they had done at New York in 1776: they now had an enemy nearer home and also had to defend Bermuda and British colonies in the Caribbean. Moreover, the enlistment of the French navy on the American side robbed Britain of what had been a considerable military advantage. In the past, the British, with virtually uncontested control of the American Atlantic coast, had little trouble holding American ports—indeed, in the course of the war, they held every major American port at one time or another—but experienced great difficulty controlling territory in the interior. If that situation had continued, the war would probably have ended with a negotiated peace by which, in one way or another, the Americans would return under Crown rule. The French navy made possible an American victory that would confirm independence and allow a continuation of the republican political revolution that accompanied it.

THE ROAD TO YORKTOWN

In 1778, the British government assessed the changed situation and adopted a third plan of war, one distinctly different from those of 1775 and 1776. It decided to cut its commitments in the North, evacuating Philadelphia and using its bases at New York and Newport to mount attacks at various points along the Atlantic coast to break the will of the "rebels." The Crown also encouraged its Indian allies to mount deadly raids on the western frontier.

In 1776, the Declaration of Independence had accused the king of having "endeavoured to bring on the inhabitants of our frontiers, the merciless Indian Savages, whose known rule of warfare, is an undistinguished destruction of all ages, sexes and conditions." Now frontier regions from New York south suffered devastating violence in which both sides were guilty of the "undistinguished destruction of all ages, sexes, and conditions." George Rogers Clark, an Indian-hating Kentuckian whom the Virginia legislature sent west in 1778 to defend its frontier, imitated the Indians he fought, dressing in a hunting shirt and breech cloth, blackening his face, and inspiring his men by shouting out a war whoop. Clark demonstrated his ruthlessness by publicly tomahawking to death Indian prisoners within sight of the British garrison under siege at Vincennes in the Illinois Country. Raids in western New York under General John Sullivan destroyed Indian crops, cut down fruit trees, and burned towns, forcing thousands of hungry Iroquois to seek refuge during the winter of 1777–78 with the British at Fort Niagara. Not all Indians sided with the British, but American frontier fighters

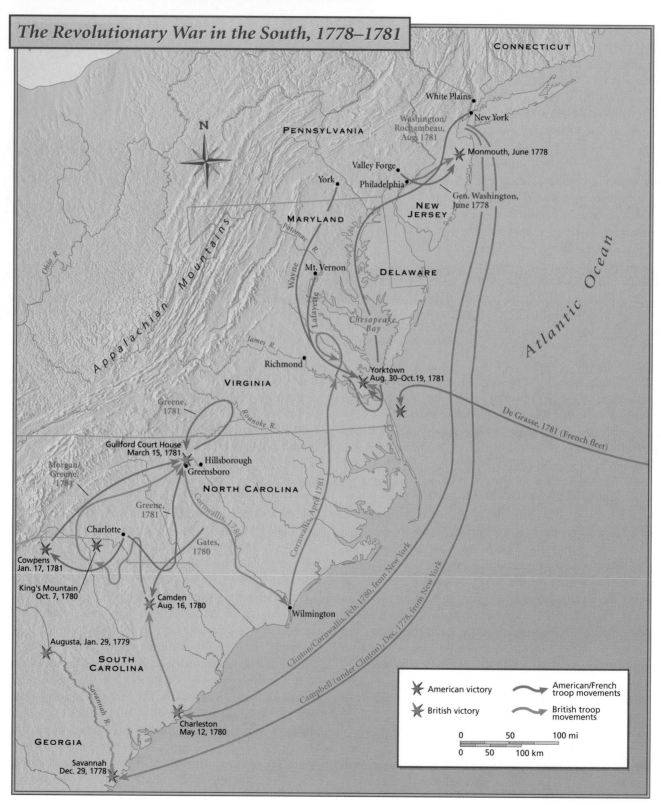

The Revolutionary War in the South, 1778–1781

CONNECTICUT

White Plains

New York

Washington/
Rochambeau,
Aug. 1781

PENNSYLVANIA

Monmouth, June 1778

Valley Forge

York

Philadelphia

Gen. Washington,
June 1778

NEW
JERSEY

MARYLAND

Potomac R.

DELAWARE

Wayne

Mt. Vernon

Lafayette

Chesapeake
Bay

Ohio R.

James R.

Richmond

Yorktown
Aug. 30–Oct.19, 1781

VIRGINIA

Appalachian Mountains

Greene,
1781

Roanoke R.

De Grasse, 1781 (French fleet)

Guilford Court House
March 15, 1781

Hillsborough

Greensboro

Morgan/
Greene,
1781

NORTH CAROLINA

Cornwallis 1781

Greene,
1781

Cornwallis, April 1781

Charlotte

Gates,
1780

Cowpens
Jan. 17, 1781

King's Mountain
Oct. 7, 1780

Camden
Aug. 16, 1780

Wilmington

Clinton/Cornwallis, Feb. 1780, from New York

Augusta, Jan. 29, 1779

SOUTH
CAROLINA

Savannah R.

Campbell (under Clinton) Dec. 1778, from New York

Charleston
May 12, 1780

GEORGIA

Savannah
Dec. 29, 1778

Atlantic Ocean

Legend

✶ American victory

✶ British victory

American/French
troop movements

British troop
movements

| 0 | 50 | 100 mi |
| 0 | 50 | 100 km |

found it hard to distinguish one Indian from another: in 1782, for example, militiamen murdered ninety-six men, women, and children at the Delaware town of Gnadenhuetten, all of whom were Moravian Christians and determinedly neutral in the Anglo-American war. Indian raiders were no kinder. Neither side held a monopoly on savagery; neither sought anything short of the enemy's total destruction.

The main British objective after 1778 was, however, not the West but the South, where it expected substantial Loyalist support. If New England and the middle colonies were lost, perhaps the Crown could at least salvage this part of its American empire. The South seemed the most vulnerable part of the United States, divided as it was into slave and free, and with white colonists along the Tidewater often at odds (and even, as for a time in North Carolina, at war) with those in the interior. The British also tried to apply a lesson they had learned during earlier campaigns in the North. Victory in this war required more than defeating the enemy on the battlefield and taking nominal control of territory. It demanded winning and holding the allegiance of the people in territories Britain hoped to retain.

King George marked the change in strategy by replacing William Howe as head of the British forces in America with Sir Henry Clinton, the third general to hold that position since the war began. By contrast, the American army still remained under its first commander, George Washington. His bedraggled 11,000 soldiers—2,000 of them without shoes—spent the cold and snowy winter of 1777–78 at Valley Forge, eighteen miles northwest of Philadelphia, where Howe was waiting out the season in comfort. A breakdown of the American supply system left men at Valley Forge without inadequate food or clothing, and huddled in what the twenty-year-old Marquis de Lafayette, one of an important set of Europeans who joined the American fight, described as "little shanties." Perhaps a quarter left or died in the course of that winter; but those who stayed and survived were better prepared for combat as a result of their rigorous drilling under the command of "Baron" Frederick von Steuben, a Prussian and onetime aide-de-camp of Frederick the Great, who arrived at the camp in February.

Von Steuben's impact became clear in June 1778, when Washington broke camp to pursue Clinton, who evacuated Philadelphia on the 18th and began marching across New Jersey toward New York City. General Charles Lee, who had been freed in exchange for British prisoners and returned to military service in May, attacked the British at Monmouth (New Jersey) Court House on June 28, then strangely ordered a retreat, for which he was subsequently court-martialed. Washington was able to rally the men, who then stood their ground through repeated attacks. In the end, Clinton escaped, and Washington marched his men north back to White Plains, New York. But the Continental soldiers' performance had given the commander reason for satisfaction.

Not much else went right. An effort to retake Newport by a coordinated action of Continental troops and the French fleet, which absorbed most of the summer of 1778, failed. The following December, Clinton took Savannah and, a month later, Augusta, Georgia. In October 1779, he evacuated Rhode Island further to concentrate his forces in the South, and in May 1780 finally seized Charleston and, with it, a 5,400-man American garrison under General Benjamin Lincoln. Then Clinton returned north, leaving behind 8,000 British troops under Lord Cornwallis, confident that Georgia and South Carolina had essentially been rewon and that Cornwallis would easily take the upper South.

As Cornwallis seized new territory, the British organized Loyalist militia companies to assure continued submission to British rule. But once the British army left an area, supporters

American Commissioners of the Preliminary Peace Negotiations with Great Britain, an unfinished painting by Benjamin West (1782). From left, John Jay, John Adams, Benjamin Franklin, Henry Laurens, and Franklin's grandson William Temple Franklin.

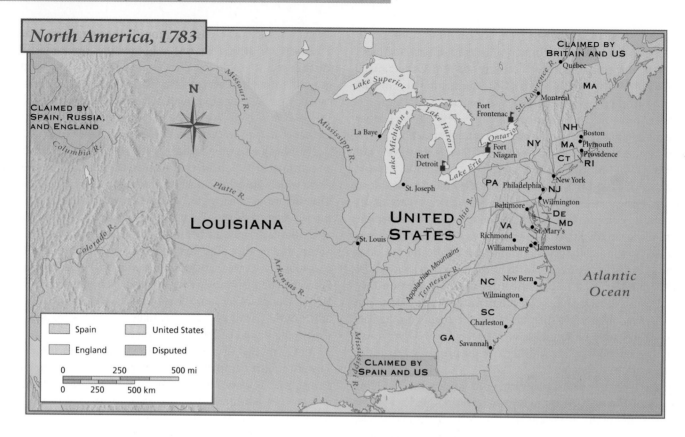

of the Revolution crawled out from the swamps and other hiding places and turned the war in the South into a bitter, nasty civil war, in which the lines of division sometimes echoed nothing more than long-standing local rivalries. Meanwhile, the British incapacity to control plundering and terrorism at the hands of British officers such as the hated Banastre Tarleton drove throngs of previously uncommitted persons into the American camp, which went far to undo Clinton's triumph.

In June 1780, Congress commissioned General Horatio Gates to lead a new American army in the South. But Gates's leadership (and army) soon came to an end at Camden, South Carolina, where in mid-August he lost almost 2,000 men (about 900 killed and another 1,000 captured); he personally fled all the way to Hillsboro, North Carolina, 160 miles away, his military career in tatters. Again there was no Continental army in the South, but the war continued nonetheless. During that bizarre, ugly, irregular phase of the fighting, American riflemen sometimes came into their own.

For example, at the Battle of King's Mountain, North Carolina, on October 7, 1780, the marksmanship of American frontiersmen led to the defeat of a 1,100-man Loyalist force. Meanwhile, Congress appointed General Nathaniel Greene to succeed Gates, and in December 1780 Greene began piecing together a third American army in the South.

Lacking the men to attack Cornwallis's camp, Greene used what resources he had to nibble away at the enemy. The American general Daniel Morgan cleverly employed "unreliable" militiamen at a battle near Cowpens, South Carolina, in January 1781, sending those "irregular" troops against Tarleton, then bringing up regulars to the redcoats' surprise as they chased the retreating militiamen. By spring, reinforcements enlarged Greene's army to 4,400. He technically lost the battle at Guilford Court House on March 15, where he applied a battle plan much like Morgan's at Cowpens, but Cornwallis's 500 casualties were so costly that he retreated to Wilmington, North Carolina, and then in April to Virginia, seeking reinforcements. There, Cornwallis could join forces with, strangely enough, Benedict Arnold. The previous fall, Arnold had conspired to deliver the American post at West Point, New York, to the British, but the plot was dramatically discovered in September 1780. Arnold escaped capture, made it to British lines, and thereafter fought for the king. Moved by resentments of real and imagined injustices, a man who had once seemed destined to become a great American military hero became instead the new nation's foremost traitor.

While Greene and a set of skillful subordinate officers gradually reclaimed most of South Carolina, Cornwallis swept through Virginia, almost capturing Governor Thomas Jefferson and the Virginia legislature at Charlottesville in June. Finally, seeking a place where he could receive reinforcements from Clinton in New York, Cornwallis settled in at Yorktown on the southern shore of the York River near the Chesapeake Bay.

When Washington learned that a French fleet under the Marquis de Grasse would be available for action in the Chesapeake between August and October, he saw his chance. With French ships in the bay preventing Clinton from sending support, Washington could move his forces to Cornwallis's rear, enclosing him in a trap. By early September 1781, de Grasse controlled the Chesapeake, and Washington and the Compte de Rochambeau, who commanded a French army of 5,000, moved rapidly to Virginia and began siege operations. By mid-October, Cornwallis's position at Yorktown was hopeless, and on the eighteenth he surrendered. Tradition has it that the next day, as the 8,000 captured British soldiers laid down their arms, a band played a British tune, "The World Turned Upside Down."

THE PEACE

There was no military reason for the war to end at Yorktown. The British still held Savannah, Charleston, and New York. But when news of Yorktown reached London on November 25, 1781, the king's minister, Lord North, exclaimed, "Oh God, it is all over." A restive Parliament and a nation tired of paying ever-increasing taxes to sustain an increasingly pointless war made it impossible to replace Cornwallis's army. In March 1782, North resigned his office, and his successor, Lord Rockingham—the same man who had orchestrated the repeal of the Stamp Act—opened peace negotiations. On Rockingham's death four months later, that responsibility fell to a ministry under the Earl of Shelburne, who had defended the Americans in parliamentary debates of early 1776.

The politics of peace were different from those of war. With Britain's empire effectively dismembered, the main French war objective had been realized. The Comte de Vergennes, the French minister who had negotiated the Franco-American alliance and now participated in negotiating the peace, had no interest in the creation of a strong American republic with capacious western lands. France, moreover, was obliged by an agreement with Spain to continue fighting until Spain won Gibralter. The United States had no particular obligations to Spain, and no interest whatsoever in delaying peace. But Congress had instructed its peace commissioners to agree to no terms without France's prior consent, as the alliance treaty specified.

The commissioners—John Adams, John Jay, and Benjamin Franklin, later joined by Henry Laurens—assessed the situation and decided to ignore those instructions. They signed preliminary articles of peace with Britain on November 30, 1782, then presented the terms to Vergennes as a fait accompli. In that way, they won British recognition of American independence and a generous territorial settlement by which the postwar United States extended south to the 31st parallel (the northern border of Florida), which reverted from British to Spanish control, and west to the Mississippi, except for New Orleans, which remained in Spanish hands. Congress promised to recommend that the states treat Loyalists fairly, and to honor its debts. The final peace treaty was signed at Paris on September 3, 1783, and ratified by Congress on January 14, 1784.

The trans-Appalachian West, whose delivery to "British liberty" New England's clergymen had celebrated some twenty years before, became part of the United States. Would American rule lead, at last, to an era of unprecedented growth, with "towns enlarged, settlements increased, and this howling wilderness become a fruitful field which the Lord hath blessed"? The havoc left in the West by a war far more brutal than tradition recalls made fulfillment of that expansionist dream more likely. The once-powerful Iroquois confederation, long an obstacle to the westward movement, was

> *"The great losers in the American war for independence were not the British, who went on to build another empire, but the Indians, who had nowhere else to go."*

1765	Parliament passes the Stamp Act (repealed March 1766).
1767	The Townshend Revenue Acts.
December 16, 1773	The Boston Tea Party.
1774	Parliament passes the Coercive, or "Intolerable," Acts.
September 5, 1774	The First Continental Congress convenes in Philadelphia.
April 19, 1775	The Revolutionary War begins with the Battles of Lexington and Concord.
May 10, 1775	The Second Continental Congress convenes.
July 4, 1776	Congress approves the Declaration of Independence.
October 17, 1777	Burgoyne surrenders at Saratoga.
February 6, 1778	France sides with the colonies against Britain.
October 18, 1781	Cornwallis surrenders at Yorktown.
1783	Treaty of Paris: British recognize American independence, and trans-Appalachian West becomes part of United States.

Chronology

Suggested Reading

John Richard Alden, *The American Revolution, 1775–1783* (1954)

Bernard Bailyn, *Ideological Origins of the American Revolution* (1992)

M. L. Brown, *Firearms in Colonial America: The Impact on History and Technology, 1492–1792* (1980)

Merrill Jensen, *The Founding of a Nation: A History of the American Revolution, 1763–1776* (1968)

Pauline Maier, *From Resistance to Revolution: American Radicals and the Development of Intercolonial Opposition to Britain, 1765–1776* (1972), and *American Scripture: Making the Declaration of Independence* (1997)

Jerilyn Greene Marston, *King and Congress: The Transfer of Political Legitimacy, 1774–1776* (1987)

Jack N. Rakove, *The Beginnings of National Politics: An Interpretive History of the Continental Congress* (1979)

Charles R. Ritcheson, *British Politics and the American Revolution* (1964)

John Shy, *A People Numerous and Armed: Reflections on the Military Struggle for American Independence* (1990)

now divided in two, with a Loyalist segment in Ontario and another in the state of New York. Elsewhere, too, devastation destroyed old ruling structures and scattered Indian peoples far from their familiar homelands, with ripple effects that extended all the way to the lands of the Comanches and Apaches far to the southwest. The great losers in the American war for independence were not the British, who went on to build another empire, but the Indians, who had nowhere else to go.

QUESTIONS

■ **What were the political innovations embodied in the first state constitutions?**

■ **What were the advances and limits to social change in the years after the Revolution?**

■ **What were the important economic innovations of the 1780s?**

The Anglo-American war was not itself revolutionary. Except for the attacks on British soldiers as they marched from Concord to Boston on April 19, 1775, and the irregular fighting later in the South and the West, the Americans fought in the traditional way that General Washington preferred, depending primarily on a regular army. And they finally won, at Yorktown, with a conventional siege operation.

Not that there was a lack of interest in innovative military techniques or devices. In 1777, the Second Continental Congress asked the states to forward information on any "discoveries and improvements in the arts of war." David Bushnell of Connecticut, a farm boy and Yale graduate given to tinkering, devised an ingenious "Turtle," a primitive submarine propelled by foot-driven paddles, with which he planned to fire torpedoes—which he also developed—into the bottoms of British ships. But nothing came of the idea, nor, it seems, of other clever proposals, except perhaps for the chains and other obstacles employed to block British ships from American rivers. Even standard military tasks such as designing forts and breastworks or river defense systems were challenging for the Americans because they lacked military engineers, having relied on the British for that service in previous wars. With the arrival in 1777 of European engineers such as Thaddeus Kosciuszko and Philippe Charles Tronson du Coudray, that problem was partially overcome. Their coming coincided with Baron von Steuben's effort to teach Continental soldiers drill routines adapted from Prussian precedents. In one way after another, Americans struggled to approximate European military standards. Improving on those standards lay well beyond their capacity.

Meanwhile, the war checked Americans' emerging strength in science. Earlier promising trends peaked in 1768 with the establishment of the American Philosophical Society in Philadelphia. The first volume of the society's *Transactions* (1771), which reported Americans' remarkably accurate observations of the 1769 transit of Venus across the sun, won extensive acclaim in Europe. Later, John Adams proposed the founding of a sister society in Boston. The American Academy of Arts and Sciences, chartered by the Massachusetts legislature in 1780, published the first volume of its *Memoirs*—the French-inspired name was a sign of the times—three years later. In the meantime, however, the American Philosophical Society, and American science in general, had sunk into a certain lassitude. The problem lay partly in the deaths of prominent figures such as John Bartram (1777) and Harvard Professor John Winthrop (1779). A handful of others, including Charleston's Alexander Garden and one of the most promising members of the next generation, Benjamin Thompson, from Rumford (now Concord), New Hampshire, became Loyalist exiles; Thompson—later Count Rumford—did virtually all of his scientific work, including pioneering studies on the nature of heat, abroad. However, several distinguished American scientists became absorbed in activities on behalf of the American cause. They included Pennsylvania's young David Rittenhouse, a clock maker and self-taught Newtonian remembered mainly for the orreries—mechanical devices that accurately represent the motion of planets around the sun—he constructed in the 1770s, and Benjamin Franklin, the dean of American scientists. When Franklin wasn't representing the United States abroad, he sat in the Second Continental Congress, presided over the convention that designed Pennsylvania's constitution of 1776 (which Rittenhouse also attended), and later, after returning from France, participated in the federal Constitutional Convention.

The creation of a workable republic became, in fact, the most fascinating challenge of the age, a form of innovation that outdistanced all others. "You and I, dear friend," John Adams wrote the Virginian George Wythe in 1776, "have been sent into life at a time when the greatest lawgivers of antiquity would have wished to live. How few of the human race have ever enjoyed an opportunity of making an election of government, more than of air, soil, or climate, for themselves or their children! When, before the present epocha, had three millions of people full power and a fair opportunity to form and establish the wisest and happiest government that human wisdom can contrive?" His friend Thomas Jefferson was in full agreement. The creation of a good government was, Jefferson said, "the whole object of the present controversy," and a task so interesting that every individual would want to have a say in it.

In the end, Americans' contributions to the science of government transformed the independence movement into a revolution. Years later, in *The Rights of Man*, Thomas Paine concluded that "the independence of America, considered merely as a separation from England, would have been a matter of but little importance." The Americans' struggle with Britain acquired broad historical significance only because it was "accompanied by a revolution in the principles and practise of governments." The Revolution also set in motion social and economic transformations whose effects would be felt far into the future. In those ways, too, the American Revolution became a revolution in the modern sense of the word, not an occurrence that moved a people back along a cyclical path like the revolution of the sun or the moon, which the word previously implied, but a traumatic event that shifted the course of history in a radically new direction.

The first steps toward revolutionary change—institutional, social, and economic—occurred within the several states, since it was there that power rested once Americans cut loose from Britain.

> *"'You and I, dear friend,' John Adams wrote the Virginian George Wythe in 1776, 'have been sent into life at a time when the greatest lawgivers of antiquity would have wished to live. . . . When, before the present epocha, had three millions of people full power and a fair opportunity to form and establish the wisest and happiest government that human wisdom can contrive?"*

rate document South Carolina adopted the following March. Both of those states' new governments were emergency measures, created to preserve "peace and good order" and provide for the people's security until, as New Hampshire put it, the "present unhappy and unnatural contest with Great Britain" was settled.

In the meantime, colonists there and in other states where royal authority collapsed discovered that self-government had unexpected charms. No longer were Americans forbidden to trade in markets or manufacture goods when they competed with the mother country. And no longer did they have to endure royal governors who were ignorant of their laws and interests, answerable to the Crown alone, and against whom redress was impossible, as South Carolina's chief justice, William Henry Drayton, put it in April 1776, "by any peaceable means." In South Carolina, the people could choose officials from among themselves and raise "the poorest man" to the highest office if he had "virtue and merit." Even the makeshift government that Congress suggested for Massachusetts back in June 1775, with an assembly and council organized according to its charter of 1691 but no royal governor, a government entirely under the control of the people, seemed by early 1776 "more free and happy" than the government of their ancestors. Suddenly, and surprisingly, the colonists discovered that the persons best qualified to govern them were themselves.

That was, of course, the message of Thomas Paine's *Common Sense*. Until the colonists shook off monarchy and hereditary rule and placed power in republican institutions that depended on popular choice, Paine argued, they would find no lasting peace or freedom. Republics, however, were by no means problem-free. By reputation, they were prone to "tumult and riot" (if the people rule, who will be ruled?) and had a nasty habit of giving way to despotism as people embraced strong leaders to end the disorder. None of the great republics of the past—those of Rome or Athens or England's own Commonwealth of the 1650s—had survived, which gave reason for pause. But as the war persisted, grievances mounted, and reconciliation came to seem an impossible dream, it became increasingly difficult to maintain civil authority

The First State Constitutions, 1776–1780

 The process of redesigning government began with the very short constitution New Hampshire implemented in January 1776 and the more elabounder the makeshift, part-legal, part-revolutionary governments in place. That was why, in its resolutions of May 10 and 15, 1776, the Second Continental Congress recommended that colonies in which "no government sufficient to the exigencies of their affairs has been hitherto established" break with the past and "adopt such government as shall, in the opinion of the representatives of the people, best conduce to the happiness and safety of their constituents in particular and America in general." In the months that followed, the people of one state after another began designing new governments for themselves and their children.

On May 15, 1776, the same day that Congress finally approved its resolutions on government, the Virginia convention (the state's revolutionary legislature) authorized the preparation of a Declaration of Rights and "a plan of government . . . to maintain peace and order in this Colony, and secure substantial and equal liberty to the people." George Mason drafted the declaration, which the convention revised and then adopted on June 12. Finally, on June 29, the convention enacted a constitution that, unlike its predecessors in New Hampshire and South Carolina, was permanent (that is, it was to continue indefinitely, until the people chose to replace it). In fact, the preamble to the Virginia constitution, written by Thomas Jefferson, formally declared the state independent of Britain, which gave Virginia a short jump on Congress.

Before the "United States in Congress Assembled" finally declared independence, New Jersey also produced a new constitution, and other states followed. In the course of 1776, all but three states either wrote new constitutions or, in the cases of Connecticut and Rhode Island, adjusted their colonial charters to fit more exactly an independent republic. Then, in 1777, New York and Georgia adopted new constitutions. So did Vermont, which was trying to break off from New York and become the fourteenth state—an ambition it would not realize until fourteen years later. Finally, in 1780, Massachusetts enacted the last of the first state constitutions and, by common consent, the best of the lot, in part because Massa-

An 1800 portrait (artist unknown) of Thomas Paine, author of *Common Sense*.

chusetts could draw on the experience of others. Before long, states began replacing their first, flawed efforts: South Carolina, for example, replaced its constitution of 1776 in 1780, New Hampshire in 1784, Pennsylvania in 1789.

The fact that men were creating the governments that would bind them was, as John Adams noted, itself remarkable. The details of how they executed that task are even more fascinating. The first constitutions included an array of peculiar devices: electoral colleges, vetoes that could be overridden, limits on terms in office, councils of one

This portrait of John Adams was done by Benjamin Blythe at Salem in 1766, when Adams was at the start of his long political career. It is the earliest known portrait of Adams.

sort or another. In the course of a few short years, the variety declined; patterns emerged, and certain solutions to nagging institutional problems won an enduring place in American government. The states served as a laboratory for the nation as a whole: in 1787, a federal constitution would be built in good part from state precedents. But the governments established for the states remained important in themselves, since the states were by far the more powerful agencies of government. It was they who made most of the decisions that shaped and regulated Americans' day-to-day lives. And so it would remain on into the twentieth century.

THE PROBLEM OF DESIGN: SIMPLE OR COMPLEX?

The first problem confronted by state constitution writers was one of basic design. Should governments be simple or complex, with constituent parts that were separated and balanced against one another? Britain's unwritten constitution, for example, distributed power among the king, House of Lords, and House of Commons, each of which represented a component of British society—the monarch, aristocracy, and people. On critical issues, such as collecting taxes or maintaining an army, no one part of government could act without the consent of the others, which explained, according to the wisdom of the time, why liberty survived in the British world.

Thomas Paine disagreed. "The Constitution of England is so exceedingly complex," he wrote in *Common Sense,* "that the nation may suffer for years without being able to discover in which part the fault lies." His concept of good government came from what he described as "a principle in nature which no art can overturn, viz. that the more simple any thing is, the less liable it is to be disordered, and the easier repaired when disordered." There Paine, an enthusiast of popular science who would later claim fame for designing an iron bridge, revealed the technical bent of his mind: the rule he stated remains today a basic principle of engineering known as the "kiss" rule (Keep it simple, stupid). Two of the three parts of the British constitution—the king and Lords—represented for him "*constitutional errors*" that contributed nothing but trouble to British freedom. What liberty Britons had, he said, was due to the republican part of their constitution, the elected House of Commons, and the "Constitution of England" was "sickly" because the Crown had corrupted and now controlled the Commons, as it always would if it got the chance. It was best, then, to get rid of monarchy and, for good measure, any equivalent of the House of Lords, and to build anew on a republican, or popular, base. Paine's proposal for state government was simple in the extreme: it consisted of an annually elected assembly with a "president only," that is, a presiding officer. He added that representation in the assemblies should be equal, their business "wholly domestic," that is, confined to matters internal to the state, and that they should be subject to the authority of a Continental Congress.

John Adams was appalled. By its "crude, ignorant Notion of a Government by one assembly," he lamented, *Common Sense* would "do more Mischief . . . than all the Tory Writings together." Paine was a powerful writer, but he remained "very ignorant of the Science of Government." Adams explained his own position in *Thoughts on Government* (1776). If all the powers of government were entrusted to one body of men, he said, it would become too powerful and in time would "not scruple to exempt itself from the burdens which it will lay without compunction on its constituents." It would also become ambitious and, in time, vote itself perpetual. Moreover, no single body was competent to exercise all the powers of government. An assembly couldn't be an effective executive because it was too cumbersome and open; it couldn't be a judiciary because it was "too numerous, too slow, and too unskilled in the laws."

Adams agreed that there was "no good government but what is republican," but he believed that a single, all-powerful assembly such as Paine proposed would make, execute, and enforce laws arbitrarily, to serve the interests of its members. The powers of a republic had to be more carefully arranged to assure "an impartial and exact execution of the laws." Under the scheme of government Adams proposed, the people would annually elect a lower house of assembly, which should be "in miniature an exact portrait of the people at large." The assembly would then choose an upper house, or council. Those two parts of the legislature would together elect a governor, also annually, who would be able to act on his "free and independent" judgment. The governor could nominate and appoint other government officials including judges, and he could veto acts of the legislature, although his implementation of those powers might require the advice and consent of a "privy council" of advisers. To assure that the judiciary remained independent, Adams insisted that judges be given fixed salaries and hold office during good behavior—that is, indefinitely.

The rough plans of government that Paine and Adams threw out for discussion in 1776 provided stark alternatives that had rough counterparts in the state constitutions actually adopted. At first, the simple "Paineite" model won out, which made sense given Americans' experience. In most colonies, governors had represented an alien power, answerable to the king. Although there were some popular royal governors, the likes of Virginia's Lord Dunmore or Thomas Hutchinson of Massachusetts came more quickly to mind in the mid-1770s, so it seemed best to eliminate powerful, independent executives. The Crown also appointed the members of most colonial upper houses, which meant that the lower houses of assembly were the only institution of provincial government elected by and responsible to the people. Moreover, in the immediate past, after royal governments had collapsed, many states were governed with reasonable success by assemblies or congresses or conventions that consisted of an elected body of delegates with a presiding officer. As a result, although no state simply enacted Paine's model government, the constitutions states adopted in 1776 tended to entrust power to elected assemblies and either to eliminate separate executives or to hamstring their power.

> *"The states served as a laboratory for the nation as a whole: in 1787, a federal constitution would be built in good part from state precedents."*

That was the case even where constitutions established an apparently complex set of institutions not so different from Adams's plan. Take the Virginia constitution of 1776. Under its terms, the people elected annually a House of Delegates from the resident freeholders of counties and towns. The people also elected an upper house, or "senate"—a word borrowed from the American republic's Roman ancestor—from the resident freeholders of twenty-four special districts. Senators had to be twenty-five years of age or older and, unlike members of the House of Delegates, held office for four years. The House of Delegates and senate together were called the General Assembly, which the constitution described as a "complete Legislature." The governor was elected by the General Assembly, as were almost all other executive officers as well as the judges of various state courts.

Virginia's governor was kept on a short leash: he had to be reelected each year, and after three years in office was disqualified for four years. The purpose of that provision, known as rotation in office, was, as the Virginia Declaration of Rights explained, to restrain public officials from oppression by returning them for fixed periods to a "private station," where they would share and so feel "the burdens of the people." The governor's powers were also severely limited. He could not prorogue or dissolve the assembly, nor could he make appointments as royal governors had done. To exercise what executive powers he possessed required the consent of a Council

Portrait of Thomas Jefferson by Charles Willson Peale (c. 1791).

of State whose eight members were, again, chosen by the assembly and could hold office for no more than three years out of six. With all those restrictions, it's hard to see the governor as a threat to anything. But just in case, the constitution gave the assembly power to impeach him. It could also impeach judges accused of "mal-administration, corruption," or other acts "by which the safety of the State may be endangered."

The Virginia constitution placed so much power in the General Assembly that it was subject to the same objections Adams had raised to Paine's plan of government. Thomas Jefferson complained that in Virginia "all the powers of government, legislative, executive, and judiciary," were invested in the legislature, which was "precisely the definition of despotic government." And despotism, Jefferson said, would be as oppressive in the hands of 173 men—the number of Virginians in the General Assembly—as in those of one.

Pennsylvania offered an even clearer example of an unbalanced government. The Continental Congress's resolutions of May 10 and 15 were designed specifically to bring down the old elitist, proprietary government of Pennsylvania, which stood determinedly against independence, and to enfranchise the Philadelphia artisans and backcountry farmers who were ardent opponents of Britain. The resolutions succeeded: the old government fell; Pennsylvania voted for independence and began the process of writing a new, republican state constitution, which it adopted in September 1776. That "radical" constitution placed power firmly in a unicameral (single-chamber) legislature like that Paine had prescribed—but in truth, Pennsylvania had a unicameral legislature through most of the eighteenth century, so the change was less dramatic than it might seem. Members of the new assembly were annually elected by an unusually broad electorate consisting of male taxpayers resident in the state for at least one year. The assembly then chose a council, which was the closest Pennsylvania came to an executive power. No plural executive can act with the effectiveness of a single person, and the Pennsylvania Council was so weak

Thomas Jefferson's pencil drawing of the Virginia Capitol's front elevation, which he did around 1785.

that it couldn't even elect its own presiding officer without the assembly butting in.

The only real check on the Pennsylvania Assembly was the people—and their countervailing force was extraordinarily powerful. Assemblymen came up for reelection every year, and could serve only four years out of seven. All votes were public, and the assembly's sessions were normally open to the public. The assembly, moreover, could not enact laws in a single session: an election had to intervene between their introduction and enactment so the people could have their say. Pennsylvania, in short, gave the assembly what power it was willing to entrust to government, but its constitution of 1776 came close to creating a direct democracy (rule directly by the people). And the Pennsylvania constitution was influential: in 1777, both Vermont and Georgia based their constitutions on the Pennsylvania model.

It took time to unlearn the experience of the past—to realize that the people could rule through institutions other than assemblies, that governors in a republic need not be as dangerous as those appointed by a king, that there were ways of separating and balancing powers that did not simply mimic Britain. After a time, Americans turned toward more complex governments in which power was, as Jefferson (and Adams) advocated, "so divided and balanced among several bodies of magistracy, as that no one could transcend their legal limits without being effectually checked and restrained by the others." The New York constitution of 1777, for example, set up an assembly and senate, which together, as in Virginia, constituted the colony's legislature, and also a governor. Since the people directly elected all three units of government, each was supported by an independent base of power. Assemblymen came up for election every year, but senators were elected to a four-year term, and the governor held office for three years before facing the electorate again. New York's governor wielded far more power than his counterpart in Virginia: he could command the state's armed forces, convene the legislature and also prorogue it for limited periods, and recommend acts of legislation. He could also veto laws "inconsistent with the spirit of this constitution, or with the public good"—acting there in conjunction with a Council of Revision—although his vetoes could be overridden by a two-thirds vote of the legislature. With a Council of Appointment, he could make appointments, including that of judges to the state supreme court. Those pesky councils showed that confidence in executive power was not entirely restored. Still, New York went a long way toward building countervailing forces, or checks on power, into its government.

Massachusetts traveled farther down the same road. John Adams drafted the Massachusetts constitution of 1780, which was the last of the first state constitutions, and it suggests how his thinking had developed since 1776. Just the form indicated a certain documentary maturity. Where Pennsylvania's "Plan or Frame of Government" consisted of forty-eight numbered provisions, and Virginia's constitution of unnumbered provisions that were simply listed one after another, the Massachusetts constitution was broken down into chapters and sections and articles. Chapter I covered the legislative power, Chapter II the executive, Chapter III the judiciary, Chapter IV delegates to Congress. Two additional chapters provided for Harvard College, the "U. Mass." of its time, and various other miscellaneous issues. The constitution invested power in an assembly elected by the towns, a senate elected from special districts set up according to the proportion of public taxes residents paid, and a governor, all of whom were elected annually. The governor had to act in conjunction with a council of eight members chosen from the cohort of forty senators by joint ballot of the senators and assemblymen sitting "in one room." Once elected to the council, however, an individual could no longer serve in the senate. The governor had the power to adjourn and prorogue the General Court—a term for both houses of the legislature that was carried over from Massachusetts's colonial charters—and could appoint judges as well as a large number of other officeholders. He could also veto acts of the General Court, although a two-thirds vote of the legislature could override that veto. The governor was commander in chief of the state's armed forces and received "an honorable stated salary, of a fixed and permanent value," which, in times past, the legislature had absolutely refused to grant the colony's royal governor.

Since the Massachusetts constitution was generally considered the best of the first state constitutions, it became a model when other states began revising their original constitutions. The New Hampshire constitution of 1784 was clearly based on Massachusetts's, although the state's chief executive was called not governor but president. Already in 1784, the word "president," which originally designated a weak executive, a person who presided over meetings of delegates, was being used for a strong, elected executive with independent power, capable of checking even the legislatures, which were deeply established in the affections of the American people.

MIXED GOVERNMENT OR SEPARATION OF FUNCTIONS?

To say that the constitutions moved from simple or unbalanced to complex and balanced raises the issue of what was being separated and balanced. The British system of mixed government pitted against each other king, Lords, and Commons, which represented different social groups. There were some efforts to follow that model in early American state governments, using devices such as property qualifications for office or differential voting qualifications to make assemblies, senates, and governors speak for different social groups. Under the New York constitution, for example, persons qualified to vote for senators had to satisfy a freehold qualification five times greater than that for persons qualified to vote for assemblymen. And in Massachusetts, governors were required to have at least a £1,000 freehold (that is, real estate) and be a resident of the state for seven years; senators needed a £300 freehold or a total estate (which included personal as well as real property) of £600 and to be a five-year resident; while members of the assembly were required to have a freehold of only £100 or a total estate of £200 and could be residents of the state for as little as a year. The question arose, however, whether those requirements were appropriate in a republic. Didn't they create social divisions among citizens who should have been equal before the law? Differential property requirements for officeholding surely undercut the capacity of meritorious poor people to hold the highest offices of the state, which Judge Drayton had described as a strength of South Carolina's first republican government.

American governments gradually dropped differential property requirements and other remnants of mixed government except for age or residency requirements, which excluded no one from the highest offices of the land on a permanent basis, and could be understood as indications of experience and knowledge—that is, of merit. As the fixation with balancing social groups waned, attention turned increasingly toward separating and balancing governmental functions.

The constituent elements in separation of functions—which, again, had roots in the English past—were not the two houses of the legislature and the king or governor, but the legislative, executive, and judiciary. Those were the divisions separated out in the first three articles of the Massachusetts constitution of 1780. Four years earlier, in fact, the Virginia Declaration of Rights had proclaimed "that the legislative and executive powers of the State should be separate and distinct from the judiciary." The Virginia constitution, however, seemed to violate that principle right and left, particularly in giving the General Assembly so much control over the executive branch.

What, then, did separation of functions mean? For one thing, it meant that the same person could not hold offices in more than one division of government—that is, that there could be no plural officeholding. A governor could not also serve in the legislature or the judiciary; a legislator could not serve in the executive or judiciary; a judge could not serve in the executive or legislative branches. That system differentiated American postrevolutionary governments from those of the past. In colonial Massachusetts, for example, Thomas Hutchinson had served simultaneously as lieutenant governor, a member of the upper house of legislature, and a judge of the supreme court, which annoyed ambitious young men like John Adams who would have liked to hold at least one of those offices. The rule also durably distinguished American from British government, where cabinet members were also (and still are—indeed, must be) members of Parliament.

Separation of functions provided a way of checking the all-powerful legislatures created by many of the first state constitutions. Those legislators, it turned out, had a way of riding roughshod over restraints—even those in the constitutions, which they honored or disregarded almost at will. The assemblies also passed stay laws, which delayed the collection of

A view of the Maryland State House at Annapolis in 1789.

debts, and tender laws, which forced creditors to accept depreciated paper currency even for debts contracted in hard money. Such measures did more damage to property rights than any action the British had taken before 1776, complained creditors such as Maryland's outspoken Charles Carroll of Annapolis (father of Charles Carroll of Carrollton, who signed the Declaration of Independence). The rights of unpopular minorities such as Loyalists were also violated, as occasionally were those of religious minorities. In short, the unbridled power of elected legislatures raised the unanticipated specter of majoritarian tyranny.

What could be done? Revive the power of governors, as was done in New York and Massachusetts; give them independent power bases and the veto power so they could check legislative wrongdoing. And establish a judiciary independent of both the legislative and the executive branches. Breaking the bond between the judiciary and the executive went against elementary logic: the execution of laws, after all, includes the trying and punishing of those who violate the law. The independence of the judiciary was, however, an English tradition that the Crown had violated in America by forcing judges to hold office on the king's pleasure. Now state after state gave judges their offices on good behavior and provided that they receive, as the Virginia constitution put it, "fixed and adequate salaries," which shielded them from manipulation by legislative paymasters as well as from the executives who had appointed them. Of the major players in state government, however, the judges alone were appointed, not elected; and they alone had tenure in office. Were they then, in effect, "life peers," a throwback to an elitist past deserving more suspicion than trust? Until the republican character of the judiciary was more firmly founded, it would remain notably weaker than the executive or legislative parts of American government.

THE PROBLEM OF AUTHORITY

Another problem faced by the creators of the first American constitutions was more basic than the overall design of government. It concerned nothing less than the nature of a constitution's authority. What exactly was a constitution? What was the source of its power? And how could it be made different from ordinary laws?

The concept of a constitution in American heads was unlike anything that existed in Great Britain—which had caused no end of confusion before 1776, when colonists condemned acts of Parliament as "unconstitutional." The British constitution was nothing more than a term for the way British government was constituted; that is, for the set of institutions, laws, and customs by which Britain was governed, a system whose principles of organization were not laid out on paper. How then, the British wondered, could an act of Parliament be unconstitutional?

For Americans, however, a constitution was written. A constitution was also a statement of fundamental law, which was different from the ordinary rules that governed traffic or trade or liquor sales. A constitution underpinned the legitimacy of those ordinary laws by granting specific powers to government and defining the way those powers were to be exercised. The colonists' concept of a constitution no doubt drew on their experience with charters or instructions to governors: after all, such documents were written, and they defined the structure of colonial government and limited the powers exercised by various officials. To ideas based on the past, however, the Americans added another: for them, constitutions corresponded to the original compact by which individuals in a state of nature formed a society and government, a process that had been described in John Locke's *Second Treatise of Government* and a host of other writings of the seventeenth and eighteenth centuries. To say an act of government was unconstitutional meant, then, that it violated those basic rules of the state that the people had made a condition of their allegiance. An unconstitutional act therefore had no legitimate binding force. By mid-1776, the Americans were past trying to explain to the British what they meant by "constitutional." Instead, they had to create constitutions that realized in fact the somewhat odd notions in their heads. How could they do that?

Some states held special elections before their legislatures drew up a constitution, so the legislators received authorization from the people for executing that task. Delaware declared that certain "fundamental rules" in its constitution could not be changed, while others could be altered only with the consent of five-sevenths of the assembly and all seven members of its legislative council, far more than was required for ordinary purposes of legislation. That was as far as the states went toward differentiating constitutional provisions from other laws. None of the state constitutions written in 1776 and 1777 were, for example, submitted to the people for approval. All were drafted and then enacted by elected legislatures. And what the assemblies created, they could change (or, more worrisome, simply ignore), which they did when constitutional edicts cramped their style or impeded their will.

A copy of the first draft of the Virginia Declaration of Rights, written by George Mason and adopted in 1776.

The problem, then, was how to write a constitution that bound the legislators. The answer came not so much from prominent leaders like John Adams as from ordinary people who were also thinking through the most challenging issues of their time. Massachusetts towns such as Concord and, above all, Pittsfield in the remote western reaches of the state insisted that the process had to begin at the bottom, with the people themselves, who would elect delegates to a special convention whose sole purpose would be to form a "Constitution of Government." The draft constitution the convention produced would then be submitted back to the people, who could reject or ratify it. A constitution enacted in that way would be different from other laws; it would be a direct act of legislation by the people, a way by which they created, charged, and limited the government that would henceforth order their lives.

In 1778, the people of Massachusetts rejected a proposed constitution in part because it had been drafted by the General Court. The constitution submitted for their approval two years later was the work of a constitutional convention—another invention of the revolutionary era—elected by the people in town meetings. Later, the people again met in town meetings to ratify the document proposed by the convention. Finally, theory and practice went hand in hand. "The body politic," explained the constitution's preamble, "is formed by a voluntary association of individuals: it is a social compact, by which the whole people covenants with each citizen, and each citizen with the whole people, that all shall be governed by certain laws for the common good." The critical enacting clause of the constitution followed from that theory. "We . . . the people of Massachusetts," it read, ". . . do agree upon, ordain, and establish, the following *Declaration of Rights, and Frame of Government,* as the CONSTITUTION OF THE COMMONWEALTH OF MASSACHUSETTS."

An elected legislature could violate such a document only at its peril. It would have to face the people and, as it happened, the judiciary. Written constitutions had the advantage of being enforceable in the courts. And so the creation of constitutions by the sovereign people gave the judiciary a popular function. Someone, after all, had to watch over a constitution, making certain that its provisions were honored. In 1776, the Pennsylvania constitution had established a Council of Censors—another of those odd devices in the early constitutions—to meet every seven years and perform precisely that task. In Massachusetts, the regular courts took on that function, assuring that constitutional provisions were honored by all who were bound by them. Judges became, in short, protectors of the will of the sovereign people as stated in constitutions that the people had proposed and ratified.

DECLARATIONS OF RIGHTS

Seven states—eight counting New Hampshire in 1784—also adopted declarations or bills of rights either as separate enactments or as integral parts of their constitutions. What was their function? Whom did they bind? And what was the source of their power?

The American **declarations or bills of rights** took their name from an English ancestor. In February 1689, the Lords and Commons, acting as a convention (which at that time indicated that Parliament was imperfect or incomplete since James II had fled the country), adopted a Declaration of Rights that included three parts. The first formally ended the reign of James II, who, it charged, had endeavored to subvert the established Protestant religion "and the Lawes and Liberties of this Kingdome." The second part stated in positive terms the "undoubted Rights and Liberties" that the king had supposedly violated. And the final part declared that William of Orange and his wife, Mary, the Protestant eldest daughter of James II, who would preserve the British people "from the violation of their rights which they have here asserted and from other attempts upon their Religion Rights and Liberties," should be "declared King and Queen of England." Once William and Mary were established on the throne, Parliament revised and reenacted the declaration as England's Bill of Rights.

The American declarations or bills of rights corresponded to the second section of the British document. Indeed, the 1776 Virginia Declaration of Rights repeated some phrases from the British declaration, such as its clause against cruel and unusual punishments, almost word for word. Since the states generally adopted their declarations of rights before enacting constitutions or made them an opening part of the constitutions, their declarations of rights were, as in 1689, a statement of rights that the new regime created by the constitution was supposed to protect more faithfully than the regime that preceded it.

Beyond those apparent similarities, however, lay some critical differences. William and Mary were bound by the English Declaration of Rights because they had agreed to its terms in accepting the Crown. In effect, the declaration stated the terms of a contract between them and the nation represented by the House of Lords and House of Commons. All the great British constitutional documents such as the Magna Carta and the 1628 Petition of Rights were the same, agreements between the king and representatives of the nation, and their provisions limited what the king could do. The Americans, however, had no king, and their declarations of rights were not the texts of agreements between officeholders and the people since there were no officeholders in place when they were adopted. What, then, gave those documents authority? Ratification by state assemblies? If so, were the declarations of rights ordinary or fundamental law? They bound, it seemed, the government, but their wording sometimes made their demands sound less than mandatory. For example, the Virginia Declaration of Rights stipulated, like the English one, "that excessive bail ought not to be required," and also that in certain legal cases "the ancient trial by jury is preferable to any other, and ought to be held sacred." The Pennsylvania Declaration of Rights even said that elections "ought to be free" and that freedom of the press "ought not to be restrained." Were those provisions suggestions or requirements? And what if governors or legislators chose to ignore them?

To add to the complications, several American declarations of rights asserted a series of basic political principles that went unmentioned in British antecedents. There they followed the example of the Virginia Declaration of Rights, which many American newspapers printed in a form that emerged from the convention's drafting committee without the modifications that the Virginia assembly later made. As a result, that draft—written by George Mason, one of the most underappreciated members of the founding generation—exerted a far greater influence than the official Virginia Declaration of Rights. According to the draft, "all men are born equally free and independant [sic], and have certain inherent natural rights, of which they cannot, by any compact, deprive or divest their posterity; among which are the enjoyment of life and liberty, with the means of acquiring and possessing property, and pursuing and obtaining happiness and safety." The words seem familiar today because Thomas Jefferson adapted them in drafting the second paragraph of the Declaration of Independence. More important, however, they made their way, with minor variations, into several state bills of rights, including those of Pennsylvania, Vermont, Massachusetts, and New Hampshire, as well as Virginia. Did such rights get their force from the law of nature or because the states enacted them? Perhaps the rights to life, liberty, "the means of acquiring and possessing property, and pursuing and obtaining happiness and safety" could be understood as natural rights. But what about the assurances in the Pennsylvania Declaration of Rights that a person accused of crimes "had a right to be heard by himself and his council, to demand the cause and nature of his accusation, to be confronted with the witnesses," and to have "a speedy public trial, by an impartial jury of the country"? Those rights emerged, it would seem, not from nature but from English legal tradition.

The planter George Mason, who in 1776 drafted Virginia's Declaration of Rights and also its first state constitution.

The foundations of the first American bills of rights were, in fact, a confused jumble of conflicting possibilities. In practice, however, those documents gradually assumed an authority essentially like that of the constitutions. In Massachusetts, both the Declaration of Rights and constitution were formally agreed upon, ordained, and established by the people, which made them statements of fundamental law. And since declarations of rights were written, they, too, could be enforced by the courts. It took time before their legally binding character was everywhere established. But when that happened, the fact that they could be enforced in the courts served not only to provide a strong undergirding for an American tradition of rights, but to give the judiciary an honored, republican function as the guardian of the people's rights and liberties. In short, the institutional implementation of ideas about basic rights served again to shore up the weakest of the three parts of American government, making not just the separation but a balance of functions more substantive.

RELIGIOUS FREEDOM

Aside from the recognition of bills of rights as a common part of states' fundamental laws, the revolutionary era brought substantial progress in the definition and establishment of specific individual rights, particularly freedom of religion. That transformation occurred at the state level. In the seventeenth and eighteenth centuries, most colonies had established religions, which in New England (except for Rhode Island) meant that people were required to attend and contribute to the Congregational Church, and in the South to the Church of England. Religious freedom took the form of religious toleration, by which certain sects were granted exceptions to the rules: dissenters—the adherents of churches other than the established church—might, for example, be allowed to support their own teachers and preachers rather than those of the established church, or to vote and exercise other civil functions despite their unorthodox religious affiliations. Toleration, however, was not a right but a privilege, one granted only to religious groups that, in the opinion of secular authorities, taught good morals and in general was "regular enough" to be granted exemptions from the standing religious laws. Catholics, for example, were denied toleration: they could not vote, hold office, or practice law, and even in Maryland, originally founded as a Catholic refuge, they could attend mass or give their children religious instruction only in the most private and unobtrusive circumstances. Some Protestant groups, such as Baptists in Massachusetts, were also denied the privilege of toleration and so had to keep supporting the Congregational Church.

In the course of the Revolution, some states moved toward implementing a new and more radical religious freedom by separating church and state. One force for change lay unsurprisingly among Baptists and other "irregular" religious groups whose membership had multiplied during the religious ferment of the mid–eighteenth century and who found it outrageous that they had to request exemption from standing religious laws and have their practices judged by secular authorities. These dissenters found a powerful spokesman in the Baptist leader Isaac Backus, who skillfully played on the rhetoric of the Revolution, charging with hypocrisy those who were "filling the nation with the cry of LIBERTY and against *oppressors*," because they themselves were "violating that dearest of all rights, LIBERTY of CONSCIENCE." Year after year, Baptists and other religious minorities were "taxed without their consent" to "uphold a worship which they conscientiously dissent from." According to Backus, the state had no claim to judge religious beliefs since church and state were by nature different: the state was governed by majority rule, but God said that only "a *few* find the narrow way, while *many* go in the broad way." During the Revolutionary War, Baptists in several Massachusetts communities refused to pay taxes to support a church whose teachings they opposed, creating divisions at a time when colonial unity against Britain seemed essential. Even between colonies, religion could cause painful divisions—as the Massachusetts delegates to the First

Patrick Henry, one of the most eloquent orators in revolutionary America, first made his name opposing the Stamp Act. By the mid-1780s, he had become an advocate of state support for religion, although not for any one church or sect. Without religion, he feared, the morals of the people would decline, and that would inevitably bring down the American Republic.

Continental Congress discovered when they were taken to task by a set of Quakers for the colony's oppressive religious establishment. The question necessarily arose whether the benefits of religious establishments were worth their cost.

The front line of change was not, however, Massachusetts but Virginia, where religious dissenters joined hands with Thomas Jefferson and James Madison, men of the Enlightenment who saw religion as a matter of opinion that, like all forms of thought, should be free of legal restraint. Their first victory came with the Virginia Declaration of Rights (1776), which proclaimed "that religion, or the duty which we owe to our Creator, and the manner of discharging it, can be directed only by religion and conviction, not by force or violence," and that therefore "all men are equally entitled to the free exercise of religion, according to dictates of conscience." No longer would the Anglican Church receive exclusive state support. But could Virginia levy a "general assessment" and use the funds it collected to sustain a variety of religious groups? Since a republic depended on the morals of the people, argued Patrick Henry and others like him, the Revolution made the moral instruction of religion more important than ever. From that perspective, to end state support for so essential a service seemed mad.

Madison and Jefferson would have none of it. Finally, in January 1786, with the support of many religious dissenters, they successfully secured passage of the Virginia Statute of Religious Freedom. "Almighty God hath created the mind free," the statute declared, and all attempts to influence it by punishments or civil incapacities bred only "hypocrisy and meanness." The statute ended clearly and forcefully all laws that compelled individuals to support a religion or ministry or punished them in any way because of their religious beliefs, and it provided "that all men shall be free to profess, and by argument to maintain, their opinion in matters of religion" with no effect on their civil capacities. The act also stated that the rights it declared were "of the natural rights of mankind," and so any future legislative effort to repeal or narrow its provisions would be "an infringement of natural right."

Virginia showed the way to the future, but the future didn't arrive all at once. Even Pennsylvania, long the center

"Few of the Revolution's innovations were accomplished in a minute. They happened over time, gradually effecting transformations that few if any foresaw when the first cries went up against parliamentary taxation."

of American religious liberalism, whose Declaration of Rights assured that citizens' civil rights could not be denied or abridged because of their religious beliefs or "peculiar mode of religious worship," confined that protection to men who acknowledged "the being of a God." Atheists need not apply. Then the Pennsylvania constitution required members of the assembly to take an oath of office that not only acknowledged their belief in God but proclaimed both the Old and New Testaments to be the work of "Divine inspiration." That provision effectively excluded Jews from the assembly despite the Declaration of Rights—which one set of Philadelphia Jews protested, not because they "perticularly" wanted to hold office, but because exclusion from office made them less than equal citizens of the republic.

Similarly, the Massachusetts Declaration of Rights (1780) protected individuals' right to worship God according to the dictates of conscience so long as they did not "disturb the public peace, or obstruct others in their religious worship." But it also authorized towns to provide for public worship and "public Protestant teachers of piety, religion, and morality" and to require attendance at the instructions of such "public teachers," although, as before, some religious groups were allowed to support their own teachers instead. It required another half century before church and state were finally severed in Massachusetts.

Few of the Revolution's innovations were, in fact, accomplished in a minute. They happened over time, gradually effecting transformations that few if any foresaw when the first cries went up against parliamentary taxation, and with which some of the most ardent defenders of colonial rights—Patrick Henry, for example—were not entirely happy. Even the "improvements" in the science of government worked out between 1776 and 1780 were implemented only gradually, since many states kept their first state constitutions, warts and all, for substantial periods of time. New York retained its constitution of 1777 for forty-five years. Virginia clung to its first constitution for fifty-four years, Maryland for sixty-five, New Jersey for sixty-eight, North Carolina for seventy-five. The Massachusetts constitution of 1780, although heavily amended, is still in effect, making it the oldest still-functioning written constitution in the world. Now many countries have written constitutions, and all those countries have, in that way at least, been touched by the American Revolution.

Society: The Meanings of Equality

Innovations in government were part of a broader story of change that penetrated virtually every aspect of life. The rules that governed society were among the first to come under question. Colonial Americans had expected that, over time, America would come to look more and more like Britain, and even produce its own aristocracy. Then, almost overnight, "aristocrat" became a derogatory term. In 1776, Americans rejected social ranks determined by birth, indeed all "artificial" or man-made distinctions. Only those "distinctions of nature" or "of heaven," as Paine put it in *Common Sense,* were worthy of respect. The result was a more "equalitarian" society. But what exactly did that imply?

The Declaration of Independence had proclaimed that "all men are created equal." That phrase, like Mason's "all men are born equally free and independent," referred originally to the state of nature, before governments were established. It meant that neither God nor nature had granted some people authority to rule others; all persons were equal in that they were, in effect, self-governing in the state of nature. All legitimate authority was, as the Declaration also said, founded on the consent of the governed.

What, then, about American society once it had an established government? Equality was traditionally considered necessary for a republic, and many Americans argued that the absence of great disparities of wealth as well as of fixed social ranks made their society peculiarly well suited for a republican government. Widespread ownership of freehold property, moreover, gave Americans an independence, a freedom from manipulation by others, that was essential for a self-governing people. But could economic equality be sustained in the future? Respect for property rights ruled out any simple redistribution of property, or "agrarian law." Instead, hopes for an egalitarian society came to rest on a system of partible inheritances by which even the greatest fortunes would be divided in equal parts among a deceased person's children, causing a "revolution" in property holding with the passing of each generation.

Republican equality also had a more immediate meaning for the supporters of independence, as one public body after another testified in the spring and early summer of 1776. The Virginia convention, for example, specified that the state's new constitution should "secure substantial and equal liberty to the people." Grand juries in South Carolina took delight in establishing a new government whose benefits extended "generally, equally, and indiscriminately to all," and under which "the rights and happiness of the whole, the poor and the rich, are equally secured." And, as noted earlier, South Carolina's Judge William Henry Drayton took pride in the fact that his state's new, republican government allowed voters to raise even "the poorest man" to the "highest dignity" if he had "virtue and merit."

None of these statements suggested that individuals would be alike in all ways or that society would be without ranks of any kind. But they insisted that government treat everyone alike and that status reflect merit, not privilege. Eighteenth-century Americans were not, in fact, alike in all regards; an array of distinctions—regional, religious, and racial, as well as of wealth, occupation, education, and sex—marked one group off from another and sometimes designated lines of power and subordination. Just how important would those differences be in the new equalitarian social order? And which traits gave evidence of the "virtue and merit" that appropriately distinguished one person from another in a republic?

THE EQUALITY OF ADULT WHITE MEN

The first order of business was to determine what distinctions were legitimate among adult white men, who constituted the political community and thus "the people" as that term was generally used in the late eighteenth century. It was in this area that some of the greatest battles were won, some so successfully that they hardly seem victories any longer. Religious divisions, for example, marked powerful social cleavages in colonial America, as indeed they do today in many parts of the world. To be sure, the extreme conflict between Quakers and Congregationalists, or Puritans and Anglicans, of the seventeenth century became muted after the 1680s, as different Protestant groups linked arms against the "Catholic powers" in one war after another. The division between Protestants and Catholics remained, however, deep and impassioned. The independence movement was itself militantly Protestant. That it opened the way for a new order in which Catholics such as the younger Charles Carroll could hold office was indeed to create a "world turned upside down."

In a republic, rank rewarded merit, or ability, and also virtue, which often implied to Americans little more than conforming to the standard rules of Christian morality. Some suggested that wealth provided a rough index of ability, which justified the differential property qualifications for office in the first state constitutions, but wealth soon came into dispute as a measure of merit. Virtue and rectitude could be found, as even some conservative spokesmen observed, in men "destitute of property." A wealthy man might be less tempted to act dishonestly than a poor one, but wealth also fostered an "aristocratic" idleness and luxury, and it could lead to unbecoming vices such as avarice. Benjamin Franklin once volunteered that "some of the greatest rogues" he had known were "the richest rogues." If so, to prefer men of wealth simply because they were wealthy made no sense. To give them legal recognition or privileges was even worse, for it would foster a European class system and so move away from the republican ideal. Ending legal privileges based on property did not, however, end the Americans' wild scrambling for wealth, which not only continued to distinguish man from man, but had immediate personal benefits as well.

If rank in a republic depended on merit and virtue, it was within reach of large numbers of ambitious young men. What equality meant for a substantial part of the population was, in short, opportunity—to raise their personal, economic, and social status, and build better lives for themselves and their children. The shattering of class ceilings meant that every honor, every attainment worth having, lay within reach for the able. The result was a great outpouring of energy fired by personal ambition and often by a confidence that private quests for betterment contributed to the nation's development.

The end of British rule, moreover, increased the opportunities available to America's new and ambitious men, who frequently sought to acquire traditional signs of status. The possession of land, for example, had always conferred respectability. And since the American victory ended British efforts to contain westward expansion, with the end of the war settlers poured into the once-bloody fields of Kentucky and what would become the state of Tennessee. The white population of the area immediately to the south of the Ohio River soared from 12,000 in 1783 to over 100,000 by 1790. Indian resistance still blocked expansion north of the Ohio until 1795, when, after the Battle of Fallen Timbers, the Treaty of Greenville (Ohio) defined boundaries between the territories of the Indians and the United States. Then a new group of settlers left New England for richer lands in the West, often ignoring those hard-won and carefully negotiated borders. The societies the migrants founded were different from those in the East. The West could boast no established families or confining traditions and fewer persons of great wealth. There, a talented man of modest means could make his mark far easier than, say, in Virginia, New York, or Massachusetts.

Holding public office was also considered an honor; and there opportunities for upward mobility expanded even in the eastern states because of an increase in the number of offices filled by election and the departure of Loyalists. Among the roughly 100,000 white Americans who went into exile

The Cheney family of New England, c. 1795. In the early Republic, boys in such families, if they were able, enjoyed more opportunities to raise their economic and social status than their fathers had.

This 1792 painting by Samuel Jennings of *Liberty Displaying the Arts and Sciences* shows Liberty as a woman with a "liberty cap" on a stick, sitting beside a table with books on philosophy and agriculture while African Americans look on with awe. Chains—shackles—lie at Liberty's feet. Learning would thrive in a free country, the artist assumed; and the truth would make blacks as well as whites free.

the top; nothing so radical happened. Nevertheless, the social requisites of power broadened. Legislatures that were once filled by "gentlemen" became, in a word, democratized, which in turn brought a raucous, interest-based politics on a scale unknown in colonial America.

If future leaders of the Republic were to be drawn from the best qualified in the population at large—and the size of the pool from which republics could choose their leaders was frequently described as one of their greatest strengths—the people in general would need to be better educated. In the late eighteenth century, tracts, proposed laws, even provisions in state constitutions called for a broad dissemination of knowledge. Schools could at once prepare talented boys for public office, teach them how to manage their affairs and contribute to economic development, and inculcate morals that sustained public order. Schemes for comprehensive systems of public education nonetheless came to little. The revolutionary era did, however, bring a dramatic increase in private academies

during the War for Independence (some to England, others to the West Indies or Canada), men who had held appointed offices under the Crown were represented far out of proportion to their incidence in the population as a whole. They included everyone from justices of the peace to judges, members of the upper houses of legislature, and governors. The departure of so many experienced officeholders created openings for others. And as men who would once have spent their lives as legislators moved to higher positions, the legislatures were filled with others from a notch or two down the social scale in terms of wealth, education, and other marks of traditional respectability.

Such opportunities were reinforced, moreover, by reforms that brought a fuller and fairer representation of the people, including those in remote towns and counties where the richest men were at best of middling status by the standards of the Atlantic Seaboard. The bottom of society did not rise to

and in colleges and universities: indeed, more institutions of higher education were founded in the last two decades of the eighteenth century than in the entire colonial period.

Newspapers were perhaps a more effective way of educating the public. The Massachusetts printer Isaiah Thomas calculated that there were 37 weekly newspapers in the American colonies on the eve of independence; by June 1810, they had grown to 360, and many were published daily. The same period saw a change in the papers' contents, as an emphasis on news gave way to informative essays on topics from politics to literature and science. The press became, as Thomas observed, a way "of conveying, to every class in society, innumerable scraps of knowledge." That development was all the more impressive because it was market-driven, supported by hundreds of thousands of ordinary Americans ready to spend their pennies and time to increase their knowledge and improve their minds.

210

Such people were unlikely to yield to others who may have had greater wealth, better established families, even university degrees, but whose arguments were unpersuasive. And that, with the opportunities afforded by a more fluid social system, was what republican equality implied for white men—an end to the deference, the instinctual bowing of "inferiors" to their "betters," that had been part of the America's British past, and a chance to become themselves a bit better than others in an equalitarian America where rank remained but was always up for grabs. The Revolution changed the conditions of their lives, and the energy they invested in taking advantage of the new reign of opportunity created ripple effects that, in turn, further transformed American life in one way after another.

THE FIRST EMANCIPATION

Did equality cross the color line? Certainly the Revolution touched the lives of **African Americans,** awakening hopes and providing circumstances in which they, too, might become free. Some 50,000 slaves, or 10 percent of the total slave population, fled their masters in the course of the Revolutionary War. Many of them, particularly in the South, headed for British lines. Sometimes they were recaptured; sometimes the need for food and shelter forced them to return to their former homes. Many who did reach the "protection" of the British army succumbed to the diseases that haunted eighteenth-century army camps, or were forced to work as laborers in ways that resembled slavery but lacked the self-interested, paternalist protection that was one of slavery's meager comforts. At Yorktown, for example, General Cornwallis used ex-slaves to build his fortifications, but then, as the siege continued and his food supplies dwindled, drove the blacks out of the camp, forcing them, as one German officer noted, "with fear and trembling . . . to face the reward of their cruel masters." Only about 20,000 ex-slaves left with the British at the war's end, finding new homes in places such as Jamaica, London, or, ultimately, Sierra Leone, the colony Britain founded for former slaves. There, on Africa's west coast, they reenacted the "dying times" of America's own early colonies.

For blacks who stayed in North America, freedom was a more realistic immediate goal than racial equality. It was difficult to deny the legitimacy of blacks' striving for freedom in a country that had, after all, made liberty its cause. Those whites who ignored the inconsistency of slaveholders opposing British political "slavery" were reminded of their hypocrisy by the slaves themselves as well as by American Loyalists and British observers such as the writer Samuel Johnson, who wondered why the greatest "yelpers" for freedom were drivers of slaves. The assertions in the Declaration of Independence and many state bills of rights that men were created or born equal and that all legitimate authority derived from consent also undermined a slave system in which status was inherited, and mastership had no foundation in consent. That's why the Virginia convention modified George Mason's draft Declaration of Rights to say that men were not "born equally free and independent" but were "by nature equally free and independent" and possessed inherent rights of which they could not deprive their posterity "when they enter into a state of society." The revised text did not deny that slaves were men or that they had inherent rights. But it freed the commonwealth of Virginia from an obligation to protect those rights since, as everyone in the convention agreed, slaves had never entered Virginia's all-white society.

Elsewhere, however, many Americans decided instead to resolve the inconsistency between principle and practice. As a result, the Revolution brought the first widespread effort to dismantle the American system of black chattel slavery, which was then still a young institution, having begun to take legal

Two young Virginians, Alexander Spotswood Payne and his brother John Robert Dandridge Payne, appear with their dog and black nurse in this late eighteenth-century painting. Slaves continued to provide domestic service as well as field and other labor to wealthy white Virginians after independence, despite an increase of antislavery sentiment.

211

form in isolated acts of provincial legislation during the late seventeenth century. The first assault was on the slave trade, which, in fact, several colonies had tried to discourage before independence, but found their efforts blocked by royal vetoes. The Continental Association established a ban on slave imports that several states later incorporated into their laws or constitutions: the Delaware constitution of 1776, for example, declared that no person brought into the state from Africa "ought to be held in slavery under any pretense whatever; and no Negro, Indian, or mulatto slave ought to be brought into this State, for sale, from any part of the world."

Next, the assault turned against slavery itself. The Pennsylvania legislature adopted a gradual emancipation act in 1780, and soon thereafter some Massachusetts slaves successfully won their freedom in the state courts by arguing that slavery was inconsistent with a provision in the state's Declaration of Rights that said all men were "born free and equal." Then several other northern states passed gradual emancipation laws—Connecticut and Rhode Island (1784), New York (1799), then New Jersey (1804). Not surprisingly, emancipation came most easily in northern New England, where there were few slaves. It met greater resistance and took a more grudging form in states with substantial slave populations that performed basic economic functions, such as New York, New Jersey, and also Pennsylvania (whose gradual emancipation acts freed no slaves until far in the future). Emancipation laws provided that all slaves born after a certain date (March 1, 1780, in Pennsylvania; July 4, 1800, in New York) would become free when they reached a certain age (in New York, twenty-eight for men, twenty-five for women). Slaves born before the magic date remained enslaved unless they or, more often, networks of family members purchased their freedom.

Slaves could also run away, as many—particularly young males—did not only during but after the war. Perhaps a half to three-quarters of Philadelphia's young slave men escaped during the 1780s. If recaptured, they ran away again; or perhaps retaliated against their oppressors by setting the waves of fires that northerners generally attributed to blacks, and that indicated how costly to white security it would be to maintain slavery. What freedom blacks gained was, moreover, often incomplete

What's for Dinner?

January 20, 1779:
"It is the poor negroes who alone work hard, and I am sorry to say, fare hard. . . .

"They are called up at day break, and seldom allowed to swallow a mouthful of homminy, or hoe cake, but are drawn out into the field immediately, where they continue at hard labour, without intermission, till noon, when they go to their dinners, and are selcom allowed an hour for that purpose; their meals consist of homminy and salt, and if their master is a man of humanity, touched by the finer feelings of love and sensibility, he allows them twice a week a little fat skimmed milk, rusty bacon, or salt herring, to relish this miserable and scanty fare. The man at this plantation [the Jones plantation, near Charlottesville, Virginia], in lieu of these, grants his negroes an acre of ground, and all Saturday afternoon to raise grain and poultry for themselves. After they have dined, they return to labor in the field, until dusk in the evening. . . .

"As I have several times mentioned homminy and hoe-cake, it may not be amiss to explain them: the former is made of Indian corn, which is coarsely broke, and boiled with a few French beans, till it is almost a pulp. Hoe-cake is Indian corn ground into meal, kneaded into a dough, and baked before a fire, but as the negroes bake theirs on the hoes that they work with, they have the appellation of hoe-cakes. These are in common use among the inhabitants, I cannot say they are palateable, for as to flavor, one made of sawdust would be equally good, and not unlike it in appearance, but they are certainly a very strong and hearty food."

Thomas Anbury, "Lieutenant in the Army of General Burgoyne," in *Travels Through the Interior Parts of America* since whites could and did require blacks to sign long-term work contacts as a condition of manumission or employment.

Meanwhile, white indentured servitude gave way to wage labor, and apprenticeships to other forms of training, so legal forms of unfreedom for white adult men (except convicted criminals) gradually disappeared. That made restrictions on black freedom all the more invidious. Nonetheless, by 1804 all northern states had accepted some scheme of emancipation. There, at least, the slave system's end was in sight.

In the South, the story was different. Virginia and Maryland passed laws that facilitated private emancipations, but reversed that modest step well before the last of New York's or New Jersey's slaves became free. The problem was not that whites in the Chesapeake particularly liked their slave system or thought it consistent with the principles of the Revolution. But, since their states included far more slaves than most northern states, emancipation would leave them with a higher number of free blacks, which they did not want. Whites in the upper South were therefore open to arguments for emancipation only when coupled with plans for the "colonization," or deportation, of ex-slaves. And in the lower South, not even colonization found many supporters. Having lost a large portion of their slave workforce during the desperate fighting in the last stages of the Revolutionary War and unable to imagine a plantation economy without slaves, planters in Georgia and South Carolina were desperate for more slaves, not less. Before long, their spokesmen would begin defending the slave system; and then, only a few years into the nineteenth century, Georgia and South Carolina would again begin importing African slaves. And so, gradually, as emancipation spread in the North, slavery became what it had never been before: a distinctively southern institution.

One of the most important results of revolutionary emancipation was the emergence of a free black community within the United States. In 1790, that community included some 60,000 people, many of whom were in the Chesapeake, and it grew to over 108,000 within the next decade. Everywhere, however, the presence of free black Americans raised questions about their status and rights. Inequality ruled: in the North, free blacks were seldom offered good jobs; they could not purchase properties in certain neighborhoods; they did not serve on juries or (except for a brief, exceptional period in New Jersey) vote. At first they found shelter in the households of whites who employed them as domestic ser-

vants; later they clustered in their own neighborhoods and founded their own clubs, schools, and charities. Emancipation, in short, brought the beginning of segregation.

It also brought the beginnings of racism in the sense of a systematic, quasi-scientific assertion of whites' natural superiority over blacks. The future was forecast by Thomas Jefferson, who found himself, in *Notes on the State of Virginia* (written in 1781, published in 1785), trying to explain his proposal that Virginia free its slaves, send them to Africa, and import Europeans to do their work. Why not just keep the freed slaves and pay them for their labor? Because of old resentments, Jefferson said, and because of the "real distinctions which nature has made" between blacks and whites, distinctions that were hardly confined to skin color and, he suggested, affected intellectual capacities as well.

Benjamin Banneker, a free black surveyor and mathematician, produced his own almanac. His accomplishments, he argued, disproved Thomas Jefferson's suggestion in his *Notes on the State of Virginia* (1785) that blacks were incapable of doing mathematics.

In the next century, American "scientists" worked hard to confirm what Jefferson advanced as a suspicion. Their research was of particular interest to a nation that had rejected all artificial social distinctions but accepted and indeed reaffirmed those decreed by nature. If race involved differences that went beyond superficial skin color, it could become an acceptable mark of rank and subordination, a way of explaining why free blacks were beneath whites as much as the slaves were subordinate to their masters. In time, in fact, the "natural" category of race would prove far more confining and demeaning a designation than those class categories that the Revolution made "un-American."

Among the most outspoken opponents of the emergent racism were the free blacks. In 1791, Benjamin Banneker, a free black surveyor and mathematician, sent Thomas Jeffer-

213

Digital History

LIFE WITHOUT LIBERTY:

MASTER AND SLAVE AT GEORGE WASHINGTON'S MOUNT VERNON PLANTATION

Above: A page from the ledger of Washington's estate, with payments for the support and burial ("coffin for Old Molly") of former slaves. Center: George Washington and his family, joined by General Lafayette, at Mount Vernon, in a painting by Thomas Pritchard and Louis R. Mignot. Right: An engraving of Mount Vernon.

"Sir: I have received your letter of today, and in answer to it must inform you that I have no inclination to purchase the Negro fellow which you mention as I have already as many Slaves as I wish, and I cannot engage to give another, or others in exchange for him, because I do not think it would be agreeable to their inclinations to leave their connexions here, and it is inconsistent with my feelings to compel them."
        —*George Washington to John Fowler, February 2, 1788*

George Washington became a slaveholder at the age of eleven, in 1743, when he inherited 10 slaves from his father's estate. Thereafter he added to his slaveholdings by purchase and through his marriage in 1759 to Martha Dandridge Custis, who brought with her 84 slaves from the estate of her first husband, Daniel Parke Custis.

Washington came to understand that slavery contradicted the ideals espoused by the American Republic and, in years after independence, expressed support for the cause of emancipation. Nonetheless, by the time of his death in 1799, 316 slaves lived on the grounds of his plantation, Mount Vernon.

Through the sources on the *Inventing America* CD-ROM, you can explore life at Mount Vernon in the late eighteenth century. How did Washington organize and manage his slave workforce? What tasks did the slaves perform, and how did they live? Did they help shape the circumstances of their lives? The slaves were consigned to a life without liberty, but was Washington also shackled by the fact that his workers were slaves? What changes in policy did Washington adopt as a result of his reservations about the slave system? Why didn't he free his slaves until he wrote his last will and testament?

As you explore the "Life Without Liberty" feature on *Inventing America*'s Digital History CD-ROM, consider the following:

■ How would you assess the material conditions of life for the slaves at Mount Vernon?

■ In what ways were the slaves at Mount Vernon able to exercise a degree of control over their lives?

■ How would you evaluate Washington's beliefs and actions as a slaveholder?

son a copy of an almanac that included astronomical calculations he had made and that would have seemed to answer Jefferson's suspicion that mathematics lay beyond black capacities. Later, others would join in the attack on Jefferson's statement, which became a powerful symbol of all that black (and white) advocates of racial equality opposed. Free blacks were also among the most active advocates of a complete emancipation of slaves and of black rights. Like Isaac Backus, they made good use of revolutionary rhetoric on behalf of their cause. The existence of a free black community was, after all, itself a product of the Revolution, an event whose heritage was, by later lights, a mixed bag—bringing at once the beginnings of emancipation, segregation, and an explicit racism, but which shaped the future of American politics and society nonetheless.

WOMEN'S PLACE

If nature determined rank in the American republic, not just "inferior races" but also the "weaker sex" faced a future of permanent subordination. Age, too, helped determine who wielded power, but childhood was at least impermanent. Race, sex, age: those were the biological, or natural, differences that readily came to mind, and the last two seemed the least problematic. Only when women and children were left out, John Adams once observed, could individuals in a state of nature be described as "equal, free, and independent of each other." If the subordination of women and children was firmly established in the law of nature, how could they be anything but subordinate under formal governments?

 The best-known effort of a woman to mobilize revolutionary rhetoric on behalf of her sex is **Abigail Adams**'s letter asking her husband, John, to "remember the ladies" in drafting laws for the new Republic and to take from husbands the "unlimited power" they had over their wives. At the time, married women did not have a legal existence apart from their hus-

This stunning portrait of Abigail Adams was done by Benjamin Blythe in 1766, when Blythe painted a companion portrait of John Adams. She became her husband's most loyal political supporter and adviser.

bands and so had little protection against men's attempts to use them "with cruelty and indignity." Her plea for ending men's "absolute power over Wives" seems modest enough in retrospect, although there was the hint of a larger agenda in her statement that women would not "hold ourselves bound by any Laws in which we have no voice, or Representation."

Some women, like free blacks, contested the significance of superficial biological differences. Judith Sargeant Murray, the daughter of a wealthy merchant from Gloucester, Massachusetts, and the wife of John Murray, a Universalist minister, drafted an essay, "On the Equality of the Sexes," as early as 1779, although it was published only in 1790. The apparent difference in the minds of men and women, she wrote, came from differences in their education—from nurture, not nature. If they received the same opportunities as men, women would be equally accomplished, as had been proven by those women in history who "towered above the various discouragements by which they have been so heavily oppressed." Women should not be educated, she argued, as if their whole purpose lay in becoming wives; they should be taught skills that allowed them to be independent.

Such arguments for women's equality had little effect. Far more influential were the insights of Benjamin Rush, whose "Thoughts on Female Education" argued that the women of the American Republic should be so educated that they could instruct their sons "in the principles of liberty and government." The Revolution did, in fact, bring expanded educational opportunities for the girls who would become "republican mothers." In 1789, Massachusetts required that towns provide elementary education for girls as well as boys. The late eighteenth century also saw the founding of many private academies for girls, particularly in New England, where young women studied not just needlework but subjects such as history and mathematics. The middle-class female graduates of the academies were prominent among those nineteenth-century feminists who demanded a more substantive equality than was possible for women confined to the domestic sphere.

What didn't happen is, in retrospect, as striking as what did. Women had done a lot to support the American cause: they wore clothes made from homespun yarn and drank herb concoctions rather than tea during the time of the nonimportation agreements; they ran the farms when their husbands went off to fight, and some even tramped behind the army, doing laundry, taking care of the wounded, preparing food. But the Revolution had little immediate impact on women's

A series of miniature portraits of American women painted by the artist John Trumbull in the early 1790s. Note that they are identified by their relationship to notable men: Harriet Wadsworth, for example, was "Daughter of Col. Jeremiah Wadsworth," Faith Trumbull the "wife of Gov. Jonathan Trumbull." The era of women known for their own accomplishments remained in the future.

subordinate status. Men's "absolute power over Wives" remained as much in place after the Revolution as before. Even small steps toward requiring women's consent to the laws that governed them proved ephemeral. In 1790, New Jersey adopted an electoral law that referred to voters explicitly as "he" or "she" with no restriction on race, enfranchising women and free blacks. But seventeen years later, the state reversed course and once again confined the vote to white men.

At most, educational reforms effected after 1776 led toward transformations realized later, when the equality among men made women's dependency particularly invidious and humiliating. Did legal equality for women imply a transformation of private relationships more disturbing to the country's male republican legislators than black emancipation? Few of the social transformations the Revolution brought about were anticipated when the event began, and most took time to work out. But women's emancipation, it seems, went beyond what seemed compatible, if not with justice and ideological consistency, with social order.

The Economy: Adversity and Innovation

By all appearances, the Revolution was an economic disaster, one so severe that, by modern estimates, the per capita gross national product declined by almost half—from $804 (in 1980 dollars) in 1774 to $437 in 1790. The reasons are not hard to find. The war was long—longer than any other in American history until the Vietnam War—and was fought on American soil. The implications for future productivity were especially great in the South, where property lost or destroyed included a substantial part of the region's labor force—the thousands of slaves who fled to the British or otherwise disappeared in the course of the war. Commercial restrictions by the Continental Congress and Parliament prevented the sale of American goods abroad in the early years of the war; thereafter, the presence of the British navy and its attempt to blockade major American ports made even coastal trade perilous. Independence, moreover, ended the bounties that had supported the production of goods such as indigo and naval stores; and after the peace, the British excluded Americans from their old and familiar markets in Britain and the West Indies.

This $5 bill, decorated with some tobacco leaves, was issued by Virginia. Both the states and the Continental Congress issued money during the revolutionary era—which inevitably produced inflation, though at different rates from place to place.

Paper money at first made economic transactions easier and so encouraged a specialization that was all but impossible with the modified forms of barter common in colonial America. But the advantage was short-lived, since Continental currency rapidly lost value: the amount of hundredweight units of flour that £100 in paper currency could buy in Pennsylvania dropped from 143.3 in 1776 to .71 in 1781. Barter, by which useful products were exchanged for other useful products, seemed attractive compared with exchanges for money whose usefulness declined almost by the minute. In March 1780, the state of Virginia even imposed a "specific tax" payable in grain, hemp, or tobacco!

In England, corporations had often been given monopolistic grants or other special advantages: the Virginia Company of London, for example, had received an exclusive right to colonize a defined part of North America. As a result, corporations came under attack as privileged institutions, an accusation that should, logically, have made them anathema in revolutionary America. "No man, or set of men, are entitled to exclusive or separate emoluments or privileges from the community, but in consideration of public services," the Virginia Declaration of Rights proclaimed; and one state after another repeated the principle. By the time of the Revolution, in fact, the British, who sustained a strong antimonopolistic tradition, had ceased to develop the corporation for profit-seeking ventures and would not revive that institution until well into the nineteenth century. In Britain, the partnership became the characteristic legal form of business during the early industrial era. But not in the United States. Here, corporations began to multiply in the 1780s, and the trend continued thereafter, as one nineteenth-century jurist put it, almost incurably, as if Americans lacked a "moral means to resist it."

Most corporations in the 1780s were *not* formed for business purposes. Those created by the Massachusetts General Court, which led the nation in the development of corporations, generally incorporated towns, districts, or other units of local government, religious groups, educational institutions, or charities and similar nonprofit organizations. The basic advantages incorporation brought—a defined structure, the capacity to protect assets in the courts, persistence through time—were as important for those types of organizations as for profit-seeking companies. At the time, no distinction was drawn between, as a later period would have it, public and private corporations. In the eighteenth century (and, indeed, the nineteenth), no organization could be incorporated unless it served a public purpose, which many acts of incorporation carefully specified. In chartering the Potowmack Company, for example, the Virginia legislature stated that "the extension of the navigation of the Potowmack river, from tide water to the highest place practicable . . . , will be of great public utility." The Maryland legislature also chartered the Potowmack Company, and Virginia and Maryland each purchased 50 shares of its stock, which together accounted for a fifth of all outstanding shares. Although private investors bought the remaining 400 shares, which sold for $440 each, the Potowmack Company remained a quasi-public enterprise. Indeed, all corporations were quasi-public bodies whose creation allowed money-strapped state legislatures to enlist private individuals in carrying out work that governments themselves might otherwise do—building roads, improving rivers, constructing bridges, founding schools, and sponsoring projects for the economic development of the state.

Efforts to incorporate cities such as Boston, or to reincorporate Philadelphia, which had been a chartered city before independence, inspired some of the most divisive controversies of the time. Opponents attacked incorporated cities as bastions of privilege and impediments to economic growth because they entrusted power to a favored few "freemen" and had historically imposed restrictions on who could trade and practice crafts within their boundaries. Moreover, because corporate charters could not be breached by legislatures, corporations were condemned as *imperia in imperio*—that is, as governments within the government—and as institutions whose creation reduced the power of the sovereign people as embodied in the legislatures.

But the proponents of corporations, inspired by the creativity recently invested in state constitutions, insisted

The magnificent Charles River Bridge made travel between Cambridge and Boston much easier. It was built by the Charles River Bridge Company (1785), one of Massachusetts's first postrevolutionary for-profit corporations.

that there was no reason American-incorporated cities had to be like those of times past. The corporations they designed allowed for elected officials who held office for limited terms and often broad electorates. Moreover, city charters, like state constitutions, set up increasingly complex governments with bicameral legislatures separate from the executive and judiciary. Cities were incorporated for only limited terms: they had regularly to return to the state legislature for renewals, which kept them firmly under legislative control. By the late 1780s, the fourteen incorporated cities of colonial America had grown to thirty-four. The redesigning of city charters pioneered in the 1780s so successfully reshaped American urban government that by the nineteenth century they came to seem the least objectionable of any type of corporation.

The handful of immediate postwar incorporations for profit-seeking ventures included the Potowmack Company (1784), Massachusetts's Charles River Bridge Company (1785), the Beverly Cotton Manufactory (1789), and banks, including the Bank of North America (1782), the Massachusetts Bank (1784), and the Bank of New York (organized in 1784, chartered in 1791). These were relatively large-scale efforts, requiring capital beyond the means of individual Americans. Incorporation allowed such projects to be financed by a large number of investors, who became members of the corporation by buying shares in a public subscription. Later, any profits would be divided on a per-share basis. Such a way of massing capital was well suited to the United States, where wealth was relatively broadly distributed and even the greatest fortunes were modest compared with those of Europe. Investors also probably felt more comfortable committing their assets to organizations with defined governing structures and firm, written rules of procedure. In short, the corporation provided a way of addressing Americans' need for capital just as machines gave hope of addressing their perennial labor scarcity.

In truth, many profit-seeking corporations were modest in scale, and not all states proved equally at home with the institution. Even for mining and manufacturing, some states, particularly Pennsylvania, preferred individually owned companies or proprietorships. Almost everywhere, however, the great bulk of profit-seeking corporations were formed to improve internal transportation. River-improvement projects were among the earliest examples. Later, states incorporated vast numbers of companies to build bridges, turnpikes, and the like. Occasionally states developed such projects themselves.

Nonetheless, the transportation infrastructure that made possible the creation of a broad domestic market was in good part the work of corporations.

Everywhere incorporation was critical to the early development of banks, which, by increasing the flexibility and sophistication of financial transactions, made a powerful impact on economic development. In 1781, Robert Morris organized the first major American commercial bank, the Bank of North America (BNA), as a way of rebuilding the finances of the United States, for which it served as a creditor and a bank of deposit. At the time, Americans had little if any experience with commercial banks. Thomas Willing, a former Philadelphia merchant who directed the BNA's daily operations, described the undertaking as like entering a "pathless wilderness" for which there were no books of directions to follow; only accident, he suggested, led the bank to replicate English precedents. The purchase of shares gave the bank its initial assets. It also received deposits, on which depositors could write checks—then a novelty in America—and it issued banknotes, redeemable at the bank in specie (gold or silver), which served as a circulating medium. With that capital, the BNA provided merchants with short-term loans, which were relatively safe, but which merchants needed so desperately that the bank was able to declare a 8.74 percent dividend in 1782, its first year of operation. The BNA's usefulness and profitability soon inspired imitators elsewhere.

The creation of business corporations was often controversial. And, as with incorporated cities, controversy led to the development of charters that answered critics' objections. Widespread hostility toward privilege guaranteed, for example, that early charters allowed corporations no privileges that individual entrepreneurs lacked, such as limited liability, which limited shareholders' responsibility for corporate debts. Charters often included complex voting requirements to limit the power of large shareholders and enhance that of smaller investors. They also defined exactly what corporations could lawfully do, limited the amount of real and movable property corporations could hold, and either remained valid for only a limited term of years or explicitly reserved the legislature's right to amend or repeal the charters they granted. Even the most famous battles, such as one that took place over the Bank of North America and culminated with the Pennsylvania legislature's canceling its charter in 1784, were fought over specific provisions in charters. Pennsylvania reincorporated the BNA in 1787, but its new charter included several constraints on the bank's duration, activities, and

1776	Thomas Paine's *Common Sense* and John Adams's *Thoughts on Government* published.
May 10, 15, 1776	Second Continental Congress approves resolutions on government.
June 1776	Virginia Declaration of Rights.
1776–80	Each of the thirteen colonies adopts a constitution; seven also adopt declarations or bills of rights.
1780	Pennsylvania adopts a gradual emancipation law.
1782	Bank of North America established.
January 1786	The Virginia Statute of Religious Freedom.
1789	Massachusetts requires elementary education for girls as well as boys.
	Brown and Almy found spinning mills in Rhode Island.

holdings that together "new modeled" the bank so it would better "harmonize with the government of this country," as one contemporary writer put it.

Charters and constitutions were, in fact, similar: both described the governing structure and set the basic rules of organizations that had been formed by a mutual agreement (or compact) among a set of people. Where corporations participated in activities beyond those specified in their charters, their acts could be declared null and void in the courts, much as acts of government could be declared unconstitutional. The familiarity of their structure probably contributed to the popularity of corporations. To work within carefully constructed organizations, whose management structures and rules of procedure were defined in a written founding document, came to be an American way of doing business of any kind, whether for profit or not.

The emergence of corporations therefore had a powerful effect on the form as well as the development of American society. The Revolution did not, it seems, produce a nation of independent individuals acting alone, as myth would have it. Individuals soon learned that effectiveness demanded joining forces with others, and if the associations they created were, as became increasingly common, legally incorporated, they were clearly placed under the control and supervision of the state legislatures. In that way, the associations avoided the frequent contemporary charge of being "self-created," free-floating mini-governments that exercised prerogatives that belonged more properly to the people as a whole or to the state. And so American society gradually became a web of organizations, all formed voluntarily from below, that penetrated the most local day-to-day activities; it became a series of corporations bound together in a federal system.

The newly independent states had moved rapidly, establishing not only the world's first republican governments organized under written constitutions but reforms that ranged from religious freedom and emancipation through a reorganization of cities and business associations. They did what they could to channel the energies released by the Revolution and the relatively small caches of American capital into activities that would sustain a dramatic economic expansion in the future. Here and there—with patents and copyrights in particular—the states acted in areas that demanded regulation on a national scale. But in early 1787, the federal system of organizations that the states were constructing step by step lacked a capstone, a national government that might serve as what one contemporary called a "great corporation, comprehending all others." That deficiency would, however, soon be remedied.

Suggested Reading

Willi Paul Adams, *The First State Constitutions: Republican Ideology and the Making of the State Constitutions in the Revolutionary Era,* translated from German by Rita and Robert Kimber (1980)

Ira Berlin, *Many Thousands Gone: The First Two Centuries of Slavery in North America* (1998)

Bruce W. Bugbee, *Genesis of American Patent and Copyright Law* (1967)

Sylvia R. Frey, *Water from the Rock: Black Resistance in a Revolutionary Age* (1991)

Brooke Hindle, *The Pursuit of Science in Revolutionary America, 1735–1789* (1956)

David J. Jeremy, *Transatlantic Industrial Revolution: The Diffusion of Textile Technologies Between Britain and America, 1790–1830s* (1981)

Linda Kerber, *Women of the Republic: Intellect and Ideology in Revolutionary America* (1986)

Pauline Maier, "The Revolutionary Origins of the American Corporation," *William and Mary Quarterly,* 3d series, 50 (1993): 51–84

Mary Beth Norton, *Liberty's Daughters: The Revolutionary Experience of American Women* (1980)

Gordon S. Wood, *The Creation of the American Republic, 1766– 1787* (1969)

QUESTIONS

■ **What were the achievements and weaknesses of the Confederation government?**

■ **What were the main divisions at the Constitutional Convention, and what were the compromises that resolved them?**

■ **What enabled the Federalists to succeed in the battle over ratification of the Constitution?**

In the best of summers, Philadelphia is an uncomfortable city, and the summer of 1787 was, some said, one of the worst in almost forty years. Might the lightning rods erected throughout the city have robbed the clouds of electricity, they wondered, and so prevented the thunderstorms that usually broke the heat?

In May, before the sweltering weather settled in, delegates to a new convention began to arrive from one state after another. In the end, all but Rhode Island sent representatives. Together, the convention members were a living *Who's Who* of revolutionary America. The Virginia delegation included George Washington, already first in the hearts of his countrymen; George Mason, author of the state's constitution and much-imitated Declaration of Rights and a man who hated leaving home; Governor Edmund Randolph; the esteemed jurist George Wythe; and the young James Madison. South Carolina sent John Rutledge and two Pinckneys who, as if to confound later generations, were named Charles and Charles Cotesworth. Benjamin Franklin came from Pennsylvania; John Dickinson, the beloved "Pennsylvania Farmer" of two decades earlier, now represented Delaware; and Washington's old aide-de-camp, Alexander Hamilton, sat for New York. Most of these distinguished men—fifty-five in all—remained through the summer, when, according to a French visitor, the heat and humidity made breathing a challenge and "the slightest movement" painful. The delegates had a mission. They were going to design a new and more powerful national government that would, as they saw it, save the American Revolution from imminent failure.

The task they undertook was among the most difficult of the revolutionary era, one that was impossible when the country first declared its independence. In 1776, Americans were understandably unwilling to recreate a central authority like that of Britain or to grant a central government powers they had denied to Parliament, such as the power to tax and to regulate commerce. In 1776, moreover, Americans had relatively little experience with a domestic national government. The several colonies had begun coordinating political action only in the 1760s, and the Continental Congress first became a national government in 1775, after Lexington and Concord. That inexperience made initiatives toward the creation of a new national government relatively hesitant and tentative. The political systems of the states, by contrast, had been established as far back as the early seventeenth century; there, Americans knew what worked and what didn't and so could begin redesigning their governments with some confidence.

Americans well-read in history and the emerging science of politics saw still another problem. Republics were traditionally considered appropriate only over small areas such as Athens or Sparta. Large republics, so the common wisdom went, included so many different interests that agreement upon the common good became all but impossible. Eventually, persistent internal conflict led to the rise of a strong ruler and the death of the republic. It seemed, then, much better to keep power firmly on the state level. This theoretical consideration went hand in hand with a final, practical obstacle to the creation of a strong nation: the states, having recently acquired unprecedented power, were unwilling to give away much more than they already had conceded to the Second Continental Congress.

The first "permanent" central government, under the Articles of Confederation (ratified in 1781), was the best Americans could agree upon at the time. In many ways, it made substantial improvements over the Second Continental Con-

customs houses between Nev
tween any other states. The
stab at defining the division c
and the state, giving Congress
sive power" to determine pea
relations, and making it "the
putes . . . between two or mor

Progress continued once t
the original system of gove
clearly inadequate, Congress
for war, foreign affairs, and fi
ficial who was not a member
it replaced the retiring sup
Morris, with a Board of Trea
able entrusting its funds to a :
nized a national post office a
order to the national debt,
chaos, having been contracte

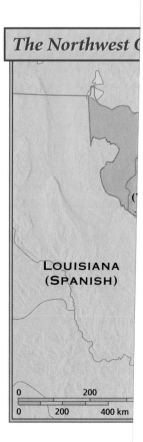

The Northwest C

LOUISIANA
(SPANISH)

gress, its predecessor. By the late 1780s, however, the weakness of the Confederation and the conviction that some check
on the states' exercise of power had become necessary led to
calls for a new and stronger national government. The
Philadelphia Convention of 1787 wrote a Constitution to fill
that need. But old questions came up again: was the Constitution the convention proposed a step forward in the science
of politics or a throwback to the form of government Americans had rejected in 1776? Could a republican government
survive over so extensive a nation? As a result, ratification of
the Constitution was itself an extraordinary political accomplishment—a victory, against the odds, over deep, articulate,
and widespread opposition.

A 1779 watercolor sketch of American flags. Although the flag had
not yet taken on a standardized form, each of these flags included
thirteen stars and stripes to represent the number of states in the
Union at that time.

From Confederation to Constitution

In the spring of 1776, the job of writing and ratifying a plan
of government for the United States probably seemed no
more challenging than many others before the Continental
Congress. In fact, the task proved surprisingly difficult, and
absorbed more time than any individual state required to
perform the same task.

The resolutions Richard Henry Lee moved on June 7,
1776, which called on Congress to declare independence, also
asked it to have "a plan of Confederation . . . prepared and
transmitted to the respective Colonies for their consideration
and approbation." A committee appointed to draft a plan of
union then submitted for Congress's consideration a document written mainly by John Dickinson. Although Congress
was able to consider, revise, and adopt the Declaration of Independence in two days, it took over a year to agree on the Articles of Confederation. Finally, on November 15, 1777, it
approved a much-revised version of the Dickinson draft and
asked the states to act quickly (by March 10, 1778), since ratification was "essential to our very existence as a free people."
But the states did not finally ratify the Articles of Confederation for three and a half years, during which time the old Second Continental Congress continued to act as the nation's
government. The Articles finally went into effect in March
1781, less than eight months before the war's end. By then,
the government they established was, in the eyes of some informed critics, already outmoded.

THE CONFEDERATION

Why did the Articles of Confederation remain so long in
Congress? Distractions caused by the war in 1776 and 1777
played a part. The Articles also raised issues of substantive detail that were destined to recur in future debates on national
government, such as representation. The Dickinson draft
continued the old Congress's system of giving each state one
vote. But populous states such as Virginia wanted representation in Congress proportioned to population, especially since
the Dickinson draft also specified that state contributions to
the Confederation would be "in Proportion to the Number of
Inhabitants of every Age, Sex and Quality, except Indians not
paying Taxes." The large states lost on representation but
succeeded in getting requisitions (state contributions to the

Plan of an American New Clea...
or, on the left, using a pole to...
considered the most promising...
worm, or snake, fence, which 1...
seventeenth-century Delaware...
Possession of the West was a n...

national treasury) proport...
veyed and granted within...
of how much land was ec...
into consideration buildin...
provision, however, was s...
Confederation ended up...
states roughly according to...

Then there was the issu...
claimed on the basis of "s...
grants from the Crown. N...
the basis of concessions i...
Another six states, howe...
The latter, especially Pe...
the western territory to...
whole, for which the Dicl...
final Articles of Confede...
deprived of territory for...
Then Maryland refused to...

trans-Appalachian West, Congress appointed a committee "to Prepare a Plan for the Temporary Government of the Western Territory." The committee and its chairman, Thomas Jefferson, proposed a plan for dividing the territory into states (not colonies, as some previous documents called them) and provided names for ten of them—Sylvania, Michigania, Cherronesus, Assenisipia, Metropotamia, Illinoia, Saratoga, Washington, Polypotamia, and Pelisipia. The plan stated that settlers should be allowed to adopt the constitutions of any already established state as the basis for their temporary governments and then, when a state contained 20,000 "free inhabitants," Congress could authorize it to call a convention and adopt a permanent constitution. States could then become full members of the federal Union, subject, however, to certain restrictions. They could not, for example, leave the Union, and the committee draft declared that "after the year 1800 . . . there shall be neither slavery nor involuntary servitude in any of the said states," except as punishment for crimes of which an individual was "duly convicted." Congress revised the proposed resolutions before adopting them in April 1784, eliminating the names suggested for the new states and also the restriction on slavery.

 The Land Resolutions of 1784 never went into effect. Three years later, Congress replaced them with the **Northwest Ordinance**, which provided for the organization of three to five states—eventually Ohio, Indiana, Illinois, Michigan, and Wisconsin—from the territory north of the Ohio River and west to the Mississippi. That meant there would be fewer states larger in size than Jefferson preferred. In an initial "territorial" stage, those future states would be governed by officials appointed by Congress, and not entirely self-governing, as under the earlier resolutions. This change reflected the conviction of several influential observers, including George Washington, that westerners were ignorant, semisavage "banditti" who honored the laws of neither God nor man and had no respect for Indian titles. Settlers of that sort would have to be taken firmly in hand or they would involve the United States in one Indian war after another. When the population of a territory included 5,000 free adult men, according to the ordinance, resident freeholders could elect representatives to an assembly, which in turn would nominate 10 men from whom Congress would choose 5 as an upper house. The governor, whom Congress appointed, would have an absolute veto over legislation. However, when the free population reached 60,000, the territory could establish a republican

government under institutions like those of the original states and apply for admission to the Union.

The Northwest Ordinance solved the old problem of how to make the people of colonial settlements free and equal with those in the "mother country" by abandoning altogether old ideas of imperial organization. There would be no dependent colonies, and no difference among the peoples of the United States that depended on where they lived, since all new states would enter the Union "on an equal footing with the original states in all respects whatsoever." The ordinance also included provisions that assured the residents of a territory of basic civil rights, including freedom of religion and trial by jury, provided that the "said Territory" and the states formed therein "shall forever remain a part of . . . the United States of America"; and unlike Congress's earlier Land Resolutions, the ordinance declared that "there shall be neither slavery nor involuntary servitude in the said territory, otherwise than in the punishment of crimes whereof the party shall have been duly convicted."

The ordinance applied only to the Ohio Territory, and its binding power ceased once that area was organized into states. However, it provided a model and precedent for organizing all future states, particularly in assuring that they would be free and equal members of the Union. For that reason, it is probably the single most important piece of legislation in the entire history of the United States.

THE CASE FOR CHANGE

Why was it necessary to replace the Articles of Confederation? Because, since the Confederation could not impose duties, it could not retaliate against nations such as Britain that put up barriers against American trade. Congress asked the states in 1781 and again in 1783 to "vest a power in Congress" to impose duties on imports, but because amendments to the Articles required unanimous consent, the refusal of a single state to ratify—little Rhode Island in 1781, and then New York—prevented that modest change.

Nor could the Confederation act effectively in foreign affairs. It could not persuade Great Britain to leave its posts in the West because, the British said, the American states had not respected Loyalist rights under the Treaty of Paris. It could neither retaliate against nor buy off pirates on the Barbary Coast of North Africa, who attacked American ships and sold their crews as slaves. And it could do nothing when Spain refused to recognize the 31st parallel as the southern

TOWARD

The natio
Nine state
interstate
(an invita
egations h
hardly en
Rather th
conventio
the states
which wo
May 1787
stitution
cies of the

The ca
to the oth
which ha
earlier in
impossibl
amend th
nally, on
saying it
sole and
eration."
New Jers
Carolina.

SHAYS'S

Meanwh
conventi
opposite
to meet
requisitio
within th
were levi
regardles
1780–81
only gol
paid in h
in weste
1784–86
where re
. . . was

John Jay of New York, secretary of foreign affairs from 1784 to 1790. His 1785 attempt to negotiate an agreement with Spain that would have barred American trade on the Mississippi for twenty-five years provoked massive opposition in the West.

border of the United States. Negotiations between John Jay and the Spanish minister, Don Diego de Gardoqui, broke down in 1786 when, after a bitter debate, Congress barely authorized Jay to "forbear" American navigation rights on the Mississippi for twenty-five years in return for a favorable commercial treaty. Only seven states voted in favor of Jay's proposal, and five opposed it. Under the Articles of Confederation, nine affirmative votes were necessary to ratify treaties, so the vote doomed Jay's efforts.

That Congress came so close to giving up navigation of the Mississippi alienated settlers of the trans-Appalachian West, whose future development required free access to the river. Could the United States hold the West? Would Kentucky leave the United States and join Spain? Would Vermont, over which New York was unwilling to release its claims, join British Canada? Indeed, could the Confederation even bind the old states together when peace made union less imperative than it had been during the war?

In December 1783, when the Continental army was disbanded, even Jefferson thought Congress should cease meeting constantly. Instead, he proposed that after holding brief meetings to discuss whatever issues arose, it should leave the Confederation's limited business in the hands of a committee of states and so "destroy the strange idea of their being a permanent body, which has unaccountably taken possession of the heads of their constituents." By the late 1780s, Congress was occasionally incapable of doing any business whatsoever

because the states neglected to send delegates with sufficient regularity to assure that a quorum was present. The states also frequently failed to pay their requisitions to Congress. Instead, they began taking over payment of the federal debt by converting federal securities into state bonds. That made nationalists uneasy. To men like Alexander Hamilton, a national debt was a national bond, a common obligation that held a people together. By that reasoning, for the Confederation to abrogate responsibility for paying off its debts was nothing less than a blow to the foundations of national identity.

Hamilton was one of the most active supporters of a stronger central government. Born in 1757 on Nevis, one of the Leeward Islands in the West Indies, he was the illegitimate child of a Scottish merchant of aristocratic descent and the daughter of a French Huguenot doctor and planter. His parents had separated before his mother died in 1768, leaving him essentially an orphan. Four years later, at age fifteen, Hamilton came to North America, alone, after some generous supporters had recognized his extraordinary intelligence and arranged for him to attend King's (Columbia) College in New York. Before long, he began writing pamphlets on behalf of the American cause, and later joined the Continental army, becoming an adjutant and near-surrogate son to the childless George Washington. Ambitious and self-confident to the point of arrogance, Hamilton had a way of rubbing people the wrong way. But there were few native-born Americans who invested so much effort and intellect on behalf of their country.

Hamilton's loyalties were not to a state but to the nation. That was common enough among certain immigrants— including Thomas Paine— who joined the revolutionary movement soon after arriving, and so developed a primary

Alexander Hamilton, in a portrait painted by the American artist John Trumbull in 1792, when Hamilton was secretary of the treasury.

dedication to the United States rather than to one of its members. It was also common among the officers of the Continental army who had suffered from Congress's incapacity to

provide
stronge
howeve
Contin
    Jame
Princet
tive tha
with th

James Madison
Charles Willson
when Madison
Virginia's repr
Continental C

    For
much
a mem
Politic
ble exa
croach
with e
negoti
They
comm
ships
paper
which
those i
    The
an org

WE the People of the States of New-Hampshire, Massachusetts, Rhode-Island and Providence Plantations, Connecticut, New-York, New-Jersey, Pennsylvania, Delaware, Maryland, Virginia, North-Carolina, South-Carolina, and Georgia, do ordain, declare and establish the following Constitution for the Government of Ourselves and our Posterity.

ARTICLE I.

The stile of this Government shall be, "The United States of America."

II.

The Government shall consist of supreme legislative, executive and judicial powers.

III.

The legislative power shall be vested in a Congress, to consist of two separate and distinct bodies of men, a House of Representatives, and a Senate; each of which shall, in all cases, have a negative on the other. The Legislature shall meet on the first Monday in December in every year.

IV.

Sect. 1. The Members of the House of Representatives shall be chosen every second year, by the people of the several States comprehended within this Union. The qualifications of the electors shall be the same, from time to time, as those of the electors in the several States, of the most numerous branch of their own legislatures.

Sect. 2. Every Member of the House of Representatives shall be of the age of twenty-five years at least; shall have been a citizen in the United States for at least three years before his election; and shall be, at the time of his election, a resident of the State in which he shall be chosen.

Sect. 3. The House of Representatives shall, at its first formation, and until the number of citizens and inhabitants shall be taken in the manner herein after described, consist of sixty-five Members, of whom three shall be chosen in New-Hampshire, eight in Massachusetts, one in Rhode-Island and Providence Plantations, five in Connecticut, six in New-York, four in New-Jersey, eight in Pennsylvania, one in Delaware, six in Maryland, ten in Virginia, five in North-Carolina, five in South-Carolina, and three in Georgia.

Sect. 4. As the proportions of numbers in the different States will alter from time to time; as some of the States may hereafter be divided; as others may be enlarged by addition of territory; as two or more States may be united; as new States will be erected within the limits of the United States, the Legislature shall, in each of these cases, regulate the number of representatives by the number of inhabitants, according to the provisions herein after made, at the rate of one for every forty thousand.

Sect. 5. All bills for raising or appropriating money, and for fixing the salaries of the officers of government, shall originate in the House of Representatives, and shall not be altered or amended by the Senate. No money shall be drawn from the public Treasury, but in pursuance of appropriations that shall originate in the House of Representatives.

Sect. 6. The House of Representatives shall have the sole power of impeachment. It shall choose its Speaker and other officers.

This first version of the Constitution was the work of a Committee of Detail that met between July 26 and August 6. The committee used the twenty-three propositions on which the convention had agreed as well as the New Jersey Plan and a proposal by Charles Pinckney of South Carolina. After the committee submitted its report, the convention began amending the draft, which was printed for delegates' consideration with wide margins in which they could mark changes agreed on by the convention. The notes and changes on this printing were made by South Carolina delegate Pierce Butler.

Confederation was a beginning, but Congress also received power "to lay and collect taxes," "to regulate commerce," and to make all laws "necessary and proper" for carrying out the powers the federal government received under the Constitution. "To promote the progress of science and useful arts," Congress was given the power to grant authors and inventors "the exclusive right to their respective writings and discoveries" for a limited time. The convention did not give Congress power to grant charters of incorporation, which Madison proposed in order to facilitate the chartering of interstate canals or roads; controversies over the Bank of North America and the Bank of New York suggested that such a provision would increase opposition to the Constitution, whose ratification was no sure thing. The states, however, were explicitly denied the right to "coin Money; emit Bills of Credit," or "make anything but gold and silver Coin" legal tender. Nor could they pass laws "impairing the Obligation of Contracts." The property of creditors would be more secure with than without the new Constitution.

Should Congress also have power to prohibit or discourage the importation of slaves? That issue provoked divisions comparable only to those over representation. One of the most ardent opponents of the slave trade was, interestingly, a Virginian, George Mason, who said that slavery was "inconsistent with the principles of the revolution and dishonorable to the American character." Delegates from South Carolina and Georgia, however, insisted that they needed more slaves and would not ratify a Constitution that outlawed the slave trade, although a modest tax on slaves, as on other im-

The Constitution, Patrick Henry added, "squints toward monarchy."

More specifically, the Antifederalists, George Mason among them, complained that the Constitution lacked a bill of rights. They said its provision that the number of representatives in Congress "shall not exceed one for every thirty thousand"—which, of course, had been even worse (one for every forty thousand) before the convention's final day—was inadequate to provide a full and free representation of the people. (The Massachusetts constitution, by contrast, allowed towns an additional representative whenever their population grew by 250 adult white men.) The Constitution, Antifederalists insisted, created a "consolidated government" inconsistent with the persistence of the states, a government that would assume all powers of legislation and whose laws would be "supreme and controul the whole."

The checks and balances built in to the Constitution were inadequate in the Antifederalists' eyes: the government's powers would soon be grotesquely expanded at the cost of liberty. Congress's right to change the places of elections for members of the House of Representatives (Article I, Section 4) would allow it to "say that the election for all the states might be had in New York." Congress's exclusive jurisdiction over the new nation's capital (Article I, Section 8) would give it the freedom to hang "any who shall act contrary to their commands" and offer asylum to would-be tyrants and others who oppressed the people. And the lack of religious qualifications for office meant that "Papists and Pagans might be introduced into office; and that Popery and the Inquisition may be established in America."

The debate raged not only on the convention floor but in pamphlets and newspapers. The well-known *Federalist Papers* by Madison, Hamilton, and John Jay of New York, a series of eighty-five essays first published in New York City newspapers between October 1787 and the following spring, offered a particularly thorough analysis and defense of the Constitution, but not the only one. Both sides produced a torrent of essays, speeches, and manifestos during the ratification contest, and both sides advanced compelling arguments. If the Federalists had no monopoly on wisdom, they did enjoy certain other distinct advantages over the Antifederalists. Most newspaper printers favored the Constitution, and the cities and rural areas served by navigable rivers tended to fall in their camp. The people in these regions were not only involved in trade, which the Constitution would benefit, but re-mained in touch with the larger world and were on the whole open to new ideas. Antifederalists tended to be from more remote regions, which (like the "Shaysite" interior sections of Massachusetts) sometimes had good reason to fear that a strong central power would be used against them.

The most prominent Antifederalist spokesmen—men like Lee or Henry—had been leaders of the independence movement, which is probably why they so readily saw the shadow of British tyranny in the Constitution. Fear, sometimes exaggerated to outlandish dimensions, dominated their arguments. However, they had nothing to propose as an alternative to the Constitution, since most Antifederalists admitted that the Articles of Confederation had failed. That alone weakened their position considerably.

Some veterans of 1776 such as Franklin and Washington supported the Constitution, but the core of Federalist leadership lay with a younger generation possessed less with fear than with hope for the future. Born in the late 1740s and 1750s, those young men of the revolution had entered politics with the elected extra-legal governments of the 1770s, not under the old regime, and by 1787 had mastered tricks of

This banner of the Society of Pewterers was carried in the Federal Procession in New York, which celebrated ratification of the Constitution on July 23, 1788. In general, artisans such as the pewterers favored ratification. They believed that a stronger federal government would bring an expansion of trade and an economic prosperity from which they, and the country in general, would benefit.

James Wilson, a Pennsylvania delegate to the Constitutional Convention and a man who, more than any other, laid the intellectual foundations of American Federalism by locating sovereignty firmly in the people.

democratic politics in ways that alarmed their opponents as much as the Constitution itself. The Federalists had organized a ratification campaign before their opponents knew what was happening, and they pushed for a rapid ratification without regard for large minorities left behind—so unlike the independence movement, which unfolded slowly and insisted on unanimity.

Having less of the old regime to unlearn, the young Federalists could also push the radical insights of 1776 further, advancing the science of politics beyond what the previous generation had accomplished. British imperial and American federal government, they insisted, were different, and fears appropriate for a monarchical government an ocean away were inappropriate in a government of elected persons chosen from among the people and who held office for limited terms. James Wilson responded to charges that the Constitution created a consolidated government by providing an intellectual foundation for American Federalism. In the United States, he said, the people were sovereign (that is, held ultimate power), and from that pool of power they could create two levels of government to perform distinct tasks on their behalf. There was no more reason those governments should conflict than that parallel lines would meet. And James Madison took on the old chestnut about republics working only in small areas. He argued in the tenth *Federalist Paper* that small democracies were particularly subject to the violence of majoritarian tyranny and so to turbulence and contention. The solution lay in greater size. "Extend the sphere and you take in a greater variety of parties and interests" and make it less likely that "a majority of the whole will have a common motive to invade the rights of other citizens." Moreover, in large republics, the people's voice fed into legislation not directly but filtered through representatives who had to speak for several sets of interests at once. The substantial populations of large republics also made it more likely that persons capable of performing that task could be found.

In the end, however, the Antifederalists shared much with the Federalists. Both wanted the Revolution and the Republic it founded to succeed; both recognized the inadequacies of the Articles of Confederation; both thought the Constitution less than perfect. If the flaws in the Constitution were as grave as its critics claimed, they could be repaired by a peaceful process of amendment that was now in the realm of the possible since amendments no longer required unanimous consent. And if the Constitution proved thoroughly inadequate, it could be replaced, as some states had already done with their first constitutions. But before repairs could be made, before a better design could be drawn, the Constitution of 1787 needed to be tried and its weaknesses confirmed by actual experience.

And so, once the Constitution was ratified, the Antifederalists took not to the swamps, like southern guerrillas in the last days of the Revolutionary War, but to the polling places and legislative halls, lending their hands to make the new government work. That willingness, with their insistence on a federal bill of rights, was perhaps the greatest of their contributions. It meant that the new government could be organized and given a fair try, that the experiment would be run.

A late eighteenth-century print suggesting that men of all classes—farmers and artisans as well as gentlemen—supported the new Constitution and the rule of law under its authority.

Chronology

March 1781	Articles of Confederation ratified.
December 1783	Continental army disbanded by Congress.
1786–87	Shays's Rebellion.
1787	The Northwest Ordinance.
May 25, 1787	The Constitutional Convention convenes in Philadelphia.
May 29, 1787	Edmund Randolph presents the Virginia Plan.
September 17, 1787	Convention delegates sign the Constitution.
October 1787	*Federalist Papers* appear in New York newspapers.
June 21, 1788	The Constitution becomes law when New Hampshire is ninth state to ratify.

Suggested Reading

Christopher and James Lincoln Collier, *Decision in Philadelphia: The Constitutional Convention of 1787* (1986)

Max Farrand, *The Framing of the Constitution of the United States* (1913)

Merrill Jensen, *The Articles of Confederation* (1966), and *The New Nation: A History of the United States During the Confederation, 1781–1789* (1950)

Cecelia M. Kenyon, ed., *The Antifederalists* (1966, 1985)

James Madison, *Notes of Debates in the Federal Convention of 1787*, ed. Adrienne Koch (1966)

Jackson Turner Main, *The Antifederalists: Critics of the Constitution, 1781–1788* (1961, 1974)

Jack Rakove, *James Madison and the Creation of the American Republic* (1990)

Robert Allan Rutland, *The Ordeal of the Constitution: The Antifederalists and the Ratification Struggle of 1787–1788* (1966)

Gordon S. Wood, *The Creation of the American Republic, 1766–1787* (1969)

ESTABLISHING THE NEW NATION:

1789-1800

View of New York from the "Jupiter," attributed to painter Archibald Robertson (1794).

Focus QUESTIONS

■ How did the new Congress and president begin to put flesh on the bare bones of the Constitution?

■ What were the main sources of economic change in the 1790s?

■ What were the major political divisions that marked the 1790s?

Once New Hampshire had cast the deciding vote for ratification, the Continental Congress began making arrangements for setting the new government in motion. The First Federal Congress, it decided, would meet on March 4, 1789, at New York, "the present seat of Congress." New York's city council, hoping to enhance its bid to become the permanent capital, promptly began remodeling the old City Hall at Nassau and Wall Streets into Federal Hall, an elegant meeting place for Congress.

Bells, flying flags, and cannon fire welcomed the day appointed for the delegates to assemble. Unfortunately, only thirteen representatives out of fifty-nine from the eleven states then in the Union had arrived, and only eight of the twenty-two senators. Not until April 1—April Fools' Day, a bad sign—did the House have a quorum of members present. Five days later, the Senate also had a quorum, so it could finally count the presidential electoral votes that had been cast the previous February. George Washington, with 69 votes, became the unanimous choice for president, as expected; and John Adams, with the next highest number of votes, 34, became his vice-president.

And so began one of the most formative and also one of the most tumultuous decades in American history. The new president and Congress had to put flesh on the bare bones of the Constitution—to transform the institutional structure outlined at Philadelphia in 1787 into a working government. Whether the federal government acted in foreign or domestic affairs, however, it fomented fears and divisions that threatened at times to bring the Americans' experiment with substantive central government to a quick end. In fact, the greatest achievement of the federal government in its opening years was the simplest of all. It survived.

Federal Hall in New York City, where the First Federal Congress met in April 1789.

Getting Started

If the new Congress's slow start recalled the old Continental Congress and its waning attendance, a surge of action soon made clear that this was, indeed, a new game. Most of the senators and representatives were men experienced in public service who had favored ratification of the Constitution; now they were ready to organize the new government and set it on a solid foundation. But the past kept haunting their proceedings: in one way after another, the new American government seemed to recall British imperial rule, which rekindled old fears and hostilities.

POLITICAL RITUAL

Nowhere was the problem more apparent than in the realm of ritual, the ceremonies and procedures that signaled the relationship of one part of the government with another. Since the Constitution said little about how intragovernmental affairs should be conducted, the political rituals of the American Republic had to be invented. But were they to be modeled on British precedents or created anew in ways more appropriate to a republic? The distinction wasn't always obvious. The only way some loyal Americans could imagine executing certain acts was in the way the British did them, so the conflict began almost immediately.

Because Washington was a firm republican, he requested that the eight-day journey by horse-pulled coach from his Virginia plantation, Mount Vernon, to New York be free of monarchical ostentation. But in towns all along the way, people came out to pay honor to the new president. They fired cannons, rang bells, shouted out acclamations. On the last leg of the journey, as Washington crossed Newark Bay and, exhausted, made his way toward his living quarters on Manhattan's Cherry Street, young girls tossed flowers in his path while the strains of "God Save the King" drifted through the air.

Already some began to suspect that such ceremonies presaged the transformation of the president into an elected monarch. And the presidential inauguration on April 30, 1789, did nothing to calm their anxiety. Robert R. Livingston, chancellor of the State of New York, administered the oath of office to Washington—who wore for the occasion a relatively simple, American-made brown suit—from an open portico at Federal Hall. Then Livingston turned to the assembled crowd outside on Wall Street and cried out, "Long live George Washington, President of the United States!"—just as the British shouted, "Long live the king!"

The Senate, according to Pennsylvania's William Maclay, whose notes provide the fullest surviving account of Senate debates, discussed at length British precedents in deciding issues such as how to receive the president on Inauguration Day or how to communicate with the House of Representatives. After Maclay objected, the Senate removed from its official minutes a reference to Washington's "most gracious speech," which, as Maclay observed, were the words "usually placed before the Speech of his Britannic Majesty" and so would give offense to the American people, who found "odious" everything related to "Kingly Authority." Some senators nonetheless advocated bestowing titles on high-ranking officials. "All the world, civilized and savage," had titles, argued Virginia's Richard Henry Lee, and without them officeholders would command no respect. There, Lee had the determined support of Vice-President Adams. Only the objections of the House of Representatives undercut a Senate committee's recommendation that the president be addressed as "His Highness the President of the United States of America, and Protector of their Liberties." In the interest of congressional harmony, the Senate finally agreed that the proper address

A print showing the triumphal arches erected near Philadelphia to welcome George Washington on his way to New York and his inauguration as first president of the United States, April 1789.

would be "'the President of the United States,' without addition of title." In this matter, at least, the view prevailed that British practice was "of no rule to us," as Maryland's Senator Charles Carroll of Carrollton put it. Instead, the American Republic adopted as its stylistic model Roman simplicity—which conveyed the fact, as Maclay said, that elected officials were "the Servants not the Lords" of their constituents.

In some areas, questions of ritual and procedure had long-term consequences for the relationships of national institutions. In the course of setting its rules, for example, the Senate tried to establish itself as superior to the House of Representatives by proposing that bills and other messages from the Senate be delivered to the House by the Senate's Secretary, but bills from the House would have to be delivered by two House members and other messages by one member. The House, Maclay reported, just laughed and the proposal died, which had the effect of establishing a certain equality between the two houses.

Or take the constitutional provision that the president could make treaties "with the Advice and Consent of the Senate." Did that imply that the president had to consult the Senate before concluding treaties, perhaps visiting its chamber in person? Washington thought it did, and in August 1789 he went to the Senate to consult on a treaty he hoped to negotiate with the southern Indians. The procedure seemed awkward and, in the end, proved unsatisfactory to both sides. Some senators sensed that they were being coerced into rubber-stamping proposals determined by the executive branch, and Washington found disconcerting the Senate's hesitation simply to give its consent on the spot. He never again sought the Senate's consent in person, and later abandoned even written communications before negotiating a treaty. Instead, he submitted finished documents for the senators' consideration. In that way, the Senate became less of an executive body, advisory to the president, and the president became less like a prime minister who executed the will of the Senate and more of an independent executive.

THE EXECUTIVE BRANCH

In other areas, the First Federal Congress resolved institutional issues in a more direct manner. Article II, Section 2, of the Constitution referred to "executive Departments," each under a "principal Officer," but said nothing about the number or responsibilities of those departments. The Constitution focused on the president and vice-president, leaving Congress

the task of fleshing out the executive branch. Soon after convening, Congress passed laws creating three separate departments for foreign affairs, war, and the treasury. Washington appointed Thomas Jefferson to head the first of those departments, but until Jefferson took office—which occurred six months later, in March 1790—John Jay supervised the nation's foreign affairs. Washington selected Henry Knox, a veteran officer from the Revolutionary War, to head the War Department, and Alexander Hamilton as secretary of the treasury. Soon Washington began treating department heads as a board of advisers, or "cabinet."

Some advocated the establishment of a fourth executive department for domestic, or "home," affairs, with responsibility for encouraging scientific and technological advances and internal improvements, as well as more standard functions such as taking the constitutionally mandated census, conducting relations with Indians, and keeping federal records. Instead, in September 1789, Congress changed the Department of Foreign Affairs into a State Department and entrusted it with several of those duties.

The supervision of federal patents and copyrights was among the new tasks assigned to the renamed State Department. The Constitution explicitly granted Congress power "to promote the Progress of Science and the useful Arts, by securing for limited Times to Authors and Inventors the exclusive Right to their respective Writings and Discoveries." Congress had no more than met when it began receiving petitions from writers and inventors who understood that federal patent and copyright laws would make unnecessary multiple applications to the states (whose number, moreover, would soon begin to multiply as the West was settled and organized politically). A committee of the House of Representatives drafted a general patent and copyright law in 1789, but the House repeatedly postponed consideration of the law so it could debate more urgent issues. Finally, in 1790, Congress enacted and, on April 10, the president signed a federal patent law that gave inventors "sole and exclusive right and liberty" for a period "not exceeding fourteen years" to make and sell inventions under a federal patent. On May 31, Washington signed a similar measure "for the encouragement of learning" by securing federal copyright to the authors or creators of "maps, charts, and books."

Both measures underwent subsequent revisions, but the advantage of a single national patent or copyright was so obvious that the system itself remained firmly in place. For a time, Jefferson, who had an interest in technical devices, personally scrutinized patent applications submitted to the State Department, and he testified that the patent law gave "a spring to invention beyond my conception." Many proposals were "trifling," but some described inventions "of great consequence which have been proved by practice, and others which if they stand the same proof will produce great effect."

While Congress was at work establishing the first three executive departments, James Madison, a member of the House of Representatives, raised another important issue. The president needed the Senate's consent in appointing department heads, but Madison proposed that Congress explicitly grant the chief executive power to remove department heads without consulting the Senate. Some representatives argued that there was no need to grant the president the power of removal since the Constitution gave him an implied authority to do so, a position that Madison eventually adopted. As a result, the first House bill creating an executive department said nothing about the power of removal, which prompted intense debate in the Senate. Some argued that to allow the president unchecked power over department heads was to take a major step toward the consolidated government that Antifederalist critics of the Constitution had predicted. In the end, the Senate's vote was tied—but Vice-President Adams cast his tie-breaking vote in favor of the president's power to fire officials without the Senate's consent. Congress established the other executive departments in the same way, with no provision on the removal of their heads from office. The result, again, was to enhance the power of the president and to make the executive branch more independent of the Senate than it might otherwise have been.

The creation of executive departments led to the establishment of a federal bureaucracy. The president thereby received powers of appointment that, along with the power of granting contracts and financial favors, had helped the British king secure followers in the House of Commons and so, as the Americans saw it, to undermine what checks on power had been built in to the British constitution. The prospect of similar "corruption" haunted certain members of the First Federal Congress such as the old Massachusetts Antifederalist Elbridge Gerry, who wanted the treasury headed by a three-person board. To put so powerful a department under one man, Gerry insisted, was a "perfect plan . . . for promoting peculation & speculation in the public funds."

Congressional actions affected regional as well as personal interests, which further complicated the houses' decisions. Legislation for a federal postal system, for example, foundered

The first patent issued by the U.S. government under the federal patent law of 1790. It was given on July 31, 1790, to Samuel Hopkins, who had devised a new process for leaching wood ashes to produce pearl and potash, products used for making soap.

in many a session because of squabbling over the location of post roads, which were likely to become economic arteries and would therefore affect the fates of communities they passed through as well as those they bypassed. The mail nonetheless was delivered, since Congress renewed for short periods of time the old postal service of the Confederation. Congress also established the office of postmaster general and put the incumbent under the direction of the president (who delegated that task to the secretary of the treasury).

Finally, in 1792, Congress enacted a Post Office Act that was worth waiting for, a law justly described as an agent of change rivaled by few others of the time. It prohibited public officials from using their power over the mail as a surveillance technique, which protected American freedom. Equally important, the act permitted newspapers to travel through the mail on extremely favorable terms and established procedures that encouraged the expansion of mail routes from the Atlantic Seaboard into the trans-Appalachian West. That privilege fed the already expansive growth of newspapers and allowed the news to penetrate remote parts of the nation. Four decades later, a French visitor discovered that a farmer in the Michigan Territory enjoyed more access to nonlocal

NEWS! NEWS!!

AARON OLIVER, *Post-Rider,*

WISHES to inform the Public, that he has extended his Route; and that he now rides thro' the towns of *Troy, Pittstown, Hoosick, Mapletown,* part of *Bennington* and *Shaftsbury, Petersburgh, Stephentown, Greenbush* and *Schodack.*

All commands in his line will be received with thanks, and executed with punctuality.

He returns his sincere thanks to his former customers; and intends, by unabated diligence, to merit a continuance of their favours.

O'er ruggid hills, aud vallies wide,
He never yet has fail'd to trudge it:
As steady as the flowing tide,
He hands about the NORTHERN BUDGET.
June 18, 1799.

A newspaper advertisement for Aaron Oliver, who offered his services as a post rider in the vicinity of Troy, New York.

information than the inhabitants of more densely populated sections of metropolitan France. In such ways, the Post Office Act undercut local isolation, supported commercial development, and allowed informed, popular political participation on a scale unanticipated by any of the wise men who had gathered at the Philadelphia Convention in the summer of 1787.

THE JUDICIARY

The Constitution vested federal judicial power "in one Supreme Court, and in such inferior courts as the Congress may from time to time ordain and establish." That left many blanks for Congress to fill in. Early in its first session, the First Federal Congress set up a committee with one member from each state to prepare a judiciary bill. The proposed bill was then printed, and members of Congress sent copies to their constituents, particularly lawyers and judges, for comment.

After further debates and amendments, the Federal Judiciary Act of 1789 specified that the Supreme Court would consist of a chief justice and five associate justices. The act also set up a system of federal district courts and circuit courts. State courts were granted original jurisdiction in most

civil cases involving federal questions, although the decisions of the highest state courts could be appealed to the Supreme Court. Section 25 of the act was especially important. It allowed the Supreme Court final say in all cases that involved constitutional issues; indeed, the Supreme Court could overturn state laws and court rulings if they conflicted with the Constitution, federal laws, or treaties of the United States. Southerners immediately took alarm, realizing that federal courts could force them to pay debts owed to British creditors, as the 1783 Treaty of Paris specified. In general, however, the Judiciary Act defined the jurisdiction of federal courts more narrowly than the Constitution allowed. There were practical reasons for this: by giving state courts a degree of concurrent jurisdiction, the Judiciary Act saved the country the cost of establishing and maintaining an extensive federal court system while undercutting fear that state courts would lose power to an expanding federal judicial leviathan.

The Judiciary Act provided for the appointment of an attorney general who would serve as a legal adviser to the president and the heads of executive departments and "prosecute and conduct all suits in the supreme Court in which the United States shall be concerned." Edmund Randolph of Virginia accepted that position, and John Jay became the first chief justice of the Supreme Court. The First Federal Congress also adopted a Punishment of Crimes Act, which defined as federal crimes treason, counterfeiting federal records, and murder, disfigurement, and robbery if committed within a federal jurisdiction or on the high seas. The act also authorized judges to sentence convicted murderers to be dissected after being executed for purposes of medical research, and even defined punishments for persons attempting to "rescue" bodies from dissection. Scientific advance, it seems, was a congressional objective from the beginning—even, in this case, against intense popular opposition to the practice of dissection.

A BILL OF RIGHTS

What sometimes seems to latter-day Americans the most important accomplishment of the First Federal Congress—the federal Bill of Rights—had trouble just making it onto Congress's agenda. To most congressmen of 1789, that proposal seemed far less pressing than the establishment of a federal revenue or the organization of executive departments or any of a host of other issues that commanded their attention. Even the measure's most vocal advocate, James Madison, became its champion more from political necessity than from profound conviction. Madison's observations of state conduct in the 1780s had convinced him that "parchment barriers" to power such as the state bills or declarations of rights were ineffectual; only institutional checks and balances, like those built in to the new federal Constitution, provided reliable protection for the people's liberty.

 Thomas Jefferson, however, offered some powerful reasons for a bill of rights in **private letters to Madison** after the Philadelphia Convention had ended. Jefferson pointed out, for example, that a bill of rights could be enforced in the courts. Equally important, during the ratification controversy, the Antifederalists had condemned the Constitution because it lacked a bill of rights and proposed literally hundreds of amendments for the new Congress to consider. Antifederal sentiment ran high in Virginia, and some Antifederalists, including Patrick Henry, blocked Madison's election to the Senate and threatened to prevent his election to the House of Representatives, too. Had he not promised to support constitutional amendments, Madison might well have sat at home through the first years of the new government in whose design and ratification he had played so important a role. It occurred to him, moreover, that the enactment of a few provisions protecting those basic liberties on which everyone agreed would undercut Antifederalist antagonism and perhaps prevent passage of the more destructive amendments they proposed, amendments that cut into substantive federal powers including the power to tax.

Madison took his promises seriously. In June 1789, he moved in the House of Representatives that a "declaration" be "prefixed to the constitution" as several states had done, and that it assert some familiar-sounding principles:

> *That all power is originally vested in, and consequently derived from the people.*
> *That Government is instituted, and ought to be exercised for the benefit of the people; which consists in the enjoyment of life and liberty, with the right of acquiring and using property, and generally of pursuing and obtaining happiness and safety.*
> *That the people have an indubitable, unalienable, and indefeasible right to reform or change their government, whenever it be found adverse or inadequate to the purposes of its institution.*

Those lines were essentially a watered-down version of the Virginia Declaration of Rights that lacked any statement of men's original equality, their possession of inherent natural rights, or their right to abolish (as opposed to reform or

change) their government. The changes were perhaps meant in part to offset the hostility of slaveholders, who by 1789 understood clearly that assertions of men's equality and inherent rights were at odds with the institution of slavery. Madison also proposed other changes in the body of the Constitution: he wanted to insert provisions protecting several basic civil rights among the restrictions on Congress in Article I, Section 9, and add to the next section a statement that "no state shall violate the equal rights of conscience, or the freedom of the press, or the trial by jury in criminal cases."

Madison's proposals were too much for his congressional colleagues, who saw no pressing need for a bill of rights—hadn't the people demonstrated that they liked the Constitution as it was by electing so many Federalists to the Senate and House?—and were certainly unwilling to begin fiddling with the Constitution's wording so early in its history. They eliminated Madison's "prefix" and, in September 1789, sent to the states twelve proposed amendments to the Constitution, which were to be listed at its end like the afterthoughts they were. Of those twelve, the states ratified ten, and on December 15, 1791, that Bill of Rights became part of the Constitution. The Bill of Rights was another bare-bones legal document, a lawyer's list of basic civil and judicial rights, one of which (the Ninth Amendment) declared that the rights enumerated did not "deny or disparage others retained by the people," and another (the Tenth) that reserved powers "not delegated to the United States by the Constitution, nor prohibited by it to the States, . . . to the States respectively, or to the people."

Because neither the federal Constitution nor the Bill of Rights included any statement about men's fundamental equality or possession of inherent rights, persons who found those old revolutionary ideas relevant to some cause in national politics turned to the Declaration of Independence. By 1789, that document was remembered mainly for its association with independence. Soon, however, the Declaration took on new life not as a revolutionary manifesto, but as a statement of principles for the guidance of an established nation. As that happened, attention began to turn from the document's last paragraph, which declared independence, toward the second, which had previously gone all but unnoticed. It read: "We hold these truths to be self-evident; that all men are created equal; that they are endowed by their Creator with certain inalienable rights; that among these are life, liberty, and the pursuit of happiness; that to secure these rights, governments are instituted among men, deriving their just powers from the consent of the governed."

In its original form, that single, long sentence went on to say that "whenever any form of government becomes destructive of these ends" (the protection of rights), the people had a right "to alter or abolish it" and to substitute a new government "as to them shall seem more likely to effect their safety and happiness." It asserted, in short, the right of revolution, which the people were exercising in 1776. After being chopped off in the middle, however, the sentence became a statement of the government's fundamental obligation to secure the people's "inalienable rights," of which "life, liberty, and the pursuit of happiness" were only a few examples. In this form, the sentence operated like a bill of rights, proclaiming the government's obligation to honor and protect certain rights. Once it assumed that function, the Declaration of Independence seemed to become part of the nation's basic constitutional order.

More immediately, Congress's adoption of a Bill of Rights led North Carolina (November 21, 1789) and Rhode Island (May 29, 1790) to ratify the Constitution and rejoin the Union. For the short run, that was benefit enough; and before the eighteenth century was over, Vermont (1791), Kentucky

The room in New York's Federal Hall where the House of Representatives met at the time it approved those amendments to the Constitution that became the federal Bill of Rights.

(1792), and Tennessee (1796) expanded the Union from thirteen states to sixteen. In the long run, the Bill of Rights, that half-hearted act of the First Federal Congress, would assume an importance beyond anything its unenthusiastic creators had imagined. But it took about a century and a half for its significance to be felt. In the meantime, the document's relative unimportance fully justified Madison's original low expectations.

A SYSTEM OF FINANCE

Achieving financial integrity and economic development was among Congress's primary objectives, and one of the first tasks to which it turned in its opening session. With relatively little squabbling, Congress approved an impost, or tariff, of 5 percent on all imported goods except those on a special list, which were subject to specific duties. It also approved a Tonnage Bill that levied charges on ships entering American ports according to their carrying capacities as measured in tons. The charges were less on American-built and -owned ships than on "all other ships." That was a welcome encouragement to American shippers, who suffered from the discriminating regulations of other nations but had previously watched ships flying foreign flags sail freely into American ports.

Other acts of 1789 set up prescribed forms for registering and clearing ships from American ports and established ports of entry where federal customs officials, with the power of search and seizure, would set up shop, much as their unpopular British predecessors had done. The United States also assumed ownership and responsibility for the lighthouses, buoys, and beacons that the states had established to facilitate coastal navigation, which ruffled some feathers. All of these acts were modified, replaced, or extended in future years, but they made a powerful point: the new federal government was going to be a presence in people's lives, particularly people who lived along major waterways.

The government would also be fiscally responsible. The Federal Appropriations Act for 1789 consisted of a single paragraph authorizing the expenditure of $639,000 to cover the current cost of the federal government. The sum was based on reports from the treasury that listed all the recipients of federal moneys and the sums owed them, down to the penny.

Fiscal responsibility also demanded paying the country's revolutionary debts. Article VI of the Constitution specified that

"All Debts contracted and Engagements entered into, before the Adoption of this Constitution, shall be as valid against the United States under this Constitution, as under the Confederation," but how exactly should the debt be retired? The problem was sufficiently vexing that on September 21, 1789, ten days after Hamilton became secretary of the treasury, the House of Representatives asked him to prepare a plan for supporting the public credit. The following January 9, Hamilton submitted his first report on the public credit, one of four epic reports he prepared for Congress. A second report focused on the creation of a national bank (December 13, 1790), a third on the establishment of a mint (January 28, 1791), and the fourth on American manufactures (December 5, 1791). Together, they provided a comprehensive plan for a national financial system and the economic development of the United States.

Hamilton's approach to the debt issue was characteristically ambitious. He proposed not only that the United States pay in full the principal and accrued interest on the debt owed to foreign nations ($11,710,378), but that it pay at par (the original face value) the nation's domestic debt ($44,414,085 with arrears of interest) and, moreover, assume responsibility for paying off the remaining Revolutionary War debt of the states (estimated at about $25 million). Holders of debt certificates would turn them in and receive in return new, interest-paying federal government bonds for the principal and 4 percent interest for the period since the original certificate was issued. As a result, moneyed people would not only be more willing to lend money to the government in the future, which was one point of "securing public credit," but they would see a close connection between their interests and that of the federal government, which was what Hamilton wanted.

Hamilton's proposal that the United States pay its debt to foreign nations raised no dispute. The recommendation to pay the domestic debt was controversial, since most of the original holders of the debt—often soldiers or suppliers of the Continental army—had sold the certificates they had received in return for services or goods during the hard times of the 1780s for substantially less than par value. Moreover, once word of Hamilton's proposal got out, speculators began buying up all the certificates of government indebtedness they could lay their hands on, expecting to make a handsome

"The Federal Appropriations Act for 1789 consisted of a single paragraph authorizing the expenditure of $639,000 to cover the current cost of the federal government."

profit when the government paid for them at par. Madison, who found that offensive, proposed that the government pay current holders of the debt "the highest price which has prevailed in the market" and distribute the difference between that price and the (higher) par value to the "original sufferers." The idea, though it won sympathy, was soundly rejected because it undercut the goal of demonstrating that the government would faithfully support its creditors. Executing Madison's proposal was probably also beyond the capacity of the Treasury Department, which lacked the manpower and the records necessary to identify and locate the original owners of all notes of federal indebtedness. It didn't hurt that many members of Congress had themselves scrambled to buy shares of the federal debt, and so stood to profit from government funding at par so long as the return went entirely to those who actually held debt certificates.

The assumption of state war debts was the most controversial of all the Hamilton proposals. States whose debts were small (Georgia, North Carolina, Maryland) or that had already paid off much of their debts and expected to extinguish them entirely in the near future (Virginia) resented the prospect of having to help retire the unpaid debts of other states, which in some cases (Massachusetts, New Jersey, New York, South Carolina) remained substantial. With passions high, Congress came to an impasse so stubborn that all legislative business nearly stopped. Sides tended to follow sectional lines, with most southern states opposing assumption and northern states favoring the measure. Southern rancor increased when northern Congressmen proved willing to consider petitions against slavery and the slave trade submitted by Quakers in early 1790. The strain was so severe that some observers predicted that the Union itself would split, then collapse in civil war.

Another compromise averted that dire fate and also settled an issue that had bedeviled Congress: where the new government would permanently reside. Under the compromise, which was worked out through a complex set of maneuvers by Hamilton, Jefferson, Madison, and Pennsylvania's Robert Morris, southerners (Madison in particular) agreed to accept the assumption of state debts in return for locating the nation's permanent capital on the shores of the Potomac River. Morris threw in his support in return for a promise that the temporary capital would be moved from New York to Philadelphia—where, he hoped, it would somehow remain after 1800, when the new federal capital was supposed to be occupied. The votes in Congress were nonetheless close, turning on the changed position of a few critical senators and congressmen. But the measures passed, one after another. And so in December 1790, the First Federal Congress met in Philadelphia, and planning for the new capital replaced fears of secession.

Hamilton's proposal for a national bank passed Congress with large majorities despite Madison's insistence that Congress had no constitutional right to charter a bank or, for that matter, to create any corporation. That was an important turnabout for Madison, who as recently as 1789, during discussions of the president's power to dismiss cabinet members, had accepted the constitutional legitimacy of implied powers. His objection bothered Washington, who consulted his secretary of state and attorney general, Jefferson and Randolph, on the issue. Both, like Madison, believed a national bank was unconstitutional because the Constitution did not explicitly give Congress the power to charter a bank. Then Washington turned to Hamilton, who had the advantage of seeing Jefferson's and Randolph's opinions before composing his own. Hamilton's argument was the most forceful and well

The Bank of the United States, which opened for business in Philadelphia during 1791. Hamilton's proposal for a national bank had provoked strong opposition since the Constitution did not explicitly give Congress power to establish a bank.

argued of the set. He asserted that the bank *was* constitutional under the provision authorizing Congress to make laws "necessary and proper" for executing its other powers, such as the collection of taxes and regulation of trade. Moreover, no provision precluded Congress from chartering banks. Although it seems that Washington was not fully persuaded, he sided with Hamilton because the issue came within Hamilton's sphere of responsibility. The president signed the Bank Bill, and so averted a confrontation with Congress that would surely have followed had he—for the first time—exercised his veto power.

Hamilton's report on the mint, a technical document concerned with the weight and value of American coinage, also went against the preferences of Secretary of State Jefferson, who in 1786 had himself prepared a report on weights and measures for Congress. Both men supported a decimal system of coinage, but by the 1790s Jefferson was hoping to establish a monetary system by which an ounce—defined as the weight of a thousandth of a cubic foot of rainwater—would correspond to the weight of silver in a dollar, so that the American systems of weights and currency would have a certain natural (but otherwise unnecessary) symmetry. Hamilton was more practical: he sought to define the weight of a silver dollar in relation to that of other coins already in circulation and to establish a reasonable ratio between silver and gold coins. No doubt Jefferson was disappointed by Hamilton's willingness to sacrifice natural harmony to the demands of the market, but in April 1792 Congress adopted Hamilton's proposals with little opposition.

Hamilton's report on manufactures, prepared after the House of Representatives requested a plan "for the encouragement and promotion of such manufactories as will tend to render the United States independent of other nations for essential, particularly for military supplies," fared less well. Hamilton provided an economically sophisticated case for the development of a mixed economy, with vital manufacturing and commercial sectors. Such an economy, he argued, would increase American prosperity and make the United States less dependent on foreign nations for critical products. The report did not disparage agriculture: "the cultivation of the earth," it read, had "intrinsically a strong claim to pre-eminence over every other kind of industry," and would itself benefit from greater economic diversity. Traditional barriers to the development of manufacturing, Hamilton argued, could now be overcome by mobilizing machines, immigrants, women, and children to offset the high cost of adult male labor, and using banks, foreign investment, and a funded debt as sources of capital.

References to banks and the funded debt pointed up the interconnectedness of Hamilton's reports, each of which supported his ambitious vision for the American future. The last report also surveyed the current state of American manufactures and listed policies that would encourage their further development. Some of those policies, particularly federal patents, were already in place. However, Congress was not ready to adopt protective duties and bounties. For one thing, high tariffs would discourage imports and thus lower the revenue from customs fees, which provided a major part of the federal government's income. Spokesmen for agricultural interests also feared that protective tariffs would spur retaliatory measures abroad and so reduce foreign purchases of American agricultural products. As a result, the federal government failed to take an activist role in encouraging manufacturing, a role that states such as Massachusetts

A plan of Washington, D.C., in 1800 that shows the grid pattern of streets with crosshatched "transverse avenues" proposed by Major Pierre-Charles L'Enfant.

had already enthusiastically assumed (see Chapter 6). The report remains therefore a repository of information on the state of American manufactures at the time and a reflection of Hamilton's thought rather than the beginning of a major change in federal policy.

THE PROBLEM WITH DREAMS: THE PASSAIC AND THE POTOMAC

Hamilton found a more direct way to realize his dreams of development through the Society for Establishing Useful Manufactures (SUM), which set out to establish a large manufacturing complex along the Passaic River at the present site of Paterson, New Jersey. The SUM won a charter from the New Jersey legislature in the fall of 1791, just before Hamilton issued his report on manufactures. Hamilton was neither an officer nor a shareholder in the society, although he probably drafted both its prospectus and its charter and was among its most enthusiastic supporters.

The scheme for the complex was nothing if not grand: the SUM purchased 700 acres on which it planned to found a town with lodgings for employees. It also began to acquire machinery to manufacture a vast variety of goods, including several types of cloth, paper, clothing, pottery, and metal wire. The planned complex would even include "a brewery for the supply of the manufacturers." The initial authorized capital stock was $500,000, although under the corporation's charter its capital could later be expanded to $1 million. The first stock issue of $100,000 sold out within days. But beginning in 1792, things started to go wrong. Investors began selling shares for profits once their price started to rise, preferring quick gain to long-term growth. Even some of the original directors were so anxious for a quick buck that they not only sold their own shares but embezzled company funds. The machinery the company purchased was poorly designed and unreliable; and the laborers recruited from abroad—because, it seems, too few Americans with appropriate skills were available—turned out to be, according to some reports, lazy, ignorant louts. Most important, an enterprise on the scale Hamilton and his associates hoped to create was far beyond the management skills of Americans at that time, so the SUM lacked effective, capable leaders who could mold the operation into an effective means for generating profits. Some manufacturing processes nonetheless continued until 1796, when the directors decided to close them down to prevent further losses. The SUM then took on another life as a real estate operation. At least there, in the management and sale of land, Americans of the 1790s were something more than rank amateurs.

The other great dream of the time, a dazzling new American capital on the shores of the Potomac, fared much the same. Its location was chosen to satisfy Virginians, for whom it was both convenient—as it was not for many others—and offered a certain moral assurance that the federal government would not stray too far from their influence. The idea of erecting the city of Washington in the District of Columbia on boglands carved from Maryland and Virginia was, however, impractical in the extreme, and plans for its execution compounded the problem.

Jefferson envisioned an impressive federal capital built according to a master plan. His dream was taken to still greater lengths by a French engineer, Major Pierre-Charles L'Enfant, who in August 1791 presented a plan for the capital every bit as ambitious as the proposals for the SUM. L'Enfant envisioned 160-foot-wide "transverse avenues" that would cut across a more simple grid of streets, 30-foot-wide walkways,

A watercolor of the U.S. Capitol painted in the mid-1790s by William Thornton, who won the prize for its design. What Thornton painted was a dream: it took seventy-one years for the Capitol to be built.

great public squares, and massive public buildings connected by long vistas across carefully cultivated parklands. His plan recalled Versailles, the French town where he had lived as a child, which King Louis XIV once hoped to make the capital of France. Jefferson and Washington liked L'Enfant's plans, but they were wildly inappropriate for the capital of a republic that was to be built on an almost uninhabited stretch of land. Some people, George Washington among them, dreamed that the Potomac would one day become a mighty highway to the West, but the river was in fact unsuited for that role. That meant the city of Washington was unlikely to develop a commercial life capable of attracting and sustaining a substantial population.

How, then, would the development of the capital be financed? Virginia and Maryland together contributed $192,000, hardly more than a beginning. The rest, Jefferson insisted, had to come from land sales in the federal district itself; President Washington could not ask for congressional appropriations, or the whole location issue might be reopened. But land auctions failed to draw buyers, and in 1796—when the SUM ended manufacturing operations—the president finally had to ask Congress for authority to borrow $500,000. Congress promised to "make good the deficiency" if the sale of lands pledged as collateral proved insufficient to repay the loan, which they almost certainly would. The president's language so understated the problems that it did little to sustain the honor of "honest George." In the meantime, financial troubles contributed to conflicts that, in turn, led to L'Enfant's dismissal in early 1792, less than a year after he began working on the new capital. His successors suffered similar fates.

There was a real question, in fact, whether the Americans were capable of executing so ambitious a scheme as L'Enfant proposed. Take the problem of designing the Capitol, for which competitors were asked to submit designs. The prize went to a Dr. William Thornton, who had no expertise in architecture and whose plan, based on classical models, turned out to include major technical deficiencies when, finally, a person who knew something about architecture examined it. Too bad we didn't know that earlier, Washington commented; but some plan, any plan, had to be adopted and, "good or bad, it must be entered upon." The Capitol's cornerstone was laid before the building plans were complete; several supervising architects in succession lost their jobs; and it took seventy-one years before the Capitol was completed. By then, the country could boast architects and engineers of its own, and manufacturing enterprises that fulfilled visions not so different from that of a great industrial complex on the banks of the Passaic. Rome wasn't built in a day, nor was the United States, and all the wishes of its most ardent supporters could not make up for the broad-based managerial and technological inadequacies that held back development on several fronts.

The failure of the SUM and the pathetic beginnings of the national capital reflected a larger truth. The United States began as a nation of amateurs; that was a source of its energy and remains part of the early Republic's charm. Sometimes amateurs are capable of astounding innovations. The eighteenth century was in general kind to men like Benjamin Franklin, who turned his attention from one field of interest to another, making significant contributions in several; and the early nineteenth would also offer opportunities aplenty to ingenious amateurs. But already in the 1790s, the realization of many grander ambitions required specialized skills. Until Americans could acquire them, the fulfillment of those dreams was necessarily postponed into the future.

> *"The United States began as a nation of amateurs; that was a source of its energy and remains part of the early Republic's charm."*

Prosperity

The bleak scenes on the banks of the Passaic and Potomac were not repeated everywhere. Consider, for example, the story of Boston, a town that had once been the leading port of British North America but lost considerable ground through much of the eighteenth century. First the heavy death toll among men who helped fight Britain's wars with France checked the town's population growth, then she suffered severely from Britain's exclusion in 1783 of American ships from her old markets in the British West Indies. Boston's merchants tried desperately to open new trade routes, and, although trade with Portugal increased, initiatives in the Mediterranean came to a halt once the Barbary pirates of North Africa turned loose on American ships. But on August 9, 1790, almost three years after leaving Boston, the *Columbia* under Captain Robert Gray became the first American ship to circumnavigate the globe, bringing the prospect of a profitable trade between the Pacific Northwest, China, and the United States. The tariffs and other legislation enacted by the

First Federal Congress also gave Bostonians hope, since they allowed American ships distinct advantages in both transoceanic and coastal trade. Even so, progress was slow: only in 1792 did Boston's per capita exports exceed those of the mid-1770s.

Then, suddenly, the port sprang to life. Between 1790 and 1800, Boston's population grew from just over 18,000 to almost 25,000—an increase of about 40 percent—and most of the increase came after 1793. In 1790, the town looked much as it had forty years earlier, but now it underwent a major physical transformation. Banks and insurance companies started to cluster along State Street, and striking new buildings appeared, some designed by Charles Bulfinch, a native Bostonian and 1781 Harvard graduate. Bulfinch studied architecture in France and England, then returned home in 1787, just in time to become an investor in the *Columbia*'s voyage. He built an elegant string of brick townhouses—the Tontine Crescent— along a curved street at Franklin Place, and massive Georgian houses with bowed fronts on Boston's Beacon Hill. The Boston State House, built in 1795 with a distinctive gilded dome, was perhaps the most eloquent early sign of Boston's new prosperity. Soon the town would literally outgrow its colonial boundaries, filling in coves and straightening out the harbor front, beginning a process of expansion that allowed a seventeenth-century peninsula to become home to a modern city.

In other Atlantic ports, the story was much the same. In fact, other towns and cities along the East Coast outstripped Boston's **population growth** both in percentage gain and in absolute numerical growth: Baltimore almost doubled in size between 1790 and 1800, to a population of 26,000, and Philadelphia, still the largest American city, grew by over 50 percent to 69,500. New York's expansion was even more impressive. From 1790, when it held just over 33,000 people, New York added 27,000 more within a decade, reaching a population of 60,500 by 1800, and its growth was far from over. With access via the Hudson River to a rich backcountry as well as a fine ocean harbor, New York's imports and exports already exceeded those of Philadelphia in 1797, although it took a bit longer for New York to become the nation's most populous city. In each case, as in Boston, population growth accompanied physical expansion, new construction, and other signs of prosperity. That sudden, explosive growth began a process of urbanization that would continue in the next centuries.

What explained these transformations? Not a major departure from old activities, but a revival of what merchants in Boston and other ports had long been good at: commerce and trade. "The harbor of Boston is . . . crowded with vessels," one observer reported in late 1794. "Eighty-four sail have been counted lying at two of the wharves only," and "it is reckoned that not less than four hundred and fifty sail of ships, brigs, schooners, sloops and small craft are now in this port." That was quite a change from ten years earlier, when American trade languished under the force of British restrictions. The reason for the difference was simple: in 1793, the major powers of Europe were at war over events stemming from the French Revolution. And the war opened a major opportunity for the carriers of neutral nations such as the United States, one that American shippers—now with the support of a viable national government—were prepared to exploit as much as possible.

Philadelphia's Delaware River front in the 1790s, full of ships at dock, with their masts down; painted by Thomas Birch.

EXPORTS AND THE "CARRYING TRADE"

The United States stood to profit from Europe's war in two ways. Belligerents needed products the Americans could supply, including wheat and other foodstuffs. They also needed the services of neutral shippers to carry goods from their colonies and other parts of the world, since ships flying the flags of warring nations faced attack by their enemies. France saw the situation clearly and in February 1793 formally opened its colonial empire to American ships. Spain did not follow suit until 1797, and England still excluded American ships from her West Indian colonies. However, as the war in Europe strained the capacities of the Royal Navy, Britain's restriction on trade with its colonial dependencies often went unenforced, which allowed American ships great freedom of movement. As an early nineteenth-century American observer explained, the European war "created a demand for our exports, and invited our shipping for the carrying trade of a very considerable portion of Europe; we not only carried the colonial productions to the several parent states, but we also became the purchasers of them in the French, Spanish and Dutch colonies." Such goods—sugar, for example, or coffee and cocoa—were brought into the United States, then reexported to Europe, where "the demand . . . for foreign merchandise, especially for that of the West Indies and South America, secured to all these cargoes a ready sale, with a great profit." On the return voyage, ships carried goods of European origin to the United States, from which many were again reexported to markets in the Caribbean or other parts of the Americas.

The percentage growth of reexports in the period was, in fact, truly spectacular: while the value of American exports went up about three and a half times between 1793 and 1801 (from $26.1 to $94.1 million), that of reexports rose from $300,000 in 1790 to $1.7 million three years later and reached $46.6 million by 1801. American consumption of imported goods—

often finished manufactured products—more than doubled in these years, from $30.8 million in 1793 to $66.7 million in 1801, but, unlike the early 1780s, the sale of American goods and services more than offset their cost. The result was an explosive increase in wealth, which lay behind the fine homes and public buildings appearing in one port city after another. In the 1790s, trade offered enticements enough for profit. It remained to be seen whether the situation would reverse again and a European peace threaten to return the United States to the plight it had faced in the 1780s. If that happened, merchants' capital assets might well be invested in less customary activities such as manufacturing.

RIPPLE EFFECTS

The beneficiaries of this dramatic expansion in trade were not confined to merchants or to port cities. As more and more vessels put to sea, the demand for seamen rose, and there is some evidence of a resulting rise in wages. For instance, ordinary Boston seamen who signed on for the *Columbia*'s first voyage to China in 1787 were paid $5 a month, and skilled seamen $7 a month. By 1799, some merchants were paying boys $8–$10, ordinary seamen $14–$17, and skilled seamen $18 a month. (For purposes of comparison, a contemporary army private received $3 a month.)

The demand for ships also rose. Before the Revolution, Americans, particularly in New England, had manufactured a substantial volume of ships, but shipbuilding foundered in the 1780s, when Britain precluded its citizens from buying American-made vessels and British insurance rates also discouraged the use of American-made ships. Once commerce revived, however, so did shipbuilding, since now the purchasers were often Americans. Ships were built on the Delaware River near Philadelphia and at towns along the Atlantic coast south of Boston such as Cohasset, Duxbury, Hingham, or Scituate, and in Amesbury and Newburyport on the north shore of Massachusetts. Shipbuilding facilities in Maine and New Hampshire, which contained huge lumber reserves and an abundance of sawmills, also hummed with activity, bringing increased prosperity and, again, population growth to that once-remote region. Ships needed not just wood but ropes and sails, spurring increased business and income among suppliers and their employees, who were sometimes farmers looking for work in the agricultural off-season.

Similarly, the expansion of seaborne trade promoted the development of ancillary services such as docks and warehouses, insurance companies and banks. The growing urban populations, drawn to ports by the opportunities they offered, also had to be fed, which required moving foodstuffs from the countryside into towns and cities. That explains in part the 1790s' enthusiasm for turnpikes, which were characteristically built on a wagon-wheel pattern, like spokes protruding from a hub out into the hinterland, along which crops traveled into urban centers. River improvements, bridges, early canals, and other, similar projects also aided transportation. And transportation and communications improvements accelerated the spread of a market economy (that is, of an area within which people buy and sell with each other frequently) whose development was already underway during the 1780s. And since a market economy serves to guide resources "to their most productive uses," its spread encouraged further economic development.

THE NEW AMERICAN PRACTICAL NAVIGATOR

Navigation itself was open to improvement in this age of sailing ships, when skill and chance—or the blessing of God—contributed as much as science to a voyage's success. Knowing a ship's location was a big help, especially when it sailed not just on familiar jaunts along the coast or to the West Indies, but around the world.

By the 1790s, the problem of fixing location by determining longitude had been solved—by John Harrison, a self-taught English clockmaker, who, beginning in the 1730s, constructed a series of innovative "sea clocks," or chronometers, that could keep accurate time despite variations in conditions at sea. Among other innovations, Harrison used different metals in such a way that one counteracted the tendency of another to expand with temperature changes. A navigator could determine local time at sea by setting his ship's clock to twelve when the sun reached its midday height; then, with another accurate clock that told him the time at his point of departure, he could compare the two. Since the earth takes twenty-four hours to turn 360 degrees, each hour of difference amounted to 15 degrees of longitude. (What that meant in terms of distance traveled varied with latitude: a degree of longitude translates to sixty-eight miles at the equator, but almost nothing at the North or South Pole. However, once a mariner knew both his latitude and longitude, he could calculate the distance he'd come.)

Harrison embarked on his inventive odyssey in an effort to win a prize of £20,000—millions of dollars in modern currency—that the British Parliament offered in 1714 for a "Practicable and Useful" means of determining longitude. He readily won the acclaim of the Royal Society, which gave him its Copley Prize in 1749, a few years before giving it to Franklin, and tests of his clocks allowed longitude to be determined with even greater accuracy than Parliament had required. However, the Board of Longitude, which Parliament set up to administer its prize and allot funds to hopeful contenders, did not officially award him the prize money, and only grudgingly gave him a substantial part of it in 1773, after George III intervened on his behalf.

There was, in fact, a problem with Harrison's solution: chronometers were extremely expensive. As a result, in the 1790s few American vessels carried one. The chronometers of the day were also frail and, unlike Harrison's amazing cre-

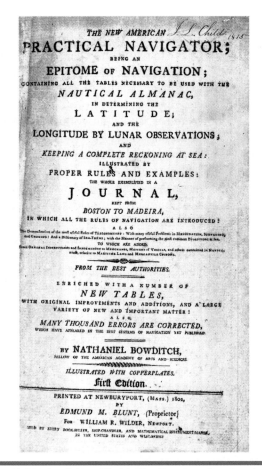

The cover of Nathaniel Bowditch's *The New American Practical Navigator*, 1802.

ations, so unreliable that even in later times, when their use became more common, ships sometimes carried three chronometers to avoid misreadings. But there was an alternative method of calculating longitude that had been favored by Harrison's critics—including the royal astronomer, Nevil Maskelyne (whose opposition to giving Harrison the prize while on the Board of Longitude provides a classic case of self-serving scientific politics). For a relatively modest price, navigators could acquire a reflecting quadrant, invented in 1731 by an Englishman, John Hadley, and almost simultaneously by a Philadelphia glazier named Thomas Godfrey. By using paired mirrors, the quadrant allowed navigators to measure lunar distances, the angular distances between the moon and some visible fixed star, even on a bobbing ship. They could then compare the results with tables in Greenwich time (the time at the Royal Observatory in Greenwich, England) to determine local time, and, using that figure, calculate their location. The method became fairly common after Maskelyne published lunar tables in the *Nautical Almanac* (1767). Reading "lunars" required care, since an error of even one minute (that is, one-sixtieth of a degree) would cause a thirty-mile miscalculation of location. To make matters worse, the tables published by Maskelyne and also the "improved" tables of his successors included many errors.

A solution to that problem came from Salem, Massachusetts, in 1790 the sixth largest town in the United States. Nathaniel Bowditch was born there in 1773 to the family of a local sailor and cooper (a barrel maker) who had trouble supporting his family. Although his unusual talent for mathematics appeared early, Bowditch's formal education ended at age ten, when he went to work with his father and later as a ship chandler, or supplier. Meanwhile, he educated himself, making good use of a local Philosophical Library that had managed to buy the library of a major Irish scientist after it was seized by a privateer during the Revolutionary War. The library included not just the *Transactions of the Royal Society of London* and the works of such towering British scientists as Robert Boyle and Isaac Newton, but scientific and mathematical treatises in German and French. Anxious to unlock their secrets, young Bowditch learned the languages necessary to read those works of continental science.

Then, in 1795, he went to sea on the first of five voyages to China and the East Indies, in the course of which he rose from clerk to captain. During dull days, Bowditch studied mathematics, including the work of the great French mathematician and theoretical astronomer Pierre Simon Laplace. He also

Nathaniel Bowditch, as painted by Charles Osgood in 1835, when Bowditch had become a prosperous businessman.

checked the available charts and tables of navigation against his own observations and later against the manuscript records of the East India Marine Society at the East India Museum in Salem, which included logs kept by its members. He found some 8,000 errors in the standard tables, many of which could lead to shipwrecks. Fortunately, Bowditch caught the attention of a publisher in another Massachusetts coastal town, Newburyport. Together they published an improved version of an English text, John Hamilton Moore's *The New Practical Navigator,* in 1799, informing readers only that the changes had been made by "a skillful mathematician and navigator." A second edition appeared in 1800.

Then, in 1802, the first edition of Bowditch's own book, *The New American Practical Navigator,* appeared simultaneously in England and the United States. It included twenty-nine tables as well as hundreds of pages of text that explained the uses of geometry and trigonometry, various specific mathematical calculations critical to navigation, as well as navigational tools such as the compass, quadrant, and sextant. It also included a glossary of terms related to the sea and information on business devices such as bills of exchange and marine insurance. The book was, in short, a complete handbook of navigation, and became the seaman's bible as it went through one edition after another. In fact, the book (although, of course, heavily revised) remains in print today; and the 1966 edition disclosed that some 700,000 copies had been printed since the first edition appeared.

The New American Practical Navigator was not a scientific achievement on the order of Benjamin Franklin's work with electricity, but Bowditch resembled Franklin both in being self-educated and in his commitment to using science for practical purposes. His book saved not just lives but ships and cargoes, and so made commerce more profitable. Bowditch's approach also fed the rage for self-education that followed the Revolution and made American crews, who were

known to spend their downtime studying Bowditch, more technically sophisticated navigators. Bowditch himself demonstrated the utility of scientifically informed navigation when, on the last voyage of his seafaring career, he guided the 260-ton ship *Putnam* safely into port through a dense snowstorm. Contrary to legend, he had managed to glimpse one landmark to confirm his position, but otherwise depended entirely on "scientific navigation."

Then, just over thirty years of age, Bowditch took up another career—as president of the Essex Fire and Marine Insurance Company, one of the new corporations chartered in postrevolutionary Massachusetts. During his twenty years in that office, while he continued his studies of mathematics and astronomy, the firm paid average annual dividends of 10 or 12 percent. Nathaniel Bowditch was a man of his time.

COTTON

In 1790, the United States included some 3.9 million people, including 700,000 slaves. About 200,000 Americans lived in the trans-Appalachian West, and their numbers almost doubled by 1800. The westerners knew that their future depended on their ability to get goods to market, which is why they tended to settle near rivers. The great bulk of the population, however, remained east of the mountains, with roughly half in the North, half in the plantation South.

Except for Baltimore, which assumed importance with the growth of trade in grains, southern cities did not share in the urban growth spurred by trade. Charleston, for example, grew at a much slower rate than ports to its north, indeed, at a rate lower than that of overall American population growth. Charleston did not reap substantial benefits from the reexport trade, since it lacked a substantial merchant community. The town was mainly an export center, but merchants from elsewhere carried most of South Carolina's products to market, and its exports were not thriving. Rice had once made South Carolinians rich; but rice exports actually declined between the 1770s and 1790s. States in the Chesapeake, whose tobacco—which had accounted for as much as a third of all exports from the British North American colonies—could no longer be shipped to Britain, faced a similar dilemma, which many planters solved by growing wheat instead. But wheat did not grow well in the warmer regions of the South. What could they produce?

Cotton was the answer. As a crop, it could be successfully grown anywhere south of the 37th degree north latitude (which crosses Virginia from a point just north of Norfolk), and the ecology of regions farther south were ideally suited for its cultivation. Cotton needed 200–210 frostless days and 20–25 inches of annual rainfall. In the South, rain tended to fall more in the spring and midsummer than later in the season, an ideal situation that could be replicated in few other places before the use of artificial irrigation. The sea islands off the coast of Georgia and South Carolina already grew a form of long-staple cotton (cotton with a long fiber), but another variety, with a short staple, could be grown inland, even in upland regions. Moreover, although cotton could be grown on small family farms, it could also be cultivated profitably in large units, allowing southern plantation owners to use the slave labor force they already had at hand and which accounted for a substantial part of their wealth.

To whom would the cotton be sold? To American cotton manufacturers? Applications for incorporation from companies such as the Beverly Cotton Manufactory in Massachusetts stressed that they would use American raw materials, but the textile industry had barely begun in the United States during the 1790s, and its beginning was full of failures. For example, a "very Compleat" carding and spinning mill built in 1795 on the Brandywine River north of Wilmington, Delaware, burned to the ground in 1797, a victim, some charged, of British arson.

The one apparent success, a factory Samuel Slater constructed for the firm of Almy and Brown in Pawtucket, Rhode Island, in 1793—a signal year for the American economy—was essentially a spinning mill with, at first, only 100 spindles. There, a labor force of women and children produced cotton thread that Almy and Brown sold to weavers and knitters who worked elsewhere. In the period 1793–1803, the operation managed to make a profit of $18,000. That, like the first voyage of the *Columbia* (which actually made no profit at all), was promising. Two-thirds of the mill's $100,000 in expenditures had gone for raw cotton, but such a sum was hardly enough to encourage an expansion of southern production. Moreover, the firm preferred to buy West Indian long-staple cotton because it was cleaner than the American product. In the southern states, Moses Brown wrote in 1791, "the present production in the mixed manner in which it is Brought to Market does not answer good purpose," so he chose to import West Indian fiber despite "the Discouragement of the Impost, rather than Work our Own production." By the late 1790s, Almy and Brown had begun using cotton from Georgia, but the cost of raw cotton remained high.

Clearly it would take time, and perhaps also a reduction in cotton prices, before American production could absorb a substantial volume of raw cotton.

But cotton, recently a luxury product imported from India or Egypt, had a future. Cotton cloth was more comfortable than wool in warm weather and could be more easily laundered; indeed, the appearance of cotton clothing signaled a revolution in personal hygiene and comfort. By 1801, Almy and Brown were receiving orders for their cotton thread faster than the firm could fill them. And by then, the cotton industry was already well established in Britain. Since theirs was not a climate in which cotton could be grown, the British had to import the raw material they processed. In 1780, Britain imported less than 7 million pounds of cotton, but then, owing to a series of technological innovations (which the Americans were trying to imitate), both production and imports rose meteorically. Britain imported 22 million pounds of cotton in 1787; fifty years later, the United Kingdom (including both Great Britain and Ireland) would import 407 million pounds. That market was a star worth catching.

There was one problem. The long-staple cotton that could only be grown in limited areas along the southeastern coast of the United States was much easier to clean than the short-staple cotton of the inland South. Bolls of long-staple cotton could simply be passed through two grooved rollers turned by a crank, as on old-fashioned mechanical clothes wringers. The smooth black seeds caught in the rollers' grooves and fell out. But the short-staple, green-seeded cotton that could be grown over most areas of the South had fuzzy fibers that clung tenaciously to the seeds. If short-staple cotton was put through rollers, the seeds held tight and came out the other side, or broke into pieces that scattered through the fiber, making the problem worse. Once successfully cleaned, however, upland cotton was a high-quality product, strong and smooth. Some technical device was needed to solve the problem of separating seeds from fibers, and the state of Georgia—where 2 or 3 million pounds of short-staple cotton were grown in anticipation of such a solution—appointed a commission to encourage inventive geniuses to propose an answer. One person who succeeded at that task was a New Englander who happened to be in Georgia when the need for a new cotton "gin" (short for "engine") was the stuff of common conversation.

Eli Whitney came from inland Worcester, Massachusetts, and spent his youth in his father's workshop doing jobs like making nails, hatpins, or canes, or fixing violins. After graduating from Yale at age twenty-six, in 1792, Whitney went

South expecting to take up a job as tutor to the children of a family in South Carolina. His ship sailed from New York to Georgia, where he visited Mulberry Grove, the home of General Nathanael Greene's widow, near Savannah. There, as he later wrote his father, he "heard much said of the extreme difficulty of ginning Cotton, that is, seperating [sic] it from its seeds," and how "if a machine could be invented which would clean the cotton with expedition, it would be a great thing both to the Country and the inventor." When "involuntarily . . . thinking on the subject," he came up with "a plan of a Machine," and "in about ten days," he said, "I made a little model, for which I was offered, if I would give up the right and title to it, a Hundred Guineas." So rather than continuing on to South Carolina, he remained in Georgia, "perfecting the Machine." By April 1793, he had built a functioning "**Cotton Gin**."

Whitney's machine used wire teeth arranged on a cylinder within a box-like container to tear cotton fiber from the seeds. The wire teeth picked up raw cotton and pulled it through slots on an iron bar that were too narrow for the seeds to pass through. As the seeds dropped into a box, brushes on smaller cylinders, which moved in the direction opposite that of the major cylinder, pulled the fiber off the teeth. This was not a high-tech device that required mathematical or scientific sophistication; it was a relatively simple machine, operated by belts that were turned by a crank, such as any reasonably skilled mechanic with access to shop tools and common building materials could construct. And it was easy to operate. One man could turn the crank of the prototype machine, Whitney explained to his father, and clean ten times as much cotton as could be done by any earlier process, and also "cleanse it much better than in the usual mode"—maybe even enough for the Moses Browns of the world. Moreover, the machine could be turned by water or a horse. That made the labor of cleaning cotton "fifty times less" than with "the old machines," and, Whitney added, "without throwing any class of People out of business."

Assured that he would "make a Fortune" by his machine, Whitney secured a federal patent in 1794, but was never able to protect his rights against imitators. It's possible, in fact, that he was not the only inventor of the cotton gin. Some forty years earlier, a community of Salzburger settlers in Georgia devised a "little machine that costs a couple of shillings, through the help of which a single person, even a child of six years," could quickly remove the seeds from "four to six pounds" of short-staple cotton "and not get even the least bit

The drawing of a cotton gin that Eli Whitney included in his original application for a federal patent.

tired." The invention was too much in advance of market demand for cotton to catch on, and when the right time came, other people could also have devised such machines. History offers examples aplenty of both premature and simultaneous inventions. In any case, the use of cotton gins revolutionized southern agriculture in a remarkably short period of time. The United States exported only 488,000 pounds of cotton in 1793; in 1794, the amount more than tripled, to 1.6 million pounds, and by 1801 reached almost 21 million pounds. Within a generation, the American South became the world's dominant producer of raw cotton.

In later years, southerners might have asked whether cotton was a blessing or a curse. It shackled the region to slave labor, and changed the relationships between white southerners in ways that would have unforeseen consequences. Since cotton soon far outdistanced the production of grains, rice, and sugar, it also transformed the South from a producer of many raw materials to a section that grew essentially one crop for export. The economic consequences of that change also became apparent only in the future. For the moment, however, faced with lagging markets and a workforce of black slaves who, it seemed, could neither be freed without unacceptable social conse-

267

quences nor profitably employed, prominent white southerners harbored few if any misgivings about rushing into a cotton economy. Cotton for them was a great and welcome blessing.

A New Party System?

In retrospect, Congress was divided from its opening days. The disputes over civil titles, between men who thought practices learned from the British past necessary and those who scoffed at the idea, seem to mark the first appearance of two political groups that became, over the course of the 1790s, reasonably settled and even organized. Whatever those differences represented, the groups (or parties) did not simply continue previous divisions over ratification of the Constitution. Richard Henry Lee, a supporter of titles, had been an ardent Antifederalist; William Maclay, who could hardly contain his disgust at such tomfoolery, had been a firm Federalist. Indeed, most members of the First Federal Congress had been Federalists in 1787 and 1788, and the two most active organizers of the ratification movement, Hamilton and Madison, became leaders of opposing groups in the politics of the later 1790s. The emergent divisions were over new issues, new situations, new antagonisms.

The divisions in Congress, moreover, were not the same as the party system of forty or fifty years later. By then, politics was a great national game between two "teams," each with a devoted electoral following that it carried to the polls year after year, winning sometimes, losing others, and never suffering a sense that victory or defeat had an effect more lasting than the distance between one election and the next. Such a political system lay in an inconceivable future. The ethics of the 1790s demanded that patriotic men devote themselves to the public good, upon which every rational, informed person not "corrupted" by a desire to serve his immediate self-interest would agree. To solicit votes was not a respectable practice: voters were supposed to support candidates for their qualifications, not because their votes were courted. And to organize a following with the intention of seizing power from a standing government, even through the ballot box, was a form of sedition. Political divisions therefore seemed to portend the onset of anarchy, which had killed off many a republic in the past.

So long as these convictions held, there could be no simple formation of a party system. Each stage in the development of political divisions during the 1790s brought denials that any such thing was happening. The parties that did emerge, moreover, could not serve the beneficial function that two-party systems usually perform—regularizing and moderating opposition as contenders move toward the center in the struggle to win the middle ground between them. The parties of the 1790s, in fact, were more like those of the 1770s than those of later times: the "Republicans" modeled themselves on the revolutionary movement and resisted government policies that, in their opinion, echoed those Great Britain had adopted between 1765 and 1776; the Federalists, on the other hand, struggled to uphold the government born of the Revolution against internal subversion. Both saw themselves as fighting to save the Republic; each denied the other's legitimacy. And the conflict between those parties often seemed as real a threat to the future of the United States as the threat their predecessors had posed to British rule.

BEGINNINGS

The record of congressional voting tells the story: divisions in the First Federal Congress were irregular, with alliances shifting from issue to issue. Hamilton and Jefferson both served as department heads in Washington's administration and remained on good terms for several years. Indeed, Jefferson helped construct the compromise of 1790 that allowed federal assumption of state debts, a critical part of Hamilton's program. Madison, too, supported the administration from his place in the House. But gradually Jefferson—and also Madison—developed a deep dislike of Hamilton and all he stood for, causing a split in the cabinet. Meanwhile, voting patterns in Congress showed two groups, later called Federalists and Republicans, taking different stands more consistently. The two sides also began trying to increase their strength by intervening in state elections and by appealing to the public through the press. The Federalist, pro-administration position was defended by John Fenno's *Gazette of the United States*; then, in October 1791, those who opposed the direction taken by the Washington administration established a paper that presented their position—the *National Gazette*, edited by the poet Philip Freneau, an admirer of Jefferson.

Before long, those who shared Jefferson's and Freneau's views came to call themselves Republicans because they saw themselves as defending the Republic against enemies who were working to undermine the accomplishments of the

American Revolution. The local groups that formed to support Republican views and candidates for office, known as "democratic" or "republican" clubs or societies, modeled themselves on the Sons of Liberty, who had resisted British policies before independence, and again for good reason. From the vantage point of people who remembered all too well the provocations that led to independence, the Washington administration gave persistent cause for worry.

Consider, for example, its use of military power. In May 1792, Congress passed a Militia Act, which authorized the states to organize men between the ages of eighteen and twenty-four into militia units. The troops were needed against Indians in the Northwest who were hostile to Euro-American expansion, but were later used against farmers in western Pennsylvania who opposed an excise tax on whiskey passed by Congress in 1791 to supplement federal revenues from tariffs. Excise taxes were never popular in either England or America; and this particular excise tax posed a particular hardship on farmers west of the Appalachians, who transported and sold their grain to eastern customers in the more portable form of whiskey. Rather than pay the tax and cut into their already meager profits, the farmers resisted, first peacefully, then with violence—for example, by tarring and feathering tax collectors, which itself recalled revolutionary opposition to Britain. In September 1794, Washington finally ordered the repression of the so-called Whiskey Rebellion. With Hamilton at his side, he personally led 15,000 militiamen into western Pennsylvania. Resistance had crumbled by the time the troops arrived, and Washington pardoned the two main insurgents after they were convicted of treason.

For people who remembered old adages against standing armies, it was disquieting to see the United States sending troops against its own people. Just as resistance to the whiskey tax recalled opposition to the Stamp Act (another excise tax), Washington's use of troops recalled British efforts to suppress civilian opposition in Boston before the Boston Massacre and again beginning in 1774.

A late eighteenth-century painting depicting General George Washington setting out to repress the Whiskey Rebellion.

Although political divisions first emerged over domestic issues, they deepened during a series of crises over foreign policy that reopened the nagging issue of America's relationship with Great Britain. Domestic and foreign policy were, however, never entirely separate, since decisions in one area frequently carried implications for the other.

FOREIGN AFFAIRS UNDER WASHINGTON

Hamilton saw much to admire in Britain. He modeled his financial policies in part on those of William Pitt the younger, a great British minister who took office in 1783, when Britain was so burdened with debt that it seemed on the verge of bankruptcy, and whose reforms restored his country's financial health. The success of Hamilton's financial program, moreover, depended on smooth relations with Britain: duties on imports provided a major source of federal revenue, and most American imports came from Britain. Hamilton did not advocate returning the Americans to British rule; he had, after all, fought for independence as an officer of the Continental army. Nor did he seek to establish a monarchy in the United States. But he thought an amicable

A view of Detroit by an unknown British officer in 1794, a year before Jay's Treaty finally brought to an end British occupation of its former posts in the West.

the reexport trade, lifeblood of the urban Northeast's new prosperity.

A treaty that asked so much of the United States and gave so little provoked widespread hostility in a country that, in any case, harbored few kindly feelings toward Britain. The Senate struck out the provision on the West Indies trade but accepted the rest of Jay's Treaty. Despite an uproar in the press and large popular meetings in several cities, Washington approved the treaty, which was finally signed on November 19, 1795. The opposition proceeded to carry the battle into the House of Representatives, which, under the leadership of James Madison, asserted its right to examine treaties before granting funds for their implementation. Washington refused House demands for the government's correspondence with Jay, which he saw as a violation of the executive branch's prerogatives. That decision set another important precedent. In the end, even the House granted the appropriations necessary to execute the treaty (on April 30, 1796). It knew the United States could not afford a war with Britain.

If Jay's Treaty was a mixed blessing, the Washington administration soon scored a few less ambiguous triumphs. One was over the Indians, although it took some doing. Efforts to make Indians recognize the territorial claims of the United States under the 1783 Treaty of Paris had failed: not surprisingly, the Indians insisted that they were unaffected by Europeans' treaties. Washington at first tried to follow a policy, proposed by Secretary of War Knox, of recognizing Indian claims and restraining white expansion except on lands the Indians sold voluntarily. That would work, Knox thought, because as farms spread westward, the population of wild animals that sustained Indian life would decline, and then the Indians would willingly give up large tracts of land. Best of all, by avoiding war, the policy would save money.

Knox was wrong. The administration succeeded in purchasing Indian title to lands in Kentucky and part of Tennessee, but north of the Ohio members of the Miami Confederation (which encompassed eight western tribes) resisted the spread of settlements that threatened their hunting grounds. Gradually, to protect frontier settlers and gain title to the Northwest, the administration went back to using force against the Indians. At first the policy failed miserably: in 1790, Indians crushed an invasion of the Ohio Territory by some 1,400 U.S. troops, and the next year they destroyed an even larger army (which included many inexperienced militiamen) on the banks of the Wabash River. Finally, Congress, in an effort to "pacify" the West, authorized the creation of a 5,000-man regular army, which General Anthony Wayne rigorously trained before leading it into Indian territory. On August 20, 1794, Wayne soundly beat the Indian forces at the Battle of Fallen Timbers on the Maumee River, just south of what is today Toledo, Ohio. It took a year to negotiate the Treaty of Greenville (August 3, 1795), by which the Indians ceded title to the southeastern corner of the Northwest Territory and a few enclaves farther inland (including the sites of Detroit and Chicago) and received annuities of about $10,000 in return. That victory and news of Jay's Treaty, under which the British, who had encouraged Indian resistance, would finally leave their western posts, led to a new surge of western settlement. Within four years, some 45,000 people had moved into what became, in 1803, the state of Ohio.

Soon the Treaty of San Lorenzo, sometimes called Pinckney's Treaty after the American negotiator, Thomas Pinckney, settled American problems with Spain. Under its terms, Spain accepted the Mississippi River and 31st parallel as the western and southern borders of the United States and allowed Americans to deposit goods at New Orleans (where they would be reloaded on oceangoing ships) for three years, and at some other point thereafter. Both nations agreed to prevent Indians in their territory from invading the other's lands. The treaty was signed at Madrid on October 27, 1795. It remained a major accomplishment of the Washington administration, which, through a time of unprecedented turmoil, succeeded in securing both British and Spanish recognition of American sovereignty over the vast stretch of land it had received in 1783 under the Treaty of Paris.

THE ELECTION OF 1796

The presidential election of 1792 was a near nonevent. Washington ran unopposed. Three electors abstained, but Washington received all of the remaining 132 electoral votes. George Clinton of New York opposed John Adams's reelection as vice-president, but Adams nonetheless won by a healthy margin. The election of 1796 promised to be far less predictable, particularly if Washington chose to retire, as many observers anticipated. But no announcement confirmed their speculation until, finally, on September 19, 1796, Philadelphia's *Daily American Advertiser* carried the text of the president's "Farewell Address," dated September 17.

That address, which Washington never presented orally, had long been in the works: Madison contributed to a draft in 1792, when Washington first contemplated retiring from the presidency. Hamilton, who remained close to Washington after leaving the treasury in January 1795, made more recent textual changes. Because the Farewell Address was understood as Washington's parting advice to his country, it was widely read and remains one of the most frequently reprinted documents in American history.

It was a moving document, beginning with expressions of the sixty-four-year-old Washington's gratitude to his "beloved country" for the honors and confidence it had invested in him and a reference to "the increasing weight of years" that admonished him "more and more, that the shade of retirement is as necessary to me as it is welcome." Then the president offered advice, based on "much reflection," that might "contribute to the permanency of your felicity as a People." He urged his countrymen to support the public credit, to "observe good faith and justice towards all Nations" while avoiding permanent alliances with any, and to disdain "overgrown Military establishments," which were always "inauspicious to liberty." But the thrust of his message concerned the country's political divisions.

Washington considered any opposition to an established republican government seditious. He saw himself not as the head of a ruling party but as the head of government, and considered all organized opposition to the government a threat to the rule of law—a view that not everyone shared. In a message to Congress of November 1794, he had referred to the democratic clubs—organizations that worked peacefully on behalf of republican policies—as "self-created societies" whose support contributed to the violence in western Pennsylvania and which were as objectionable as actual insurrections. After Washington's condemnation, the societies dissolved, but Thomas Jefferson was furious. Not only had Washington (under the influence of Hamilton, "the servile copyist of Mr. Pitt") used a "military force for civil purposes," Jefferson said, but in attacking the democratic societies he had violated the freedom "of association, of conversation and of the press" in a way not even England, though "advancing to the establishment of an absolute monarchy, has yet been bold enough to attempt."

Now, in his Farewell Address, Washington offered a full-force attack on political parties: the "alternate domination of one faction over another" was itself "a frightful despotism" and led to a more "formal and permanent despotism" by allowing "cunning, ambitious, and unprincipled men ... to subvert the Power of the People and to usurp for themselves the reins of Government." To Washington, in short, the "baneful spirit of Party" was a real and present threat to the future of the American Republic.

The election of 1796 was nonetheless shaped by partisan politics. Adams ran for president as Washington's successor, but Hamilton tried to get Thomas Pinckney—who had just successfully negotiated the Treaty of San Lorenzo—elected instead. Under the procedures stated in the Constitution, each elector cast two votes without specifying which was for president and which for vice-president. The person who won the highest number of votes became president, and the candidate with next-highest number became vice-president. Hamilton attempted to persuade southern Republicans, who favored Thomas Jefferson, to cast their second vote for Pinckney. Then, with a full share of the Federalists' votes, Pinckney would outrank Adams.

Hamilton's scheme failed: Adams's supporters in the North anticipated the danger and scattered their second votes among several vice-presidential candidates. In the end, Adams became president with 71 votes, 3 more than Jefferson; Jefferson in turn received 9 more than Pinckney and so became Adams's vice-president.

THE ADAMS ADMINISTRATION

It seems strange in retrospect, this administration with a president from one party (Federalist) and vice-president

273

American shipping, Congress had authorized the construction of six new frigates—smaller than the ships of the line, the largest and most powerful ships in the great navies of the era, but faster and more maneuverable. Part of the order was canceled the next year, when the United States signed a peace treaty with Algeria, but three ships remained in production. They were built according to technologically innovative plans that are generally attributed to Philadelphia master shipbuilder Joshua Humphreys, although others contributed to the designs. Humphreys conceived of a ship that combined heavy firepower, approaching that of ships of the line, with the speed of a frigate, characteristics thought to be mutually exclusive. These "super frigates"—the Concordes of their day—would have distinctively long, sleek hulls and towering sail rigs to enhance speed, and carry an unusually large number of heavy guns mounted on two decks. According to Humphreys, that design would make the American ships "superior to any European frigate" and allow them to avoid action except "on their own terms."

But by increasing the length and armament (and hence weight) of the ships and by providing sleek hulls, the new designs made the ships susceptible to a bending of the keel (the lowest part of the ship's bottom, or hull), known as "hogging" because the keel's curvature resembled the arch of a hog's back. The phenomenon was a well-known obstacle in wooden ship design and the reason why speed and heavy armament were considered incompatible. Hogging occurs because upward water pressure is greatest at the center of a ship, where the hull is widest, and that pressure increases with the ship's weight. Moreover, the ship's heavy, gun-laden decks, which extended forward and backward over the narrow keel, brought tremendous downward pressure on its outer ends. These forces on the keel—up at its center, down at its ends—increase with the length of a ship, because length has a leveraging effect. Hogging at first slows a vessel's speed, and can eventually cause the keel to crack, sinking the ship.

But the frigates' designers proposed a solution: an integrated system of interlocking beams and immense internal braces with diagonal "riders" made of live oak—a particularly dense wood native only to North America and parts of Cuba—that carried the guns' weight down to the most vulnerable part of the keel and so counteracted the stress that led to hogging. The builders also constructed unusual, three-layered hulls of live oak with cross planks of white oak, another extremely dense, rot-resistant wood. At points, the hulls of the new ships were as much as twenty-five inches thick,

which made them virtually impervious to enemy fire. Their construction, a massive project carried out by shipbuilders in three different ports for political reasons, with sawyers (some of whom were slaves) in Georgia cutting and shipping timber and Humphreys overseeing the whole operation, was like nothing Americans had accomplished before.

The new super frigates—USS *United States*, USS *Constellation*, and USS *Constitution* (later dubbed "Old Ironsides" after a sailor watched enemy cannonballs bounce from its surface and shouted, "Huzzah! Her sides are made of iron!")—were launched in 1797, although the assembling of crews and other preparations prevented their taking to sea until the next year. They provided a fine beginning for the new U.S. Navy. Stoddert worked to acquire by one means or another an additional six frigates as well as some forty smaller ships. He also encouraged the indigenous development of techniques for rolling copper to sheath the ships' bottoms, a challenge that was finally met by Boston's Paul Revere, the onetime revolutionary express messenger; the domestic manufacture of carronades, short-range guns first developed by the British for splintering wood; and the creation of American sources of hemp, canvas, and other articles needed by the navy. And Stoddert built, virtually from scratch, a respectable naval officers corps and established a program for the recruit-

The gun deck of the USS *Constitution*. The heavy cannons on the ship brought great pressure down on its keel. Without countervailing measures, the pressure would have helped cause a misshaping of the keel known as "hogging."

ment and training of promising young midshipmen. Within a relatively short period of time, the United States possessed a navy capable of providing American merchant ships substantial protection and offsetting wildcat fears of a French invasion, mounted from the West Indies, of the American southern seaboard. All this Stoddert accomplished during a trying two-year period, from 1798 to 1800, while American and French ships engaged in an undeclared war on the seas that threatened continually to blossom into a regular declared war.

THE ALIEN AND SEDITION ACTS

As the war fever grew, Adams fell into Washington's old position, regarding critics of his government as seditious people who put their confidence in France rather than their own government. Federalists in Congress went further, passing a series of laws for the suppression of the Republicans and the Republican press. Three Alien Acts, passed in June and July of 1798, moved against immigrants, who were often members of the Republican Party. The first, an Alien Enemies Act that allowed the president to arrest or banish enemy aliens, would take effect only if war was declared. Another Alien Act allowed the president to deport any foreigners he considered dangerous to the public peace and safety, and a Naturalization Act increased the time of residence before immigrants could become citizens—and thus acquire voting rights— from five to fourteen years. Both of those laws would expire in 1802. Finally, a Sedition Act provided punishments including imprisonment for persons who combined "to oppose any measure or measures of the government of the United States" or who wrote, printed, spoke, or published "any false, scandalous, and malicious writing or writings against the government of the United States, or the President of the United States, with intention to defame . . . or to bring them or either of them, into contempt or disrepute." That law would expire on March 3, 1801, when the next presidential administration took power.

The Sedition Act was a reformed version of earlier English sedition laws: it allowed truth as a defense, and specified limited, not open-ended, punishments. But the act was administered in a violently partisan way. Among the victims were Matthew Lyon, an outspoken Republican congressman from Vermont remembered for a raucous fight on the floor of Congress with Federalist Roger Griswold, who was up for re-election. Lyon's attacks on Federalist policies won him a

A cartoon depicting the fight of Republican representative Matthew Lyon and the Connecticut Federalist Roger Griswold on the floor of Congress in 1798.

four-month jail sentence (during which he was reelected) and a $1,000 fine. The editors of Republican newspapers, who spent their lives trying to make the Adams administration and its policies objects of contempt, were also attacked and forced to cease publication, even to go into hiding.

THE VIRGINIA AND KENTUCKY RESOLUTIONS

Thomas Jefferson was alarmed by the Alien and Sedition Acts. So was James Madison. His old theory that there was no danger in placing power at the center of a confederated government had proven wrong. Neither the checks and balances built in to the Constitution nor the "parchment barriers" in the Bill of Rights had kept the Federalists from violating the basic freedoms of assembly, speech, and the press.

Jefferson anonymously drafted a set of resolutions that the Kentucky legislature adopted on November 16, 1798, asserting that, "as in all other cases of compact among parties having no common Judge, each party has an equal right to judge for itself" when the compact was violated and to determine the appropriate "mode and measure of redress." On that basis, Kentucky proceeded to declare several acts of Congress, including the Alien and Sedition Acts, unconstitutional and therefore "void and of no force." The Kentucky legislature sent its resolutions to the state's U.S. senators and representatives with a request that they work to repeal "the [aforesaid] unconstitutional and obnoxious acts." It also sent copies of the resolutions to the other states, asking that they similarly declare the specified acts "void and of no force" and request their repeal. The laws in question, Kentucky maintained, amounted to an "undisguised declaration" that the federal government intended to assume power to bind the states "in all cases whatsoever"—a clear reference to the British Declaratory Act of 1766. And unless arrested, that effort could "drive this state into revolution" and strengthen those ene-

mies of the Republic who believed "that man cannot be governed but by a rod of iron."

Madison drafted another set of resolves that the Virginia legislature adopted on December 24, 1798. They, too, condemned the Alien and Sedition Acts as "alarming infractions" of the Constitution and saw in congressional legislation an effort to "consolidate" the states by degrees and "transform the present republican system of the United States into an absolute, or, at best, a mixed monarchy." Virginia asserted that in the case "of a deliberate, palpable, and dangerous exercise" of

American Journal

What if You Get Sick?

"On Thursday Decr 12th [1799] the General [George Washington] rode out to his farms. . . . Soon after he went out, the weather became very bad. . . . A heavy fall of snow took place on friday, which prevented the General from riding out as usual. He had taken cold (undoubtedly from being so much exposed the day before) and complained of having a sore throat. . . .

"About two or three o'clk Saturday Morning he awoke Mrs Washington & told her he was very unwell, and had had an ague [fever]. She observed that he could scarcely speak. . . . As soon as the day appeared . . . he desired that Mr Rawlins, one of the Overseers who was used to bleeding the people, might be sent for to bleed him before the doctors could arrive. . . . I found him breathing with difficulty—and hardly able to utter a word intelligibly. . . . A mixture of Molasses, Vinegar & butter was prepared, to try its effect in the throat; but he could not swallow a drop. . . . Mr. Rawlins came in soon after sun rise—and prepared to bleed him. When the Arm was ready—the General, observing that Rawlins appeared to be agitated, said, as well as he could speak, *'don't be afraid,'* and after the incision was made, he observed *'the oriface is not large enough.'* . . . Mrs. W being . . . uneasy lest too much blood should be taken, it was stop'd after about half a pint was taken from him. Finding that no relief was obtain'd . . . I proposed bathing the

throat externally with Salvalaltita. . . . A piece of flannel was then put round his neck His feet were also soaked in warm water. This, however, gave no relief."

In the meantime, several doctors arrived. They "put a blister of cantharides on the throat & took more blood . . . and had some Vinegar & hot water put into a Teapot, for the General to draw in steam from the nozel." They also gave him "sage tea and Vinegar to be mixed for a Gargle," but when the general "held back his head to let it run down [his throat], it put him into great distress and almost produced suffocation." In the afternoon, he was "bled again, and the blood ran slowly . . . and did not produce any symptoms of fainting." They also administered "calomil & tarter em." but "without any effect." Around 6 P.M., the general told his physicians, *"'I feel myself going . . . let me go off quietly; I cannot last long.'"* Two hours later, the doctors "applied blisters to his legs, but went out without a ray of hope." About 10, with great difficulty, Washington said, *"'I am just going. Have me decently buried, and do not let my body be put into the Vault in less than two days after I am dead.'* I bowed assent." A little while later, "he expired without a struggle or a Sigh!"

Tobias Lear's journal entry on the death of George Washington at Mount Vernon, December 15, 1799 unconstitutional powers by the federal government, the states as parties to the federal compact "have the right and are in duty bound to interpose for arresting the progress of the evil."

Both the Kentucky and Virginia Resolutions failed. The state legislatures that replied—essentially all those from Maryland north—disavowed Kentucky's and Virginia's constitutional arguments. Some, like Rhode Island, argued that the power of judging the constitutionality of acts of Congress was vested exclusively in the Supreme Court of the United States, not in state legislatures. Kentucky, however, stuck to its guns, and passed another set of resolutions on February 22, 1799, that restated its previous position and added that a "nullification" by the states of all acts of Congress unauthorized by the Constitution was the "rightful remedy" while promising to oppose violations of the Constitution "in a constitutional manner."

Virginia took another approach. Madison drafted a "Report" that reexamined the constitutional issues under debate. The problem, he said, was that the word "states" had several meanings. The power to judge the constitutionality of federal laws lay in the states not as territories nor as governments, but as "the people composing those political societies, in their highest sovereign capacity," because it was the people—not the legislatures—who had ratified the federal Constitution. The Supreme Court's power was not superior to that of the people, since the courts were the people's creation. Like other branches of the government, the judiciary could violate the Constitution and so must remain subject to scrutiny. Moreover, "the authority of constitutions over governments, and of the sovereignty of the people over constitutions, are truths . . . at no time, perhaps, more necessary than at present." Finally, since the people exercised their sovereign power through conventions, not legislatures, the Virginia Resolutions were just a statement of opinion, not an effort to nullify federal laws. That was a clever but theoretically sophisticated effort to answer those who accused the legislature of acting improperly.

Still, the basic powers of government had not been the subject of such searching debate since the time of the Revolution. That precedent was not reassuring.

PEACE

John Adams ended the crisis. He fought off demands from ardent Federalists for a declaration of war, and listened instead to a stream of reports from Europe suggesting that France had become more open to conciliation. In February 1799, without consulting his cabinet, Adams nominated William Vans Murray as minister to France. That alone eased tensions by offering a prospect of peace. Murray did not set out until October, when he was accompanied by two other commissioners, Chief Justice Oliver Ellsworth and William R. Davie of North Carolina. When the three arrived, Napoleon Bonaparte had seized power and was ready to repair France's relationship with the United States. Napoleon was unwilling to compensate the Americans for past losses, but agreed to respect the rights of neutral ships in the future and ended France's campaign against American ships. The scare was over.

Adams's appointment of Murray was an act of courage, one that drew on the skills and instincts he had developed earlier as a diplomat. But it alienated a substantial part of his Federalist supporters and cast into doubt his reelection as president. In May of 1800, Adams finally dismissed McHenry and Pickering from his cabinet and took control of his administration. It was too late. So was news of the peace agreement, which arrived only after the election.

THE ELECTION OF 1800

Republicans organized for the election as no political group had done before, with local and state committees directed by a caucus of Republican congressmen in Philadelphia. Meanwhile, Republican newspapers attacked the government for its violations of basic liberties, its creation of a navy and army, and the taxes levied to support them. Their own candidate for president was Jefferson, and Aaron Burr for vice-president. Charles Cotesworth Pinckney was Adams's running mate. Once again Alexander Hamilton tried, as in 1796, to manipulate the vote so that Pinckney outranked Adams, and once again he failed. Considering the circumstances, Adams did well, winning 65 electoral votes—only 6 fewer than in 1796—and Pinckney 64. But both Jefferson and Burr received 73 votes, and it took thirty-six ballots in the House of Representatives, in which each state had for this purpose one vote, to break the tie. Jefferson finally won, ironically, through the intervention of Hamilton, who persuaded some of Burr's supporters to cast blank ballots. Compared with Burr, Hamilton concluded, Jefferson was the lesser evil.

THE END OF A CENTURY

Jefferson's inaugural, on March 4, 1801, was the first to take place in the nation's new capital on the Potomac. If Washington, D.C., was a symbol of the nation's future, or even the future of the federal government, the prospects looked grim indeed. There was no sign there of the prosperity that touched the government's previous homes in New York and Philadelphia: Washington was a backwater, a "city" with unpaved streets that turned to dust in the dry days of summer and into mud streams when it rained. The executive residence, first occupied by the Adamses, remained, like the Capitol, unfinished. What was built had been constructed so poorly that chunks of ceiling fell and pillars split within a few years of their installation. There were no streetlights, no street signs; grand avenues became cow paths. The city was home to flies and mosquitoes, frogs and also hogs, who happily gobbled up garbage in the roadways. An uninformed visitor witnessing the scene could only wonder whether some disaster had occurred. Was Washington half built, or half destroyed?

The new president, at least, looked to the future with confidence. He thought of his election as the "Revolution of 1800" because it brought to an end the repressive policies of

April 1789	First Federal Congress meets in New York; George Washington elected president.
April–May 1790	Federal patent and copyright laws passed.
1790–91	Hamilton submits plans for financial system and economic development.
December 15, 1791	The Bill of Rights added to the Constitution.
1792	The Post Office Act.
April 1793	Eli Whitney invents the cotton gin.
1794	Whiskey Rebellion.
1798	The XYZ Affair.
June–July 1798	The Alien and Sedition Acts.
November/December 1798	The Kentucky/Virginia Resolutions.
1802	Nathaniel Bowditch's *The New American Practical Navigator* appears.

Chronology

This campaign banner of 1800 reads, "Thomas Jefferson, President of the United States" and also, "John Adams no more."

the Federalists. Through the ballot box, Americans had averted the bloody revolution that the Kentucky Resolutions predicted. Now that constitutional government had been reestablished, the new president suggested, the threats to freedom and republicanism that he saw in the policies of the Federalists and also the political divisions that answered them would, along with the eighteenth century, disappear forever. He reminded his listeners that "every difference of opinion is not a difference of principle. We have called by different names brethren of the same principle. We are all Federalists; we are all Republicans." Anyone who wished to dissolve the Union or end the Republic should henceforth "stand undisturbed as monuments of the safety with which error of opinion may be tolerated where reason is left free to combat it."

The new president spoke of "a rising nation, spread over a wide and fruitful land," crossing the seas "with the rich productions of their industry," conducting commerce with foreign nations and "advancing rapidly to destinies beyond the reach of mortal eye." Would an honest patriot, "in the full tide of successful experiment, abandon a government which has so far kept us free and firm"? Some said "that man cannot be trusted with the government of himself. Can he, then, be trusted with the government of others? Or have we found angels in the forms of kings to govern him? Let history answer this question."

Jefferson had no doubt of history's answer. The election showed that men could be trusted with their own self-government. The Republic would survive.

Suggested Reading

Charlene Bangs Bickford and Kenneth R. Bowling, *Birth of the Nation: The First Federal Congress, 1789–1791* (1989)

Stanley Elkins and Eric McKitrick, *The Age of Federalism* (1993)

David J. Jeremy, *Transatlantic Industrial Revolution: The Diffusion of Textile Technologies Between Britain and America, 1790–1830s* (1981)

Douglass C. North, *The Economic Growth of the United States, 1790–1860* (1966)

Douglass C. North, Terry L. Anderson, and Peter J. Hill, *Growth and Welfare in the American Past: A New Economic History* (1983)

Douglass C. North and Robert Paul Thomas, eds., *The Growth of the American Economy to 1860* (1968)

Michael A. Palmer, *Stoddert's War: Naval Operations During the Quasi-War with France, 1798–1801* (1987)

Merritt Roe Smith, "Eli Whitney and the American System of Manufacturing," in Carroll W. Pursell Jr., ed., *Technology in America: A History of Individuals and Ideas,* 2nd ed. (1990)

Dava Sobel, *Longitude: The True Story of a Lone Genius Who Solved the Greatest Scientific Problem of His Time* (1996)

Dirk J. Struik, *Yankee Science in the Making* (1948)

Helen E. Veit et al., eds., *Creating the Bill of Rights: The Documentary Record from the First Federal Congress* (1991)

Conrad Edick Wright, ed., *Massachusetts and the New Nation* (1992)

Gavin Wright, *The Political Economy of the Cotton South: Households, Markets, and Wealth in the Nineteenth Century* (1978)

James Sterling Young, *The Washington Community, 1800–1828* (1966)

PROSPERS

New Orleans in 1803, the largest city west of the Appalachian Mountains and gateway to the enormous trade of the Mississippi Valley.

Focus QUESTIONS

■ **How did the nation move in major new directions during Jefferson's first term?**

■ **How did the embargo spur new developments in the economy?**

■ **How did the War of 1812 arise, and what were its major events?**

■ **What significant economic developments resulted from the War of 1812?**

As Thomas Jefferson took office at the dawn of a new century, there was a sense of change and anticipation all about. One indicator came from the Census Office, which announced in 1801 that the population of the United States stood at 5.3 million, a 35 percent increase since 1790. The Republic's population would continue its steep increase, nearly doubling by 1820 and more than doubling again by 1840. This meant a growth rate of more than 33 percent each decade over a fifty-year period, far exceeding that for any country in Europe. The rapid growth was powered mainly by an unprecedented commercial and geographic expansion, the leading edge of which emanated from the bustling cities of New York, Philadelphia, Boston, and Baltimore. Seaborne trade built the wealth of these port cities and the resources to invest in new ventures like textile manufacturing.

With a population of 70,000, Philadelphia was America's largest city in 1800, standing second in the world only to London in the value and volume of trade that passed through its harbor. Ten years later, New York City would eclipse Philadelphia in population and trade, and by 1821 New York would attract 37 percent of all imports entering the United States. In 1820, there were twelve U.S. cities with populations exceeding 10,000, and only two of them, New York and Philadelphia, had more than 100,000 people. Forty years later, 101 cities (most of them located in the Northeast and Midwest) boasted populations of more than 10,000, with eight surpassing 100,000. By then, New York was in a league of its own with over 1 million inhabitants.

Despite the rapid growth of New York and other seaboard cities, the United States remained overwhelmingly agricultural and rural in 1800. Most of the population, 75 percent, lived in the countryside and made their living from farming, while only 5 percent lived in cities. The remaining 20 percent lived in towns and villages that serviced the rural population. Beneath the surface, however, even the agrarian economy was changing. People were on the move: with the increasing scarcity of good farmland in the East, the distribution of bounty lands to veterans of the American Revolution, the opening of Ohio to white settlement, and the speculative activities of numerous land companies, Americans were heading westward, eventually crossing the Appalachians into the Ohio and Mississippi River valleys. Kentucky (1792) and Tennessee (1796) had already entered the Union as states, soon to be followed by Ohio in 1803. As the western migrations continued, the demographic center of the United States would move from a point twenty-three miles east of Baltimore in 1800 to a point twenty miles south of Chillicothe, Ohio, by 1860. This change reflected not only a **geographic shift in population** but the gathering momentum of an industrial economy.

The lure of the West was unmistakable in other ways as well. As the region's population grew, a western market emerged as the largely agrarian population looked eastward for manufactured goods and other hard-to-obtain supplies. Northeastern merchants, aware of escalating tensions in Europe and the threat they posed to overseas trade, began to cultivate trade with western outposts from Lake Erie to Memphis. But this alternative posed its own problems, the most serious of which was transportation. In 1800, the best trade route to the American West was by water along the Atlantic coast into the Gulf of Mexico and up the Mississippi River to New Orleans. The river floated pig iron, lumber, and nonperishable farm products like whiskey and salted pork downstream from as far north as Monongahela, Pennsylvania, while pack horses and small river craft brought trade goods upstream. The problem was that the Spanish con-

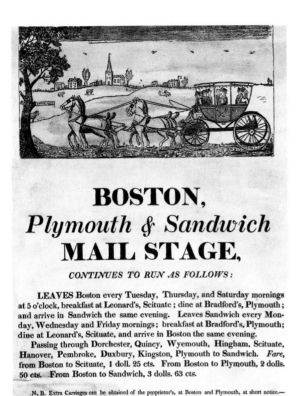

An 1810 advertisement for stagecoach service from Boston to Cape Cod. The bus lines of the eighteenth and nineteenth centuries, stagecoaches carried people, cargo, and the mail. As the fee schedules indicate, stagecoach service was not cheap. Most workers earned less daily than it cost to ride the local stage.

bridges. Stagecoaches, the fastest land conveyances of the day, rarely did better than four or five miles an hour. Larger and heavier freight wagons moved at an even slower pace, often taking weeks to cover 100 miles. Inland transportation throughout the country was not only slow but prohibitively expensive. The lack of well-maintained roads and canals was choking commercial development by hindering western farmers from sending their surplus goods to eastern population centers and eastern merchants from tapping western markets. Both groups expressed frustration, while rumors spread that the states and territories of the trans-Appalachian West might abandon the Union, form their own republic, and align themselves with the Spanish at New Orleans.

Setting a Course

Such was the state of affairs when Jefferson became president in March 1801. Well educated, the fifty-seven-year-old Virginian was a lawyer by training, with a distinguished political and diplomatic record. He was also a respected amateur scientist who counted among his friends some of the world's leading authorities on natural history (encompassing botany and zoology), geology, geography, meteorology, and astronomy. "Science is my passion, politics my duty," he explained to a correspondent in later life. His "fondness for philosophical studies," however, did not prevent him from engaging in practical pursuits. Always interested in agricultural improvements, he had used his mathematical and mechanical skills in 1788 to design a moldboard for turning soil that improved the efficiency of the common plow. As the American ambassador to France (1784–89), he had informed the United States about the latest European innovations in textile machinery, steam engines, and other technological improvements of the age. On at least one occasion, he had tried to persuade a talented French armorer to emigrate to America in order to build and equip a factory for manufacturing firearms with interchangeable parts. Although the attempt failed, Jefferson's correspondence alerted public authorities to

Thomas Jefferson, third president of the United States (1801–09).

trolled the port of New Orleans and, through it, all trade that passed up and down the Mississippi from Tennessee, Kentucky, Ohio, western Virginia, and western Pennsylvania. Given the uneasy situation in Europe, this route could be closed to American traffic at any time.

The other option, to ship goods westward via a series of connecting roads, rivers, and canals, was still unformed in 1800. No canal system connected the East Coast with the so-called western waters. Roads became little more than rutted paths after 50 or 60 miles, virtually impassable during mud seasons and always excruciatingly slow and bumpy to travel even in good weather. No one knew this better than Thomas Jefferson, who, on his way from Washington, D.C., to his plantation near Charlottesville, Virginia, had to travel unkept dirt roads and cross five rivers, only two of which had the new technology and attracted entrepreneurs like Eli Whitney to the idea. "I am not afraid of new inventions or improvements," Jefferson later wrote the artist-inventor Robert Fulton. "Where a new invention is supported by well-known principles, and promises to be useful, it ought to be tried."

JEFFERSON'S SOCIAL VISION

What Jefferson did fear were cities. His reading of classical history suggested that the early republics of Greece and Rome had succumbed to despotism when propertyless people crowded into cities. During his diplomatic stay in Europe, he had witnessed the grinding poverty that existed in Paris and London. Indeed, he was in Paris on July 14, 1789, when, much to the fright of his family, angry mobs armed themselves, stormed a prison called the Bastille, and initiated the first phase of the French Revolution. Like Benjamin Franklin, Jefferson believed that "manufactures are founded in poverty." It was the poor without land who had to "work for others at low wages or starve." Since most of Europe's manufacturing operations were located in cities, he took a dim view of both. "While we have land to labor," he cautioned, "let us never see our citizens occupied at the work-bench. . . . Let our work-shops remain in Europe. . . . The mobs of great cities add just so much to the support of pure government as sores do to the strength of the human body."

The key element in Jefferson's social theory was freehold agriculture. He once wrote, and continued to believe, that the "cultivators of the earth are the most valuable citizens . . . the most independent, the most virtuous, and they are tied to their country and wedded to its liberty and interest by the most lasting bonds." So long as people owned their own farms and worked hard to provide the basic necessities of life, the Republic would survive, even flourish. In order to ensure that sufficient land would be available for freeholders to occupy, Jefferson envisioned the United States expanding relentlessly across the continent. As early as 1792, he proposed an expedition to map the vast territories west of the Mississippi River to the great "Stony Mountains" and beyond to the Pacific. Mapping the country and expanding what he referred to as "the empire of liberty" would not only preoccupy him as president but remain a goal to his dying day.

Agriculture and expansion constituted the essence of Jefferson's vision for the young Republic. Yet despite his stature as the primary author of the Declaration of Independence and spokesman for democracy in America, his vision had limits. Native Americans, blacks, and other people of color were excluded. Although he frequently decried slavery and called for the gradual emancipation and recolonization of slaves back to Africa, he owned as many as 223 slaves and, according to recent DNA evidence, is very likely to have fathered at least one child by a slave concubine, Sally Hemmings. As for machine-based manufacturing, Jefferson was enough of a realist to recog-

View of Ezekiel Derby's farm near Salem, Massachusetts, c. 1800. The orderly appearance of the farm, especially its whitewashed fences, large house, and numerous barns and outbuildings, indicates that the Derbys were prosperous. Most farmers were not as well off.

nize that it had to be developed to lessen America's dependency on foreign goods and to establish a dynamic domestic economy. But he continued to cast a wary eye on large-scale enterprises that employed massive labor forces. His politics thus reflected a conservative social philosophy that would come increasingly in conflict with the economic and social currents of the times. Moreover, as president, he himself became an agent of changes that would fundamentally alter the course of the Republic and set the terms for political debate for at least two generations.

Jeffersonian Economy

Jefferson entered office determined to undo the centralizing program of the Federalists and to return governing power to the states. Public finance assumed a high priority, because Jeffersonians believed that the Federalists had enacted protective tariffs and excise taxes that favored eastern merchants and discriminated against their main base of support, farmers and planters. In 1801, most of the nation's $112 million debt accrued from the federal government's assumption of state debts. Jefferson deeply regretted "the dinner table bargain" struck with Alexander Hamilton some ten years earlier that had led to the federal government's assumption of state debts in exchange for locating the national capital on the banks of the Potomac. Whereas Hamilton considered the assumption of debts a national blessing that tied the states closer to the federal government, Jefferson viewed it as a burden and a corrupting influence on government at all levels. As someone whose personal affairs frequently teetered at the edge of bankruptcy, Jefferson was well acquainted with the evils that could flow from indebtedness. For example, as much as he may have wanted to free his slaves, his indebtedness prevented him from doing so because slaves, according to Virginia law, were a form of capital that could be used as collateral for loans. Paying off the national debt thus seemed as much a matter of personal redemption as national redemption for the president.

When Jefferson asked Secretary of the Treasury Albert Gallatin to develop a plan for retiring the debt, Gallatin responded by proposing an austerity program that earmarked

> *"Agriculture and expansion constituted the essence of Jefferson's vision for the young Republic."*

$7 million a year toward total payment of the debt by 1816. Since the federal government's annual income hovered around $9 million, this left about $2 million for its annual expenses. To stay within such a lean budget, Gallatin proposed making drastic cuts in the number of federal employees, particularly those in the military. The intended reductions sought to kill two birds with one stone. Not only would they lower the national debt, they would also diminish the size of the federal government—something Jefferson considered essential if the United States was to recapture the pristine, states-oriented republicanism of its revolutionary past. "We are hunting out and abolishing multitudes of useless offices," the president wrote with satisfaction to his son-in-law, "striking off jobs, lopping them down silently."

Albert Gallatin, secretary of the treasury in the Jefferson and Madison administrations (1802–14).

Since Jefferson and Gallatin considered the navy the largest drain on the treasury, they slashed its budget by more than half, intending to leave only one frigate and several smaller gunboats in active service. This action led to many layoffs among enlisted men, commissioned officers, and civilian employees as the administration severely curtailed work at navy yards, dry docks, and other shore installations. Although a bothersome conflict with Barbary pirates in the Mediterranean Sea and eastern Atlantic forced the administration to increase the navy's budget between 1802 and 1806, Jefferson and his successor, James Madison, resumed the austerity program as soon as the conflict ended. After 1807, the American navy became a downsized fighting force consisting mainly of small, fifty-foot gunboats that served to patrol American harbors. During the same period, most of the navy's largest fighting vessels, like the thirty-six-gun USS *Constellation*, lay rotting in nearly abandoned naval installations such as the Washington Navy Yard.

Compared with the reduced condition of the navy, the army fared better during the Jefferson administration because of its value to American expansion into Indian territory. The president was particularly sensitive to this issue, since some of his strongest support came from western and southern states, where land hunger and expansionism tended to drive politics. Jefferson nonetheless reduced the size of the regular army to 3,350 officers and enlisted men and stationed them either along the western frontier or at East Coast forts remote from large cities. As long as the army remained isolated and out of sight, its existence seemed less troubling to Jeffersonians, who distrusted standing armies as a threat to liberty.

THE COURT SYSTEM

In the highly partisan environment following the election of 1800, one of the most vexing questions facing the Jefferson administration was the judiciary. Republicans controlled both houses of Congress, but Federalists held the vast majority of federal judgeships, and in the eyes of Jeffersonians, virtually all of them were arrogant, undemocratic, and opposed to anything that smacked of republicanism. To make matters worse, the passage of the Judiciary Act early in 1801 created sixteen new circuit court judgeships, allowing the lame-duck president John Adams to pack them with Federalists shortly before he left office. In addition to allowing for these "midnight appointments," the Judiciary Act also reduced the number of Supreme Court justices from six to five, threatening to delay and perhaps even prevent Jefferson from appointing anyone to the Court. And when Oliver Ellsworth resigned as chief justice, Adams nominated and the Senate approved Secretary of State John Marshall—a bitter Jefferson enemy—to the post. Jefferson never forgave Adams for these affronts, nor could he tolerate them. At Jefferson's urging, Senator John Breckinridge of Kentucky introduced a bill in January 1802 to repeal the Judiciary Act and thus do away with the midnight judges and restore the number of Supreme Court justices to six. The bill squeaked through the Senate by only one vote, passed the House, and was quickly signed into law by the president.

John Marshall, chief justice of the U.S. Supreme Court (1801–35).

While the Jeffersonian Republicans succeeded in halting the Federalist effort to expand their control over the federal court system, the repeal of the Judiciary Act did nothing to check Federalist judges who held earlier appointments. Jefferson and his supporters in Congress decided to use impeachment as a means of removing the most troublesome Federalist judges from office. Their first victim, a federal district judge from New Hampshire named John Pickering, was a chronic alcoholic with serious mental problems, and so made a relatively easy target. The Republican-dominated House of Representatives moved the case for impeachment, and the Senate convicted and removed him from office in March 1804.

The same day that the House issued its verdict against Judge Pickering, it initiated another major impeachment proceeding. This time, the intended victim was Associate Justice Samuel Chase of the Supreme Court. Well-known as a signer of the Declaration of Independence, Chase was an arch-Federalist who, in the view of many Jeffersonians, had exhibited "oppressive and disgusting" partisanship on the bench. Although the case for impeachment was made in the House of Representatives, Republicans failed to muster the necessary two-thirds majority in the Senate to convict Chase. Federalists hailed the acquittal as a great victory, while most Republicans reacted bitterly to the verdict. Chase returned to his place on the Supreme Court and continued to vilify his Republican opponents until the day he died in 1811. Although the Supreme Court remained intact with a five-to-one Federalist majority, Jefferson would nonetheless have the opportunity to appoint three Republicans to the bench before he left office.

The most irksome of Adams's appointments, in Jefferson's opinion, was that of John Marshall as chief justice of the Supreme Court. Although distant cousins, Jefferson and Marshall genuinely disliked each other, and over time their mutual dislike grew into open hatred. The tall, thin, black-eyed Marshall was an avowed Federalist who possessed an uncanny ability to construct elaborate arguments that sounded impartial but invariably turned back on his opponents. This stealthy quality, coupled with his "lax lounging manners" and "profound hypocrisy," made Jefferson extremely wary of him. Jefferson considered Marshall a more formidable political opponent than that other champion of federalism, Alexander Hamilton. "When conversing with Marshall," he confided, "I never admit anything. . . . So great is his sophistry you must never give him an affirmative answer or you will be forced to grant his conclusion. Why if he were to ask me if it were daylight or not, I'd reply, 'Sir, I don't know, I can't tell.'"

Marshall showed his genius for subtlety in the 1803 case of *Marbury v. Madison*. William Marbury was a minor figure who had been named a justice of the peace in the District of Columbia by President Adams. However, Marbury's letter of appointment had not been delivered to him before Adams left office, and upon Jefferson's inauguration, Secretary of State James Madison refused to deliver it. Marbury hired a lawyer who went to the Supreme Court to compel Madison to perform his "duty."

The resulting decision, written by Marshall, made two points. On the one hand, it asserted that Marbury had a right to his commission and publicly chided the Jefferson administration for refusing to deliver it. However, after lecturing the president and unquestionably embarrassing him, the decision stated, on the other hand, that the Court had no authority to order Madison to deliver Marbury's commission, because the congressional legislation that had granted that authority under the Judiciary Act of 1789 exceeded the constitutionally defined powers of the judiciary and was therefore null and void.

The decision revealed Marshall's genius at its maddening best. On the surface, the Supreme Court appeared to hand the president a victory by refusing to force Madison to deliver Marbury's commission. At a deeper level, however, the Marshall Court, while seemingly constricting its authority, was actually expanding it in a substantial way. In *Marbury v. Madison*, the Court relinquished a relatively minor power regarding the delivery of commissions in order to assert a much greater power in nullifying an act of Congress as unconstitutional. In doing so, it established not only the precedent for judicial review but also the Supreme Court's right to interpret the meaning of the Constitution.

THE LOUISIANA PURCHASE

As America's population grew and increasing numbers of white settlers looked westward for affordable land, events were unfolding that would dramatically change the map of America and influence the nation's political, economic, and social development for much of the nineteenth century. At issue was the so-called Louisiana Territory, a vast area that stretched from the Mississippi River in the East to the Rocky Mountains in the West and north to Canada. Like most Americans, Jefferson harbored the belief that Louisiana would some day belong to the United States. It was thought that control of Louisiana, long considered a natural extension

of the United States, loomed critical in defending the country's expanding frontier against Indian raids and foreign adventurers as well as serving as a valuable source of raw materials—most notably the lucrative western fur trade. Most important, in Jefferson's view, the Louisiana Territory would be America's ultimate safety valve: a seemingly limitless territory to which Indians could be removed ahead of white settlement and, above all, a place where landless immigrants from the East might move to carry on the American agrarian tradition that he deemed so essential to the well-being of the Republic.

Controlled for most of the colonial period by the French, Louisiana had been ceded to Spain in 1763, following France's defeat in the Seven Years' War. So long as Spain, now the "sick man of Europe," held Louisiana, Jefferson was content to wait for the inevitable day when American settlers would sweep into the trans-Mississippi West and take it by default. Contentment turned to concern, however, when news reached Washington in May 1801 that Spain, with its colonial empire in shambles, had secretly ceded the Louisiana Territory as well as the city of New Orleans back to France. Spanish control of the Louisiana region was one thing; French control was quite another—especially because Napoleon Bonaparte had recently come to power and had designs on reestablishing a French empire in North America. Jefferson learned in the fall of 1802 that officials in charge of New Orleans had suddenly closed its port as well as the entire lower Mississippi to American commerce. Outraged westerners, who shipped their products to eastern markets through New Orleans and numbered among Jefferson's strongest supporters, began to call for military action against the French. Jefferson responded by urging Congress to appropriate funds for raising an army and constructing a fleet of riverboats for possible military action against New Orleans. He even went so far as to suggest that the United States might have to "marry ourselves to the British fleet and nation" in order to rid itself of the French threat to its western expansion. In the meantime, he instructed the American ambassador to France, Robert Livingston, to approach Napoleon about selling New Orleans to the United States and sent his old friend and ally Governor James Monroe of Virginia to join the negotiations.

Then came even more staggering news. No sooner had Monroe arrived in Paris than Napoleon—confronted with a disastrous slave revolt led by Toussaint-Louverture in Haiti and the need to finance a renewed war with Britain—abruptly decided to sell not just New Orleans but all of Louisiana to the

United States for the sum of $15 million (80 million francs). Presented with the prospect of nearly doubling the area of the United States at the price of three cents an acre, Livingston and Monroe moved quickly to seal the bargain before Napoleon could change his mind. They decided to proceed without Jefferson's formal approval and signed an agreement with the French government on April 30, 1803.

Once the official documents reached Washington, Jefferson, though pleased with the deal, faced a dilemma. As someone who believed in a strict interpretation of the Constitution, he knew that the nation's governing document contained nothing about the acquisition of new territory. The proper procedure would have been to amend the Constitution before making the purchase, but time was of the essence. With overwhelming public approval and the urging of his closest advisers, Jefferson decided to send the treaty forward to Congress for approval. After all, he had the power to make treaties, and by doing so in this instance, he was avoiding war. Although Louisiana's $15 million price tag amounted to about twice the government's annual revenue, Congress quickly sanctioned the treaty and appropriated the money. Even leading Federalists like John Adams, Alexander Hamilton, and John Marshall approved of the action. For his part, Jefferson never held that the purchase was constitutional. He

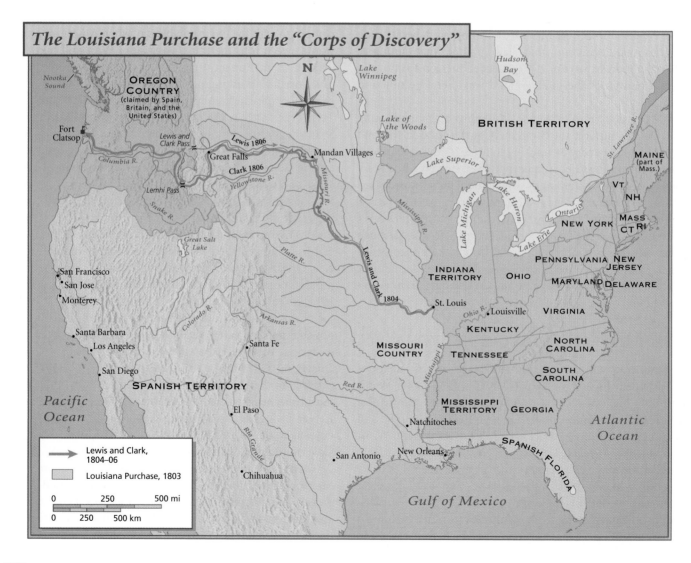

The Louisiana Purchase and the "Corps of Discovery"

would later observe that "it is incumbent on those who accept great charges to risk themselves on great occasions," adding that "to lose our country by a scrupulous adherence to written laws, would be to lose the law itself." Jefferson was willing to take the risk, even if it meant compromising his principles. On December 20, 1803, Spanish officials at St. Louis turned over control of upper Louisiana to an American delegation. At New Orleans, the French tricolor flag was lowered and the Stars and Stripes raised in its place.

The timing of the Louisiana Purchase could not have been better, for Jefferson had already decided to send a "Corps of Discovery" across the continent in search of a northwest passage to the Pacific Ocean. To carry out this mission, he selected Meriwether Lewis, a young Virginian who had served with General Anthony Wayne in the Old Northwest (the area including the present-day Ohio, Indiana, Illinois, Michigan, and Wisconsin) and most recently as his private secretary. Lewis's "talent for observation" coupled with his army service and knowledge of the "Western country" (including its plants and animals) made him the perfect candidate for the job. Lewis, in turn, asked that an old Army friend, William Clark, join him as joint commander of the enterprise, and Jefferson approved.

LEWIS AND CLARK

Secrecy surrounded the expedition until news of the Louisiana Purchase became public. In the meantime, Jefferson gave Lewis access to his large personal library of scientific works and tutored him in meteorology, geography, surveying, and paleontology (fossil study) as time permitted. He also sent Lewis to Lancaster and Philadelphia, Pennsylvania, for an intensive two-month period of more formal training with some of the nation's best-known natural scientists. In addition to studying botany, paleontology, medicine, mathematics, and navigational astronomy, Lewis also learned how to use sextants and other scientific instruments necessary for making observations and plotting his course as the Corps of Discovery made its way across the Great Plains and into the high country. Before leaving Philadelphia in late June 1803, he purchased navigational instruments (including a $250 chronometer, the most expensive item carried on the expedition) and standard reference books on astronomy, mineralogy, botany, and other subjects as well as a supply of medicines for the journey. Provided with an order from the secretary of war, he also had rifles and muskets as well as an iron boat

Meriwether Lewis, Jefferson's choice as leader of the Corps of Discovery (1803–06).

frame made at the Harpers Ferry National Armory. All told, Lewis assembled over 2,300 pounds of supplies and equipment, enough to fill two large Conestoga wagons for the difficult overland journey to Pittsburgh and, from there, by keelboat down the Ohio River toward the Missouri Country.

On July 5, 1803, the day after news reached the capital that France had formally agreed to sell the Louisiana Territory to the United States, Lewis quietly departed Washington on the first leg of his western journey. After experiencing a lengthy delay near Pittsburgh while a drunken group of workmen completed his keelboat, he finally rendezvoused with Clark at Louisville, Kentucky, in November, and the two set off for their winter encampment about eighteen miles north of St. Louis, near the entrance to the Missouri River. In May 1804, the Corps of Discovery, comprising twenty-nine carefully selected men, boarded their keelboat and proceeded to row, pole, and pull their way up the Missouri.

William Clark's sketch of the fifty-five-foot keelboat made at Pittsburgh for the expedition. Capable of carrying twenty-two men and twelve tons of supplies and equipment, the boat proved difficult to manage in the fast-flowing currents of the Missouri River.

 It was a **treacherous and dangerous journey.** Several of their original calculations proved wrong. Having planned to cross the continent primarily by water, Lewis and Clark assumed they would have to carry their boats only a short distance from the headwaters of the Missouri River to the headwaters of the Columbia River and believed that the whole trip would take from eighteen months to two years. They had no idea that the terrain would be so difficult or that they would have to forage off the land in order to avoid starvation. The available technology of 1803–06 did not allow for any single mode of transportation to be used by such a large party: they started with boats, then switched to horses, then back again to boats. Besides foraging for food, the men depended on trade with local Indian tribes, not all of whom were friendly.

The party slowly ascended the Missouri River, taking over five months of back-breaking labor to reach their winter quarters with the Mandan people about sixty miles above the present-day site of Bismarck, North Dakota. They continued the following spring (1805) into Montana, located passes through the Rocky and Cascade Mountains, and descended down the Columbia River to the Pacific Ocean, where they spent the winter of 1805–06. In March, the Corps of Discovery began their return trip, going up the Columbia and recrossing the mountains, where they divided into two parties to explore parts of present-day Montana. They rejoined one another at the junction of the Yellowstone and Missouri Rivers, excited about the prospect of returning home and not realizing that many at home had given them up for lost. The party moved quickly down the Missouri, sometimes covering seventy to eighty miles a day, until they reached St. Louis on September 21, 1806, nearly two and a half years after setting out. A triumphant reception awaited them as they put in to St. Louis. As shots rang out, nearly every one of the town's 1,000 residents lined the riverfront to greet them with shouts and cheers. One eyewitness reported excitedly that "they really have the appearance of Robinson Crusoes—dressed entirely in buckskins."

Throughout their travels, Lewis and Clark followed Jefferson's detailed instructions to the letter, making daily observations of climatic conditions, collecting hundreds of specimens, and keeping detailed journals that recorded not only the plants, minerals, and wildlife of the regions visited but also ethnographic information about the native peoples they encountered. They also noted the topographical "face of the country" and took "observations of latitude & longitude, at all remarkable points" during their journey. Above all, they heeded the president's injunction to make their observations "with great pains & accuracy" so that they would be of use "for others" as well as themselves.

Newspapers from Kentucky to New York hailed the return of Lewis and Clark, emphasizing their bravery and pointing to the national benefits of the expedition. Yet beyond its immediate popular impact, the expedition proved important for other reasons. Although Jefferson had initially characterized the expedition as a "literary" venture, its real purpose was to locate "the most direct and practicable water communication across this continent for the purposes of commerce" and to solidify American claims not only to the Rocky Mountain region but also to the Oregon Country beyond. The most immediate beneficiaries of the expedition's discoveries were the fur companies, who straightaway used the knowledge accumulated by Lewis and Clark to extend their network of trading posts deep into the upper reaches of the Missouri River. In the process, they would trap beaver to near extinction.

But Jefferson had more in mind than the fur trade. In his view, the maps Lewis and Clark prepared would also serve to guide white settlers into these areas and thus extend the "empire of liberty." For him, the West represented America's future. Even before Lewis and Clark returned home, three other federally sponsored expeditions (two military, one civilian) had headed up the Red River to explore the still-disputed southern boundary of the newly acquired Louisiana Territory. And there would be many more, owing primarily to Lewis and Clark's resounding success. In effect, they created a model for army exploration of the American West that would continue throughout the nineteenth century.

Lewis and Clark also established themselves as pioneering naturalists by contributing to a better scientific understanding of the regions they explored. Along the way, they collected botanical, mineral, and animal specimens as well as Indian artifacts, which they transported in crates back to the president in Washington. Jefferson kept some of these materials for his personal collection at Monticello, his Virginia plantation, but most of them ended up in Philadelphia, adorning the collections of the American Philosophical Soci-

American Journal

What's for Dinner?

As Lewis and Clark made their way up the Missouri River during the fall of 1804, they encountered numerous tribes with whom they sought to establish friendly relations. One group was the Teton Sioux, whom the expedition met at the mouth of the Bad River near present-day Pierre, South Dakota. Although their four-day stay (September 24–28) began and ended with tense moments, the intervening two days were spent feasting and dancing, as Lewis and Clark described in their diaries.

"September 26th. Captains Lewis and Clark, who went on shore one after the other, were met on landing by ten well-dressed young men, who took them up in a robe highly decorated and carried them to a large council-house, where they were placed on a dressed buffalo-skin by the side of the grand chief. The hall or council-room was in the shape of three-quarters of a circle, covered at the top and sides with skins well dressed and sewed together. Under this shelter sat about 70 men, forming a circle round the chief, before whom were placed a Spanish flag and the one we had given them yesterday. This left a vacant circle of about six feet diameter, in which the pipe of peace was raised on two forked sticks, about six or eight inches from the ground, and under it the down of the swan was scattered. A large fire, in which they were cooking provisions, stood near, and in the center about 400 pounds of buffalo meat as a present for us. As soon as we were seated, an old man got up, and after approving what we had done, begged us take pity on their unfortunate situation.

To this we replied with assurances of protection. After he had ceased, the great chief rose and delivered a harangue to the same effect; then with great solemnity he took some of the most delicate parts of the dog which was cooked for the festival, and held it to the flag by way of sacrifice; this done, he held up the pipe of peace, and first pointed it toward the heavens, then to the four quarters of the globe, then to the earth, made a short speech, lighted the pipe, and presented it to us. We smoked, and he again harangued his people, after which the repast was served up to us. It consisted of the dog which they had just been cooking, this being a great dish among the Sioux, used on all festivals; to which were added [pemmican], a dish made of buffalo-meat, dried or jerked and then pounded and mixed raw with grease; and a kind of ground potato, dressed like the preparation of Indian corn called hominy, to which it is little inferior. Of all these luxuries, which were placed before us in platters, with horn spoons, we took the [pemmican] and the potato, which we found good, but we could as yet partake but sparingly of the dog. We eat and smoked for an hour, when it became dark. Everything was then cleared away for the dance, a large fire being made in the center of the house, giving at once light and warmth to the ballroom."

Elliott Coues, ed., *History of the Expedition under the Command of Lewis and Clark* ety, the Academy of Natural Sciences, and painter Charles Willson Peale's well-known museum of natural history. Among the more notable specimens sent back were the hides and skeletal remains of a bighorn sheep, a pronghorn antelope, several elk, and a grizzly bear. There were also numerous bird skins, and 216 sheets of dried, pressed plants comprising 173 different species, 70–75 of which were completely new to the world of science.

Largely as a result of Lewis and Clark's collecting activities, Philadelphia became the leading center in America for the study of natural history. Before the arrival of these specimens, the trans-Mississippi West was "an area of rumor, guess, and fantasy" about as remote to Americans then as Mars is today. Lewis and Clark's artifacts and specimens began to put a face on the West, greatly stimulating public interest. Aspiring artists, explorers, and scientists began making plans to visit the "high country" in order to collect, record, and make discoveries of their own. Leading them all were units of the United States Army, whose wagon roads, topographical surveys, maps, and fortified settlements paved the way for the many "crossings" that would follow.

> *"Before the arrival of these specimens, the trans-Mississippi West was about as remote to Americans then as Mars is today."*

Troubled Times

With his party's popularity at an all-time high, Thomas Jefferson easily won reelection in 1804: he carried every state but two (Connecticut and Delaware) and overwhelmed his Federalist opponent, Charles Cotesworth Pinckney of South Carolina, in the electoral college by a count of 162 to 14. The election not only signaled the decline of the Federalist Party, it also revealed how personal ambition and extremist political maneuvering continually threatened the fragile Republic. Already in turmoil, the Federalist Party suffered a crushing blow before the election when Vice-President Aaron Burr shot and killed Alexander Hamilton in a July 1804 duel at Weehawken, New Jersey. Burr had always been a political schemer. He had long since parted ways with Jefferson over the 1800 election deadlock, and was dumped from the Republican ticket long before the 1804 election. He became involved with an extremist Federalist faction (known as the "Essex Junto") that advocated the establishment of a separate nation called the "Northern Confederacy," consisting of the New England states as well as New York and New Jersey. Urged on by separatist friends in the Federalist Party, Burr ran for governor in New York in February 1804 and was denounced by Hamilton as a traitor and "despicable" character. Burr lost. He blamed his defeat on Hamilton, and the deadly duel was the result.

With Hamilton's death, the Federalist Party deteriorated, and Burr became a political outcast. Forced to flee New York and New Jersey to avoid prosecution for murder, he became involved in yet another political intrigue that involved capturing Mexico, separating part of the newly acquired Louisiana Territory from the United States, and establishing a western empire under his rule. Although Jefferson knew of Burr's activities, he did not take action until word reached him in November 1806 that Burr and a group of armed supporters had boarded a boat on the Ohio River and were heading downstream to attack New Orleans. Jefferson ordered Burr's arrest for treason and had him returned to Richmond, Virginia, for trial. When a jury presided over by Chief Justice Marshall acquitted Burr, an irate Jefferson had him rearrested on other charges and sought to move the trial to a friendlier court in Ohio. Before he could do that, however, the wily Marshall freed Burr on bond and the former vice-president escaped to Europe, his career in shambles.

WINDS OF WAR

The same escalating tensions in Europe that had initially benefited the United States with Napoleon's decision to sell Louisiana soon led to a quagmire in foreign affairs. American overseas trade had prospered since the mid-1790s. Owing to their status as neutral carriers, Yankee shippers enjoyed a lucrative trade with Great Britain and the British West Indies as well as a rapidly growing reexport trade in tropical produce (coffee, sugar, indigo, leather hides, etc.) with French and Spanish colonies in the East and West Indies, Latin America, and the Philippine Islands. America's merchant marine was rapidly becoming the largest in the Atlantic, something that did not go unnoticed by British merchants, who longed to tap into the markets of Spain's vast but weakening Latin American empire. Conditions began to change in 1803, however, when the perennial enemies France and England went to war for the fourth time in fifty years. This time, hostilities would not cease until the defeated Napoleon was permanently banished to the island of St. Helena in 1815.

During the first two years of the so-called Napoleonic Wars, world prices for farm goods (like cotton and wheat) rose, and the American carrying trade boomed as England and France slugged it out on land and at sea. By 1805, the two powers had become virtually stalemated with England in command of the sea and France firmly in control of the European Continent. At that point, the two belligerents began to supplement direct military action with indirect economic warfare in order to damage each other in any way they could. Britain acted first by issuing a series of Orders in Council that, in effect, sought to blockade Napoleonic Europe by ordering all vessels going there to stop first in English ports, submit to inspections of their cargoes, pay certain fees, and obtain clearance papers to proceed. Not to be outdone, Napoleon responded with a series of decrees that threatened the seizure of any vessel that complied with the British blockade.

The United States repeatedly protested the warring countries' violations of America's rights as a neutral nation, but to no avail. Of the two, Britain posed the greater threat to American commerce because its navy controlled the sea lanes and could pounce on merchant ships almost at will. Much to America's consternation, British forces frequently halted American ships within sight of the U.S. coastline as well as on the high seas. Moreover, the British seized not just contraband cargoes but also seamen who were suspected of either deserting from the British navy or being British subjects and therefore liable to impressment (forcible enlistment) in the British navy. Yet despite continued harassment by England and France, American seaborne trade experienced a healthy 12.5 percent increase between 1805 and 1807. Even in the midst of wartime prohibitions and seizures, merchants stood to make considerable profits if only one ship in three evaded its pursuers.

Of all the depredations committed on American commerce, the most controversial were the British navy's impressment procedures. Between 1793 and 1811, nearly 1,000 seamen were forcibly removed from American vessels and pressed into British service. Although estimates vary, foreigners (many of whom were Englishmen) constituted between one-third and one-half of the labor force in the American merchant marine. Merchantmen thus became a primary target of the press gangs. Desperately short of manpower, officers

of the Royal Navy paid little attention to naturalization papers that claimed American citizenship and took anyone they suspected of being British. On at least two occasions between 1798 and 1805, British warships even stopped vessels of the United States Navy and took off suspected deserters. Such actions aroused public indignation. In the spring of 1806, for example, a riot broke out in New York after an American seaman died when hit by a shot fired from the British HMS *Leander*. Although Thomas Jefferson retaliated by ordering the arrest of the *Leander*'s captain and banning it and its sister ship from taking on water and provisions in American ports, British searches and seizures continued unabated.

THE EMBARGO OF 1807

The crisis came in the summer of 1807, when news arrived from Norfolk, Virginia, that the British ship *Leopard* had fired on the American frigate *Chesapeake* and inflicted twenty-one casualties before British officers boarded the American vessel and hauled off four suspected deserters. The country pulsed with anger as reports of the *Chesapeake* affair filled the newspapers. "Never since the battle of Lexington have I seen the country in such a state of exasperation," Jefferson noted. With a majority in Congress behind him, he probably could have secured an immediate declaration of war. But recognizing that the United States was ill prepared for conflict with a major European power, he instead closed all American ports to the Royal Navy and instructed the American ambassador in England to demand reparations as well as a complete renunciation of impressment on the part of the British government. Although Prime Minister George Canning agreed to recall the officer responsible for firing on the *Chesapeake*, return three of the four captured sailors (one had already been hanged for desertion), compensate the families of those killed or wounded in the incident, and promise not to board American navy vessels in the future, he reasserted his government's right to use force in retrieving deserters from the Royal Navy.

Rebuffed yet again, Jefferson had three options. He could call for a declaration of war, do nothing, or impose trade sanctions on Great Britain. In the Non-Importation Act of 1806, Congress had already authorized him to prohibit the importation of certain products from the British empire. Although Jefferson implemented the act on December 14, 1807, he had come to believe that even stronger measures were needed. He therefore called on Congress to pass a bill that

This 1808 Federalist cartoon satirizing Jefferson's embargo policy shows American ships bottled up in port by a wall of proclamations issued by the quill-pen-sword-wielding president, referred to by the cartoonist as "King Quilldriver." In the upper-right-hand corner, a seemingly angelic Napoleon blows the winds of war against the windmill on Jefferson's hat.

the Embargo Act, and Jefferson signed it into law on December 22, 1807.

The embargo represented an eighteenth-century response to a nineteenth-century crisis. Remembering the various boycotts and nonimportation agreements employed during the revolutionary era, Jefferson and the Republican Congress turned to them again in the hope that they would force Britain and France to recognize American rights as neutral traders. However, much had changed since the Revolution. During the quarter century since 1781, the United States had assembled one of the largest merchant marines in the world—one that operated on a global scale. The trade that flowed from it put hard cash in the pockets of easterners and brought unprecedented prosperity not only to the Eastern Seaboard but also to inland areas that participated in its larger mercantile network. By imposing a complete trade embargo on the nation, Jefferson and his Republican colleagues seemed out of step with the times and unable to recognize the larger economic implications of their political actions. In this respect, the embargo represented a mismatch between the expanding economy and the eighteenth-century ideas that informed the Jeffersonian approach to political economy.

The Embargo Act brought almost immediate economic disaster. In 1808 alone, trade plummeted by more than 80 percent, and prices for leading farm exports like cotton and wheat fell by 23 percent. America's mercantile sector, a primary source of national income and economic growth, stood in shambles. Upon visiting New York, a British traveler observed that "the port indeed was full of shipping, but they were dismantled and laid up. . . . Many of the countinghouses were shut up, or advertised to be let; and the few solitary merchants, clerks, porters, and laborers that were to be seen were walking about with their hands in their pockets." Similar scenes could be found in virtually every city and seaport in America.

Jefferson had anticipated that the embargo would be painful for merchants, but he had no idea that it would hit farmers hard as well. While traveling through the Virginia countryside on his way home to Monticello during the summer of 1808, he discovered just how bad things were. Wheat prices had fallen from a high of two dollars a bushel to less than ten cents, and tobacco was practically worthless. Once-prosperous planters and farmers found themselves saddled with debt and the value of their property swept away. Yet, bad as things were, Jefferson clung tenaciously to the hope that England and France would eventually yield and recog-

would impose a total trade embargo not only on England and France but on all nations. In effect, the United States would wall itself off from the rest of the world; no ships would leave the country, and none would enter. Convinced that neither England nor France—but especially England, since the United States absorbed nearly 45 percent of its exports—could do without American trade, Jefferson expected that both countries would abandon their seizure policies and come to terms. Although merchants strongly protested the measure and Secretary of the Treasury Gallatin remained skeptical that any sort of economic coercion would bring favorable results, the Republican Congress nonetheless passed nize America's rights as a neutral country. In the meantime, he prepared for the worst by calling for more congressional appropriations to build coastal fortifications, construct gunboats for the navy, and procure arms and equipment for the regular army and state militias.

As the depression worsened, evasions of the embargo grew more and more numerous. From Maine through upstate New York and all along the Canadian border, smuggling operations rapidly expanded. At one point, the president declared certain areas of Vermont and New York in a state of insurrection in order to justify sending federal troops to the Canadian border to curtail smuggling. Even greater evasions took place along the Atlantic Seaboard as ships slipped out to sea and headed for foreign ports under the pretense of engaging in coastal trade with other American cities. By August 1808, Gallatin had become convinced that the embargo was a failure. "The embargo is now defeated," he wrote gloomily to the president, "by open violations, by vessels sailing without any clearances whatever." Still, Jefferson persisted in the belief that England and France would relent. "If they repeal their orders," he wrote to James Madison in September 1808, "we must repeal our embargo. If they make satisfaction for the Chesapeake, we must revoke our proclamation. . . . If they keep up impressments, we must adhere to non-intercourse, manufactures & a navigation act."

Willing to use "all means . . . by force of arms or otherwise" to suppress popular resistance to the embargo, Jefferson came dangerously close to subverting civil liberties in the interest of enforcing the law. Indeed, there was much that seemed distinctly Hamiltonian in his policies by the end of his second term. He seemed unconcerned that the embargo contradicted Republican principles by concentrating unprecedented power in the hands of the chief executive and by allowing him to deploy the army and navy against civilians for purposes of enforcement. Nor did he overly concern himself with the protections against unreasonable searches and seizures granted by the Fourth Amendment.

The Emerging Factory System. With the embargo, Jefferson, the apostle of agrarianism, unwittingly opened the door to a fundamental change in the American economy. Adventuresome entrepreneurs seized on unexpected advantages that the embargo dropped into their laps. With overseas commerce at a virtual standstill and British products cut off from American markets, entrepreneurs shifted their capital into machine-based manufacturing and, in some cases, expanded earlier operations. Such was the case with Samuel Slater of Pawtucket, Rhode Island. Having established a pioneering cotton-spinning mill with two Providence merchants (Almy and Brown) in 1790, Slater struck out on his own in 1799 and expanded his holdings to three different textile mills by 1811. He would become involved with at least a dozen other businesses related to textile manufacturing before he died in 1835.

Nor was Slater an exception. Between 1807 and 1810, the number of textile mills in the United States jumped from fifteen to eighty-seven. All along the Atlantic Seaboard from Massachusetts to Maryland, new manufacturing ventures in textiles and other consumer products took up the slack created by the exclusion of British manufactures. The significance of this new market was unmistakable not only to

> *"With the embargo, Jefferson, the apostle of agrarianism, unwittingly opened the door to a fundamental change in the American economy."*

An 1807 Federalist cartoon contrasting the patriotic virtues of George Washington and the evil associations of Thomas Jefferson with the French Enlightenment and Revolution. Washington is shown surrounded by a burst of sunlight, a victor's wreath, a reclining lion, and the American eagle, and Jefferson by the candle of Enlightenment, murky smoke, a hissing snake, and an alligator.

own cabinet, Thomas Jefferson had no desire to seek a third term in the election of 1808. When friends urged him to run, he declined, maintaining that he wanted to follow the precedent set by George Washington and retire to Monticello. Jefferson was tired. His second term had been as troubled as his first had been triumphant. He was thus relieved when his old friend and ally James Madison received the Republican nomination for president.

Madison handily won the election, but not by the resounding majority that had reelected Jefferson four years earlier. The Federalist candidate, again Charles Cotesworth Pinckney, made a much stronger showing this time, and his party gained twenty-four seats in Congress, even though Republicans continued to control both houses. The election campaign revealed the extent of division the embargo had left behind. Although Jefferson continued to defend the measure, he recognized that it had failed to serve its purpose. A few days before leaving office, he supported a congressional motion to repeal the embargo and replace it with the Non-Intercourse Act, which reopened trade with all nations except Great Britain and France. Convinced that war would soon follow, Jefferson spent his last days in Washington taking care of personal affairs and awaiting Madison's inauguration. "Never did a prisoner, released from his chains feel such relief as I shall in shaking off the shackles of power," he wrote a close friend.

War *would* follow, but not as quickly as Jefferson had anticipated. In 1810, when the Non-Intercourse Act expired, Congress replaced it with Macon's Bill Number Two. This law restored commerce with both Britain and France while promising that if one of them repealed its restrictions against American commerce, the United States would immediately cease trading with the other. Seeing an opportunity to turn America against England, Napoleon announced that France would revoke its decrees against neutral shipping, adding shrewdly, "it being understood that the English are to revoke their orders in council." Although John Quincy Adams, son of the former president and the American ambassador to Russia, cautioned Madison that Napoleon was setting a trap "to catch us in a war with England," the president took the bait and announced that nonintercourse would be reinstated against Great Britain.

Much to Madison's chagrin, Napoleon showed promptly that he had no intention of living up to the bargain. During the next two years, the French continued to seize American merchant vessels, while relations between Britain and the United States deteriorated to the point of all-out war. Ironically, two days before Congress formally approved a declaration of war in June 1812, the British government, under pressure at home, suspended its orders in council against American shipping. But this news, brought by sailing vessel, came too late to Washington. By then, other events had occurred to hasten the conflict.

Mr. Madison's War

The first shots in the **War of 1812** were fired not on the high seas but rather along America's trans-Appalachian frontier. There, the continuing incursions of white settlers and the aggressive behavior of their political leaders brought conflict with Indians from the Great Lakes to the Gulf of Mexico. Indian tribes east of the Mississippi River had long-standing grievances against whites. Beginning in 1783 with the Treaty of Paris, Great Britain had abandoned its Indian allies by failing to reserve any tracts of land for them and instead granted all the territory from the Atlantic coast to the Mississippi to the United States. Thereafter, many tribes had been pressured or even forced at gunpoint to relinquish huge tracts to the federal government. During the administrations of Jefferson and Madison, for example, fifty-three treaties of cession were signed with various Indian leaders, through which the United States obtained millions of acres of land in return for annual payments and promises not to intrude further into their hunting grounds. But treaties signed were almost always broken, as white settlement continued to spread during the early decades of the nineteenth century. In Indiana alone, the white population surged from 5,600 in 1800 to 24,500 in 1810 and to over 147,000 by 1820. Similar trends could be found throughout the Old Northwest as well as farther south in the Mississippi Territory, where the influx of white settlers and their slaves, attracted by lands suited for raising cotton, soon outnumbered the native inhabitants.

As far as the U.S. government was concerned, nothing was allowed to stand in the way of territorial expansion. Even Jefferson, who wrote with admiration about Native Americans and greeted their leaders with respect, frankly acknowledged in a letter to the governor of Ohio that "our settlements will gradually circumscribe and approach the Indians and they will in time either incorporate with us as citizens of the United

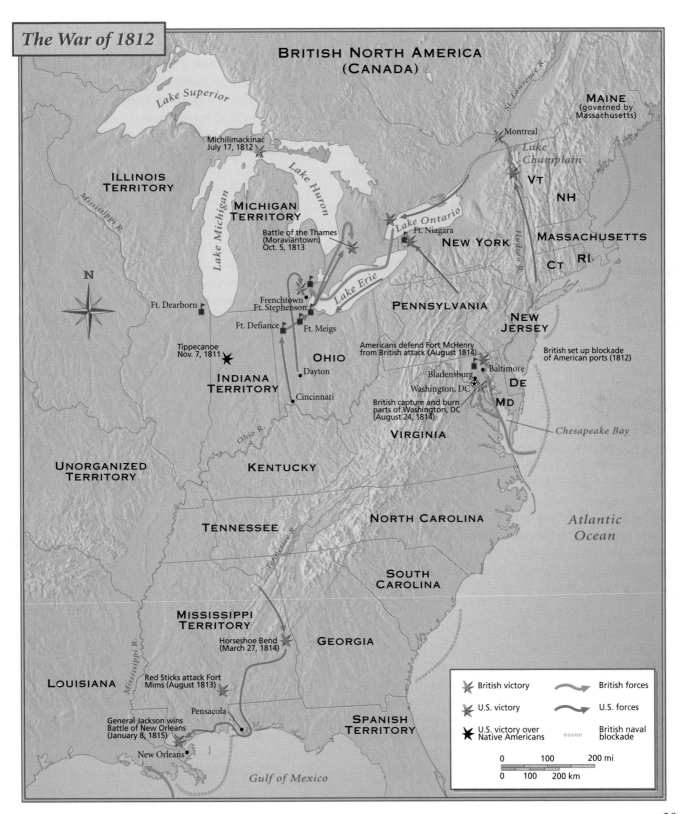

The War of 1812

BRITISH NORTH AMERICA
(CANADA)

MAINE
(governed by
Massachusetts)

Lake Superior

Michilimackinac
July 17, 1812

ILLINOIS
TERRITORY

Lake Huron

Montreal

Lake Champlain

VT

NH

MICHIGAN
TERRITORY

Lake Michigan

Battle of the Thames
(Moraviantown)
Oct. 5, 1813

Lake Ontario

Ft. Niagara

NEW YORK

MASSACHUSETTS

Hudson R.

CT

RI

Frenchtown
Ft. Stephenson

Lake Erie

PENNSYLVANIA

NEW
JERSEY

Ft. Dearborn

Ft. Defiance

Ft. Meigs

Mississippi R.

N

Tippecanoe
Nov. 7, 1811

OHIO

Dayton

Americans defend Fort McHenry
from British attack (August 1814)

British set up blockade
of American ports (1812)

Baltimore

Bladensburg

DE

INDIANA
TERRITORY

Cincinnati

Washington, DC

MD

British capture and burn
parts of Washington, DC
(August 24, 1814)

Ohio R.

VIRGINIA

Chesapeake Bay

UNORGANIZED
TERRITORY

KENTUCKY

NORTH CAROLINA

*Atlantic
Ocean*

TENNESSEE

Tennessee R.

SOUTH
CAROLINA

MISSISSIPPI
TERRITORY

Horseshoe Bend
(March 27, 1814)

GEORGIA

Mississippi R.

Red Sticks attack Fort
Mims (August 1813)

LOUISIANA

Pensacola

SPANISH
TERRITORY

General Jackson wins
Battle of New Orleans
(January 8, 1815)

New Orleans

Gulf of Mexico

⚹ British victory	➔ British forces	
⚹ U.S. victory	➔ U.S. forces	
★ U.S. victory over Native Americans	British naval blockade	

0   100   200 mi

0   100   200 km

A patriotic American cartoon published during the war, showing the American snapping turtle "Ograbme" ("embargo" spelled backward) attacking a British merchant.

States or remove beyond the Mississippi. . . . They must see that we have only to shut our hand to crush them, and that all our liberalities to them proceed from motives of pure humanity only." These remarks capture not only Jefferson's personal attitude but also his policy as president. In his view, Native Americans were doomed regardless of whether they abandoned their nomadic, hunting-oriented ways and assimilated into white culture or were driven by force beyond the Mississippi. Eventually their history would be terminated by the inexorable march of white civilization. Although Jefferson denied that he had ordained this fate, he felt no compunction about implementing strategies that would bring it about.

Other than the use of force, federal officials—Jefferson among them—devised sophisticated schemes for securing land from various Indian groups. One of the most effective ways was to establish government trading posts on or near Indian lands. At these outposts, blankets, cloth, ammunition, and iron tools were exchanged for beeswax, deerskins, and other animal pelts. But the trading posts also existed to extend credit to tribal leaders and draw them into debt. Although he didn't invent this strategy, Jefferson encouraged it. The essential idea, as he put it, was "to establish among them a factory or factories for furnishing them with all the necessaries and comforts they may wish (spirituous liquors excepted), encouraging these and especially their leading men, to run in

debt for these beyond their individual means of paying. . . . Whenever in that situation, they will always cede lands to rid themselves of debt." By entangling Indians in a chronic cycle of indebtedness, the federal government, often working with private trading companies and land speculators, acquired vast tracts of Indian land at a pittance.

THE PROPHET AND TECUMSEH

Given the ongoing tensions that existed between white settlers and Native Americans, it was only a matter of time before the Indians' festering resentments hardened into widespread resistance. During the summer of 1805, a Shawnee holy man named Tenskwatawa ("the open door"), having fallen into a trance and experienced a spiritual awakening, began to call on his people to reject the evil influences of white civilization and return to their traditional ways. Among other things, Tenskwatawa—who became known as "the Shawnee Prophet"—instructed his followers to cease all contact with whites and stop using any clothing, tools, or food produced by white people. The only exception to this rule was of firearms, which the Prophet permitted for self-defense but not for hunting. All game had to be taken by bow and arrow or other traditional methods. The Prophet promised that if his people followed these precepts and kept themselves pure, "the Master of Life" would restore them to happiness and prosperity.

As Tenskwatawa's message spread to other tribes, hundreds of Indians journeyed to his village on the Tippecanoe River in the Indiana Territory, called, appropriately, Prophetstown. There they met the Shawnee mystic and heard his elder brother Tecumseh speak of forming an Indian confederacy aimed at stopping white expansion and even regaining lands that had already been lost. Arguing that the land "belongs to all," Tecumseh condemned previous treaties as fraudulent because they had been validated by a few corrupted village chiefs and not all the people. At the same time, the Prophet castigated white Americans as children of

Tecumseh, the Shawnee war chief and champion of an Indian confederacy, wanted to stop American settlement in the Midwest.

a "Great Serpent" that "grew from the scum of the great water when it was troubled by the Evil Spirit." Convinced that all whites were devils, converts from the Delaware tribe returned to their villages and initiated a witch hunt that resulted in the deaths by burning of four kinsmen who had converted to Christianity and adopted white ways. Alarmed by news of these excesses as well as an upsurge of Indian raids on white settlements, Governor William Henry Harrison of the Indiana Territory decided to call out the militia and march on Prophetstown to disperse the Prophet's followers and end Tecumseh's fledgling confederacy.

What became known as the Battle of Tippecanoe occurred on November 7, 1811, at Prophetstown, while the warrior chief Tecumseh was in the South recruiting allies among the Creek, Chickasaw, and Choctaw nations. The Prophet made the mistake of telling his warriors that they would be invulnerable to the white men's bullets and would easily secure a victory. When the promise of victory turned to defeat, the Prophet's influence quickly dissipated, and along with it went Tecumseh's vision of a dominant Indian confederacy. Upon returning to Indiana early in 1812, Tecumseh found Prophetstown burned to the ground, its provisions destroyed, and his allies scattered. He would spend the next two years trying to rebuild his shattered confederacy and fighting the hated Americans. In the meantime, warfare continued along the frontier from Michigan to Mississippi as warriors from numerous tribes, still eager for combat, wreaked havoc on white settlements and terrified their inhabitants. In the Old Northwest, William Henry Harrison emerged as a popular hero. Widely known as "Old Tippecanoe," his military victory propelled his political career, culminating in 1840 with his election to the presidency.

News of Harrison's victory at Prophetstown reached Washington not long after the Twelfth Congress had assembled for its first session in November 1811. Among its members were a number of younger congressmen led by the new Speaker of the House and master political tactician, Henry

View of Amherstburg and Fort Malden on the Canadian side of the Detroit River, where Tecumseh and his Indian allies joined the British in the War of 1812.

Clay of Kentucky, and the equally talented John C. Calhoun of South Carolina. Like Clay, many members came from the western sections of the country and had lost family members and friends in the Indian wars. They seemed unable to recognize that the aggressiveness of their constituents had anything to do with ongoing violence on the frontier; in their view, Great Britain was the culprit. Upon learning that English-made firearms had been found on the battlefield at Tippecanoe, they became all the more convinced that British agents were inciting Indians against the United States and that something had to be done to eliminate their suspected base of operations in Canada.

Nor was that all. Clay, Calhoun, and their colleagues—collectively known as the "War Hawks"—were fed up with Britain's belligerent and condescending treatment of the United States as well as President Madison's seemingly endless attempts to find a diplomatic solution. Angry at Britain's continued assaults on the high seas and arrogance at the bargaining table, they were determined to take a stand even if it meant going to war. "Something besides dollars and cents is concerned," an American diplomat wrote in 1812, "and no alternative left but war or the abandonment of our right as an independent nation." That "something" was national pride and the refusal by the War Hawks and a growing number of other Americans to submit to further British humiliations.

THE CLASH

By May 1812, even Madison had concluded that further diplomatic efforts were useless, and he began to draft a war message to Congress. In it, he claimed that Britain was already in "a state of war against the United States," citing the continuing impressment of sailors, violations of neutral rights, the presence of British warships in American waters, the incitement of Indians, and the refusal to negotiate. Although Congress approved the measure, its vote was divided, with the strongest opposition coming from the commercially oriented Federalist strongholds of Connecticut, Massachusetts, and New York. On June 18, Madison formally signed the bill declaring war against Great Britain. To his Federalist opponents, the conflict would become known as "Mr. Madison's War," and they made the most of it in the presidential election of 1812. Although Madison soundly defeated the "peace party" candidate and Republicans retained control of both houses of Congress, a persistent antiwar clamor—fanned by merchants angry about the loss of overseas trade—continued in New England and New York.

The War of 1812 lasted two and a half years and took place primarily in three regions of the country: along the Canadian-American border from Lake Erie in the west to the St. Lawrence River valley and Lake Champlain in the east; in the deep South from the Mississippi Territory along the Florida panhandle to New Orleans; and in the Chesapeake Bay area. From the outset, weak executive leadership and poor preparations plagued the war effort. The Madison administration, particularly its inept leaders at the War Department, had no clearly defined strategy other than striking at Canada—the one British possession that American troops could reach—and attacking Britain's Indian allies, most notably the rebellious Tecumseh. Since a majority of people in upper Canada (today the province of Ontario) originally came from the United States, many Americans concluded that it could be easily taken—"a mere matter of marching," as Thomas Jefferson put it. They soon found out otherwise.

After two years of vicious fighting along the Canadian border and numerous failed attempts to invade one another's territory, American and British forces remained stalemated in virtually the same positions they had occupied at the outset of the war. One significant event in the border war occurred in October 1813, when an American army commanded by General William Henry "Old Tippecanoe" Harrison and consisting primarily of Kentucky militia invaded upper Canada east of Detroit and defeated a combined British and Indian force at Moraviantown on the Thames River. Reported among the dead was the Shawnee leader, Tecumseh, although his body was never found. Tecumseh's death brought an abrupt end to his Indian confederacy, delivered a crushing blow to hopes for an independent Indian territory in the Great Lakes region, and secured the Old Northwest for the final stage of white settlement.

In the South, hostilities began with an Indian war and ended with a belated American victory at New Orleans. Thanks in large part to Tecumseh's influence, Indian resistance to continued white expansion into the Mississippi Territory grew dramatically after 1811. By 1813, civil war had broken out among the Creek Indians as militant tribesmen in the northern part of the territory called "Red Sticks" clashed with those "Lower Creeks" who had become more assimilated into white culture as planters and slave owners. The so-called Creek War came to a head in August 1813, when the Red Sticks, in retaliation for a previous attack by a joint force of white militia and their Lower Creek allies, assaulted Fort Mims and killed 250 men, women, and children. In response, an army consisting of 1,400 whites, 500 Cherokees, and 100 Lower Creeks under the command of Andrew Jackson pursued the Red Sticks and ultimately defeated them at the Battle of Horseshoe Bend on March 27, 1814. Over 800 Red Sticks died at Horseshoe Bend. The few who survived escaped to Spanish Florida, where they joined runaway slaves and Seminole tribesmen in raiding ever-expanding American settlements.

Andrew Jackson, a Tennessee planter and land speculator as well as a military leader, ignored the support he had been given by friendly Creeks and proceeded to impose a treaty on the Creek nation that exacted 14 million acres of land from them—over two-thirds of their territory and more than half of the present state of Alabama. When his Creek allies protested, Jackson bluntly responded by telling them that "the great body of the Creek chiefs and warriors did not respect the power of the United States—They thought we were an insignificant nation—that we would be overpowered by the British. . . . we bleed our enemies in such cases to give them their senses."

Jackson's military subjugation of the Creeks boded ill for other Indian tribes in the South and east of the Mississippi River. The Creeks not only lost huge chunks of land but also were systematically squeezed into ever smaller enclaves. The same fate awaited other tribes like the Choctaws, Chickasaws, Cherokees, and Seminoles. By the late 1830s, all of them would be forcibly "removed" to lands beyond the Mississippi.

While Jackson's army moved on to secure Mobile and a portion of western Florida from Britain's ally Spain before converging on New Orleans, events in the Chesapeake Bay area went far less well. With the defeat and (temporary) exile of Napoleon to the island of Elba in 1814, Britain was free to focus the full force of its military power on the United States. Although the American navy had enjoyed considerable success in single engagements with British warships and raiding British commerce, it was no match for the Royal Navy in an all-out sea war. When a large British flotilla appeared in the Chesapeake in August 1814 and disgorged an army of 4,500 combat-proven veterans, American commanders could do little but adopt a delaying action and hope for the best. When it became apparent that the invaders were heading for Washington, a feeble attempt to stop them at Bladensburg, Maryland, resulted in a rout. Critics of the debacle accused Madison and his cabinet of cowardice in the face of the enemy. On August 24, the British army entered Washington and set fire to the Capitol building and the presidential mansion (which, when subsequently repainted, became known as the White House). One of the few government buildings left untouched was the U.S. Patent Office, whose commissioner persuaded the British to spare it in the interest of humanity.

Having humiliated the Madison administration and the Congress, the British forces next set their sights on Baltimore. Encountering a spirited resistance there, they assaulted Fort McHenry at the entrance to the harbor with a bombardment of incendiary and case-shot rockets and cannon shells. Although the British failed to capture Baltimore, the assault threw a scare into the city's inhabitants. Having personally witnessed the night-long bombardment of Fort McHenry, with "the rockets' red glare" and "the bombs bursting in air," a lawyer named Francis Scott Key composed the verses that subsequently became known as "The Star-Spangled Banner."

At the very time that British forces were wreaking havoc on Washington and Baltimore, peace negotiations had already begun in the Belgian city of Ghent. The British delegation initially made heavy demands, insisting on control of the Great Lakes, the cession of a substantial portion of Maine, and the establishment of a neutral Indian state to serve as a buffer zone between the United States and Canada. However, when news arrived that the British had failed to take Baltimore and another invading army had been repelled by the Americans at Plattsburgh, New York (on the western shore of Lake Champlain), the British government instructed its envoys to move toward compromise. Great Britain had been at war for more than two decades and had suffered an enormous loss of lives as well as a spiraling national debt. Moreover, Europe remained restive as rumors spread that Napoleon was about to return from his exile at Elba and attempt to reestablish his lost European empire. After months of negotiating, the British and American commissioners signed the Treaty of Ghent on Christmas Eve 1814.

On paper, the accord amounted to little more than an armistice, leaving matters about as they had stood before the war. Although the United States retained the section of west Florida it had seized from Spain, no other significant territorial cessions were made, nor did the treaty mention impressment, neutral rights, or the Indian menace, grievances for which the Americans had originally gone to war. But to war-weary Americans, that did not seem to matter. By and large, the public greeted the news of peace with bonfires, ringing bells, and a great sense of relief that the conflict had ended.

A wartime cartoon showing America's "Brother Jonathan" bloodying the nose of Britain's King George III, also known as "John Bull."

POLITICAL AFTERMATHS

Although generally viewed as a diplomatic and military draw, the War of 1812 had significant political consequences. It greatly weakened the military and political power of Native Americans from the Appalachians to the Mississippi and opened the floodgates for further white incursions into unsettled territory. The war also made heroes of William Henry Harrison and Andrew Jackson, the two military leaders most responsible for subduing the Indian resistance, and propelled their political careers. Finally, the war and its immediate aftermath sounded the death knell of the Federalist Party and led to a period of realignment when American politics was dominated by a single but amorphous political party.

On January 8, 1815, two weeks after the Treaty of Ghent was signed, Andrew Jackson inflicted a devastating defeat on a large British army at the Battle of New Orleans. While assuring Britain's ratification of the peace accords, news of Jackson's triumph provided a tremendous boost to the Madison administration and excited patriotic fervor throughout the country. Just as William Henry Harrison's name had become associated with Tippecanoe, Jackson's became associated with New Orleans. Despite the fact that he, like Harrison, was a man of wealth and a Tennessee politician, admiring publicists and political allies depicted him as a frontier farmer/freedom fighter fresh from the plough and committed above all else to defending the nation's honor against British tyranny. As one popular jingle proclaimed,

> He's none of your old New England stock,
> Or your gentry-proud Virginians,
> But a regular western fighting-cock
> With Tennessee opinions.

Such characterizations pleased Jackson, and he did his best to cultivate them.

While Jackson's political prospects soared at war's end, those of the Federalist Party came crashing down. The great stronghold of Federalism lay in the northeastern seaboard states, especially New England. Leading businessmen and clergy of the region had long criticized the domestic and foreign policies of Jefferson and Madison as being anticommercial and biased toward the French. Hard-line Federalists even accused Republican leaders of purposely setting out to destroy the maritime carrying trade of New England and New York and of going to war with England in order to assure Madison's reelection in 1812. When the war came, Federalists not only denounced it but also tried to embarrass the Madison administration by refusing to make loans to the U.S. government, opposing callups of state militias, and defying wartime restrictions by openly trading with the enemy. Some even talked of seceding from the Union.

Convinced that Republican blundering during the war would soon return their party to power, New England Federalists convened at Hartford, Connecticut, in the fall of 1814 to plot their strategy. Although a few extremists continued to call for secession, the majority of delegates settled on a plan aimed at curbing the power of republicanism in the South and West. They endorsed a series of amendments to the Constitution that, among other things, would eliminate the three-fifths method of counting slaves for the apportionment of seats in the House of Representatives, prevent the president from serving more than one term, and require a two-thirds majority in Congress for the admission of new states to the Union, embargoes on trade, and declarations of war.

> *"The conflict greatly weakened the military and political power of Native Americans from the Appalachians to the Mississippi and opened the floodgates for further white incursions into unsettled territory."*

This cartoon, entitled "The Hartford Convention," shows three New England states (Massachusetts, Connecticut, and Rhode Island) about to leap into the arms of Britain's King George III.

Whatever hope members of the Hartford convention had for the future were dashed, however, when news of Jackson's victory at New Orleans and the Treaty of Ghent arrived almost simultaneously. Already angered by Federalist obstructionism during the war, Republicans accused their opponents of conspiracy, sedition, and outright treason. The Federalist Party quickly became the object of public scorn. Although the party would linger on into the 1820s, the election of 1816, which swept James Monroe into the presidency, revealed that the Federalists were no longer a viable force in American politics. Monroe was Madison's handpicked successor and the fourth Virginian to hold the nation's highest office since 1789. The presidency was becoming known as the "Virginia Dynasty."

An early view of Fulton's *Clermont* steaming up the Hudson River from New York to Albany, c. 1810. Note the vessel's resemblance to traditional sailing ships of the day.

Toward a New Mechanical Age

The War of 1812, like other major conflicts, brought with it far-reaching economic, technological, and social changes. The war and its aftermath began a major shift in the economy from an agrarian base toward an increasingly industrial one, characterized by the widespread adoption of machinery. There were a number of precedents for this change. One, already noted, was the innovative work of Samuel Slater and other talented English immigrants in establishing the American textile industry. Another was the introduction of the steamboat, arguably America's first significant contribution to world technology.

> *"The steamboat arguably was America's first significant contribution to world technology."*

STEAM POWER

The application of steam power to transportation marked one of the entering wedges of the industrial revolution in America. The best known of the inventors of the steamboat was Robert Fulton. Although not the first person to apply steam power to the propulsion of water craft, he was the most successful. Fulton launched his "*North River* steamboat" (later renamed the *Clermont*) at New York City in August 1807. An unorthodox-looking vessel, the boat measured 150 feet long and 13 feet wide, with straight sides and a flat bottom that drew only 18 inches of water. It had two masts fore and aft for carrying square sails. What was new and noteworthy, however, was the *North River*'s source of power—a large, vertically standing, low-pressure, English-built steam engine situated beneath the deck and attached through a diamond-shaped crank to 15-foot paddle wheels on each side of the boat amidship. A boat that belched smoke, hissed steam, and thudded from the motion of its crankshaft and piston! It presented a strange sight to the crowds that gathered along the shore to watch its first run up the Hudson River from New York City to the state capital at Albany and back. A few spectators ran away as the boat approached, but many others "waved their handkerchiefs and hurrahed for Fulton" and his invention. Although he heard some sarcastic remarks about "Fulton's folly" before the *North River* got underway, Fulton was cheered by the result. "I overtook many sloops and schooners to the windward and parted with them as if they had been at anchor," he wrote triumphantly to a friend. "The power of propelling boats by steam is now fully proved."

The invention proved to be so popular and profitable that Fulton and his partners proceeded to build more vessels and, for a time, monopolized the steamboating business in New York waters and on the lower Mississippi from New Orleans to Natchez. Once successfully deployed in and around these port cities, **steamboating**—especially passenger and, to a lesser degree, mail packet service—spread quickly to other rivers as well as to the Great Lakes region. By 1817, 17 steamboats were operating on western rivers. Thereafter, the number of steam-powered vessels plying the Ohio, Mississippi, and their tributaries grew steadily from 69 in 1820 to 187 in 1830 and 536 in 1850. The rivers became the capillaries of a vast system of water-based transportation.

The great advantage of the steamboat over older craft was its speed, especially when moving upstream. Whereas early steamboats averaged around 50 miles a day, keelboats and other handpoled and pulled vessels could do no better than 20 miles a day and substantially less under adverse conditions. Equipped with more powerful engines and improved hulls, steamboats were capable of averaging 100 miles a day by the mid-1820s. Neither keelboats nor wagons could come close to managing those speeds even under the best of conditions. We have seen how long it took for the National Road to reach its western terminus at Vandalia, Illinois. One reason why construction proceeded sporadically after the road reached Wheeling, Virginia, in 1818 was that steamboats were waiting there to carry passengers and cargo speedily either upriver to Pittsburgh or, more likely, downriver to ports along the Ohio and Mississippi Rivers, and, by the 1840s, in a westerly direction along the Missouri, Red, and upper Mississippi Rivers and their tributaries. More than any other conveyance, the steamboat hastened the movement of white settlers into Indian territory and, as such, served as a vehicle of conquest as well as economic change. As one American journalist put it in 1841, "Steam navigation colonized the West."

Steam power and steam engineering proved to be particularly important to the developing economy of the Ohio Valley. In a region richly endowed with timberlands and coal deposits but with few good water-power sites, steam engines quickly found applications in manufacturing as well as river transportation. Owing mostly to the construction of steamboats, the manufacture of steam engines became one of the earliest and most important industrial products of Pittsburgh, Wheeling, Cincinnati, and Louisville. In 1814, Pittsburgh alone possessed some of the best mechanical talent in America. The remarkable assemblage of skilled machinists, ironworkers, and carpenters initially attracted to these cities by the steamboat business helps to explain their emergence before the Civil War as centers of transportation and industry.

Oliver Evans's "Columbian" steam engine, first patented in 1804, was used to power steamboats as well as sawmills, flour mills, and industrial machinery. Compared with earlier British-built Boulton and Watt steam engines, they were more compact, cheaper to build, and easier to operate and maintain. But they also ran at much higher steam pressures and thus were more dangerous to operate.

Farther east, especially in Philadelphia and New York, a thriving machine-building industry arose even earlier. In Philadelphia, for example, Oliver Evans, perhaps the most brilliant American inventor of the early nineteenth century, established his Mars Works in 1806 to manufacture the high-pressure steam engine he had patented two years earlier. While other shops like Nicholas Roosevelt's Soho Works near Newark, New Jersey, continued to make large pumping engines based on earlier British designs, Evans-type engines soon became the technology of choice in powering steamboats on western rivers.

Because finished engines were so expensive, early builders felt lucky if they received three or four orders a year. This meant that they had to supplement their income by executing less ambitious work, such as hand tools and decorative ironwork, for smaller customers. European visitors often commented on the versatility of American machine shops, noting that their lack of specialization exposed them to a wider variety of technical problems and, as a result, greater opportunities for innovation. Moreover, early steam-engine works like those of Evans and Roosevelt served an educational purpose. Long before the first engineering schools came into being, these shops trained a cadre of steam engineers and mechanics who went on to build ever larger machine shops and foundries. "Graduates" of these shops played a pivotal role in introducing the next generation of steam engines, railway locomotives, and other types of heavy industrial machinery in America.

The appearance of steamboats on America's rivers provided the most visible evidence of the new mechanical age ushered in by the war years. But the textile and firearms industries also grew rapidly in this period, following a similar trend toward mechanization. From Boston in the North to Richmond in the South and Pittsburgh and Cincinnati in the West, the war spurred a surge of manufacturing activity to meet the demand caused by wartime shortages of British manufactures. Cincinnati, little more than a frontier village

The steamboat *Ouishita* on the Red River, in the Louisiana Territory, 1836. By the 1810s, steamboats operating on western rivers had taken on a different appearance from their eastern counterparts. In addition to using more compact, American-made, "high pressure" steam engines, western river steamers were built with flatter bottoms, which allowed them to navigate in as little as three feet of water.

of 750 people in 1800, nearly quadrupled its population by 1810 and grew into a small city of almost 10,000 by 1820. When the War of 1812 ended, this "Queen City" had four cotton mills, a woolen factory, a white-lead works for making paint, flour and lumber mills, a barrel factory, glassworks, and furniture shops. Elsewhere around the country during the war, hundreds of mill hamlets and small manufacturing villages sprang up along the fall lines of rivers and streams. For example, textile manufacturing expanded along the Brandywine Creek some three miles west of Wilmington, Delaware, from two small mills in 1810 to nine by war's end. The war also stimulated a variety of manufacturing activities ranging from small blacksmith and machine shops that served the needs of local manufacturers to larger mills for making everything from flour to gunpowder.

In rural enclaves like the Brandywine Valley, water rather than steam provided the driving force behind industry. Indeed, manufacturing centers in outlying areas of rural America like the Brandywine Valley outpaced the developments of industry in larger cities like New York and Philadelphia.

View of waterpowered paper mills on the Brandywine Creek, c. 1830. Similar mills existed on the Brandywine and elsewhere for manufacturing cotton and woolen cloth and making gunpowder.

Cities such as these boasted good harbors and strategic locations, but they lacked ready access to adequate water power. So steam engines tended to be an urban phenomenon, and the engine works of Oliver Evans, Nicholas Roosevelt, and others arose in the big northern cities. But the technology of waterwheels was better understood by early factory masters and cheaper to install than steam engines. And waterwheels could convert the rushing waters along rural fall lines into usable power. So it was in the countryside, not the city, where the factory system experienced its fastest growth. Mechanization transformed the rural landscape even as it spurred the growth of cities.

THE BOSTON MANUFACTURING COMPANY

The most important factory to appear during the War of 1812 was the Boston Manufacturing Company in rural Waltham, Massachusetts. The enterprise began when a group of twelve Boston merchants, headed by Francis Cabot Lowell, decided to divert a portion of their capital from shipping to manufacturing after the British blockade of American ports had virtually halted overseas trade. Lowell and his associates chose to focus on the production of cotton cloth because they had previous trade experience with cotton and believed that a lucrative market existed in North America for the right kind of product. Lowell had spent two years in Britain between 1810 and 1812 visiting mills and noting what he saw. The experience fed his vision of what might be accomplished in America.

Historians would later refer to Lowell's initial group of merchant investors as the "Boston Associates." They were a tight-knit group, some related to one another by marriage or connected through previous business relationships. Prudent businessmen, they relied on Lowell for information about cotton manufacturing, particularly about the tools and machinery employed by English factory masters, whom they sought to emulate.

Early in 1813, Lowell and his closest associate and brother-in-law, Patrick Tracy Jackson, decided to go forward with the cotton venture. They obtained a charter from the Massachusetts legislature incorporating the Boston Manufacturing Company and raised the unparalleled sum of $100,000 (soon to grow to $300,000, then $600,000) in initial stock subscriptions from their mercantile associates. They then acquired a mill site on the Charles River some eight miles west of Boston in the village of Waltham, where they built the first of two large waterpowered factories for the production of a plain, multipurpose cloth called "sheeting."

Lowell hired an able master mechanic named Paul Moody to superintend the operation. Moody was not only an exceptional machinist but also a superb organizer with many connections throughout the mechanical community. Between his arrival at Waltham in 1813 and the beginning of production two years later, Moody devoted most of his time to equipping the mill with machinery for producing cotton cloth. His primary concern was the construction of a full-scale power loom for weaving. Using a model provided by Lowell and assisted by workers from the company's newly established machine shop, Moody succeeded in the fall of 1814 in building a loom that worked. Lowell was thrilled with the result. Years later, merchant Nathan Appleton, one of the original Boston Associates, recollected "the state of admiration and satisfaction with which we sat by the hour, watching the beautiful movement of this new and wonderful machine, destined as it evidently was, to change the character of all textile industry."

The power loom was the rock on which the Boston Manufacturing Company built its business strategy. Elsewhere in the United States, weaving was conducted separately from spinning. But Lowell and his partners aimed at making the entire product under one roof. Building an integrated manufacturing facility was a risky move, completely novel in the textile industry. In effect, it meant that raw cotton would enter the mill at one end and come out the other as finished cloth. In between, a series of machines attended by young female workers (of whom more will be said in Chapter 12) took the raw material, cleaned and carded (combed) it, spun it into thread, and wound the thread onto bobbins, which fed banks of power looms that wove it into cloth. To Lowell and

Moody, the power loom provided the missing link in the manufacturing process. By bringing power weaving into their mill rather than sending thread out to local weavers, they achieved control over the entire manufacturing process. This gave them a decided advantage over other textile manufacturers, and allowed their enterprise unlimited possibilities for growth.

In a continuous manufacturing operation such as this, one mechanical process depended on the smooth execution of another, and success depended on having threads spun to virtually uniform sizes. Any irregularities in a machine-based system of production could cause managerial nightmares, especially when economic efficiencies and, ultimately, profit depended on consistently making a product with uniform weights and dimensions. Early manufacturers like Moody and Lowell became single-minded in their pursuit of uniformity and control over every aspect of production. As we shall see, this compulsion had a significant impact on those who worked on the shop floor.

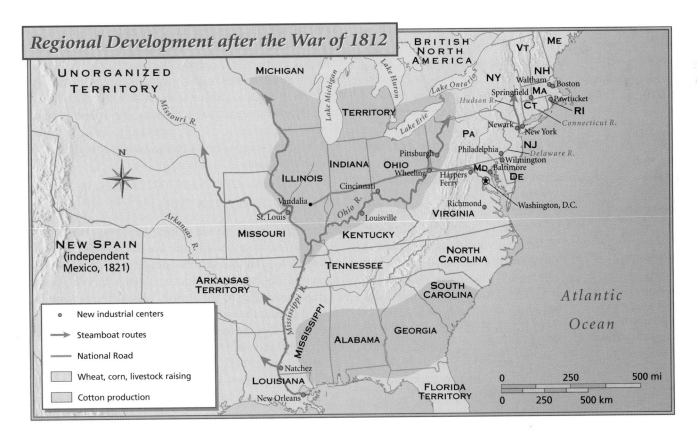

Regional Development after the War of 1812

The Boston Manufacturing Company's decisions on the types of cloth to produce were influenced by market considerations, but also by labor policy. From their visits to textile mills in England and the United States, Lowell and Moody learned that skilled workers—particularly mule spinners (workers who tended large spinning machines called "mules") and hand-loom weavers—could be independent, troublesome employees. Moody therefore did everything he could to avoid the use of skilled labor by breaking cloth production down to its simplest elements, assigning only one element to each worker, and devising "stop motions" that would automatically disengage machines if something went wrong. Given the state of textile technology in 1814–15, only coarse goods—such as garments for slaves—lent themselves to such a specialized degree of mechanization, and these became the focus of production at Waltham.

View of the Boston Manufacturing Company mills at Waltham, Massachusetts, c. 1825. As the rural scenery indicates, the city of Waltham grew around textile manufacturing and, later, the production of world-famous "Waltham" pocket watches and clocks.

Paul Moody, the Yankee mechanic responsible for building the Boston Manufacturing Company's mills at Waltham. Moody would eventually move to Lowell to establish the Boston Associates' Lowell Machine Shop.

The decision to produce cheap fabrics at Waltham proved to be a stroke of genius. While scores of small mills producing finer goods faltered and often failed in the face of renewed British competition after the War of 1812, the Boston Manufacturing Company prospered. The Waltham mill began to turn out its first cotton sheeting in a piecemeal way in 1814, and production began to hit stride two years later, after a number of mechanical kinks and bottlenecks had been worked out. Once underway, annual sales sky-rocketed from about $34,000 in 1817 to nearly $350,000 in 1822. By then, the Boston Associates had added a second mill to its Waltham complex and had increased its investment in the property to $771,000.

With their mills churning out three miles of cloth a day and their Boston marketing house selling every yard of it with calls for more, stockholders enjoyed extremely good returns on their investments. In 1817, the company paid its first dividend of 20 percent. During the next decade, annual dividends maintained this remarkable rate and sometimes exceeded it. Lowell and his partners had expected to make a profit, but not even in their wildest dreams had they imagined that it would be so great.

REGIONAL SPECIALIZATION

As machine-based manufacturing began to take hold in the Northeast, cotton became the South's most valuable commodity. In 1810, plantations located mainly in South Carolina and Georgia had produced 178,000 bales of cotton for markets primarily in the British Isles. Although production flagged during the war years, the coming of peace and the re-opening of European trade prompted a great surge in cotton cultivation and, with it, the expansion of slavery. In 1815, planters sent 209,000 bales—each weighing generally from 500 to 600 pounds—to market. As the world textile industry expanded and the price of raw cotton increased, more and more planters got into the business. This growth, in turn, set off what became known as "Alabama fever": hundreds of white settlers and their slaves streamed into the Mississippi Territory (comprising mainly the present states of Alabama and Mississippi), intent on making their fortunes and, in the process, displacing the region's Indians. By late 1817, the year the state of Mississippi entered the Union, cotton production approached 272,000 bales. Two years later, when Alabama came into the Union, it stood at 349,000 bales. By the 1820s, the South had become the world's foremost supplier of cotton, and southern politics began to reflect the dominant economic influence of "King Cotton."

Compared with the cotton culture of the deep South, a more diversified economy developed in the area west of the Appalachian Mountains that comprised the Old Northwest Territory and parts of the upper South bordering the Ohio and Mississippi Rivers. There, agriculture was also the dominant occupation. But owing to differences in climate and the length of the growing season, farms focused mainly on the production of wheat, corn, and livestock products. These were shipped downriver to New Orleans for distribution to southern buyers as well as markets located in the Northeast and, later, Europe. As with the spread of cotton cultivation in the deep South, rising prices for agricultural goods induced mass migrations of white settlers into the rich lands of Ohio, Indiana, Illinois, Michigan, Iowa, Wisconsin, and Missouri after the War of 1812. In 1816, Indiana entered the Union, followed by Illinois in 1818 and Missouri three years later. Thereafter, the region developed rapidly. And as fast as the white population grew, Native American culture declined.

Given the long-standing reliance of western farmers on the Ohio and Mississippi Rivers to get goods to market, the region's commerce moved mostly southward. But with the opening of the National Road after the War of 1812 and especially with the advent of an east-west network of canals and railroads several decades later, western trade became more directly connected with growing markets in the Northeast. The east-west trade received further impetus when the discovery of rich deposits of lead in Missouri, copper in Michigan, and coal and iron ore in western Pennsylvania, southern Ohio, and northern Kentucky attracted eastern capital to the region.

> *"By the 1820s, the South had become the world's foremost supplier of cotton, and southern politics began to reflect the dominant economic influence of 'King Cotton.'"*

Cities such as Cincinnati, Louisville, St. Louis, and Pittsburgh experienced rapid growth after the war. In the South, by contrast, only New Orleans was a fast-growing city.

As the West became more diversified after the War of 1812, the economy of the Northeast—like that of the South—became more specialized. But as the Northeast's economy developed increasingly toward manufacturing and heavy industry, older pursuits like shipping, the mercantile trade, and even agriculture continued to play important roles. Although the number of city and town dwellers grew in proportion to farmers, farming continued to be a leading occupation. Farm families adjusted to the growth of urban-industrial markets and the influx of nonperishable western foodstuffs by supplying perishable items such as milk, butter, eggs, fruit, and vegetables. They also supplemented their farming income by making palm-leaf hats, weaving cloth, and doing other "outwork" for local merchants and manufacturers during the winter months.

Steamboats, factories, and regional specialization—these important shifts in the economy indicated that Thomas Jefferson's cherished social vision of America as a nation of farmers was breaking down. Life as he had known it would never be the same. Jefferson's vision would remain a powerful influence in American politics and culture for generations

This sketch of the Union Manufactories on the Patapsco Falls near Baltimore (c. 1815) provides an excellent example of an early waterpowered textile factory and the company housing that surrounded it.

Chronology	1803	*Marbury vs. Madison.*
		Napoleonic Wars begin.
	December 20, 1803	The Louisiana Purchase.
	May 1804–September 21, 1806	Lewis and Clark's Corps of Discovery.
	August 1807	Robert Fulton launches the first steamboat.
	December 22, 1807	Embargo Act signed into law.
	November 7, 1811	Battle of Tippecanoe.
	June 18, 1812	War declared against Britain.
	1813	Boston Manufacturing Company founded in Waltham, Massachusetts.
	December 24, 1814	Treaty of Ghent ends War of 1812.
	January 8, 1815	Battle of New Orleans.
	1817	Milling machine introduced.

to come, but it no longer represented the driving force of American life. The United States was experiencing the initial stages of an industrial revolution, and like all fundamental changes, this one brought tensions that soon manifested themselves not only in business and labor relations but also in sectional strife. In all of this, the War of 1812 stood as a watershed.

Suggested Reading

Stephen F. Ambrose, *Undaunted Courage: Meriwether Lewis, Thomas Jefferson, and the Opening of the American West* (1996)

Donald R. Hickey, *The War of 1812* (1989)

John Lauritz Larson, *Internal Improvement: National Public Works and the Promise of Popular Government in the Early United States* (2001)

Walter Licht, *Industrializing America* (1995)

Richard White, *The Middle Ground: Indians, Empires, and Republics in the Great Lakes Region, 1650–1815* (1991)

Joseph Ellis, *American Sphinx: The Character of Thomas Jefferson* (1997)

In September 1848, photographers Charles Fontayne and William S. Porter set up their camera on a rooftop along the Ohio River in Newport Kentucky, to get a panoramic shot of Cincinnati. They panned their camera across Cincinnati's waterfront, capturing separate segments of the growing city's skyline. The resulting images from that day, eight whole-plate daguerreotypes, are known as *The Cincinnati Panorama*. By this time, Cincinnati was well known for its steamboat-building and meatpacking enterprises. The latter proved so important that Cincinnati also became known as "Porkopolis."

Focus QUESTIONS

■ **How was the American population changing in this period?**

■ **How did the Madisonian Platform represent a new vision of the federal government as a catalyst of change?**

■ **What developments were strengthening the forces of sectionalism in this period?**

■ **How did American foreign policy become more assertive in this period?**

■ **How were the tides of American politics shifting after the election of 1824?**

"We stand at this moment," an observer in New York declared in 1821, "on the brink of fate, on the very edge of the precipice. . . . We are no longer to remain plain and simple republics of farmers, like New-England colonists, or the Dutch settlements on the Hudson. We are fast becoming a great nation, with great commerce, manufactures, population, wealth, luxuries, and with the vices and miseries that they engender." Speaker of the House Henry Clay of Kentucky agreed, declaring, "A new epoch has arisen." Political leaders of Clay's generation knew that this new epoch was closely related to the mechanical technologies on the rise around them.

The three most debated political issues of the day—banks, tariffs, and internal improvements—were all tied to the new mechanical age. Four of the five leading political figures of the time—Clay, John C. Calhoun, John Quincy Adams, and Daniel Webster—all took up the cause of "industry and improvement." Even the fifth, Andrew Jackson, stood for the expansion and progress of American industry, although his views on the role of the federal government in the economic arena often put him at loggerheads with the others. Like most Americans, all five leaders had emerged from the war with strong nationalist and patriotic feelings. But as the pace of change quickened during the postwar period, they repeatedly found themselves challenged by constituents who feared the central government, placed regional economic and social interests ahead of national interests, and, accordingly, held different views about the relationship of individual states to the nation. The emerging tension between national and sectional interests would alter the structure of American politics and infuse it with a dangerous divisiveness.

Population Growth

In 1815, the United States counted roughly 8.4 million inhabitants, up 58 percent since 1800. Overwhelmingly white, agrarian, and Protestant, nearly three-quarters of the population came from an English, Scottish, or Scotch-Irish background. The remainder of the white population were primarily German, Irish Catholic, French, Spanish, or Dutch. Next in numbers came involuntary immigrants, namely African slaves, and free blacks. In 1790, blacks constituted nearly 20 percent of the population, but their numbers were declining in proportion to whites. By 1840, the total black population numbered around 2.9 million souls, but its percentage of the total population had fallen to 17 percent. In the next decade, it would decline to 16 percent.

People of Native American ancestry were not even listed on the census returns, a clear indicator of their irrelevance to the U.S. government. One estimate for 1790 placed them at roughly half a million, spread thinly around the country. Relatively few Indians remained in the Northeast. In New England, the once-mighty Abenakis, Pequots, Mohegans, Penobscots, Narragansetts, Passamaquoddies, and Wampanoags had been reduced to hundreds. While they retained their ancient languages and continued to practice some of their impressive crafts, they nonetheless became increasingly absorbed into a part of the dominant white culture that, according to one observer, "resemble[s] that of the lower orders in our cities." The same fate awaited other native peoples in other parts of the country as land-hungry white Americans used political trickery and often military force to remove them from their lands.

A striking feature of the census data is the changing regional distribution of the population over time. In 1815, nearly 50 percent lived in the northeastern part of the United States comprising the New England states, New York, New Jersey, Pennsylvania, Delaware, and Maryland. A little more than one-third lived in the southern states of Virginia, North Carolina, South Carolina, Georgia, Louisiana, and the future states of Florida, Alabama, Mississippi, Arkansas, and Texas. The fastest-growing region was the trans-Appalachian West, consisting of Kentucky, Tennessee, Ohio, and the future states of Indiana, Illinois, Missouri, Michigan, Iowa, and Wisconsin. Growth was nothing less than spectacular in the five states—Ohio, Indiana, Illinois, Michigan, and Wisconsin—that once comprised the Old Northwest Territory. In 1800, about 51,000 white people, or 1 percent of the nation's total population, inhabited the Old Northwest. By 1850, that number would balloon to 4.5 million, about 20 percent of the national total.

A burst of immigration after the War of 1812 ignited the country's population explosion. What appeared to be a modest influx in the 1820s grew tremendously by the mid-1840s. The national census of 1820, the first since the war, revealed that 8,385 individuals had entered the country that year. Of that number, the vast majority came from northwestern Europe. Irish migrants headed the list with 3,614, followed by 2,410 English and 968 Germans. Ten years later, the number of immigrants nearly tripled to 23,322, with Irish, Germans, and English leading the way. By 1840, the number had swelled to over 84,000, more than tripling again. Then, owing to political turmoil in Europe and a devastating famine in Ireland, the floodgates opened. In 1848, for example, over 226,000 foreigners entered the country. Again, Irish, German, and English immigrants headed the lists. During the next six years, from 1849 to 1854, the numbers soared to over 2 million, reaching an all-time pre–Civil War high with 427,833 in 1854, when for the first time Germans replaced Irish as the leading immigrant group in America.

Dramatic changes in the organization of oceangoing commerce and ship technology paralleled, and to a certain degree prompted, the swelling tide of immigrants after 1815. A particularly important development was the appearance in 1818 of trans-Atlantic "packet ships" that, in contrast to more common tramp vessels, ran on fixed schedules between ports. The earliest company, the Black Ball Line, owned by Quaker merchants, sent two vessels a week between New York and Liverpool, England. By the mid-1820s, New York had emerged as the center of a thriving packet-line industry that emphasized speed and regularity of service, factors that significantly improved passenger travel as well as the delivery of overseas mail. Operating initially with traditional sailing vessels, the packets introduced regular steamship service in 1838. After a slow start, the number of steamships plying the Atlantic grew dramatically after 1847 as a number of new companies headed by Cunard, the Ocean Navigation Company,

View of the Miami Canal at Dayton, Ohio, 1831–32. Before the coming of railroads, canals served briefly as the primary carriers of people, raw materials, and commercial goods from the East Coast to the Midwest.

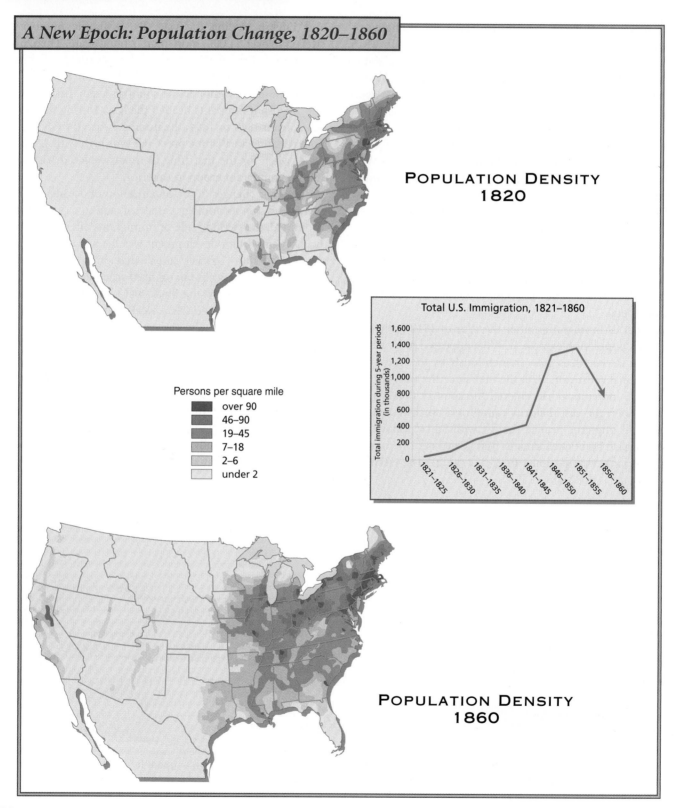

A New Epoch: Population Change, 1820–1860

POPULATION DENSITY
1820

Persons per square mile

over 90
46–90
19–45
7–18
2–6
under 2

Total U.S. Immigration, 1821–1860

Total immigration during 5-year periods (in thousands)

1,600
1,400
1,200
1,000
800
600
400
200
0

1821–1825
1826–1830
1831–1835
1836–1840
1841–1845
1846–1850
1851–1855
1856–1860

POPULATION DENSITY
1860

and the Collins Line competed for passenger and freight service on the high seas. Packet service would eventually spread to other American seaport cities, but none rivaled the port of New York. Already linked to the west by the Erie Canal and excellent steamboat lines on the Hudson River, New York became, with the introduction of packet ships, America's leading commercial center and port of entry for European immigrants.

All told, more than 5 million people came to the United States between 1819 and 1860—over half of them during the 1850s. Observers who were aware of these dizzying numbers had trouble comprehending fully what they meant. To some, they bespoke progress, expansion, and unbounded optimism about the future. To others, they signaled the breakup of old ways, the threat of alien religions and undue foreign influences, and apprehension about the future. To still others, they conveyed mixed messages that changed as their personal experiences changed. One thing seemed clear to all: the rapid population growth was bringing considerable change to all sectors of American society.

The Madisonian Platform

When the War of 1812 ended, James Madison was nearing the end of his second and final term as president of the United States. Although criticism of his wartime leadership had taken its toll, he entered the postwar period uplifted by the widespread nationalistic feeling that permeated the land. Madison was intent on redeeming his tarnished reputation and charting a course for the country that would secure the prosperity everyone so eagerly hoped for.

After consulting with congressional leaders and reviewing proposals that had been set aside during the war years, Madison unveiled his plan on December 5, 1815, in his Seventh Annual Message to Congress. In it, he urged legislative action on five fronts: military affairs, banking and currency, protective tariffs, internal improvements (particularly roads and canals), and a national university. Altogether, the agenda became known as the "Madisonian Platform."

The message conveyed a vision that captured the imagination of both the public and Congress. Each of the five proposals had, in fact, been made before, most notably by former Secretary of the Treasury Albert Gallatin, Speaker of the House Henry Clay, and Madison himself. What made the

A poster advertising the schedules and fees of packets and steamers from Liverpool, London, and Glasgow to New York in 1840.

message so different—indeed, innovative—was Madison's combination of all five proposals into a coherent program of political action that constituted nothing less than a blueprint for national economic development. Implicit in the message was the idea of moving the federal government from periphery to center stage as a catalyst of change—something that challenged the very core of Jeffersonian beliefs.

MILITARY REFORM: THE UNIFORMITY SYSTEM

The Madisonian agenda began with the military. Despite the widespread popular belief that the United States had won the War of 1812, insiders knew that the conflict had been a logistical and strategic nightmare. From the outset, faulty arms, insufficient supplies, erratic deliveries, and outright subterfuges had plagued the war effort. Even before the war ended, Con-

Simeon North, one of numerous private arms makers who got their start in business by taking U.S. government contracts. A gifted inventor of tools and machinery, North willingly relinquished his patent rights in order to retain his government contracts.

gress, at the president's urging, passed legislation aimed at improving the organization of the regular army and its relationship to state militia units. In February 1815, for example, Congress enacted a law that placed the national armories at Harpers Ferry, Virginia, and Springfield, Massachusetts, as well as all private arms contractors under the direct supervision of the U.S. Army Ordnance Department. Influenced by former French officers in the American army, the chief of ordnance (arms and munitions) and his assistants had long been calling for greater "system and uniformity" in the manufacture of firearms. With the passage of the "Act for the better regulation of the Ordnance Department," they quickly announced a program to establish standardized patterns for all small arms supplied to the U.S. government and eventually to manufacture weapons with uniform parts. Although their definition of uniformity remained purposely vague, everyone knew that their goal was to produce firearms with interchangeable parts that could easily be repaired on the battlefield.

As it turned out, interchangeable manufacturing methods developed incrementally over thirty years, not dramatically and fast. Scores of talented machinists, army ordnance officers, and private entrepreneurs cooperated in developing the new technology. An important benchmark occurred around 1816, when Simeon North, a private arms contractor to the federal government from Middletown, Connecticut, succeeded in making the lock, or firing mechanism, of horsemen's pistols with interchangeable parts. Another important stage was reached ten years later when John H. Hall, a New Englander working at the Harpers Ferry National Armory, was able to produce a patented breech-loading rifle bearing his name, with interchangeable parts. By 1831, Hall and North reached another plateau when, after considerable difficulty, they successfully (and separately) made Hall rifles at Harpers Ferry and Middletown (some 400 miles apart) whose parts would interchange. The final stage took place at the Springfield National Armory, where, during the early 1840s, the government's workshops were retooled with the latest gauges and machinery to produce 20,000 to 30,000 muskets annually with fully interchangeable parts. Springfield would again demonstrate its prowess during the Civil War when, in 1864, it reached the unprecedented production level of 276,000 rifle-muskets a year. Such manufacturing capability would not be surpassed until Henry Ford introduced the mass-production assembly line for making Model T automobiles at Highland Park, Michigan, in 1913.

The Upper Water Shops of the Springfield Armory, 1830. Here, iron components of muskets and pistols were forged before being transported by wagon to another set of shops about a mile away to be machined for assembly. By the 1840s, Springfield had become a leading center of interchangeable manufacturing and machine-tool building in America.

322

*How did the Madisonian Platform
represent a new vision of the federal
government as a catalyst of change?*

The Springfield Armory's leadership in the mechanical arts depended as much on its assimilation of techniques invented elsewhere by private arms contractors as on in-house activity. As early as 1825, it became known as "The Grand National Armory," the mecca of the American arms industry. But its influence went beyond the manufacture of arms: it became a clearinghouse for the dissemination of mechanical know-how. The Army Ordnance Department opened the national armories at Springfield and Harpers Ferry to all callers and made technical information available free of charge. Private arms makers or any other manufacturers seeking to learn about the latest developments in metalworking invariably visited Springfield. There, they could examine the most advanced tools and machinery, make notes and sketches, and discuss common problems with the master armorer or the master machinist. Visitors might then arrange to replicate whatever they needed at machine shops

A Hall breech-loading rifle made at Harpers Ferry in 1826. The irregular shapes of the parts that made up the breechblock, or firing mechanism (lower right), indicate the level of mechanical difficulty Hall faced in making guns with interchangeable parts. He solved the problem by applying specially designed machinery to the manufacture of his gun and carefully measuring each part with standardized gauges as it moved through the production process.

nearby, which likewise had access to the armory's patterns and drawings. Such easy movement from one shop to another contrasted with more closely guarded practices in Europe. Openness and accessibility proved to be one of the earmarks of the small arms industry as it developed and refined methods that became known abroad by the 1850s as "the American system" of manufacturing.

By the mid-1840s, manufacturing methods pulled together at the national armories began to spread to all sorts of factories and machine shops turning out metal products. Helping to push this change were former ordnance officers who left the army and assumed managerial posts with privately owned firearms businesses, foundries, and railroads. But skilled workers counted for more than managers. "Armory practice," as it came to be called, was usually transmitted by skilled workers who received their early training at one of the public or private armories and then moved on to new positions as master machinists and production supervisors at other manufacturing establishments. Countless firms, large and small, followed this pattern, thereby acquiring the latest armory

know-how—faster and cheaper than they could by learning it all over by themselves.

More often than not, those who borrowed the new technology had to adapt it to different uses, leading to further refinements and inventions. By the 1850s, armory methods could be found in factories making sewing machines, pocket watches, padlocks, railway equipment, shoes, wagons, and hand tools. And the key transmitters of these methods were New England machine-tool firms closely connected with the Springfield Armory.

UNIFORMITY AT WEST POINT AND THE POST OFFICE

Since precision production was expensive, most businessmen contented themselves with manufacturing products with standardized but not necessarily interchangeable parts. Only the U.S. government could afford the luxury of complete interchangeability. The person who presided over the early stages of the uniformity project was South Carolina's John C.

Calhoun. An avid nationalist, Calhoun possessed a first-class mind, enormous energy, and driving intensity. During the War of 1812, he had been an outspoken critic of the Madison administration's management of the war effort, accusing the president and his cabinet of incompetence. Although Madison recognized Calhoun's talents, he also knew that the South Carolinian had ruffled too many feathers to serve in his cabinet. But after Madison retired in 1817, his successor, James Monroe, asked Calhoun to take over the War Department.

Leaving the House of Representatives in November 1817, Calhoun entered his new office determined to reorganize the military and eradicate the mismanagement he had denounced. Early on, he endorsed the Ordnance Department's budding uniformity program and emphasized the need for discipline and systematic control over everything in the army, from the training of cadets at the U.S. Military Academy at West Point, New York, to more mundane matters such as record keeping and accounting practices. Above all, Calhoun envisioned the army as something more than a fighting force. At a time when people eyed standing armies with suspicion, he felt that the U.S. Army could and should be used for constructive civil purposes.

One of Calhoun's first actions as secretary of war was to appoint Captain Sylvanus Thayer as superintendent of the

LEFT: John C. Calhoun, James Monroe's secretary of war (1817–25).
RIGHT: Captain Sylvanus P. Thayer, superintendent of the U.S. Military Academy and educational innovator.

academy at West Point. Established by act of Congress in 1802, West Point was intended to be as much an engineering school as a military academy—the first of its type in America. But it suffered from a lack of discipline and, more seriously, only sporadic congressional support. Thayer's mission was to reinvigorate the academy. He had visited Europe on a tour of inspection, returning to the United States greatly impressed with the training of French military engineers at the famous École Polytechnique in Paris. French educational practices had influenced West Point's curriculum since its founding, but only incompletely. Upon assuming command in 1817, Thayer patterned the academy's program more closely after the French model by borrowing its syllabi, adopting its textbooks, and hiring former French officers to teach at West Point. His goal was to produce not just competent soldiers but "soldier-technologists" who could master the level as well as the sword. Under his leadership, the Military Academy would emerge as the nation's leading engineering school. Its only serious rival before the Civil War was the Rensselaer Polytechnic Institute established at Troy, New York, in 1824.

Grounds of the U.S. Military Academy at West Point, New York, 1828.

Thayer's emphasis on tests, grades, disciplinary demerits, and class rankings made West Point cadets particularly conscious of the importance of accountability in their lives. This ethos, coupled with formal training in mathematics, science, and engineering as well as more traditional military subjects, tended to produce officers who put great emphasis on precision measurement, calculation, and the establishment of objective norms through rational analysis. The best graduates of the Military Academy went into the elite army corps of engineers, ordnance, and artillery intent on bringing greater system and uniformity not just to the manufacture of firearms but to every aspect of military affairs.

"West Point was intended to be as much an engineering school as a military academy—the first of its type in America."

While Thayer revamped West Point's curriculum, Calhoun reorganized the War Department, issuing in 1821 a set of regulations that established clear lines of authority from his office to every branch of the army. The earmarks of Calhoun's new approach—accountability, precision, control—were the same as Thayer's at West Point. Moreover, both schemes meshed with the emphasis that the Ordnance Department placed on uniformity in the sphere of manufacturing. Under the new rules, every army unit (from infantry regiments in the West to the national armories in the East) was required to prepare monthly, quarterly, and annual reports that detailed what they were doing, the condition of their equipment, and how they had spent funds allocated to them. Secretary Calhoun and his staff used these reports not only to account for expenditures, but also to compare the performances of individual officers, army units, and army installations, including the national armories. Above all, the new regulations allowed the War Department to exercise greater control over the army's far-flung, multiunit operations. In effect, the War Department under Calhoun's leadership created a bureaucratic management structure that would become a model not only for other government institutions but also for private enterprise.

An early beneficiary of Calhoun's innovations was the U.S. Post Office. In operation since 1775, the postal system had grown as the population grew. By 1816, the system employed more than 3,000 postal officers, a number that embraced 69 percent of the entire federal civilian workforce. By 1828, the United States had 74 post offices for every 100,000 people, a ratio that vastly exceeded those for Great Britain and France. Equally impressive, the U.S. Post Office served an area spread over 116,000 square miles, delivering nearly 14 million letters and 16 million newspapers annually. More than any other branch of the federal government, it had the most frequent contact with the general public and their everyday lives. "For the vast majority of Americans," one writer observes, "the postal system *was* the central government."

The person who presided over the expansion of the Post Office during the 1820s was John McLean, a politically ambitious lawyer-politician from Ohio. A friend and protégé of Calhoun, McLean drew on Calhoun's experience as secretary of war in bringing greater system and efficiency to the operations of the Post Office. Like Calhoun, McLean distributed a detailed set of regulations that covered everything from ac-

Interior view of the U.S. Post Office at New York (1844), showing the system used for sorting letters, newspapers, and packages for distribution to all parts of the United States and abroad.

counting and inventory methods to the sorting and distribution of mail. He and his competent staff oversaw the scheduling of mail deliveries around the country and negotiated contracts with privately owned post-rider, stagecoach, and steamboat lines for carrying the mail.

Of all these conveyances, stagecoaches were the most important until railroads superseded them during the Civil War. In 1828, McLean estimated that the Post Office had under its direct control 17,584 horses, 2,879 carriages, and 243 smaller wagons. As Calhoun had at the War Department, he strongly supported the construction of roads, bridges, and other internal improvements and sponsored the production and distribution of maps that hung in virtually every post office in the United States, reminding the public how important good roads were to the prompt delivery of the mail. Because he headed the country's largest organization and controlled more jobs—public or private—than any other individual in America, McLean was a formidable force in American politics and a perennial contender for the presidency.

"The organizational reforms instituted by Calhoun helped power the expansion of the American economy."

The organizational reforms instituted by Calhoun and McLean helped power the expansion of the American economy. These new methods traveled with former army officers (many of them West Point graduates) and

A Boston and New York mail coach, 1820. In addition to transporting passengers, an important part of the stagecoach business was carrying the U.S. mail.

postal officials who, after serving the U.S. government, entered private business as consultants, engineers, plant superintendents, and company presidents. With them went the skills, habits of mind, and penchant for system and control that characterized the emerging industrial economy and the modern technological age.

BANKING REFORM

The most pressing domestic problem facing the federal government in 1815—and the second major item on the Madisonian Platform—was the chaotic state of the country's **money and banking system.** Although the U.S. Mint had issued a limited number of gold, silver, and copper coins each year, the U.S. had no national currency. Whatever paper money existed came from state-chartered banks. Before the War of 1812, the First Bank of the United States had served as an effective brake on unregulated state banks that issued worthless paper currency by collecting and returning suspect bills and demanding that they be redeemed in gold or silver coin. With the failure of Congress to renew the bank's charter in 1811, that brake was removed, and it did not take long for unbacked paper money to flood the market and prompt runaway inflation. Wary of currency presented to them from banks whose credit ratings they knew nothing about, merchants and manufacturers either refused to accept such money or, more often, discounted its value by as much as 30 or 40 percent.

The situation had grown so bad by 1814 that the U.S. Treasury, which by law had to accept tax payments and other debts owed the government in either specie or paper currency, stood on the verge of bankruptcy. Since people invariably chose to pay the government in depreciated paper money rather than hard specie, the treasury became a dumping ground for state banknotes of suspicious worth. Saddled with currency worth significantly less than its stated face value, federal officials experienced considerable difficulty using funds collected in one part of the country to pay debts owed elsewhere. The government moved to correct the problem by chartering a Second Bank of the United States. Finding themselves in a situation reminiscent of Jefferson's when debating the constitutionality of the Louisiana Purchase, James Madison and other leading members of the Republican

Party quietly set aside questions about the constitutionality of the bank in the interest of solving the currency crisis and placing the treasury on firm financial footing at a time of rapid national expansion.

Once proposed, legislative action came quickly. In January 1816, the House Committee on National Currency introduced a bill calling for the establishment of the Second Bank of the United States. In dramatic fashion, House Speaker Henry Clay, who had strenuously opposed rechartering the First Bank in 1811 on constitutional grounds, stepped down from his podium to admit his mistake and endorse the bill. "The force of circumstance and the lights of experience" had persuaded him that Congress did indeed possess the right to incorporate such an institution. The bank bill subsequently passed the House by a healthy margin and, with certain amendments—the most important of which mandated that all government debts be collected in legal U.S. currency (gold or silver) or in banknotes redeemable, on demand, inspecie—moved through the Senate to become law on April 10, 1816.

In its final form, the new law provided the Second Bank of the United States with a twenty-year charter and established it as a semiprivate corporation with a capital stock of $35 million, approximately 80 percent of which came from private investors and the remaining portion ($7.5 million) from the federal government. The bill also stipulated that, like its predecessor, the Second Bank's headquarters would be in Philadelphia, with branch banks located throughout the country as its twenty-five directors saw fit. Equally important, the bank was obligated to pay the U.S. government a fee, or "bonus," of $1.5 million in three installments over the first years of its operation. This last point, the so-called Bonus Bill, would soon become a bone of contention when Congress turned to the subject of internal improvements.

Compared with the hundreds of state-chartered banks that existed throughout the country, the Second Bank of the United States was an extraordinarily powerful institution. Simply put, they were small and it was big—very big. In addition to its capital stock of $35 million, the Second Bank also became the repository of all federal monies. The paper currency it issued and the loans it made had the full weight of the federal treasury behind them. The bank could also wield considerable influence over interest rates throughout the country. With branches in every important commercial city, it could do exactly what it was chartered to do, namely act as a stabilizing influence on a rapidly growing economy. No private bank could come close to exercising that sort of clout.

Headquarters of the Second Bank of the United States in Philadelphia, a prime example of what became known as Greek Revival architecture. The building still stands near Independence Hall in Philadelphia and currently serves as an art museum.

But stability came at a price. The Second Bank of the United States sometimes used its power to stop certain state-chartered banks from issuing paper currency of questionable worth, thereby reducing their ability to make loans. With state banks facing such competitive disadvantages, it did not take long for them to level charges against the Second Bank as an unconstitutional monopoly that favored eastern monied interests. Although the bank survived such accusations throughout the 1810s and 1820s, a political boiling point would come in 1832 with the reelection campaign of President Andrew Jackson. Ironically, the bank's very economic strength became the source of its greatest political vulnerability.

PROTECTING AMERICAN MANUFACTURERS

As soon as the War of 1812 ended, British manufacturers, eager to undermine U.S. manufacturing and tap the expanding North American trade, began dumping goods in New York and other eastern ports at low prices that threatened to damage, if not destroy, the infant industries that had taken root in the United States during the embargo and war years. In response to calls for government protection from manufacturers centered in Pennsylvania but supported by kindred groups in New England, Ohio, and Kentucky, the Madison administration proposed a tariff bill that offered moderate protection to American manufacturers but fell short of equaling the virtually complete protection they had enjoyed during the war years. On imports of cotton and woolen textiles, for example, Madison's secretary of the treasury recommended taxes of 33$\frac{1}{2}$ percent and 28 percent, respectively, on the value of goods being imported. When the bill reached the House Ways and Means Committee, however, the rates for both products were slashed to 20 percent, even though the same committee (which had a large southern contingent) ratcheted up the duty on imported sugar to a whopping 56 percent. The setting of tariff rates clearly involved sectional economic interests and, accordingly, sectional politics. In 1816, after considerable debate, Congress finally settled on a tariff that levied duties of 30 percent on textile imports for two years, followed by 25 percent for two more years, and finally leveling off in the fifth year at 20 percent.

The idea of scaling down rates over a five-year period came from Daniel Webster, a representative from New Hampshire and an opponent of the protective tariff. Webster, as well as many others in Congress, believed that five years of protection should be enough to place American manufactures on an equal footing with foreign competitors. House Speaker Clay, however, felt differently. His unstinting efforts on behalf of high protective tariffs for all American products made him a hero to many manufacturers. The Delaware gunpowder maker and outspoken protectionist E. I. du Pont became a close friend of Clay's at this time and a staunch supporter of the Kentuckian's subsequent races for the presidency. So, too, did other budding industrialists.

When Madison stepped down from the presidency in March 1817, it seemed a foregone conclusion that Clay would emerge as the foremost spokesman for the Madisonian Platform. In fact, by the mid-1820s, the platform would become

Eleuthère Irénée du Pont. The son of a French intellectual leader, du Pont came to America in 1799 to escape the ravages of the French Revolution. Having worked at a Parisian gunpowder factory under Antoine Lavoisier (the founder of modern chemistry), young du Pont established a similar business on the family farm near Wilmington, Delaware.

better known as Clay's "American System." Whatever the label, they stood for the same thing: protective tariffs, internal improvements, and a strong national bank, all of which assumed an activist role on the part of the federal government as a catalyst of economic growth in advance of free-market forces. Viewed in this light, the Tariff of 1816 served as a critical inducement for industrial development.

Considerable maneuvering went on behind the scenes as the tariff bill took shape. No one proved more effective a lobbyist than the Boston Manufacturing Company's Francis Cabot Lowell. As a producer of cheap cotton cloth, Lowell sought the best possible competitive advantages for his product. He advocated a tariff that would afford greater protection to cheap cotton goods made by his company than to goods of finer quality from places like Pawtucket, Rhode Island, or Philadelphia. Moreover, Lowell helped persuade Calhoun and other representatives from the cotton-growing regions of the South to support the measure because, he maintained, it protected growers as well as manufacturers from cheap Indian cottons that were beginning to compete with American goods.

Calhoun supported the tariff primarily for patriotic rather than economic reasons. Even though the United States emerged from the war with its independence intact, Calhoun remained wary of the continuing threat posed by England. National defense and national unity were his primary concerns, but he also realized that economic barriers had to be erected if the United States was to achieve economic independence from Britain. Other southern politicians felt the same; with little or no interest in manufacturing, they voted in favor of protectionism out of an avid nationalism. In 1816, they could afford to be broad-minded because they controlled the Republican Party and with it the machinery of government. But that attitude would soon change. While the North veered increasingly toward an industrial economy, the South remained steadfastly agrarian. Cotton was its primary cash crop, and it was dependent on foreign trade for the export of cotton, tobacco, and other raw materials and the import of European manufactured goods. On strictly economic grounds, its leaders recognized that the new tariff threatened foreign trade while increasing the prices southerners had to pay for European imports. With the North and South developing in different directions, it was only a matter of time before their economic differences became manifest in increasingly bitter political clashes.

INTERNAL IMPROVEMENTS

The most ambitious part of the Madisonian Platform—and the keystone of Clay's American System—concerned internal improvements. Scarcely 100 miles of canals existed in the United States in 1816. Roads in most parts of the country were little more than rutted wagon paths that often became impassable during wet weather. Well-maintained turnpikes and toll roads existed in eastern Pennsylvania, New Jersey, New York, and southern New England, but they often proved prohibitively expensive for the transportation of commercial goods. The National Road, the one federally funded project that sought to link the East with the West, had not yet reached Wheeling on the Ohio River. Every well-informed person recognized that an interconnecting system of roads, canals, steamboat lines, and (later) railroads was essential to economic and geographic expansion. Three questions, however, stood foremost in their minds: Who would be in charge of building such a system? Where would the projects be placed? And who would benefit most from them? At issue was the economic survival of some communities and regions over others.

"Clay's 'American System' stood for protective tariffs, internal improvements, and a strong national bank."

Although Madison initiated the idea of internal improvements and Clay vigorously supported it, Calhoun took the lead in pressing the issue before Congress. Early in 1817, before he became secretary of war, he sponsored a bill that proposed using the $1.5 million bonus and the dividends from the government's stock in the Second Bank of the United States for the construction of roads and canals. In doing so, he sidestepped the tricky constitutional issues raised by the Bonus Bill by pointing to the military significance of internal improvements and appealing to nationalist sentiments. "Let it never be forgotten," he argued in one of his most impassioned speeches, "that the extent of the republic exposes us to the greatest of calamities—*disunion*. . . . Whatever impedes the intercourse of the extremes with this, the centre of the republic, weakens the union. . . . Let us, then, bind the republic together with a perfect system of roads and canals. Let us conquer space."

When New England Federalists and old-line Jeffersonian strict constructionists questioned the constitutionality of the Bonus Bill, Calhoun replied that the "general welfare" clause made it constitutional. When they continued their opposition, Calhoun appealed to practicality and common sense. "If we are restricted in the use of our money to the enumerated powers [stated in the Constitution], on what principles can the purchase of Louisiana be justified?" he asked. For Calhoun, as well as for other nationalists in Congress, a national transportation system was essential—"the condition of our greatness," as he put it.

Despite Calhoun's eloquence, the Bonus Bill encountered rough sledding: after squeaking through Congress, the bill was vetoed by Madison on constitutional grounds. Nor could the best efforts of Calhoun and Clay revive it. Madison's veto delivered a blow to postwar nationalism and signaled the abandonment of his expansive economic platform. When he retired and Calhoun moved to the War Department, Henry Clay assumed the mantle of leadership on internal improvements and, as mentioned, made them a central feature of his American System. Yet, as much as he tried, even the dynamic Clay could not resurrect the Bonus Bill. President Monroe stood firm in his opposition to using the bonus and dividends from the Second Bank of the United States to create a permanent fund for internal improvements.

The Baltimore and Ohio Railroad's British-built "Tom Thumb" steam locomotive racing a horse-drawn car, 1830. Within ten years, British locomotives would be replaced by American-designed locomotives that were better adapted to the sharper curves and higher grades of the American landscape.

329

An American-designed locomotive from the 1850s.

All was not lost, however. After declining to sign a bill to extend the National Road into Ohio in 1822, President Monroe issued a lengthy paper entitled "Views of the President of the United States on the Subject of Internal Improvements," in which he admitted that Congress had "the unlimited power to raise money" and appropriate it "to the purposes of common defense and of general, not local, national, not State benefit." This gave congressional nationalists the opening they needed, and they moved quickly to test the president by passing an appropriations bill to repair the National Road, which, cast in the appropriate language of national defense, Monroe signed. Although Clay and his followers rejected the president's logic, they gladly accepted the result and even hailed it as a victory for the American System.

In the meantime, Calhoun kept pressing his views on Monroe about the strategic importance of roads and canals for national defense. Intent on making the War Department the locus of an internal improvements empire, he recommended that the Army Corps of Engineers conduct surveys for roads and canals throughout the nation and, when finished, be placed in charge of their construction. With Calhoun at the peak of his popularity and Clay steering the legislation as Speaker of the House, it did not take long for the first phase of Calhoun's plan to materialize in the General Survey Act of 1824. The bill's emphasis on national defense again enabled President Monroe to sign it into law without hesitation. Although Clay was troubled by this military emphasis as well as Calhoun's ambition, he also recognized that half a loaf was better than none and that, in any event, the successful implementation of the General Survey Act could lead to a more comprehensive program of internal improvements that he, himself, would lead. While the Kentuckian continued to campaign for greater federal involvement in internal improvements, his vision would never materialize. In the end, America's transportation network would be financed primarily by private, state, and municipal capital.

The General Survey Act nonetheless served an important purpose. The legislation permitted the president to assign army engineers to privately owned transportation companies for the purpose of conducting land surveys of possible routes, estimating costs, and actually supervising construction. Between 1824 and 1828, members of the Army Corps of Engineers worked on ninety-six different projects, most of which were surveys of either state or privately owned roads and canals. After 1828, railroad surveys began to claim an increasing proportion of the engineers' work. One of the earliest and most important was the Baltimore and Ohio Railroad, which originated in the eastern seaport of Baltimore in 1828 and branched westward across the Appalachians into the Ohio Valley at Wheeling and from there on to Cincinnati and St. Louis. By the time the Corps of Engineers wrapped up its work under the General Survey Act in 1840, nearly fifty new railroads had been surveyed—a remarkable accomplishment. As with the development of interchangeable manufacturing, the silent workings of the federal government exercised an enormous influence on industrial development while fostering private enterprise.

> *"The silent workings of the federal government exercised an enormous influence on industrial development while fostering private enterprise."*

Toward Sectionalism

At a time when the future of the United States seemed boundless, two events cast a pall over the nation and shifted the tide from nationalism to sectional interests and bitter political debate.

THE PANIC OF 1819

While Republican Party leaders struggled over implementing the Madison-Clay platform, the country experienced its first economic depression since the 1780s. Instability set in when the Napoleonic Wars precipitated a spiraling European demand for American farm products. As prices for corn, cotton, flour, beef, and pork soared, an immense speculation in land took place as enterprising Americans scrambled to take advantage of the opportunities for gain presented by Europe's woes.

Cotton proved to be the most volatile commodity. In January 1815, the price of ginned cotton stood at less than 20 cents a pound. By June 1816, it had jumped to the unheard-of level of 30 cents a pound, reaching an all-time high of 33.5 cents a pound in January 1818. The boom was on. As planters and farmers rushed to buy and cultivate more land, the production of agricultural goods—led by cotton—rose accordingly. Since the best opportunities for land acquisition existed in the trans-Appalachian West, the greatest speculations occurred there. Encouraged by policies that allowed the purchase of land on credit, banks—including, for a time, the Second Bank of the United States—eagerly jumped into the burgeoning market, making loans to buyers with little or no money down and often no collateral.

What American speculators did not count on was the resilience of the overseas economies. As European agriculture began to recover and as British textile manufacturers turned to India for cheaper cotton, prices for cotton and other staples began to fall. In November 1818, the bubble burst as prices for all goods plummeted. By July 1819, the price of raw cotton stood at less than 15 cents a pound, exactly half the price for the same month a year earlier. Farmers who had bought tracts of land expecting that prices would at least stay the same found themselves deep in debt. Lending banks, which had often issued paper currency far in excess of their specie holdings to support the boom, now teetered on the brink of disaster as the value of their assets dried up with falling prices. When the Second Bank of the United States, which had been lax in its oversight of the currency system, finally began in 1819 to present these banks with their notes and demand payments in hard cash, a full-scale panic ensued. Hundreds of banks, unable to redeem their notes, failed, and thousands of speculators—particularly in the Midwest and South—lost their property to foreclosures.

The Panic of 1819 depressed the American economy for nearly six years, with farmers and planters in the Midwest and Southwest particularly hard hit. Once underway, the panic also caught merchants, manufacturers, and working people in its spiraling fall. Suddenly everyone from farmers and laborers to merchants and craftsmen found themselves thrust into bewildering discussions about the nature of money,

the meaning of credit, and what to do about their straitened circumstances. One response was a widespread call for "stay laws" aimed at protecting debtors in danger of losing their property to creditors. Ten states, including Maryland, Pennsylvania, and Vermont, passed stay laws. Another response was the appearance of trade unions that protested deteriorating working conditions and called for the abolition of imprisonment for debt, an end to fraudulent payments in paper money worth less than its stated value, prohibitions on government-licensed monopolies, and other workplace and social reforms. Within ten years, the union movement would gather momentum, coalesce into the Working Men's Party, and run candidates in the presidential election of 1828. But

A coach-makers' union charter from the 1840s. The elaborately engraved scenes surrounding the charter illustrate the nature of craft labor, with its emphasis on highly skilled handwork over less skilled machine work.

more broadly, and especially in the West, people blamed the panic and resulting depression on the Second Bank of the United States and wanted it dismantled.

The bank had been badly mismanaged before 1819, but it could hardly be held responsible for the global economic readjustments that followed the Napoleonic Wars and the speculative greed they sparked in America. Western critics like Andrew Jackson and Missouri's Thomas Hart Benton nonetheless believed that the bank had caused the depression because it had tightened credit at the wrong time, setting the downturn in motion. As property values fell and bankruptcies mounted, western cities from Pittsburgh to New Orleans suffered immensely. In some cases, growing manufacturing centers, like Henry Clay's own Lexington, never recovered from the blow. The Second Bank found itself the owner of all sorts of defaulted property and, in the words of Benton, became "the engrossing proprietor of whole towns." In the minds of westerners like Benton, the Philadelphia-based bank had become a "Monster" because its strict money policy favored eastern creditors who devoured everything in sight.

They would not forget what happened to them in 1819. The panic exacerbated sectional divisions within the Republican Party and made the Second Bank of the United States a burning political issue during the next decade.

THE MISSOURI COMPROMISE

In the midst of the panic, a second crisis traumatized the nation. Late in 1819, the territory of Missouri applied for admission to the Union as a slave state. Earlier that year, when Missouri was being organized as a territory out of the original Louisiana Purchase, Representative James Tallmadge of New York had attached an amendment to a bill that sought to prohibit the further introduction of slaves into Missouri and provide for the gradual emancipation of those already there. The amendment was defeated in the Senate, as was a similar one regarding the Arkansas Territory. But they presaged a bitter debate in both houses of Congress between December 1819 and March 1820 over the expansion of slavery and Missouri's admission to the Union.

The Missouri Compromise, 1820

Legend:
- Territory closed to slavery by the Missouri Compromise
- Free states and territories
- Territory opened to slavery by the Missouri Compromise
- Slave states and territories

Before the Missouri controversy, an implicit understanding between the North and South had allowed new states to enter the Union generally in pairs, so that an equal balance between free and slave states could be maintained in the Senate. In 1820, the United States consisted of twenty-two states, evenly divided between free and slave. Missouri's request for admission ignited controversy because, as the first state other than Louisiana (1812) to be carved out of the immense Louisiana Purchase, it was viewed as setting a precedent concerning the future of slavery in other newly admitted states. Politicians from the North and East had never been happy with the "three-fifths" compromise made in the Constitutional Convention of 1787 (which counted nonvoting slaves in apportioning the seats in the House of Representatives), because it gave slave states a voting advantage over free states. They therefore expressed strong feelings about extending such apportionment schemes beyond the Mississippi into places like Missouri. As much as he may have been affronted by slavery, Tallmadge made himself clear on the subject. The trans-Mississippi West "had no claim to such an unequal representation," he argued, because it was "unjust in its results upon the other States." Power politics, it seems, was as much at play during the Missouri debates as any humanitarian concern with the future of slavery in the territories.

Thanks to some skillful maneuvering by Clay, the deadlocked Congress worked out a compromise that settled the Missouri controversy. The agreement had three components. First, Missouri came into the Union as a slave state. Second, Maine, formerly a part of Massachusetts, was admitted as a free state, thereby preserving the balance between free- and slave-state votes in the Senate. Finally, slavery was thereafter prohibited in all territories north of latitude 36°–30′, the southern boundary of Missouri. With the approval of both houses, President Monroe quietly signed the Missouri Enabling Bill into law on March 6, 1820.

The Missouri Compromise, as it came to be called, received mixed reactions. Nationalists in the North and South hailed the agreement and lauded Henry Clay for his statesmanship as the great "Pacificator." Northern enemies of slavery, however, condemned the compromise because it served southern interests by allowing slavery in Louisiana Purchase territories south of 36°–30′. While generally applauding the compromise, pro-slavery southerners nonetheless felt uncomfortable because it established the precedent that Congress might, in the future, enact laws regarding slavery. They also viewed the Tallmadge Amendment and subsequent attempts to restrict slavery in Missouri as a plot on the part of northern politicians to disrupt the Virginia-led "Republican Ascendancy" fashioned by Thomas Jefferson and his successors and to build a new northern party on its ruins. In such ways, sectional allegiances were becoming a source of divisive feelings. For his part, the elderly Jefferson viewed the Missouri controversy as "a firebell in the night" that threatened to sound "the knell of the Union." "We have the wolf by the ears," he wrote pessimistically to a friend, "and we can neither safely hold him, nor safely let him go." In Jefferson's mind, the Missouri Compromise may have temporarily banked the fires of sectionalism, but it did not put them out. Events would prove him right.

> *"The elderly Jefferson viewed the Missouri controversy as a 'firebell in the night' that threatened to sound 'the knell of the Union.'"*

Adams's Nationalist Foreign Policy

The Panic of 1819 and the Missouri controversy revealed the clashing interests that divided North from South, East from West. But nationalism remained the major theme of the Monroe administration's foreign policy. Between 1817 and 1824, the United States adopted a bold posture in foreign affairs under the leadership of Monroe's secretary of state, John Quincy Adams. Rarely was American diplomacy pursued with greater bravado than during Adams's eight years at the State Department.

As the eldest son of President John Adams, John Quincy Adams was raised in the corridors of power. He had spent most of his distinguished career in the diplomatic service representing the United States in Britain, Russia, the Netherlands, and Prussia before becoming secretary of state in 1817. Possessed of a sharp tongue and even sharper mind, Adams shared a number of traits with his equally talented colleague at the War Department, John C. Calhoun. Both were well educated, highly disciplined, and intense individuals. Both could be cold and austere. Both held the Enlightenment view that the world worked according to fixed, scientific laws and that one could discern those laws through systematic study. Both embraced the Madisonian Platform, believing that the

James Monroe, fifth president of the United States (1817–25), and the last of the so-called Virginia Dynasty of presidents.

federal government should play an activist role in advancing science, technology, and economic growth. Above all, both were outspoken nationalists who believed that America had a God-given destiny to establish, as Adams put it, "our proper dominion . . . [over] the continent of North America."

Four interrelated concerns defined Adams's foreign policy strategy. First and foremost was his determination to expand American territory. Second was the realization that Spain's Latin American empire was crumbling in the wake of the Napoleonic Wars and that newly independent states like Colombia and Mexico were seeking both diplomatic recognition and trade relationships with other nations. Third was Adams's conviction that Great Britain, through its possession of Canada, its powerful navy, and its interest in dominating trade in both North and South America, posed the greatest economic as well as military threat to the United States. British ambitions therefore needed to be contained if the United States was to realize its desire for expansion in the Americas. Fourth, and closely related to the second and third concerns, was Adams's view that, with the rapid growth of American manufactures and the loss of privileged access to British West Indian markets, trade with Latin American republics was becoming increasingly important to the United States. If the British could be kept at bay, the United States stood to dominate the Latin American trade and profit enormously.

"Foremost in Adams's foreign policy strategy was his determination to expand American territory."

Adams's commitment to American expansion became explicit in **the treaties he negotiated.** A case in point is the Anglo-American Convention of 1818, in which he succeeded in establishing perpetual fishing rights for American vessels off the shores of Newfoundland and designating the 49th parallel as the boundary between the United States and Canada from the Lake-of-Woods (in northern Minnesota) to the Rocky Mountains. The latter agreement proved to be particularly important because it brought British recognition of the Louisiana Purchase and all U.S. territorial claims that went with it, including American control over the present states of North

Dakota, Montana, and Idaho. The convention also declared that the "Northwest Country" of Oregon beyond the Rockies would remain "free and open" to the subjects of both the United States and Britain for ten years. While this proved to be less than what he wanted, Adams felt confident that in ten years American settlers would pour into the Oregon Country and eventually secure it peacefully for the United States.

Adams's greatest diplomatic coup proved to be the so-called Transcontinental Treaty (also known as the Adams-Onis Treaty) with Spain in 1819. For years, Americans had coveted the Spanish province of Florida. At the time of the Louisiana Purchase, the region included not only the present state of Florida but also the southern portions of Alabama and Mississippi. Exactly what Adams predicted for Oregon had already occurred in Florida. In 1810, American settlers who lived in the region seized the westernmost part of the Florida panhandle. Then during the War of 1812, American forces took another chunk, including the strategically important port of Mobile. For Adams and many other Americans, it was only a matter of time before the United States would gather in all of Florida.

A turning point came in December 1817, when President Monroe ordered forces under General Andrew Jackson to the Florida border to suppress the activities of Seminole Indians who were raiding American settlements and providing a haven to escaped slaves. Previous orders to another general had instructed the army to pursue the Seminoles into Florida, but not to engage them if they took refuge in Spanish forts. Although Jackson had seen these orders, some confusion existed, because Secretary of War Calhoun also told him to "adopt the necessary measures to terminate . . . [the] conflict." "Great interests are at stake," President Monroe added in an accompanying note. Jackson, who had no love for either the Spanish or the Indians, interpreted his orders in the broadest possible terms and invaded Florida, laying waste to Seminole villages and seizing Spanish strongholds at St. Marks and Pensacola. In the process, he also arrested and hanged several Seminole chiefs as well as two British subjects—one of them an army officer—whom he accused of supplying the raiders and inciting them to war against the United States.

When news of Jackson's invasion reached Washington in July 1818, the Spanish and French ministers to the United States immediately descended upon the State Department to protest and to demand an apology. Most in Monroe's cabinet, including Calhoun, favored disavowing and disciplining Jackson. Adams, for his part, urged his colleagues to stand behind the general because he saw an opportunity to use the raid as a bargaining chip in negotiations with Spain. After heated discussion, the president and his cabinet decided to support the popular military leader, who by that time had added another big feather to his political cap.

Having won the day, Adams proceeded to draft a memorandum to the Spanish ambassador in which he argued that Jackson's invasion of Florida was justified because Spain had failed to keep its subjects under control, as specified some twenty-three years earlier in Pinckney's Treaty (1795). He also warned that "if the necessities of self-defense should again compel the United States to take possession [of Florida], another unconditional restoration . . . must not be expected." Then came the ultimatum: if Spain could not control its territory, the United States would; either relinquish Florida immediately, or "Spain would not have the possession of Florida to give us."

Knowing that his country was in no position to rebuff Adams's threat and knowing as well that Britain did not intend to take action against the United States, the Spanish ambassador came to terms. On February 22, 1819, a date that Adams purposely chose to commemorate Washington's birthday, the Transcontinental Treaty was signed. Spain ceded all of Florida to the United States and relinquished all claims to territories north of the 42nd parallel, including the Oregon Country. The United States, in turn, acknowledged Spanish ownership of Texas and agreed to assume all claims made by American merchants against Spain for damages suffered during the Napoleonic Wars, to an amount not exceeding $5 million.

SPANISH CLAIMS AND THE BIRTH OF LOWELL

All told, the Transcontinental Treaty represented a landmark in America's territorial expansion and one of the great triumphs of John Quincy Adams's long diplomatic career. To carry out the monetary settlements stipulated by the agreement, Congress established a Spanish Claims Commission in 1821 to compensate those with claims against the Spanish government. In effect, the money doled out by the commission during the next three years represented the purchase price of Florida. But they played another role as well. As a strong proponent of the Madison-Clay platform and a native of Massachusetts, Adams found further satisfaction when a sizable chunk of the Spanish claims moneys ended up going to his home state and helping to build what, by the 1840s, would become the most extensive manufacturing town in America.

The person who secured the Spanish claims funds for Massachusetts industry was Daniel Webster. A native of New Hampshire and an avowed Federalist, Webster was already well-known as a friend of business and a gifted orator. "He was a . . . raven-haired fellow with an eye as black as death, and as heavy as a lion's," an admirer remarked. "And no lion in Africa ever had a voice like him." At a time when conflict of interest had little meaning in American society, Webster served simultaneously as a U.S. congressman (and later senator from Massachusetts) and as the chief lobbyist and legal representative of the Boston Associates in Washington. With careful coaching from Francis Cabot Lowell and others, he had played an important role, beginning in 1816, in preparing tariff and patent legislation that favored the interests of the associates but not necessarily all textile manufacturers. Of all his work on behalf of the associates, however, none proved more impressive than his involvement with the Spanish Claims Commission.

Since the bulk of American claims against Spain involved vessels and cargoes lost by merchants during the Napoleonic Wars, a number of Boston Associates as well as several marine insurance companies owned by them became eligible to seek reimbursement. They consequently engaged Webster to represent them before the Spanish Claims Commission, paying him a commission of 5 percent on every dollar they were awarded. Webster proceeded to win over $1 million for them, fully 20 percent of the total claims disbursements.

But that's only part of the story. Webster presented his claims to the commission between 1821 and 1824, the very

Senator Daniel Webster of Massachusetts, the era's best-known orator and political spokesman for American industry, particularly the Boston Associates.

> "The person who secured the Spanish claims funds for Massachusetts industry was Daniel Webster."

335

time that the Boston Associates decided to expand their textile operations beyond Waltham by acquiring a site some twenty-five miles northward, where the Merrimack River fell thirty-five feet in the space of one mile and had the capability of generating over 9,000 horsepower. After naming the new center after the recently deceased Francis Cabot Lowell, the associates incorporated the Merrimack Manufacturing Company in 1822 and the Hamilton Manufacturing Company in 1825 at a total cost of $1.2 million—almost exactly the same amount that came to them from the Spanish Claims Commission. While it can't be proved that the claim funds were applied directly to the construction of Lowell's early mills, at the very least they had the effect of freeing up venture capital for investment there. Moreover, Webster was rewarded for his services by being allowed to purchase four shares in the highly profitable Merrimack Manufacturing Company, an opportunity usually reserved for those in the associates' innermost circle. The price of these shares came close to the commissions he received from his Spanish claims work. In 1831, Webster won additional payments for the Boston Associates from a French Claims Commission, which corresponded with a second wave of mill building that took place at Lowell between 1832 and 1837.

In just seventeen years (1822–39), Lowell grew from a quiet agricultural village of 200 people into a thriving industrial city of over 18,000. By 1839, America's "city of spindles" had outdistanced the famous mills of Manchester, England, to become the world's leading producer of textiles. The city's nine textile corporations employed over 8,500 workers, three-quarters of whom were young women between the ages of eighteen and twenty-five. Each week its twenty-nine mills churned out over 1 million yards of cloth while consuming 890 bales of cotton. In 1830, in order to satisfy the mills' voracious appetite for cotton, the Boston Associates built one of America's earliest railroads (the Boston and Lowell Railroad) to move the raw material more expeditiously inland from the port of Boston. Businesses from machine shops to dry-goods stores sprang up in Lowell to serve the daily needs of the textile corporations and their employees. But above all, there was the city's primary product, cheap and sturdy cotton cloth. Lucrative markets beckoned not only in the United States but also in Asia and especially Central and South America. To that end, the Boston Associates strongly supported an aggressive foreign policy that thrust open the doors to markets around the world.

> *"By 1839, America's 'city of spindles' had outdistanced the famous mills of Manchester, England, to become the world's leading producer of textiles."*

THE MONROE DOCTRINE

Trade and territorial expansion were central to American foreign policy. This was especially so in the declaration that became known as the Monroe Doctrine. Two developments keyed President Monroe's declaration. One was the potential threat of the so-called Holy Alliance—Russia, Prussia, and Austria—to restore Spain's lost American colonies. The other was an imperial decree in 1821 by Czar Alexander I of Russia, who ruled Alaska, asserting that all lands in the Pacific Northwest above the 51st parallel belonged to Russia and that no foreign vessels would be permitted within 100 miles of its coastline. In effect, the Russian announcement denied the rights to the Oregon Country that the United States had recently obtained from Spain in the Transcontinental Treaty, as well as the right of American

View of Lowell, Massachusetts, America's most famous textile-manufacturing center, c. 1844.

merchants to trade in the area. Great Britain and the United States, not surprisingly, protested the action. Secretary of State Adams, who was particularly upset, curtly informed the Russians that "the American continents are no longer subjects for *any* new European colonial establishments."

In the fall of 1823, British prime minister George Canning proposed that Great Britain and the United States issue a joint declaration against European intervention in Latin America. President Monroe seemed to favor the idea, especially when former presidents Jefferson and Madison recommended it. But not so John Quincy Adams. Canning's proposal offended Adams's nationalist sensibilities and aroused his suspicions. Once more he bucked the political winds in Monroe's cabinet to argue that such a joint declaration would make the United States appear "as a cock-boat in the wake of the British man-of-war." Since the British navy would see to it that other European nations stayed out of Latin America anyway, said Adams, what purpose would a joint declaration serve other than to forestall America's future interests in the region? Instead, he recommended that the United States issue a unilateral declaration, thereby asserting its independence from Europe and maintaining complete freedom of action in the Western Hemisphere.

Adams's argument again won the day. On December 2, 1823, the president issued the doctrine that became associated with his name in his annual address to Congress. The message established three basic principles: noncolonization, isolation, and nonintervention. Concerning the first, Monroe forthrightly stated that "the American continents . . . are henceforth not to be considered as subjects for future colonization by any European powers." As for the second, "in the wars of the European powers," Monroe declared, "we have never taken part, nor does it comport with our policy to do so." Finally, he warned Europe about intervening in American affairs. "We should consider any attempt . . . to extend their system to any portion of this hemisphere as dangerous to our peace and safety," he concluded. America was for Americans; Europeans were to keep their hands off.

The language of the declaration as well as the decision to release it publicly rather than privately through the usual diplomatic channels came from Monroe. But the crucial ideas behind the message originated with John Quincy Adams. In the short run, the Monroe Doctrine had little immediate effect because the Holy Alliance, in the face of British

> *"The Monroe Doctrine, along with Washington's Farewell Address, became the foundation on which American foreign policy rested for over a century."*

opposition, had already abandoned any intention of intervening in Latin America. Moreover, Adams's repeated protests had induced the czar to renounce his claims to all territory south of 54°–40′ in the Pacific Northwest. Nonetheless, the Monroe Doctrine made Americans feel as if they were standing up to European bullies and asserting themselves in hemispheric politics. And in the long run, the Monroe Doctrine, along with Washington's Farewell Address, became the foundation on which American foreign policy rested for over a century.

As it turned out, the principles enunciated in the doctrine proved more of a challenge to the industrial, seaward-oriented British, whose merchant marine controlled a substantial portion of the Latin American trade, than to any other European power. The noncolonization aspect particularly irked Canning and other British leaders. But England nonetheless continued to pursue its commercial interests in the Americas as if nothing had happened. A race was on to see who would control the commerce, if not the territory, of the Pacific Northwest and all of Latin America, and this time the key players were Britain and the United States, the most rapidly industrializing nations in the world.

The Election of 1824

The sectional divisions generated by the Missouri crisis and the Panic of 1819 set the stage for the presidential **election of 1824**. The Virginia Dynasty was coming to an end, and the Republican program for national economic development was dissipating into bitterly contested personal and sectional agendas. In previous administrations, the office of secretary of state had served as a stepping-stone to the White House. Thomas Jefferson's secretary of state had been James Madison, and Madison's secretary of state had been James Monroe. John Quincy Adams therefore seemed the logical choice to succeed Monroe, and he certainly wanted the job. But others did, too: two of them were Monroe's secretary of war, John C. Calhoun, and secretary of the treasury, William Crawford of Georgia. Calhoun quickly dropped out of the race to run successfully for the vice-presidency. He was only

"A Foot Race," an 1824 election cartoon depicting the presidential candidates in a dead heat. On the left, John Quincy Adams, William Crawford, and Andrew Jackson are virtually tied at the finish, while on the right, Henry Clay—out of the running—scratches his head over which candidate to support in the House of Representatives' deciding vote.

forty-two years old in 1824, and could afford to be patient. Crawford, a giant of a man and an early favorite to win, won the endorsement of Jefferson and stayed in the race even though he was gravely ill. The two most serious challengers, to Adams, however, were Henry Clay and Andrew Jackson.

The dynamic and resourceful Clay lusted for the presidency. As Speaker of the House, he was well-known to Washington insiders. Unlike the other candidates, he offered a clearly defined program in his American System of internal improvements, protective tariffs, and a strong national bank. The trouble was that sectional interests were becoming so strong that virtually no region embraced the whole system. The Kentuckian's stand on internal improvements, for example, won little support in New York and New England, while his position on high tariffs won him even less support in the cotton South. Clay's strongest backing came from the border states and the Midwest. But even there, his stand on the national bank encountered stiff opposition from supporters of Andrew Jackson in neighboring Tennessee.

Of all the candidates, the volcanic Jackson, known as "Old Hickory," enjoyed the greatest popularity. Standing second only to George Washington as an American military hero, he was generally admired and respected. His personal appearance, especially his tall build and strong features, proved to be another attraction; he *looked* presidential. As early as February 1823, a popular convention of Jackson supporters meeting in Harrisburg, Pennsylvania, chose him as their candidate to succeed Monroe. Unlike Clay, Jackson had no clear program of action. Even though he had served in the House of Representatives and the Senate, he remained a Washington outsider. In Congress, he had voted in favor of the General Survey Act and a new protective tariff. As a slaveholder, he also opposed federal efforts to restrict slavery. But first and foremost, he was a military man and a nationalist, and this made him attractive to a growing number of voters, particularly in the expanding West and South.

When the results of the election came in, Jackson won nearly as many popular votes as Adams and Clay put together. However, he failed to win a majority in the electoral college, which meant that, for a second time, the election was thrown into the House of Representatives. Under the Twelfth Amendment, only the three top electoral vote getters remained eligible. Clay was eliminated from the contest, but as Speaker of the House and victor in the states of Kentucky, Missouri, and Ohio, he was, ironically, placed in the position of kingmaker. He threw his support to Adams.

Clay's choice seemed logical enough. Apart from their natural rivalry as the West's leading political figures, Clay and Jackson had been bitter enemies ever since Clay had condemned Jackson's invasion of Florida in 1818. William Crawford, for his part, was seriously ill and, in any event, was an outspoken states' rights opponent of Clay's beloved American System. By a process of elimination, only Adams remained. Although the freewheeling Clay and the somber Adams had little in common personally, both were avid nationalists who saw eye to eye on the need for the American System. Thus Clay, in total disregard of Jackson's popular vote as well as the Kentucky legislature's instructions to support Old Hickory, used his considerable power as House Speaker to see to it that Adams was elected on the first ballot.

At this point, Adams made an honest but costly mistake. Soon after his election, he announced Clay's appointment as his secretary of state and, it appeared, heir apparent. Howls of protest immediately erupted from Jackson's camp to the effect that Adams and Clay had struck a "Corrupt Bargain." Jackson excoriated Clay as "the Judas of the West" and asserted that "corruption and intrigues at Washington . . . defeated the will of the people." Others, like the irascible Jeffersonian John Randolph of Virginia, sneered at the unholy alliance between "the Puritan [Adams] and the black-leg [Clay]." "It was impossible [for Jackson] to win the game," he claimed, because "the cards were packed." An outraged Clay subsequently challenged Randolph to a duel over these remarks. Although three shots were fired, neither man was injured. But the political damage had been done.

DISRUPTION OF THE AMERICAN SYSTEM

For the next four years, Adams labored under the shadow of the election of 1824. Hard as he tried, he could not neutralize the criticism that came from the Jacksonian camp and its growing league of supporters. Nor could he deflect the country from a decided turn away from postwar nationalism toward states' rights and sectionalism. In his inaugural address, Adams emphasized that "the spirit of improvement is abroad upon the earth" and summoned the country to a full-blown program of federally sponsored public works. Among other things, he recommended the founding of a national university, the construction of an astronomical observatory, the establishment of a uniform standard of weights and measures, the reform of the patent system, the creation of a new Department of the Interior, the exploration of western territories, and the construction of a vast system of roads, canals, and harbor facilities that would accelerate the growth of commerce. Even Clay seemed taken aback by the president's ambitious vision. Although he "approved the general principles," he told Adams that he "scrupled a great part of the details." In fact, of all of Adams's cabinet members, only Secretary of the Treasury Richard Rush approved of "near the whole."

Jacksonians seized on Adams's inaugural address to criticize his administration. His concluding remark admonishing Congress not "to slumber in indolence" or be "palsied by the will of our constituents" allowed them to resurrect the old accusation that "all Adamses are monarchists" and to argue that this Adams, in particular, cared not at all about the will of the people. Tarred first by the brush of corruption and

now with the brush of antidemocracy, the president seemed at a loss as to how to explain himself.

Years later, an embittered Adams reflected on the cause of his stillborn presidency. "The great effort of my administration," he wrote a friend in 1837,

was . . . the application of all the superfluous revenue of the Union into internal improvement which . . . would have afforded high wages and constant employment to hundreds of thousands of laborers, and in which every dollar expended would have repaid itself fourfold in the enhanced value of public lands. With this system . . . the surface of the whole Union would have been checkered over with railroads and canals. It may still be done half a century later and at the limping gait of State legislature and private adventure. I would have done it in the administration of the affairs of the nation. . . . When I came to the Presidency the principle of internal improvement was swelling the tide of public prosperity, till the Sable Genius of the South saw the signs of his own inevitable downfall in the unparalleled progress of the general welfare in the North, and fell to cursing the tariff and internal improvement, and raised the standard of free trade, nullification, and state rights. I fell and with me fell, I fear, never to rise again in my day, the system of internal improvement by means of national energies.

Adams's grand plan fell victim to more than the accusations of Jacksonians and "the Sable Genius of the South," a

John Quincy Adams, son of former president John Adams and sixth president of the United States (1825–29).

reference to slavery. Deepening sectional divisions throughout the country had already dampened the prospects for his federally centered program. First Virginians (including Thomas Jefferson), then other southerners objected to the idea of a national university and an astronomical observatory as a scandalous waste of money. How were such institutions to be financed? By higher tariffs? Although James Madison urged Jefferson not to join the southern attack, the elderly Jefferson was convinced that Adams and his supporters were "openly marching by the road of construction in a direct line to that consolidation which was always their real object." To southerners, consolidation meant the expansion of the federal government and its encroachment on the states. Time and again, they warned that if the central government could build canals, schools, and observatories, it could interfere with slavery. Did Adams's "federative fraternity," one of them pointedly asked, include "a system of emancipation"? Many thought so.

Equally worrisome to Jacksonians from all parts of the country was the growing size of the central government and the patronage power of officials who oversaw large bureaucracies like the Post Office, the Second Bank of the United States, and internal improvement projects. Since Jackson was the only major candidate who lacked access to such patronage in the election of 1824, Jacksonians railed against it. Although Adams refused to use patronage appointments to reward supporters, plenty of others did.

"Southerners warned that if the central government could build canals, schools, and observatories, it could interfere with slavery."

But these were not the only complaints. Adams's commitment to use the sale of public lands as a source of revenue for internal improvements alienated many who lived west of the Appalachians. They feared that this would mean higher land prices, which in turn would slow western settlement. James K. Polk of Tennessee ably conveyed westerners' sense of alarm and the social as well as sectional antagonisms it generated. "The policy," he argued before Congress in 1830, "is, to sell your lands high, [and] prevent thereby the inducements to emigration, retain a population of paupers in the East, who may, of necessity, be driven into manufactories to labor at low wages for their daily bread." In Polk's mind, Adams and his northern cronies were conspiring not just against western farmers but against working people everywhere. Such a policy showed Adams for what he was: an elitist puppet of eastern monied interests. Again, sectional politics was rearing its disruptive head.

Adams's demeanor as president did little to defuse these attacks. Part of the problem rested with his flinty personality; part stemmed from his inability to surround himself with trusted and able cabinet members; and part arose from his unwillingness to use the spoils system to reward loyal supporters. His supporters consequently drifted away, and with them went any semblance of a strong party organization capable of defending and advancing his political agenda.

All these factors worked against Adams's form of federalism and in favor of states' rights. The latter, in turn, quickly became identified with grassroots democratic reform under the banner of Andrew Jackson. Old Hickory's managers shrewdly cultivated his image as a heroic military commander while proclaiming him "a uniform and consistent democrat." He was a man of the people leading a revolt against not only political corruption but also corrupt politicians' control of politics. Most important, he would return power to where it rightfully belonged: the states and, through them, the people.

Chronology

December 5, 1815	The Madisonian Platform introduced.	
1816	Tariff of 1816.	
April 10, 1816	Second Bank of the United States chartered.	
December 1817	Andrew Jackson attacks Seminoles in Florida.	
1819	Panic leads to six-year depression.	
February 22, 1819	Transcontinental Treaty (Adams-Onís Treaty) signed with Spain.	
March 6, 1820	The Missouri Compromise.	
1822	Textile mills established at Lowell, Massachusetts.	
December 2, 1823	Monroe Doctrine issued.	
1824	General Survey Act.	
1831	Hall and North produce rifles with interchangeable parts.	

Adams lacked such management. Despite his intellectual ability and impressive national vision, he lacked the political skill to be an effective president. His personal failings, however, were only part of the story. Fundamental changes were taking place in the structure of American politics, changes that placed new demands on presidential leadership. Politics was being reconfigured in response to the increasing regional specialization of the economy. The unfolding of these changes marked the arrival of an expansive but also tension-filled era in American history.

Suggested Reading

Daniel Feller, *The Jacksonian Promise: America, 1815–1840* (1995)

Forest G. Hill, *Roads, Rails, and Waterways: The Army Engineers and Early Transportation* (1957)

Merrill D. Peterson, *The Great Triumvirate: Webster, Clay, and Calhoun* (1987)

Merritt Roe Smith, ed., *Military Enterprise and Technological Change* (1985)

George R. Taylor, *The Transportation Revolution, 1815–1860* (1951)

G. Edward White, *The Marshall Court and Cultural Change* (1991)

Chapter 11

POLITICAL INNOVATION IN A MECHANICAL AGE:

1828-1840

An 1836 painting of the upper village at Lockport, New York, showing a massive, five-tiered set of locks on the Erie Canal (right) as well as another canal to supply waterpower to the various mills (center left). This image reveals how local industries developed along the canal throughout upstate New York.

- How did sectional interests affect the alignment of parties in the 1820s?

- What were the main political and social innovations of the Jacksonian period?

- How did the issue of state vs. federal authority emerge under Jackson?

- What were the central issues in the controversy over the Bank of the United States?

- How was the legal basis for commercial expansion established in this period?

- How did the policy of Indian removal come about?

- How did a new party system emerge in the 1830s?

The most significant political issues of the 1820s—tariffs, banks, and internal improvements—were directly tied to the country's shift toward industrialization and the sectional antagonisms it generated both in the halls of Congress and in the courts. Equally important, political parties experienced major organizational innovations, similar to those happening in the business world. Such fundamental changes altered the structure of American politics and resulted in the two-party system we know today.

Jacksonian Democrats

For nearly a decade after the War of 1812, the United States had only one major political party. The demise of the Federalists left the Jeffersonian Republican Party as the dominant force in politics. Yet rather than being a highly centralized organization with a clear chain of command, the Jeffersonian Republicans consisted of numerous factions dominated by local personalities who operated primarily at the state level, with little interest in a coordinated national organization. The party's fragility became apparent during the bitter political skirmishes that occurred during and after the election of 1824. After the election, followers of John Quincy Adams and

Henry Clay formed the National Republican Party, and in 1834 its successor, the Whig Party, while those who favored Andrew Jackson eventually coalesced into the Democratic Party. Both parties were driven more by a thirst for office than by high-minded political principles—"a contest of office and nothing else," as one contemporary put it. Of the two parties, the Jacksonian Democrats put together the most formidable national organization. Critical to its success were party-sponsored newspapers that attacked the opposition, promulgated party positions, kept the membership together, and organized campaigns. Newspaper editors accordingly served as party managers and often as local party leaders.

Atop the Democratic Party leadership stood Andrew Jackson. During the 1820s, he had gone from being a nationalist who quietly supported higher tariffs and internal improvements to a presidential candidate who increasingly adopted a states' rights platform and questioned the constitutionality of federally funded internal improvements and, most of all, the federally chartered Second Bank of the United States. Jackson found an important ally in New York's Senator Martin Van Buren, who had actually voted against him in the election of 1824. The son of a tavern owner from the small upstate town of Kinderhook, Van Buren possessed captivating personal charm and a genius for political organization. Viewing himself as a disciple of Thomas Jefferson, he steadfastly opposed a strong central government and a loose construction of the Constitution. This also meant that he opposed Henry Clay's American System as well as John Quincy Adams's expanded version of it. Like Jackson, he believed that the foundation of a free society rested on "good old jeffersonian Democratic republican principles." More than anyone else, Van Buren was responsible for assembling the coalition of eastern, southern, and western interest groups that, in the late 1820s and early 1830s, resulted in the Democratic Party.

THE SOUTH CAROLINA EXPOSITION AND PROTEST

One person Van Buren recruited to Jackson's cause was John C. Calhoun. No one had been more blatantly nationalistic during and immediately after the War of 1812 than Calhoun. Yet between 1824 and 1828, he adopted an increasingly vehement states' rights position in domestic matters while continuing as a nationalist in military and foreign affairs.

Calhoun's retreat from economic nationalism stemmed from frustrated ambitions for the presidency as well as changing political circumstances in his home state of South Carolina. He could not abide the election of John Quincy Adams, because he believed that "bargain and corruption" had tainted the process. In the support South Carolina had given Jackson, Calhoun recognized a shift away from his brand of economic nationalism. This became evident in 1825, when states' righters in the South Carolina legislature—irked by higher tariff rates on European imports at a time of falling cotton prices—passed resolutions declaring the protective tariff (passed in 1824) and internal improvements unconstitutional and accused Calhoun of being a party to both measures. "He was the advisor to that fool Monroe," one radical critic wrote; "he is a national internal improvements man; he is a fortification man; he spends the money of the South to buy up influence in the North." With cotton prices continuing to fall and

planters blaming their misfortunes on the protective tariff, Calhoun began to draw back from economic nationalism and turn toward states' rights in an effort to salvage his political career.

Knowing of Calhoun's alienation from the Adams administration and his political difficulties at home, Van Buren courted the South Carolinian throughout 1826. At this time, Calhoun openly broke with Adams and Clay over the American System as well as their conciliatory policy toward slave revolts that were erupting in Latin America. Underlying these conflicts were long-standing personal animosities between Clay and Calhoun. The final break came in 1826 when Van Buren and Calhoun agreed that Calhoun would join forces with Jackson and become his vice-presidential running mate in the election of 1828.

As the election approached, Calhoun became increasingly drawn into the tariff debate. As president of the Senate, he had already revealed his opposition to protective tariffs in 1827, when he cast the deciding vote against a bill that would have raised duties on imported woolen goods. However, a far more serious challenge occurred the following year when Congress, largely at Van Buren's instigation, passed and Pres-

Andrew Jackson speaking to a crowd of well-wishers.

ident Adams signed a new tariff bill that jacked up duties on foreign imports to the highest levels since the War of 1812. Van Buren pushed for the new Tariff of 1828 because he wanted to whip up backlash support for Jackson from the Northeast and Midwest in the upcoming election. But in doing so, he touched off a storm of protest from southern politicians, including Calhoun, who felt that they had been duped by the wily "Red Fox of Kinderhook."

Throughout the South, the Tariff of 1828 became known as the "Tariff of Abominations." South Carolina took the lead in condemning the law when a special committee of the state legislature asked Calhoun to prepare a document setting forth the wrongs done by the federal government and how they could be remedied. He agreed to undertake the task, so long as his authorship remained secret.

Calhoun had good reason for wanting to remain anonymous. Because Jackson had publicly stated that he favored a judicious tariff, Calhoun hoped that once elected, Old Hickory would be true to his word and sponsor a tariff bill that would be more favorable to southern interests. Jackson, after all, was a westerner with southern roots. Moreover, as Jackson's running mate and possible successor, Calhoun was concerned that his critique of the tariff might embarrass the general and jeopardize his election. Calhoun therefore saw to it that the document would not be published until after the election.

The product of his labors was entitled *The South Carolina Exposition and Protest*. In it, he argued that the Tariff of 1828 levied an unjust tax on the South because its high rates not only helped northern manufacturers but also invited retaliatory measures by European countries—particularly Great Britain—who exported manufactured goods to the United States. Since cotton was America's leading export and since southerners benefited economically from access to cheaper European imports, the higher tariff meant that they were saddled with a double burden: already low prices for cotton and now higher prices for manufactured goods. A constitutional remedy for such an intolerable law had to be found, and Calhoun discovered it in what he referred to as the "compact" theory of government. Since the Constitution represented a compact between the original thirteen states, it followed that sovereignty ultimately rested with the people of the individual states, not the federal government. Calhoun therefore rea-

> "*The* Exposition and Protest *struck forcefully at federal power and placed state sovereignty at the center of the American political system.*"

soned that a state had the right to nullify any federal law that operated against its best interests until three-fourths of all the states decided the question in a special convention. If the federal government persisted in enforcing the law within the nullifying state or used force against it, that state in turn had the right to secede from the Union.

The *Exposition and Protest* struck forcefully at federal power and placed state sovereignty at the center of the American political system. Calhoun admitted that he had crafted a harsh solution to the sectional problem. But he saw it as something of a compromise. He loved the Union, but he feared for his state. He believed that a strongly worded statement on nullification would offset the demands of radical "fire-eaters" within his state who were calling for immediate secession, bring all parties to their senses, and, in effect, save the Union.

In the short run, South Carolina's nullification movement had little impact because no other state joined the protest. But the publication of the *Exposition and Protest*, after the 1828 election, put Calhoun on a collision course with Jackson. Nor would southerners forget the document. Calhoun had made his point brilliantly, and his ideas would become a rallying point for those who would eventually break from the Union in 1861.

A good deal more was at stake than tariffs, however. By the late 1820s, many South Carolinians had grown fearful of the rise of antislavery groups in the North and blamed them for slave unrest like the alleged 1822 conspiracy of Denmark Vesey, a free black in Charleston who supposedly plotted to seize ships and take off for Santo Domingo. They used every opportunity to excoriate the activities of radical abolitionist groups as well as the more conservative American Colonization Society, founded in 1816 and dedicated to the removal of free blacks from the United States to Africa. As much as protective tariffs galled southerners, they represented "the occasion rather than the real cause" of southern discontent.

Calhoun put the issue succinctly. If the northern majority who controlled Congress could use "the right of laying duties, not only to raise revenue, but to regulate the industry of the country," what was to prevent it from acting on "any purpose that the majority think to be for the general welfare"? The answer seemed perfectly obvious to South Carolina fire-eaters like Judge William Harper. "In contending against the Tariff," he observed in 1831, "I have always felt that we were combatting the symptom instead of the disease. [Federal] Consolidation is the disease. . . . Tomorrow may witness . . . [an attempt] to relieve . . . your free negroes, first; and afterwards, your slaves." The vulnerability felt by slaveholders in 1828 would soon become the source of bitter divisions in American politics.

THE ELECTION OF 1828

As early as December 1827, John Quincy Adams privately acknowledged that he would probably not be reelected to a second term. Having lost majorities in both houses of Congress the previous fall, his political future looked grim. Nonetheless, Adams determined not to go down without a fight. His chief opponent was Andrew Jackson, whose managers depicted him as a Washington outsider who stood for the common man against privileged elitists like Adams.

While he did indicate an antipathy toward the Second Bank of the United States, Jackson was vague about issues like the tariff and internal improvements. Like Adams, he remained silent about the provision of free public schools, the abolition of imprisonment for debt, the establishment of a ten-hour workday, and other egalitarian reforms called for by Working Men's parties that appeared in towns and cities from New England and the Middle Atlantic states as far west as Ohio. Instead, the campaign degenerated into mud slinging and personal invective. Still lacking an official party label, "friends" of Jackson took to accusing Adams of elitism, corruption, and intrigue while characterizing their own candidate as an honest and forthright "man of the people." As the campaign wore on, the negative contrasts seemed endless: Jackson the war hero versus Adams the closeted intellectual; Jackson the self-made man versus Adams the silver-buckled aristocrat; Jackson the democrat versus Adams the monarchist, and so on.

When the results came in, **Jackson won a convincing but not overwhelming victory.** Adams captured 44 percent of the popular vote and carried all of New England, as well as Delaware, New Jersey, and most of Maryland. New York divided between the candidates, but Jackson carried everything else, including Henry Clay's home state of Kentucky. The victory meant that, for the first time, a westerner would occupy the White House.

The election also signified a transfer of power from the East to the West. Recognizing this, northerners and southerners vied to strengthen their economic and political ties to the West. With the new president a southerner by birth, southern politicians looked to Jackson to protect their section's vital interests, most notably slavery. They also counted on the support of his vice-president, Calhoun, who in 1828 considered Jackson an ally and fully expected to succeed him.

Among the most important questions of the day was who would control the burgeoning trade west of the Appalachians. New York, with the Erie Canal and excellent steamboat service down the Hudson River to the sea, held a decided advantage, but other states from Massachusetts and Pennsylvania in the North to Maryland, Virginia, and South Carolina in the South hurried to challenge New York's lead. Jackson's election coincided not only with the beginning of an extended period of prosperity and economic growth, but also with the building of canals, roads, and railroads that would tap the trade of the Ohio and Mississippi Valleys. Efforts to secure economic connections with the West also meant

Slanderous accusations came from both camps during the election of 1828. This anti-Jackson "coffin bill" lists the names of three American militiamen and accuses Jackson of unjustly executing them during the War of 1812.

building South-West and North-West political alliances. The resulting maneuvering over national legislation pertaining to tariffs, banks, roads, rails, and waterways brought sectional differences to the very center of American politics.

Jackson and the Expansion of Democracy

Andrew Jackson's inauguration on March 4, 1829, was unlike anything Washington had ever seen. Thousands of supporters converged on the Capitol to see the "old hero" sworn in. Amid thunderous applause, Jackson moved to the podium, bowed to the "majesty of the people," and delivered a brief speech in which he promised to protect states' rights, pay off the national debt, and adopt "judicious" policies concerning tariffs and internal improvements. He also promised to return power to the people by reforming the civil service and correcting "those abuses that have brought the patronage of the Federal Government into conflict with the freedom of elections, and . . . have placed or continued power in unfaithful or incompetent hands." Although Jackson did not mention the Adams administration by name, few listeners missed the meaning of his remarks. "*They really seem to think that the country is rescued from some dreadful danger,*" a chagrined Daniel Webster observed.

A satirical view of Jackson's inaugural celebration entitled "The President's Levee, or All Creation Going to the White House." The artist, no Jackson supporter, clearly wished to portray the mob-like behavior of the throngs that attended the party.

Once the swearing-in ceremony ended, the scene shifted to the other end of Pennsylvania Avenue, where a great throng of people—many of them office seekers—from the "highest and most polished, down to the most vulgar and gross," descended on the White House and proceeded to lay waste to its furnishings in a riotous celebration. "The *Majesty of the People* had disappeared," the wife of one senator noted with disgust. "The President [was] nearly pressed to death & almost suffocated & torn to pieces by the people in their eagerness to shake hands with Old Hickory." While anti-Jacksonian critics like Supreme Court justice Joseph Story roundly condemned the proceeding as "the reign of KING MOB," Jackson supporters relished the scene for what it symbolized. "It was a proud day for the people," a western newspaper reported. "General Jackson is *their own* President . . . [and] he was greeted by them with an enthusiasm which bespoke him the Hero of a popular triumph."

If any single principle informed Jackson's politics, it was his commitment to democratic majority rule. He repeatedly declared that "the people are the government, administering it by their agents; they are the Government, the sovereign power." To Jackson, the people included free adult white males but not blacks, Indians, or women. Nonetheless, for its time, his conception of democracy marked a significant departure from the ideas of his predecessors in the White House. Jackson believed that key government officials should be directly elected "by the people," not indirectly elected by state legislatures (as were U.S. senators) or appointed (as were federal judges). He advocated an end to elitism and special privilege in government; any reasonably intelligent person could manage the "plain and simple" tasks associated with most government offices. Arguing that "more is lost by the long continuance of men in office than is generally to be gained by their experience," he demanded "a general extension of the law which limits [all government] appointments to four years." The system should be changed through "rotation of office."

Although he did not coin the phrase, Jackson believed in the dictum "To the victors belong the spoils." His oft-stated objective was to reduce, if not totally eliminate, a growing "class" of government bureaucrats who, in his view, seemed to think that they should hold their offices for life. During his first eighteen months in office, he removed 919 federal appointees, virtually all of whom held well-paid supervisory positions. In the largest bureaucracy—the U.S. Post Office—the housecleaning began at the top when Jackson replaced the postmasters general, his chief clerk, and the first and second postmasters general, followed by over 400 postmasters. Those dismissed tended to be the highest paid, and most came from those parts of the country—New England, the mid-Atlantic, and Midwest—where the Jacksonian party was weakest. There were relatively few dismissals in the South and Southwest, where the Jacksonian movement was strongest.

> *"The right to vote expanded so dramatically after the war because of changes in America's social structure."*

In short, the Jacksonians used patronage positions to install people loyal to the party and to consolidate their political base in areas where it needed strengthening. By removing competent people from office, the spoils system challenged the meritocratic government agencies that Calhoun and John McLean presided over during the 1820s. Its impact would become even more widespread as Jackson's successors expanded it during the next thirty years.

VOTING RIGHTS

How much did Andrew Jackson influence the expansion of democracy in America? Although his new political party would become known during the 1830s as the Democratic Party, and as much as he touted "the sovereignty of the people," called for majoritarian rule, and cultivated his image as a "man of the people," Jackson was more of a symptom than a cause of democracy in America. Before he became a candidate for president, democratic impulses were already sweeping the country, and they came from all corners of the Republic. The War of 1812 was an important benchmark.

Before the conflict, most state constitutions restricted the right to vote to free adult white males who either owned property or paid taxes in their communities. But when it came to actually voting, enforcement of the rules varied from state to state and often from one community to another within the same state, depending on who oversaw elections. In many communities, legally ineligible males voted. The prevailing rule seemed to be that so long as you were a white male and a recognized member of the community, you could vote.

It was only a matter of time before property-oriented restrictions gave way to broader voting rights. The new state of Ohio, upon being admitted to the Union in 1802, pointed the way when it adopted a constitution that extended the franchise to all white males who either paid taxes or worked them off by devoting a certain amount of time each year to building and maintaining public roads. The movement toward universal white male suffrage gathered further momentum after the War of 1812, when five new states—Indiana, Illinois, Alabama, Missouri, and Maine—adopted constitutions that opened up the franchise. Soon Connecticut, Massachusetts, and New York jettisoned all property qualifications for voting and adopted minimal tax-payment standards. By the 1850s, virtually all white males could vote. Although certain restrictions continued to exist in some states, lax enforcement tended to be the norm.

The right to vote expanded so dramatically after the war because of changes in America's social structure brought on by a rapid population growth and the onset of industrialization. Between 1820 and 1850, the population of the United States more than doubled to over 20 million people, cities grew, and vast new territories came under the American flag. As machine-based manufacturing spread, a growing proportion of the population owned little or no property at all. From these artisans, mechanics, small shopkeepers, tenant farmers, and laborers came grassroots pressure to enlarge the franchise in the form of petitions to state legislatures and state constitutional conventions. A Louisianan aptly captured

George Caleb Bingham's painting *County Election* reveals the public culture of elections in early America. Election days were often festive occasions, a time when businesses closed and voters were treated to drinks by their employers. Voters, as Bingham's piece suggests, were exclusively male.

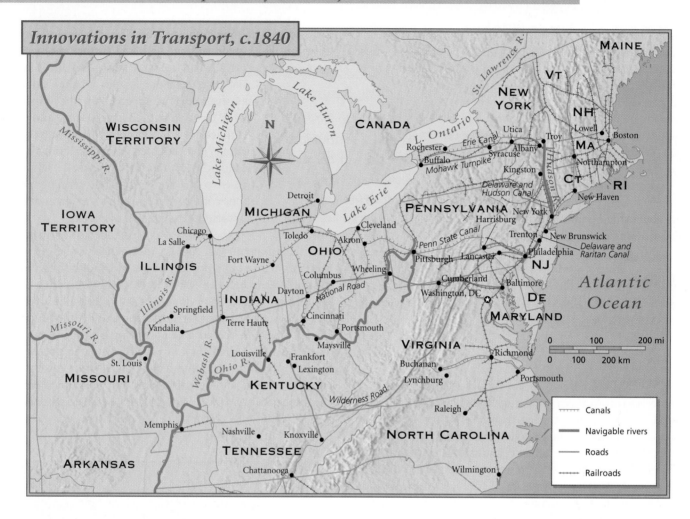

Innovations in Transport, c.1840

the spirit of the age when he observed, "If a man can *think* without property, he can *vote* without property." Political values were inclining in the direction of democracy.

Economic and political self-interest also played a role in expanding the electorate. In sparsely populated regions of the country, voters supported white male suffrage because they believed that doing so would encourage settlement, raise property values, and stimulate economic development. In the highly partisan ferment of the 1820s and 1830s, politicians supported the expansion of the franchise because it gave them the opportunity to win new voters and gain an edge over opponents. Even employers tended to support the new democracy because it allowed them to influence the outcome of local elections by swaying their employees.

In industrial communities, not only did workers seek to vote, factory masters urged them to go to the polls. Near

Wilmington, Delaware, for example, the gunpowder manufacturer E. I. du Pont and his sons regularly closed their Brandywine works on election day and gave their men the day off with pay. On several election days during the 1810s and 1820s, the du Ponts, along with other local manufacturers, actually gathered their workers together (many of whom were foreign-born Irish who had yet to become citizens) and paraded them en masse to the polls at a nearby tavern, where they were treated to free drinks after voting.

Political adversaries frequently accused the du Ponts of illegally interfering with elections by encouraging their employees to vote and even handing them ballots for favorite candidates as they entered the polling place. The voting took place in the open, and with different political parties using different-colored ballots, it was easy for the du Ponts or anyone else to see what candidates a person supported. No evidence exists that the Du Pont Company fired anyone for voting the wrong ticket, although evidence from other communities suggests that such retaliations did occur. More than likely, the need rarely arose: Du Pont workers, as much out of self-interest as self-preservation, probably voted the way their employers did. Not until the widespread adoption of the secret ballot in the 1880s and 1890s would voter intimidation cease to be a factor in American politics.

INNOVATIONS IN TRANSPORTATION

Although he had indicated his desire to limit the scope of the federal government and return power to the people at state and local levels, no one knew exactly where Jackson stood on the American System at the time of his election. As a U.S. senator, he had supported the General Survey Act and the higher Tariff of 1824, but he became suspiciously elusive about both subjects as a presidential candidate. The first clear sign of his different course occurred in May 1830, when he vetoed a bill that would have provided partial federal support for the construction of a turnpike from Lexington to Maysville, Kentucky.

With its northern terminus located just across the Ohio River from Cincinnati, the so-called Maysville Road was intended to link up with the National Road in Ohio and extend it southward through Kentucky and Tennessee to the Gulf of Mexico. Unlike the ill-cared-for dirt roads that passed for highways in most parts of the country, this was to be a macadam road consisting of tar and crushed stone compressed on a graded and drained gravel bed. Such a cost-effective, lower-maintenance technology of road building promised to speed the flow of horse-drawn wagons and place inland towns like Lexington in closer contact and competition with the prosperous trade of the Ohio River valley.

Given the road's interstate connections and national scope, nearly everyone expected approval. But Jackson thought otherwise. In his veto message, he specifically questioned the national character of the road: the funds being appropriated were intended to connect two points within the same state. Like Madison and Monroe before him, he believed that federal aid to such intrastate projects was not sanctioned by the Constitution. What's more, he voiced general opposition to any federal funding of internal improvements within the United States.

Jackson's message stunned Congress and angered many of its members, including the president's arch enemy, Henry Clay of Kentucky. Clay felt certain that Jackson had intended to punish his state out of personal enmity. He became even more convinced when he learned that Jackson had left unsigned (thereby exercising what became known as the "pocket veto" for the first time in American history) two other internal improvement bills, one of which was for a canal around the falls of the Ohio River near Louisville, Kentucky. But the real picture was more complicated. Standing behind Jackson, and urging him on was Secretary of State Martin Van Buren, a staunch opponent of federally supported internal improvements.

Even though Jackson ended up endorsing more internal improvement bills than any of his predecessors, on the whole he opposed federal involvement in the building of roads, canals, railroads, and waterways. In 1831, for instance, he announced that he was ending the army's participation in internal improvement projects under the General Survey Act. Two years later, he made a similar decision to turn over completed sections of the National Road to the states through which it passed. His support mainly went to projects that lay either outside or at the borders of state jurisdictions, such as the dredging of rivers and harbors or the building of wagon roads in territories that had yet to become states. Jackson thus did not completely reject the American System, but he recast its guiding principles, although with little logic or consistency.

Paved roads were uncommon in early America, as this view of a stagecoach making its way from Trenton, New Jersey, to Philadelphia suggests.

The Maysville Road controversy took place during a period of innovation in the ways Americans transported themselves and their goods. It began during the Jefferson administration, when construction started on the great National Road project and steamboats began operating on eastern and western rivers. It hit full stride with the completion of New York's state-financed Erie Canal in 1825, and would culminate during the 1850s with the completion of several large "trunk line" railroads, so called because they originated in Eastern Seaboard cities and connected with various branch lines as they moved westward.

 Of all these developments, the **Erie Canal** had the greatest immediate impact because it provided the first all-water route directly connecting the Great Lakes and the rapidly growing Midwest to the major eastern seaport at New York City. The canal proved so successful that it set off a wave of canal building across the country: cities like Baltimore and Philadelphia and states from Virginia to Illinois eagerly sought to emulate New York and tap into the profitable trade that was flowing across its upstate region from Buffalo to Troy and down the Hudson River to New York City.

> *"The Erie Canal provided the first all-water route directly connecting the Great Lakes and the rapidly growing Midwest to the major eastern seaport at New York City."*

This view of the Erie Canal at Lockport, New York, shows workers (center) operating gates that controlled the flow of water from one elevation to another, thus allowing canal boats to ascend and descend elevations along the route. At Lockport, the Erie Canal dropped 571 feet, requiring a series of five locks to raise and lower boats.

The Erie Canal not only carried manufactured goods westward and transported western produce eastward; it also became the passageway for thousands of native-born white Americans and European immigrants into the upper reaches of New York and Pennsylvania and, beyond that, into the burgeoning midwestern states of Ohio, Indiana, Illinois, and Michigan. Along its course, boomtowns like Utica, Syracuse, and Rochester, New York, sprang up to supply the great migration and take advantage of the growing trade that flowed back and forth along its heavily traveled towpaths. All three towns had become important manufacturing centers by the time of Jackson's Maysville Road veto. As New York's success invited emulation, members of Congress and the Jackson administration were besieged with requests for federal funding to help build roads, canals, and railroads in other parts of the country. Most of these requests were turned down with the reminder that New York had constructed its canal system with its own state funds.

The canal craze slowed appreciably by the late 1830s. Canals were costly to build ($20,000–$30,000 per mile and upward) and maintain. Both winter weather and recurrent flood damage interrupted the flow of traffic. Revenues were inadequate. Most significant of all, **steam-powered railroads** appeared just a few years after the canals. When boom times ended with the Panic of 1837 (see p. 369), followed by six years of economic depression, Pennsylvania and Indiana stood virtually bankrupt, while states like Ohio found themselves in financial difficulty because of their overextended investments in canal building. The canal boom halted around 1840, by which time the United States had built 3,326 miles of canals at a cost of roughly $125 million, or $37,580 per mile. Railroad construction, by contrast, had already reached 3,328 miles at an average cost of $17,000 per mile. Although most lines existed in the Northeast, railroads could be found in all parts of the country by the 1840s, and no end was in sight. By then, no one questioned that the "iron horse" represented the wave of the future.

In addition to costing less to build, rail lines could serve areas that could not be reached by boats and barges in either the drought of summer or the freezing of winter. And although canals and steamboats could ship goods more cheaply, railroads provided much faster service. Whereas

Anxious to challenge New York for the flourishing "western trade," states like Pennsylvania introduced lotteries to raise money for constructing canals.

horse- and mule-drawn freight wagons and canal boats averaged around two miles an hour, freight trains and steamboats averaged around twelve. More important, because railroads, unlike steamboats and canals, could be built more directly from one geographic point to another, they saved even more time than their traveling speeds suggest. During the 1850s, for example, a trip from Cincinnati to New York City by freight wagon could take forty to fifty days or more, depending on weather conditions. The same goods shipped down-river by steamboat to New Orleans and then by packet ship to New York required twenty-eight days, while those shipped on the Ohio canal system across Lake Erie to the Erie Canal and down the Hudson took eighteen. Railroads, by contrast, required only six to eight days, thus cutting the time by more than half that of their closest water-borne competitors.

The sight and sound of a steam locomotive pulling a train of cars across varied landscapes made deep impressions on the public, as numerous works of art and poetry attest. The imposing size of the "iron horse," the powerful chugging of its steam engine, the rhythmic clickity-clack of its cars moving over segmented rails, the shrill shrieks produced when iron wheels engaged iron rails in sharp curves, the high, lonesome sound of the locomotive's whistle as it passed over hill and dale—such images helped make the railroad the primary symbol of the nation's technological progress in nineteenth-century America.

Although the railway system would experience its greatest growth after the Civil War, many of its defining features were introduced during the Jacksonian era. Of these, the most important were the management practices introduced by West Point–trained engineers. From the outset, these "soldier technologists" recognized that large-scale enterprises like railroads required systematic management. Accountability and

control proved all the more important on single-track railways that had several trains running daily in different directions as well as scores of stations along the way selling tickets, shipping freight, and collecting revenues. In addition to engineering and overseeing the construction of railroads, the engineer-managers set up rules for their operations. Like the army regulations on which they were based, these rules established clear lines of authority from top to bottom, codified everyday operating procedures and accounting practices, determined train schedules, and spelled out practices for employees at every level, from repair-shop machinists to gandy dancers (a slang term for crowbar-wielding maintenance crews who chanted and moved rhythmically as they pried heavy iron rails into place on the roadbed).

The engineers based their rules on an accumulated fund of experience that went back to their early training at West Point and included working under the military model introduced at the War Department during the early 1820s by Secretary Calhoun. All told, more than 120 West Pointers worked on American railroads before the Civil War, almost always as supervisors or consultants. On projects like the Baltimore and Ohio Railroad, they were joined by engineers from other backgrounds. As the industry grew during the

Named after the governor of New York responsible for building the Erie Canal, the *Dewitt Clinton* made its first trip from Albany to Schenectady, New York, on August 9, 1831. Note the influence that stagecoaches had on the design of a train's passenger cars.

This lithograph by the New York firm of Currier and Ives (c. 1849–50) indicates how railroad carriage and locomotive designs had changed during the previous decade. Instead of resembling stagecoaches, the passenger cars had become larger and more rectangular. Likewise, the steam locomotive had evolved from a smaller British design into what became known as the "American" type, with four drive wheels, a four-wheel "lead truck" to help negotiate sharp corners, and a "cow catcher" in front to move obstructions off the rails.

1830s and 1840s, more and more young men learned their engineering by working, in apprentice fashion, on canals and railroads. Such was the case for Benjamin Henry Latrobe, chief engineer of the Baltimore and Ohio, Daniel C. McCallum, general superintendent of the New York and Erie Railroad, and J. Edgar Thompson, president of the Pennsylvania Railroad. All three refined and extended the West Point paradigm by creating increasingly sophisticated administrative structures to operate their railroads. By the late nineteenth century, these railroads would number among the largest and most powerful corporations in America.

Personal Tensions and Sectional Politics

By the time Jackson issued his Maysville Road veto in May 1830, he was already facing a serious crisis within his cabinet. The problem was his growing alienation from Vice-President Calhoun.

The crisis had three sources. One was a growing tension between Calhoun and Martin Van Buren over who would be Jackson's designated successor if, as many anticipated, he de-

cided to serve only one term. A second and related source was the old information, brought to Jackson's attention by Van Buren, that Calhoun had been among those members of Monroe's cabinet who sought to discipline and punish the general for invading Florida and attacking the Seminole Indians back in 1818. Although he initially learned of Calhoun's perceived betrayal during the election campaign of 1828, Jackson remained silent rather than openly confront Calhoun and thus damage his chances for election. But inwardly his blood boiled at the thought that a political ally was capable of such treachery.

Still, Jackson may have gotten over the Seminole affair had it not been for another run-in with Calhoun. This time the problem centered on Peggy O'Neale, an attractive young widow who married Jackson's close friend and secretary of war, John H. Eaton, in 1828. When rumors spread that the Eatons had been having an affair long before Peggy's first husband died, several cabinet families—led by Mrs. Floride Calhoun—snubbed them. Jackson, whose late wife had been similarly slandered during the 1828 campaign, came to Mrs. Eaton's defense and insisted that his cabinet members include the Eatons in their social gatherings.

When the Calhouns as well as three other cabinet families refused, an enraged Jackson stopped holding official cabinet meetings and began to rely almost exclusively on a "kitchen cabinet" of informal advisers that included his closest allies—among them Van Buren, who sided with him in the Eaton affair. With the executive branch hopelessly divided, the entire cabinet resigned in April 1831. By now, Calhoun had reached a point of no return. Banished from the inner circles of the Jackson administration and with his chances for the presidency growing ever dimmer, he withdrew further into the cocoon of states' rights.

THE WEBSTER-HAYNE DEBATE

Just as the Eaton affair was coming to a boil, Calhoun became involved in one of the most memorable debates in American history. The confrontation began in the Senate when Connecticut's Samuel A. Foote, in a routine economizing measure, introduced a motion in January 1830 that would temporarily suspend the sale of any new public lands in the West until the federal government had disposed of some 72 million acres already on the market. Foote's resolution elicited an immediate reaction from Senator Thomas Hart Benton of Missouri, who angrily accused Foote and his New England colleagues of seeking to check the growth of the West in order to prevent the migration of workers that eastern manufacturers needed at home for factories and mills. In Benton's view, Foote's resolution, coupled with an already high protective tariff that benefited northern manufacturers, amounted to "a most complex scheme of injustice, which taxes the South to injure the West, to pauperize the poor of the North!" Convinced that the measure was a giant eastern conspiracy, Benton called on his southern colleagues to join him in defeating it.

At this point, South Carolina's senior senator, Robert Y. Hayne, came forward to support Benton in an effort to forge a stronger political bond between the South and the West. Assailing the Foote resolution as nothing more than an adjunct of the American System, he leveled a withering attack on its eastern proponents as unprincipled tyrants who sought to subjugate not only their workers but also the rest of the country, so they could reap huge profits.

Daniel Webster, who happened to stroll into the Senate chamber in the midst of Hayne's speech, could hardly believe

Legendary orator Senator Daniel Webster replying to Senator Robert Hayne, 1830.

This political cartoon, entitled "The Rats Leaving a Falling House," shows a stunned Andrew Jackson sitting in a collapsing chair as members of his cabinet scurry like rats to avoid the fallout of the Peggy Eaton affair.

his ears, especially in view of Hayne's request only a day earlier that Webster present a petition for federal aid from a South Carolina railroad. Hayne wanted the railroad, but prevailed on Webster to take the case forward because he didn't want to compromise his states' rights principles. Now Hayne was attacking the very people Webster represented, and Webster asked to be heard. "The East!" he began, "the obnoxious, the rebuked, the always reproached East! . . . Sir, I rise to defend the East." And defend he did—so vigorously that the original resolution that had ignited the debate receded into the background. The two men confronted each other over two different philosophies of government: Hayne defended "the Carolina doctrine" of state sovereignty and nullification, while Webster defended national power, which he captured in the famous phrase "Liberty *and* Union, now and forever, one and inseparable!"

The Webster-Hayne debate unfolded over a period of eight days in early 1830 and attracted large crowds to the Senate chamber. Not surprisingly, both sides claimed victory. Webster's brilliant oratory catapulted him into national prominence and made him an instant, though unlikely, candidate for the presidential election of 1832. Although Calhoun did not participate directly in the oratorical clash, he nonetheless carefully coached Hayne. The debate, after all, was as much about Calhoun and his doctrine of nullification as anything else.

What remained to be seen was how Jackson would react to the debate. That moment came on April 13, 1830, at a dinner organized by Benton, Hayne, and their supporters in honor of Thomas Jefferson's birthday. Hayne gave the keynote address, in which he sought to link Jefferson's role in the Virginia and Kentucky resolutions of 1798 with South Carolina's nullifiers. Warned ahead of time by Van Buren about Hayne's speech, Jackson came to the dinner prepared. When asked to propose a toast, he rose from his chair, looked directly at Vice-President Calhoun, and declared, "Our *Federal* Union—*It must be preserved.*" Calhoun came next. Upset by the president's toast, his hand trembled as he held up his glass and replied, "The Union: Next to our Liberty the most dear."

The die was cast. A month later, Jackson confronted Calhoun about his involvement some twelve years earlier in the Seminole affair. The South Carolinian attempted to vindicate himself by soliciting letters of support and eventually publishing them in a Washington newspaper favorable to his cause. But the more he tried, the more Jackson was convinced of his guilt. Finally, in 1831, Jackson denounced Calhoun as "fit for any act of human depravity" and unceremoniously read him out of the Democratic Party.

NULLIFICATION AND THE TARIFF OF 1832

Sectional tensions worsened during the presidential election campaign of 1832. At issue was tariff protection for northern manufacturers versus southern concern over the tariff's effects on the South's economy and the future of slavery there. With Clay challenging Jackson for the White House under the banner of National Republicanism, Congress passed a compromise tariff bill that modified but did not significantly reduce the high rates of the 1828 Tariff of Abominations. Calhoun pinned his hopes for a presidential veto on Jackson's states' rights leanings and earlier campaign promise to support a "judicious" tariff. But Jackson dashed these hopes when he signed the bill, and the Tariff of 1832 became law.

For Calhoun, this was the last straw. Having been drummed out of the party and lost the opportunity to be Jackson's designated successor, he resigned the vice-presidency, ran for the U.S. Senate in South Carolina, and proceeded to put his theory of nullification into practice. At his urging, South Carolina's governor called a special session of the state legislature, which in turn took the grave step of calling for an election of delegates to a state convention that would take action on the new tariff. Secessionist sentiments ran high as the convention met on November 19, 1832, at the state capitol and, within a matter of days, passed an Ordinance of Nullifi-

cation by an overwhelming margin. Declaring the Tariffs of 1828 and 1832 null and void in South Carolina, the ordinance established February 1, 1833, as the date when the collection of federal duties would be prohibited within the state. It also warned that if the federal government tried to force the collection of duties, South Carolina would secede from the Union.

Fresh from a hard-fought victory over Clay and the National Republican Party at the polls, President Jackson responded to the South Carolina ordinance in his message to Congress on December 4, 1832. His tone seemed conciliatory. He even acknowledged that the new tariff was not only too high but also inequitable, and that he favored a substantial reduction. But privately he seethed at the rebellious South Carolina "nullies."

Less than a week after his message to Congress, Jackson issued a "Proclamation to the People of South Carolina" in which he scorned the idea of nullification and denied that any state had the right to secede from the Union. "The laws of the United States must be executed," he warned. "My duty is emphatically pronounced in the Constitution. Those who told you that you might peaceably prevent their execution deceived you. Their object is disunion. But be not deceived. . . . Disunion by armed force is *treason.*"

To show that he meant business, Jackson placed a naval squadron on alert, ordered several thousand troops to the South Carolina border, sent ammunition to Forts Moultrie and Pinckney in Charleston Harbor, and notified commanders there to prepare for hostilities. He then sent a message to Congress on January 16, 1833, asking for quick passage of a bill authorizing the use of military force against the rebellious South Carolinians. The so-called Force Bill quickly made its way through Congress and was immediately signed into law by the president.

Jackson's proclamation, followed by the Force Bill, as well as the president's personal threats to hang Calhoun, came like claps of thunder before a dangerous storm. They surprised many northerners and sobered South Carolinians, the most radical of whom called for immediate secession from the Union. The nullifiers had seriously misjudged Old Hickory's commitment to states' rights as an equally strong commitment to state sovereignty. If anyone had doubted Jackson's nationalism, they had no cause to doubt it now. Much as he sought to shift domestic affairs from the federal to the state level, he was unmistakably committed to the Constitution as the supreme law of the land.

While nationalists like Daniel Webster hailed the president's stand, his closest advisers—particularly his new vice-president, Martin Van Buren—feared a political disaster. Jackson's hard line toward the nullifiers, they feared, might jeopardize the coalition of "southern planters and plain republicans of the North" that they had worked so hard to consolidate into the Democratic Party. Considerable support existed in both parties for some sort of compromise. Henry Clay advanced a plan to lower the Tariff of 1832 over a period of ten years until all duties reached a moderate rate of 20 percent on the value of imported goods. Calhoun would have preferred more radical cuts over a shorter period of time, but he realized that it was either this deal or none at all. Continuing to balance his love for the Union with his sectional loyalty and desirous

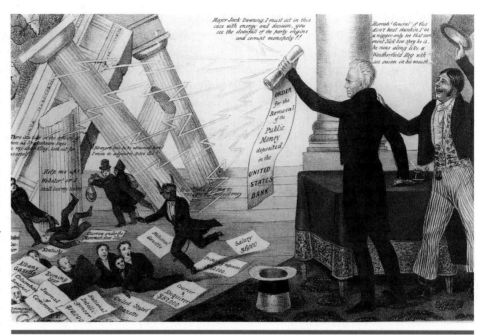

"The Downfall of Mother Bank," a pro-Jackson cartoon showing the bank crumbling and Jackson's opponents in flight in response to his removal of government deposits.

to head off a confrontation, Calhoun agreed to the compromise. Jackson signed the compromise tariff into law on March 2, 1833. The South Carolina convention reconvened and repealed its Ordinance of Nullification, but in a final act of defiance it enacted another ordinance declaring the Force Bill null and void. This time, Jackson did not respond. Satisfied with the outcome, he declared that "nullification is dead." "The next pretext," he ominously predicted, "will be the negro, or slavery question."

The Bank War

Of all the issues that heightened political tensions during the 1830s, none had greater long-term economic implications than the so-called Bank War of 1832–33. At the center of the controversy was the Second Bank of the United States (BUS). Established by act of Congress in 1816, the bank was headquartered in Philadelphia with branch banks scattered around the country. Although it made short-term loans to other banks and businesses, its primary purpose was to maintain monetary stability in the economy by controlling the

amount of credit state-chartered banks could extend. It could do so because it was the repository of all funds collected by the U.S. government, including the paper money issued by state banks and used by citizens to pay their taxes.

The BUS thus became a creditor of state banks and at any time could insist on redeeming their notes in specie—hard currency. The threat of such calls for payment forced state banks to limit the amount of paper money they issued and, accordingly, the amount of credit they could extend. Not surprisingly, state bankers took a dim view of the BUS's regulatory power and frequently accused it of discriminatory practices and restraining the country's economic development. Complaints about the bank tended to divide along an east-west axis, with capital-starved westerners the most vehement critics.

As a westerner who blamed the BUS for causing the Panic of 1819, Andrew Jackson had indicated after his election in 1828 that he intended to oppose renewing the bank's charter. The BUS represented everything he disliked about the eastern monied establishment. This elitist institution, with its access to all government funds, had far too much power over the economy to suit Jackson. Moreover, he was convinced that the bank had contributed money to his opponents and actively campaigned against him in the election of 1828. In fact, the bank's president, Nicholas Biddle of Philadelphia, had voted for Jackson in 1828 and would do so again in 1832.

The spark that ignited the Bank War, though, came not from Jackson but rather from his opponent in the 1832 election, Henry Clay. Convinced that the pressure of an upcoming election might push Jackson to change his mind and support the BUS, Clay persuaded Biddle to seek an early renewal of the bank's charter. Biddle learned from Senator Daniel Webster, one of the bank's legal counsels, that he favored the idea. Biddle also knew that every member of Jackson's cabinet except Attorney General Roger Taney was pro-BUS and that both houses of Congress were well disposed toward it as well. The time seemed right to go forward.

"KING ANDREW'S" VETO

As expected, the recharter bill moved through Congress and arrived on President Jackson's desk around the Fourth of July 1832. Without blinking, Jackson vetoed it. In a blistering message to Congress, he assailed the bank as an unconstitutional monopoly that favored eastern monied interests over less affluent westerners, corrupted the political process, and

BORN TO COMMAND.

OF VETO MEMORY.

HAD I BEEN CONSULTED.

KING ANDREW THE FIRST.

"King Andrew the First," c. 1832.

served "to make the rich richer and the potent more powerful" at the expense of "the humble members of society—the farmers, mechanics, and laborers—who have neither the time nor the means of securing like favors to themselves." The federal government, he concluded, must provide "equal protection" under the law to all segments of society. Aghast at the vehemence of Jackson's message, Biddle observed that "it has all the fury of a chained panther biting the bars of his cage."

Jackson fully intended to politicize the bank with his veto, and he succeeded. Friends of the BUS—especially those in Congress—railed at the imperious tone of the message. Biddle castigated it as a "manifesto of anarchy," while Clay denounced it as "a perversion of the veto power." Webster got to the heart of the matter when he accused Jackson of claiming "for the President, not the power of approval, but the primary power of originating laws."

What really shocked Jackson's adversaries, however, was his frontal assault on the Supreme Court. In the 1819 case of *McCullough v. Maryland*, the Court under Chief Justice John Marshall had ruled in favor of the bank's constitutionality. Jackson disagreed. In his veto message, he asserted that the chief executive and Congress "must each be guided by its own opinion of the Constitution." If he had stopped at this point, little might have been made of the remark. But what followed landed like a bombshell: "The opinion of the judges has no more authority over Congress than the opinion of Congress has over the judges, and on that point the President is independent of both. The authority of the Supreme Court must not, therefore, be permitted to control the Congress or the Executive when acting in their legislative capacities, but to have only such influence as the force of their reasoning may deserve."

The implications were clear. As the directly elected representative of the people, Jackson believed that the president should exercise legislative as well as judicial authority. He was taking a position radically different from that of previous presidents. "We have arrived at a new epoch," Webster exclaimed in disgust. "We are entering on experiments with the government and the Constitution, hitherto untried, and of fearful and appalling aspect." Clay and Calhoun, in an uncommon union of sentiments, agreed. All three expressed concern over "the rapid strides of Executive power," as Clay put it, and Calhoun warned of "the approach of despotic power." Opposition cartoonists began to depict Jackson as "King Andrew" the imperial president, wearing a crown, decked out in ermine robes, carrying a scepter, and trampling on the Constitution.

Buffeted by criticism from political opponents and members of his own party alike, Jackson fought back. He persuaded a majority of voters that the "Monster Bank" deserved to be scorned and exterminated. His reelection victory in 1832 was decisive. Clay carried only five states and part of another. All others except Vermont, which voted for a third-party candidate, went to Old Hickory and his Democratic Party.

THE END OF THE BANK OF THE UNITED STATES

Bolstered by the election results, Jackson informed his cabinet in November 1832 that he intended to kill the "hydra-headed monster" by withdrawing all federal funds from the BUS and withholding any further deposits. Fearing that such action would shake public confidence and cause a financial panic, two successive secretaries of the treasury refused to remove the funds and were immediately fired by Jackson. These were the first dismissals of cabinet officers by a president, and they led to further howls of protest from congressional critics like Clay and Webster. Jackson's third choice for the treasury, the outspoken anti-BUS attorney general, Roger Taney, promptly executed the president's order by withdrawing government funds from the bank and depositing all incoming funds in privately owned, state-chartered "pet banks" around the country.

With the resources of the BUS shrinking, Nicholas Biddle began to take precautionary measures by calling in loans and tightening credit. The action seemed justified at first, in view of Jackson's intentions. But Biddle continued his tight money policy into the winter and spring of 1833–34, long after it was needed to safeguard the bank. His aim was to cause enough financial distress to force Jackson to recharter the bank. The resulting recession brought tremendous pressure on the administration from all parts of the country. But Jackson refused to budge. "I will never restore the deposits," he told a group of New York businessmen. "I never will recharter the United States Bank, or sign a charter for any other bank, so long as my name is Andrew Jackson." When the House of Representatives passed a series of resolutions censuring Biddle and his bank for their actions, Jackson knew that he had won the Bank War. When its federal charter expired in 1836, the BUS was incorporated as a state bank under the name United States Bank of Pennsylvania. The institution eventually went bankrupt and closed its doors in 1841.

Jackson's fight against the bank unleashed a torrent of consequences he neither expected nor sought. The shifting of federal funds to pet banks led to a flood of paper money from unregulated state banks and fostered a speculative boom not unlike the one that had helped trigger the Panic of 1819. Recognizing this, Jackson sought to slow down the overheated economy by issuing a Specie Circular in July 1836, which required gold and silver coin in payment for the sale of public lands. Rather than slowing the inflationary spiral, however, Jackson's well-intentioned order had the opposite effect. Land purchases became more difficult for people of limited means, while wealthy land speculators continued to buy. In the process, speculators drained specie from eastern banks to make their purchases in the West.

With the national debt paid off and government coffers overflowing, Jackson also agreed to a bill sponsored by Henry Clay calling for the distribution of the federal surplus to the states in proportion to their representation in Congress. Although the legislation called these distributions "loans," no one expected them to be paid back, and the recipients quickly spent the funds, mainly for the construction of roads, canals, and railroads. While playing an important role in expanding America's transportation system, the so-called Distribution Act also contributed to growing inflation. As specie drained out of the pet banks, the banks began to tighten credit, raise interest rates, and call in loans. Like the Specie Circular, the Distribution Act tended to exacerbate rather than lessen a serious economic problem.

In the long run, the Jackson administration's fiscal policies, particularly the destruction of the Second Bank of the United States, ended efforts to introduce a central banking system and caused considerable economic instability. More than twenty-five years would elapse before the Legal Tender Act (1862) and the National Banking Act (1863) would seek to take up where the BUS had left off. In the meantime, the rapidly expanding country suffered from the absence of federal regulation, a sound credit policy, and a uniform currency.

Industry and the Law

At no time in its history has the United States had a laissez-faire economy—that is, completely free from government intervention. At the national level, the government supported industrial development through tariff, patent, and banking legislation and periodic subsidies to build roads, canals, and railways. Under the auspices of the U.S. Army, the federal government not only spurred the development of interchangeable manufacturing methods but also provided engineers and managers to guide the early stages of the transportation revolution. But that's only part of the story. States and local communities wrote most of the laws and provided much of the monetary support for developing industries. And courts as well as legislatures enthusiastically promoted industry and business. It could not have been otherwise. Public opinion after the War of 1812 agreed that America needed to establish once and for all its economic independence from Europe.

> *"States and local communities wrote most of the laws and provided much of the monetary support for developing industries."*

STATE CHARTERS

The number of chartered corporations in the United States began to rise in the 1780s and then multiplied beyond all precedent in the early nineteenth century. The advantages of incorporation remained in the 1830s much the same as they had been a half century earlier: a charter made a group into a "body politic," an artificial legal person, that could regulate its internal affairs, protect its assets in court, and persist over time. Many legislators resisted giving corporations privileges denied to individual citizens, such as limited liability, which restricted stockholders' responsibility for a company's debts to the size of their initial investment. Nonetheless, as competition for the business of incorporating companies increased, more and more states felt compelled to include limited liability clauses in the charters they issued.

Charters generally defined not only the form of a company's internal government but the activities in which it could engage, the extent of its property, how stockholders voted, and even the distribution of dividends. Charters were usually granted for a limited period of time or gave legislatures the right to amend or repeal them; but given their enthusiasm for growth, legislatures were less likely to crack down on corporations that violated restrictions in their charters than to encourage promising companies with reduced taxes or rights to public lands. If the weakness of regulation gave the United States the appearance of having a laissez-faire economy, the government's active support of development made clear that it did not.

The most consistent supporter of federal intervention was the National Republican Party of Henry Clay and John Quincy Adams. But Jacksonian Democrats often pushed for federal aid to pet projects as well. Even leading states' rights advocates from South Carolina, as we have seen, sought federal aid for the construction of a railroad at the height of the nullification crisis. Political principles mattered, but sometimes they mattered less than immediate local needs. Successful politicians had to be willing to bend to the wishes of their constituents, and their constituents often called for government intervention to improve economic conditions.

State and community governments went to considerable lengths to support industrial development. The Erie Canal, representing an investment of more than $7 million, was wholly owned by the state of New York. Other major canal systems in Pennsylvania, Ohio, Indiana, and Illinois were also state-owned. Pennsylvania spent the most: $68.5 million for public works between 1825 and 1860. As a result of their investments in the Baltimore and Ohio Railroad, the city of Baltimore and the state of Maryland chose eighteen of the company's thirty directors. Virtually every other state acted similarly. Ohio's Loan Law of 1837, for instance, provided matching funds to any internal improvement company (canal, turnpike, or railroad) that satisfied certain specifications. Although the Loan Law was repealed five years later, Ohio's legislature nonetheless passed more than 100 special laws between 1836 and 1850 authorizing loans to railroads within the state.

THE SUPREME COURT AND THE OBLIGATION OF CONTRACTS

In the great government-stimulated rush toward mechanization and economic expansion after the War of 1812, disputes about contracts and property rights proliferated. The responsibility for sorting them out fell to the nation's judicial system. While most litigations came under the jurisdiction of state and local courts, those involving larger constitutional issues ended up before either the Supreme Court or one of the sixteen U.S. circuit courts. Under Chief Justice John Marshall, the Supreme Court boldly asserted its prerogatives and, by extension, those of the federal government over the states. A disproportionate number of precedent-setting cases bore directly on business and economic affairs. Four in particular deserve attention.

In *Fletcher v. Peck* (1810), the Court struck down a Georgia statute that sought to reclaim state lands along the Yazoo River that had been sold to land speculators who had bribed members of the state legislature. Since the speculators had already sold a large part of the Yazoo tract to unsuspecting buyers who evidently were unaware of the fraud, the Marshall Court ruled in favor of the buyers because they had acted in good faith and, in the Court's view, had valid sale contracts. For Marshall and his colleagues, the key issue in the *Fletcher* case was the constitutional provision (Article I, Section 10) that prohibited states from "impairing the Obligation of Contracts." In two 1819 cases, *Dartmouth College v. Woodward* and *Sturgis v. Crowenshield*, the Court likewise invalidated state laws that impaired the obligation-of-contracts clause and ruled in favor of those who held prior contracts.

For all its aggressiveness in expanding federal power at the expense of the states, the Marshall Court's emphasis on established property rights and the sanctity of contracts revealed a fundamentally conservative political philosophy. The Court stood behind commercial development, but it did so with the conviction that real economic growth could only take place in a stable, orderly political and business environment. Given this philosophy, the Court proved hostile to state-sponsored bankruptcy and stay laws enacted during depressions and business downswings that, in effect, protected debtors at the expense of their creditors. Such laws, in the Court's view, struck at the heart of the obligation of contracts. What's more, they fostered a free-for-all competitive atmosphere that threatened not only to disrupt the economy but undo the Republic. That was intolerable to the Marshall Court.

The Court's positions drew praise from business groups and their representatives, such as the Boston Associates and Daniel Webster, but to the state governments—whose rights were often being challenged—they were high-handed, undemocratic, and unconstitutional. The last of the Marshall Court's major decisions was handed down in 1824. In *Gibbons v. Ogden*, a case concerning steamboat travel in New York Harbor, the court decisively established federal over state power in the regulation of interstate commerce. Thereafter, an antifederalist reaction set in. With the disputed presidential election in 1824, the political winds began to shift as a growing number of voters embraced the egalitarian, states' rights philosophy of Andrew Jackson and the newly emerging

Democratic Party. Marshall's influence began to recede even before Jackson's election, when the composition of the Supreme Court changed and it began to soften its stance on the obligation of contracts and sustain state bankruptcy laws.

The Charles River Bridge Case.

The Court's "federalist era" ended with John Marshall's death in 1835. His successor as chief justice was Roger B. Taney of Maryland, a strong believer in free competition who, as Jackson's attorney general, had removed federal funds from the BUS. Taney soon took the Court in a different direction. The extent of the shift away from Marshallian principles was revealed in the 1837 case of *Charles River Bridge Company v. Warren Bridge Company.*

As the sole bridge between Boston and Cambridge, the Charles River Bridge Company had long enjoyed monopolistic privileges. In response to a public outcry against the company's high toll charges, the Massachusetts legislature granted a corporate charter to the Warren Bridge Company with the stipulation that its bridge over the Charles River would eventually become public once the builder paid for its construction costs and made a modest profit. Having failed to win its suit against the Warren charter before Massachusetts tribunals, the Charles River Bridge Company, represented by Senator Daniel Webster, appealed to the Supreme Court, claiming that the Massachusetts law that established the Warren Bridge Company violated the obligation-of-contracts clause of the Constitution.

Roger Brooke Taney, chief justice of the U.S. Supreme Court (1835–64).

John Marshall would doubtless have sided with the Charles River Bridge Company. But not Roger Taney. A firm believer in equal rights (at least for adult white males), Taney had little tolerance for monopolies and special privileges that, under the old federalist system, had been an essential part of the business world. "While the rights of private property are sacredly guarded," he wrote in the Court's majority opinion, "we must not forget that the community also have rights." To deny the Warren Bridge Company its charter, he reasoned, would be tantamount to denying the Boston community its rights. Taney also thought that a decision in favor of the Charles River Bridge Company's monopoly would encourage other monopolies, which in the long run could stifle the country's economic development.

To Marshall, the obligation of contracts was a stabilizing influence on the economy; to Taney, it was a means of blocking competition and, therefore, economic prosperity. By 1837, the Marshallian idea of stability had given way to a more powerful concept—the idea of progress. The Taney Court agreed with the larger public that industrial and technological progress was an essential engine of democracy. More and more goods and services were becoming available to more and more people. Nothing—not even the obligation of contracts—should stand in the way.

THE COURTS AND BUSINESS

The Supreme Court under both Marshall (1801–35) and Taney (1836–64) was consistently friendly toward business. Marshall's Court helped bring stability to the economy when it was buffeted by war, embargo, and a severe panic. Taney's Court, on the other hand, sought to provide greater flexibility within the law, and thus more opportunity for capitalists, during a period of dynamic growth. Although Taney and a majority of his colleagues embraced a states' rights view of the law, they never made it a hard-and-fast rule. Instead, they followed their predecessors in developing a reasonable approach to commercial law that could be uniformly enforced throughout the nation.

Federal circuit courts also played an important role in the country's economic development. At one level, they opened their chambers to distant parties so that citizens of one state or region could settle business differences with citizens of others. At another, more mundane level, they served as arbitrators in local disputes over property rights. Inventors, for example, frequently turned to federal courts to protect their patent rights against infringers. The same courts likewise played a significant role in settling disputes between mill owners over rights to water power. The disputes often hinged on technological details. At Woonsocket, Rhode Island, in 1836, for instance, after a flurry of suits and countersuits, a circuit court judge appointed a local engineer to take measurements and establish dam levels for all to see so that water power on the Blackstone River could be equitably distributed to ninety-six mill sites in the neighborhood. In cases

"The Supreme Court under both Marshall and Taney was consistently friendly toward business."

such as these, the courts relied heavily on the expertise of hydraulic engineers in determining a policy of "reasonable use." Even the law, it seems, could not escape the growing momentum of technological change.

Trails of Tears

Whether measured in terms of industrial output, population growth, or new territory, expansion became a dominant theme in early nineteenth-century America. And nowhere was the country's expansionist impulse more evident than along its western borders. Between the 1790s and 1830s, thousands of white migrants streamed across the Appalachians to settle in the Ohio and Mississippi Valleys and beyond. By 1812, Kentucky, Tennessee, Ohio, and Louisiana had already entered the Union. During the next twenty-five years, seven out of the eight new states came from the trans-Appalachian West. For many, rapid territorial expansion meant progress; but for Indians, it was a different matter.

Of all the politicians who supported national expansion, none was more determined than Andrew Jackson. Long before he became president, Jackson had advocated removing all Indians who lived between the Appalachians and the Mississippi River, forcefully if necessary, to lands west of the great river. His reasoning was bound by the racial assumptions and political concerns of the time. First, he considered the continued presence of native peoples in these areas a threat to the security of the United States. Memories of trouble-making by the British and their Indian allies during and after the War of 1812 weighed heavily on Jackson, and he was determined not to let them wreak havoc on white settlers again. Second, he viewed the territorial claims of various tribes as totally bogus from a legal standpoint. Just because Indians claimed certain lands as their hunting grounds did not give them right of ownership, he argued, because "they have neither dwelt nor made improvements" on them.

Finally, Jackson cited humanitarian reasons for removal. Noting that "some of the tribes have become extinct and others have left but remnants [of their culture] to preserve," he believed that the same fate awaited all native peoples who

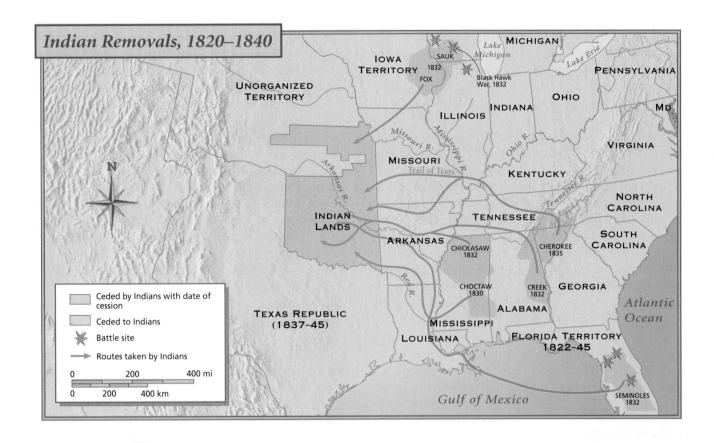

Indian Removals, 1820–1840

Legend:
- Ceded by Indians with date of cession
- Ceded to Indians
- Battle site
- Routes taken by Indians

Scale: 0 | 200 | 400 mi; 0 | 200 | 400 km

came in contact with the forces of white civilization. Having been raised in a society that justified slavery on grounds of racial inferiority, Jackson, like many of his contemporaries, also thought that Indians could never be fully "civilized." He believed they possessed certain racial "deficiencies" that could not be altered through education or cultural assimilation. For him, race determined culture, not the other way around. So the humane thing to do so was to remove the Indians to an isolated territory beyond the Mississippi where they would be free to follow their own traditions and not be "surrounded by the whites" with their alien technologies and institutions.

Jackson also took issue with a long-standing federal policy of recognizing native peoples as separate nations with their own governments. Such a position was unacceptable because, as he put it, the Constitution held that "'no new State shall be formed or erected within the jurisdiction of any other State' without the consent of its legislature." In Jackson's view, all Indians were subjects of the United States, and Congress there-

fore had the right not only to "legislate their boundaries," but also to seize their lands and make them part of the public domain. The Indians had only two choices: they could "emigrate beyond the Mississippi or submit to the laws of those States."

THE INDIAN REMOVAL ACT

By the time Jackson assumed the presidency, Indian removal had become a hot political issue in the South, where Georgia and the Cherokee people contested a large expanse of territory within the state's northwestern boundary. The Cherokees, who numbered around 20,000, claimed that they were a separate nation independent of the state of Georgia. In 1827, they had adopted a written constitution that provided for a bicameral legislature, a judiciary, and an elected executive known as "the principal chief." Contrary to Jackson's thinking, many Cherokees had adopted the trappings of white civilization by becoming successful farmers, businessmen, and plantation owners. Some of the wealthiest Cherokees had even acquired African American slaves and lived in mansions that rivaled those of the wealthiest whites in the region. This doubtless fostered resentment on the part of many less affluent white Americans. The already tense situation worsened during the 1820s, when gold was discovered on Cherokee lands.

Georgia claimed that its colonial charter as well as a compact signed with the U.S. government in 1802 gave it sole authority over the Cherokee people as well as their lands. To make its position clear, the Georgia legislature passed a resolution in 1827 stating "that the Indians are tenants at [Georgia's] will, and [Georgia] may at any time she pleases, determine that tenancy by taking possession of the premises." The legislature put the Cherokees on notice that if they continued "to turn a deaf ear to the voice of reason," harsh consequences would follow. "The lands in question *belong* to Georgia," the resolution concluded. "She *must* and she *will* have them."

Jackson's public statements on the subject encouraged the legislature to take further action against the Cherokees. Between 1828 and 1831, it passed a series of laws that divided Cherokee territory into five counties and placed them directly under Georgia's governance, invalidated all laws passed by the Cherokee legislature, forbade it to meet, and created a "Georgia Guard" police force to make sure its directives were executed. In the meantime, Jackson urged federal legislation to establish a formal mechanism for removing Indians to the West. The bill passed, but only after a bitter debate during which anti-Jacksonian congressmen from the Northeast accused the bill's sponsors of instrumenting a land grab.

John Ross, the principal Cherokee chief who adamantly opposed removal to the Oklahoma Territory.

The Indian Removal Act of May 1830 established a specially designated Indian Territory in the present state of Oklahoma and provided $500,000 for negotiating with Indian tribes, paying them for any improvements (houses, mills, businesses, etc.) made on lands they currently occupied, and relocating them in the West. The act also guaranteed that each tribe would receive an amount of land in the new Indian Territory equivalent to what they had surrendered in the East. During the first year in the West, they would be given food and tools in order to help them get settled. Federal troops would protect the émigrés "against all interruption and disturbance." Each tribe would function independently in its new terrain without interference from the United States.

Faced with pressure from the Georgia legislature and the Jackson administration to cede their lands and move west, Cherokee leaders sought to protect their rights by turning to the Supreme Court. They knew that Chief Justice Marshall was no friend of Jackson, and so they might have a reasonable chance of success. The Court issued an ambiguous ruling in *Cherokee Nation v. Georgia* (1831), but a year later, in *Worcester v. Georgia*, it clearly recognized Cherokee independence by declaring that Georgia had no right to legislate for the Cherokees because they were a separate sovereign nation.

The Cherokee victory proved fleeting though. Upon learning of the Supreme Court's verdict, Jackson is said to have retorted: "Well, John Marshall has made his decision: *now, let him enforce it!*" Recognizing that the Court could do nothing without the president's support, Georgia defied the ruling and continued making preparations for a state lottery that would distribute Cherokee lands to its white citizens.

THE TREATY PARTY

While some 4,000 Cherokees had moved west before 1832, the vast majority refused to abandon their ancestral lands and bitterly resented those who did. But Cherokee solidarity began to fracture in the aftermath of the *Worcester* decision. Several prominent Cherokee leaders, depressed by the growing hopelessness of their situation, changed their minds and began to support the idea of removal. Although viewed as traitors and expelled from the tribe's governing councils, this rump group, known as the Treaty Party, continued to claim legitimacy. In December 1835, they signed the Treaty of New Echota with the U.S. government, ceding all Cherokee lands in return for $5 million, an equivalent amount of land in the new Indian Territory, transportation to the West, and the promise of food and tools for one year. The Cherokees would have two years to prepare for their departure, after which they would be forcibly removed from their lands. Although the Cherokee Nation's legitimate leaders vehemently protested the treaty as fraudulent, the U.S. Senate nonetheless ratified it in the spring of 1836, whereupon it went into effect.

Confusion and disbelief reigned among the Cherokee people as the fateful deadline approached. When federal troops

This 1830s engraving expresses outrage over the massacre of hundreds of white settlers in Florida at the hands of Indians and escaped slaves. Such publicity inflamed white antagonism toward the Seminoles in Florida and, after seven years of bloody conflict, eventually led to their removal to the Oklahoma Territory.

under the command of General Winfield Scott began to arrive in May 1838 to enforce the treaty, few were prepared for what followed. In mid-June, the troops, assisted by Georgia militia, began to round up thousands of Cherokees and herd them into hot, crowded stockades to await deportation to the West. Writing from one of the deportation camps, a Baptist missionary reported, "The Cherokees are nearly all prisoners. . . . They have been dragged from their houses . . . [and] were allowed no time to take any thing with them, except the clothes they had on. . . . Many of the Cherokees, who, a few days ago, were in comfortable circumstances, are now victims of abject poverty. Some, who have been allowed to return home, under passport, to inquire after their property, have found their cattle, horses, swine, farming-tools, and house-furniture all gone." Years later, a Georgia militiaman recollected, "I fought through the Civil War and have seen men shot to pieces and slaughtered by the thousands, but the Cherokee removal was the cruelest I ever saw."

Thus began what became known among the Cherokees as the **"Trail of Tears,"** a grueling 1,000-mile journey—mostly on foot—that lasted more than five months. Some 16,000 persons began the trek; fewer than 12,000 survived it. To make matters worse, a bloody civil war broke out among the Cherokees as "Old Settlers" who had moved west before 1838 insisted that the newcomers live under their government and as the embit-

tered newcomers, in turn, exacted revenge on the Treaty Party by killing three of its most prominent leaders. Nearly seven years elapsed before peace came to the fractured nation.

THE BLACK HAWK WAR

The Cherokees were only one of many tribes that faced removal beyond the Mississippi during the 1830s. Some went peacefully; others resisted. In Florida, for example, efforts to remove the Seminole people provoked a conflict that lasted seven years and cost thousands of lives. Even then, some Seminoles evaded federal troops by moving deep into the Florida everglades, where they remained unmolested for decades. Farther north in Illinois, an embittered Sauk chief named Black Hawk led a short-lived effort in 1832 to take back lands that had been lost to white settlers as a result of a questionable treaty signed years earlier that had ceded 50 million acres to the United States for a pittance. The so-called Black Hawk War lasted less than four months and resulted in a devastat-

Black Hawk, Sauk war chief and Indian leader of the war that assumed his name.

Osceola, famed Muskogee Seminole war leader who engineered major victories over American troops during the Second Seminole War in Florida. Captured under a flag of truce in 1837, he died of malaria in a South Carolina prison the following year. The Second Seminole War (1835–42) proved to be the longest and costliest Indian war in U.S. history.

The Jacksonian Legacy

The U.S. Senate ratified the Treaty of New Echota, making the Cherokee removal a political reality, near the end of Jackson's second term as president. Jackson's presidency was largely focused on domestic issues, especially those called forth by America's economic development and expansion. His attacks on internal improvements and the Bank of the United States were designed to redistribute power in domestic economic affairs from federal to state levels. But Jackson established a clear demarcation between states' rights, which he supported, and state sovereignty, which he rebuffed during the South Carolina nullification crisis. His appointees to the Supreme Court, notably of Roger Taney as chief justice in 1836, steered the Court away from the federalist positions of John Marshall. Yet despite his desire to hold the power of the federal government in check, Jackson enhanced the power and prestige of the presidency. He imprinted his strong personal character on the office—a feisty, direct, no-nonsense style allied to nationalism and a commitment to American territorial expansion.

ing defeat for Black Hawk and his outnumbered group of Sauk and Fox warriors. Although he managed to evade capture after an army of federal troops and Illinois militia (one of whom was a young Abraham Lincoln) decimated his band, he was eventually betrayed to federal authorities by a group of neighboring Winnebagos with whom he had sought refuge. The reward was twenty horses and $100.

Black Hawk spent the next year in a federal prison near Washington, D.C. Upon his release, Andrew Jackson paraded him throughout the Northeast so people could see the rebellious "savage" and so he could "see the strength of the white people." Black Hawk finally returned in disgrace to what remained of his people in the remote reaches of present-day Iowa. Thus ended the last impediment to white settlement in the Old Northwest.

"Jackson established a clear demarcation between states' rights, which he supported, and state sovereignty, which he rebuffed."

Before Jackson left office in 1837, over 45,000 Indians had been removed to the trans-Mississippi West, and many others had died. In the process, they relinquished about 100 million acres of land to the United States in return for 32 million acres of western land and $68 million in payments and subsidies. As one congressman who supported the removals put it, "What is history but the obituary of nations?" Should the United States, he continued, "check the course of human happiness—obstruct the march of science—stay the works of art, and stop the arm of industry, because they will efface in their progress the wigwam of the red hunter, and put out forever the council fires of his tribe?" To Jacksonians and a majority of white Americans in 1837, the answer was clear.

Some challenges Jackson avoided. He detested the rapidly growing antislavery movement but ducked the whole question of slavery and its expansion into new territories. When American settlers in Texas revolted against Mexico in 1836 and sought their independence as a slave-holding republic, Jackson moved cautiously. He feared igniting controversy in a critical election year that saw his longtime ally and heir apparent, Martin Van Buren, running for the presidency. Despite his close friendship with the Texas revolutionary leader, Sam Houston, he delayed recognizing the new republic until a few days before he left office.

THE MODERN POLITICAL PARTY

It was during the Jacksonian period that **the modern political party** came into existence, complete with new organizational methods for selecting candidates and conducting campaigns. These campaigns became lively contests that involved open-air rallies, torchlight parades, candidate debates, periodic violence, and a broader level of participation not only on the part of white male voters but also nonvoting female lobbyists and activists.

Such political innovation paralleled important social, institutional, and technological changes during the 1820s and 1830s. As the white population grew exponentially, the geographic expanse of the nation widened, and industrialization began to take off, American society became increasingly infused with immigrants from different ethnic and religious backgrounds, many of whom voted. Politicians soon recognized that ethno-cultural and class distinctions could be used for cultivating new constituencies: cultural identities could reinforce political identities. To spread their political messages, party leaders took advantage of a rapidly expanding communications network fostered by the U.S. Post Office, distributing millions of party newspapers, campaign documents, and other sources of political propaganda to all corners of the country. Within a few years, parties could turn out even more material on steam-driven printing presses and, by the mid-1840s, speed communication via the telegraph. Influenced by the new technology, political activists began during the 1830s to use machines and factories as metaphors to describe their new organizations. To control public opinion in an increasingly pluralistic society, they were forced to build political coalitions, ultimately forming the first fully institutionalized political parties that placed party loyalty ahead of ideology. All this depended on having the institutions and technology that could disseminate information on a massive national scale.

Newspapers proved particularly important in building party organizations and shaping public opinion. Between 1790 and 1828, the number of newspapers published in the United States went from 92 to 861, and by 1840 had jumped to over 1,400—a phenomenon that reflected the introduction of high-speed printing technologies. Editors and publishers became the field mar-

> *"Newspapers proved particularly important in building party organizations and shaping public opinion."*

shals of their parties and played prominent roles in selecting candidates and devising electoral strategies in their states. They also influenced who received patronage jobs in local post offices and other government agencies after successful elections. Nothing was more important than the distribution of political patronage. It was the glue that held parties together and a defining feature of the new party system that emerged during the 1830s and 1840s.

Early glimmerings of the new system appeared in New York after the War of 1812, when Martin Van Buren led a dissident faction called the "Bucktails" against an elite that had been running the state government for years. After creating a strong state organization, Van Buren went on to join Jackson in the campaign of 1828 and became one of the chief architects of the Democratic Party. From the outset, Van Buren maintained that political partisanship enhanced democracy by allowing issues to be openly debated and challenging voters to make important choices. Rejecting the views of Thomas Jefferson, George Washington, and other "founding fathers,"

The press room of a Boston publishing house, c. 1852. Note the women workers operating the long line of steam-powered printing presses.

Van Buren believed that division and conflict were constructive and should become a permanent feature of American politics.

WHIGS VERSUS DEMOCRATS

The new Democratic Party soon had a rival in the Whig Party, which conducted its first campaign in the congressional elections of 1834. Formed by leaders such as Henry Clay and Daniel Webster, and composed of old-line Federalists, National Republicans, moral zealots, and social reformers, the Whigs were slower to assemble a national organization owing to their heterogeneous origins. What initially united them was their determined opposition to Jackson and especially what they perceived to be his high-handed manner in waging the Bank War and in undermining Supreme Court decisions (as in the Cherokee removal case) he disagreed with.

Genuine philosophical differences separated the Whigs and Democrats. The Whigs, like their Federalist and National Republican predecessors, emphasized national issues and

> *"In many areas, ethnic and religious tensions divided the electorate."*

supported a strong federal government. By contrast, the Democrats, like the Jeffersonian Republicans, emphasized state issues and the need for limited government and local autonomy. While the Whigs believed in a hierarchical society that promoted a general "harmony of interests" and supported trickle-down economic policies aimed at achieving prosperity as well as social order, the Democrats generally touted the "common man" and distrusted "the aristocratic wealthy," who, they believed, often profited at the expense of the majority.

While Whig politicians were more pro-bank and pro-tariff than their Democratic counterparts, little separated the two parties concerning internal improvements. When it came to the construction of canals, turnpikes, and railroads, voting patterns tended to reflect local interests as Whigs and Democrats from the same district often joined forces in supporting or opposing such legislation. The two parties disagreed more on issues pertaining to social and economic reform. Whigs tended to be more interested in humanitarian reform. A higher percentage of Whigs supported public education than Democrats. Likewise, a much higher percentage of Whigs supported the antislavery movement than Democrats. Yet more Democrats than Whigs favored an end to imprisonment for debt. Here, as elsewhere, Whigs and Democrats differed fundamentally on the proper role of government. Whigs generally favored an activist government that would foster reform, while Democrats viewed most humanitarian reform efforts as "meddlesome interferences."

Why did men vote the way they did? In many areas, ethnic and religious tensions divided the electorate. Catholic immigrants often tended to vote Democratic, while free blacks, Protestant immigrants, and native-born evangelical Christians supported Whig candidates. At the same time, the wealthiest citizens frequently split their vote between Democratic and Whig candidates. For all concerned, personal rivalries and friendships as well as kinship connections made a difference, as did economic interests and moral considerations such as one's views on slavery.

Besides the Democrats and Whigs, fraternal groups like the Working Men's Party became a political force during the late 1820s, a result of the country's turn to industrialization. The most important third party to emerge, however, was the Anti-Mason Party, a movement that originated in western New York state and quickly spread to other parts of the coun-

This lithograph, entitled "Politics in an Oyster House," shows two citizens, one grasping a newspaper, engaged in discussion. Foreign visitors frequently commented on the American addiction to newspapers and politics.

try during the late 1820s in response to the mysterious disappearance of a former Freemason who threatened to expose the secret practices of the order. Convinced that the Masons had conspired to cover up his murder, the Anti-Mason Party set out to undermine the Masonic Order by opposing any Mason who ran for office.

As it turned out, the Whig Party profited greatly from the anti-Masonic frenzy. Since Jackson and Van Buren were Masons, the Democratic Party quickly became tainted by anti-Masonic attacks, even though prominent Whigs like Henry Clay also had Masonic ties. Whig Party leaders deftly implied that their Democratic opponents were conspiratorial and anti-democratic. As the 1830s went on, the Whig Party forged alliances with the Anti-Mason Party in local and national elections and eventually absorbed it. But the Anti-Masons permanently influenced both Whigs and Democrats by pioneering such novel practices as open-nominating conventions and the publication of party platforms.

A Working Men's Party cartoon from the 1830s accusing a wealthy businessman (left) of conspiring with the devil to buy votes, while the honest worker (right) casts his ballot for "Liberty and the Rights of Man." Such cartoons provide evidence of class tensions in antebellum America.

The essence of the new party system, which historians now refer to as "the second party system," was open and unrepentant partisanship. Party leaders emphasized the need for discipline and unity in supporting the party ticket, regardless of personal preferences, and came to believe that a strong organization held the key to electoral success. "ORGANIZE, ORGANIZE," the editor of the Seneca Falls (New York) *Democrat* exhorted his readers in 1842. "The enemy is in the fields. Be you up and doing. Now is the time for action." "Parties in our republic . . . may be compared to contending armies," another Democratic editor observed five year later; "there must be system, discipline, order, regularity, union, and concert of action."

The new party system that emerged during the 1830s redefined American politics and changed the very meaning of the word "party." In the Federalist-Republican era, "party" carried the negative connotation of "faction." By the late 1830s, a party was thought to be an organization rather than a zealous attitude. The new approach was characterized by well-organized national parties that disseminated information on a massive scale and used the spoils system to reward loyal party workers. This represented a new era in which parties dominated politics as they never had before.

Panic and Depression

In the midst of these political realignments came the election of 1836. Since Jackson had long since indicated his desire to see Van Buren succeed him as president, it came as no surprise when the Democratic national convention meeting in Baltimore quickly nominated the New Yorker as the party's standard bearer. The interesting question was who would contest Van Buren for the presidency.

Meanwhile, distrust and ill feeling swirled within the ranks of the newly formed Whig Party as its leaders sought a presidential nominee. Henry Clay wanted the nomination, but his loss to Jackson four years earlier made him an unlikely choice. It soon became evident that the Whigs had neither the organi-

Martin Van Buren, eighth president of the United States (1837–41).

zation nor party unity to match the Democrats. The leaders ranged from New England industrialists to conservative southern planters who favored commercial development, to younger northern politicians who not only embraced anti-Masonry but also antislavery and temperance. While they agreed on the need to expand federal power and revitalize the American System, Whigs often differed over the details and spent more time bickering among themselves than challenging their Jacksonian opponents. When it became apparent that they could not agree on a single candidate, they ended up nominating three—General William Henry Harrison of Ohio, Senator Daniel Webster of Massachusetts, and Hugh Lawson White of Tennessee. The Whigs hoped that each candidate might draw enough votes from each of their respective sections of the country to deny Van Buren a majority and throw the election into the House of Representatives, where they stood a better chance of success.

As it turned out, the Whig strategy nearly worked. Although Van Buren won a convincing majority in the electoral college, the popular vote proved to be much closer, with Van Buren winning by a margin of less than 2 percent. Although he had been one of the primary organizers of the Democratic Party and possessed considerable personal charm, Van Buren lacked Old Hickory's charisma. He was too much of a political insider, too much an organization man. Without Jackson's strong endorsement, he might have lost. His base of support in the South and Southwest was shaky. Van Buren thus emerged from the election victorious but lacking momentum. The new Democratic Party was vulnerable in the new two-party system that had emerged.

Less than two weeks after the inauguration, the financial crisis that Jackson had sought to avert broke with a fury on his successor. The causes of the Panic of 1837—speculation in western lands, overextensions of credit, and mountains of debt backed by inadequate specie and too much paper money—were similar to those that had precipitated the economic crash some eighteen years earlier. In March 1837, the New Orleans cotton market collapsed in response to a severe depression in Europe. A chain reaction then caused the failure of mercantile firms and banking houses from Louisiana to Massachusetts. As concern mounted, nervous investors, eager to unload suspect banknotes for hard cash, started a run on the banks that forced many into bankruptcy. By May, the run had become so draining that New York banks suspended specie payments. Like dominos, banks in other parts of the country soon followed suit. Bad went to worse as prices fell, speculators defaulted on their loans, and thousands of small farmers, beset by crop failures, lost their land to foreclosures. By the fall of 1837, unemployment lines lengthened as hundreds of shops and factories, unable to sell their products, closed their doors, never to reopen again. In many parts of the country, the shake-out left property values at a fraction of their original value. The United States teetered at the edge of total financial collapse.

An anti-Jacksonian cartoon depicting the effects of the depression of 1837: a bank panic and beggars in the street.

From the outset, the Van Buren administration seemed helpless in the face of the panic and ensuing six-year depression. Adhering to the Jeffersonian adage that that government governs best which governs least, Van Buren warned citizens not to look to the federal government for relief. Relief must come from the states and local communities, where, to his way of thinking, essential power resided. He limited himself to proposals for protecting the federal government's holdings. In a reversal of Jacksonian policies, he urged that distributions of the federal surplus to the states be postponed and that all federal monies be transferred from pet banks to federal treasury vaults (an independent treasury).

Van Buren's two proposals encountered bitter criticism from Whig politicians, who argued that both measures would take federal funds out of public circulation at the very time they were most needed. Although the postponement bill quickly moved through both houses of the Democratic Congress and became law, the Independent Treasury Act faced much tougher sledding as Whigs and maverick Democrats in the House of Representatives refused to support the measure. When the nation's private banks suspended specie payments for a second time in 1839, enough votes shifted to pass the Independent Treasury Act in June 1840. But, as Whig opponents had predicted, it did nothing to ease the depression. Serving only as the government's strongbox for keeping and disbursing funds, the independent treasury played no real regulatory role. The banking business remained completely decentralized and unregulated for more than two decades.

The economic disaster was a political disaster for Van Buren, who had virtually no chance for reelection in 1840. Yet he was no political failure. More than anyone other than Andrew Jackson, Van Buren was the architect of the Democratic Party. He was a master political organizer who saw the value to a democracy of having a vigorous two-party system. As one of Jackson's closest advisers, he played a key role in formulating the party's states' rights philosophy and putting in place policies that shifted power away from the federalist agenda of Henry Clay and John Quincy Adams. By 1837–38, this shift had become so pervasive that even Clay—the foremost spokesman of the American System—began to relax his position. He had already accepted a lower tariff as part of the compromise of 1832. As he sought to win southern support in making yet another bid for the presidency in 1840, Clay reiterated his flexibility on the tariff while agreeing not to press

1825	The Erie Canal completed.
1828	Calhoun's *The South Carolina Exposition and Protest* published.
	"Tariff of Abominations."
January 1830	Webster-Hayne debate.
May 1830	Indian Removal Act.
1832	Black Hawk War.
November 1832	South Carolina's Ordinance of Nullification.
1832–33	Bank War.
1837	*Charles River Bridge Company v. Warren Bridge Company.*
	Financial panic.
June 1838	Cherokees' "Trail of Tears."

too hard for a national bank. Even more remarkable, he appeared to abandon his main plank by admitting that federal sponsorship of internal improvements no longer remained a great national issue. That the chief spokesman of the American System would retreat from the statist policies he had so vigorously championed for more than twenty years speaks volumes about the larger impact of the Jacksonian political economy. Younger up-and-coming politicians, like Abraham Lincoln of Illinois, would not forget the essential ingredients of Clay's vision. But for the time being, the American System had receded from the public's eye. By the late 1830s, other issues pressed for attention.

Suggested Reading

William W. Freehling, *Prelude to Civil War: The Nullification Controversy in South Carolina, 1816–1836* (1966)

Albert Hurtado and Peter Iverson, eds., *Major Problems in American Indian History* (1994)

Edward Pessen, *Jacksonian America: Society, Personality, and Politics* (1978)

Robert V. Remini, *Andrew Jackson*, 3 vols. (1977–84)

Carol Sheriff, *The Artificial River: The Erie Canal and the Paradox of Progress* (1996)

QUESTIONS

■ How was farm life changing in the antebellum North?

■ What were the main features of the slave system in the antebellum South?

■ What were the main features of the factory system in the antebellum period?

■ How did the widespread use of clock time affect work in this period?

Before the Civil War, most Americans still lived on small, family-owned farms and followed the agrarian life-style idealized by Thomas Jefferson. But other types of labor were becoming more visible and, as it turned out, more controversial. As cotton became America's primary export to Europe, plantation agriculture spread slavery across the South and subjected slaves and their masters to a strange and cruel way of life. At the same time, mechanized factories and large mill complexes emerged as an alternative to farming while fanning the development of mass transportation systems and the growth of urban areas. The new employment opportunities attracted a growing proportion of European immigrants entering the United States. Particularly in the northeastern states, industrial capitalism had begun, and with it dawned the modern age.

Whether on the farm, on the factory floor, or under the tyrannical bonds of slavery, the world of work experienced major changes. And some of these changes—mechanization, increased regimentation, and adherence to clock time—eventually reconfigured the face of politics, society, and the economy.

A Nation of Farmers

In one of his most frequently quoted statements, Thomas Jefferson proclaimed that "those who labour in the earth are the chosen people of God, if ever he had a chosen people." Over the years, Jefferson continued to believe that agriculture and the agrarian way of life were not only central to America's special character but essential to the survival of the Republic. In his view, those who led a country life were more honest and industrious, independent and responsible, than city people. Because land ownership gave individuals a

propertied stake in society, Jefferson considered landholders "the most precious part of a state." "I think our governments will remain virtuous for many centuries as long as they are chiefly agricultural," he wrote, adding that "this will be as long as there shall be vacant lands in any part of America." "When [people] get piled up upon one another in large cities, as in Europe," he warned, "they will become corrupt as in Europe."

Jefferson's outspoken agrarianism fit with his times. In 1800, the year of his election as president, rural people outnumbered city people by more than 15 to 1. Although the ratio would narrow to 5.5 to 1 in 1850 and 4 to 1 in 1860, family farms were still common in all parts of the United States during this period. One English traveler observed from a hilltop outside Utica, New York, in 1819: "Certainly I had more than a thousand farms spread before me, . . . many hundreds could be seen at one glance." Artists of the time captured the grandeur of America's natural environment in their paintings. Asher B. Durand's panoramic view of *Dover Plains, Dutchess County, New York* (1848), for instance, conveys a sense of the beauty, peacefulness, and wholesomeness of rural life. By the 1850s, New York firms like Currier and Ives began to mass-produce such views as color lithographs and made them available at cheap prices. Extremely popular, the lithographs did much to romanticize the agrarian tradition long after it ceased to be the primary influence on American life and politics.

FARM LIFE

Farms varied in size and orientation depending on their geographic location and time of settlement, and the interests, ambition, and good fortune of their owners. In sparsely settled areas along the frontier, the main objective was to build a cabin, clear the land, and plant enough basic crops (like corn) so that the farmer could "get by." Later, he might plant various vegetables, fruit trees, and grain crops as well as raise cattle, horses, hogs, sheep, turkeys, chickens, and geese. Clearing the land required back-breaking labor. Since heavy rocks and stumps had to be removed and brush piled and burned to create a field, neighboring farmers often relied on one another for help. They also loaned each other tools and sometimes even small amounts of money.

Most farms in the antebellum (pre–Civil War) period generally raised the same types of crops and livestock. Virtually all farms had milch cows, for example. Whereas dairy farmers might own a herd of sixteen to forty milkers, other farmers—whether they raised cash crops or remained at a subsistence level—kept a cow or two to feed their families. Most farmers raised hay, oats, corn, grain, potatoes, garden vegetables, fruits, chickens, hogs, and cattle, and they all owned oxen or horses for fieldwork and basic transportation. Farms differed in emphasis and the proportion of their crops and livestock, not in their methods.

Everyone in farm households had certain responsibilities, divided up along gender lines. Men's work included plowing, seeding, and cultivating the fields, clearing the land and hauling rocks, building and repairing fences, chopping wood, and caring for larger livestock such as horses, oxen, cattle, and sheep. Women, in addition to keeping house, preparing meals, and caring for children, did the milking, tended gardens, raised chickens, spun woolen yarn and wove homespun cloth, and made soap and candles as well as butter, cheese, and other dairy products. Cheese making required considerable skill, and in many households it became an important source of income, as did surpluses of grain, livestock, eggs, and butter. During the winter months, northern farm women often supplemented the family income by making palm-leaf hats and other items for local merchants who supplied them

"Northern farm women often supplemented the family income by making palm-leaf hats and other items for local merchants."

with the raw material and paid them either in cash or, more likely, credit at their general stores.

Given the many tasks that farming entailed, farm couples often had large families. Beginning at the age of six or seven—sometimes earlier—both boys and girls were expected to feed the chickens, gather eggs, slop the hogs, weed plants, sweep the house, and keep wood boxes full. As children reached puberty, they began to take on gender-related chores: young men joined their fathers in the field, and young women helped their mothers in the house. Depending on the size of the farm and the ages of children, farm families frequently employed live-in "hired hands" to lighten their toils. Sometimes these workers were relatives who stayed for the season; sometimes they were unmarried aunts or uncles who resided permanently with the family.

Farm life required a considerable degree of flexibility. Men helped out with the milking, gardening, and feeding of livestock, while women and their daughters often joined the men in the field during the haying, harvesting, and butchering seasons, when time was of the essence to prevent spoilage. During such periods of intense labor, neighbors and kinfolk assisted one another. The sheer drudgery of stacking hay in one-

Asher B. Durand, *Dover Plains, Dutchess County, New York* (1848).

hundred-degree barn lofts or the trauma of hearing hogs frantically squeal as their throats were being cut during the late-fall slaughter suggests that farming could be a hard life. To be sure, it had its compensations in the form of land ownership, personal independence, a generally healthy work environment, close-knit neighborly acts of helping and sharing, and communal activities such as barn dances and quilting bees. But for those who worked hard to keep up and perhaps even get ahead, it was a demanding life.

Early nineteenth-century farmers generally established business relationships with local merchants who owned general stores and dealt in a range of goods. There, farmers exchanged home-grown produce for such essential goods as salt, sugar, harnesses, nails, tools, finished cotton cloth, and "fancy goods" like fine woolens, brass buttons, and ladies' hats. Relatively little cash changed hands in these barter-type relationships. Instead, farmers and merchants "settled up" periodically, paying what they owed in hard cash.

As the transportation revolution broadened trade networks, farming became more cash oriented and commercial-

> *"As the transportation revolution broadened trade networks, farming became more cash oriented and commercialized."*

ized. As early as the late 1820s, agents from business firms in the cities traveled the countryside buying livestock, grain, cheese, and other farm commodities. If an exchange of goods took place on the spot, the farmer or his wife usually received an immediate cash payment. If a contractual agreement was drawn up, as was often the case regarding cheese, grains, or other goods to be delivered at a later date, the farmer received a cash advance on signing the contract and full payment either on delivery or soon thereafter. In either case, farm families were pulled into market relationships of increasing complexity.

Old ways persisted, however. Farmers tended to be conservative people who felt uneasy about establishing business relationships with distant companies whose owners they neither knew nor fully trusted. They generally steered a middle course between the rising, impersonal market economy and the more traditional "moral economy" with its face-to-face relationships and long-standing personal business associations. A German immigrant living in Illinois conveyed a sense of the shifting moral economy in rural America when he wrote in 1851 that "the Americans living around us are thoroughly good neighbors, ready and willing to be of help. But in business they are just as crafty as all their countrymen. When doing business they have no conscience at all."

PLOWS AND REAPERS

Just as the manufacturing economy moved increasingly toward more standardized products for growing markets, so too did agriculture—though more slowly. The shift from subsistence to more commercially oriented farming first occurred in areas that were experiencing industrial development and urban growth. In New York, for example, the completion of the Erie Canal in 1825 and the attendant growth of manufacturing centers along its path from Troy to Utica, Syracuse, Rochester, and Buffalo stimulated the rise of dairy farming throughout the

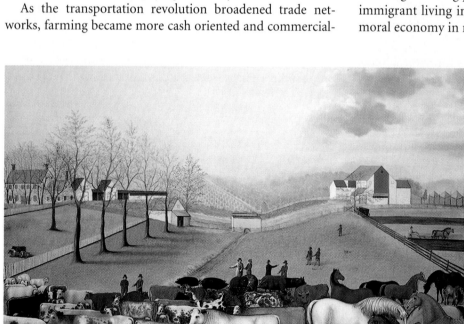

Edward Hicks, *An Indian Summer View of the Farm and Stock of James C. Cornell of Northampton, Bucks County, Pennsylvania* (1848). Mr. Cornell, like most farmers who could afford to have their properties recorded by an artist, was likely a leading citizen of Bucks County.

region. Rather than focusing on wheat as a cash crop (as they previously had), New York farmers turned increasingly to the production of milk, butter, and cheese for the growing city trade in the Northeast. These products were initially processed on the farm by women, but the demand grew, so that factory production eventually replaced home production, and, in the process, men took over the industry. With the coming of railroads during the 1850s, the dairy zone spread beyond New York, New England, and Pennsylvania into northern Ohio and Indiana and eventually into large expanses of the Midwest, notably Wisconsin, Illinois, Minnesota, and Iowa. By 1880, dairy farming would become, in the words of a prominent spokesman, "the greatest single agricultural interest in America."

But compared with the rapid spread of mechanization in industry, farmers adopted new technologies slowly. Before the 1850s, milking, planting, cultivating, and harvesting were largely done by hand. The symbol of agriculture in popular

American Journal

Where Do You Live?

Log cabins dotted the rural landscape in nineteenth-century America. A product of the earliest colonial settlements, examples can still be found from the East Coast to the far West.

As she traveled in southwestern Ohio near Cincinnati in 1830, British writer Frances Trollope (mother of novelist Anthony Trollope) recorded her impressions of an isolated small family farm and the "country people" who occupied it. While Trollope admired the family's independence, she also noted that "there was something awful and almost unnatural in their loneliness."

"We visited the farm which interested us particularly from its wild and lonely situation, and from the entire dependence of the inhabitants upon their own resources. It was a partial clearing in the very heart of the forest. The house was built on the side of a hill, so steep that a high ladder was necessary to enter the front door, while the back one opened against the hill side: at the foot of this sudden eminence ran a clear stream, whose bed had been deepened into a little reservoir, just opposite the house. A noble field of Indian corn stretched away into the forest on one side, and a few half-cleared acres, with a shed or two upon them, occupied the other, giving accommodation to cows, horses, pigs, and chickens innumerable. Immediately before the house was a small potato-garden, with a few peach and apple trees. The house was built of logs, and consisted of two rooms, besides a little shanty or lean-to, that was used as a kitchen. Both rooms were comfortably furnished with good beds, drawers, etc. The farmer's wife, and a young woman who looked like her sister, were spinning, and three little children were playing about. The woman told me that they spun and wove all the cotton and woollen garments of the family, and knit all the stockings; her husband, though not a shoemaker by trade, made all the shoes. She manufactured all the soap and candles they used, and prepared her sugar from the sugar-trees on their farm. All she wanted with money, she said, was to buy coffee, tea, and whiskey; and she could 'get enough any day by sending a batch of butter and chicken to market'. They used no wheat, nor sold any of their corn, which, though it appeared a very large quantity, was not more than they required to make their bread and cakes of various kinds, and to feed all their live stock during the winter. She did not look in health, and said they had all had ague [*fever*] in 'the fall'; but she seemed contented and proud of her independence; though it was in somewhat a mournful accent that she said: 'Tis strange to us to see company. I expect the sun may rise and set a hundred times, before I shall see another *human* that does not belong to the family.'

"I have been minute in the description of this forest-farm, as I think it the best specimen I saw of the back-woods independence, of which so much is said in America."

Frances Trollope, *Domestic Manners of the Americans*

iconography, the plow, provides a good example of the pace of **change in farm technology.**

Although plows had been used for centuries, the process of plowing remained one of the most physically demanding and skilled jobs on a farm. The common plow of the 1820s consisted of a wooden moldboard and a wrought-iron plowshare attached to a simple wooden beam with handles that the farmer grasped as he shouted commands to a team of oxen or horses pulling the device. By the 1830s, the wrought-iron plows made by local blacksmiths began to give way to cast-iron plows with standardized parts, produced in large quantities in foundries from Worcester, Massachusetts, to Pittsburgh. Although simple, cheap, and easily repaired, cast-iron plows nonetheless had shortcomings. Cutting a straight furrow proved difficult under any circumstances. Worse, plowmen had to stop constantly and back up in order to scrape away sod that stuck to the iron blade and wooden moldboard. Made from a relatively brittle metal, cast-iron plowshares (the cutting part) frequently broke in tough soils, and they proved all but unusable on the heavy, damp prairie soils of the Midwest.

Inventors sought to develop improved plows, but not until the late 1830s did one appear that made a significant difference. First introduced in Illinois by John Deere and several competitors, the new plow replaced the wooden moldboard with one of wrought iron with a hardened steel cutting edge.

Unlike most early manufacturers, Cyrus H. McCormick excelled at marketing his product. Here, a company advertisement recreates McCormick's first demonstration of his horse-drawn reaper in 1831.

It became known as the "singing plow" because it made an audible vibration as it cut through (or scoured) the soil and delivered the furrow without any need to clean the blade. With this new steel plow, an average farmer could go from plowing eight acres a season to plowing as many as eighty. The new problem was how to increase the speed and capacity for harvesting crops.

The 1830s and 1840s witnessed other advances in the mechanization of farming, the most notable being the development of horse-drawn reaping machines for harvesting grain. Although all the elements of a successful mechanical reaper for cutting and bundling wheat existed in England by 1820, more than two decades elapsed before two Americans—Cyrus H. McCormick and Obed Hussey—working independently of each other, came up with competing reaper designs that actually worked. Of the two inventors, McCormick achieved more commercial success, primarily because he continued to improve his machine and developed an innovative marketing strategy that included advertising, trade-in allowances for older models, flexible payment plans, and fast service for breakdowns. In 1848, McCormick chose to build his factory in Chicago because it was not only located in the midst of the Ameri-

Harvest time on Ralph Wheelock's farm in Southbridge, Massachusetts, c. 1822. The harvesting was done by men, women, and children wielding sickles, rakes, and pitchforks. In this instance, the crop appears to be wheat, which was cut, piled, and bound for carriage to the barn floor, where it was winnowed to separate the wheat from the chaff. The wheat kernels were then bagged and taken to a local gristmill to be ground into flour.

can wheat belt but also emerging as a key railroad hub that served as one of the gateways to the West. Like John Deere, McCormick prospered, and both companies went on to rank among the largest and most successful agricultural equipment makers in the world.

As important as the innovations of Deere and McCormick were, the mechanization of American farming nonetheless proved to be a long-term process. Before the Civil War, most farmers simply could not afford to buy expensive farm equipment other than the all-essential plow and perhaps a harrow for breaking up freshly plowed soil. That would change during the war years as labor shortages and higher prices for farm products prompted more farmers to acquire reapers, mowers, and other labor-saving equipment. Yet even then, the vast majority of small farmers continued to plant, cultivate, and harvest their crops primarily by hand, and would do so well into the twentieth century.

THE PROCESSING OF FOOD

Like the mechanization of farming, the application of scientific knowledge to agriculture also proceeded slowly. In the eighteenth century, a number of "gentlemen farmers" like George Washington and Thomas Jefferson kept abreast of developments in Europe by joining agricultural societies and corresponding with leading agricultural reformers. They also experimented with new seed varieties, practiced crop rotation, and imported purebred animals, such as Merino sheep. But such farmers were a small minority. By and large, farmers remained ignorant of "scientific agriculture," even though important discoveries in soil chemistry during the 1840s pointed to the importance of using fertilizers and rotating crops.

Food processing picked up speed before the Civil War. The fully automated mills that Oliver Evans had developed during the mid-1780s for grinding grains into flour (see Chapter 6) evolved into large commercial mills that could

be found throughout the United States in the 1820s. Rice milling developed along similar lines, with enterprising South Carolina planters, anxious to reduce losses caused by erratic hand-processing methods, adapting Evans's automated methods to the shelling, cleaning, polishing, and packing of rice.

In most parts of the country prior to the Civil War, long before refrigeration, the meat trade centered on small, locally owned slaughterhouses that served local customers with fresh, smoked, pickled, and salted pork, mutton, and beef. The one major exception was Cincinnati, which emerged during the 1830s as the largest pork-packing center in North America. Two factors established Cincinnati's reputation as "Porkopolis." One was its location on the Ohio River, with access both upstream and down to large markets and plentiful sources of hogs. The other was the development of an in-

Cutaway view of Oliver Evans's patented automated mill for grinding and processing wheat and other grains. Powered by a water wheel, Evans's mill consisted of a series of hoppers, grinding wheels, and screens connected to one another by Archimedean screws (for moving the grain in a horizontal plane) and bucket chains (for moving it in a vertical direction). Thus, the man standing in the wagon on the right simply dumps his sacks of grain into a receiving hopper (2), where it is weighed and then moved without human intervention through the automated machinery until finished flour comes out at the other end of the mill in barrels ready for shipment.

An early view of pigs being slaughtered by hand. By the 1860s, meatpackers in Cincinnati and Chicago were hanging gutted pigs from hooks attached to pulleys running on overhead rails, so that the carcasses could be moved systematically from one butcher to another for the removal of various body parts. Such disassembly procedures would later influence Henry Ford's development of the moving assembly line for automobiles.

genious disassembly system of butchering. The process began with the dead hogs hung face down from hooks attached to a large rotating horizontal wheel suspended from the ceiling of the plant. Apprentice butchers then cleaned, gutted, and delivered the carcasses to adjacent tables, where master butchers severed the heads and feet and cut up the remains into hams, shoulders, and sides. These were further divided into smaller cuts and graded before being taken to the packing rooms to be smoked, pickled, and salted before shipment.

Over the years, Cincinnati's meat packers also became proficient in making use of what had been waste products. Pig bristles became brushes; bones, hooves, and other body parts were made into glue; and lard was rendered from discarded pig heads, feet, backbones, ribs, and fatty material. Procter and Gamble, the internationally known twentieth-century company, originated in Cincinnati when William Procter, a candle maker, and James Gamble, a soap maker, formed a partnership in 1837 to manufacture Neat's foot oil from pigs' feet and soap from the vast quantities of lard that came from local slaughterhouses. The factory system had come to agriculture.

Even small farmers felt the effects of the factory system. Farmers who contracted with large processing firms to de-

liver livestock, grain, fruits, vegetables, and raw milk became enmeshed in a time- (and profit-) oriented system as they pressed to meet schedules and avoid late-delivery penalties. Farm machinery was introduced not only to save labor but also to bring greater regularity and uniformity to planting, cultivating, and harvesting. Agricultural reformers who called for the adoption of purebred animals did so primarily because they sought to achieve higher yields and better standards of quality. By the 1850s, American agriculture was being significantly influenced by the policies of the rapidly growing manufacturing and transportation industries, especially the railroads. Although no one realized it at the time, the stage was being set for the scaling up and ultimately the incorporation of agriculture. In the long run, the new agricultural regime would spell the end of the small family farm.

The Peculiar Institution

In the antebellum years, no region of the United States was more oriented toward agriculture than the South. Indeed, agriculture thrived there almost to the exclusion of everything else. Other than New Orleans, the South had no large cities to compare with those in the North. And relatively little mechanized manufacturing existed in the region. As late as 1860, for example, only the Tredegar Iron Works in Richmond, Virginia, boasted foundry facilities equal to "best practice" firms located in the North. Even then, the Tredegar Works—and most southern manufacturing and agricultural processing firms generally—relied largely on New England, mid-Atlantic, and Ohio Valley machine shops for their basic operating equipment. The same was true of southern railroads. Although cotton textile factories could be found throughout the South, their size paled in comparison with those in the North. Massachusetts alone possessed more cotton mills in 1860 than did all eleven southern states that eventually formed the Confederacy.

Yet owing primarily to the soaring industrial demand for raw cotton, the southern economy prospered during the antebellum period. The region's per capita income ranked fourth in the world in 1860, ahead of France, Germany, Russia, and Denmark and behind only Australia, England, and the northern United States. The cotton crop had exploded eightfold from 335,000 bales in 1820 to 2,799,000 bales in 1850, and then nearly doubled to an all-time pre–Civil War high of 5,387,000 bales in 1859. Throughout the antebellum period, cotton not only represented America's largest single foreign export, it also dwarfed all other exports in dollar value. As one Louisiana planter noted, cotton growers were making "oceans of money," and the largest of them ranked among the wealthiest individuals in America. As many white southerners proclaimed, "Cotton is King!"

Southern prosperity rested on the backs of black slaves. And by the mid–nineteenth century, the emancipation movement that began in the North during the revolutionary period had completed its work, eliminating black chattel slavery altogether above the Mason-Dixon line and making slavery a southern institution. Known among southerners as the "peculiar institution," slavery expanded rapidly during the early nineteenth century as the cotton culture pressed in from the Atlantic coast first to inland South Carolina and Georgia, and then to new states farther west and south. In 1790, the national census reported just under 700,000 slaves in the United States, the vast majority of whom lived in the South. By 1810, their numbers had increased by more than 70 percent to almost 1.2 million, and by 1860 they had more than tripled again to nearly 4 million. New arrivals accounted for only a tiny part of that number: in 1808, Congress passed legislation to outlaw further imports of slaves, although international slave traders continued to smuggle small numbers of slaves into the South. The rapid expansion of the slave population came, for the most part, from natural increase.

In 1860, slaves constituted roughly one-third of the South's 12.3 million population. Some parts of the South had heavier concentrations than others. In border states like Delaware, Maryland, and Missouri, for example, their numbers were far smaller than in South Carolina and Mississippi, where slaves outnumbered whites; and in Georgia, Alabama, Louisiana, and Florida, they approached 45 percent of the population. Slaves were concentrated in the deep South because that's where cotton, rice, and sugar were grown. As the demand for slaves grew in response to the expansion of cotton cultivation, older states like Virginia became important sources of supply for the prospering do-

mestic slave trade. Slave trading became one of Virginia's largest income producers after the War of 1812.

While slaves could be found in such occupations as domestic servants, skilled craftsmen, and industrial workers, the majority worked as field hands. Three types of farming existed in the antebellum South. Most numerous were small farmers who were too poor to own slaves and lived off the land primarily to support themselves. Next came middle-class farmers who owned larger spreads and often grew cotton as a cash crop to supplement the usual run of corn, oats, hogs, and livestock. Depending on the extent of their holdings, members of this group might own anywhere from one or two to forty or fifty slaves. However, not all of them grew cotton. In Kentucky, for example, farmers employed slaves to grow hemp as a cash crop, while their counterparts in Virginia and North Carolina focused mainly on tobacco. In the great Valley of Virginia, moreover, wheat became a favored cash crop, while some enterprising slaveholders combined farming with the production of iron for commercial sale.

Large plantations made up the third and most visible type of southern agriculture. Varying in size from hundreds to tens of thousands of acres and owned by a small but politically powerful planter elite (some 10,000 families), they commanded 50 or more slaves. The largest of these estates were located in the deep South, and most, though not all, grew

A cotton plantation, probably in Louisiana, c. 1850–65.

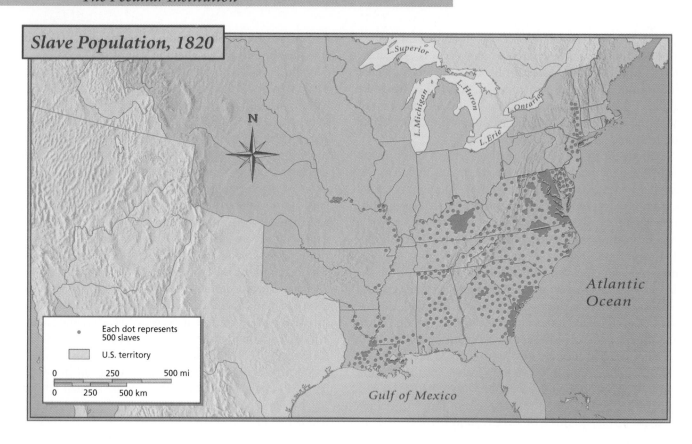

Slave Population, 1820

Each dot represents 500 slaves

U.S. territory

0   250   500 mi

0   250   500 km

Atlantic Ocean

Gulf of Mexico

cotton. Of the eighty-eight planters who owned more than 300 slaves in 1860, for example, twenty-nine grew rice, among them the one individual in the South who owned more than 1,000 slaves. Altogether a quarter of the slave population lived on large estates consisting of 50 or more slaves; half lived on medium-size plantations of 10–49 slaves; and the remainder lived on farms of 1–9 slaves. Most slaves lived on moderately sized estates that grew cotton as a cash crop. Slave ownership not only represented an enormous capital investment but also indicated social status in the white community. As one southerner put it, "A Man's merit in this Country, is estimated according to the number of Negroes he works in the field."

MASTERS AND SLAVES

On some plantations, including those technically advanced rice plantations along the Atlantic coast, masters would sometimes absent themselves from the premises and might even leave slaves in charge of the operation. There, the old task system of colonial days survived for a time: slaves, who were often highly skilled, had to perform a set amount of work per day, and then their time was their own. That system gave slaves an incentive to perform their assigned tasks even in the absence of white supervision. By contrast, owners generally lived on the new upland plantations that grew cotton, and so could supervise and discipline slaves. There a gang system of labor took hold that allowed slaves little free time—and, in its early years, caused considerable tension in the master-slave relationship.

The system of gang labor functioned in various ways. On farms and plantations with fewer than ten slaves, owners tended to work alongside their slaves and to superintend them directly. On those with more than ten but less than thirty slaves, masters seldom worked in the fields except at harvest time. In both cases, however, owners knew their slaves by name and interacted with them personally. Slaves on such modest-sized plantations were rarely specialized: they had several different work assignments and experienced relatively little regimentation. Still, their workday

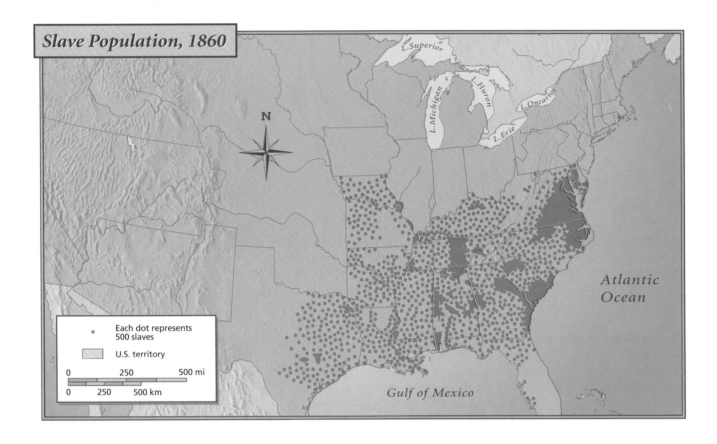

Slave Population, 1860

Each dot represents 500 slaves

U.S. territory

0   250   500 mi

0   250   500 km

L. Superior
L. Michigan
L. Huron
L. Ontario
L. Erie

Atlantic Ocean

Gulf of Mexico

N

lasted from sunrise to sunset and included few sanctioned breaks in between.

On large plantations with fifty or more slaves, conditions were more rigid. Masters might periodically inspect the fields, but they rarely if ever supervised or directly participated in the work. Instead, they hired white overseers to take charge of the plantation workforce. The overseer, in turn, divided the slaves into gangs, each headed by a "driver" who supervised work in the fields and, more often than not, was an older slave in whom the overseer placed some modicum of trust.

In the summer of 1854, a traveler in Mississippi described a slave gang as it returned from the field after a day's labor. "First came, led by an old driver carrying a whip, forty of the largest and strongest women I ever saw together; they were all in a simple uniform dress of a bluish check stuff, the skirts reaching little below the knee; their legs and feet were bare; they carried themselves loftily, each having a hoe over the shoulder, and walking with a free, powerful swing, like chasseurs [light infantry] on the march." Next came plow hands leading their mules, "the cavalry, thirty strong, mostly men,

but a few of them women. . . . A lean and vigilant white overseer, on a brisk pony, brought up the rear."

This description conveys the degree of organization and specialization that characterized slave labor forces on large plantations. A sense of military regimentation in the description of the women in uniform dress with hoes slung over their shoulders is typical: plantation masters and agricultural writers throughout the South frequently used military and factory metaphors to describe the ideal type of plantation that owners sought to run. When a reporter for a leading southern agricultural journal visited the enormous 20,000-acre Louisiana plantation of Colonel J. A. S. Acklen in 1852, he noted that the vast operation was divided into six plantations with six overseers, a general agent, a bookkeeper, two physicians, a master carpenter, a tinsmith, and a preacher—all of them white males. "Every thing," the writer stressed, "moves on systematically, and with the discipline of a regular trained army."

Another article in the same journal argued that "a plantation might be considered as a piece of machinery; to operate successfully, all of its parts should be uniform and exact, and

An 1842 drawing entitled "Hauling the Whole Week's Picking" suggests that small children as well as adult slaves went to the fields at harvest time.

the impelling force regular and steady." That these ideas penetrated directly into the daily operations of large plantations is readily apparent from the published accounts of work regimens at numerous sites. In each instance, the chain of command from master to overseer to drivers to field hands closely resembled the system found in both the military and private industry.

 Few, if any, plantations actually ran with clockwork precision. The real world of **chattel slavery** rested on a regimen of forced labor that revealed all sorts of tensions, evasions, compromises, and confrontations. To be sure, many masters sought to encourage their slaves by rewarding them for work well done. Incentives included garden plots (from which they could keep or sell what produce they raised), permission to raise chickens and, occasionally, hogs or a cow, extra holidays, and special privileges such as passes that allowed them to travel to nearby plantations and towns to visit friends and relatives. Some masters established work quotas for their labor gangs; anything done beyond the required amount resulted either in cash payments or, more often, credit at the plantation store. Others went so far as to establish profit-sharing agreements, such as the Louisiana sugar planter who paid his slaves a dollar for each hogshead (large barrel) of sugar they prepared. In one instance, a Virginia ironmaster even permitted his most valued slave to open a savings account at a local bank for the astonishing amount of $100. Such practices, another Virginian noted, served as "a powerful lever . . . to enforce obedience and fidelity."

But behind the carrot always loomed the stick. Every aspect of a slave's life was circumscribed by rules that dictated when to get up in the morning, when to eat, when to go to work, how to do the work, when to take breaks, when to quit, and when to go to bed. Rules also governed activities that lay be-

A slave gang hoeing on a plantation with the driver and overseer, whips in hand, looking on (1839).

yond the immediate realm of work, such as hunting, fishing, keeping garden plots, obtaining permission to get married, selling or trading goods, and leaving the plantation premises for whatever reason. Such rules, which were enforced according to the whims of the masters, supplemented state laws that prohibited slaves from learning to read or write, conducting public assemblies of any sort, possessing liquor or firearms, hiring themselves out, or moving about without a pass from their owner. Like plantation rules, the state "slave codes" aimed at subordinating slaves to white authority, although they tended to be inconsistently enforced.

Slaves who transgressed the rules could expect to be punished. Some masters refused to discipline them with physical force. If slaves broke the rules, they were denied certain privileges. If they persisted in unruly behavior, the ultimate—though reluctantly reached—solution was to turn them over to a slave trader to be sold. Most slaveholders, however, did not agree with this "persuasion doctrine," nor did they believe in unrestrained brutality. Instead, they adopted a paternalistic approach that viewed slaves as children who needed the threat as well as the occasional application of disciplinary measures in order to assure good order and correct behavior.

Depending on the temperament of the owner and the seriousness of the offense, slave punishments could entail public humiliations (like making men wear women's clothing and do women's work) or confiscating garden crops and livestock and reducing their rations. Slaves could be put in stocks, confined with iron-pronged collars on their necks, or branded and mutilated. The most-used method of punishment proved to be the whip, the ultimate symbol of the master's power. On large plantations that employed overseers, masters often prescribed the number of lashes for each offense. "The highest punishment," a Georgia planter-politician wrote in his plantation manual, "must not exceed 100 lashes in one day and to that extent only in extreme cases. . . . In general, 15 to 20 lashes will be a sufficient flogging." Other planters devised other strategies. "Had to administer a little rod to Bob this morning," a Virginian noted in his diary. "Have seen for more than three months [that] I should have to humble him some, hope it may benefit him." Another Virginian agreed. "A great deal of whipping is not necessary," he wrote; "*some* is."

Floggings, more often than not, were communal affairs intended to intimidate those who witnessed the event as well as

> *"The most-used method of punishment proved to be the whip."*

punish the person being whipped. The severity of punishment depended on the type of whip being used. Slaveholders who wished to make an impression but not seriously injure the person used a "stout flexible stalk" covered with leather that had a thin "buckskin cracker" attached to it; this whip, according to one observer, made "a very loud report, and stings, or 'burns' the skin smartly, but does not bruise it." Slaveholders ordinarily avoided the use of shorter and thicker rawhide whips because they severely lacerated the skin, which besides being life threatening left disfiguring scars that lowered a slave's market value. Still, many a slave—both men and women—could be found with "large raised scars or whelks" four to six inches in length on their shoulders, buttocks, and lower backs. After flogging a slave, particularly brutal masters and overseers would pour brine on the wounds to increase the painful effects. Whether or not they were on the receiving end of a whip, people who witnessed a flogging never forgot its excruciating physical and psychological effects.

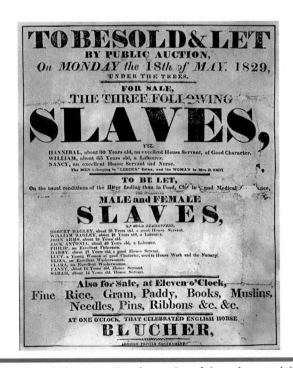

An 1829 broadside announcing the auction of three slaves and the rental of eleven others (five females, six males), along with the sale of "that celebrated English horse Blucher."

A slave auction house in Atlanta, c. 1865.

Slaves also lived in perpetual fear of being sold and separated from their families and friends. Any number of circumstances—personal pique, financial need, the settlement of an estate after a master's death—could result in a slave's being sold. During the half century before the Civil War, hundreds of thousands of slaves from the upper South were sold "down river" to cotton-producing states in the deep South. "All the time we would see 'nigger traders' coming through the country," a former slave recalled. "I have seen men and women cuffed to 60-foot chains being took to Lynchburg, Va., to the block to be sold." "On New Year's day we all were scared," another remembered. "That was the time for selling, buying, and trading slaves. We did not know who was to go or come."

Masters interfered with the lives of their slaves in many other ways. Some insisted on naming slave children. Others, who considered religion a stabilizing force, would assemble their slaves for Bible readings and to hear white preachers, yet forbade them to conduct their own religious services. Still others demanded that slave couples secure their permission before getting married and punished those who sought a divorce or engaged in extramarital affairs. Yet often the very masters who demanded moral rectitude of their slaves forced themselves on slave women. "How many have fallen before this temptation!" a Virginian wrote in disgust. "So many that it has almost ceased to be a temptation to fall!"

RELIGION AND FAMILY LIFE OF SLAVES

The slave quarter was far enough away from the "big house" that slaves were able to find some measure of privacy and interact with one another more or less on their own terms. There, people did everything from eating and sleeping to fighting, praying, and making love. Two activities in particular—religion and family life—proved especially important in shaping the slave's inner world. Most masters approved of them because they saw them as stabilizing influences on the slave population.

Although some of the largest plantations retained white preachers on their staffs, most slaves "got religion" by hearing the Christian gospels read to them by their masters, responding to calls from itinerant white missionaries, and attending Sunday services at white churches with white congregations. Slaves gravitated more to the evangelical, and often highly emotional, services of Baptists and Methodists than to the more reserved Episcopalians and Presbyterians. Even then, slaves remained leery about sermons they heard from white ministers that emphasized the virtue of obedience. "Dat ole white preacher," a former slave recalled, "jest was telling us slaves to be good to our masters. We ain't keer'd a bit 'bout dat stuff he was talling us 'cause we wanted to sing, pray, and serve God in our own way."

The desire to serve God in their own way led to the development of a new religious tradition in the slave community that blended elements of white evangelical Christianity and African culture. What ultimately emerged was a distinctive African American style of Christianity that took evangelical religion to a new level of intensity while substituting themes of oppression and deliverance for the slaveholder's theology of obedience and trust. Subtle expressions of protest against enslavement were embedded in the sermons of self-styled (and mostly illiterate) black preachers and in the songs that slave congregations sang. The Old Testament story of Moses delivering his people from bondage proved particularly meaningful, as did deeply moving **spirituals** like "Nobody Knows the Trouble I've Seen" and "Lord Keep Me from Sinking Down." Whether sermons and songs expressed lament at the slave's deplorable condition or joy in the knowledge that salvation awaited every person, the new religion provided slaves with a spiritual life that transcended the drudgery and pain of their daily toils and gave hope that better times were coming.

If religion provided hope and consolation, family life proved a fragile buffer against the daily abuses of slavery. Although masters encouraged their slaves to marry and have children, slave marriages had no legal standing because these people were property, not citizens. Married slaves faced the constant threat of being separated either by sale or, if the couple were owned by different masters, by a move. Other intrusions, particularly the unwanted sexual advances of white masters and overseers, further complicated slave marriages. Yet family life persisted and even flourished.

Slave housing was crude by any standard. The usual family accommodation consisted of a one-room log structure measuring sixteen by eighteen feet with an unfinished interior. On prosperous plantations, better units housed single families of three to seven people and had stone chimneys and plank floors. On poorer plantations, however, living conditions could be far more spartan and crowded. Many cabins had no chimneys and rested on dirt floors.

With their husbands often owned by other masters and residing elsewhere, the task of nurturing and raising children fell primarily to the women. Always eager to increase the number of slaves they owned, white masters expected slave women to have plenty of children—the more the better. Motherhood conferred status within the slave community and heightened a woman's monetary value to the master. Barren women were disparaged, made to work harder, and often sold off. Compared with male slaves, whose value fell with age and declining physical stamina, women generally maintained their value into their elderly years by working as house servants, cooks, midwives, seamstresses, or weavers. By and large, slave women led trying lives that saw their husbands and children mistreated and degraded before their eyes, and themselves victimized by hard work, physical violence, and sexual exploitation.

Slaves received annual allocations of clothing consisting of a "winter issue" and a "summer issue." For men, the winter issue included heavy pants, a shirt, a coat, socks, a pair of shoes, and a blanket. Summer clothing consisted of a lighter pair of pants, a shirt, and a second pair of shoes. Women received several dresses, petticoats, a blanket, and two pairs of shoes, while children were given long shirts but little else. The

> *"If religion provided hope and consolation, family life proved a fragile buffer against the daily abuses of slavery."*

shoes usually fit so poorly that often slaves chose to go without them. One trick was to wade in water with the new shoes on so that the leather would soften and subsequently dry to better conform to the person's foot. Though some clothing consisted of homespun cloth spun by slave women, more was made from "Negro cloth"—coarse but sturdy denim-like fabrics made in northern textile mills. Slaves often supplemented their owner-distributed clothing with fancier fabrics acquired either by trading for them at the plantation store or, if permitted, buying them from local merchants with what little savings they may have accumulated.

Although far from excellent by twentieth-century standards, the typical slave diet was relatively healthy. In addition to their usual rations of cornmeal and pork (or bacon), slaves supplemented their diets with vegetables and chickens grown in their garden patches and wildlife taken by fishing, trapping, or hunting. Luxury items such as sugar, salt, and coffee were sometimes distributed by owners and sometimes obtained at the plantation store in exchange for produce. There is evidence that the general health of adult slaves was probably no worse than that of many southern whites. The death rate among slaves was slightly higher than for whites. Infant mortality rates among slaves proved much higher, however, mainly because slave

This African American dance was drawn by artist Lewis Miller during a trip to Virginia in 1853. The banjo and bones are African instruments, while the fiddle is European.

387

women were forced to work up to the moment of giving birth and forced back to work too soon afterward. Slaves succumbed to the same diseases as whites, although, owing to the sickle-cell trait, they suffered less from malaria. On the other hand, they suffered more from pulmonary disease, cholera, tetanus, and other common diseases. Because they were considered valuable investments, they received more medical attention than did most southern whites, who rarely if ever visited a physician. Given the primitive state of medical knowledge before the Civil War, though, that may have been more of a disadvantage.

SLAVE RESISTANCE

As slave parents struggled to endure, they did the best they could to raise their children in a loving environment and to pass on certain customs and values that would serve them well in later life. Since the vast majority of slaves could not read or write, children learned mainly through verbal instruction. Storytelling and songs proved important not only in conveying moral values and religious beliefs but also in describing the outside world and offering practical advice about how to interact with whites. So-called trickster tales, like the story of "Br'er Rabbit," were filled with charming characters and great humor yet at the same time conveyed lessons about the need for quick-wittedness, wariness, and even deceit when dealing with whites. Such tales often parodied white society, holding its double standards, hypocrisy, and injustices up to ridicule. They revealed a spirit of protest that often eluded the white community and, in doing so, gave slaves a degree of satisfaction.

In addition to trickster tales, plaintive songs, and other forms of passive protest, slaves found additional ways to resist their masters. The most common included everyday acts of noncooperation and "silent sabotage" such as pretending to misunderstand orders, working carelessly or at a slow pace, "accidentally" breaking tools, feigning illness, stealing, mistreating animals, and, in extreme cases, setting buildings on fire. While some slaveholders attributed such acts to inherent laziness and stupidity, others considered them nothing but sheer "rascality." A northerner observing a gang of slaves on a South Carolina plantation noted that the overseer was "constantly directing and encouraging them, but . . . as often as he

"The most common forms of resistance included everyday acts of noncooperation and 'silent sabotage.' "

visited one end of the line of operations, the hands at the other end would discontinue their labor, until he turned to ride towards them again." "Hands won't work unless I am in sight," a Virginia planter wrote in anger and exasperation. "I left the Field at 12 [with] all going well, but very little done after."

Despite their servile condition, slaves exercised a degree of leverage over their masters that allowed them some leeway in what they would do and how and when they would do it. Plantation records are filled with notations about slaves who "took off work" during the heat of summer or "went away" to fish, hunt, or simply to "play" for days at a time without being punished. In the eyes of masters, slaves of both sexes frequently feigned illness in order to get off work. Such was the case in 1859, when a Valley of Virginia ironmaster noted in his journal that three skilled forge hands, one of whom was appropriately named Tooler, stayed away from work for several days because of illness. When Tooler failed to return the following Monday, the owner wrote, "Tooler sick, *Hum.*" When Tooler remained out the rest of the week, he simply entered "loafing" under the slave's name but evidently did nothing about it. The master was dependent on his artisans and could not risk more serious disruptions for fear of closing down the ironworks altogether and facing even greater monetary losses.

Running away and outright resistance constituted more direct challenges to the slave master's authority, and resistance occurred far more frequently than most slave owners wished to admit. Although premeditated murders and other acts of slave violence sometimes took place, most confrontations involved spur-of-the-moment blowups in which an angry slave reacted to some intolerable situation such as persistent browbeating or repeated whippings. Because harsh words and blows were often exchanged, slaves who confronted masters or overseers often took flight immediately afterward in order to avoid punishments administered in a fit of rage. More often than not, they returned on their own after a day or so once tempers had cooled and the likelihood of brutal retaliation had diminished.

The decision to run away permanently took some serious planning. More men than women ran away, and more from the upper South than the deep South, which was hundreds of miles from free territory. The journey from slavery to freedom required resourcefulness and a great deal of luck. Most fugitives made their way north on their own. Once they reached the border areas between free and slave states, sympathetic blacks and whites sometimes fed and sheltered them and conducted them to other safe havens. Such individuals became collectively known as the "Underground Railroad," but their operations were much less systematic than the railroad analogy suggests. Even with the help of antislavery sympathizers, a fugitive's likelihood of success remained slim. In addition to paid slave catchers hired by owners, white "slave patrols" roamed every southern state pursuing runaways and stopping suspicious blacks and demanding to see their owner-issued travel permits. Capture by a slave patrol was one of the worst things that could happen to a fugitive, because, unlike the owner or paid slave catcher who had a financial stake in the slave's condition, the patrol couldn't care less whether they returned the subject dead or alive.

With shorter distances to travel, runaway slaves from border areas like Maryland or Kentucky stood a better chance of success. Still, escaped slaves had to be constantly on guard for fear of being betrayed in exchange for a slave catcher's reward. Such concerns extended to fellow blacks, for, as one es-

American Journal

What's for Dinner?

The escaped slave and abolitionist leader Frederick Douglass published several autobiographical accounts of his experience as a slave on the plantation of Colonel Edward Lloyd in eastern Maryland. The following describes the slave diet, which consisted mainly of ground corn, pork scraps, and locally caught fish, like herring. Elsewhere in his writings, Douglass noted that slaves supplemented this sparse diet by fishing, hunting, and tending small garden plots whenever time allowed.

"As a general rule, slaves do not come to the quarters for either breakfast or dinner, but take their 'ash cake' with them, and eat it in the field. This was so on the home plantation; probably, because the distance from the quarter to the field, was sometimes two, and even three miles.

"The dinner of the slaves consisted of a huge piece of ash cake, and a small piece of pork, or two salt herrings. Not having ovens, nor any suitable cooking utensils, the slaves mixed their meal with a little water, to such thickness that a spoon would stand erect in it; and, after the wood had burned away to coals and ashes, they would place the dough between oak leaves and lay it carefully in the ashes, completely covering it; hence, the bread is called ash cake. The surface of this peculiar bread is covered with ashes, to the depth of a sixteenth part of an inch, and the ashes, certainly, do not make it very grateful to the teeth, nor render it very palatable. The bran, or coarse part of the meal, is baked with the fine, and bright scales run through the bread. This bread, with its ashes and bran, would disgust and choke a northern man, but it is quite liked by the slaves. They eat it with avidity, and are more concerned about the quantity than about the quality. They are far too scantily provided for, and are worked too steadily, to be much concerned for the quality of their food. The few minutes allowed them at dinner time, after partaking of their coarse repast, are variously spent. Some lie down on the 'turning row,' and go to sleep; others draw together, and talk; and others are at work with needle and thread, mending their tattered garments. Sometimes you may hear a wild, hoarse laugh arise from a circle, and often a song. Soon, however, the overseer comes dashing through the field. *'Tumble up! Tumble up, and to work, work,'* is the cry; and, now, from twelve o'clock (mid-day) till dark, the human cattle are in motion, wielding their clumsy hoes; hurried on by no hope of reward, no sense of gratitude, no love of children, no prospect of bettering their condition; nothing, save the dread and terror of the slave-driver's lash. So goes one day, and so comes and goes another."

Frederick Douglass, *My Bondage and My Freedom*

caped slave put it, "twenty-one years in slavery had taught me that there were traitors even among colored people." And once a fugitive entered free territory, there were no guarantees of work. Racism was rampant throughout the North as well as the South. Former slaves were sometimes even driven out of town. Yet even against these daunting odds, tens of thousands of slaves sought to break their bonds and achieve freedom during the pre–Civil War years. Only about 1,000 a year succeeded.

Slavery, with its environment of suspicion and fear, was the foundation of antebellum southern society. Slaves lived in constant fear of their masters' godlike authority to interfere in every aspect of their lives. Masters, in turn, feared slave recalcitrance, random acts of violence, and the loss of runaways. Even the nearly three-quarters of the South's white population who did not own slaves were touched by the peculiar institution. Slavery was the scaffold of their social status and economic well-being. The desire to keep blacks in their place thus became the cement that held an otherwise segmented society in the South together. "I reckon the majority would be right glad if we could get rid of the niggers," a poor white informed a northern traveler. "But it wouldn't never do to free 'em and leave 'em here. I don't know anybody, hardly, in favor of that. Make 'em free and leave 'em here and they'd steal every thing we made. Nobody couldn't live here then." "From childhood," the same northerner concluded, "the one thing . . . which has made life valuable to the mass of whites has been that the niggers are yet their inferiors." "It is African slavery that makes every white man in some sense a lord," a southern editor asserted, adding, "Color gives caste."

Southern whites' greatest fear was of a massive slave rebellion. Reports of slave conspiracies circulated throughout the South, but only one revolt resulted in widespread violence in the three decades before the Civil War. It occurred in August 1831 and was led by Nat Turner, a slave preacher from Southampton County in southeastern Virginia, who claimed that God had called him to strike down the "Serpent" that held his people in bondage. Convinced that "the first should be last and the last should be first," Turner gathered a small force and initiated his crusade by killing his master as well as the master's family. The rebellion lasted two days and embraced a twenty-mile area of Southampton County. During that time, his seventy-some followers killed fifty-nine whites—men, women, and children—before being routed by a better-

> *"Southern whites' greatest fear was of a massive slave rebellion."*

armed white force consisting of local guards and state militia. In the days that followed, the white community took its vengeance. "Many negroes are killed every day," a local minister wrote, "the exact number will never be known." Although Turner initially eluded his pursuers, he was eventually captured, tried, and hanged. In the end, over one hundred blacks died in Southampton's reign of terror.

Long after Nat Turner went to his grave, the governor of Virginia remained "fully convinced that every black preacher in the whole country east of the Blue Ridge . . . was in" on Turner's "secret." Fear of further uprisings lingered as well. Another Virginian was more explicit. "These insurrections have alarmed my wife so as really to endanger her health," he lamented to an associate in Ohio. "I have not slept without anxiety in three months. . . . There has been and there still is *panic* in all this country. . . . There is no principle of life. Death is autocrat of slave regions." These words suggest, as well as any can, the degree to which southern whites, having constructed the machinery of slavery, had become caught in its very works.

Industrial Labor and the Factory System

Compared with farming, industry represented an altogether new type of labor in early nineteenth-century America. Two characteristics distinguished the factory system as it evolved in the United States: one was its sheer extent, and the other its presence in the countryside. European observers frequently commented on how widespread was the adoption of machinery in the United States. And wherever they traveled, they found the most visible outcroppings of machine-based industry not in cities but in rural areas close to waterfalls. This was so because the earliest mechanical enterprises in the seventeenth and eighteenth centuries—gristmills, sawmills, iron furnaces, iron forges, woolen-fulling (thickening) mills—were closely tied to agriculture and relied exclusively on waterpower. Unlike England, where steam power was widely used by the late eighteenth century, the United States possessed thousands of streams with falls of water capable of driving machinery. Many nineteenth-century factories stood on spots formerly occupied by colonial grist-, fulling, and sawmills. Steamboats and steam railroads carried the great bulk of passengers and freight in early industrial America, but waterwheels drove its factory system. American industry relied on waterpower well into the 1860s. Not until the Civil War did steam power begin to gain ascendancy.

Most small waterpowered mills in early nineteenth-century America generated no more than a few horsepower, and were owned, operated, and often built by local farmers with the assistance of a local carpenter or millwright. Most processed grain and lumber for local customers. Larger mills, numbering in the thousands, focused on manufacturing goods for regional and national markets. Often both types of mill evolved out of local agricultural pursuits. A case in point is E. I. Du Pont de Nemours and Company, a gunpowder manufacturer established on the family farm near Wilmington, Delaware, in 1803. During the nineteenth and early twentieth centuries, it grew into one of the nation's largest corporations.

Rural mills were also the seedbeds of villages and larger communities. A gristmill might cause an original farmstead to expand into a small village with several houses, a general store, blacksmithy, church, and post office. Larger mill complexes often attracted other businesses and, before long, grew into towns. Some, like Lowell, Massachusetts, developed into flourishing industrial cities. In fact, one authority notes that of the nearly 500 townships that existed in the New England states of Connecticut, Massachusetts, and Rhode Island in 1840, "it would have been difficult to find 50 . . . which did not have at least one manufacturing village clustered around a cotton or woolen mill, an iron furnace, or a carriage shop." Although there was a concentration of mill communities in New England and the Middle Atlantic states, the pattern spread across the United States.

More often than not, a mill was a community's largest employer, and mill owners frequently had other business investments in the neighborhood such as general stores, real estate, and residential properties. They helped found

> *"Rural mills were also the seedbeds of villages and larger communities."*

and direct local banks. In local politics, mill owners often urged their employees to support candidates who favored their business interests. In the establishment of local churches and public schools, they served not only as benefactors but also as deacons, vestrymen, and trustees. Most were well aware, as the Lowell textile magnate Patrick Tracy Jackson put it, that "the village steeple is the unfailing companion of the waterwheel." They firmly believed, as did most people, that churches and schools fostered values of virtue, honesty, and thrift that carried over into the workplace. Early factories even looked like churches.

Although their backgrounds varied, mill owners and factory masters were almost exclusively male. One exception was Rebecca Lukens (1794–1854) of Coatesville, Pennsylvania. The daughter and designated heir of a Quaker forge master, the thirty-one-year-old mother of three young daughters suddenly found herself thrust into the business when her physician husband, who managed the family's Brandywine Iron

This lithographic rendering of the Crown and Eagle cotton mills at North Uxbridge, Massachusetts, provides a panoramic view of a small factory village c. 1830, with its worker housing, company store, and requisite mill stream for waterpower. A fine example of the Rhode Island system of small- and medium-size mills influenced by Samuel Slater, the Crown and Eagle contrasts with the much larger mills built by the Boston Associates at Waltham, Lowell, and other northern New England sites.

Although falling water remained the primary source of industrial power up through the end of the Civil War, increasing numbers of factories turned to steam power with the disappearance of good waterpower sites. The Haywood Rubber Company at Colchester, Connecticut, provides an early example (1832) of a manufacturing plant powered solely by steam.

Works, died unexpectedly in 1825. Although friends urged her to dispose of the financially strapped enterprise, Mrs. Lukens, with the help of two brothers-in-law, ran the operation for the next twenty-two years and turned it into a highly profitable operation. When she finally relinquished the business to her sons-in-law in 1847, the waterpowered Lukens rolling mill employed two dozen workers, had been completely rebuilt, and was producing some of the finest iron for steam-engine boilers in America. (Rolling mills, like rolling pins with pie dough, squeeze red-hot iron bars into plates of uniform dimensions.) Under her leadership, the mill had gone from making nails and barrel hoop iron for local customers to making much heavier pieces of rolled iron for a growing national market. The firm's list of customers included two leading locomotive builders, several shipyards, and a number of machine shops and stationary steam engine manufacturers. As an entrepreneur in an age of change, Rebecca Lukens proved more than able.

PROFITS AND PATERNALISM

Early American factories came in all shapes and sizes. They ranged from Lowell's mass-production textile mill complexes with their all-female workers to more modest enterprises like Rebecca Lukens's Brandywine Iron Works. All shared the same fundamental objectives. One was a straightforward economic interest in making a profit. Another was to manufacture a product that would find and hold a niche in the market. A third was to create an environment that would encourage the making of a profitable product—and this objective presented the most formidable challenge to manufacturers, for on it rested the success of the other two. A successful work environment not only involved building and equipping mills and hiring workers, but also establishing the divisions of labor and the rules of conduct governing the employees. To handle their most vexing daily issue, the organization and control of workers, manufacturers resorted to traditional paternalistic practices.

In the context of early American industry, the controlling idea behind paternalism was that workers should show proper deference to their employers and unhesitatingly comply with their commands. There was no room for democracy on the factory floor. Indeed, early factory masters resembled southern plantation owners in the lofty social positions they occupied. Along with impressive property holdings and high social standing, they often held political offices and headed local militia units. A wide circle of people depended on them for jobs, housing, loans, and business patronage. Yet despite these dependencies, life and labor in early industrial communities revealed subtle patterns of reciprocal social relationships.

The Brandywine Iron Works. Let's return to Rebecca Lukens's Brandywine Iron Works. Although this family-owned firm never posted formal work rules, there was no question about who was in command and what was expected. Throughout the nineteenth century, Lukens and her descendants demanded loyalty and respect, if not abject obedience, from their workers. "To manage so large a number of men, many of them much older than thee and who have known thee as a boy will be a nice matter," her daughter counseled a son who had just entered the business. "Many of these men," she continued, "are accustomed to being guided by their passions,

Rebecca Pennock Lukens, a successful ironmaster at a time when women rarely became involved in the business world.

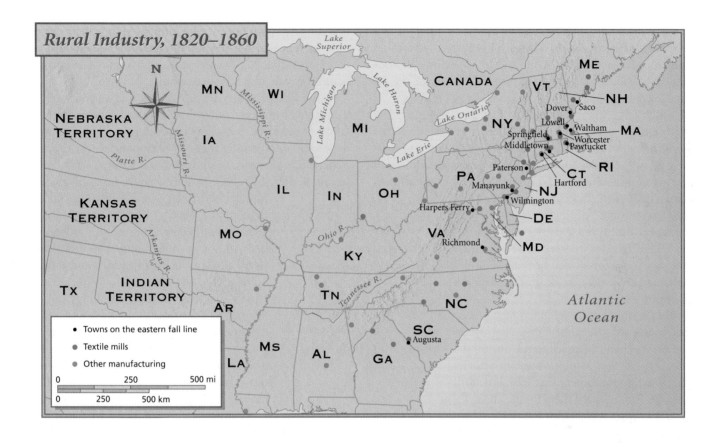

Rural Industry, 1820–1860

- Towns on the eastern fall line
- Textile mills
- Other manufacturing

paying little attention to principle, still these men respect it when they see it and the rule of 'kindness with firmness'—which I have found so efficacious with employees will be a good one for thee."

Kindness with firmness proved efficacious indeed. Few ironworkers failed to live up to the Lukens family's paternalistic code. Those who fell short, after several warnings, were eventually fired and even blacklisted. But in exchange for their labor and loyalty, the workers at Brandywine Iron Works had certain expectations of their bosses. It was understood, for instance, that a forge worker could occasionally ask a comrade to fill in for him and leave work early without incurring the owner's wrath. It also was understood that furnace and forge crews did not have to work on days of excessive summer heat. While the Lukens family frowned on the use of alcohol, workers knew that they would not be fired for occasional drunkenness or misconduct. There seemed to be no stated rule about how many times a person might transgress the owner's authority before he was disciplined or

dismissed. Although these understandings remained vague, they seemed to function well. There is no evidence that the owners ever suddenly fired a worker.

The Lukens brand of paternalism extended workers a safety net as well. Mill workers knew that they would keep their jobs and company-owned housing even during hard times. They counted on the Lukens family to provide them with food, fuel, and other supplies "on account" at reduced prices. The record suggests that the Lukens family ran the rolling mill at no profit during economic downturns in the 1850s and 1860s in order to keep their hands employed and presumably to keep from losing them. On other occasions when the forge was idle, the family put the mill hands to work on its farms. To be sure, hard times for the mill spelled serious hardships for the workers. But on at least two occasions, in 1837 and 1854, workers received bonuses to partially compensate them for the lower wages they had been paid during slack times. From time to time, they even drew wages in advance for work not yet performed.

Women Workers at Lowell. Paternalism wore a different face at Lowell, Massachusetts. There, the Boston Associates sought to govern their mills through more stringently enforced rules and regulations. Lowell specialized in the manufacture of cotton cloth rather than boilerplate, and its mills were much larger than those of the Lukens family. In 1836, Lowell boasted twenty mills with 6,000 workers, while the Lukens operation consisted of one rolling mill with approximately 20 workers. Even more striking was the social makeup of the two communities' working populations. In contrast with Lukens's male workers, 85 percent of Lowell's labor force consisted of single women between the ages of fifteen and twenty-nine. Whereas most of the Lukens workers lived with their families in company-owned housing, Lowell's female workers lived apart from their families in dormitories.

From the outset at Lowell, the Boston Associates continued the policy they had established at Waltham, Massachusetts, during the War of 1812: they equipped their factories with self-acting machinery that took little skill to operate. This allowed them to hire cheap female labor rather than skilled but more expensive and potentially troublesome male workers. To attract a workforce, they had to reassure young women and their families that Lowell was a good place to work. In the words of a New York mill owner, they had "to convince the enemies of domestic manufactures that such establishments are not 'sinks of vice and immorality,' but, on the contrary, nurseries of morality, industry, and intelligence." To the associates, Lowell and its mills were more than a place of labor and production; they constituted a great social experiment, moral gymnasiums where employees would not only earn wages—sometimes saved for dowries—but also experience moral and spiritual growth. The mill owners' emphasis on "moral instruction" fit nicely with their desire to exercise complete control over every aspect of production.

Company regulations required girls to "board in the Company's boarding houses," "attend public worship . . . and to conform strictly to the rules of the Sabbath," and to refrain from "frivolous and useless conversation." In an apt statement of its social vision, one company urged its employees to recognize "that where objects are to be obtained, by the united efforts and labor of many individuals, that some must direct and many be directed. That their religious and political

> *"In 1836, Lowell boasted twenty mills with 6,000 workers; 85 percent of Lowell's labor force consisted of single women between the ages of fifteen and twenty-nine."*

opinions need not however be influenced, nor their personal independence, or self-respect, or conscious equality lost sight of or abandoned." These last words would come back to haunt the company a few years later.

Besides their factory work rules, Lowell's textile corporations sought to weave other threads into the moral fiber of its female labor force. Boardinghouse tenants, another company declared, "will consider themselves responsible for the order, punctuality of meals, cleanliness, and general arrangements for rendering their houses comfortable, tranquil scenes of moral deportment, and mutual good will." Echoing the factory rules, the house rules also admonished against the use of "ardent spirits." An honor code bound all boarders to report "all cases of intemperance and dissolute manners" to the company's agent. Other offenses included Sabbath-breaking and foul language. In the interest of self-denial and discipline, boardinghouses were to close their doors every evening at ten o'clock. "We must give up some portion of what may be deemed our privileges, for the sake of enjoying the remainder in greater purity," the company's agent explained. As much as visitors admired the spirit of moral vigilance and hard work that pervaded Lowell, there is no denying that company regulations completely circumscribed the workers' world. Former mill girls frequently remi-

The Middlesex Company Woolen Mills in Lowell, c. 1848. Although the company manufactured woolen goods, the mill complex closely resembled the majority of other Lowell mills, which focused on cotton textiles.

nisced about the "pleasant life" they had experienced while working in Lowell, but they also acknowledged that the powerful corporations could be oppressive.

Despite its awesome economic success, Lowell's tight social fabric began to fray by the mid-1830s, when feverish expansion gripped the textile industry. In the Northeast alone, hundreds of firms sprang up hoping to capture lucrative markets for cotton goods in the South, the West, the Caribbean, and various U.S. cities. As competition increased and technological improvements expanded the capacity of textile machinery, prices and profits began to fall. At the same time, the gradual sale of their stock holdings by aging members of the Boston Associates led to a more broadly based ownership that seemed intent on maintaining the

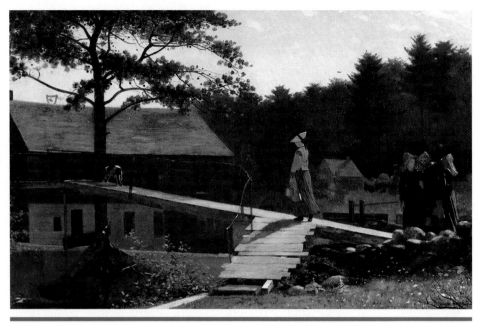

Winslow Homer's *The Morning Bell* (1872) provides an idyllic view of mill girls on their way to work in a New England textile factory.

same profit margins as in earlier days. Caught in a competitive spiral, Lowell companies and others like them in New Hampshire, Maine, and Massachusetts began to adopt cost-cutting measures, the brunt of which fell on their workers. The managers at Lowell installed new and faster machinery, speeded up the pace of machinery, stretched out workloads by assigning additional machines to mill girls, and lowered the piece rates (rates paid for work done by the piece). Within a few years, output per worker nearly doubled, while wages increased only slightly.

The first sign of trouble at Lowell occurred in February 1834, when 800 women walked off their jobs to protest a 12.5 percent wage reduction. Although the strikers comprised less than one-sixth of Lowell's labor force and the incident lasted only a few days, emotions ran high. Reflecting tensions of gender and power in the community, male factory agents condemned the protest as an "amizonian [sic] display," arguing that the strikers were both unfeminine and ungrateful. The female workers, on the other hand, felt wronged by the mill owners' high-handed treatment as well as by the "unjust and unreasonable" cut in their wages. In the end, the strike failed, but the workers found some solace in the fact that they had reminded the "purse proud ARISTOCRATS" that they were equal in birthright if not in economic power.

Another strike took place in 1836, this time in response to mill owners' raising the price for room and board at boardinghouses. This action involved more workers (some 1,500 to 2,000) than the earlier strike, and succeeded in getting the companies to rescind their charges. The victory nonetheless proved fleeting. In 1837 and again in 1840, Lowell's mill women experienced further wage cuts. With the United States in the midst of a serious depression, they had little choice but to accede. In the meantime, speedups and stretch-outs continued to take their toll on both the earnings and nerves of the workers.

Confronted by relentless pressure to increase their productivity and aware that their earlier methods had been less than successful, Lowell's women workers adopted a different strategy during the 1840s. In December 1844, they founded the Lowell Female Labor Reform Association with the intent of mitigating the ill effects of factory work through political action. Instead of staging strikes and protests, they joined other labor and reform groups to organize a massive but ultimately unsuccessful petition campaign to get the Massachusetts legislature to limit factory work to ten hours a day (they normally worked twelve to fourteen hours a day). In the months that followed, leaders of the association testified at hearings about the polluted air in cotton mills and the unreasonably short pe-

Digital History

CITY OF SPINDLES

THE TEXTILE MILLS OF LOWELL

"You wish to know . . . of our hours of labor. We go in at 5 o'clock; at seven we come out to breakfast; at half-past seven we return to our work, and stay until half-past twelve. At one . . . we return to our work, and stay until seven at night. Then the evening is all our own, which is more than some laboring girls can say, who think nothing is more tedious than a factory life."

These words were written in June 1844 by "Susan," a Lowell mill girl. They invite us into the world of the mills and the women who tended the weaving, spinning, and carding machines that powered production at Lowell.

Now we can enter Susan's world at Lowell through the Digital History program of *Inventing America*. Enter the Boott mill and experience the noise; sense the vibrations of the vast room's machinery working at full throttle. See the boarding-house rooms where the women lived, and hear their voices through the letters they wrote to family and friends. Explore the rivers and canals that supplied the power to drive the machines of Lowell. Consider Lowell from the perspective of the investors as well as the workers, the industrialists who wrote its rules and shaped its policies. Judge for yourself in the disputes between the workers and the owners and managers. Understand the significance of the Lowell enterprise for the development of industry in America.

Above: Two mill girls at Lowell, Massachusetts.
Center: The Merrimack Corporation mills and boarding houses in Lowell, 1850.
Right: A weaver drawing in warp ends, c. 1855.

As you explore the "City of Spindles" feature on *Inventing America*'s Digital History CD-ROM, consider the following:

■ For the New England women and later the immigrants who worked at Lowell, what were the attractions and drawbacks to life there?

■ How successful were the Lowell founders in their economic and social experiment?

■ What were the innovations introduced in the industrial process at Lowell, and what was their significance?

MERRIMACK CORPORATION

to human progress. But like many other intellectuals, Emerson became ambivalent about the changes taking place, at times hailing the "mechanic arts" as a great liberating force for mankind and on other occasions expressing concern about their negative implications. He seemed, moreover, to grow more pessimistic with the passage of time. "What have these arts done for the character, for the worth of mankind?" he asked in 1857. "Are men better?" The answer seemed clear. "Tis too plain," he concluded, "that with the material power the moral progress has not kept pace."

Henry David Thoreau.

Similarly, in *Walden* (1854), Emerson's Transcendentalist student and friend Henry David Thoreau denigrated his neighbors in Concord for leading "lives of quiet desperation" connected with trade and factory work. "Men have become tools of their tools," he lamented. He also characterized the railroad that passed by Walden Pond on its way from Boston to Concord as "that devilish Iron Horse," noting at one point that "we do not ride upon the railroad; it rides upon us." Yet on another occasion, even as the whistle of the locomotive penetrated his woodland retreat "like the scream of a hawk," he admitted that "I feel refreshed and expanded when the freight train rattles past me."

Such ambiguities lie at the heart of Thoreau's Walden experience. For him as well as for other writers, the problem was not the technology, but the uses to which it was being put. This question runs through Nathaniel Hawthorne's allegorical short story "The Celestial Railroad" (1846), in which a steam locomotive and its cars are depicted as a satanic instrument following a path straight to hell, and Herman Melville's *Moby Dick* (1851), the story of Captain Ahab's relentless pursuit of a great white whale, and one of the great American novels.

Unlike the nation's leading artists and writers, newspaper editors, journalists, and other popular writers openly celebrated the advent of the machine age and the "inventive genius" that made it possible. Whether in eulogistic biographies or shorter sketches in journals, writers sought to enshrine inventors with the nation's leading military and political heroes. Just as George Washington became known as "the father of his country," so famous inventors like Eli Whitney,

Robert Fulton, and Oliver Evans were considered "artists of their country." At a time when the word "technology" was rarely used, people associated invention with the "mechanical arts" and placed inventors on the same plane as the country's other artists—its writers and painters. And many inventors considered themselves key players in the ongoing effort to reform society.

The Second Great Awakening

The spread of democratic and technological change took place at a time of tremendous religious ferment. The "Second Great Awakening," a religious revival that began in the 1790s, reached a crescendo during the 1820s and continued well into the 1840s. Drawing particularly on the evangelical methods of the rapidly expanding Baptist and Methodist denominations, the Second Great Awakening first took root in western regions of the United States, where circuit-riding evangelists attracted converts in unprecedented numbers. In Kentucky, Ohio, and Tennessee alone, the number of conversions soared to well over 50,000 souls between 1800 and 1812. The evangelical movement spread like a wildfire to all parts of the country. Fearful of losing their own members to the newer churches, older Calvinist denominations—notably the Presbyterians and Congregationalists—began to use the "new measures" as well.

The Second Great Awakening offered an optimistic and democratic theology. In contrast to the older Calvinist viewpoint that people were predestined to heaven or hell and could be saved only if God had "elected" them, the new evangelical theology emphasized individual free will and, most important, the idea that everyone was equal in the eyes of God. It followed that each individual could gain salvation by "seeing the light"; the choice between heaven or hell was in their own hands. Rather than embracing a stern God of judgment as many "old light" Calvinists did, adherents of the Second Great Awakening believed in a God of love and free, saving grace for all. Many of them were affiliated with denominations that exercised local governance, elected their own ministers, and believed in "a priesthood of all believers." These democratic religious ideas helped to advance political democracy in America.

Revivalism was another key feature of the Awakening. When an evangelist arrived in a small town, local business often came to a standstill for days. A significant social event, exciting and personally intense, a revival could touch virtually everyone in the community. Surviving records reveal the emotional swings that people experienced as they underwent conversion. Such experiences, called "exercises," included everything from blackouts and fainting spells to trances and visions, uncontrollable laughing, jerking, barking, and rolling on the ground. Not all revivals exhibited these behavioral extremes, however. Congregationalist and Presbyterian ministers often frowned on these physical exercises and the mass hysteria they generated. Yet even the most controlled preachers frequently filled their sermons with references to hellfire and brimstone and, as one critic put it, threatened their listeners with "*instant and eternal damnation . . . unless they repent forthwith.*"

Most evangelicals associated with the Awakening were millennialists and perfectionists. They believed that God had chosen America to lead the world into the final thousand years of peace and prosperity before the Second Coming of Christ, and that American culture needed to be unified under evangelical Protestantism and cleansed of evil before the day of final judgment. Such ideas had important political implications. They reinforced the old Puritan belief that America was "the New Jerusalem," destined to occupy a special place in world history. This theme had justified American territorial expansion in the past, and it would soon reappear in a more virulent form under the banner of Manifest Destiny. Furthermore, evangelical Protestants advocated moral reforms aimed at ridding society of such sinful practices as drunkenness, idleness, Sabbath-breaking, prostitution, war, and (in the North) slavery, each one a subject of political controversy. Moral progress melded nicely with the technological progress of the age; in millennialist thought, both provided clear evidence of America's redemptive world mission.

The Second Great Awakening gathered momentum just as Congregationalism was disestablished in Connecticut (in 1818) and Massachusetts (in 1833), marking the end of state-supported religions in America and the final separation of church and state in public affairs. As religious sects multiplied, denominationalism (the phenomenon of many reli-

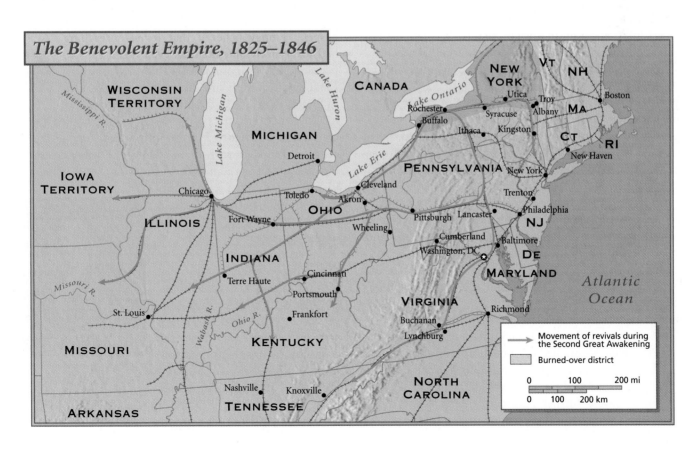

The Benevolent Empire, 1825–1846

Movement of revivals during the Second Great Awakening

Burned-over district

This early nineteenth-century view of a camp meeting shows well-dressed listeners, mostly women, experiencing conversion "exercises" in response to the preacher's powerful exhortations.

gious groups competing with one another for members) imprinted itself on American culture in unprecedented ways. This was most apparent in upstate New York, where the Erie Canal and the rapid industrial transformation that accompanied it helped to kindle one of the most momentous religious revivals in all of American history (see p. 415). There, the fires of religion burned with such intensity that the region became known as "the burned-over district."

Along the towpaths and boomtowns of the Erie could be found all the kinds of people that white evangelical Protestants most feared and wanted to "reform": Catholics, immigrants, paupers, and other "heathens," and sometimes even the primary agents of material progress, merchants and manufacturers. Then, as the transportation revolution spread westward into Ohio, Kentucky, Indiana, Illinois, and beyond, the agencies of Protestant religion and moral reform, collectively known as the "Benevolent Empire," moved with it. The geographies of religion, reform, and the market economy were part of the same westward-expanding process. Industrialization and reform were closely aligned with the new technologies of the era, especially what Daniel Webster referred to as "that mighty agent, steam." Both impulses carried with them the older civil and cultural institutions of the East into new territories and laid the foundations for new states that, they hoped, would further harmonize material and moral progress and ultimately achieve a more perfect society.

FINNEY'S REVIVALS

The person best known for kindling the fires of revivalism in the burned-over district as well as elsewhere in the Northeast and Midwest was Charles Grandison Finney. A lawyer whose religious conversion in 1821 resulted in his becoming a Presbyterian minister, Finney became the most sought-after preacher in America. Like other "new light" evangelists, he held that everyone had the God-given ability to achieve salvation if they would only repent, believe in Jesus Christ, and strive to perfect their lives in accordance with Christian precepts.

Standing six feet two inches tall with blond hair and ice-blue eyes, Finney cut a handsome figure. Observers always commented on his "great staring eyes" and how his imposing physical presence coupled with a penetrating tenor voice contributed to his effectiveness as a preacher. Characterized as "one of the Brigadier Generals of Jesus Christ with a special commission from the court of heaven to preach the gospel," Finney believed that revival preaching had to be lively and exciting, even theatrical. He peppered **his sermons** with everything from personal reminiscences and heart-wrenching stories to threats of hellfire and damnation in order to jar his listeners from a state of "betweenity," as he called it, into a conversion experience. He also introduced some of the procedures of modern revivals: in addition to daily prayer meetings, he usually preached three times on Sunday and three nights a week, often over a four-to-six-month period. "Anxious seats" were provided at the front of the congregation, where Finney invited those on the verge of professing their faith to sit so that he and his assistants could counsel them and pray for their conversion. In an effort to enliven services and get away from the dirge-like hymns that filled more traditional Presbyterian and Congregational services, he supported choir singing and encouraged his assistants to introduce more

The Reverend Charles Grandison Finney, a leading figure of the Second Great Awakening.

View of Rochester, New York, around the time of Finney's memorable revival there.

Finney's greatest impact was felt in the manufacturing districts of America, where the response was as enthusiastic as it had been at Rochester. Manufacturers and master workmen usually converted first, followed by workers. Thousands of workers and their families responded to the call in the late 1820s and 1830s, during which years church attendance rose to an all-time high. Whereas one in twenty adults maintained some sort of church affiliation in the 1790s, three out of four did so by 1835. Moreover, through his support of theological schools in upstate New York, Ohio, and Illinois, Finney came into contact with young men training for the evangelical ministry who were receptive to his emphasis on Christian perfectionism, and to his message that believers "should set out with determination to aim at being useful in the highest degree possible." Being useful meant leading a Christian life, diligently conducting revivals, and seeking not only to save individual souls but to reform all of society. This last goal,

modern music into the services. One of them, Thomas Hastings of Utica, New York, composed the melody for "Rock of Ages," one of the greatest of all nineteenth-century hymns.

Roughly between 1825 and 1837, Finney conducted revivals in factory towns and villages throughout the burned-over district and, once his reputation was established, moved on to preach to large assemblies in the seaboard cities of Wilmington, Philadelphia, Boston, and New York. One of his most successful revivals took place between September 1830 and March 1831 in the Erie Canal boomtown of Rochester, New York. Called there by merchants and manufacturers concerned about the lawlessness and raucous behavior that accompanied the town's spectacular economic growth, Finney conducted a six-month crusade aimed not only at gaining converts but also at purging the community of its sinfulness, particularly drunkenness.

The results of Finney's Rochester crusade were impressive. During the 1830s, hundreds of workers joined churches and, in the process, adopted their perfectionist sentiments. Conversion bred piety, and piety bred self-restraint; workers became more sober, industrious, and obedient. In the long run, voluntary conversions proved far more powerful in controlling worker behavior than any paternalistic work rules promulgated by factory masters. News of the Rochester revival spread Finney's fame far and wide. Invitations to conduct revivals came from all parts of the country as well as from Europe, and he led two major ones, in Boston and New York, before moving permanently to Oberlin College near Cleveland, Ohio, in 1835.

The "Finney Tent," erected at Oberlin College to house the large crowds that came to hear Finney preach and to experience conversion.

Finney's students believed, would perfect humanity and set the stage for a thousand years of peace.

VISIONS OF UTOPIA

Joining Charles Finney's revivalists in their mission to refashion society were the founders of so-called utopian communities. These communities were extraordinarily diverse: some were deeply religious, others were secular; some were well integrated into their surrounding cultural landscapes, while others remained isolated and in constant tension with their neighbors. Virtually all of them, however, held the common American belief that people could achieve a perfect society given the correct set of guiding principles, and had faith that science (and what would soon be identified as technology) could propel them toward this society. To utopian perfectionists, history was neither static nor cyclical but progressive in character.

Robert Owen and New Harmony. One of the best-known utopian communities was Robert Owen's settlement at New Harmony, Indiana. A native of Wales who set out for London at age ten to "seek his fortune," Owen moved through the ranks of the working class to become one of the most successful textile manufacturers in England. Having personally experienced the injustices of the British factory system, he committed himself to finding ways of ensuring that machinery would benefit workers rather than exploit them. For him, "the momentous question" of the age was "whether this vast gift of labour-saving machinery is to result in mitigation of the toil and melioration of the condition of the millions who have acquired it."

Owen's first attempt at reform occurred at his New Lanark mill in Scotland, where he erected worker housing with improved sanitation facilities, instituted an eight-hour (in place of the usual twelve-to-fourteen-hour) workday, provided his employees with health insurance and retirement benefits, and established a free school for their children rather than putting them to work at an early age. After these innovations proved successful, he sought a larger arena for his reforms by lobbying for national legislation to limit child labor, provide health and injury benefits, and establish an inspection system to reduce hazardous working conditions. When his proposals met opposition in Parliament, Owen decided to redirect his efforts to America by purchasing the 20,000-acre site at New Harmony from a German religious sect headed by George Rapp. There, he reasoned, the less class-bound environment might be more hospitable to his vision of a "Village of Cooperation" in which the residents lived and labored as equals.

Owen arrived in America late in November 1824. His celebrity prompted invitations to speak before President James Monroe, President-elect John Quincy Adams, and both houses of Congress. There, he outlined his plans for the New Harmony community and revealed the essence of his philosophy. "Make a man happy and you make him virtuous—this is the whole of my system," he told the packed audiences. "To make him happy," he continued, "I enlighten his mind and occupy his hands, and I have so managed the art of instruction that individuals seek it as an amusement. Two of the most powerful moral agents I use are music and dancing." Further, Owen told his listeners, "I am come to this country to introduce an entire new state of society; to change it from the ignorant, selfish system, to an enlightened, social system, which shall gradually unite all interests into one, and remove all cause for contest between individuals." Until the "selfish system," based on private property and the pursuit of profit, was replaced by communal property ownership, Owen saw little hope for "permanent improvement in the condition of the human race."

The New Harmony experiment initially attracted more than 800 individuals, ranging in background from prominent intellectuals to working-class families. From the outset, however, there was little harmony at New Harmony. Disputes arose almost immediately over property rights, work assignments, levels of compensation, and how the backwoods utopia should be governed. Owen, who was frequently absent from New Harmony, proved incapable of reconciling the divergent personalities that splintered the community. His indecisive leadership coupled with the community's growing financial problems, as well as public criticism of his unorthodox ideas about private property, organized religion, and even marriage, brought about the dissolution of New Harmony in 1828. After disposing of the financially encumbered property, Owen returned to Britain with less than one-fifth of his original fortune. Although more than twenty smaller

> *"Until the 'selfish system,' based on private property and the pursuit of profit, was replaced by communal property ownership, Robert Owen saw little hope for 'permanent improvement in the condition of the human race.'"*

Owenite communities elsewhere in North America and Great Britain survived the failure of New Harmony, they, too, encountered internal problems and eventually disappeared.

The North American Phalanx. Just as the Owenite movement was fading, another group had begun to capture the utopian imagination. Based on the writings of the French socialist Charles Fourier and his American disciple Albert Brisbane, the new movement held out the promise of a perfect new world by establishing communities called "phalanxes" (or "phalanges"), in which the participants held stock and found personal fulfillment by selecting occupations that best suited them. Twenty-eight Fourierist phalanxes were set up in the United States between 1841 and 1858, ranging as far west as Iowa and as far south as Texas. One of the best known, the North American Phalanx near Red Bank, New Jersey, was founded in 1843. Its ninety residents engaged primarily in agriculture, with each person choosing work that seemed the most satisfying. Despite difficulties in getting members to do all the tasks that needed to be done, the North American Phalanx by and large succeeded. It received considerable publicity through one of its benefactors, Horace Greeley, the reform-minded owner of the *New York Tribune.* Visitors to the phalanx often noted its friendly atmosphere and wholesomeness. Yet when a fire destroyed the gristmill in 1854, the members voted to dissolve the community rather than rebuild it, even though they had the resources to do so. After ten years, the novelty of the experiment in "plain living" and "high thinking" had worn off.

The Shakers. Of the hundred or more communitarian societies established in America between the Revolution and the Civil War, the greatest success financially and socially was the Shakers. Unlike the secular Owenites and phalangists, the Shakers drew inspiration from their religious beliefs. The sect's founder, Mother Ann Lee, came from a poor, working-class family in Manchester, England. As a child, she labored in a cotton mill; as a young woman, she claimed to have experienced "religious impressions" that gave her "great light and conviction concerning the sinfulness and depravity of human nature, and especially concerning the lusts of the flesh." These mystical visions, coupled with her association with a radical group of Quaker dissenters, led her to claim that the millennium was at hand and that God had ordained her to be the Christ spirit that would initiate the "new dispensation," or Second Coming, on earth. Because Mother Ann's

As this contemporary engraving suggests, set pattern dancing was an integral part of Shaker religious services.

message attracted few believers in England, she decided to carry the gospel to America, where, she hoped, the ground for conversions would be more fertile.

"Ann the Word" and a small contingent of believers arrived in America in 1774. The sect grew steadily, reaching a high point during the 1850s with some eighteen communities (called "societies") spread across the country from Maine to Kentucky. The name "Shaker" derived from a contemporary reference to "Shaking Quakers" and the physical intensity of their services, especially their dancing, the purpose of which was to "shake sin from the body through the fingertips." Admirers considered their sacred songs and dances highly synchronized and beautiful, though others were appalled by what they saw. Alexis de Tocqueville wrote that Shaker dancing reminded him of "trained dogs who are forced to walk on their hind legs."

The Shakers believed in universal salvation, practiced celibacy, and sought to live apart from the world in order to achieve Christian perfection. But they did not divorce themselves from worldly economic activities, which they often described as "consecrated industry." "We believed we were debtors to God in relation to Each other, and all men," an elder explained, "to improve our time and Tallents in this Life, in that manner in which we might be most useful." This meant that "all things made for sale ought to be well done, and suitable for their use," and Shaker products met very high standards for quality and workmanship. Shakers developed thriving businesses in the sale of garden seeds, medicinal herbs, tanned goods, brooms and brushes, leather whips, baskets, straw and palm leaf hats and bonnets, and all sorts of kitchen products—applesauce, apple butter, dried apples and corn, maple syrup, and relishes and sauces.

Their best-known products came from their woodworking shops and stood in a class by themselves. Shaker-made furniture—slat-back chairs, cabinets, tables, clock cases, and the like—reveal a lightness and simplicity of design that is unmatched in the annals of American craftsmanship. Ornamentation and other "superfluities" were considered sinful because they revealed "the pride and vanity of man." "The beautiful," one elder stated, "has no business with us." Yet in Shaker hands, simplicity exemplified elegance and beauty.

"In Shaker communities, technology was a natural ally of religion."

Upon visiting a Shaker village in 1849, a British writer commented on the sect's technical creativity, noting that "here machinery of every kind is always among their greatest blessings." Shaker artisans readily availed themselves of the latest mechanical know-how. After making forays into the outside world to examine machinery and manufacturing methods, they tended to replicate what they saw in-house rather than make outright purchases. Their most important innovations included a washing machine (reflecting a rare concern for lessening women's labor), a circular saw that was widely adopted throughout the country, and machines for planing and machining boards. In Shaker communities, technology was a natural ally of religion.

The Rappites. Other religious sects espoused principles similar to those of the Shakers. The Harmony Society, founded by German immigrant George Rapp and known as the Rappites, were, like the Shakers, millennialists who believed in celibacy, universal salvation, and communal property ownership. They, too, lived in separate communities while participating in the general economy. Between Rapp's arrival in America in 1804 and the sect's demise one hundred years later, the Rappites established three settlements: first in western Pennsylvania from 1805 to 1815; second on the Wabash River in southern Indiana, the settlement Rapp sold to Robert Owen in 1824; and finally back to western Pennsylvania, where they built the village of Economy some fifteen miles north of Pittsburgh, a settlement that became well-known for its high-quality leather goods, cotton and woolen textiles, cutlery, and distilled alcoholic beverages.

Oneida Perfectionists. A later group, the Oneida Perfectionists, were far more radical than either the Rappites or the Shakers. Founded during the 1830s by a college-educated lawyer and evangelical clergyman, John Humphrey Noyes, the sect originated in Putney, Vermont, and in 1847 moved to Oneida, in upstate New York. Noyes and his followers believed that a person achieved perfection through a conversion experience, after which the believer was no longer capable of sinning. From this theology flowed a number of practices considered extreme in nineteenth-century America, most notably the idea of "complex marriage," whereby a sanctified man and a sanctified woman could have sexual relations regardless of their marital status. Such beliefs prompted a host of critics to condemn Noyes as a false prophet and Oneida as his den of iniquity.

Accused of adultery and pursued by the law on numerous occasions, Noyes persisted in following the dictates of Christian perfectionism and speaking his mind on public issues. In 1837, he accused the U.S. government of being nothing more than a "bloated, swaggering libertine, trampling on the Bible—its own Constitution—its treaties with the Indians—the petitions of its citizens: with one hand whipping a negro tied to a liberty pole, and with the other dashing an emaciated Indian to the ground." Renouncing "all allegiance to the government of the United States," he asserted "the title of Jesus Christ to the throne of the world" and endorsed temperance, the abolition of slavery, and universal peace.

Despite the hostility that Oneida's political radicalism and unorthodox sexual practices aroused, the community prospered. Like the Rappites and Shakers, the Perfectionists combined manufacturing with farming in order to generate income. Logging provided some support during the early years, but a turning point came in the mid-1850s when the community took up the manufacture of steel traps. After reaping large profits, the Perfectionists turned to manufacturing silk thread, canned fruit, and silver tableware. This tableware, their one lasting material legacy, can be found in stores today as "Oneida silver plate."

In the end, the Shakers, Rappites, and Oneida Perfectionists met similar fates in spite of their economic success. After experiencing a period of spiritual growth and vitality, all three societies eventually disappeared. Escalating problems over Noyes's controversial leadership and a falling away from religious ideals led to the decline of the Oneida community. Celibacy proved to be the undoing of the Rappites and Shakers. With no offspring to carry on the founders' traditions, both sects declined in numbers and gradually died out. The significance of these communities lies in their pursuit of human perfection through separatist religious practices, and in their eager embrace of the new machine technology as a way of lightening their daily chores so that they could devote more time to spiritual fulfillment. All three groups reflected the larger society's growing commitment to social progress and to technology as a means of achieving that progress.

Most of the other American utopian experiments appeared after the War of 1812 and had relatively short lives. In New England, for example, Brook Farm, a secular community near Boston, became famous during the 1840s as a center of progressive education and high-minded discourse that was closely associated with the Transcendentalist movement. It attracted some of America's leading intellectual figures, among them Margaret Fuller, Ralph Waldo Emerson, and Nathaniel Hawthorne. Yet it lasted little more than six years. The individualism spawned at Brook Farm and other secular com-munities contrasted with the more spiritually oriented and disciplined religious communities. This discipline accounts more than anything else for the longevity of the Shakers and Rappites.

> *"The significance of these communities lies in their pursuit of human perfection through separatist religious practices, and in their eager embrace of the new machine technology as a way of lightening their daily chores so that they could devote more time to spiritual fulfillment."*

THE MORMONS

The most successful new denomination to emerge in New York's "burned-over district" was the Church of Jesus Christ of Latter-Day Saints, also known as the Mormons. The Mormons originally came together around a charismatic leader, Joseph Smith, and a sacred book. While living in upstate New York, Smith claimed to have discovered and translated, through divine revelation, a series of gold tablets detailing the ancient history of the Americas. Published in 1830, Smith's translation of *The Book of Mormon* was not meant to replace the Bible, but rather made the Western Hemisphere an additional source of revelation by identifying the American Indians as descendants of the ancient Israelites. While this "biblical" account proved satisfying to converts, it appeared blasphemous to other Christians, who hounded the Mormons from one settlement after another. When an anti-Mormon mob in Illinois lynched Smith and his brother in 1844, Mormon leaders prepared to move to the far West, beyond the reach of their enemies.

The exodus from Illinois, led by Joseph Smith's associate and elected successor, Brigham Young, was a feat of careful planning and organization. Aided by army maps that pointed them in the direction of the Great Salt Lake Basin, the lead party, consisting of some 1,500 refugees called "the Camp of Israel," set out in February 1846. By June, their 540 wagons had reached the Missouri River near Council Bluffs, Iowa. Following them were another 2,500 wagons divided into five or six companies and organized in pyramidal groups of tens, fifties, and hundreds of families. Each group had its own leaders and armed guards. All followed detailed regulations on the rigors of overland travel and the proper use of essential foodstuffs and other provisions as they made their way across the continent.

As the lead group blazed a wagon road along the northern side of the Platte River across Nebraska into eastern Wyoming and, from there, into the rugged high country that led through the South Pass to the Great Salt Lake Basin, they established way stations and planted crops for those following them. Despite these preparations, though, life on what became known as the Overland Trail was difficult. Wagons broke down, animals became lame, food supplies ran short, and people fell ill; some 200 died along the treacherous route. But under the determined leadership of Brigham Young and his circle of advisers, the Mormon exodus continued, with the first contingent of settlers arriving in the Salt Lake region in July 1847. Within three months, nearly 3,000 people had entered the valley, and within two years they would establish the Provisional Government of the State of Deseret, the theocratic Mormon domain in the West. By 1850, the Mormon population in Utah approached 12,000, and reached 40,000 a decade later.

The Mormons were vilified more than any other utopian community

Brigham Young, Joseph Smith's successor and leader of the Mormon trek to their "New Jerusalem" in the Great Salt Lake Basin.

of the period. *The Book of Mormon* was considered inflammatory in a society molded by evangelical Christianity, as was the Mormon practice of polygamy. But non-Mormon "gentiles" came to view the Mormons as dangerous outsiders as much because of their political economy as their religious or social doctrines. From the beginning, the "Saints," as they called themselves, not only lived apart from their neighbors but also preferred to trade among themselves. In local politics, they tended to vote as a block, undermining democratic government and the separation of church and state in the eyes of critics. Moreover, many Mormon converts were poor, and they maintained generally friendly relations with native Americans, whom they attempted to convert to the faith. In the border state of Missouri, rumors spread that they were attempting to convert black slaves.

The Mormons were one of the first groups of white Americans to live in the radically different ecology of the Rocky Mountain West. The difficulties of surviving as agricultural-

ists in an arid land without the familiar resources of water, wood, or machine-made goods likely strengthened their commitment to community and theocratic rule. For a time, Mormons endured preindustrial conditions, wearing woolen homespun and getting by with only a few machine-made tools. They succeeded in setting up local gristmills, sawmills, tanneries, and light industries for making soap, brooms, hats, and the like. But more ambitious plans to recreate the mines, ironworks, and factories of the East largely failed owing to the scarcity of capital, skilled labor, and equipment.

The defining technology of Mormon Utah became elaborate irrigation systems, which supported eastern-style farming. With arable land scarce, Mormon settlers learned early on how to convey water from distant mountain streams by building canals and tapping them with sluice gates and ditches that distributed water by gravity flow to farms and home lots. Each farmer was allocated specific hours of water once or twice a week. Everything depended on having adequate water for cultivation. Without it, green fields soon wilted, and the landscape returned to sagebrush. Survival in the desert depended on community participation and cooperation. Only with the coming of the transcontinental railroad—which Brigham Young welcomed and even invested in—would the farming culture of the Mormons begin to integrate with the larger national economy, and parts of Utah take on the character of an industrial landscape.

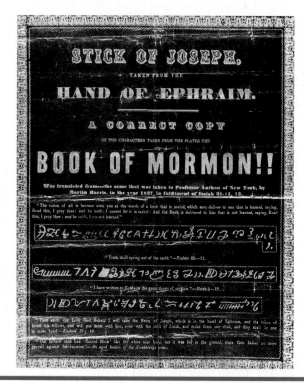

A flyer advertising Joseph Smith's translation of the Book of Mormon.

Evangelical Roots of Abolitionism

One of the striking features of the Second Great Awakening was a belief in religious equality, the ability of every soul to attain salvation. But as the evangelical movement spread to the South, it bumped up against the greatest example of inequality the nation could offer—slavery. The resulting tension between religious equality and slavery soon fed older antagonisms between the North and South to inflame the nation's most divisive issue.

THEODORE DWIGHT WELD

The potential for conflict was high in Cincinnati, the rapidly growing city in southwestern Ohio. With its strategic location on the Ohio River, adjacent to slaveholding Kentucky, and its

Theodore Dwight Weld.

stature as a meatpacking center and leading builder of steamboats, the city maintained strong trade and social contacts with farmers, planters, and businessmen in the South. In 1833, a group of young men assembled at the Lane Theological Seminary in Cincinnati under the leadership of Theodore Dwight Weld, a Finney convert from western New York. After working as one of Finney's assistants during the mid-1820s, Weld had enrolled at the Oneida Institute near Utica to study for the ministry. Once there, however, he found himself slowly drifting away from his ministerial calling toward a life of activism. By the time he arrived at Lane, Weld was already well-known as an advocate of temperance, Sabbath-keeping, and the advanced education of women. During a two-year stint as the general agent of the evangelically sponsored Society for the Promotion of Manual Labor in Literary Institutions, he traveled over 4,500 miles to all parts of the country, including the deep South, where he witnessed first-hand the abuses of plantation slavery.

Weld had long been against slavery. Before going to Ohio, he had supported the idea of gradual emancipation and had even sympathized with the American Colonization Society, which favored shipping all blacks, slave or free, back to Africa. Yet the colonization scheme never fully satisfied him: its assumption that blacks were inferior to whites and could not prosper in America ran against his belief that all people, regardless of race, were equal in God's eyes. In the end, this conviction, coupled with an introduction to the writings of the Boston newspaper editor William Lloyd Garrison, made an abolitionist of Weld. His call for an immediate end to slavery and the granting of equal rights to freedmen caused considerable turmoil at the Lane Seminary and shocked local white society. Rather than submit to disciplinary action at the seminary, Weld and seventy-five of his comrades, called the "Lane Rebels," left in October 1834, many embarking on careers devoted to abolitionism. Virtually all of them maintained their ties to evangelical religion.

Elizabeth Cady Stanton. Like the Grimké sisters, Stanton was a feminist abolitionist and a founder of the women's rights movement.

Weld himself had come to believe that the abolitionist cause "not only *overshadows* all others, but . . . absorbs them into itself. Revivals, moral Reform etc. will remain stationary until the temple is cleansed." He consequently declined Finney's offer of a professorship at Oberlin College and became instead an agent of the Ohio Antislavery Society. When he heard this news, fellow abolitionist James G. Birney wrote in his diary, "I give him one year to abolitionize Ohio." Although off by eight months, the prediction proved essentially correct. By 1836, Weld, a magnetic figure, had moved through much of Ohio as well as parts of western Pennsylvania, impressing audiences with his magnificent oratory and helping to establish local abolitionist societies.

Others followed similar paths to the abolitionist cause. Among them were Weld's long-time friend and fellow Lane rebel Henry B. Stanton and his wife, Elizabeth Cady Stanton—soon to achieve renown as a leader in the emerging women's rights movement. Like the Stantons, many of these reformers came from middle-class backgrounds in the Northeast, especially New England and the burned-over district of upstate New York. But not all. James G. Birney, one of the movement's most courageous leaders, was a prominent

Sarah M. Grimké.

Angelina M. Grimké.

lawyer-politician and former slave owner from Alabama and Kentucky. Of equal stature were Sarah and Angelina Grimké, daughters of a wealthy, conservative slaveholding family in Charleston, South Carolina, who became outspoken abolitionists and controversial advocates of women playing roles usually reserved for men. In 1838, Angelina Grimké married Theodore Weld.

WILLIAM LLOYD GARRISON

As much as Weld, Birney, the Stantons, the Grimké sisters, and countless others energized **the abolitionist movement,** its best-known leader—indeed, its animating force—was Boston's William Lloyd Garrison. A Baptist by conviction and a printer by trade, Garrison was working in Baltimore when his Quaker employer, Benjamin Lundy, and members of the city's free black community converted him to "the cause of the slave" and immediate emancipation. Lundy, an early abolitionist, had adopted a moderate tone in his newspaper, *The Genius of Universal Emancipation.* Young Garrison did not. Militant in his demands for the immediate emancipation of slaves, he set out to break the "conspiracy of silence" that surrounded slavery. After being jailed in Baltimore for libel, he returned to his native New England and, with the financial support of New York merchants Arthur and Lewis Tappan, published the first issue of *The Liberator* in January 1831. In it, he announced that "I will be as harsh as truth, and as uncompromising as justice. On this subject, I do not wish to think, to speak, or write, with moderation. . . . I am in earnest—I will not equivocate—I will not excuse—I will not retreat a single inch—AND I WILL BE HEARD."

William Lloyd Garrison.

The Liberator never achieved a large circulation in the North, nor did its message attract many adherents there. Published as a weekly newspaper, it had only 50 white subscribers in its first year and no more than 400 two years later. Most of those who read it were already true believers. But the publication found an enthusiastic audience among free blacks and fugitive slaves in the North, who in 1833 constituted over 60 percent of its readership. The escaped slave Frederick Douglass became one of its most ardent champions and, in 1848, went on to publish his own abolitionist newspaper, *North Star,* at Rochester, New York, the heart of the burned-over district. Only a handful of southerners actually read *The Liberator,* but southerners heard plenty about it through commentary in their own press. And what they heard infuriated them. Many blamed the Bostonian for the bloody slave revolt led by Nat Turner in Southampton County in southeastern Virginia, shortly after *The Liberator* first appeared. Garrison never represented the whole of abolitionism, a diverse and decentralized movement. In fact, most northerners considered him a fanatic.

Lewis Tappan.

THE AMERICAN ANTI-SLAVERY SOCIETY

Three factors—commitment, organization, and technology—propelled the abolitionist movement to the forefront of American society during the mid-1830s. In most cases, commitment to this cause came after a conversion experience not unlike those of religious revivals—a period of intense soul-searching and eventual acceptance of the doctrine that slavery was morally wrong. Then, like good evangelicals, abolitionists worked ceaselessly to convert others to the cause.

In 1833, the American Anti-Slavery Society, the first national organization of its kind in the United States, was established. William Lloyd Garrison composed the society's governing "Declaration of Sentiments," an ingenious document that drew on the precedents of the American Revolution to demand immediate emancipation and to argue that "our fathers were never slaves—never bought and sold like cattle—never shut out from the light of knowledge and religion—never subjected to the lash of brutal taskmasters." The declaration went on to condemn slavery as a sin "unequalled by any other on the face of the earth" and to attack the idea of deporting blacks to Africa. All those who signed the Declaration of Sentiments pledged to oppose racial prejudice in all its guises and to "secure to the colored population . . . all the rights and privileges that belong to them as men and as Americans." The signers also agreed that the method of achieving these ends should be through the old revivalist mode of "moral suasion" rather than the use of violence or other "carnal weapons." To this end, they pledged themselves to organize antislavery societies in every city, town, and hamlet and to circulate pamphlets and broadsides (large sheets printed in bold letters) throughout the country to win over public opinion. In almost every instance, evangelical ministers and their churches became the organizing agencies of abolitionism at the local level.

Although abolitionists often drew on the language of the Revolution for justification, their movement was directly influenced by the British Anti-Slavery Society, which, after half a century of struggle, had convinced Parliament in 1833 to outlaw slavery in the British West Indies, including the Bahama and Virgin Islands. The abolition of slavery in these British islands, which were closely related historically and geographically to the American South, further isolated the South, making it appear all the more backward and uncivilized. British antislavery churchmen also influenced northern clergy who might safely have ignored Garrison and Weld.

Since most funding for the American Anti-Slavery Society came from wealthy New York merchants like the Tappan brothers, its main office was located in New York City. Weld and other agents working throughout the country received their instructions, literature, and paychecks from New York. The society also took advantage of the city's position as the center of the publishing trade. With important innovations occurring in high-volume printing, the leaders of the society were able to take advantage of this new technology when they decided in 1835 to mount a national campaign of moral suasion.

Called "the great postal campaign," the project aimed at peppering the country with all sorts of abolitionist literature. Heading the mailing list were leading citizens of the South. The recent development of steam-driven rotary presses (aptly called the "Lightning" machine) speeded the printing process. In 1833, for example, the average New York newspaper, using hand presses, could print around 200 impressions an hour; with the introduction of steam-driven rotary presses in 1835, output jumped to 5,500 copies an hour. Printing costs fell so much that the American Anti-Slavery Society went from distributing 122,000 pieces of literature in 1834 to 1.1 million pieces the following year. Other reform groups—notably the American Temperance Union, religious tract societies, and state and local abolitionist associations—had resorted to pamphleteering before 1835, but none of them achieved the massive distribution of the great postal campaign. The new printing technology strengthened the abolitionist cause by making mass distribution possible.

Although the great postal campaign had an immediate and lasting impact, public reaction took a different turn than expected. Instead of recognizing the sinfulness of slavery and repenting, as abolitionists had anticipated, southerners exploded in rage and tried to suppress the mailings. On July 29, 1835, for instance, a crowd descended on the Charleston, South Carolina, post office and seized mailbags containing abolitionist literature. The next evening, the mob reappeared to burn effigies of William Lloyd Garrison and Arthur Tappan, using as fuel the material they had seized a day earlier. Elsewhere in the South, community leaders, prompted by large-plantation owners, established vigilance committees to seize any incoming mail that contained "incendiary literature." President Andrew Jackson, himself a slave owner, encouraged these actions by publicly denouncing the postal campaign and urging Congress to pass legislation aimed at banning abolitionist literature from the mails. Although nothing came of it, southerners redoubled their efforts to

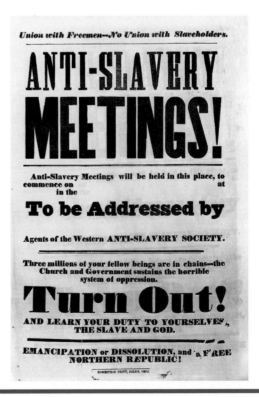

An 1850 poster announcing an antislavery meeting in Salem, Ohio, and urging all readers to "Turn Out! And learn your duty to yourselves, the slave and God."

Lucretia Coffin Mott, an abolitionist and women's rights advocate who, along with Elizabeth Cady Stanton and other reform-oriented feminists, organized the first women's rights convention in Seneca, New York, in 1848.

snuff out dissent against the "peculiar institution." And they were supported by northern merchants and manufacturers who enjoyed lucrative trade relationships in the South. In the end, only Connecticut—a leading manufacturing state—responded with an actual gag law banning abolitionist speakers.

But the opposition to abolitionism continued. Many northern whites were unable to support the movement because it challenged the common belief in white supremacy. From New England to Ohio, "gentlemen of property and standing" took the lead in mounting attacks on abolitionist leaders while tapping deep veins of racism within the white community. In October 1835 at Utica, New York, a mob of workers and community leaders broke up an abolitionist state convention and roughed up its delegates. In Cincinnati, irate antiabolitionists repeatedly attacked a print shop owned by James G. Birney, while in Boston another mob seized Garrison and dragged him through the streets at the end of a rope. The violence frequently spilled over against communities of free blacks. One abolitionist agent reported that he faced mobs on more than seventy occasions while working in Ohio and Pennsylvania. In the southern Illinois town of Alton on November 7, 1837, a mob set fire to a building where the abolitionist editor Elijah Lovejoy was guarding his press and murdered him as he ran, pistol in hand, into the street. The cause had its first martyr.

The American Anti-Slavery Society responded by mounting yet another major campaign, this time in the form of petitions to Congress. In northern states, petitions protesting slavery had begun in the eighteenth century and continued sporadically into the 1830s. The volume grew so drastically, however (by 1835 there were over 30,000), that in May 1836 the House of Representatives adopted a "gag resolution" that immediately tabled all antislavery petitions before they could reach the House floor for debate. Nevertheless, the American Anti-Slavery Society decided the following year to increase pressure on Congress by conducting a petition campaign the likes of which had never been seen before. Some petitions

aimed at ending slavery in the District of Columbia; others called for outlawing interstate trade in slaves; and still others sought to prevent new slave states from entering the Union. Women such as Elizabeth Cady (soon to be Elizabeth Cady Stanton), Angelina Grimké, Lucretia Mott, and Susan B. An-

A proslavery lithograph from 1850 that favorably contrasts the easygoing life of southern plantation slaves with the harsh realities of "factory slavery" in England and, by implication, the northern United States. The fact that this poster was printed in Boston indicates that many northerners opposed the abolitionist movement.

thony assumed key roles in organizing the campaign and gathering signatures. Her involvement in the effort led Grimké to observe that "the investigation of the rights of the slave has led me to a better understanding of my own." Indeed, the antislavery movement helped kindle debate over the right of women to participate in politics. After a year of intensive effort, the American Anti-Slavery Society announced that 415,000 petitions had been sent to Washington. Over half of the petitions contained the signatures of women.

Unlike the great postal campaign, which targeted newspaper editors, politicians, and civic leaders throughout the South, the petition campaign of 1837–38 was more of a grassroots operation that focused exclusively on the North. Still, it elicited angry responses from militant slave owners and "Northern men with Southern principles." And the more the "slave power" sought to silence abolitionists through gag rules, illegal mail searches, and mob violence, the more it drew attention to the movement while raising concerns over the safety of America's civil liberties. To many northerners with little sympathy for the antislavery cause, it seemed that essential rights of free speech, free assembly, and free press were being trampled by slave masters and their allies. "Our opposers are doing everything to help us," an elated supporter wrote to Garrison. Nothing had been "ever so much talked about as slavery is everywhere."

A cartoon satirizing the gag rule in the House of Representatives. On the ground cowering over a pile of abolitionist petitions is John Quincy Adams. Standing above him behind a barrel is Congressman Waddy Thompson Jr., a Whig defender of slavery from South Carolina. Crouched next to Thompson are two slaves, one of whom whispers, "Abolition is down flat!"

Political Abolitionism

ADAMS AND THE 1836 GAG RULE

By 1838, a growing number of abolitionist leaders openly acknowledged that their strategy of moral suasion was taking a new direction. The pamphleteering effort and the violent opposition it elicited was moving abolitionism away from its evangelical base toward a more ideological and political orientation. This shift became apparent in the controversy that rocked the House of Representatives over the 1836 gag resolution.

In the eye of the storm was former president John Quincy Adams, who had been elected to the House in 1830. Adams had never supported the abolitionist movement. Content to tolerate slavery wherever it existed, he had even confided to his diary his belief "that the general treatment of slaves is mild and moderate." He nonetheless harbored deep resentments toward southern slaveholders who, he believed, had been instrumental in preventing his reelection in 1828. When the southern-controlled House of Representatives adopted the gag rule in 1836, Adams saw an opportunity to stand for a fundamental principle of free government—the right of petition—and to skewer old enemies. He therefore drew on his considerable skill as a parliamentarian to present petitions in defiance of the gag rule and to attack slavery as "a sin before the sight of God" during House floor debates. By the late 1830s, most southerners would have agreed with a Virginia congressman's remark that Adams had become "the acutest, the astutest, the archest enemy of Southern slavery that ever existed." After eight years of unstinting effort, Adams would finally see the gag rule repealed in 1844.

Several new congressmen joined Adams in opposing slavery, the gag rule, and the values of the planter class. Among them were Joshua R. Giddings from the western reserve region of northern Ohio, Seth Gates from New York's burned-over district, and William Slade from western Vermont. Like Adams, they came from hotbeds of antisouthern and antislavery feeling that stretched from Boston westward into the Berkshire Mountains and along the Erie Canal into northern Ohio, northern Indiana, and southern Michigan. They had a mandate from their constituents to challenge the institution of slavery, even if it meant bolting against party discipline.

> *"Garrison sympathized with the Grimké sisters' growing realization that black slavery and male domination over women had much in common."*

As the political storm over slavery gathered force, the American Anti-Slavery Society began to fracture. Personalities clashed while members differed over future tactics. Frustrated with the public opposition to the society's efforts at moral suasion, Garrison blasted away at religious and political leaders in *The Liberator*. He also began to attack the federal government itself, damning the U.S. Constitution as "a covenant with death and an agreement with hell" and urging his followers not to vote or in any way become involved with an institution that supported human bondage and maintained it by force. Garrison would eventually call for even more drastic measures, including outright disunion. The only way the North could cleanse itself of the sin of slavery, he came to believe, was to expel the slave states from the Union. But such ideas were too radical for many other members of the American Anti-Slavery Society.

WOMEN'S RIGHTS

Another source of conflict among abolitionists centered on the place of women in the movement. Some younger women, active in the 1837–38 petition campaign, had openly defied their "appointed female sphere" by speaking before audiences that included males as well as females. Such "promiscuous" behavior appalled older, more straight-laced members of the American Anti-Slavery Society, such as James G. Birney and the Tappan brothers. When Angelina and Sarah Grimké undertook a lecture tour of New England in 1837, they encountered as much abuse from within the society as they did from antiabolitionists. Congregationalist ministers circulated a *Pastoral Letter* denouncing the sisters for speaking in public and admonishing them to obey men rather than lecturing to them. As one abolitionist leader put it, the "tom turkies ought to do the gobbling," not the hens.

William Lloyd Garrison sympathized with the Grimké sisters' growing realization that black slavery and male domination over women had much in common. When they and other women abolitionists began to push for gender equality within the American Anti-Slavery Society, Garrison wholeheartedly supported them. In his view, they had done as much as, if not more than, male members to advance the cause during the 1830s. They therefore deserved not only recognition and thanks but also the right to vote, hold office, and participate fully in the society's affairs. Other society members, however—including a number of women—took a dim view of the "open platform" that extended full rights to all regardless of

Cover to "I'll Be No Submissive Wife," a feminist ballad of 1835. Sample lyrics: "Should a humdrum husband say / That at home I ought to stay, / Do you think that I'll obey? / No no no, not I."

Where Do You Live?

*In nineteenth-century America, a common painting
material was called "whitewash." Applied to
everything from fences and the exteriors of buildings
to the interiors of barns and houses, whitewash was
popular because it was cheap, readily available, and
easy to apply. In 1841, Catherine Beecher (the sister
of abolitionist Harriet Beecher Stowe), believing that
"cleanliness was next to godliness," published two
handy recipes.*

"There is nothing which so much improves the
appearance of a house and the premises, as painting
or whitewashing the tenements and fences. The
following receipts for whitewashing, have been
found, by experience, to answer the same purpose
for wood, brick, and stone, as oil-paint, and are much
cheaper. The first is the receipt used for the
President's house at Washington, improved by
further experiments. The second, is a simpler and
cheaper one, which the Writer has known to succeed,
in a variety of cases, lasting as long, and looking as
well, as white oil-paint.

Receipt.
"Take half a bushel of unslacked lime, and slack it
with boiling water, covering it during the process.
Strain it, and add a peck of salt, dissolved in warm
water; three pounds of ground rice, boiled to a thin
paste, put in boiling hot; half a pound of powdered
Spanish whiting; and a pound of clear glue, dissolved
in warm water. Mix, and let it stand several days.
Then keep it in a kettle, on a portable furnace, and
put it on as hot as possible, with a painter's or
whitewash brush.

Another.
"Make whitewash, in the usual way, except that
the water used should have two double-handfuls of
salt dissolved in each pailful of the hot water used.
Then stir in a double-handful of fine sand, to make it
thick like cream. This is better to be put on hot.
Coloring matter can be added to both, making a
light stone color, a cream color, or a light buff, which
are most suitable for buildings."

Catherine Beecher, *Treatise on Domestic Economy*

American Journal

race or sex. Such beliefs became associated with Garrison's
name, so much so that the term "Garrisonian" came to stand
for everything ultra in the way of reform.

The differences that festered within the abolitionist ranks
erupted at the society's annual meeting in July 1840, when
Garrison and his supporters succeeded in getting an outspoken feminist named Abby Kelly elected to the executive committee. Upset with the result and Garrison's leadership, his
opponents left the American Anti-Slavery Society, never to
return. Some of the dissenters immediately joined with Lewis
Tappan to form the American and Foreign Anti-Slavery Society in an attempt to redirect the abolitionist movement back
to its more conservative evangelical roots. Always a maverick,
Theodore Weld condemned both societies as morally bankrupt and self-serving, refused to join either one, and instead
assisted John Quincy Adams in his fight against the gag rule.
Others likewise abandoned both national organizations and
devoted themselves to abolitionist activities at the local level.
Still others joined James G. Birney and Henry B. Stanton in
organizing the Liberty Party as an alternative to the Democratic and Whig presidential tickets in the election of 1840.

THE LIBERTY PARTY

Third parties rarely win elections, but they can significantly influence the political process either by forcing major parties to
modify their positions on key issues or by drawing votes away
from major candidates. So it was with the Liberty Party, which
grew directly out of the abolitionist movement and sought to
call attention to the "slave power" conspiracy that dominated
American politics. In 1840, James G. Birney received the party's
nomination and ran on an "immediatist" platform that emphasized ending slavery in the District of Columbia, outlawing
the interstate and coastal trade in slaves, and prohibiting the

admission of new slave states to the Union. Urging citizens to "vote as you pray and pray as you vote," Birney and his supporters (called "Liberty men") conducted a campaign that resembled an old-fashioned religious crusade. When the results came in, the Whig party candidate, General William Henry Harrison, defeated the Democratic incumbent, Martin Van Buren, and Birney received fewer than 7,000 votes. But Liberty Party pressure on Whig and Democratic congressional candidates in Ohio, Pennsylvania, New York, and Massachusetts forced them to harden their positions against slavery. It proved to be a small but significant victory.

James G. Birney, presidential nominee of the abolitionist Liberty Party in the elections of 1840 and 1844.

By pointing to the inherent contradiction between slavery and one of the most fundamental of American values—personal freedom—the Liberty Party forced people to confront not only the morality of slavery but also its ideological implications. The dichotomies of freedom/slavery and union/disunion increasingly polarized the North and South after 1840. These sectional tensions had surged to the forefront during the Missouri debates of 1820, the South Carolina nullification crisis of 1832, and the abolitionist postal and petition campaigns of the mid-1830s, but now they divided the Whig and Democratic Parties themselves. The American political system was faced with the supreme test of resolving the problem of slavery and maintaining the Union.

The Limits of Antebellum Reform

Antebellum reformers came largely from white, middle-class, Protestant backgrounds. They thought of themselves not as social reformers but rather as Christian soldiers engaged in a war to uphold Protestant morality, republican principles, and technological progress against the forces of sin and barbarism. Their causes ranged from abolitionism, pacifism, and women's rights to temperance, public education, and prison reform. Their method of operation owed much to the evangelical religious movement, from which most of them came.

They believed initially that reform would come about as a result of moral suasion, individual repentance, and voluntary action rather than through coercive government action. Yet as much as they committed themselves to moral and social improvement, they nonetheless harbored biases that reflected the culture in which they lived.

BLACK ABOLITIONISTS

From the outset, free blacks and escaped slaves committed themselves wholeheartedly to the cause of immediate emancipation. They set up their own national society—the National Negro Convention Movement—in 1830, organized support groups within black churches, established voluntary associations aimed at educating blacks, and published newspapers devoted to abolitionism. From 1835 to 1843, they worked assiduously for the American Anti-Slavery Society.

Abolitionism even provided a forum for some African American women, a group rendered voiceless in most areas of public life. The abolitionist Sojourner Truth was born a slave in upstate New York in 1797. After slavery ended in New York in 1827, the thirty-year-old Truth, then named Isabella, became one of a small number of African American women preachers at Methodist camp meetings during the Second Great Awakening. She subsequently worked with New York prostitutes at an institution supported by the Tappan brothers and lived in two different utopian communities, the second of which—the Northampton Association in western Massachusetts—was overseen by William Lloyd Garrison's brother-in-law. It was at Northampton that Truth became involved with the antislavery movement. In the late 1840s, she joined the abolitionist circuit as a forceful speaker for the humanity of slaves and free blacks, including black women. Sharing lecture halls with **Frederick Douglass** and members of the British Parliament, Truth never shied away from taking issue with male antagonists. According to author Harriet Beecher Stowe, no one "had more of that silent and subtle power which we call personal presence than this woman."

Sojourner Truth.

By the late 1840s, many black abolitionists had become exasperated by their white colleagues' refusal to admit them to the highest levels of the movement. Not only were blacks excluded from leadership positions in the American Anti-Slavery Society, they also experienced condescending treatment. White abolitionists frequently denigrated black culture and urged African Americans to absorb their own "superior" precepts of piety, hard work, and the like. But the path of assimilation did not necessarily lead to equality. Black abolitionists like Douglass and Truth were prized for their effectiveness as public speakers, but even Douglass was once told by a white colleague, "Better have a little of the plantation speech than not; it is not best that you seem too learned."

The son of a slave woman and white man, Douglass grew up in bondage on the Eastern Shore of Maryland. After working at plantation jobs and as a ship's caulker in Baltimore, he escaped to freedom in 1838 and went on to achieve international fame as an abolitionist, orator, newspaper editor, and writer. His eloquent indictments of slavery soon made him America's most important black leader and a voice of hope for his people.

Frederick Douglass.

Douglass and other black reformers had long been among Garrison's strongest supporters and felt obligated to him for bringing them into the movement. But as Garrison's tactics changed during the late 1830s to embrace women's rights, pacifism, and nonresistance, they found themselves increasingly estranged from their white colleagues. Douglass finally broke with Garrison in 1847, mainly because of his old mentor's attempts to control what he said and the way he acted. Thereafter, black abolitionists blazed a path of their own.

WORKERS

In contrast with their opposition to slave labor, antebellum reformers showed little interest in the condition of white workers. When labor-management discord erupted during the late 1820s and early 1830s and white artisans sought to protect their rights by organizing trade unions and running political candidates in local elections, they received no support from the evangelical reform groups that composed the Benevolent Empire. In this instance, differences of class, religious belief, and ethnicity (by the 1850s, some of the most militant trade unionists were German and Irish immigrants) proved insurmountable. Protestant reformers condemned strikes and other public displays by labor groups as a threat to good order. They deplored the extent to which workers drank and "frollicked" and denounced the labor movement as antagonistic to religion. The only issue on which workers and reformers agreed was the need for free public schools, and even then they did so for different reasons. From the tradesmen's perspective, public schools gave their children an opportunity for education and advancement. For Protestant reformers, schools were places where the "correct" values of honesty, thrift, hard work, and godliness could be instilled.

Even when the working women of Lowell, Massachusetts, organized the Female Labor Reform Association in 1844 and drew on the language of the Declaration of Independence to assert their "rights and privileges" as the "daughters of freemen," they were ignored by women's rights advocates. The oppression that middle-class women like Angelina Grimké, Elizabeth Cady Stanton, and Lucretia Mott experienced in their own lives did not sensitize them to the plight of Lowell's "mill girls." Although bound by common Protestant values, these women came from different social classes and lived in different social worlds, one governed by the factory system, the other by a "cult of domesticity" that held that a woman's place was in the home. The middle-class reformers seemed unable to recognize that the inequities working people complained of had the same paternalistic roots as their own oppression.

IMMIGRANTS

Protestant social reformers displayed even more insensitivity toward another group of Americans: non-Protestant immigrants. Up through the end of the War of 1812, most foreigners who entered the United States were white Anglo-Saxon Protestants. After the war, that trend began to change, dramatically by the mid-1840s.

The vast majority of immigrants in this period were Roman Catholics from Ireland and Germany. Often destitute, the Irish tended to settle in northeastern cities like Boston, New York, and Philadelphia. Germans also settled in the Northeast—particularly in New York, New Jersey, and Pennsylvania—but many more made their way inland either to buy farms in the Midwest or to settle in thriving German communities at Cincinnati, St. Louis, and Milwaukee. Between 1840 and 1860, some 4 million people, among them

1.7 million Irish and 1.3 million Germans, entered the United States, and their arrival signaled a dramatic demographic shift. The change was especially noticeable in eastern cities like Boston and New York, where, by the 1850s, the number of foreign-born residents climbed to more than 50 percent of the total population.

The large influx of Irish Catholic immigrants, which began in the mid-1840s, stemmed mainly from a disastrous potato famine that struck Ireland in the fall of 1845. To make matters worse, the failure of the potato crop, the staple of the Irish peasantry, occurred in the midst of ongoing land enclosures and tenant evictions by largely Protestant British landlords. The displacement of thousands of peasants off the land led to widespread starvation and, ultimately, 1.5 million dead. The massive Irish emigration to America was an act of survival, although in some years as many as 20 percent died in passage or shortly after they arrived in the new land. Destitute Irish farmers who poured into eastern ports of the United States and Canada were generally condemned to a new kind of hardscrabble existence in urban slums. Men who once tilled the soil had to settle for ill-paid jobs digging ditches, foundations, and canals, while women became factory workers and servants in middle-class American homes. In a pattern that would hold through the next century, Irish immigrants were pitted against other immigrant groups and against African Americans in competing for jobs, housing, and status, by a business system increasingly aware of its ability to manipulate difference.

Public reaction to the tidal wave of immigration that began in the 1840s was varied. Manufacturers, construction contractors, and other industrial employers looked favorably on the influx of foreigners because they lowered labor costs. Native-born workers resented the competition that came from immigrants. The language and life-styles of the newcomers annoyed virtually all segments of the Anglo population. Most irksome of all, though, was the growing presence of Roman Catholicism. German and Irish Catholics were often characterized as an ignorant and superstitious lot who too easily fell under the "spiritual despotism" of Rome's papal hierarchy. The Irish in particular became caricatured as

The caption to this anti-Irish political cartoon notes sarcastically, "The balance of trade with Great Britain seems to be still against us. 630 paupers arrived in Boston in the steamship *Nestoria* . . . from Galway, Ireland, shipped by the British Government." Often overcrowded and disease-ridden, such transports became known as "coffin ships."

The Benevolent Empire sought to Americanize immigrants by teaching them Protestant values. To this end, organizations such as the American Bible Society, the American Tract Society, and the American Sunday School Union distributed millions of booklets and essays. Another goal was free, tax-supported public education. In the mid-1830s, leading public school advocates like Horace Mann of Massachusetts denounced the intemperance, profanity, violence, and ignorance of the "dangerous classes" as vehemently as any Protestant preacher. Not only would public schools teach the three R's, Mann believed, they would also "inculcate all Christian morals," encourage good behavior, and serve as a "preventive and antidote" to the dangerous classes. In fact, Mann argued that free public education "does better than disarm the poor of their hostility toward the rich; it prevents being poor." It would thus become "the great equalizer of the condition of men."

Describing himself as a "circuit rider to the next generation," Mann abandoned a successful law career to serve as secretary of the Massachusetts Board of Education. Thanks largely to his efforts, the state legislature more than doubled its appropriations for public schools, substantially increased teachers' salaries, and established the first state college (called a "normal school") for the training of teachers. By the time

drunken and dishonest ne'er-do-wells whose growing political influence threatened to destroy the Republic and undo the fabric that bound Protestant America together.

The most vehement anti-Catholic attacks came from Protestant ministers in New England, New York, Pennsylvania, and Ohio. Evangelical stalwarts like Charles Grandison Finney and Lyman Beecher considered the new immigrants a serious threat and frequently spoke out against a "papist" conspiracy in America. In the early 1830s, Beecher delivered a series of blistering anti-Catholic sermons in Boston that inflamed public animosity. Catholic churches were burned, priests assaulted, and people driven from their homes from Philadelphia to Bangor, Maine. Beecher's involvement in organizing the American Temperance Society in 1826 owed much to his growing concern over the disruptive influence of "Romanists and Infidels." Throughout the antebellum period, in fact, the temperance movement engaged as much in nativist hostility as moral reform. The American Temperance Society's activities illustrate the odd mixture of humanitarianism, intolerance, progressivism, and self-righteousness that pervaded most aspects of reform.

This 1846 temperance society print shows a reformed drunkard "Signing the Pledge."

Dorothea Dix.

Mann resigned his position in 1848 to run for John Quincy Adams's seat in Congress as an antislavery Whig, he had turned public education into one of the most popular reforms of the era. A proponent of "the glorious sphere of Benevolence," he also became a strong ally of other educational reformers. Among them was Boston's Dorothea Dix, whose tireless lobbying activities before state legislatures resulted in the establishment of prison educational facilities and state hospitals for the mentally ill.

Like other reform efforts, the public school movement had a bright side and a dark side. During the antebellum period, a growing number of northern states established public school systems that provided a basic education to millions who otherwise couldn't afford it. But reformers shaped curricula to reflect the interests of Protestant America. The Boston School Committee, for instance, described its mission among the city's Irish Catholic population as "taking children at random from a great city, undisciplined, uninstructed, often with inveterate forwardness and obstinacy, and with inherited stupidity of centuries of ignorant ancestors" and "forming them from animals into intellectual beings, and . . . from intellec-

tual beings into Spiritual beings." Concerned about such challenges to their cultural and religious autonomy, Catholics responded with a nationwide network of parochial schools, hospitals, voluntary associations, and, eventually, colleges. These institutions were staffed by Catholic clergy intent on ensuring that health, education, and welfare comported with church doctrine.

From the 1820s to the 1850s, reform-minded Americans organized numerous movements to address new causes. A thriving market economy boosted many people into the middle class or higher, and this new prosperity allowed them to devote their energies to what they perceived as progressive causes. Just as important as economic prosperity was the widespread belief that the nation's good fortune would continue. The concept of America as a land of opportunity destined for greatness captured the popular imagination and paved the way for new utopian and charitable projects. Even though prejudice and racism pervaded society, unprecedented numbers of prosperous Americans sought to share their success, redeem the less fortunate, and reshape them in accordance with traditional Anglo-American values.

The Benevolent Empire also benefited from the telegraphs, newspapers, postal service, canals, steamboats, and railroads that allowed like-minded individuals to coordinate their ideas and actions over vast distances. But even as the new technologies helped to create unity, other forces acted in the opposite direction. Sectional divisions that had long simmered below the surface of political life would soon boil over and absorb all of America in an escalating controversy that would shake the country to its very core. By the 1840s, slavery had become the great issue that divided the United States. And it would not go away.

Chronology

	1824	Robert Owen founds New Harmony.
	1826	American Temperance Society established.
	January 1831	William Lloyd Garrison publishes first issue of *The Liberator*.
	1833	American Anti-Slavery Society established.
	1835	Anti-Slavery Society mounts "great postal campaign."
	May 1836	House of Representatives' gag resolution tables all antislavery petitions.
	1845	Irish potato famine.
	July 1847	Mormon settlers reach the Great Salt Lake Basin.
	1854	Henry David Thoreau publishes *Walden*.

Suggested Reading

Robert H. Abzug, *Passionate Liberator: Theodore Dwight Weld and the Dilemma of Reform* (1980)

Julie Roy Jeffrey, *The Great Silent Army of Abolitionism: Ordinary Women in the Abolitionist Movement* (1998)

Leo Marx, *The Machine in the Garden* (1964)

James B. Stewart, *Holy Warriors: The Abolitionists and American Slavery* (1976)

Ronald G. Walters, *American Reformers, 1815–1860* (1978)

This post–Civil War painting, *American Progress,* by John Gast, shows the goddess "Liberty" (symbol of the United States) moving westward across the continent while stringing telegraph wire. Accompanying her are symbols of American progress—miners, pioneer farm families, stagecoaches, telegraph lines, and steam railroads—and fleeing from these forces are Indians, buffalo, wild horses, and a snarling bear.

435

Focus QUESTIONS

- How did Texas and Oregon become objects of American expansion?

- What were the major political issues raised by territorial expansion?

- How were American forces able to prevail in the Mexican War?

- How was the future of slavery becoming a political issue in this period?

- What was the significance of the California gold rush?

- How did the Compromise of 1850 address the issue of slavery in the territories?

Manifest Destiny

In 1839, editor John L. O'Sullivan published an article in his New York *Democratic Review* declaring that "our country is destined to be the great nation of futurity." He confidently went on, "The far-reaching, the boundless future will be an era of American greatness. In its magnificent domain of space and time, the nation of many nations is destined to manifest to mankind the excellence of divine principles."

Six years later, O'Sullivan coined the term "Manifest Destiny" to summarize his belief that the United States had "the right . . . to overspread and to possess the whole of the [American] continent which Providence has given us for the development of the great experiment of liberty and federated self-government entrusted to us." The expression quickly caught on among proponents of territorial expansion, but the basic idea was not new. From the early days of the Republic through the presidency of Andrew Jackson, political leaders had repeatedly stated that, as one Democratic congressman put it, "this continent was intended by Providence as a vast theatre on which to work out the grand experiment of Republican government, under the auspices of the Anglo-Saxon race." This self-evident truth, an article of faith, was, in John Quincy Adams's view, "the best argument we had."

O'Sullivan's phrase captured the essence of this view, and brought Jefferson's "Empire for Liberty" and Jackson's desire to extend "the area of freedom" into a new era. But this pe-

> *"If the first principle of Manifest Destiny was Anglo-Saxon expansion, the lesson was that other people—Native Americans, Mexicans—would have to give way."*

riod, in which Manifest Destiny reached its highest pitch, also brought the strains of sectionalism to a new level of tension. The counterpoint of national expansion and sectional division increasingly demanded political attention. And if the first principle of Manifest Destiny was Anglo-Saxon expansion, the lesson was that other people—Native Americans, Mexicans—would have to give way.

THE TEXAS REVOLUTION

While Americans cast covetous eyes on the Southwest and Oregon during the 1820s and 1830s, the primary object of their attention by 1838 was Texas. Eighteen years earlier, a bankrupt lead-mine owner from Missouri named Moses Austin had secured permission from Spain to act as an *empresario*, or colonization agent, in settling 300 families from the United States in Texas. When Austin died in 1821, his son Stephen succeeded him. Stephen's plans were delayed, however, when the overthrow of Spanish rule in Mexico (1821) forced him to renegotiate his father's colonization agreement with the newly independent Mexican government.

Between 1824 and 1835, Austin brought more than 8,000 Americans into Texas, more than any of the forty other *empresarios* who had negotiated colonization agreements with the Mexican government. By 1835, the Anglo-American population in Texas reached 35,000, outnumbering the Mexican population there by 7 to 1. As Texas quickly became Americanized, tensions with Mexico increased. Cultural differences between the *norteamericanos* and Mexicans lay at the heart of the problem. American settlers had originally promised to become Mexican citizens, and to convert to Mexico's state religion of Roman Catholicism. But they remained strongly attached to the United States, and continued to hold Protestant Sunday services, violating Mexican law.

A serious confrontation occurred in 1829, when Mexico's president abolished slavery throughout the country. Some 90 percent of Anglo Texans were American southerners who either owned slaves or expected to do so in the future, and they resisted abolition. Although angry protests induced the Mexi-

can government to exempt Texas from its antislavery ruling, bitterness and distrust lingered. There were continual land disputes and Anglo complaints that they lacked a voice in Mexico's government. Mexican laws prohibited further American colonization and limited all labor contracts to ten years, which, in effect, meant a gradual end to slavery. Most threatening of all, Mexico began to garrison troops in Texas communities. With each passing year, the gulf between the American community and the Mexican government grew wider. So, too, did separatist sentiment on the part of the Americans.

Discontent soon turned to open resistance. Word reached Texas late in 1834 that the recently self-proclaimed Mexican

The Texas Revolution, 1835–1836

LEFT: Stephen F. Austin.

RIGHT: General Antonio Lopez de Santa Anna.

dictator, General Antonio Lopez de Santa Anna, had decided to send an army to Texas to clamp down on the Americans. It was rumored that Santa Anna intended to disenfranchise them, abolish their local governments, and send them packing back to the United States. Aiming to preempt Santa Anna, a separatist "war party" of forty armed men led by William B. Travis seized a Mexican tariff-collection garrison at Anahuac on Galveston Bay in June 1835. Learning of the attack, Santa Anna resolved to launch an all-out military campaign to crush the rebels and teach all of Texas a lesson.

As Santa Anna's army moved north, it encountered increasing armed resistance. Yet as late as November 1835, a convention (called a "consultation") with representatives from a dozen American communities in Texas voted 33 to 15 against declaring independence from Mexico. Instead, the delegates issued a Declaration of Causes for taking up arms, condemning Santa Anna's dictatorial regime while pledging loyalty to the Mexican government "so long as that nation is governed by the constitution and laws." But the convention also established a provisional government and named Sam Houston as the commander of its army. Slowly but surely, a Texas revolution was taking shape.

The Alamo, Goliad, and San Jacinto. Angered and embarrassed by a series of military defeats, Santa Anna left Mexico City to take personal command of his army. Arriving at San Antonio late in February 1836, he struck his first blow against a contingent of Americans who had barricaded themselves behind the adobe walls of an abandoned mission called the Alamo. After ten days of fierce fighting during which his troops suffered heavy losses, Santa Anna's forces finally took the Alamo on March 6. Of the 187 Texan defenders of the Alamo, all but one died—the only survivor was a slave named Joe who belonged to Colonel Travis, the commander of the rebel garrison. Less than two weeks later, Santa Anna delivered another crushing blow. His troops surprised a rebel force of 350 men near the town of Goliad. After holding the captives for a week, Santa Anna's men marched them to a wooded area outside the town and shot them down in cold blood. Santa Anna, it was thought, personally ordered the massacre.

The Alamo and Goliad massacres united Texans as nothing had before. "Remember the Alamo," "Remember Goliad" became rallying cries that energized their revolution. Even while the Alamo was under siege, a convention of Texans issued a formal declaration of independence modeled on the American document of 1776 and formed the republic of Texas. As news of the escalating conflict filtered back to the United States, hundreds of volunteers crossed the border to join Sam Houston's army. To the consternation of the American population in Texas, Houston's outnumbered and ill-equipped forces retreated before Santa Anna's army for more than seven weeks. But all this time, Houston was drilling his troops and waiting for the right moment to strike a decisive blow. That moment arrived on April 21, when his rebel force surprised a segment of Santa Anna's army in a wooded area near the San Jacinto River. After fifteen minutes of vicious fighting, 630 of Santa Anna's soldiers lay dead on the battlefield, many of them killed out of vengeance; 730 more were taken prisoner. Texan casualties numbered 9 dead and 30 wounded. A day later, Santa Anna was captured trying to escape in the uniform of a common soldier.

> *"Of the 187 Texan defenders of the Alamo, all but one died—the only survivor being a slave named Joe who belonged to Colonel Travis, the commander of the rebel garrison."*

The Republic of Texas. The Battle of San Jacinto effectively ended the Texas revolution. Santa Anna was taken to the new government's temporary headquarters at Velasco and forced to sign two treaties: one recognizing the independence of Texas, the other pledging his support to the new republic and acknowledging the Rio Grande as its southern boundary. Although Santa Anna and the Mexican government subsequently refused to recognize the treaties, Houston and his fellow revolutionaries had what they needed. Later that year, Houston was elected first president of the republic of Texas. Of the 6,000 persons who voted, 99 percent favored immediate annexation to the United States. Upon entering office in October 1836, Houston, pledged to fulfilling that task, dispatched a special agent to Washington with instructions to "make every exertion to effect annexation with the least possible delay."

By the time President Houston's emissary reached Washington, Andrew Jackson was in the final months of his presidency. His hand-picked successor, Martin Van Buren, had just won a convincing victory over several Whig opponents, yet Jackson seemed remote and uneasy. Houston was a longtime friend and political ally, and, all things being equal, Jackson would have liked nothing better than to annex Texas. But all things were not equal in the fall of 1836. The abolitionist movement had gained considerable political momentum during the past year, and its leaders, including the wily John Quincy Adams, were bound to stir up a hornet's nest if debate over the annexation of slaveholding Texas reached Congress. Jackson was also aware that Mexico refused to recognize Texas's independence and that annexation would in all likelihood lead to war. Moreover, President-elect Van Buren, himself no friend of slavery, seemed cool to the idea of annexation. All these considerations, along with signs that the economy was about to enter a downward spiral, caused Jackson to back away from annexation. Convinced that the president would not change his mind, Houston's agent successfully lobbied Congress to fund a U.S. diplomatic representative to Texas. Although Jackson also had qualms about that idea,

The Mexican army assaulting the Alamo, 1836.

General Sam Houston, hero of San Jacinto and first president of the republic of Texas (1836–38).

on March 2, 1837, two days before he left office, he signed a document officially recognizing the republic of Texas as a sovereign state. Texas was not in the Union, but half a loaf was better than none.

THE OREGON COUNTRY

While Texans stewed over annexation, American expansionism gathered momentum in the far West. At issue was the Oregon Country, half a million square miles that lay between the Pacific Ocean and the continental divide. Oregon embraced not only the present states of Oregon, Idaho, and Washington and parts of Montana and Wyoming, but also almost half of the Canadian province of British Columbia, as far north as 54°–40′ latitude.

Before 1840, Oregon was primarily the domain of Indians, trappers, and fur-trading companies. While both Great Britain and the United States claimed the region, they had agreed in an 1818 treaty to a joint occupation of the sprawling territory. So long as settlement remained sparse and the fur trade prospered, the agreement worked reasonably well, with the British tending to stay north of the Columbia River and Americans to the south. The situation began to change, however, during the early 1840s. An increasing number of midwestern farm families down on their luck from the de-

This cartoon about the Oregon boundary dispute shows a pugnacious "America" squaring off against his somewhat bemused and larger opponent, "England."

pression of 1837–41 sold what remained of their holdings and trekked along the Oregon Trail. A tortuous three-month journey across the continent and through the Rocky Mountains brought the farmers into the fertile Willamette Valley south of the Columbia River near Portland.

The American community in Oregon numbered less than 2,000 in 1843. Yet, to the chagrin of British, it formed a territorial government with the explicit intent that "the United States of America extend their jurisdiction over us." By 1845, the American population had more than doubled to 5,000. As "Oregon fever" spread, midwestern expansionists began to petition the federal government to end its joint occupation agreement with Britain and claim all of Oregon for the United States. Their slogan became "54–40 or fight."

The Politics of Expansion

THE ELECTION OF 1844

American voters not only chose a president in 1844; they also decided the question of territorial expansion. The electoral outcome was widely viewed as a national referendum on the politics of Manifest Destiny.

Of the four candidates in the field, the most visible was President John Tyler, a former Democrat turned Whig who ascended to the office in 1841 when William Henry Harrison died suddenly of pneumonia after only a month in office. Next came Henry Clay of Kentucky, the economic nationalist and perennial Whig Party favorite who twice before—in 1824 and 1832—had run for the presidency, only to fail. Clay's Democratic counterpart was former president Martin Van Buren of New York, a staunch Jacksonian and party architect, who had been defeated in 1840 by Harrison. Last came Kentucky's James G. Birney, the candidate of the small but outspoken abolitionist Liberty Party. Of the four, only Clay and Birney would survive the nomination process.

President Tyler's chances of survival seemed remote by 1844. Democrats considered him a political renegade, and he had been drummed out of the Whig Party for vetoing several key pieces of legislation. As a politician without a party, Tyler knew that he needed a political miracle to retain his office. He thought he saw his opportunity through foreign affairs.

Thanks primarily to Tyler's secretary of state, Daniel Webster, the United States had signed a treaty with Great Britain in 1842 that settled long-standing disputes over the Canadian-American boundary from northern Maine as far west as the Lake of the Woods in northern Minnesota. Although no one

A lithographic print of presidential candidate Henry Clay in 1844. As Clay had been denied the nomination in 1840, this poster pleads for "Justice to Harry of the West."

knew it at the time, the Webster-Ashburton Treaty also secured the immensely rich Mesabi iron-ore range in northern Minnesota, which would become one of the mainstays of the steel industry after the Civil War. While negotiations over the Canadian-American boundary west of the Rockies simmered, Tyler pinned his political hopes on the annexation of Texas. But a treaty of annexation negotiated with the Texas government failed in the Senate over the issue of the extension of slavery. His defeat sealed, Tyler eventually withdrew from the race. Meantime, the Whig convention in Baltimore unanimously nominated Clay as its standard bearer. Fearful that "annexation and war with Mexico are identical," Clay opposed the annexation of Texas and called for "union, peace, and patience." In making no reference whatsoever either to expansion or Texas, the Whig platform sidestepped the issue of slavery altogether.

Not so the Democrats. Although Van Buren was the early favorite, pro-expansionist northerners as well as southerners distrusted him because of his antislavery leanings and his ambiguous stand on Texas. By the time the Democratic convention met in May, expansionist party members from the South and Midwest had engineered a revolt that deadlocked the convention and resulted in the nomination of James K. Polk. A former congressman, speaker of the House, and governor of Tennessee, Polk was a longtime supporter of Andrew Jackson, a stalwart Democrat, and an outspoken expansionist. Long before the convention met, he had indicated that he favored the immediate annexation of Texas. The Democratic Party's platform went even further, boldly declaring "that the re-occupation of Oregon and the re-annexation of Texas at the earliest possible period are great American measures." The Democrats also increased the stakes for midwestern expansionists by asserting that "our title to the whole of the Territory of Oregon is clear and unquestionable." By adopting such an aggressive stance, the Democrats

An 1844 Democratic Party cartoon satirizing the Whig Party's opposition to the annexation of Texas. Personified as a beautiful young woman, Texas is holding a cornucopia filled with flowers. Doffing his hat, James K. Polk takes Texas's hand and welcomes her, saying, "Your valor has won you liberty and independence." On the other hand, Henry Clay (arms folded) warns, "Stand back, Madam Texas! For we are more holy than thou! Do you think we will have anything to do with gamblers, horse-racers, and licentious profligates?"

sought not only to attract both northern and southern expansionist votes but also to clearly demarcate themselves from the Whigs.

The election itself featured invective and mudslinging from all sides. Long-standing economic differences between Whigs and Democrats over tariffs, banking and currency, and revenue distribution paled in comparison with the Texas question and the larger issue of territorial expansion. Although Clay softened his stance on Texas annexation as the campaign wore on, his waffling probably cost him as many votes among Whigs as he won. Polk's expansionist views on foreign policy, on the other hand, attracted strong support in the Midwest and deep South. When the election returns came in, "Young Hickory" emerged victorious, but only by about 38,000 votes. Indeed, Clay might have won the election if he had carried New York; but Birney's Liberty Party syphoned off just enough antislavery Whig support to give Polk a

5,106-vote edge and all of New York's electoral ballots. In this instance, the presence of a third party made an enormous political difference.

THE INTERNATIONAL DIMENSION

Despite his narrow victory, Polk claimed a popular mandate to fulfill America's Manifest Destiny. Convinced of the same, the outgoing President Tyler again pushed for the immediate annexation of Texas and, through some clever legislative maneuvering, succeeded at length in winning congressional approval. On March 1, 1845, three days before he left office, Tyler signed the resolution and sent it by special agent to Texas. Although Britain and France tried to persuade Texas leaders not to align themselves with the United States, popular sentiment in Texas proved overwhelmingly favorable to the idea. The congress of the Lone Star Republic voted unanimously for annexation on June 16. With President Polk's wholehearted approval, Texas entered the Union in December as the twenty-eighth state. The government of Mexico immediately severed diplomatic relations with the United States.

In the midst of the crisis with Mexico, Polk turned his attention to the Oregon boundary question. At least four times before, the United States had approached Great Britain about settling the boundary at the 49th parallel, only to be rebuffed. Bolstered by Democratic campaign slogans like "All of Oregon or none" and "54–40 or fight," Polk warned the British in his inaugural address in March 1845 that "our title to the country of the Oregon is 'clear and unquestionable.'" With threats of war rumbling on both sides of the Atlantic, the new president quietly informed the British minister to Washington that he would settle for the 49th parallel even though the United States had a rightful claim to all of Oregon. When the minister flatly refused the offer without consulting his superiors in London, Polk reasserted

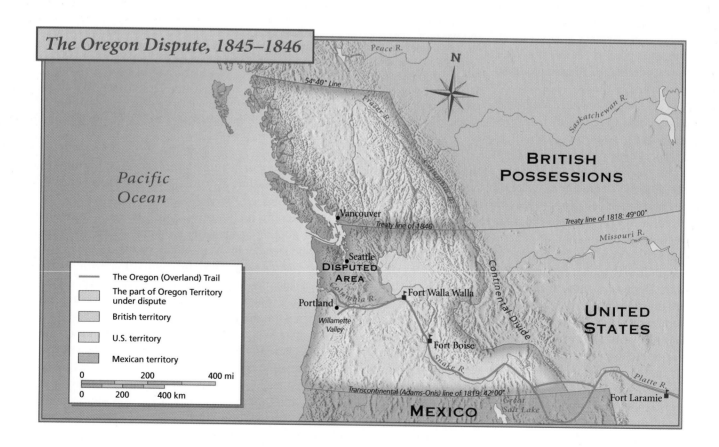

The Oregon Dispute, 1845–1846

Legend:
— The Oregon (Overland) Trail
- The part of Oregon Territory under dispute
- British territory
- U.S. territory
- Mexican territory

0   200   400 mi
0   200   400 km

Peace R.
54°40" Line
Fraser R.
Saskatchewan R.
Pacific Ocean
BRITISH POSSESSIONS
Vancouver
Treaty line of 1846
Treaty line of 1818: 49°00"
Missouri R.
Seattle
DISPUTED AREA
Fort Walla Walla
Portland
Columbia R.
Continental Divide
UNITED STATES
Willamette Valley
Fort Boise
Snake R.
Platte R.
Transcontinental (Adams-Onis) line of 1819: 42°00"
Great Salt Lake
Fort Laramie
MEXICO

James K. Polk, eleventh president of the United States (1845–49).

his original demand for all of Oregon, even if it meant war with England. In his message to Congress in December 1845, he even reintroduced the Monroe Doctrine to warn the British that "no future European colony or dominion shall with our consent be planted or established on any part of the North American continent."

The United States and Great Britain came dangerously close to war during the spring of 1846. Determined to follow "a bold & firm course," Polk notified the British in May of his intention to end the joint occupation of Oregon. Equally determined not to relinquish all of Oregon to America, Britain began to outfit thirty warships for action against the United States. But serious political problems at home caused the British to alter their position and offer to settle the boundary at the 49th parallel. Polk's cabinet urged him to accept the deal. Reluctant at first but aware that war with Mexico was imminent, Polk decided to submit the treaty to the Senate. Although a few radical expansionists protested his "surrender" to the British and demanded "every foot or not an inch" of Oregon, the Senate ratified the agreement on June 15, 1846.

By the time the Oregon Treaty was signed, the United States had already declared war on Mexico, which refused to recognize Texas's independence and its subsequent annexation by the United States. Texas, in turn, insisted that its southern border lay along the Rio Grande rather than its original Mexican boundary at the Nueces River. And with expansionist sentiment widespread, Americans now sought to acquire the Mexican province of California.

American merchants and sea captains involved in the fur, whaling, and China trades had long known about the scenic beauty and commercial potential of California. But political leaders did not notice the area until a navy expedition under Captain Charles Wilkes sailed into San Francisco Bay in 1838 and subsequently reported that "Upper California may boast one of the finest, if not the very best harbour in the world." The publication of Wilkes's report in 1845 heightened the

American appetite for California. Reflecting the business interests that some of his most important Massachusetts constituents had in the "Pacific trade," Senator Daniel Webster declared that "the port of San Francisco would be twenty times as valuable to us as all Texas." Although he differed with Webster on Texas, President Polk nonetheless recognized the value of California. Convinced that the British had designs on the region, he confided to a friend that "in reasserting Mr. Monroe's doctrine I had California and the fine bay of San Francisco as much in view as Oregon." Polk wanted California. It was the richest prize yet in North America.

OUTBREAK OF WAR

The spark that ignited the war with Mexico came not from California, however, but Texas. In June 1845, Polk ordered General Zachary Taylor and a small army of 1,500 men to move into Texas and occupy the disputed territory between the Nueces River and the Rio Grande, claimed by both Mexico and Texas. By July 25, Taylor had reached Corpus Christi on the Gulf Coast but decided not to move closer to the Rio Grande for fear of provoking war. While Taylor encamped on the south side of the Nueces near Corpus Christi, Polk received word that the Mexican government was willing to discuss the boundary question. He dispatched John Slidell of New Orleans to Mexico City with instructions not only to resolve the disputed boundary, but also to offer Mexico $25 million for California and another $5 million for the territory of New Mexico, plus the cancellation of $6 million in claims by American citizens against Mexico for the loss of property suffered during its many political upheavals.

When Slidell arrived in Mexico City in December 1845, the Mexican government refused to receive him, ostensibly because his appointment had not been officially confirmed by the U.S. Senate. By the time Slidell's Senate confirmation reached the Mexican capital, a new government had come to power that refused either to negotiate the Texas boundary or to receive Slidell. When news of Slidell's treat-

General Zachary Taylor, whose exploits during the Mexican War resulted in his election as twelfth president of the United States (1849–50).

ment reached Washington, Polk readied for war by ordering General Taylor and his enlarged force of 4,000 to move farther south to the banks of the Rio Grande. Taylor reached the north side of the river just across from the Mexican town of Matamoros on March 26, 1846, and reported that all was quiet. But by April 11, the first elements of the Mexican army began to arrive in Matamoros, and their numbers grew to 5,700 troops. The inevitable clash occurred when a Mexican cavalry unit crossed the Rio Grande on April 24, and the next day exchanged fire with a smaller scouting party of American mounted infantry sent out to investigate its movements. By the time the engagement broke off, 16 dragoons were either dead or wounded. "*War has commenced*," an American soldier wrote excitedly in his diary, "and we look for a conflict within a few days."

News of the clash near Matamoros arrived the day after a disgusted John Slidell had returned to Washington and counseled the president "that nothing is to be done with those people, until they have been chastised." Convinced that he had no alternative, Polk sent a war message to Congress on May 10 in which he claimed that despite "every ef-

fort at reconciliation," Mexico "has passed the boundary of the United States, has invaded our territory, and shed American blood upon the American soil." Although both houses responded by passing war resolutions by large majorities, there was considerable dissent from the outcome. Abolitionist and antislavery Whigs denounced Polk's actions, claiming that he had purposely provoked the Mexicans into hostile action in order to satisfy the interests of "Land Jobbers and Slave-Jobbers." At the same time, an obscure Whig congressman from Illinois named Abraham Lincoln challenged the Polk administration to point to the exact "spot" on American soil where American blood had been shed. Implicit in young Lincoln's "spot resolution" was the denial that Texas's boundary extended as far south as the Rio Grande as well as the charge that President Polk had maneuvered the United States into a war.

THE WILMOT PROVISO

The Democratic Party was also divided over the war and its implications. A large majority of Democrats had initially supported Polk's expansionist policies, but they soon split over the future of slavery in the new territories. The flash point came when David Wilmot, a freshman representative from Towanda, Pennsylvania, introduced an amendment to an appropriations bill in August 1846 that excluded slavery from any territory that might be acquired from Mexico. Wilmot's "Proviso" shocked the Polk administration. Wilmot had consistently supported the president's legislative agenda, including the annexation of Texas, but he now pointed the way for "free-soil" Democrats who opposed the expansion of slavery into new territories. Free-soilers did not necessarily sympathize with blacks or support abolition. To the contrary, Wilmot himself viewed the West as a white man's preserve where "the sons of toil, of my own race and own color" could establish new roots without having to compete against either slave or free black labor.

"The Issue Joined." In June 1846, Senator Daniel Webster accused Polk of purposely provoking a war with Mexico. This cartoon plays on that confrontation, showing Webster, fists held high, challenging Polk to a fight. Serving as seconds to Polk are Thomas Ritchie (second from left) and James Watson Webb (far left), two well-known Democratic newspaper editors. Webster is seconded by an unidentified person and Horace Greeley (far right), the reform-oriented editor of the *New York Tribune*.

Representative David Wilmot, author of the highly controversial proviso that prohibited slavery in any territory acquired from Mexico.

Wilmot's amendment, which passed in the House but failed in the Senate, nevertheless had momentous consequences. By focusing public attention on the future of slavery in new territories, it pulled politics away from issues of national expansion toward the widening sectional differences between the North and the South. The issue of slavery in the territories would be debated and voted repeatedly over the next fifteen years. And as slavery increasingly dominated the political agenda, sectional antagonisms grew more intense. These tensions altered the structure of American politics by undermining old parties and lifting up new ones.

"Jimmy Polk's War"

The Mexican War was fought mainly on three fronts: from the Rio Grande southwest toward Monterrey and Buena Vista; in California and the inner reaches of New Mexico; and from the coastal city of Vera Cruz westward to Mexico City.

THE MAJOR CAMPAIGNS

From the outset, President Polk played a direct role in coordinating U.S. forces. Sending Zachary Taylor to secure Texas's southern boundary on the Rio Grande, he ordered a naval blockade of Mexico's east coast, hoping that it would force the Mexican government to accede to his territorial demands. Although the blockade succeeded militarily, it failed to bring Mexico to the bargaining table. If anything, it hardened Mexican determination not to yield to the bullying of the United States. Convinced that their army was stronger than the largely volunteer American force, that their country's rugged terrain would create logistical nightmares for the invaders, and that European nations—particularly England and France—would come to their aid, Mexican leaders brimmed with confidence.

But they soon had cause for doubt. At the Battles of Palo Alto and Resaca de la Palma in May 1846, Taylor's smaller army inflicted heavy casualties, forcing their Mexican opponents to retreat across the Rio Grande. Occupying Matamoros in mid-May, Taylor slowly carried his invasion of Mexico toward Monterrey, a heavily fortified regional capital. Taylor was outnumbered and outgunned, and his poorly executed attack nearly led to disaster. But after two days of fighting, the badly mauled American forces penetrated the walls of Monterrey. The Mexican commander surrendered on condition that he and his troops could leave and that Taylor would not pursue them for eight weeks. Learning of the capture—and the armistice—an angry Polk ordered Taylor to abrogate the agreement and continue his march into the interior of Mexico. Taylor followed orders, stopping in November 1846, in Saltillo, convinced that going farther into the heartland of Mexico would stretch his supply lines to the breaking point.

While Taylor's army rested at Saltillo, a much larger force of 15,000 men under the command of General Santa Anna marched north to confront it. When Santa Anna drew near on February 20, 1847, Taylor withdrew from Saltillo to a stronger defensive position just south of Buena Vista. At this time, his army numbered 4,500, mostly ill-trained volunteers with no battle experience. Well aware of Taylor's desperate situation, Santa Anna urged him to surrender. When Taylor refused, the Mexican army began its attack. Two days of repeated assaults failed to dislodge the Americans, however. Finally, with casualties on both sides heavy, the Mexican force retreated, in effect ending the war in northern Mexico. Taylor remained with his army until October 1847, when he returned to New Orleans to a tumultuous welcome. A national hero, he began to contemplate a run for the presidency in the upcoming election of 1848.

Elsewhere, American forces were attempting to establish U.S. control over California and New Mexico. As in Oregon, several thousand Americans arrived in California during the early 1840s, most of them settling in the Sacramento Valley near a place called Sutter's Fort. Even before they learned that war with Mexico had been officially declared, a group of Americans revolted against local Mexican authorities in June 1846 and set about establishing an independent republic at Sonoma, replete with their own flag that carried one star and the symbol of a grizzly bear. The rebels were soon joined by Captain John C. Frémont and a group of heavily armed U.S. soldiers who purportedly were in the region to conduct a topographical survey. Frémont, the politically ambitious son-in-law of Senator Thomas H. Benton of Missouri, became a leader of the Bear Flag Republic. On July 7, Commodore John D. Sloat's U.S. naval squadron seized Monterey on the California coast and established control over the San Francisco, Sonoma, and Sutter's Fort areas. Two days later, the American flag was raised at Sonoma, bringing to an end the short-lived Bear Flag Republic. Later that month, Sloat's successor, Commodore Robert F. Stockton, announced the annexation of California to the United States with himself as

governor and Captain Frémont as commander of "the California Battalion of United States troops."

While Stockton and Frémont sought to extend American control over all of California, a 1,400-man army under Colonel Stephen Watts Kearny marched westward from Fort Leavenworth (in present-day Kansas) with orders from President Polk to seize New Mexico and then move on to assist in the annexation of California. Following a seven-week march

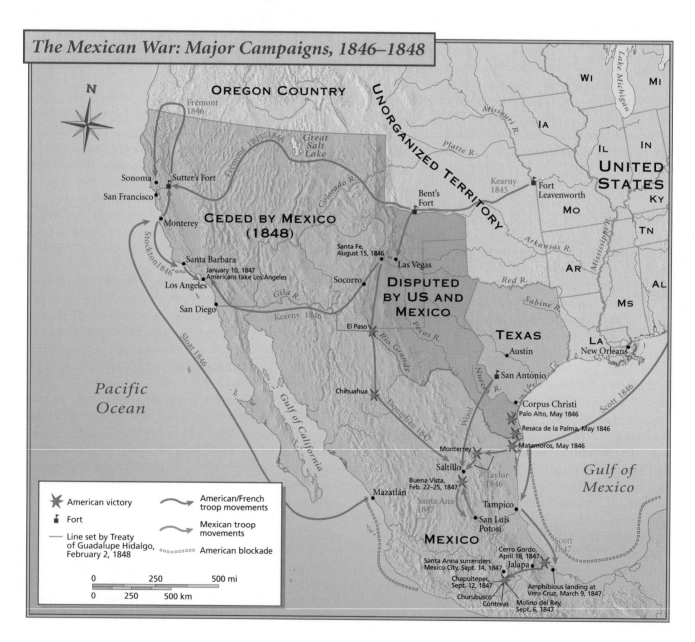

The Mexican War: Major Campaigns, 1846–1848

San Francisco, gateway to the California gold fields, was little more than a small town in 1849, with as many tents and shacks as houses. Telegraph Hill is in the background, as are dozens of ships bringing miners and supplies to the boomtown.

that covered over 850 miles, Kearny's force took Santa Fe on August 15, 1846, without firing a shot. After establishing a territorial government and posting most of his troops to hold New Mexico, Kearny set out with 100 men on the second leg of his campaign on September 25. Eleven days out of Santa Fe, he met the explorer-guide Kit Carson, who brought news from Commodore Stockton about the seizure of California. Kearny prevailed upon Carson to serve as his guide, and after a grueling ten-week march through hot and inhospitable desert country, his weary contingent reached southern California just in time to help Stockton and Frémont quell Mexican forces in the Los Angeles area. The struggle for California ended on January 10, 1847, when the victorious Americans entered Los Angeles with their band playing and raised the Stars and Stripes over the town's Government House. With the fall of Los Angeles, Polk's fondest desire was realized.

The third major American campaign began in October 1846. Polk and his advisers decided to attack Mexico's most important port at Vera Cruz and, from there, move an American army inland against Mexico City. The president turned to General Winfield Scott to lead the invasion. Commonly known among military associates as "Old Fuss and Feathers," Scott was an experienced senior officer and a superb organizer. Yet Polk was uneasy because he knew that Scott, like Zachary Taylor, had ties to the Whig Party and would proba-

bly use his military exploits as political capital once the war ended.

Calling for an amphibious landing of 15,000 troops, Scott ordered the attack on Vera Cruz in early spring before the deadly yellow fever season began. Much to Taylor's consternation, Scott also transferred more than half of Taylor's battle-tested veterans to the Vera Cruz expedition—a decision that prompted Santa Anna's ill-fated attack on Buena Vista in February 1847. Scott's strategy was to land American forces south of heavily fortified Vera Cruz, envelop it with artillery, and lay siege to it. The amphibious landing—the first of its type in American history—took place on March 9, 1847, when 10,000 troops went ashore in specially designed "surf-boats" requisitioned by Scott. Since the Mexican commander chose to remain behind the walls of Vera Cruz, the Americans experienced virtually no opposition. Blockaded by sea and cut off by land, the city surrendered less than three weeks later.

With Vera Cruz secured, the way inland lay open for Scott's army. Santa Anna attempted to stop the invaders at Cerro Gordo, but, thanks to astute reconnoitering on the part of Captain Robert E. Lee, Scott's troops outflanked the Mexican defenders and overcame them on April 18. The next day, they entered Jalapa, almost 5,000 feet above sea level and well beyond the coastal yellow fever zone.

447

The most challenging phase of Scott's invasion began early in August, when he set out with more than 10,000 men on the final push toward Mexico City. At this point, he made a bold decision. Convinced that he did not have the manpower to maintain a supply and communication line to Vera Cruz, he decided "to render my little army a *self-sustaining machine*" by foraging off the land. European observers were convinced that Scott had committed a fatal error and that he and his men would soon be swallowed up in the Mexican terrain. "Scott is lost," the Duke of Wellington—perhaps the most famous soldier of the age—concluded. "He can't take the city, and he can't fall back upon his base."

Lithographic view of Los Angeles in 1857.

But superb planning and leadership helped Scott's little army to endure and triumph. By August 20, 1847, the American forces had reached the outskirts of Mexico City. Outnumbered by more than three to one, Scott wisely decided not to attack the Mexican army under Santa Anna head-on. Relying on the advice of young engineering officers like Captain Lee and Lieutenant P. G. T. Beauregard, he instead resorted to diversionary tactics and flanking movements to secure hard-fought victories at Contreas and Churubusco. He was not deflected by the Battle of Molino del Ray on September 8, which resulted in the heaviest casualties (781) suffered by American troops during the entire war. The last remaining obstacle was the fortified castle of Chapultepec with its summer palace and the buildings of Mexico's military academy. After an intense artillery bombardment and hand-to-hand fighting, the castle fell on September 12. Later that day, the first American troops streamed down an eastward causeway and entered Mexico City. The following day, Scott's 7,000-man army marched in. Santa Anna surrendered unconditionally on September 14.

THE TREATY OF GUADALUPE HIDALGO

Although Scott's troops occupied Mexico City, a peace accord did not come immediately. Guerrillas posed a serious threat to the American invaders, and the Mexican government refused to negotiate. The war's cost in blood and treasure mounted, as did opposition to the conflict at home. A frustrated President Polk increased his territorial demands from Mexico, while ardent expansionists within the Democratic Party began calling for "All Mexico." Adding to Polk's irritation was his belief that a state department official named Nicholas P. Trist, sent the previous spring to open negotiations with the Mexican government, had botched the job and, even worse, had become a political ally of General Scott. Polk recalled him. Trist ignored Polk's order, however, and contin-

Scott's troops assaulting the fortress of Chapultepec, which led to the capture of Mexico City on September 14, 1847.

ued to represent himself as the official diplomatic agent of the U.S. government in Mexico City. At length, on February 2, 1848, he signed the Treaty of Guadalupe Hidalgo, in which he committed the United States to pay Mexico $15 million and assume $3.25 million in claims of American citizens against Mexico—in return for the cession of California and New Mexico and the recognition of the Rio Grande as the southern boundary of Texas.

Although Polk was exasperated by Trist's conduct, the terms of the treaty largely fulfilled his original goals. He therefore decided to submit the document to the Senate for approval rather than heighten tensions festering within his party between southern "All Mexico" proponents and northern advocates of the Wilmot Proviso. Ratification came quickly. "The desire for peace, and not the approbation of its terms," John C. Calhoun observed, "induces the Senate to yield its content." A disgruntled Whig critic was less kind. "The treaty negotiated by an unauthorized agent, with an unacknowledged government, submitted by an accidental President to a dissatisfied Senate," he wrote, "has . . . been confirmed." Although he would have liked more from Mexico, Polk seemed satisfied with the outcome. California and New Mexico, he told Congress in July 1848, "constitute of themselves a country large enough for a great empire." The United States now spread from the Atlantic to the Pacific. For the time being, America's Manifest Destiny had been satisfied.

"By 1846, the United States stood second only to Great Britain as the leading industrial nation of the world."

THE TECHNOLOGY OF WAR

A key to the U.S. victory lay in military leadership and superior technology. Although he lacked organizational ability and tactical sophistication, Zachary Taylor earned his battlefield nickname of "Old Rough and Ready" through sheer determination and coolness under fire. Winfield Scott, on the other hand, was a prickly and proper individual, as his nickname "Old Fuss and Feathers" suggested. Yet he proved to be a master planner and, in the Mexico City campaign, a brilliant field commander. Both men surrounded themselves with capable subordinates. In addition to Scott's Captain Lee and Lieutenant Beauregard, dozens of West Point graduates served in the Mexican War, many of them in the elite engineering, artillery, ordnance, and topographical engineering corps. Among them were Braxton Bragg, Ulysses S. Grant, Henry W. Halleck, Joseph E. Johnston, James Longstreet, George B. McClellan, George G. Meade, William T. Sherman, and George H. Thomas—all of whom would become renowned commanders some fifteen years later during the Civil War. The Mexican War thus served as an important training ground for the subsequent conflict.

The war previewed a number of new technologies that gave American forces a distinct advantage over their Mexican adversaries. By 1846, the United States stood second only to Great Britain as the leading industrial nation of the world. Railroads and steamboats, two prominent technologies of the industrial era, were used to transport troops and supplies to the battlefront. Even the **electric telegraph,** only two years old in 1846, helped to facilitate the communication of military and diplomatic messages from Washington, D.C., to American outposts in Mexico. The experience gained with all three technologies served as a useful prelude to their massive deployment during the Civil War.

Of more immediate importance were the weapons used by American forces. By 1846, American armories were producing some of the most sophisticated small arms in the world. Regular infantry troops carried percussion muskets that were not only faster to load and more reliable than the older flintlock models used mainly by Mexican soldiers but also more easily repaired in the field, thanks to their interchangeable parts. Some troops, like Colonel Jefferson Davis's First Mississippi Volunteer Regiment, were armed with highly accurate (and interchangeable) rifles, while others, like Captain Samuel H. Walker's First Texas volunteer "rangers," carried the new six-shot revolving pistols invented by Samuel Colt of Hartford, Connecticut. Owing largely to their use during the Texas revolution and the Mexican War, Colt's six-shooters quickly became popular sidearms throughout the American West. All of these weapons traced their origins to the uniformity system of interchangeable manufacturing developed after the War of 1812 in America's armories.

In addition to the excellence of American small arms, the outcome of many important battles fought during the Mexican War hinged on the effective use of artillery. Thanks to design and manufacturing improvements introduced before the war, American artillery units were equal to any in the world. Although the American arsenal included howitzers and mortars for siege purposes, the basic weapon for use in battle was a "six-pounder gun," so-called because it fired a standard projectile weighing six pounds. Often referred to as "light" or "flying" artillery because of its impressive mobility, the six-pounder had greater range (1,500 yards) and fired a larger variety of projectiles than comparable Mexican guns. Gun crews could load and fire the piece in less than a minute, often three to eight times faster than their Mexican opponents. Under the supervision of West Point–trained officers, the flying artillery proved highly effective against numerically superior Mexican forces. Altogether, the success of American arms during the Mexican War verified the capability of the uniformity system of manufacturing introduced by the U.S. Army Ordnance Department at armories and arsenals before the war.

The Election of 1848

The euphoria of victory could not dispel the tensions of a divisive war and a developing sectionalism. With the 1848 presidential election looming, President Polk, owing to declining health, chose not to seek a second term. Both major parties experienced the turbulence caused by the Wilmot Proviso and its sanctions against the spread of slavery into new territories. In New York state, for example, the Democratic Party had split into two hostile camps. The Barnburners, led by former president Martin Van Buren, supported the Wilmot Proviso. Their name came from their opponents, who charged that like the proverbial farmer who burned his barn to get rid of the rats, they were destroying the party in order to keep slavery out of new territories. The opposing Hunkers were conservative Democrats who "hunkered down," putting office-seeking ahead of political principle and taking a pro-South stand on the expansion of slavery. The two factions were also divided by personal feuds that went back to 1844, when Hunker Democrats abandoned Van Buren's candidacy for the presidency and supported Polk.

Similar divisions also beset the Whig Party, with antislavery "conscience" Whigs squaring off against conservative "cotton" Whigs who did not want to rock the boat concerning slavery. Whigs and Democrats from the South often joined together in defending slavery, and their northern counterparts also acted together. These divisions and realignments beset Congress, where bitter feelings and at least one

"As positions hardened over the expansion of slavery, Congress became a battle arena that pitted sectional antagonists against each other rather than a meeting place for working out common problems."

challenge to a duel fueled debate over a bill organizing a territorial government for Oregon. A bill excluding slavery from the Oregon Territory passed in August 1848, but only after nine months of debate and over the vehement protests of southern congressmen who believed that masters should be allowed to take their slaves into any new territory. All sense of decorum seemed to ebb away during the Oregon debates. As positions hardened over the expansion of slavery, Congress became a battle arena that pitted sectional antagonists against each other rather than a meeting place for working out common problems that faced the nation.

With tensions high, the parties held their nominating conventions. Meeting in Baltimore in May, the Democrats nominated New Hampshire–born senator Lewis Cass of Michigan. A party stalwart, Cass had distinguished himself in the War of 1812, served eighteen years as the governor of the Michigan Territory, and served another six years as Andrew Jackson's secretary of war. An ardent expansionist as the southerner Polk was, Cass had called for all of Oregon up to 54°–40′, supported Texas annexation, and pushed for territorial expansion as far south as the Yucatán peninsula. He openly opposed the Wilmot Proviso, proposing instead that the inhabitants of each territory determine whether or not they would allow slavery—a formula that would become well-known during the 1850s as "popular sovereignty." Cass quietly acceded to the Democratic platform, which denounced abolitionism and evaded discussion of the great political issue of the day, slavery in the territories. In the view of Horace Greeley, the reform-minded editor of the *New York Tribune*, Cass's acceptance of the platform made him "the servile pimp of Slavery . . . and the deadly enemy of Impartial Justice and Universal Freedom."

Although Henry Clay hoped to be the Whig Party's nominee, his position had weakened by the time delegates gathered in Philadelphia on June 7. More than anything else, Whig leaders wanted a victory in the upcoming November elections, and they were not confident that the seventy-year-old Clay could deliver it. Instead, they turned to "Old Rough and Ready" Zachary Taylor, the Mexican War hero. By his own admission, Taylor was apolitical. He had never joined the Whig Party; indeed, he had never voted. Even when supporters advanced his name as a possible presidential nominee, he maintained silence not only about slavery but also other traditional Whig concerns such as the protective tariff and internal improvements. But as a Louisiana planter who owned more than 100 slaves, he seemed "safe" on the slavery question and therefore enjoyed strong southern support at the convention. Content to campaign solely on Taylor's war record, the Whigs adjourned without adopting a platform. As a sop to the disappointed Clay, the vice-presidential spot went to his friend and supporter Millard Fillmore of Buffalo, New York.

The evasive positions of the Whigs and Democrats concerning slavery failed to satisfy party members who supported the Wilmot Proviso or in other ways harbored antislavery sentiments. Such disenchantment burst into the open when Van Buren's Barnburner faction walked out of the Democratic convention in protest and, at its own convention at Utica, New York, nominated Van Buren as its presidential candidate. The Barnburner revolt within New York's Democratic Party set the stage for a much larger national gathering of pro–Wilmot Proviso Democrats, "conscience" Whigs, and Liberty Party leaders at Buffalo, New York, on August 9, 1848. Calling for a new third party based on antislavery principles to challenge the Whig and Democratic nominees, the delegates established the Free Soil Party with Van Buren for president and John Quincy Adams's son Charles Francis as vice-president. In return for their support of the Barnburner Van Buren and the conscience Whig Adams, Liberty Party delegates led by Ohio's Salmon P. Chase were given a free hand in drafting the new party's platform. Insisting that "Congress has no more power to make a Slave than to make a King," the resulting document called for "No more Slave States and No more Slave Territory," adding that the federal government had to divorce itself completely from any support of slavery. "We inscribe on our banner, 'FREE SOIL, FREE SPEECH, FREE LABOR, AND FREE MEN,'" the platform declared, "and under it we will fight on, and fight ever, until a triumphant victory shall reward our exertions."

Zachary Taylor won the election with 1,360,000 popular votes to 1,200,000 for Lewis Cass, a margin of less than 5 percent. Although Van Buren ran a distant third with slightly more than 291,000 votes (or 10.1 percent of the total ballots cast), he attracted enough dissident Democratic and Whig votes in the northern states to establish the Free Soil Party as a serious political force. And since lingering political animosities prevented many conscience Whigs and Liberty Party men from supporting Van Buren, antislavery feeling in the North loomed even larger. The election demonstrated that the old issues—banks, tariffs, internal improvements—that had dominated American politics since the 1820s no longer held center stage. The future of slavery now dominated the discussion, and old-timers like Cass knew it. "My day has gone by," he wrote ruefully, shortly after the election. What remained to be seen was how Taylor, a politically inexperienced military hero and slaveholder, would respond to the political instabilities he had inadvertently helped to create.

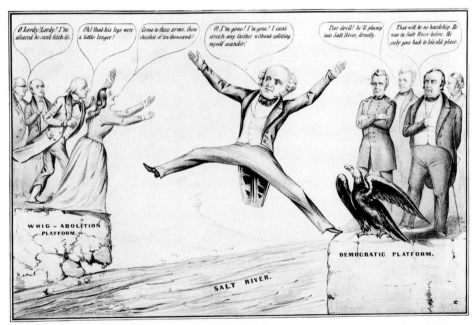

An 1848 election cartoon pointing to the difficulties Free Soil candidate Martin Van Buren faced in building an effective coalition between antislavery "conscience" Whigs, Liberty Party abolitionists, and "Barnburner" Democrats. On the far right, Lewis Cass waits for Van Buren to fall into the Salt River; on the left, abolitionists led by Horace Greeley and Abby Folsom beckon to the unsteady candidate while a concerned Charles Francis Adams (Van Buren's running mate) and William Lloyd Garrison look on.

California Gold

The one subject that attracted more attention than sectional politics was the **discovery of gold in California.** On January 24, 1848—less than two weeks before the end of the Mexican War—a worker employed by trader-entrepreneur John Sutter to build a sawmill on the American River some forty miles northeast of Sutter's Fort (soon to become the city of Sacramento) noticed a shiny golden particle in the flow of water from the mill's waterwheel. The worker reported his finding to Sutter, who tried to keep the news secret; still, word of the discovery inevitably spread through the local district and westward to San Francisco, San Jose, and Monterey. By the summer of 1848, hundreds of native "Californios" as well as recent American émigrés were rushing into the western foothills of the Sierra Nevada Mountains beyond Sacramento, hoping to strike it rich. Entire crews jumped ship upon anchoring in San Francisco Bay; soldiers deserted the army in droves; stores, sawmills, and brickyards closed; news-papers suspended publication for lack of workers; and commerce came to a standstill as merchants, lawyers, ranchers, and public officials abandoned their positions for the gold fields. In less than a month, San Francisco's population fell from several hundred to only a handful. The first phase of the California gold rush was on.

Although news of California's "gold mania" filtered back to the East Coast during the fall of 1848, it initially aroused little public interest. It wasn't until President Polk acknowledged in his annual message to Congress on December 5 "that mines of the precious metals existed to a considerable extent in California" that early skepticism gave way to enthusiastic belief. "Gold fever raged all winter," a resident of Sag Harbor, New York, noted. Groups of four to twenty pooled their resources and made ready for the arduous trip to California. From Maine to Florida and from New Orleans along the Texas coast to Corpus Christi and northward up the Mississippi to St. Louis, Louisville, Cincinnati, Pittsburgh, and the inner reaches of the Ohio, Missouri, and Tennessee Valleys, the reaction was the same. Thousands of men—young

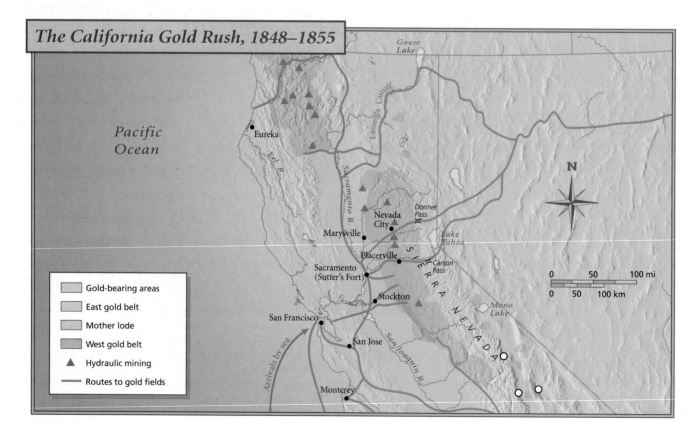

The California Gold Rush, 1848–1855

Gold-bearing areas
East gold belt
Mother lode
West gold belt
▲ Hydraulic mining
— Routes to gold fields

Pacific Ocean

Goose Lake
Eureka
Eel R.
Sacramento R.
Nevada City
Donner Pass
Lake Tahoe
Marysville
Placerville
Carson Pass
Sacramento (Sutter's Fort)
Stockton
San Francisco
Mono Lake
San Jose
San Joaquin R.
Arrivals by sea
Monterey
SIERRA NEVADA
Lassen's Cutoff

N

0   50   100 mi
0   50   100 km

NOW LOADING FOR HER FOURTH VOYAGE
TO SAN FRANCISCO.
SMALL! SHARP & FAST!!
INSURES AT EXTREME LOWEST RATES.
NEVER DAMAGES HER CARGO.
LARGE ENGAGEMENTS AND QUICK DISPATCH.
The A 1 Extreme Clipper Ship

COMMODORE
GROZIER, Commander,
At PIER 14, East River,
Being favorably known to the trade for her quick passages to
California and homeward, and being far advanced in loading,
will receive extremely QUICK DISPATCH.
SAMUEL W. OSGOOD,
88 WALL ST., Tontine Building.

Broadside offering passage to San Francisco on the ship *Commodore*. Such postings could be found in virtually every American seaport during the late 1840s and early 1850s.

and old—from all walks of life departed by land and sea for the golden West in one of the greatest mass migrations in American history. Gold seekers also came from around the world, making the rush an international event. In little more than a year, the lure of gold swelled California's population from 13,000 to well over 100,000 by the end of 1849.

THE MINING LIFE

The so-called argonauts who stampeded into California's gold district soon discovered that a miner's life could be difficult and disappointing. They worked ten to twelve hours a day up to their knees in the icy waters of rushing mountain streams while shoveling gravel and panning for gold. Since few women were drawn to the mining camps, the men also had to assume domestic chores such as cooking, washing, and housekeeping. Given the physical intensity of mining and their inexperience with domestic work, most forty-niners not only ate poorly but also lived under primitive, unsanitary conditions. Many suffered from chronic illnesses such as scurvy or, worse, killer diseases such as cholera, smallpox, and dysentery. Those who could afford to eat at local boardinghouses or roadside kitchens frequently noted that a single meal cost as much in gold as they made in an entire day. On the East Coast, you could have a hearty breakfast for 25 cents; in the mining fields of California, the same meal might cost as much as $20. At a time when miners expected to earn from $20 to $50 a day, such prices became a fact of life.

California's gold rush proved the adage about the early bird getting the worm. Gold seekers who arrived at the mines in 1848 and 1849 enjoyed considerable success. Some of them made even larger fortunes by moving into other occupations after they accumulated $1,000 or $2,000 in gold. Entertainers, merchants, doctors, and lawyers did especially well. Upon making $3,300 in less than two weeks after arriving in Sacramento, a young lawyer wrote to his parents in the East, "You have no idea of the extent of litigation in this city or the size of fees." Those who arrived at the mines after 1850 did less well. Although the annual production of gold in California soared from $10,151,360 in 1849 to an all-time high of $81,294,700 in 1852, per capita income among miners actually fell in that period. As more and more miners poured into California after 1850, they found that most of the best mining sites had already been taken up, subdivided into smaller plots, and begun to "play out."

THE TECHNOLOGY OF MINING

The earliest miners found gold mainly by washing ore-bearing gravel dug from gulches and old streambeds in large tin pans. The heavier gold settled in the bottom of the pan as a miner swirled the water, gravel, and sand over the pan's lip. In order to increase their yields, miners working in teams, or "clubs," of four to six built downward-sloping wooden boxes set on top of rockers and open at the lower end. Called "rockers," or "cradles," because they resembled rocking chairs and baby cradles in their motion, such devices followed the same principle of washing and sifting gravel employed in panning. The advantage was that rockers processed a larger volume of gravel

Three gold miners and a woman bringing them lunch pose beside their equipment in Auburn Ravine, California, in 1852.

and hence yielded more gold. The gold settled in the bottom of the rocker during the washing process and accumulated against a series of raised wooden cleats positioned there. But the cleats did not catch everything, so many smaller gold particles were lost in the process.

For efficient operation, a rocker required teamwork as well as the division of labor. While one miner dug the ore-bearing gravel and another carried and deposited it in the rocker, a third carried buckets of water from a nearby stream and dumped them into the box, while a fourth vigorously rocked the contraption in order to move the water through the gravel and shake the heavier gold to the bottom of the box. The miners would periodically stop so that they could pick particles of gold and heavier stones from the cleats and remove debris that had accumulated at the open end of the downward-sloping rocker box. Then they would alternate positions, so they would not have to perform the same repetitive labor all day long.

So long as gold remained plentiful, rockers and the similar but larger "long toms" served miners reasonably well. Men working rich deposits on the American, Yuba, Feather, and other northern California rivers in 1848–49 typically earned $25 a day and, on rare occasions, as much as $500 to $5,000. Compared with the $1 wage that day laborers in the East commanded, these were fantastic earnings, even if the work was extremely difficult. But these profitable days did not last for long. During the early 1850s, new washing technologies, consisting primarily of extended lines of sluice boxes, were introduced to rework old deposits and capture fine particles of gold that had escaped the cleats of rockers. Miners also employed the age-old method of using mercury (commonly called "quicksilver") to absorb gold embedded in sands that had escaped their washing apparatus, then heating the amalgam in a vessel to burn off the mercury. They did not realize that the escaping mercury vapors would have toxic effects on themselves as well as on the surrounding environment.

By 1850, miners who had risked all to go to California were writing home that they could barely make ends meet. "I am perfectly astounded to see so few doing well," a store owner reported from the mining village of Placerville in 1850. "I had always said these fellows who did not make out much was lazy drinking fellows but it is not so," he continued. "I have seen many a one, who worked as hard as he could ... look into his rocker to see the result of his days labor and ... find about $1.00 when his board would cost him at least $3.00." "The real truth," a San Francisco newspaper subsequently reported, "there is gold still in those banks, but they will never yield as they have yielded. The cream ... has ... been taken off. We now have the river bottoms and the quartz veins; but to get the gold from them, we must employ gold. The man who lives upon his labor from day to day, must hereafter be employed by the man who has in his possession accumulated labor, or money."

The implication was clear: miners without money to invest in new technologies stood little chance of success. The day of the small, independent miner working his own claim was passing. Taking his place were highly capitalized companies, often owned by absentee investors as far away as Boston. Such companies could afford the equipment and labor costs necessary to sink shafts deep into the earth in search of gold embedded in hard quartz rock, or build canals that would convey huge volumes of water under pressure to wash tons of earth from surrounding hillsides and deliver gold-bearing gravel to sluice boxes that sequentially washed and retrieved the precious metal. The latter method, called "hydraulicking," resulted in the construction of over 4,000 miles of canals and ditches in the Sierra foothills by 1857 at a cost approaching $11.9 million. The volume processed was enormous, as was the erosion that scarred the landscape. One Sacramento newspaper noted that

the amount of water now used by one company of four or five men, two or three years ago would have kept two or three hundred men at work.

The main difference is that then, *men did the work, using the water merely as an auxiliary, and the amount of work done depended on the number of men employed. But now, the water is used as the laboring agent, and like machinery in manufacturing, only men enough to keep the machinery properly directed, are required. . . . Banks of earth that would have kept a hundred men employed for months in its removal, will now be removed by three or four men in two weeks.*

As gold mining became increasingly industrialized, capital intensity replaced labor intensity, and miners who formerly worked their own claims became company employees. Although the resulting deforestation, erosion, and indiscriminate dumping of everything from mine tailings to personal garbage ravaged the landscape, no one seemed to mind so long as the mining operations yielded a profit. Whether owner, worker, or local merchant, the prevailing motto seemed to be "Get in, get rich, get out."

POPULATION BOOM AND ETHNIC TENSIONS

The California gold rush had ripple effects throughout North America. California gold stimulated unprecedented economic growth by pumping over half a billion dollars into the American economy during the 1850s. Such wealth changed the face of northern California from a sparsely populated

---

What Do You Do for Fun?

In early America as well as today, the 4th of July was a time of widespread celebration. Even as wagon trains made their way across the continent on the rugged Overland Trail, travelers took time off to celebrate. The following comes from the diary of William Swain, a twenty-seven-year-old farmer from western New York who, among thousands of others in 1849, was making his way to the California gold fields to strike it rich.

"July 4.   [At sunrise a salute of thirteen guns was fired.] We lay abed late this morn and after a late breakfast set about getting fuel for cooking our celebration dinner.

"Our celebration of the day was very good, much better than I anticipated. We had previously invited Mr. Sexton of the Plymouth company [which had joined the Rangers on May 29] to deliver an address, and we had appointed Mr. Pratt to read the Declaration of Independence. We had one of the tents pitched at a short distance from the camp, in which was placed a table with seats for the officers of the day and the orators. The table was spread with a blanket.

"At twelve o'clock we formed a procession and walked to the stand to the tune of 'The Star Spangled Banner.' The President of the day called the meeting to order. We listened to a prayer by Rev. Mr. Hobart, then remarks and the reading of the Declaration of Independence by Mr. Pratt, and then the address by Mr. Sexton. We then listened to 'Hail Columbia.' This celebration was very pleasing, especially the address, which was well delivered and good enough for any assembly at home.

"We then marched to the 'hall,' which was formed by running the wagons in two rows close enough together for the wagon covers to reach from one to the other, thus forming a fine hall roofed by the covers and a comfortable place for the dinner table, which was set down the center.

"Dinner consisted of ham, beans, boiled and baked, biscuits, john cake, apple pie, sweet cake, rice pudding, pickles, vinegar, pepper sauce and mustard, coffee, sugar, and milk. All enjoyed it well.

"After dinner the toasting commenced. The boys had raked and scraped together all the brandy they could, and they toasted, hurrayed, and drank till reason was out and brandy was in. I stayed till the five regular toasts were drunk; and then, being disgusted with their conduct, I went to our tent . . . in which I enjoyed myself better than those who were drinking, carousing, and hallooing all around the camp."

J. S. Holliday, *The World Rushed In*

American Journal

agricultural hinterland into a diverse economy that attracted not only miners and mine companies but also hundreds of businesses that catered to their needs. At the same time, mining camps sprouted into towns and towns into cities. San Francisco, for example, was little more than a trading outpost at the time gold was discovered at Sutter's mill in 1848. Within two years, its population would boom to 25,000 and more than double again by the end of the decade. Blessed with a great harbor, the city quickly became the West Coast's leading financial and commercial center as well as the location of foundries and machine shops that supplied the mining districts with everything from hand tools to steam engines. Similar developments occurred in Sacramento, Stockton, and leading mining towns like Marysville, although on a smaller scale. Serving as a gateway to the northern mines, Sacramento gained another advantage: it became the state capital in 1854.

California's growing population was dominated by men between the ages of twenty and forty. Unlike miners elsewhere, the forty-niners rarely brought their wives and children to California. It was too expensive, and the miners expected to get in and get out fast. In 1850, the mining town of Nevada City had a population of 2,683, 97 percent male. In the nearby mining village of Grass Valley, men constituted 94 percent of the population. Although these figures would fall slightly during the next decade, men continued to outnumber women by a significant margin in California long after gold ceased to be its primary product.

Chinese and American miners pose next to a long tom.

This San Francisco saloon, with its mix of Spanish, Mexican, Chinese, and Anglo patrons, might have been derogatively referred to as a "Spanish House."

Ethnic diversity was an early characteristic of the gold rush. Among the first to head for the gold fields were Hispanic Californios, though they were soon outnumbered by Americans. As the gold rush gathered momentum, miners arrived from all over the world—from Great Britain, Ireland, and Germany, and smaller numbers from Canada, China, Chile, Mexico, and France. Early on, this diversity brought little social tension because there appeared to be plenty of gold for everyone. But as the tide of immigrants swelled, white Americans began to complain about foreigners taking jobs and claims that should rightfully belong to them. A loud proponent of this view was General Persifor Smith of the American army that occupied California. Outraged that large numbers of Latin-American "greasers" were arriving in California on government-subsidized American steamships, he protested that "nothing can be more unjust and immeasurable than for persons not citizens of the United States . . . to dig the gold found in California, on lands belonging to the American Government." Such ideas became popular among the American inhabitants of California and soon resulted in actions, both legal and extralegal, that aimed at reducing foreign influence.

Feelings of nationalism and racial superiority drove the exclusionist movement as much as the desire for economic gain. Lacking well-organized law enforcement agencies and courts to mete out justice, American-dominated communities organized vigilance committees during the early 1850s to curb lawlessness and root out undesirable elements. Since "undesirable" tended to conflate people of foreign birth with murderers, thieves, and prostitutes, the brunt of vigilante action most often fell on groups who were neither white nor Protestant.

California Indians and Spanish-speaking people became the first targets. The former, already small in number and weakened by over a century of European intrusions into their territories, were quickly dispersed and reduced to a condition of dependence. The latter, consisting mainly of Californios, Mexicans, and Chileans but indiscriminately called "Spanish" by white Americans, were viewed as posing the greatest threat to American control. Nativist agitators condemned their Catholicism and depicted them as the dregs of society who "dabble their hands in human gore as a pastime" and kill "with fiendish delight." Moreover, nativists used the terms "Spanish woman" or "señorita" almost always to refer to a prostitute, while "Spanish house" stood for the most depraved places of entertainment, regardless of the owner's nationality. Vigilante groups raided the mining camps of Hispanics and seized their property in a spate of actions that resulted in numerous deaths, arrests, and summary executions.

Although nativists aimed their attacks at all foreign groups during the early 1850s, they did so selectively and with varying intensity. European immigrants, for instance, suffered less abuse than Chinese and "other colored races." The selectiveness of American xenophobia became particularly apparent in April 1850, when the newly organized California state legislature, at the governor's urging, enacted a law that levied a tax of twenty dollars a month on all foreign miners but then proceeded to collect the tax more consistently from Chinese and "Spanish" miners than others. Faced with loud protests—especially from French nationals—the legislature repealed the tax in March 1851, but not before it had worked enormous hardships. The levy hit Chinese miners especially hard. Because they tended to live apart from the rest of the mining community and could neither read nor write English, they remained unaware of the law until officials suddenly rode into their camps, seized their property, and auctioned it off to satisfy their debts to the state.

A year later, the California legislature reenacted the foreign miners' tax but added a new wrinkle: although the law lowered the tax rate to three dollars a month, it excluded those who intended to become American citizens. But since a federal law of 1790 prohibited all but whites from becoming citizens, Chinese and other "colored" miners had no other option than to pay the tax. "It is strange that Americans are not willing to give foreigners an equal chance, when there is so much labor required to secure the uncertain gains which fall to the lot of the laborer here," an American missionary sympathetic to the plight of the Chinese observed. In mid-nineteenth-century America, religion, skin color, and cultural tradition mattered, in every section of the country.

The Compromise of 1850

California's gold rush did not deflect national attention away from the growing controversy over slavery for long. California itself became enmeshed in sectional tensions in January 1850, when, at President Taylor's urging, its officials applied for immediate admission to the Union as a free state.

Senator John C. Calhoun as the Old Testament's "Joshua Commanding the Sun to Stand Still," an 1848 cartoon condemning Calhoun's rigid stand on slavery. In this instance, the sun stands for enlightenment and the printing press at its center for the flood of pamphlets and posters coming from abolitionists.

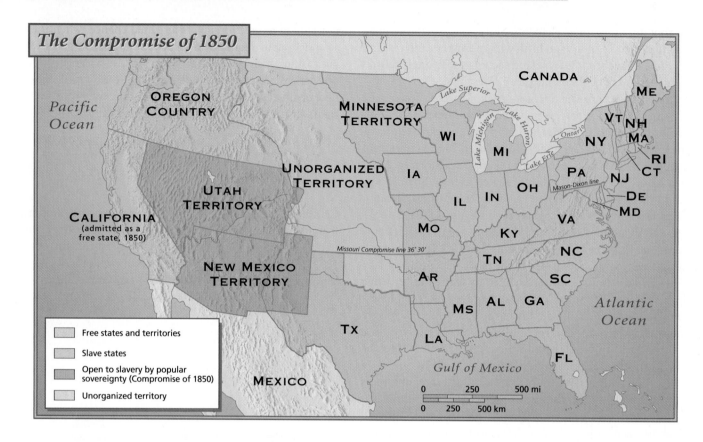

The Compromise of 1850

Free states and territories

Slave states

Open to slavery by popular sovereignty (Compromise of 1850)

Unorganized territory

Angered by what they perceived to be the president's betrayal (Taylor, after all, was a Louisiana slave owner), southern politicians vowed to stop the process. In their eyes, the issue was critical because California's admission threatened to upset the equilibrium that currently existed between the fifteen free and fifteen slave states in the Senate. Since the North's population had long since outstripped that of the South, no such balance existed in the House of Representatives; nor did anyone expect the balance to be restored. All of the Oregon Territory as well as the upper part of the Louisiana Territory lay north of the Missouri Compromise line of 36°–30′. The best southerners could hope for was an extension of the Missouri Compromise line all the way to the Pacific, with the eventual establishment of slave states from the parts of California and New Mexico that lay below the line. California's admission as a free state would dash those hopes and thrust the South into the status of a permanent political minority. A growing number of white southerners became convinced by 1850 that antislavery forces in the North intended "to make war," as John C. Calhoun put it, "on a do-

mestic institution upon which are staked our property, our social organization and our peace and safety." Their only choice, as they saw it, was either to secure their position by getting the federal government to guarantee the future of slavery or to secede from the Union before it was too late.

Other issues were also exciting sectional tensions. President Taylor was urging New Mexicans to apply for statehood as soon as possible and to decide for themselves on the future of slavery—a position southerners found troubling given the president's stance on California. A bitter boundary dispute between New Mexico and Texas threatened to degenerate into an all-out border war. And having relinquished all their customs houses to the United States, and with them their primary source of revenue, Texans (especially Texas bondholders) were upset that the federal government refused to assume the state's $10 million war debt. Southerners, moreover, deeply resented stepped-up efforts on the part of antislavery groups in the North to abolish slavery in the District of Columbia. They found even more galling the passage in northern states of "personal liberty" laws that prohibited local courts and law enforcement agencies from helping slave catchers return runaways from northern havens to their owners. Having lost thousands of slaves over the years, southerners were insisting on a more stringent federal fugitive slave law that would punish anyone who assisted runaways. Finally, every state legislature in the North except one had adopted resolutions calling for the prohibition of slavery in the territories. These grievances, and the attendant sense of crisis that gripped their districts, roused southern politicians to block the admission of California. Even moderate southerners were beginning to speak of secession. An unprecedented crisis was at hand.

CLAY'S OMNIBUS BILL

Into this angry impasse stepped Senator Henry Clay of Kentucky, the "Great Pacificator" whose name had long been associated with the Missouri Compromise of 1820 and the resolution of the nullification crisis in 1833. Clay was seventy-two years old and in failing health, but his devotion to the Union was as strong as ever. Convinced that the Taylor administration was unequal to the task of solving the sectional crisis, Clay began to search for "some comprehensive scheme of settling amicably the whole question, in all its bearings." He conferred with other Unionist stalwarts like Senator Daniel Webster of Massachusetts, and urged friends and fellow politicians to organize Unionist meetings to counter secessionist sentiments being spread by radical southern politicians called "fire-eaters."

On January 29, 1850, Clay entered the Senate chamber and asked to be recognized. "Mr. President," he began, "I hold in my hand a series of resolutions which I desire to submit to the consideration of this body. Taken together, in combination, they propose an amicable arrangement of all questions in controversy between the free and slave states, growing out of the subject of slavery." Clay then proceeded to count off the eight resolutions in his proposal:

- the admission of California as a free state;

- the establishment of territorial governments for the remainder of the Mexican Cession (encompassing all of present-day New Mexico and Utah and parts of Colorado, Arizona, and Nevada) without any restrictions on slavery (which meant, in effect, that the territories themselves would decide on the future of slavery within their bounds);

- the settlement of the New Mexico–Texas boundary dispute at roughly the present limits;

- the federal government's assumption of Texas's preannexation debt as compensation for accepting an unfavorable boundary settlement with New Mexico;

- the promise that slavery would not be abolished in the District of Columbia without the consent of its citizens as well as those in neighboring Maryland;

- the abolition of the slave trade in the District of Columbia;

- assurance from Congress that it would not interfere with the domestic slave trade elsewhere in the South;

- and the passage of a new Fugitive Slave Act that would penalize anyone who attempted to interfere with the recovery of runaway slaves.

Henry Clay presenting his California compromise resolutions to the U.S. Senate, February 5, 1850.

459

No sooner had Clay presented his "Omnibus Bill" than a number of Senate colleagues insisted on speaking against it. Southerners like Jefferson Davis of Mississippi felt that the South was getting the short end of the stick, while antislavery senators from the North, led by William Seward of New York, opposed the plan because they felt that it was too soft on slavery. A six-month debate ensued, beginning with a dramatic speech by Clay on February 5 and 6 that discussed each resolution in detail, warned southern disunionists that "war and dissolution of the Union are identical and inevitable," and ended with an emotional appeal to his Senate colleagues to draw back from the abyss and preserve the Republic as a shining example to the rest of the world.

The gravity of the situation drew crowds to Capitol Hill to hear **Clay's speech and the others that followed.** Among the most eagerly awaited was South Carolina's senior senator, John C. Calhoun, the most prominent southern politician and the acknowledged intellectual force behind the ideas of nullification and secession. Like Clay, Calhoun was not well at the time of the debates and, in fact, would not survive them. Bedridden, he dictated his speech to an assistant and on the appointed day had to be helped to his desk in the Senate chamber, where he sat in a slumped position, weak and emaciated, as a Senate colleague read the prepared text.

It was a solemn, even gloomy speech, filled with ominous references to how the constant "agitation of the slavery question" had snapped "some of the most important cords" that

Senator Daniel Webster around the time of the California debates.

bound the Union together and "greatly weakened all the others." Once the last of these cords broke, Calhoun argued, only force could maintain the Union. At the same time, the speech displayed contempt for the Taylor administration's territorial policy and Clay's compromise. Other than making a vague reference to a dual presidency—one representing the North, the other the South—with each executive armed with full veto powers, the South Carolinian offered no solution to save the Union. Yet Calhoun's warning about the South's discontent and the imminent danger that confronted the Union per-

suaded many listeners, including southern colleagues, of the need for compromise.

Three days after his speech, Calhoun left his sickbed and returned to the Senate to hear Daniel Webster's views. Considered a free-soiler by many yet also known to support Clay's resolution, no one knew exactly what the "God-like Daniel" was going to say. But the crowds packed the Senate chamber to find out. "Mr. President," Webster intoned in his deep, resonant voice, "I wish to speak today not as a Massachusetts man, nor as a Northern man, but as an American, and a member of the Senate of the United States. . . . I speak for the preservation of the Union. 'Hear me for my cause.'" He then spoke for more than three hours in favor of the compromise while urging his colleagues not to taunt the South with the Wilmot Proviso or reproach it about the extension of slavery into the territories when everyone knew that environmental conditions in those areas would exclude slavery in any case. Peace and conciliation lay at the heart of his message.

As soon as Webster sat down, reporters rushed to the nearest telegraph office to flash their reports back home. Across the country, partisan newspapers known for their criticism of Webster now hailed him as a great statesman and patriot. "He has this day exhibited a higher degree of moral courage than ever graced a great captain on the battle field," declared the Baltimore *Sun*. Even in the deep South, newspapers praised Webster for making "emphatically a great speech." In his home state of Massachusetts, however—supposedly friendly territory—the reviews were decidedly mixed. While some Whig newspapers supported him, others damned him as a traitor to the cause of free soil. Leading abolitionists were particularly upset. "He has walked for years among the gods, to descend from the empyrean heights and mingle . . . in a masquerade full of harlots and leeches," the educational reformer Horace Mann wrote in disgust. "'Liberty! liberty!' Pho!," Ralph Waldo Emerson confided to his journal. "Let Mr. Webster for decency's sake shut his lips once and forever on this word. The word *liberty* in the mouth of Mr. Webster sounds like the word *love* in the mouth of a courtezan."

In the weeks that followed, one senator after another mounted the podium to express his views on Clay's proposal. While speaking against the compromise on March 11 as "radically wrong and essentially vicious," William H. Seward of New York referred to "a higher law than the Constitution," a moral obligation that took precedence when it came to slavery. While the American Anti-Slavery Society printed 10,000 copies of Seward's speech for immediate distribution, southerners condemned the New Yorker's comments as inflammatory and irresponsible. As the debate rolled on and the hot, humid Washington summer approached, Clay and his supporters thought they had enough votes among southern Whigs and northern Democrats to pass the Omnibus Bill. But no one was certain.

President Taylor continued to press solely for the immediate admission of California. When Clay criticized him for his narrow-mindedness, the Taylor camp shot back that Clay was vain and dictatorial. In the meantime, angry Texans protested the Taylor administration's attempt to syphon off part of their state and incorporate it into New Mexico, Southern "ultraists" continued to press for an extension of the Missouri Compromise line to the Pacific, and northern free-soilers attempted to insert the Wilmot Proviso into Clay's Omnibus Bill. Then, as the political skies seemed darkest, news arrived that President Taylor had suddenly taken ill on July 4. Five days later he was dead. Thrust into the limelight, his successor, Millard Fillmore of New York, made it known that he supported the Omnibus Bill. Yet when the bill came to a vote in the Senate on July 31, it collapsed under a rain of amendments that dismantled the compromise piece by piece. Shocked and exhausted, Clay sat at his desk with a blank stare, then silently left the Senate building.

Two days later, Clay left Washington for some rest at Newport, Rhode Island, but not before he pleaded with senators to pass the compromise measures as "separate and distinct" bills. Now the initiative passed to Stephen A. Douglas, an ambitious, thirty-seven-year-old first-term Democratic senator from Illinois whom an adversary described as a "steam engine in britches." Following Clay's call, Douglas broke up the Omnibus Bill into separate pieces and presented them to the Senate one at a time. This time the strategy succeeded. By the time Clay returned to Washington on August 27, the Senate had approved all but one of the measures. Three weeks later, both houses of Congress sanctioned the measures, and President Fillmore signed them into law.

A GENERATION PASSES

The Compromise of 1850 represented a great political victory for Douglas, Webster, Fillmore, and, not least of all, Clay. All of Washington seemed to breathe a sigh of relief knowing

> " 'The question of slavery in the territories,' abolitionist senator Salmon Chase of Ohio warned, 'has been avoided. It has not been settled.' "

that Congress had successfully passed through one of its most tumultuous sessions and that, for the first time in six years, it could meet without immediately getting embroiled in clashes over slavery. In the weeks that followed, crowds gathered in the streets to celebrate the accord, while great parties took place on Capitol Hill. The halls of Congress seemed more relaxed than they had for years. Douglas "resolved never to make another speech upon the slavery question in the Houses of Congress." His Democratic colleague Senator Lewis Cass of Michigan agreed. "The question is settled in the public mind," he declared. "I do not think it worthwhile to make speeches on it."

But not everyone shared these sentiments. "The question of slavery in the territories," abolitionist senator Salmon Chase of Ohio warned, "has been avoided. It has not been settled." Chase had a point. There were fundamental ambiguities in the Compromise of 1850, not least of which was the disposition of slavery in the territories. So long as northern congressmen could tell their constituents that the people of each territory could decide for themselves on the future of slavery while, at the same time, southern congressmen could report that the Wilmot Proviso was dead and that slave owners had the right

March 6, 1836	Fall of the Alamo.
April 21, 1836	Battle of San Jacinto ends Texas revolution.
December 1845	Texas joins the Union.
April 25, 1846	Mexican War begins at the Rio Grande.
June 15, 1846	Oregon Treaty ratified.
August 1846	The Wilmot Proviso introduced.
August 15, 1846	United States takes New Mexico.
January 10, 1847	United States takes California.
September 14, 1847	Santa Anna surrenders.
January 24, 1848	Gold first spotted in California.
February 2, 1848	Treaty of Guadalupe Hidalgo.
September 1850	The Compromise of 1850 (including the Fugitive Slave Act) signed into law.

Chronology

to take their slaves into any territory, this key question remained unanswered. Moreover, it was not clear whether northern states would stand for a new Fugitive Slave Act that demanded that local bystanders assist slave catchers, denied fugitives the right to a trial by jury and to testify on their own behalf, and subjected anyone who either concealed or prevented the capture of an escaped slave to a fine of $1,000 and up to six months in prison. In these respects, the compromise measures represented more of a truce than a final settlement of the slavery question. But for the moment, many people chose to celebrate the occasion and hope for the best.

The debates leading to the Compromise of 1850 marked the last time that "the great triumvirate" of Daniel Webster, Henry Clay, and John C. Calhoun would appear together in the public arena. For nearly forty years, they had occupied center stage in American politics and had played key roles in the triumphs and failures of the era. Calhoun died in March 1850, before the debates had ended, and Clay and Webster would follow him to the grave within two years. Their passing signified a changing of the guard. From a generation who knew the founders of the Republic, experienced first-hand the threats to the new nation's survival during the War of 1812, and appreciated the expediency of compromise in the interest of preserving the Union, leadership passed to a younger, less patient generation of politicians raised in the party battles of the Jacksonian era and exposed to a new, more powerful America in the throes of industrialization, economic growth, geographic expansion, and sectional conflict. The new generation included not only Stephen Douglas, Salmon Chase, and William Seward but also Jefferson Davis of Mississippi, Robert Barnwell Rhett of South Carolina, Abraham Lincoln of Illinois, and Charles Sumner of Massachusetts. It remained to be seen how well they would navigate the uncharted political waters of the 1850s and, most important, whether they could maintain the fragile bonds of the Union.

Suggested Reading

Donald S. Frazier, ed., *The United States and Mexico at War* (1998)

Robert W. Johannsen, *To the Halls of the Montezumas: The Mexican War in the American Imagination* (1985)

Susan Lee Johnson, *Roaring Camp: The Social World of the California Gold Rush* (2000)

David M. Potter, *The Impending Crisis, 1848–1861* (1976)

Malcolm J. Rohrbough, *Days of Gold: The California Gold Rush and the American Nation* (1976)

John D. Unruh Jr., *The Plains Across: The Overland Emigrants and the Trans-Mississippi West, 1840–1860* (1979)

The north transept of the London Crystal Palace, 1851.

Focus
QUESTIONS

- How were technology and nationalism intertwined in the 1850s?

- How did an American science develop from explorations of the continent?

- What kept the slavery issue so divisive in the early 1850s?

- How did the debate over a transcontinental railroad heighten sectional divisions?

- How did the chances for sectional compromise diminish in the late 1850s?

- What was the significance of the 1860 election?

The Crystal Palace: Technology and Empire

As Americans celebrated the Compromise of 1850 and California gold poured into the nation's coffers, an event was being planned in London that would attract international attention. Formally called "The Great Exhibition of the Works of Industry of All Nations," it quickly became known as the **Crystal Palace,** after the massive, iron-framed exhibit building whose plate-glass exterior sparkled like a crystal. The great exhibition ostensibly sought to celebrate peace and good will among nations while emphasizing the benefits of free trade. But to knowledgeable observers, it was more than that. The first of numerous world fairs to be held during the next fifty years, the Crystal Palace celebrated the technological progress of the age, and the political and military might that flowed from it. Technology as an engine of economic growth and colonial expansion was the unstated but central theme of the fair, and no nation better illustrated this theme than the exhibition's sponsor, Great Britain. By 1851, the British economy and the British empire stood second to none in the world.

The exhibition opened to the public on May 1, 1851, with no less than 14,000 exhibitors—almost half of them foreigners, including many from France—mounting displays in the twenty-two-acre hall. The American exhibits, however, used much less than their allotted square footage; many cases were left half-filled or empty. The coordinator of the American section rushed back to the States seeking more exhibitors, but the effort proved fruitless.

While Austria, Belgium, and Russia sent finely crafted luxury objects embellished with jewels and precious metals, the Americans emphasized practical items such as soap and India rubber boots, as well as agricultural goods like "Henry County" tobacco and South Carolina cotton. Queen Victoria noted of the mundane American display that it was "certainly not very interesting." The British humor magazine *Punch* went further: "We could not help . . . being struck by the glaring contrast between large pretension and little performance, as exemplified in the dreary and empty aspect of the large space claimed by and alloted *(sic)* to America. . . . For a calculating people, our friends the Americans are thus far terribly out in their calculations." Although the New York editor Horace Greeley railed against such "meanly invidious and undeserved . . . slurs," even he had to admit that "the show from the United States disappoints." The *Richmond Enquirer* was more philosophical. "We often talk as if we were the only civilized nation on earth," its editor observed. "It is time that the conceit was taken out of us."

But British opinion of the American exhibits began to change once various juries started to examine the "Yankee notions" and submit them to competitive tests. The event that initially caught people's attention was a field trial in which two American-made reaping machines—one by Cyrus Hall McCormick of Chicago, the other by Obed Hussey of Baltimore—did extremely well. "The American reapers are worked by a single span of horses abreast, with a driver and a man to rake off the grain as it is cut down by moveable knives," an English observer noted. "These reapers will cut from twelve to twenty acres of wheat in a day." McCormick's reaper won a coveted gold Council Medal from the jury on agricultural implements. In bestowing the award, the jury approvingly quoted an earlier statement by the U.S. commissioner of patents that Mc-Cormick's reaper "is one of those great and valuable inventions which commence a new era in the progress of improvement, and whose beneficial influence is felt in all coming time."

Other American entries received prestigious Council Medals as well, among them Charles Goodyear's patented India rubber garments and life rafts and Gail Borden Jr.'s "patent meat biscuits," used by the U.S. Army. Altogether, American exhibitors won 159 awards at the Crystal Palace exhibition—far fewer than the British and the French but nonetheless a respectable showing. Among the winners was the New York firm of Day and Newell, manufacturers of locks. In one of the more flamboyant competitions, an employee of Day and Newell successfully picked the locks of several well-known English lock makers, while an English locksmith failed to pick Day and Newell's locks. The American won a cash prize for his efforts, while the Bank of England, whose vault he opened, subsequently placed an order with Day and Newell for a new set of locks.

American displays at the Crystal Palace.

McCormick's reaper in action. Note that the machine required two operators: one to drive the team of horses, the other to rake the cuttings into piles as the reaper moved along its path.

The ultimate Yankee victory came on August 28, when the yacht *America* defeated the British *Titania* in a race off the coast at Cowes to win what later became known as the America's Cup. Unlike the competition for medals, where judgments could be subjective and open to national bias, the yacht race was an open competition decided solely by the skill of the participants and the quality of their vessels. The *America*'s rout of its British rivals came as a stunning blow to English pride. The *Liverpool Times* declared, "The Yankees are no longer to be ridiculed, much less despised. The new world is bursting into greatness—walking past the old world, as the Americans did to the yachts at Cowes. . . . America, in her own phrase, is 'going ahead' and will assuredly pass us unless we accelerate our speed."

THE COLT PISTOL AND NATIONALIST EXPANSION

Nowhere was American ambition more evident at the Crystal Palace than in the activities of Samuel Colt. The inventor of a fast-firing six-shot pistol bearing his name, Colt went to London intent on drumming up business for his factory in Hart-

Currier and Ives's lithographic view of the victorious *Clipper Yacht "America,"* 1851.

ford, Connecticut. With a workforce of 300 men and an annual output of 55,000 pistols, Colt's Grove Street armory was already the largest and soon to be the most technologically advanced in America. As much a showman as an entrepreneur, Colt displayed more than 500 "patent revolvers" along with a few experimental repeating rifles at his booth in the Crystal Palace. Hundreds of visitors flocked to the exhibit, where they examined the inventor's pistols and listened to his promotional stories.

One of Colt's favorite tales was how, in the summer of 1844, fifteen Texas Rangers armed with his revolvers drove off about eighty Comanche Indians by "boldly attacking them upon their own ground, killing & wounding about half their number." The implicit message was that the Colt revolver had introduced a new calculus of warfare. As Colt's biographer put it, "every man armed with one of [the] weapons was armed sixfold. . . . Savages would have seen that . . . the first man of them who rushed forward with the tomahawk would rush on certain death." Colt went so far as to decorate the cylinders of his large-caliber "dragoon" revolvers with an engraving of the 1844 "Big Fight" with the Comanches.

The message was not lost on British military officials who were engaged in similar wars of colonial expansion and conquest. In their view, the Colt revolver represented Anglo-Saxon ingenuity at its best and the ultimate tool of em-

pire. Colt embraced the notion. Like so many other mid-nineteenth-century Americans caught up in the cult of technological progress and nationalist expansion, Colt could not see its racist implications. For him, the "progress of the age" meant the triumph of the Anglo-Saxon race and its associated Protestant principles, republican institutions, and business systems. "Barbarians" and "savages"—whether Indians, Mexicans, or black Americans—had to submit to the dominant white man's civilization or be annihilated. In Colt's mind, his revolver was a "peace maker," an instrument of civilization.

Colt's pistols drew interest in his manufacturing methods as well as his products. Impressed by his remarks on these methods, the British government appointed a three-man Committee on the Machinery of the United States of America, made up of ordnance and artillery specialists, to investigate what was increasingly being referred to in England as "the American system of manufactures." The committee arrived in Boston in March 1854 and proceeded on a four-month inspection tour that took them as far south as the national armory at Harpers Ferry, Virginia, and as far west as various ironworks in Wheeling, Virginia, and Pittsburgh. The primary objects of their visit, however, were the Colt Patent Arms Manufacturing Company at Hartford, the national armory at Springfield, Massachusetts, and a half-dozen private armories and machine shops that lined the Connecticut Valley from Windsor, Vermont, to Middletown and New Haven, Connecticut. Before leaving the United States in August 1854, the committee purchased over $100,000 worth of machinery

In 1851, Samuel Colt's steam-powered factory in Hartford, Connecticut, was the largest and most advanced privately owned armory in the United States and a showplace of American industry. Note the factory's Russian-style cupola, reflective of Colt's recent visit to Russia.

and tools from two machine shops connected with the Springfield Armory, one of them the Crystal Palace award–winning firm of rifle manufacturers Robbins and Lawrence.

Earmarked for use at the Royal Small Arms Manufactory at Enfield, England, this equipment represented the first large-scale transfer of American manufacturing technology to a foreign country. Before 1854, the flow of technology had been in the opposite direction, with the United States as the perpetual borrower. Now, with firms like Colt and Robbins and Lawrence pursuing international customers, American technology—particularly machine tools, firearms, sewing machines, and other products made by armory methods—began to be exported overseas on a regular basis. More than the textile mills of Lowell or the nation's railroad system, "armory practice" was the technology Europeans considered most novel, wanted to learn about, and began to acquire on an increasing scale beginning in the mid-1850s. Although the American arms industry was small compared with the textile and railroad industries, its impact throughout the world soon became significant, because its machine-based methods could also be applied to such products as pocket watches, typewriters, bicycles, business machines, and eventually automobiles. To supply the growing demand for armory-spawned technologies, a specialized machine-tool industry emerged in the Connecticut Valley during the late 1850s, led by new firms like Pratt and Whitney of Hartford. And the catalyst for all this activity had been the London Crystal Palace exhibition.

"In Europe, science had long enjoyed royal patronage as well as high social prestige, but American culture emphasized utility over purely intellectual pursuits. What counted most in the United States was empirical research that yielded practical results."

An American Science

Despite the European accolades for American engineers and manufacturers, the pursuit of science in America was looked on as an adjunct to European science. With the exception of Benjamin Franklin and possibly one or two lesser figures, Americans were considered amateurs. While Americans collected and classified natural materials, Europeans formulated grand theories. In Europe, science had long enjoyed royal patronage as well as high social prestige, but American culture emphasized utility over purely intellectual pursuits. What counted most in the United States was empirical research that yielded practical results.

Still, the United States could boast a few world-class scientists in 1851, who were determined to challenge Europe's scientific superiority. Chief among them was Joseph Henry, head of the recently established (1846) Smithsonian Institution, whose pathbreaking research on electromagnetism had led, in 1844, to Samuel F. B. Morse's invention of the electric telegraph. Joining Henry was Alexander Dallas Bache, a graduate of West Point and an expert in terrestrial magnetism (the earth's magnetic field), who headed the Washington-based U.S. Coast Survey and whose great-grandfather was Benjamin Franklin. Henry and Bache gathered around them an inner circle of a half-dozen leading scientists half jokingly referred to as the "Lazzaroni," an Italian word for "beggars." Their purpose was to campaign against sloppy scientific amateurism while emulating the professional manner in which the best European scientists worked. The Lazzaroni hoped eventually to overtake, even surpass, the Europeans in scientific productivity and sophistication.

The first meeting of the American Association for the Advancement of Science, held in Philadelphia in 1848, marked a new stage in the development of American science. Following the model of the British Association for the Advancement of Science, founded some fifteen years earlier, Henry and the Lazzaroni dedicated the American Association to a threefold mission: "to promote intercourse between those who are cultivating science in different parts of the United States; to give stronger and more general impulse, and a more systematic direction to scientific research in our country; and to procure for the labours of scientific men, increased facilities and a wider usefulness." The goals were laudable, but the new association's constitution left open the central question of who would be admitted to voting membership in the

Joseph Henry, America's leading scientist and first secretary of the recently established (1846) Smithsonian Institution in Washington.

association—all comers, or just those who were full-time scientists? Fearing a backlash in public support if they restricted membership and acknowledging that amateurs could be useful contributors, the founders opted for democracy. Still, it was the full-time scientists like Bache and Henry who would govern the association.

Another problem facing the association was locating financial support for scientific research. The support for science to be found in the universities of Germany, France, and Britain had no equivalent in the United States. American colleges in the 1850s emphasized teaching over research and, in any case, lacked the money to build laboratories and procure the necessary equipment for serious scientific investigation. Reformers thus looked to government institutions, both state and federal, to take the lead in supporting the "new science" in America.

GEOLOGICAL SURVEYS

In the states, the first support for the projects of science came from geological surveys. Spawned by the internal improvement programs of the 1820s and 1830s, these surveys reported on mineral deposits, soil conditions, and other "objects of interest" to state legislatures. Often they went beyond their immediate, practical purposes, an English geologist noted, to "collect facts and publish speculations which they deemed likely to illustrate the general principles of the science and lead to a sound theoretical conclusion." For example, a survey initiated in Pennsylvania by the anthracite-coal-mine owners of the region advanced the scientific study of mountain systems even though it proved of little practical use. Many geologists gained "practical" experience with mining on such state surveys that launched them into new careers as private consultants to the mining industry.

FEDERAL SUPPORT FOR SCIENCE

At the federal level, four agencies—the Smithsonian Institution, the U.S. Coast Survey, the U.S. Naval Observatory, and the U.S. Army Topographical Engineers—were the primary catalysts of scientific research. Under Joseph Henry, the Smithsonian, created by Congress in 1846, aspired to become the nation's leading scientific establishment. Henry, who had little use for amateurism in science, sought to fashion it into an elite institute for advanced study by providing peer-selected scientists with research grants and then publishing their findings. Doing so, he believed, would fulfill the Smithsonian's charter for increasing and diffusing knowledge. But other government officials had their own ideas about what the Smithsonian should be doing, with the result that Henry struggled throughout the 1850s to implement his vision of basic science while trying to satisfy calls for more "useful" services. "In a country like ours," he wrote sarcastically, "it will probably be found necessary to make a few oblations to Buncombe [petty government officials] [since] practical science must have its share."

One such "oblation" was a meteorology program at the Smithsonian in which observers from around the country collected daily information about weather conditions and telegraphed it to Washington. There, the data were posted daily on a national "weather map" and made available to newspapers across the country for dissemination to farmers as well as firms engaged in maritime and other weather-dependent enterprises. Another was the creation of a National Museum at the Smithsonian to house patent models and other "curiosities" from the U.S. Patent Office along with natural history specimens brought back to Washington by government-sponsored exploring expeditions. Under the curatorship of Henry's talented assistant, Spencer Baird, the National Museum soon became the Smithsonian's most important branch and a beehive of activity in zoology, botany, ornithology, and other natural history subjects. Baird not only collected and studied these materials, he also tutored and helped to equip a generation of army, navy, and civilian explorers who set out to probe the American continent and the oceans that lay beyond. Even more than Henry, he gave the Smithsonian Institution its enduring character.

The Smithsonian's Spencer Baird.

Baird's success as an institution builder and scientific impresario brought him lasting relationships with a wide circle of professional and amateur scientists. Foremost among the amateurs was George Perkins Marsh, a diplomat-politician from Vermont who coached Baird in the intricacies of Washington politics and played a key role in securing his appointment at the Smithsonian. At a time when few professional scientists paid attention to the environmental costs of the industrial age, Marsh, like his fellow New Englander Henry David Thoreau, concerned himself with changes in the land and warned that people were fast making the earth "an unfit home for its noblest inhabitants." After several decades of fieldwork, Marsh published *Man and Nature, or Physical Geography Modified by Human Action* (1864), an original, authoritative look at nature's interconnectedness. Contrary to most scientific thinking at the time, Marsh argued that even small disturbances of nature's equilibrium could accumulate to transform the land and its creatures. "Man is ever a disturbing agent," he declared. "Wherever he plants his foot, the harmonies of nature are turned to discords." Foreshadowing a basic dispute among environmentalists, Marsh and Thoreau differed on what to do about environmental deterioration. Marsh was a conservationist who believed in selective harvesting and replenishment, while Thoreau was a pure preservationist. Both are regarded as precursors of today's environmental movement.

As important as the Smithsonian Institution was in promoting science in mid-nineteenth-century America, it was not the federal government's largest scientific operation. The U.S. Coast Survey's annual appropriations dwarfed those of the Smithsonian and supported five times as many scientific projects. Mapping the shorelines of the United States, under the able leadership of Alexander Dallas Bache, the Coast Survey became the hub of geophysical research in the same way that the Smithsonian's National Museum served the natural sciences. The Coast Survey existed primarily to serve maritime navigation, but Bache extended his mandate to fund basic research in his own field of terrestrial magnetism as well as astronomy, telegraphy, and biology.

Maritime navigation was also the focus of Lieutenant Matthew Fontaine Maury, a commander of the U.S. Naval Observatory in Washington. Maury's staff gathered astronomical information as well as entries from hundreds of ships' logs on winds, currents, and general oceanographic data. From this work emerged six series of *Wind and Current Charts*, accompanied by a frequently updated book of *Sailing Directions* that proved enormously useful not only to naval commanders but also to commercial seamen engaged in whaling or the flourishing China trade. Thanks largely to Maury's analyses, ships sailing from New York to San Francisco in 1855 reduced their passage time

26 percent, from 180 to 133 days. The previous year, the Boston clipper ship *Flying Cloud* achieved a record passage time from Boston to San Francisco of 89 days and 8 hours.

WILKES'S NAVAL EXPEDITION

Of all the scientific activities sponsored by the U.S. government, military expeditions to the "western country" yielded the largest quantity of data and, arguably, the most impressive results. After Lewis and Clark's Corps of Discovery during Thomas Jefferson's presidency, the most productive of these early missions was the navy's United States Exploring Expedition between 1838 and 1842. Commanded by Lieutenant Charles Wilkes, a flotilla of six small ships embarked from Hampton Roads, Virginia, on a voyage that took it around Cape Horn, along 1,500 miles of Antarctica's coastline, into the central Pacific islands of Fiji and Hawaii, and, most important, as far north as the Columbia River, the inland waters of the Oregon Territory, and the Strait of Juan de Fuca near present-day Seattle. In addition to Wilkes, who was selected to command the expedition because of his scientific background, nine other "scientifics" endured the long, often dangerous voyage.

By the time Wilkes and his crew returned home, the voyage had cost almost $1 million and generated an impressive collection of some 160,000 zoological, ornithological, botanical, and ethnographic specimens. On this expedition, how-

Members of the Wilkes expedition measuring the girth of a redwood tree in what they described as a "primeval forest of pines" on the Columbia River.

471

Lieutenant Wilkes sketched this sophisticated Indian fishing weir on the Chehalis River in present-day Washington, 1841.

and friendly or hostile Indian tribes. The U.S. Senate had 10,000 copies of Frémont's report published and distributed to prospective western immigrants. One of them was the Mormon leader Brigham Young, who later credited Frémont's report for inspiring him to leave Illinois and lead his persecuted flock to the Great Salt Lake Basin.

Frémont's career bridged two distinct periods of American exploration. The first, which began with Lewis and Clark and ended with the Mexican War, was adventurous in style and open-ended in coverage and method. The second, between the Mexican War and the Civil War, was more specialized and systematic. Exploring the vast area acquired by the United States through the Louisiana Purchase was the primary goal of the first period. The goal of the second was economic development through western settlement and the building of roads and railroads. In both periods, the acquisition of information about the flora, fauna,

ever, as on others, discovery shaded into incursion. After natives on a Fijian island attacked and killed two of his officers, Wilkes retaliated by killing more than eighty Fijians in a bloody battle, laying waste to two of their villages and seizing some of their belongings for his collection. Wilkes's massive collection eventually made its way to the Smithsonian Institution's National Museum, forming the core of the museum's holdings.

FRÉMONT'S WESTERN EXPEDITIONS

While Wilkes steered a course homeward during the spring of 1842, army lieutenant John C. Frémont departed St. Louis on the first of five expeditions that would take him to the far West during the next ten years. A member of the U.S. Corps of Topographical Engineers and well connected politically as the son-in-law of Missouri's Senator Thomas H. Benton, Frémont became one of America's best-known agents of nationalist expansion. In 1846—shortly before he played a central role in the seizure of California from Mexico (see Chapter 14)—he prepared a series of annotated maps detailing the route he had taken along the Oregon Trail from present-day Kansas City, Missouri, to the junction of the Columbia and Walla Walla Rivers in southeastern Washington. These maps, along with Frémont's lucid report on California and the Northwest, provided detailed information about the terrain, the weather conditions, the availability of water and food,

John C. Frémont, army explorer and Republican candidate for president in 1856.

472

minerals, and native inhabitants of the West was a priority—and science benefited enormously.

THE GREAT RECONNAISSANCE

Between 1848 and 1861, the federal government sent two dozen survey parties to the West, in what historians have come to call "The Great Reconnaissance." While some of these expeditions surveyed the Mexican-American border, searched for artesian wells, and built wagon roads into the interior of the United States, the most ambitious and controversial assignments focused on a railroad route that would connect the East Coast with California. Six large survey teams went into the field between 1853 and 1854, each headed by an army topographical

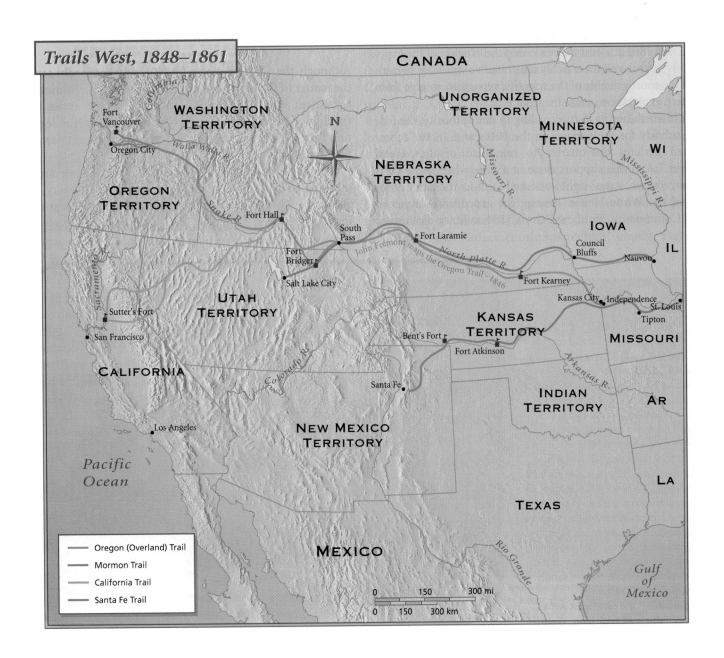

Trails West, 1848–1861

- Oregon (Overland) Trail
- Mormon Trail
- California Trail
- Santa Fe Trail

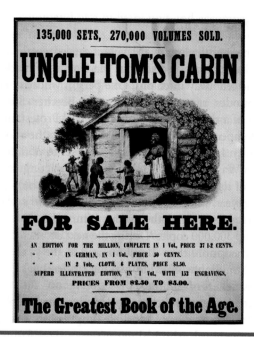

Poster advertising *Uncle Tom's Cabin*, c. 1859.

holders denounced its "falsehoods" and "distortions" and tried unsuccessfully to have it banned from the region. Some measure of the effect of this book can be gained from a supposed remark by President Lincoln in 1862, who greeted Stowe as the woman "who wrote the book that made this great war."

PIERCE AND THE OSTEND MANIFESTO

Uncle Tom's Cabin was published in 1852, a presidential election year. President Millard Fillmore's efforts to enforce the Fugitive Slave Act had won support among southern Whigs, but alienated antislavery northern Whigs who viewed him as a lackey of the slaveocracy. Dissension among Whigs became particularly apparent in Fillmore's home state of New York, where William Seward opposed his nomination and supported the Mexican War hero, General Winfield Scott, for the presidency. After fifty-two tedious roll-call votes, Scott won the Whig Party nomination. Yet even though he agreed to "acquiesce in" the Compromise of 1850—including the enforcement of the Fugitive Slave Act—he failed to generate support among southern party members, many of whom condemned the ticket and shifted their allegiance to the Democratic Party.

The Democrats also went into their convention divided between sectional candidates, but they emerged after forty-eight ballots united around a dark horse, Franklin Pierce of New Hampshire. A former U.S. congressman and senator as well as a Mexican War veteran, Pierce was one Yankee trusted by southern politicians, who considered him "sound" on slavery. One Mississippi politician pronounced him "as reliable as Calhoun himself." Even though the party endorsed a platform that stood firmly for the Compromise of 1850 (including strict enforcement of the Fugitive Slave Act) and pledged to keep slavery out of politics, it nonetheless succeeded in drawing Martin Van Buren and other free-soil Democrats back into its ranks. Such surprising unity boded well for Pierce, who carried twenty-seven out of thirty-one states in one of the most lopsided presidential victories since the War of 1812. Upon learning that Scott garnered only 35 percent of the popular vote in the South and won majorities in only two of the fifteen slave states (Kentucky and Tennessee), a Georgia congressman ominously proclaimed that "the Whig Party is dead."

Among Pierce's strongest supporters was the ultranationalistic "Young America" movement, which called for the continued territorial expansion of the United States. Many of its most enthusiastic members were southerners who believed that, as one of them put it, "the safety of the South is to be found only in the extension of its peculiar institutions." While some Young Americans spoke of America's Manifest Destiny "over all Mexico, over South America, [and] over the West Indies," the most desirable prize of all was Spanish Cuba.

President Polk had indicated shortly after the war with Mexico had ended (1848) that he was "decidedly in favour of purchasing Cuba & making it one of the States of [the] Union." The idea of acquiring Cuba, with its potential for sugar, tobacco, and cotton cultivation, proved particularly attractive to southerners interested in expanding their political representation and power in the Congress. When Spain refused to sell Cuba, several privately funded expeditions attempted unsuccessfully to seize it. The final act came in October 1854, when the Pierce administration's minister to Spain, having failed to acquire Cuba for $120 million, joined with the American ministers to Britain and France in drafting a memorandum to the State Department. Having offered Spain a price "far beyond [Cuba's] present value" and "been refused," the ministers concluded that the United States "shall be justified in wresting it from Spain if we possess the power."

The so-called Ostend Manifesto was intended as a confidential government document, but details of the statement leaked out to the European press, and in November 1854 a New York newspaper published the story. Antislavery advocates branded the ministers' declaration a "Manifesto of Brigands"—yet another southern conspiracy to "grasp, to rob, to murder, to grow rich on the spoils of provinces and toils of slaves." In response to a subpoena from the House of Representatives, an embarrassed Pierce administration released the controversial Ostend correspondence and immediately jettisoned all further plans to obtain Cuba. By then, however, the damage had been done.

Railroad Politics

Even the projected transcontinental railroad across the United States fell afoul of the widening sectional divide. As early as 1844, the New York merchant Asa Whitney had proposed constructing a railroad connecting the Atlantic with the Pacific. The federal government would finance the project through huge land grants to the builders, who in turn could sell them to settlers. Nothing came of the proposal until after the war with Mexico, when competing groups from Chicago, St. Louis, Memphis, and New Orleans began vying to construct the railroad. Where would its eastern terminus be,

in the North or the South? The stakes were high, with personal fortunes riding on the decision. Those communities through which the railroad, with its potentially vast western market, passed would enjoy a tremendous commercial boost.

Senator Stephen A. Douglas of Illinois.

Chief among the railroad politicians was Stephen A. Douglas of Illinois. Although he came from downstate, Chicago was Douglas's choice for the transcontinental terminus, with various connections from there to the East Coast. He had real estate interests in the Chicago area and believed that the city, with its excellent harbor on Lake Michigan and connecting canal facilities to the south and west, was the ideal core of the nation's transportation lines.

Douglas was convinced that the chances of gaining the railroad for Chicago would be greatly enhanced if the vast area lying west of Iowa and Missouri could be formally organized into a territory so that a legislature could be established and land expropriated from its native inhabitants for white settlement. Early in 1853, Douglas and a House colleague from Illinois introduced bills to organize most of the remaining part of the Louisiana Purchase north of 36°–30′ as the Nebraska Territory. The House of Representatives promptly passed the bill, but a group of southern senators, led by David R. Atchinson of Missouri, tabled the measure in the Senate. Their reasoning was simple: under the Missouri Compromise of 1820, the territory north of 36°–30′ outlawed slavery; hence they had no incentive to support the Douglas bill. Nor did the southerners want to give Chicago a commercial advantage over St. Louis, Memphis, Vicksburg (Mississippi), Natchez (Mississippi), or New Orleans. Knowing that Douglas needed his vote as well as those of several southern senators to pass the Nebraska bill, the proslavery Atchinson declared

View of Chicago in 1854, northern gateway to the American West.

477

that he would rather see Nebraska "sink in hell" than have it organized as free territory. He insisted that Douglas recast the bill to place "slaveholder and non-slaveholder upon terms of equality" in the new territory.

With the Nebraska legislation blocked and Douglas stewing over how to meet Senator Atchinson's challenge, Congress authorized $150,000 for the War Department to determine the best railroad route to California. Four major survey par-

ties, each commanded by an army topographical engineer, set out for the West in the spring and summer of 1853, with four more taking the field the following fall and winter. But not even these engineers could devise an impartial solution to the politically loaded railroad question.

From a scientific standpoint, the army surveys succeeded brilliantly, collecting an immense amount of specimens and data on the geology, botany, zoology, meteorology, and eth-

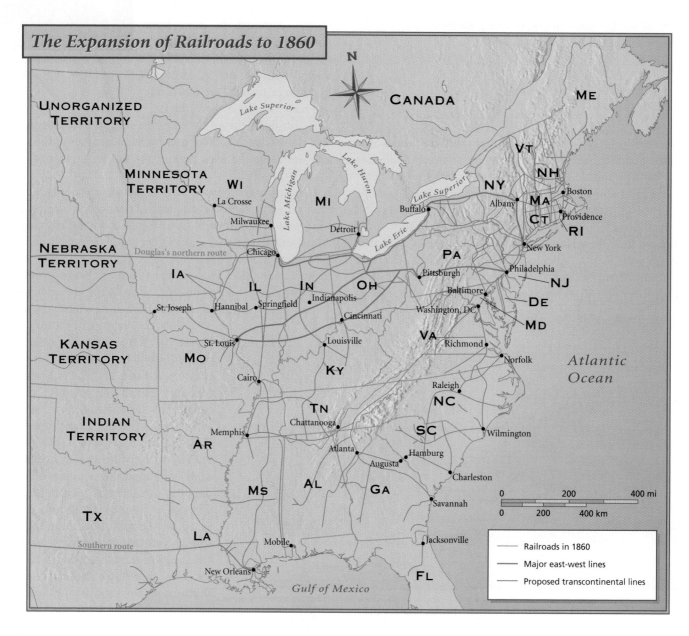

The Expansion of Railroads to 1860

The Pacific Railroad surveys produced a great fund of knowledge about the West, including some first-rate works of art. This lithographic view of a large buffalo herd near Lake Jessie in east-central North Dakota was done by the artist John Mix Stanley, c. 1853–54.

nology of the West. But from a political standpoint, the surveys failed, revealing not one but several possible routes to the West Coast. This allowed war secretary Jefferson Davis of Mississippi to hold to his favored southern route, which roughly followed the 32nd parallel westward from Natchez to San Diego. He ignored at least two routes farther north that could have won over nearly all the contending parties for the transcontinental railroad, including Douglas. To secure the land needed for his southern route, Davis orchestrated the so-called Gadsden Purchase in 1854, involving 19 million acres of Mexican land in what are now Arizona and New Mexico. Davis pushed the purchase through long before the army engineers had completed their surveys. In the end, sectional politics prevailed over science. Davis issued a report to President Pierce that recommended the southern route. The controversy over the location of the transcontinental railroad continued unabated.

DOUGLAS'S KANSAS-NEBRASKA ACT

While the topographical surveys were in progress, Douglas twice failed to fashion a Nebraska bill that would win the votes of his southern colleagues. Finally, he gave in, and on January 23, 1854, introduced a new bill that created two territories—Kansas, west of Missouri, and Nebraska, west of Iowa and Minnesota. The bill conveyed an impression of balance, with Kansas likely to become a slave state and Nebraska free. The bill also stipulated that the people of each territory, not Congress, would decide on the future of slavery through the exercise of popular sovereignty. Since Kansas lay north of 36°–30′, this provision in effect repealed the Missouri Compromise.

Douglas's Kansas-Nebraska bill fueled one of the fiercest congressional debates in American history. President Pierce initially balked at the legislation, because he considered the repeal of the time-tested Missouri Compromise line injudicious. But pressure from a delegation headed by Douglas and Jefferson Davis moved him to support the bill and make it "a test of party orthodoxy." It was a fateful decision.

Douglas's bill caught northern Whigs and Democrats by surprise, but the loudest opposition came from Free-Soilers who openly attacked the measure "as a gross violation of a sacred pledge, as a criminal betrayal of precious rights, as part and parcel of an atrocious plot" to make Kansas-Nebraska a "dreary region of despotism, inhabited by masters and slaves." Free-Soilers also condemned Douglas for placing his presidential aspirations ahead of the national interest and accused him of serving as a henchman of "slavery despotism." As the debates heated up, anti-Nebraska groups sent petitions to Washington while ten state legislatures in the North either denounced the bill or refused their support. Every northern Whig in Congress opposed the bill.

But Douglas relentlessly pushed the Kansas-Nebraska Act, and it passed the Democratic-controlled Senate in March by a vote of 37 to 14. Only five free-state Democrats broke ranks to join the northern Whig and Free Soil opposition, indicating that the Pierce administration had indeed made the bill a test of party orthodoxy. Two months later, following more heated debates, the House of Representatives passed the bill by a margin of 13 votes. On May 30, 1854, President Pierce signed it into law.

479

INNOVATIONS IN PARTY POLITICS

The Kansas-Nebraska Act was a deeply polarizing law. It killed the Whig Party by exciting already serious divisions between proslavery southerners and antislavery northerners in the party. By 1854, former Whigs were seeking new political affiliations that tied them closer to purely sectional rather than national interests.

Although the Kansas-Nebraska Act did not destroy the Democratic Party, its polarizing effects set the party on a narrowly sectional course. Evidence of the change came in the fall elections of 1854, when Democratic voters in the North deserted the party in droves to vote for other candidates. Going into the election, Democrats controlled both houses of Congress and held an overwhelming majority in the House of Representatives. The election cost House Democrats 72 percent of their seats from districts in the North and 13 percent from the South, leaving the party in a minority position. At the national level, the party lost its sectional balance as well. Beginning in 1855, southern Democrats outnumbered their northern counterparts in party councils, allowing them to steer the party in a proslavery direction. The balance that had once distinguished the "Democracy" of Andrew Jackson and Martin Van Buren was gone, and with it, the spirit of compromise.

The Thirty-fourth Congress, which met for the first time in March 1855, reflected the extent of the political realignments taking place. The demise of the Whig Party and the ex-

This 1856 campaign cartoon bitterly denounces the Democratic Party for the Kansas-Nebraska Act and the outbreak of civil war in Kansas. In the center is "Liberty" (the female symbol of the United States) imploring buckskin-clad President Franklin Pierce to "spare me gentlemen, spare me!" Pierce is surrounded by other Democratic Party leaders, notably Stephen A. Douglas (far right, who has just scalped a hapless farmer) and, next to him, the heavily armed Lewis Cass, who is licking his lips and scoffing, "Poor little Dear. We wouldn't hurt her for the world, would we Frank? ha! ha! ha!" On the left, James Buchanan is picking the pockets of another dead victim of the Kansas fighting, while Pierce's secretary of state, William Marcy (wearing the 50-cent trouser patch), assists him.

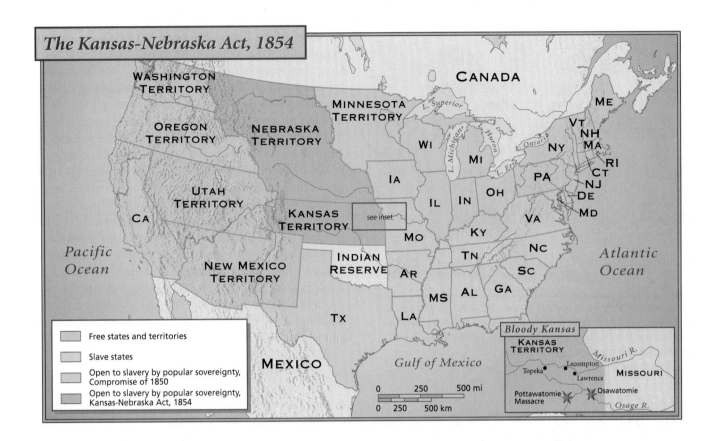

The Kansas-Nebraska Act, 1854

Free states and territories

Slave states

Open to slavery by popular sovereignty, Compromise of 1850

Open to slavery by popular sovereignty, Kansas-Nebraska Act, 1854

Bloody Kansas

odus of anti-Nebraska Democrats meant that the Democratic Party in the North now took a back seat to two new parties: the American, or "Know-Nothing," Party and the Republican Party. Although they emphasized different issues, these two parties often cooperated with each other, and eventually they would coalesce into a major party known as the Republicans.

The American Party appeared in 1854 as an expression of long-standing antagonisms between predominantly Catholic immigrant groups and the overwhelmingly Protestant native-born majority. Nativist tensions had escalated after 1845 when an unprecedented wave of immigration, led primarily by Irish Catholics fleeing the deadly potato famine, broke on U.S. shores. This pulse brought nearly 3 million immigrants—the largest number in American history—to the United States by 1854.

The nativist, anti-immigrant reaction followed the newcomers from their arrival in eastern port cities like Boston, New York, and Philadelphia to their inland destinations, such as Buffalo and Chicago. Since most of the new arrivals were impoverished peasant-laborers from Ireland and Germany,

they were soon blamed for rising crime rates and public costs in urban areas. Nativists also noticed that by the early 1850s, more and more immigrants were beginning to vote. The percentage of foreign-born voters was growing much faster than that of native-born. Immigrant voters tended to support Democratic candidates and oppose temperance, antislavery, and other reform efforts, which put them on a collision course with largely evangelical Protestants who headed these movements and, in the past, had voted Whig. The quarrel went beyond reform, when native-born white workers found themselves in competition with Irishmen and other recent immigrants for jobs. The growing resentment went both ways: the immigrants and their Catholic leaders attacked free-soilers, abolitionists, and Protestant reform groups while calling for tax-supported Catholic schools, where their children would not be exposed to the perceived heresies being taught in public schools.

Political nativism took form in secret fraternal societies such as the Order of United Americans and the Order of the Star-Spangled Banner. Their members pledged never to vote

A mid-nineteenth-century nativist cartoon showing an Irish whiskey drinker and a German beer drinker carrying off a ballot box while other immigrants riot in front of an election polling place in the background. The message is clear: immigrants are a corrupt and disruptive influence on the Republic and its long-standing traditions.

for Roman Catholics or other foreigners for public office, and supported efforts to pass temperance laws and raise the residency requirements for American citizenship to twenty-one years. When queried by outsiders about their political activities, they were instructed to reply, "I know nothing"— and so opponents derided them as "Know-Nothings." The Know-Nothing Party fielded its first slate of candidates in the congressional and state elections of 1854, and won impressive gains throughout the Northeast as well as in the border states and the deep South. "How people do hate Catholics," a Cincinnati editor exclaimed, "and what happiness it was to thousands to have a chance to show it in what seemed like a lawful and patriotic manner." The Congress that convened in March 1855 included at least fifty new House members who identified themselves as members of the American Party, and another seventy were elected with Know-Nothing support.

The Republican Party originated in the Midwest and gradually spread to former Whig strongholds in the Northeast. The party's primary concern was the expansion of slavery—especially, as Abraham Lincoln put it, the "moral wrong and

> *"Support for antislavery did not mean a belief in racial equality. Like other white Americans of the time, Republicans harbored racist ideas."*

injustice" of the Kansas-Nebraska Act in allowing slavery to expand into territory previously closed to it. Here it becomes clear that support for antislavery did not mean a belief in racial equality. Like other white Americans of the time, Republicans harbored racist ideas. Admitting that "he cared nothing for the 'nigger,'" a future Republican congressman from Pittsburgh declared that "it was not the mission of the Republican party to preach rebellion" but rather "deliverance to the white man." By this, he meant that Republicans opposed the extension of slavery into the territories as a hindrance to the ability of free white labor to earn a living wage there. This free-labor ideology could accommodate attacks on the "slave oligarchy" as well as support for legislation prohibiting free blacks from residing within certain states like Lincoln's Illinois. A hallmark of the Republican Party as it entered its first campaign in 1854, the ideology proved successful, at least in the North. Republican candidates made strong showings in state elections in the Midwest and Northeast, and won approximately 105 House seats in 1854.

BLOODY KANSAS

In the midst of these structural changes in American politics, the contest to determine whether Kansas would be slave or free began. It was a conflict that extended from the corridors of power in Washington to the rich soil of the Kansas Territory. New York's antislavery Whig (soon to be Republican) senator William H. Seward sounded the call to free-soilers. "We will engage in competition for the virgin soil of Kansas," he told his Senate colleagues, "and God give the victory to the side which is stronger in numbers as it is in right." Long before Seward made these remarks, a group of wealthy antislavery advocates headed by Amos Lawrence of Boston had raised $5 million and incorporated the Massachusetts Emigrant Aid Company "for the purpose of assisting emigrants to settle in the West." Although the incorporators originally thought that New Englanders would flock to Kansas, most of the company's support went to midwestern farmers who embraced the free-soil ideology. Slowly at first, but then in growing numbers, nonslaveholding settlers began to move into the Kansas Territory.

Determined not to be bested by Seward and his "free soil crowd," Senator David Atchinson of Missouri cautioned that "the game [for Kansas] must be played boldly." "If we win we carry slavery to the Pacific Ocean," he wrote a Senate colleague from Virginia, "if we fail we lose Missouri, Arkansas, Texas, and all the territories." When the newly appointed territorial governor called for the election of a legislature, Atchinson saw to it that supporters from Missouri flocked into Kansas to elect proslavery candidates. "There are eleven hundred men coming over from Platte County [Missouri] to vote," he boasted, "and if that ain't enough we can send five thousand—enough to kill every God-damned abolitionist in the Territory." In the legislature they elected, proslavery members outnumbered free-soilers thirty-six to three.

Appalled by the actions of Atchinson and his supporters, the territorial governor called for yet another election in certain districts where he was convinced that fraudulent voting had taken place. This time, free-soilers won most of the seats, but when they reported for duty in July 1855, they were turned away by the proslavery legislature seated at Lecompton. When the governor protested these actions in Washington, the Pierce administration removed him and appointed a successor thought to be more sympathetic with Senator Atchinson's views. In the meantime, the Lecompton legislature passed a series of laws that recognized the votes of nonresidents (thus validating the earlier elections), established strict slave codes, and imposed penalties on anyone who spoke out against slavery, assisted runaways, or in any way encouraged slave recalcitrance or revolts.

Free-soil Kansans, who now outnumbered their opponents, refused to recognize the legislature at Lecompton or obey its laws. Taking matters into their own hands, they called a convention in October 1855, drew up a free-state constitution, and elected their own governor and legislature, which they installed at Topeka. At this point, Kansas had two competing territorial governments: one representing free-soilers at Topeka, the other officially recognized by the Pierce administration and representing the proslavery constituency at Lecompton. Both sides were heavily armed and spoiling for a fight. That moment arrived in November 1855, when the murder of a free-soiler by a proslavery resident ignited a series of clashes along the Kansas-Missouri border. Only the intervention of Senator Atchinson, who urged his followers to

> *"Well known for his sharp tongue and condescending demeanor, Senator Charles Sumner referred in the speech to Senator Andrew P. Butler of South Carolina as a 'Don Quixote who has chosen a mistress . . . the harlot, Slavery' and to Butler's home state for 'its shameful imbecility from Slavery.'"*

bide their time, and the onset of a hard winter prevented a full-scale attack on the free-soil town of Lawrence by some 1,500 Missouri border raiders. But the following spring, the inevitable occurred when a large force of Missourians, purportedly armed with a warrant from a proslavery judge to arrest the leaders of the free-soil government for treason, rode into Lawrence, made several arrests, and burned and looted the town.

The Sumner-Brooks Confrontation. As civil war flared in Kansas, physical violence erupted on the floor of the U.S. Senate. There, on May 19–20, 1856, Charles Sumner of Massachusetts, one of the few outright abolitionists in Congress, delivered a blistering speech to packed galleries entitled "The Crime Against Kansas." Well known for his sharp tongue and condescending demeanor, Sumner referred in the speech to Senator Andrew P. Butler of South Carolina as a "Don Quixote who has chosen a mistress . . . the harlot, Slavery" and to Butler's home state for "its shameful imbecility from Slavery." As for that "noisome, squat, and nameless animal" Stephen A. Douglas, he was "the squire of Slavery, its very Sancho Panza, ready to do all its humiliating offices." Sumner ended his diatribe by calling for the immediate admission of Kansas to the Union as a free state.

As he had intended, Sumner's speech created a public furor. Although letters and telegrams from abolitionist supporters poured into his office praising him for his "inspiring eloquence and lofty moral tone," Sumner's closest Senate colleagues thought that he had gone too far. Lewis Cass, the dean of the Senate and Sumner's oldest acquaintance there, denounced the speech as "the most un-American and unpatriotic that ever grated on the ears of this high body."

And Sumner touched a raw nerve in Congressman Preston Brooks of South Carolina when he referred to Senator Butler, a relative of Brooks's, as the Don Quixote of slavery and made tasteless fun of a physical impediment that caused Butler to drool and "expectorate" when speaking. The enraged Brooks decided that, he would assume the "duty to relieve Butler and avenge the insult to my State."

On May 22, two days after Sumner delivered his speech, Brooks waited until the Senate had concluded its business for

This cartoon, entitled "Southern Chivalry," shows South Carolina's Preston Brooks beating Charles Sumner, who is holding a copy of his speech, "The Crime Against Kansas," in his left hand.

the day, then entered the chamber and addressed Sumner, who was writing at his desk. "Mr. Sumner, I have read your speech twice over carefully. It is a libel on South Carolina, and Mr. Butler, who is a relative of mine." Before Sumner could rise from his chair, Brooks struck him on the head with his walking stick and continued to rain down blows until Sumner became "as senseless as a corpse . . . his head bleeding copiously from the frightful wounds, and the blood saturating his clothes." "I . . . gave him about thirty first rate stripes," Brooks later boasted. "Towards the last he bellowed like a calf. I wore my cane out completely but saved the Head which is gold."

The attack made Brooks an instant hero in the South. A Richmond newspaper reported, "The only regret we feel is that Mr. Brooks did not employ a horse whip or a cowhide upon [Sumner's] slanderous back, instead of a cane." On the other side, northerners condemned the attack as "brutal, murderous, and cowardly." Some vowed that they would vote Republican because they were appalled at the unrepentant "tone of the Southern Press, & the approbation . . . of the whole Southern People." Political observers predicted that the Democratic Party stood to lose 200,000 votes in the upcoming presidential election. The most ominous comment, however, came from the pen of the Transcendentalist writer Ralph Waldo Emerson. "I do not see

> *" 'I do not see how a barbarous community and a civilized community can constitute one state,' Ralph Waldo Emerson declared. 'I think we must get rid of slavery, or we must get rid of freedom.' "*

how a barbarous community and a civilized community can constitute one state," he declared. "I think we must get rid of slavery, or we must get rid of freedom."

The Pottawatomie Massacre. The Sumner-Brooks confrontation brought sectional antagonisms to a boil throughout the United States, especially in Kansas. There, in the small, free-soil settlement of Osawatomie, a militant abolitionist and intensely religious individual named John Brown brooded over what he considered the miscarriage of justice by corrupt federal authorities as well as the atrocities committed by proslavery raiders from Missouri. Already upset about the sack of Lawrence, Brown, according to his son, "went crazy—*crazy*" when he heard about the Sumner beating. Determined to "fight fire with fire," he decided to "strike terror in the hearts of the proslavery people" by conducting a retaliation of his own. On May 24, 1856, Brown gathered a small force and rode into a proslavery settlement along Pottawatomie Creek, where in the dead of night they dragged five suspected proslavery agitators from their cabins and butchered them with broadswords specially sharpened for the purpose.

As news of the sack of Lawrence and the Pottawatomie massacre spread, southeastern Kansas became a bloody battleground. Chaos reigned during the summer and early fall of 1856. Fearing for their lives, families on both sides hastily packed their belongings and left the territory. Others joined guerrilla bands that marauded the countryside, shooting up towns, robbing stores and banks, burning settlers' homesteads, and running off their livestock. Among them was John Brown, described by a reporter from New York as "a strange, resolute, repulsive, iron-willed, inexorable old man" who quoted the Bible and believed that he was fighting a holy war against wickedness.

Thanks largely to the resolute actions of Governor John W. Geary, appointed by the Pierce administration to pacify Kansas, guerrilla warfare slowly subsided during the fall of 1856. Geary disbanded the armed groups and used federal troops as a police force. He also convinced both sides that continued violence would hurt their causes in the upcoming presidential election. Some 200 people had died during the conflict, with property losses estimated at $2 million. Yet even though Geary put a stop to the worst of the fighting, his failure to get Kansans to agree on a state constitution, coupled with a falling out with the Pierce administration, led to his abrupt resignation in March 1857.

Sporadic fighting continued over the next three years as Geary's successors sought to hold fair elections and prepare a new constitution that would reflect the views of the territory's majority. The Democratic Party divided irretrievably over the slavery issue in Kansas, with President Pierce and his successor, James Buchanan, supporting the proslavery constitution drafted by the Lecompton legislature and Stephen A. Douglas denouncing it as a travesty of popular sovereignty. Free-soil Republicans eventually gained the upper hand in the territorial legislature and adopted a constitution that brought Kansas into the Union as a free state in January 1861, but by then renewed guerrilla warfare had cost hundreds of lives and more millions in destroyed property. As for the transcontinental railroad that had caused the Kansas embroglio, it remained moribund—nothing more than a paper plan and a figment of Douglas's ambitious imagination.

Buchanan and the Politics of Disunion

The turmoil in Kansas and the intense sectional hostility that flowed from it made 1856 a critical election year. Going into the race, leaders of the newly formed Republican Party realized that they had little chance of success unless they could attract Know-Nothing support. Playing on widespread prejudice against Catholics and immigrants, anger over the repeal of the Missouri Compromise, and support for temperance legislation as well as the ouster of corrupt politicians, the American Party had attracted thousands of former Whigs and Democrats to its nativist cause. But as formidable as it appeared, the party had failed to deliver on its promises to pass anti-immigrant and temperance legislation and to reform the political system. And it was proving vulnerable to opposition charges of bigotry, undemocratic secret practices, and gang violence during elections. Above all, the party was divided on the slavery question.

The American Party finally split in two at its national convention in February 1856. Fifty northern delegates walked out after southern delegates, with support from New York, rejected a resolution calling for the repeal of the Kansas-Nebraska Act and the restoration of the Missouri Compromise. The division did not heal. "South Americans" nominated Millard Fillmore for president, and "North Americans" nominated Speaker of the House Nathaniel Banks. When Banks declined the nomi-

nation and threw his support to the Republican Party, thousands of Know-Nothings shifted their allegiance and cast Republican ballots in November. This critical realignment signaled the beginning of the end of the American Party while assuring the future of the Republicans. In less than three years, they had grown from an obscure third party to a major player in the two-party system.

The Republicans still faced a tricky electoral task. Northern Know-Nothings shared Republicans' opposition to the Democratic Party, the Kansas-Nebraska Act, and what they considered the slave oligarchy of the South. But Republicans sought to downplay Know-Nothing issues of temperance and anti-immigrant policy, while still exploiting the hatred for Roman Catholics in the electorate. In some important state races, the Republicans supported Know-Nothing candidates in return for their support of the Republican presidential nominee, John C. Frémont.

Despite a lack of political experience, Frémont made an attractive candidate. He had gained national stature as "The

An 1856 presidential campaign banner touting the candidacy of John C. Frémont, the "brave path finder," and the Republican Party's principles of "free speech, free press, free soil, and free men."

485

Pathfinder," the country's most famous living explorer. He had also been a prominent advocate of California's admission to the Union as a free state, and he supported the same for Kansas. And Frémont was married to the daughter of Senator Thomas H. Benton, the sworn enemy of Missouri's proslavery Senator David Atchinson and his "border ruffians";

James Buchanan, fifteenth president of the United States (1857–61).

Benton's endorsement promised to attract significant support among former free-soil Democrats. The ambitious Frémont wanted the Republican nomination, and he got it on the first ballot.

Faced with a three-way race and formidable opposition, Democratic Party leaders sought a candidate who was not tainted by "Bloody Kansas"—as were President Pierce and Stephen A. Douglas—and who could rally a divided party to victory. After seventeen ballots at the national convention in Cincinnati, they selected James Buchanan. A sixty-five-year-old bachelor from Pennsylvania and a longtime Jacksonian Democrat, Buchanan had served in both the House and Senate, as Polk's secretary of state, and in the diplomatic corps—safely out of the country—as the American minister to Russia and Great Britain. Well known and well liked but somewhat colorless, Buchanan presented a stark contrast with the youthful, impetuous Frémont. But in the charged atmosphere of 1856, Buchanan's attributes were viewed as advantages. His initial support came from northern Democrats, but southerners quickly accepted his nomination, confident that he would support their interests in Kansas and oppose further agitation of the slavery question.

No two party platforms could have been more different, with the Republicans denouncing the Kansas-Nebraska Act and popular sovereignty, and the Democrats embracing them. The Democratic platform also supported states' rights and limited government while opposing federally funded internal improvements (other than the transcontinental railroad), high tariffs, and a national bank. Most important, the Democratic press identified Buchanan as the only legitimate candidate in the election, a factor that weighed heavily with Democrats and former Whigs who feared for the future of the Union. Buchanan emphatically pressed the point: "The Black Republicans must be . . . boldly assailed as disunionists, and this charge must be reiterated again and again," he asserted. "This race ought to be run on the question of Union or disunion."

Buchanan won the presidency and the Democrats recaptured both houses of Congress, but hardly by a landslide: Buchanan won 45 percent of the popular vote to Frémont's 33 percent and Fillmore's 22 percent. Although Fillmore did well in the South, the only state he carried was Maryland. With Buchanan winning all of the South and Frémont all of New England plus New York, Ohio, Michigan, Iowa, and Wisconsin, the crucial contests centered on the lower northern states of Illinois, Indiana, New Jersey, and especially Pennsylvania. Buchanan managed a narrow victory in Pennsylvania largely by warning voters that if elected, Frémont and the "Black Republicans" would cause the breakup of the Union and "turn loose . . . millions of negroes, to elbow you in the workshops, and compete with you in the fields of honest labor." Although they had lost the election, Republican Party leaders considered it a "victorious defeat." They realized that they could win the presidency in 1860 if they maintained their hold on the northern states already in their camp and added Pennsylvania and either Illinois or Indiana to the fold.

THE *DRED SCOTT* DECISION

Buchanan launched his presidency on troubled political and economic waters. On March 6, 1857, two days after his inauguration, the Supreme Court exploded a judicial bombshell in the *Dred Scott* decision. Scott was an elderly Missouri slave whose master, an army surgeon, had taken him into Illinois and to Fort Snelling, in the northern part of the Louisiana Purchase (present-day Minnesota), for extended stays during the 1830s. Scott sued for his freedom on the grounds that Illinois was a free state and that Fort Snelling, under the provisions of the Missouri Compromise, was in free territory. Supported by a group of white abolitionists, Scott initially brought suit in the Missouri court system in 1846 and lost. But through a series of appeals and legal maneuvers, the case wound up before the Supreme Court in 1856.

Dred Scott.

Well aware of the case and its implications, President-elect Buchanan urged Chief Justice Roger Taney to render a decision that would effectively remove the slavery debate from Congress and quash the intensifying sectional conflict. Buchanan knew several weeks beforehand what the Court's majority opinion would be. The decision had three parts: first, the Court held that Scott was a slave, not a citizen, and therefore had no right to sue in a federal court. At this point, the Court could have thrown out the case, but it went on to make two more pronouncements. One was that Scott's four-year residence in free territory did not make him free. The other was that Congress did not have the right to ban slavery north of 36°–30′ in the Missouri Compromise or, for that matter, anywhere else because such action conflicted with Article V of the Constitution, which guaranteed that no citizen could "be deprived of life, liberty, or property, without due process of law." Since, in the Court's view, slaves were property, they could be taken anywhere in the United State or its territories—despite what Congress or the territorial legislatures might legislate.

> *"Since, in the Court's view, slaves were property, they could be taken anywhere in the United States or its territories—despite what Congress or the territorial legislatures might legislate."*

The *Dred Scott* decision pleased Buchanan and the slaveholding South. Democratic leaders throughout the country viewed it as "the funeral sermon of Black Republicanism." But events soon proved them wrong: *Dred Scott* invigorated the Republican movement. Outraged by the decision, Republican leaders attacked the Taney Court as part of a "slave power" conspiracy. Indeed, Senator William Seward of New York charged that Buchanan and Taney had conspired to render a decision favorable to the South. Although the president and chief justice denied the accusation, aroused Republicans vowed to make the case a political issue in the upcoming elections of 1858 and 1860 and, if victorious, to "reconstitute" the Supreme Court and overturn its "inhuman dicta." "The remedy," according to the Chicago *Tribune*, lay in "the ballot box." "Let the next President be Republican," its editor declared, "and 1860 will mark an era kindred to that of 1776."

THE LINCOLN-DOUGLAS DEBATES

The sectional furor provoked by the *Dred Scott* decision, coupled with the ongoing crisis in Bloody Kansas, led to one of the most famous **series of debates** in American political history. In Illinois, Senator Stephen A. Douglas, the foremost proponent of popular sovereignty and a leading contender among northern Democrats for the presidency in 1860, was up for reelection in 1858. His adversary was Abraham Lincoln, a former Whig who had emerged as a Republican leader in Illinois. Because he lacked Douglas's visibility and wanted to counter charges that he was a "Black Republican" whose abolitionist views would destroy the Union, Lincoln challenged Douglas to a series of seven debates to be held throughout the state during the late summer and early fall of 1858. It was a bold move on Lincoln's part because the dynamic Douglas was well known as a powerful speaker and quick-witted debater.

The Lincoln-Douglas debates attracted large crowds and, owing primarily to Douglas's national reputation, received widespread press coverage, including verbatim transcripts. The spectacle of the gangly and somewhat disheveled six-foot-four Lincoln trading verbal blows with the short and stocky but impeccably attired Douglas was somewhat humorous. But once the debates began, there was nothing funny about the hard-hitting tactics of the two debaters, and their focus was on slavery and the fate of the Union.

From the outset, Lincoln accused Douglas of departing from the views of the founding fathers on slavery as expressed in the Declaration of Independence. By contrast, he said that Republicans, like the founders, "insist that [slavery] should . . . be treated as a [moral] wrong, and that it shall grow no more." Douglas, in turn, accused Lincoln of being an abolitionist whose "doctrine is revolutionary, and destructive of the existence of our government." In Douglas's view, including blacks among those "created equal" in the Declaration of Independence was a "monstrous heresy." "Are you in favor of conferring upon the negro the rights and privileges of citizenship?" he asked in the first debate. "No, no," responded the crowd. "Do you de-

Abraham Lincoln at the time of the *Dred Scott* decision, 1857.

Buchanan and the Politics of Disunion

sire to strike out of our State Constitution that clause which keeps slaves and free negroes out of the State, and allow the free negroes to flow in . . . and cover your prairies with black settlements? Do you desire to turn this beautiful State into a free negro colony?" The crowd roared again, "No, no!" "If you desire negro citizenship . . . if you desire them to vote on an equality with yourselves," Douglas continued, "then support Mr. Lincoln and the Black Republican party. . . . For one, I am opposed to negro citizenship in any and every form. I believe this government . . . was made by white men, for the benefit of white men and their posterity for ever, and I am in favor of confining citizenship to white men . . . instead of conferring it upon negroes, Indians and other inferior races." The crowd cheered: "Good for you!" "Douglas forever!"

Douglas's racist barbs hit their mark. The more Lincoln tried to distance himself from abolitionism yet denounce

Cartoon depicting Stephen A. Douglas as a fearless gladiator fighting for popular sovereignty.

slavery as a "moral and political wrong," the more Douglas hammered him about being a candidate of "the Abolition party" and the dire threat such "revolutionary principles" posed to white society. By the time of the fourth debate on September 18, Douglas had Lincoln on the defensive. "I am not, nor ever have been in favor of bringing about in any way the social and political equality of the white and black races," Lincoln insisted. "I am not, nor ever have been in favor of making voters or jurors of negroes, nor of qualifying them to hold office, nor to intermarry with white people. . . . There must be the position of superior and inferior, and I as much as any other man am in favor of the superior position being assigned to the white race."

Lincoln refused to leave the issue there, however. He coupled his comments on white superiority with a plea for fairness and the inclusion of blacks in the most basic tenets of American freedom—a clear indication of the direction in which he would move so dramatically in the years that lay just ahead. "I hold that . . . there is no reason in the world why the Negro is not entitled to all the natural rights enumerated in the Declaration of Independence, the right to life, liberty, and the pursuit of happiness," Lincoln told the crowd at Ottawa, Illinois. "I hold that he is as much entitled to these as the white man. I agree with Judge Douglas that he is not my equal in many respects—certainly not in color, perhaps not in moral or intellectual endowment. But in the right to eat the bread, without leave of anybody else, which his own hand earns, *he is my equal and the equal of Judge Douglas, and the equal of every living man.*"

Even though these comments were greeted with "Great applause," according to a reporter present, it seems fair to say that, on balance, Douglas bested Lincoln on the race issue during their exchanges. If the debates revealed anything, it was the extent to which racism pervaded the culture of pre–Civil War Illinois and, by extension, all of America. Lincoln was part of this America, to be sure, but he was also capable, as he demonstrated during the debates, of rising above the cruder prejudices of his era and thinking of black men and women as human beings who deserved a chance to share in the promise of this country.

Lincoln also got in plenty of licks, none more telling than a question he posed during the second debate, held at Freeport on August 27. Suppose, Lincoln began, the people of Kansas adopted a state constitution that excluded slavery. But, he added, in the *Dred Scott* case the Supreme Court had decided that "states cannot exclude slavery from their limits." Whose position would Douglas support, the people of Kansas or the Supreme Court? Lincoln knew what Douglas's response would be: as the champion of popular sovereignty, he emphatically chose the people's position. "Whatever the Supreme Court may . . . decide as to the abstract question of slavery," Douglas insisted, "the people of a Territory have the lawful means to admit it or exclude it as they please, for the reason that slavery cannot exist a day or an hour anywhere unless supported by local police regulations . . . furnished by the local legislature." He concluded, "No matter what may be the decision of the Supreme Court on that abstract question, still the right of the people to make it a slave Territory or a free Territory is perfect and complete."

Douglas's response became known as the Freeport Doctrine. His ringing endorsement of popular sovereignty played well before his Illinois audiences and helped to get him reelected to the Senate, but it fatally damaged his standing with southern Democrats. Although Lincoln lost his senatorial bid, he emerged from the election as a Republican of national stature and a likely candidate for the presidency in 1860. Douglas likewise strengthened his position among northern Democrats and, much to the consternation of Buchanan, looked as if he would be the party's standard-bearer in 1860. Having clashed with the Buchanan administration over its support of the proslavery Lecompton constitution and, in effect, denied the efficacy of the *Dred Scott* decision, Douglas with his victory struck a blow to Buchanan and his southern supporters.

THE PANIC OF 1857

The public uproar over *Dred Scott* and Bloody Kansas was joined by a financial panic that gripped the country during the fall of 1857. The crash came unexpectedly on August 24, when the New York office of an Ohio investment bank stopped making specie (gold and silver) payments on its notes and deposits because an employee had absconded with its funds. Thousands of depositors jammed their local banks intent on closing their accounts and being paid off in gold specie. Unable to meet the sudden surge of demand for specie, some 1,400 banks closed their doors while hundreds of investment houses and manufacturing firms declared bankruptcy. Before long, unemployed workers thronged the streets of northern cities shouting, "Bread or blood!" Some of

Oil painting of New York City's *Wall Street, Half Past Two O'clock, October 13, 1857.* The Panic of 1857 put half of Wall Street's brokers out of business.

the most serious incidents occurred in New York City, where hungry workers looted the shops of flour merchants and, on November 10, threatened to seize the U.S. Customs House (containing some $20 million) before they were dispersed by a contingent of marines and infantrymen.

The panic was caused by a number of factors—growing trade deficits, rampant speculation, overinvestment, rising interest rates, and outright greed. The Crimean War in Europe (1854–56) contributed to the instability by pushing up grain prices and enticing farmers and land speculators to assume large mortgages on land in the Midwest. When the war ended, grain prices fell before farmers could recoup their investments, severely damaging them and their bank creditors.

The 1850s were also a time of expansive factory and railroad building, much of which was funded by American banks that had attracted investment capital from Europe. When the costs of the Crimean War and other colonial ventures drained specie from British and French banks, interest rates rose, causing European investors to dispose of their American holdings for higher-yielding investments in their own

In this Republican electoral cartoon, Abraham Lincoln is trying to decide which Democrat to eat first: the "hard shell" proslavery candidate, John C. Breckenridge (right), or the moderate "soft shell" candidate, Stephen A. Douglas. Well aware that the Democratic Party was divided over slavery, the cartoon exudes confidence in a Republican victory.

With the Democratic Party split down the middle, Republican leaders exulted in the knowledge that they had a good chance of winning the election. Although still limited primarily to the northern states, far more populous than the South, the Republican Party had matured since 1856. It was a stronger organization with a broad policy base that included antislavery, a strong protective tariff, a homestead act, a Pacific railroad, and internal improvements. The party now also extended a hand to foreign immigrants by favoring their "rights of citizenship." Moreover, party leaders like Senator William Seward of New York realized that they had to distance themselves from the radical abolitionist wing in order to win the election. "An Anti-Slavery man *per se* cannot be elected," Horace Greeley of the New York *Tribune* noted, "but a Tariff, River-and-Harbor, Pacific Railroad, Free-Homestead man *may* succeed *although* he is Anti-Slavery."

Seward loomed as the odds-on favorite going into the Republican convention at Chicago. As the former governor of New York and two-term senator, he was the most prominent member of the Republican Party. But he was also an antislavery advocate who shocked listeners by pointing to "a higher law than the Constitution" and an "irrepressible conflict between freedom and slavery." At the same time, Abraham Lincoln was steadily gaining momentum among midwestern Republicans. Considered a quick-witted and resourceful politician, Lincoln

by the federal government that neither Congress nor any territorial legislature could, in the words of Jefferson Davis, "impair the constitutional right of any citizen of the United States to take his slave property into the common territories." When Douglas supporters refused to back the proposal because it went against their commitment to popular sovereignty, fifty delegates from the lower South walked out of the convention. Unable to agree on a candidate after fifty-seven acrimonious ballots, the convention adjourned with the understanding that it would reconvene at Baltimore in six weeks.

The hiatus did little to cool tempers or modify positions. The continuing impasse led virtually all of the southern delegates to walk out again and organize their own convention. They then nominated Vice-President John C. Breckinridge of Kentucky on a platform that called for the protection of slave property in the territories as well as the annexation of Cuba. Not to be outdone, the original Baltimore convention nominated Douglas on a platform that emphasized popular sovereignty and, as a sop to the South, strict enforcement of the Fugitive Slave Act.

An anti-North cartoon depicting abolitionist congressman Thaddeus Stevens of Pennsylvania as the quack "Dr. North" (seated) proposing to cut off the legs of "Patient South" and replace them with wooden legs. One of the legs is labeled "Constitutional Amendment," aimed at curtailing slavery in the states.

did not have Seward's political baggage. He consequently won the nomination with the support of party leaders from key border states like Pennsylvania and Indiana, who considered him more electable.

While Douglas Democrats, Breckinridge Democrats, and the united Republicans mustered their forces, a fourth contending party appeared on the scene. Known as the Constitutional Union Party, it consisted mainly of old-line Whigs and former Know-Nothings who denounced the sectionalism that pervaded both major parties and, in the spirit of Henry Clay and Daniel Webster, appealed to the cause of the Union. Meeting in Baltimore in May 1860, these conservative nationalists refused to take a stand on the issues that divided the nation and instead adopted a platform that pledged "to recognize no political principle other than *the Constitution . . . the Union . . . and the Enforcement of the Laws.*" Well aware that they stood little chance of winning the election, party organizers hoped to carry several border states and draw enough votes away from Lincoln in key lower northern states to throw the election into the House of Representatives, where they might then exercise enough leverage to elect someone with strong unionist proclivities. Their candidate was John Bell of Tennessee, a life-long Whig and former secretary of war under William Henry Harrison. Although he owned slaves, Bell was not a fire-eater. Southern Democrats accused Bell and his party of trying to push the slavery question under the rug. "That issue," a southern editorial declared, "must be met and settled."

The election of 1860 surpassed all others to that point for tension, complexity, and excitement. Taking a page from their Whig predecessors' book, the Republicans organized a campaign that outdid their adversaries for enthusiasm and showmanship. They staged massive torchlight parades and organized "Wide Awake" clubs to provide local gatherings with plenty of vocal support. Party literature portrayed Lincoln as "Honest Old Abe," the rail splitter who was born in a log cabin and epitomized the common man. Leaders also emphasized that theirs was more than a one-issue party, a strategy that sought to moderate its radical antislavery image in order to attract voters from both slaveholding border states and lower northern states. Pennsylvania Republicans, for example, used the tariff issue to considerable effect; at the same time, they pointed to the Buchanan administration's sorry

> " '*An Anti-Slavery man per se cannot be elected,*' Horace Greeley of the New York Tribune *noted, 'but a Tariff, River-and-Harbor, Pacific Railroad, Free-Homestead man may succeed although he is Anti-Slavery.*' "

record of corruption in making government contracts, distributing patronage, and bribing members of Congress. Since Douglas as well as Breckinridge Democrats were implicated in the scandals, Republican campaigners made great political capital by pointing to all Democrats as rascals associated with the immoral "slave power."

The stakes in the election were high, for the future of the Republic weighed in the balance. Southern politicians and editorialists warned that "the South will never submit to such humiliation and degradation as the inauguration of Abraham Lincoln." Despite these warnings, Republicans refused to believe that if they won, secession and war would follow. As early as 1856, Lincoln had declared that "all this talk about dissolution of the Union is humbug, nothing but folly." Four years later, he remained steadfast in the belief, noting that "the people of the South have too much good sense, and good temper, to attempt

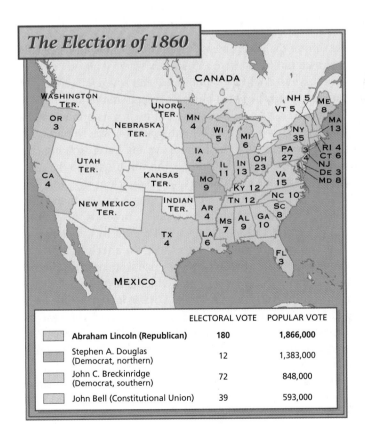

The Election of 1860

	ELECTORAL VOTE	POPULAR VOTE
Abraham Lincoln (Republican)	180	1,866,000
Stephen A. Douglas (Democrat, northern)	12	1,383,000
John C. Breckinridge (Democrat, southern)	72	848,000
John Bell (Constitutional Union)	39	593,000

1844	Samuel F. B. Morse invents the telegraph.	
1846	The Smithsonian Institution established.	
	John C. Frémont maps the Oregon Trail.	
May 1, 1851	The Crystal Palace exhibition opens in London.	
1852	Harriet Beecher Stowe publishes *Uncle Tom's Cabin.*	
1854	The Gadsden Purchase.	
	The Kansas-Nebraska Act.	
November 1855	Conflict breaks out in Kansas.	
May 24, 1856	The Pottawatomie Massacre.	
1857	Financial panic.	
March 6, 1857	The *Dred Scott* decision.	
October 16, 1859	John Brown's raid at Harpers Ferry, Virginia.	

the ruin of the government." Even though Lincoln repeatedly promised not to interfere with slavery where it already existed, his image as a "Black Republican" and inveterate enemy of slavery not only persisted but grew among southerners.

The one candidate who viewed himself as a national candidate and refused to write off either section was Douglas. Although weakened by the hard living and hard drinking that would soon take his life, Douglas threw himself into the campaign like no one else. Unlike Lincoln, Breckinridge, and Bell, who followed tradition and stayed home while others campaigned for them, Douglas personally canvassed the country from one end to the other while pointing to the danger of disunion and vowing to prevent it. Even after he learned in early October that the Republicans had won crucial gubernatorial victories in Pennsylvania, Ohio, and Indiana, he continued on the campaign trail. "Mr. Lincoln is the next President," he told his friends. "We must try to save the Union." During the next month, he conducted a whirlwind speaking tour that took him from Milwaukee to St. Louis, Memphis, Atlanta, Mobile, and other communities in the deep South. At each stop, the message was virtually the same:

"not to ask for your votes . . . but to make an appeal to you on behalf of the Union." The "Little Giant" ended his odyssey on election day, an exhausted and dying man.

Lincoln won the election with less than 40 percent of the popular vote. With the exception of New Jersey (whose electoral votes he split with Douglas), he carried all eighteen free states, which gave him 180 electoral votes and a comfortable 27-vote margin of victory. That he won the election without even being on the ballot in ten southern states spoke to the skill of his organization, but it also indicated the degree of polarization that had occurred during the campaign. By contrast, Douglas polled well over 1.3 million votes spread across the country, but he carried only Missouri, which, coupled with New Jersey's split vote, gave him a disappointing fourth-place finish with 12 electoral votes. Breckinridge, who garnered fewer popular votes but won eleven southern states, came in second with 72 electoral votes, followed by Bell's 39 from Virginia, Kentucky, and Tennessee. For the first time in the country's seventy-two-year history, a party embracing principles hostile to slavery held the presidency. But even though the Republicans won the White House, they failed to win a majority in either house of Congress; nor did they control the Supreme Court.

It remained to be seen how the South would respond to the election. Both sides recognized that these were "revolutionary times" and that, for better or worse, a Republican would soon assume the most powerful position in the country. Forty years of sectional tension now reached a climax.

Suggested Reading

Robert V. Bruce, *The Launching of Modern American Science, 1846–1876* (1987)

David H. Donald, *Charles Sumner and the Coming of the Civil War* (1961)

Eric Foner, *Free Soil, Free Labor, Free Men: The Ideology of the Republican Party Before the Civil War* (1995)

William H. Goetzmann, *Army Exploration in the American West, 1803–1863* (1959)

Michael F. Holt, *The Political Crisis of the 1850s* (1983)

William Hosley, *Colt: The Making of an American Legend* (1996)

Stephen B. Oates, *To Purge This Land with Blood: A Biography of John Brown* (1970)

David M. Potter, *The Impending Crisis, 1848–1861* (1976)

CIVIL WAR:
1861-1865

Artist's sketch of Confederate troops (right foreground) about to attack
the Union line at Chickamauga Creek, September 19, 1863.

QUESTIONS

■ **How did the Fort Sumter crisis end any chance of compromise?**

■ **What was the significance of the war at sea?**

■ **What were the military and political turning points in the course of the war?**

■ **How can the Civil War be considered the first modern war?**

■ **How did each side marshal its resources during the war?**

■ **What was the great significance of the Civil War?**

Secession was the first item on the agenda for South Carolina's legislature after the election of Lincoln. It swiftly passed a bill for the election of delegates to a state convention to consider that one issue. Gathering amid great fanfare on December 17, 1860, the convention unanimously adopted an ordinance of secession three days later. Encouraged by South Carolina's bold action, Mississippi, Florida, Alabama, Georgia, Louisiana, and Texas soon followed suit. In early February 1861, representatives from all seven states met at Montgomery, Alabama, establishing the Confederate States of America and electing Jefferson Davis of Mississippi as president and Alexander H. Stephens of Georgia as vice-president of the new republic. Asserting that Thomas Jefferson and the other founders had erred in the Declaration of Independence when they held that all men are created equal, Stephens emphasized that "our new government is founded upon exactly the opposite idea . . . that the negroe is not equal to the white man; that slavery . . . is his natural and normal condition." President Davis declared that he and his Confederate colleagues had left the Union "to save ourselves from a revolution" being perpetrated by Lincoln and his "Black Republican" allies. Confronted by a movement that "threatened to destroy their social system," they had no choice but to secede. They little thought that their actions would lead, swiftly and bloodily, to the end of slavery.

Compromise Efforts

The seven states that formed the Confederacy now looked to the eight remaining slave states—Virginia, North Carolina,

Tennessee, Arkansas, Kentucky, Maryland, Missouri, and Delaware—to join them. The speed with which the Confederacy took shape disguised the presence of a significant minority in the lower South opposed to secession. In Alabama, for example, 39 percent of the delegates to the secession convention had voted against the measure; 30 percent of Georgia's delegates did the same. Unionist sentiment proved even stronger in the upper South and border states, which were more closely linked economically to the North than to the lower South, and had smaller slave populations. When voters in North Carolina and Kentucky refused to call secession

Confederate president Jefferson Davis of Mississippi.

498

conventions, and sitting conventions in Arkansas, Missouri, and Virginia rejected secession in the early spring of 1861, Unionists saw glimmers of hope. Still, the situation remained ominous. Tennessee's legislature expressed a pervasive view in the lower South and border states when it warned of resistance to any attempt to "coerce" the Confederate states or to invade "the soil of the South." Heeding these warnings, moderate Republicans such as William Seward urged President-elect Lincoln "to be conciliatory, forbearing and patient" and to "open the way for the rising of a Union Party in the seceding States which will bring them back into the Union."

But what compromise would satisfy both sides? With his cabinet rocked by scandals and himself accused of being in league with the secessionists, lame-duck President Buchanan worked behind the scenes to bring the divided parties together. His main hope rested with getting Lincoln to support a constitutional convention in which the North and South might iron out their differences. But Lincoln vacillated and then responded that he did "not desire any amendments to the Constitution." What little hope remained turned toward

a compromise measure proposed by Senator John J. Crittenden, Henry Clay's successor from Kentucky.

CRITTENDEN'S COMPROMISE

Crittenden's compromise plan proposed to restore the Missouri Compromise line of 36°–30′ (breached by the Kansas-Nebraska Act) all the way to California and to guarantee that the national government would not interfere with slavery in states where it already existed. While Lincoln had no problem with the latter measure, as he would affirm in his inaugural address, he refused to entertain any compromise that involved "the *extension* of slavery." In December 1860, Lincoln had written to Alexander Stephens to assure him that his administration had no intention of disturbing slavery where it was. The only difference between North and South, he emphasized, was that "you think slavery is *right* and ought to be extended; while we think it is *wrong* and ought to be restricted." Since bringing back the Missouri Compromise would allow the extension of slavery south of 36°–30′, Lin-

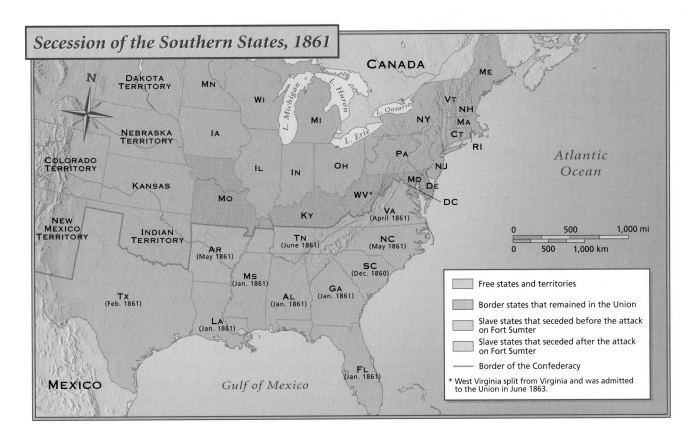

Secession of the Southern States, 1861

Free states and territories

Border states that remained in the Union

Slave states that seceded before the attack on Fort Sumter

Slave states that seceded after the attack on Fort Sumter

Border of the Confederacy

* West Virginia split from Virginia and was admitted to the Union in June 1863.

CHARLESTON

MERCURY

EXTRA:

Passed unanimously at 1.15 o'clock, P. M., December 20th, 1860.

AN ORDINANCE

To dissolve the Union between the State of South Carolina and other States united with her under the compact entitled "The Constitution of the United States of America."

We, the People of the State of South Carolina, in Convention assembled, do declare and ordain, and it is hereby declared and ordained,

That the Ordinance adopted by us in Convention, on the twenty-third day of May, in the year of our Lord one thousand seven hundred and eighty-eight, whereby the Constitution of the United States of America was ratified, and also, all Acts and parts of Acts of the General Assembly of this State, ratifying amendments of the said Constitution, are hereby repealed; and that the union now subsisting between South Carolina and other States, under the name of "The United States of America," is hereby dissolved.

THE

UNION

IS

DISSOLVED!

Headline from a Charleston, South Carolina, newspaper boldly proclaiming the dissolution and secession of South Carolina, December 20, 1860.

coln warned Republican moderates who favored Crittenden's proposal that it "would lose us everything we gained by the election. . . . The tug has to come," he concluded, "& better now, than any time hereafter." Braced by these comments, the Republican members of the Senate committee that had initiated the Crittenden compromise ended up voting against it. So did two secessionist Democrats who reasoned that no compromise was possible without Republican support. In the end, Crittenden's bill was narrowly defeated on the floor of the now-reduced Senate, 25 to 23. All 25 nays came from Republicans.

LINCOLN'S FIRST INAUGURAL ADDRESS

By the time Lincoln boarded a train in Illinois for his March 4 inauguration in Washington, he had already drafted a version of his inaugural address. Knowing that what he said could be taken as his first policy statement concerning the secession crisis, he chose his words carefully. The seven states of the new Confederacy had begun seizing federal forts, arsenals, customs houses, and treasury buildings that lay within their respective boundaries. Seven other states in the upper South and border-state areas were teetering on the brink of secession. Lincoln's first task in preserving the Union was to prevent further secessions. Then, perhaps, he could persuade the Confederate states to "reconstruct" themselves by returning to the Union.

In his inaugural address, Lincoln adopted a carrot-and-stick approach. The carrot was his oft-repeated promise not to interfere with slavery where it already existed and his assurance that the controversial Fugitive Slave Act would be strictly enforced. The stick was his determination to employ "all the powers at my disposal" to "reclaim the public property and places which have fallen; to hold, occupy, and possess these, and all other property and places belonging to the government, and to collect the duties on imports." Lincoln also assured the South that "the government will not assail *you*, unless you *first* assail *it*." (Before inauguration day, moderate advisers such as his newly named secretary of state, William Seward, persuaded him to soften these remarks by deleting "unless you *first* assail *it*" as well as his threat to "reclaim the public property.") Lincoln ended his address with an impassioned plea for the preservation of the Union. "We are not enemies, but friends," he asserted. "Though passion may have strained, it must not break our bonds of affection. The mystic chords of memory, stretching from every battlefield, and patriot grave, to every living heart and hearthstone, all over this broad land, will yet swell the chorus of the Union, when again touched, as surely they will be, by the better angels of our nature." Yet behind these words stood a president who had just taken a "most solemn" oath to "preserve, protect and defend" the Union. Viewing the Union as "perpetual" and secession as the "essence of anarchy," he intended to see to it that "the laws of the Union be faithfully executed in all the States."

As expected, fellow Republicans generally hailed the speech as statesmanlike, while southern secessionists denounced it as a "Declaration of War." In between were northern Democrats and southerners with Unionist sympathies—two groups that Lincoln most wanted to reach. Although some northern Democrats criticized the speech as either waffling or bellicose, Stephen A. Douglas considered it a "peace offering" and announced that "I am with him." Similar comments came from the upper South, where Unionists felt bolstered by the "temperance and conservatism" of Lincoln's address and reasonably confident that they might yet stem the rising tide of secessionism.

The Fall of Fort Sumter

Lincoln's biggest quandary upon entering office was what to do about federal properties that lay within the boundaries of the Confederacy. Most pressing was the status of Fort Sumter, a newly reconstructed fortification in the harbor of Charleston, South Carolina—the great hotbed of secessionism and anti-Yankee feeling. Ever since South Carolina had seceded, its newly elected governor, Francis W. Pickens, had demanded the "immediate" surrender of not only Sumter but also Fort Moultrie and Castle Pinckney, two other coastal installations that guarded the entrance to Charleston. Although accused of complying with southern demands, President Buchanan had, in fact, refused to relinquish any federal property in the South and warned Governor Pickens that "if South Carolina should attack any of these forts, she will then become the assailant in a war against the United States."

Despite Buchanan's warnings, pressure from South Carolinians continued to mount. The local Union army commander, Major Robert Anderson, expected an attack at any moment. To strengthen his position, Anderson disabled the guns at Fort Moultrie and, on the night of December 27, 1860, secretly moved his entire command to Fort Sumter. Outraged at Anderson's action, South Carolina responded the following day by seizing Fort Moultrie,

Castle Pinckney, and the U.S. Customs House at Charleston. There matters stood. While Anderson waited in his offshore stronghold, South Carolina seized other federal facilities, closed the port of Charleston to all U.S. ships, and, at one point, fired on the *Star of the West*, an unarmed vessel dispatched by the Buchanan administration with food for Anderson's beleaguered force.

The day after Lincoln took office, Buchanan's outgoing secretary of war sent the new president a sobering message. A dispatch had arrived from Major Anderson reporting that he was running short of supplies and estimating that it would take at least 20,000 troops to relieve Fort Sumter. At best, Anderson said, he could hold the fort six weeks before he and his men would be starved out and forced to capitulate. Shocked by the news, Lincoln called a cabinet meeting the following morning. Secretary of State Seward and army commander General Winfield Scott recommended abandoning Sumter in the interest of avoiding an all-out war and reassuring Unionists throughout the South of the new administration's peaceful intentions. Although the president hesitated to make a final decision, the ambitious Seward, who viewed himself as Lincoln's premier and the real head of

Lincoln's inauguration at the unfinished Capitol in Washington, D.C., March 4, 1861.

the government, began to spread the word that Sumter would soon be relinquished.

In hopes that he could keep his inaugural promise to "hold, occupy, and possess" federal property in the South while not being seen as the aggressor, Lincoln began to consider an effort to resupply Sumter. The plan was to send a fleet of warships to the outskirts of Charleston's harbor and, with smaller boats, transfer men and supplies to Fort Sumter under the cover of darkness. With the support of his cabinet, Lincoln gave the order to go ahead on April 4, 1861.

Once the relief fleet set sail for Charleston, the decision whether to allow the provisioning of Fort Sumter rested with the Confederacy's president and commander in chief, Jefferson Davis. Already under fire for not taking action against Sumter sooner and fearful that continued inaction might cost the Confederacy the support of the upper South, Davis came under pressure to "strike a blow." On April 9, Davis gave the order, and three days later General Pierre G. T. Beauregard's artillery opened fire at 4:30 A.M. The Confederate bombardment lasted thirty-three hours, pummeling Anderson's outgunned force. Although the Union relief fleet arrived outside Charleston Harbor during the fighting, a storm prevented it from intervening. Anderson and his half-starved force lowered the American flag and surrendered to Beauregard on April 14.

The fall of Fort Sumter marked the onset of civil war. The day after Anderson's capitulation, Lincoln issued a proclamation calling on northern governors for 75,000 militia troops to quell the rebellion. The president, confident that concerted action would nip the insurrection in the bud, asked that the state troops be released for national service for a period of ninety days. To his surprise, the northern governors offered him twice the number of troops called for.

While an eruption of public enthusiasm swept over the North, the governors of six slave states still in the Union condemned the president's "unholy crusade." Kentucky's governor, expressing a common viewpoint, notified Washington that his state would "furnish no troops for the wicked purpose of subduing her sister Southern States." Embers of secession burst into open flame elsewhere in the South as four more states—Virginia, Arkansas, North Carolina, and Tennessee—seceded and joined the Confederacy during the late spring of 1861.

> *"Although southern speakers and editorialists made much of state sovereignty, regional honor, and resistance to coercion, the central issue for all of them centered on the threat Lincoln and his 'Black Republican' Party posed to the right of whites to own slaves and to take them anywhere they pleased."*

Virginia, one of the original thirteen states, was the first to go. Citizens of the cradle of five presidents had strongly resisted leaving the Union. As late as March, a convention meeting in Richmond refused to adopt articles of secession despite enormous pressure from fire-eaters. But when news of Sumter reached Richmond on April 13, there was much excitement. "Great rejoicing," a resident recorded in his diary, "100 guns fired and [a] torchlight procession." Four days later, the Virginia convention finally voted—88 for secession, 55 opposed; 1 member abstained. Although the ordinance had to be ratified by a public referendum, the die was cast. Of the 161,000 voters who went to the polls on May 23, 80 percent voted in favor of secession. By then, similar conventions had set Arkansas, North Carolina, and Tennessee on their way out of the Union. Although southern speakers and editorialists made much of state sovereignty, regional honor, and resistance to coercion, the central issue for all of them centered on the threat Lincoln and his "Black Republican" Party posed to the right of whites to own slaves and to take them anywhere they pleased.

PREPARING FOR WAR

Neither the Union nor the Confederacy was prepared for war, let alone a prolonged one. Relatively few people, North or South, thought at this point that the "rebellion" would last more than a couple of months. As the crisis deepened and hopes of a reconciliation disappeared, however, both sides sought to procure not only arms and munitions but everything from army blankets and tents to wagons, horses, and mules.

On paper, the North appeared to enjoy an overwhelming advantage in resources. Northern white males of fighting age outnumbered southern whites by more than three to one. Equally daunting, the northern states commanded over 90 percent of the country's manufacturing capacity. The census of 1860 clearly revealed the North's dominance in the production of firearms (97 percent), railway locomotives (96 percent), cloth (94 percent), pig iron (93 percent), boots and shoes (90 percent), and many other items. The same was true of mass transportation facilities, with the North possessing twice the railroad mileage of the South and several times the

A poster calling for Irish volunteers to form a company in the Second Regiment of Baker's Brigade, Philadelphia, 1861.

mileage in paved roads and canals. Only in food production did the South rival the North. Yet even then, the South's inferior railway system often prevented food and other supplies from reaching war zones.

Initially, at least, one southern state appeared better prepared to wage war than others. In 1860, largely in response to John Brown's raid on Harpers Ferry, the Virginia legislature had appropriated money to rebuild the state's long-defunct "Manufactory of Arms," soon to be renamed the Richmond Armory. Moreover, on April 18, 1861—the day after the Virginia legislature voted for secession—a state militia seized the national armory at Harpers Ferry and dismantled its machinery for shipment to Richmond. All told, Virginia placed nearly two complete sets of arms-making machinery (one for rifles, the

other for longer-barreled rifle-muskets), thousands of tools, and tons of raw material at the disposal of the Confederate government. The Virginia militia also confiscated more than 4,000 finished firearms and enough components to assemble between 7,000 and 10,000 weapons of the latest design. The Harpers Ferry machinery eventually would be used to tool the two largest armories in the South, one at Richmond, the other at Fayetteville, North Carolina.

The looting of the Harpers Ferry Armory dealt a serious blow to the Lincoln administration. Even with Harpers Ferry in production, the national armories did not have the capacity to arm 75,000 militia, to say nothing of the 400,000 extra troops Lincoln would call for in July 1861. The armories at Springfield, Massachusetts, and Harpers Ferry were each capable of producing around 21,000 rifle-muskets (the standard infantry weapon of the period) a year. The largest private armory in America—Samuel Colt's works at Hartford, Connecticut—averaged around 35,000, almost all of them pistols. Although Colt offered to contract with the War Department for 500,000 rifle-muskets, he could not make immediate deliveries because he had to tool up to produce some components and subcontract for the rest with other manufacturers. Colt's predicament was typical of all private contractors in the North: they possessed the know-how but needed at least a year to equip their armories with machinery and train workers to use it. War Department officials thus could not count on domestic manufacturers to fill the volume of requests for small arms that flooded their offices during the spring and summer of 1861. So they turned to foreign sources of supply.

During the first year of the conflict, War Department officials signed over thirty contracts with European and American arms brokers for the delivery of hundreds of thousands

Imported British Enfield rifle-muskets became highly valued by Confederate troops. They were equal in quality to the Model 1861 Springfield rifle-musket and made largely by American machinery installed at the British government's Enfield Armory in 1855–58. Both firearms were referred to as "rifle-muskets" because they had longer barrels than standard military rifles of the day.

503

of foreign-made firearms. Rather than basing these contracts on "advertisement and open competition" as stipulated by law, authorities hastily adopted an open-ended method of contracting that, in effect, operated on a first-come, first-served basis. But this system worked poorly. Army ordnance officers often reported that unscrupulous "speculators and 'middle men'" had duped the government into signing loosely worded contracts that allowed them to substitute "guns of very inferior quality" for those promised. "Tens of thousands of the refuse arms of Europe are at this moment in our arsenals, and thousands more still to arrive," a government commission observed in July 1862, "not one of which will outlast a single campaign, while most of them will never be issued at all, being entirely unfit to be placed in the hands of civilized troops."

By the fall of 1862, most of the Union's needs for arms were being met by the Springfield Armory and twenty-four private contractors headed by Colt, Alfred Jenks of Philadelphia, and the Providence Tool Company of Rhode Island. Altogether, they delivered over 1,427,000 rifle-muskets during the war years, a remarkable feat of industrial production. New England armories accounted for 86 percent of these deliveries, the Springfield Armory topping all others with an output of more than 793,000. Ordnance experts touted the Springfield rifle as "the best infantry arm in the world."

Like the North, the Confederacy faced serious weapons shortages. Most of the 159,000 small arms seized from federal arsenals were obsolete or in need of repair, and gunpowder and ammunition were in short supply. Most serious of all, the Confederate states lacked the manufacturing capacity to produce such materials. To solve the problem, President Davis turned to Colonel Josiah Gorgas, a West Point graduate and head of the Confederate Ordnance Bureau. Gorgas devised a plan: to capture arms on the battlefield, build and equip arsenals in the South, and import arms and ammunition from Europe.

To get guns at once, Gorgas dispatched an army colleague, Major Caleb Huse, to London. Provided with letters of credit based on the sale of southern cotton (known as "white gold") in England, Huse made his first shipment of arms in September 1861. Within two years, he succeeded in shipping two-thirds of the Confederacy's supply of weapons, plus "large quantities of saltpeter, lead, cartridges, percussion caps, flannel and paper for cartridges, leather, hardware, &C." By war's end, 600,000 small arms from Europe had reached Confederate armies, along with critical supplies of clothing, blankets, cloth, and shoes. Gorgas's great skill as a planner and Huse's unstinting efforts as his agent in Europe go far in explaining why Confederate armies became such a formidable fighting force during four years of civil war.

The War at Sea

Transporting the weapons and supplies acquired in Europe safely to southern ports posed other problems. Within a week after the fall of Fort Sumter, Lincoln, heeding the advice of General Winfield Scott, imposed a blockade on the South

The innovative USS *Monitor* (right foreground) lent its name to other Union ironclad vessels during the Civil War. This painting depicts the battle with the Confederate ship *Virginia* on March 9, 1862.

that sought to cut off the Confederacy from all outside sources of supply. But with only forty-two ships available to patrol 189 harbors and over 3,000 miles of southern coastline, the Union blockade was ineffective during the war's first year, with nine out of ten ships getting through. Well aware of the problem, Lincoln's secretary of the navy, Gideon Welles, sought to acquire more warships and to provide them with fueling and repair bases by capturing key points along the southern coast. In August 1861, Cape Hatteras fell to a joint army-navy amphibious expedition. Shortly afterward, a navy flotilla captured Ship Island near Biloxi, Mississippi. During the next six months, successful assaults on Port Royal (South Carolina), Fort Pulaski (Georgia), Roanoke Island (North Carolina), and New Orleans threatened to bottle up every major southern port east of the Mississippi River except Mobile (Alabama) and Wilmington (North Carolina). But even then, seven out of eight blockade runners successfully evaded Union patrols in 1862.

Stillman Allen and Company's Novelty Iron Works in New York City was one of several foundries and machine shops that supplied components for the construction of the *Monitor*. The company built the ship's innovative revolving gun turret.

THE *MONITOR* VERSUS THE *VIRGINIA*

While the Union navy sought to tighten its control over southern shipping, Confederate strategists busied themselves with breaking the blockade. Since the South had no navy to speak of, much depended on the reconstruction of the *Merrimack*, a steam-powered, wooden-hulled frigate scuttled by Union forces in April 1861, when the state of Virginia seized the Norfolk Navy Yard. Newly outfitted with ten stationary guns and protected by four-inch-thick plates of laminated iron, the rechristened *Virginia* steamed out of Norfolk on March 8, 1862, and attacked the Union blockading squadron stationed at Hampton Roads, Virginia. With cannonballs bouncing harmlessly off its armor, the *Virginia* sank two Union warships, while three others ran aground trying to escape her. The action clearly demonstrated that traditional wooden vessels, no matter how many guns they carried, posed no threat to ironclads. President Lincoln and his advisers spent a sleepless night contemplating the *Virginia*'s next move, even though they realized that help was on its way to Hampton Roads in the form of a newly built ironclad called the *Monitor*. But would the smaller, two-gun *Monitor* check the larger *Virginia*?

When the *Virginia* left Norfolk on March 9 to finish off its grounded opponents, the *Monitor* was waiting. Hundreds of onlookers watched as the two vessels hammered each other for two hours at point-blank range. One cannonball after another struck armor and ricocheted into the sea. Neither ship was seriously damaged, but the *Virginia* finally broke off the contest and returned to Norfolk.

The contest ended in a tactical draw, but the North gained the strategic advantage. Stalemated by the *Monitor*, the *Virginia* was unable to do any more damage to the Union fleet, and southern hopes for breaking the blockade dissipated. Forced to abandon Norfolk two months later, Confederate officials scuttled the *Virginia* rather than allow it to fall into enemy hands. Later that year, as fate would have it, the *Monitor* sank in heavy seas off the coast of North Carolina.

Although the first ironclads were built in France and England, the *Monitor* and *Virginia* were the first to fight at sea. The two vessels made an indelible impact on naval warfare. Not counting the *Monitor*'s two steam engines, screw propellers, and iron plating, the ship was said to contain fifty patentable inventions. Most noteworthy was the revolving turret, protected by eight inches of laminated iron all around, which housed two huge bore Dahlgren guns that could be aimed anywhere during an engagement without having to turn the ship. Such innovations, coupled with the *Monitor*'s impressive performance at Hampton Roads, convinced the Lincoln administration to concentrate on building ironclads, now also called monitors, for coastal and river service. Fifty-eight were in service by war's end and had become the mainstay of the Union fleet. The advent of the new technology presaged a major shift in ship design and naval warfare.

FIGHTING THE UNION BLOCKADE

The Confederate government, short of industrial facilities to roll iron plate and manufacture steam engines, was able to commission only twenty-two ironclads. To supplement these, Confederate officials employed various types of mines (called "torpedoes"), which ended up sinking or damaging forty Union vessels, including four monitors. They also launched the CSS *Hunley*, the world's first combat submarine, in 1863. After losing its crew three times during sea trials, the *Hunley* finally succeeded in destroying a Union warship off Charleston Harbor in February 1864, but not before it sank with all on board. While Union commanders condemned "this base style of rebel warfare," they soon called for submarines, too.

Since its small navy would never seriously challenge Union forces on the high seas, the Confederate government turned to attacking merchant ships, hoping that such raids would disrupt the northern economy and force the Lincoln administration to divert warships from the blockade of southern ports. Four Confederate cruisers built in England caused significant damage to the U.S. merchant marine. The most famous of these was the *Alabama*, a converted merchant steamer that went to sea in May 1862 and took sixty-four prizes before being sunk off the coast of France two years later. Altogether the *Alabama* and her sister ships sank 257 Union ships and forced hundreds of others either to stay in port or to register under foreign flags in order to avoid the same fate. Nevertheless, commerce raiding did not have the intended effect. Northern merchants simply shifted their cargoes to foreign vessels, which enjoyed the status of neutral carriers. More important, the Union navy continued to focus on the blockade and refused to be drawn into a game of raider chasing.

Although Confederate blockade runners continued to get through, there is no question that the Union blockade significantly reduced the total volume of southern seaborne trade. Four years before the war, some 20,000 vessels entered and departed southern ports; during the war, the number fell by 60 percent to 8,000. The smaller blockade runners had less cargo ca-

pacity than prewar merchantmen, and they frequently dumped their cargoes in order to gain speed when being pursued. Total trade volume shrank. The Union blockade forced the Confederacy to scramble to build a manufacturing base with which to produce guns, ships, uniforms, and other supplies. But with its late start in industrial investment, the South never came close to rivaling the industrial colossus of the North.

The Land War

The blockade of southern ports was part of a larger Union strategy devised by General Scott, and supported by President Lincoln: to exert economic and political pressure on the South by sealing it off from the rest of the world along the coastline and up the Mississippi and slowly squeeze it into

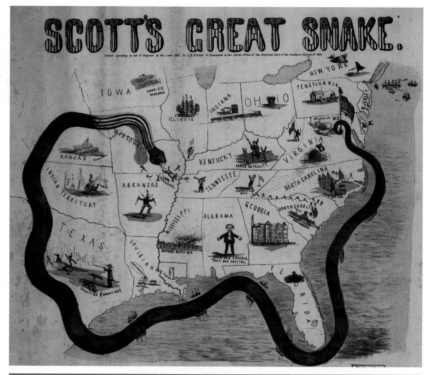

This lithograph reveals how General Winfield Scott's "Anaconda Plan" aimed at cutting off the South from outside supplies and internal trade by wrapping Union forces around the seceded states and economically squeezing them into submission.

The Civil War: Major Campaigns in the East, 1861–1862

submission. Doing so, in Scott's view, would "bring them to terms with less bloodshed than by any other plan."

But while Lincoln hoped that the contest would not "degenerate into a violent and remorseless revolutionary struggle," he knew that some sort of **large-scale invasion of southern territory** would be necessary. Even Scott admitted that the Union would have to "conquer the seceding states by invading armies." Nonetheless, he urged restraint. "Our patriotic and loyal Union friends," he cautioned, "urge instant and vigorous action, regardless, I fear, of the consequences." Most outspoken were a group of radical Republican newspaper editors, led by the *New York Tribune*'s Horace Greeley, who ridiculed Scott's "Anaconda Plan" as too plodding and slow. Pressure for an invasion of the South mounted when news arrived that the Confederate Congress had transferred its capital to Richmond, Virginia, and would meet there for the first time on July 20, 1861. "FORWARD TO RICHMOND! FORWARD TO RICH-

Casualties of War

The face of battle elicited many expressions, none more heartrending than the thoughts of a dying Union sergeant named Jonathan Stowe, of Company G, Fifteenth Massachusetts Infantry Regiment. Seriously wounded at the Battle of Antietam on September 17, 1862, Sergeant Stowe remained on the battlefield nearly twenty-four hours before Confederate troops removed him to a local field hospital, where he waited another twenty-four hours to be treated. Through all this, Stowe managed to keep a diary as he watched comrades die and waited to hear from friends at home.

September 17 (Wednesday)—"Battle Oh horrid battle. What sights I have seen. I am wounded! . . . Am in severe pain. How the shells fly. I do sincerely hope I shall not be wounded again."

September 18 (Thursday)—"Misery acute, painful misery. How I suffered last night. . . . My leg must be broken for I cannot help myself scarcely any. I remember talking and groaning all night. Many died in calling for help. . . . Carried off the field at 10 a.m. by the Rebs who show much kindness but devote much time to plundering the dead bodies of our men. . . . Water very short. We suffer very much."

September 19 (Friday)—"Rebs retreat. Another painful night. . . . By and by our boys come along. . . . Dr. looks at my wound and calls it [a] doubtful case. Get me on ambulance at 3 p.m. but do not get to hospital till nearly dark. Plenty of water. . . . Nurses worn-out by fatigue. Placed on straw near the barn."

September 20 (Saturday)—"Leg amputated about noon. What sensations—used chloroform hope to have no bad effects. There are some dozen or more [amputated] stumps near me."

September 21 (Sunday)—"Very weak and sore. . . . Hot weather by day cool at night. Hard to get nurses. . . . People come in from all parts of the country. Stare at us but do not find time to do anything."

September 22 (Monday)—"Two men died last night. . . . How painful my stump is. I did not know I was capable of enduring so much pain. How very meager are accommodations—no chamber pots & nobody to find or rig up one. How ludicrous for 2 score amputated men to help themselves with diarrhea."

September 23 (Tuesday)—"Oh what long fearful horrid nights. What difficulties we have to contend [with]. . . . Relief can hardly be found."

September 24 (Wednesday)—"One week today fought and wounded. Such a week. Suffering all around."

September 25 (Thursday)—"Such nights! Why they seem infinitely longer than days. The nervous pains are killing 2 or 3 every night. All sorts of groans & pleadings."

September 26 (Friday)—"Very cold last night. . . . This cold weather may all come for best, certainly maggots do not trouble so much and air is some purer."

September 27 (Saturday)—"Commence taking brandy none too soon. Dr. tells me I am dangerously ill and must take his prescription in order to change condition of blood."

September 28 (Sunday)—"Oh what lengths to the nights. The horrid smell from mortifying limbs is nearly as bad as the whole we have to contend [with]."

September 29 (Monday)—"Slept a little more comfortable last night. Got nice soups and nice light biscuit and tart also nice butter from Mrs. Lee. . . . How the quinine keeps me parched for water and so sleepy and foolish. . . . I recd 4 letters from friends at home but am so boozy it takes the whole a.m. to read them. Mr. Dr. Kelsey dressed my stump admirably and am quite comfortable if the quinine does not choke me to death. It is far more quiet here but begins to rain."

On Wednesday, October 1, Sergeant Stowe died at Hoffman's Hospital near Sharpsburg, Maryland.

Robert E. Denney, *Civil War Medicine*

gressional election in November, Lee hoped that a successful invasion might persuade voters to throw Lincoln's Republican supporters out of office, replace them with "Peace Democrats," and "bring [the war] to a termination." Perhaps most important, Lee knew that diplomatic efforts were underway to gain British and French recognition of the Confederacy and, accordingly, their intervention in the war on the South's side. Britain and France waited for news of Lee's invasion before making the fateful decision. Much was at stake.

Lee's invasion began on September 4, 1862, when the first of his troops crossed the Potomac River about forty miles above Washington. By then, Lincoln had fired Pope and called back McClellan to command the dispirited Army of the Potomac. Lincoln had a ready answer for those who opposed the move: even though McClellan "can't fight himself, he excels in making others ready to fight."

Lincoln visiting General McClellan and his staff at Sharpsburg, Maryland, after the Battle of Antietam, 1862.

Two weeks later, on September 17, the two armies clashed along the banks of Antietam Creek just outside Sharpsburg, Maryland. The result was a veritable bloodbath—the deadliest single day of the entire war. As darkness fell on the battlefield, over 24,000 men lay dead or wounded, more than half of them Confederates. Lee had begun the campaign with roughly 45,000 soldiers under his command. After the Battle of Antietam ended, one-third of his army was dead or disabled. All told, the Union and Confederate armies sustained twice as many casualties in one day at Antietam as the United States lost altogether during the War of 1812, the Mexican War, and the Spanish-American War (at the end of the nineteenth century).

McClellan wired Lincoln that he had won a great victory at Antietam, but in fact it was a tactical draw. Bloodied but unbowed, Lee waited for McClellan to attack on September 18, but there was no attack. That evening, Lee gave the order to withdraw and, much to Lincoln's chagrin, escaped across the Potomac into Virginia. When Lincoln asked McClellan for an explanation of his failure to pursue and "destroy the rebel army," he received one excuse after another. Exasperated by McClellan's "over-cautiousness" and "total inaction," Lincoln eventually replaced him with General Ambrose Burnside. Antietam proved to be McClellan's last campaign. Already an outspoken critic of Lincoln's war policies, he quickly became the darling of northern Democrats who opposed the war and began to present himself as the one candidate who could defeat Lincoln in the election of 1864.

Confederate dead after the Battle of Antietam, September 17, 1862.

513

THE EMANCIPATION PROCLAMATION

The Battle of Antietam ranks as one of the most decisive of the Civil War. As a result of Lee's failure to invade the North, Great Britain and France backed away from recognizing the Confederacy or entering the war on its side. Lee's retreat across the Potomac was enough of a victory for Lincoln to issue his preliminary **Emancipation Proclamation** on September 22, in which he warned the Confederate states that if they failed to put down their arms and return to the Union by January 1, 1863, all slaves within their boundaries "shall be then, henceforward, and forever free." Heeding the warnings of cabinet members that a blanket proclamation might turn loyal slaveholding areas against the Union, Lincoln exempted Maryland, Kentucky, Missouri, Tennessee, and parts of Virginia and Louisiana from his order. He also indicated that once the Emancipation Proclamation took effect, freedmen would "be received into the armed service of the United States," a revolutionary pronouncement that struck at "the heart of the rebellion" and enraged southerners.

> *"After reading the telegraph messages from Fredericksburg, a depressed Lincoln commented, 'If there is a worse place than Hell, I am in it.'"*

That Lincoln understood the larger implications of his actions is clear from his correspondence during the fall of 1862. After January 1, "the character of the war will be changed," he acknowledged to an administration official. "It will be one of subjugation. . . . The South is to be destroyed and replaced by new propositions and ideas." Less than ten months earlier, he had hoped for victory with a minimal amount of bloodshed and decried a "remorseless revolutionary struggle." But as the fighting had escalated in scope and intensity, the limited conflict had expanded into a total war aimed at destroying the Confederacy. "There is no possible hope for reconciliation," Lincoln's chief of staff wrote to General Grant. "We must conquer the rebels or be conquered by them." Lincoln had established a new agenda: unconditional surrender and the destruction of the South's peculiar institution. Abolitionists like William Lloyd Garrison hailed the new dispensation. Whether he wanted to or not, the president had joined their side.

UNION DEFEATS

While Lee's Army of Northern Virginia dominated its Union adversaries during the summer of 1862, Confederate forces west of the Appalachian Mountains launched a counteroffensive, with three aims: retaking lost ground in Tennessee, invading Kentucky, and preventing Grant's Army of the Tennessee from capturing Vicksburg and controlling the entire length of the Mississippi River. For a time, it appeared as if the strategy would succeed. Confederate cavalry under Generals Nathan B. Forrest and John Hunt Morgan wreaked havoc on Union supply lines by burning bridges, tearing up railroad tracks, and raiding supply depots. By September, an army of 30,000 under General Braxton Bragg had penetrated deeply into Kentucky and established a Confederate state government at Frankfort before being repulsed at Perryville on October 8 and forced to withdraw through the Cumberland Gap back into Tennessee. Although the Union held, the year ended in a major disappointment for the Lincoln administration: Grant's army failed to take Vicksburg. Although General William S. Rosecrans's Army of the Cumberland won a bloody contest at Murfreesboro/Stones River, Tennessee, it failed to crush Bragg's mangled forces.

Even worse news came from the East. Word arrived on December 13 that Lee's army had rebounded from Antietam to inflict a devastating defeat on the Army of the Potomac at Fredericksburg, Virginia. Outnumbering Lee's forces by nearly 40,000, the Union army mounted thirteen brigade-level assaults on the dug-in Confederates only to be "swept from the field like chaff before the wind." The extent of the loss became apparent after the battlefield was cleared and medical units reported 12,600 Union casualties to the Confederate's 5,000. After reading the telegraph messages from Fredericksburg, a depressed Lincoln commented, "If there is a worse place than Hell, I am in it."

Events of the new year did nothing to boost Lincoln's confidence. Shaken by its defeat at Fredericksburg, the Army of the Potomac hit rock bottom in mid-January when it became bogged down on muddy roads and had to call off another attempt at capturing Richmond (at this point, Joseph Hooker had replaced Burnside as commander). At the same time, Grant's army experienced difficulties maneuvering into position for an assault on the "Gibraltar of the West" at Vicksburg. In one of the most ambitious engineering efforts of the war, the Union army made several valiant but unsuccessful attempts to divert the Mississippi River out of range of the heavy artillery that guarded the bluffs of Vicksburg and pre-

The Civil War: Major Campaigns in the East, 1863–1865

PENNSYLVANIA

Chambersburg

Gettysburg,
July 3, 1863

Hagerstown

MARYLAND

NEW
JERSEY

Potomac R.

Frederick

WEST
VIRGINIA

N

Middletown

DISTRICT
OF COLUMBIA

Washington

DELAWARE

Delaware Bay

Shenandoah R.

ATLANTIC
OCEAN

Chancellorsville,
May 1863

Grant
The Wilderness,
May 5–6, 1864

Fredericksburg

VIRGINIA

Lee and Jackson

Spotsylvania,
May 8–12, 1864

North Anna,
May 22–27, 1864

Cold Harbor,
June 1–3, 1864

Richmond

Chesapeake Bay

York R.

0   25   50 mi
0   25   50 km

James R.

Lynchburg

Appomattox R.

Lee

Grant

Yorktown

Appomattox,
April 9, 1865

Petersburg siege,
June 1864

James R.

▭	Union states
▭	Confederate states

UNION FORCES
→ Advances, 1863
➤ Advances, 1864–65

CONFEDERATE FORCES
→ Advances, 1863
⇢ Retreats, 1863
→ Advances, 1864–65
⇢ Retreats, 1864–65

BATTLES
✴ Confederate victory
✷ Union victory

NORTH CAROLINA

vented gunboats and troop carriers from getting through. Indeed, everything seemed to be going wrong for the Union forces.

Amid these military failures, criticism hit the White House from all sides. Most controversial was the Emancipation Proclamation, which took effect on January 1, 1863. Enraged by the proclamation's freeing of slaves and its call for the enlistment of blacks in the Union army and navy, Confederate leaders threatened to execute any black captured in a north-

ern uniform. At the same time, northern Democrats, known as Peace Democrats among fellow party members and Copperheads by their Republican adversaries, assailed Lincoln for issuing the "wicked, inhuman, and unholy" proclamation and repeated earlier warnings that such "Black Republican" policy would result in freed slaves flooding the North and competing with whites for jobs. Some Democrats even predicted that the freedmen would commit "rapine" and murder in the streets. The Republicans had experienced a net loss in the November

515

1862 elections of two governorships and thirty-four seats in the House of Representatives, largely in response to the Emancipation Proclamation. Republican leaders in Congress, still acting on the assumption that Lincoln was William Seward's puppet, called for a shake-up in Lincoln's cabinet and a more vigorous prosecution of the war. Through all these crises, the president, though experiencing bouts of depression, steered a steady, determined course.

In the spring of 1863, after months of effort, Grant's Army of the Tennessee succeeded in surrounding and laying siege to Vicksburg. But on May 6, Lee's outnumbered army of 60,000 (about half the size of the enemy) inflicted another embarrassing defeat on the Army of the Potomac at Chancellorsville, a country crossroads some nine miles west of Fredericksburg. The victory revealed Lee at his tactical best, but it exacted a serious toll. In addition to suffering 13,000 casualties amounting to 22 percent of his total force (as opposed to 17,000, or 15 percent, for the Union), Lee lost his most trusted associate, General Stonewall Jackson, who was mistakenly fired on by his own troops.

Jackson's death cast a shadow over the Army of Northern Virginia, but his death was nothing compared with the gloom that descended on Washington in the aftermath of Chancellorsville. "All is lost," Massachusetts abolitionist senator Charles Sumner exclaimed on hearing the news. In Richmond, the Confederate high command concluded that Chancellorsville presented a new opportunity to relieve pressure on the South and seek diplomatic recognition in Europe by again invading the North. Convinced that his army was invincible and that his troops would "go anywhere and do anything if properly led," Lee began reorganizing his army into an invasion force of 75,000.

THE BATTLE OF GETTYSBURG (JULY 1863)

The Army of Northern Virginia's morale soared as it began its march up the Shenandoah Valley toward Pennsylvania early in June 1863. As with his first invasion of the North a year earlier, one of Lee's primary objectives was Harrisburg, the capital of Pennsylvania and an important railroad center that linked the East Coast with the Midwest. As it turned out,

" 'My dear general,' Lincoln wrote on July 14, 'I do not believe you appreciate the magnitude of the misfortune involved in Lee's escape. He was within your easy grasp, and to have closed upon him would, in connection with our other late successes, have ended the war. As it is, the war will be prolonged indefinitely.' "

his army clashed with the Army of the Potomac at Gettysburg, a small town some thirty-nine miles south of Harrisburg. During the first three days of July, the opposing forces slugged it out in what became the largest and most important battle of the war. On the third day, July 3, the clash culminated with one of the most famous assaults in modern history, in which nine Confederate brigades marched across a mile-wide open expanse to attack the Union line in what became known as "Pickett's Charge." The result was a Confederate disaster, with nearly half of the 14,000 who went forward failing to return. All told, Lee lost more than one-third of his army at Gettysburg (3,903 killed, 24,000 wounded or missing), the Union more than one-quarter (3,155 killed, 20,000 wounded or missing). The Army of Northern Virginia would never be the same. Blaming himself for the defeat, Lee offered his resignation to Jefferson Davis, but Davis refused.

Once again, the Union forces did not close in for the kill. Rather than pursuing Lee's crippled army, the Union commander, General George Gordon Meade, allowed Lee to retreat southward across the Potomac River and back into Virginia. Lincoln expressed his frustration in a letter he drafted but did not send. "My dear general," he wrote on July 14, "I do not believe you appreciate the magnitude of the misfortune involved in Lee's escape. He was within your easy grasp, and to have closed upon him would, in connection with our other late successes, have ended the war. As it is, the war will be prolonged indefinitely. . . . Your golden opportunity is gone." The "other late successes" were the fall of Vicksburg on July 4 and the surrender of Port Hudson—the last remaining Confederate stronghold on the Mississippi River—five days later. Both victories owed much to the generalship of Ulysses S. Grant, whose reputation rose rapidly in Washington during the summer of 1863.

It is often said that Lee's retreat at Gettysburg, coupled with the fall of Vicksburg, marked the beginning of the end of the great rebellion. While there is some truth in the statement, the war was far from over in July 1863. Although a Confederate army under General Braxton Bragg evacuated Chattanooga, Tennessee—a key railroad town and an invasion gateway to Georgia—on September 8, it suddenly reversed the Yankee advance by winning a stunning victory at Chickamauga Creek less than two weeks later and threatened to retake Chattanooga. In need of an aggressive leader, Lincoln placed Ulysses Grant in command of all Union armies operating in the western theater and urged him to take the offensive. Grant sped to Chattanooga, where his armies won the Battles of Lookout Mountain and Missionary Ridge (November 23–25). Bragg's beaten army had no choice but to fall back along the tracks of the Western and Atlantic Railroad toward Atlanta. With Chattanooga secure, Grant spent the winter of 1863–64 rebuilding his railroad supply lines in Tennessee and Mississippi, resupplying his forces, and preparing for an all-out push on Atlanta the following spring. By the end of 1863, southerners sensed that the Confederacy was in serious trouble. A Richmond diarist wrote that "gloom and unspoken despondency hang like a pall everywhere."

> *"The lesson of Fort Wagner was clear—black soldiers were willing to lay down their lives for the country that promised freedom to their people."*

On November 18, Lincoln took a train to Gettysburg to participate in the dedication of a national military cemetery for those who had fallen in the great battle some four months earlier. The ceremony lasted three hours, most of which was taken up by a well-received oration delivered by former secretary of state Edward Everett of Massachusetts. Although Lincoln's speech took less than three minutes, it captured the political meaning of the war in words that soon became immortalized: "that all men are created equal . . . and that government of the people, by the people, for the people, shall not perish from the earth." Lincoln's **"Gettysburg Address"** is widely recognized as the greatest speech ever made by an American politician.

"THE BRAVERY OF THE BLACKS"

The enlistment of thousands of black troops in the Union army following the Emancipation Proclamation marked a crucial turning point in the northern war effort. Originally considered fit only for garrison or fatigue duty, black soldiers pressed for the right to serve in combat and insisted that discriminatory practices—like lower pay and a smaller uniform allowance—be abolished. They eventually won all of these struggles. In July 1863, soldiers of the Fifty-fourth Massachusetts regiment stormed Fort Wagner near Charleston, South Carolina, in an engagement that was to reveal the courage of

black troops in unmistakable terms. Their white commander, Colonel Robert Gould Shaw, son of a prominent Boston abolitionist family, died leading his men, and the regiment suffered heavy losses in the attack.

The lesson of Fort Wagner was clear—black soldiers were willing to lay down their lives for the country that promised freedom to their people. At Milliken's Bend near Vicksburg, at Port Hudson in Louisiana, and at the Battle of the Crater during the Petersburg campaign of 1864, black troops showed the same resolute qualities in battle that white Union soldiers displayed. "The bravery of the blacks" at Milliken's Bend, said Assistant Secretary of War Charles A. Dana, "completely revolutionized the sentiment of the army with regard to Negro troops. I heard prominent officers who formerly in private had sneered at the idea of negroes fighting express themselves after that as heartily in favor of it," he added. By the end of the war, some 190,000 African Americans had served in the Union army and navy and had made a significant contribution to northern victory.

A Union volunteer corporal proudly holding his Model 1849 Colt revolver. This soldier's uniform, with its brass oval "U.S." belt, dark-blue woolen jacket, light-blue pants, and dark-blue "kepi" hat, illustrates what "standard issue" military garb looked like in the Union army by 1863. No such uniformity existed among units in the Confederate army.

517

GRANT AND SHERMAN "PULLING TOGETHER" (1864)

With the urging of Congress, in March 1864 Lincoln promoted Grant to lieutenant general, the highest-ranking officer in the Union army, and summoned him to Washington. On the way, Grant met in Cincinnati with his friend and trusted subordinate General William Tecumseh Sherman, to devise a strategy for crippling the Confederacy and ending the war. Sherman would take command of the Union armies in the western theater, while, in accordance with Lincoln's wishes, Grant would make his headquarters with the Army of the Potomac. Knowing that the forces they commanded were much larger and better supplied than their adversaries, they decided to push simultaneous offensives against the two largest remaining Confederate armies in Georgia and Virginia. No longer would they, as Grant put it, act "independently and without concert, like a balky team, no two ever pulling together." From now on, the pressure on the rebels would be relentless. Lincoln heartily approved of the plan.

Grant began his part of the joint campaign early in May by moving against Confederate strongholds in Virginia. Some of the heaviest fighting of the war broke out, but now it was sustained. Once again the battle was joined in an area just west of Chancellorsville known as the Wilderness. True to form, Lee's 64,000-man Army of Northern Virginia halted the advance of the 115,000-strong Army of the Potomac. But Grant kept moving, refusing to admit defeat. Again and again, he attempted to outflank Lee's smaller army only to be met by spirited Confederate defenders who fought from behind an elaborate system of trenches and log fortifications. In quick succession, the Battles of Spotsylvania (May 8–12), North Anna (May 22–27), and Cold Harbor (June 1–3) exacted a terrible toll; the casualty lists shocked both North and South.

William Tecumseh Sherman, Union general who, after taking Atlanta, left for his famous "March to the Sea."

Finally Grant's relentless counterclockwise movement took him southward across the James River to the outskirts of Petersburg, an important railroad and industrial center that supplied Richmond some twenty miles to the north. Now Lee's forces were held in what Lincoln called a "bulldog grip." Knowing that if he could take Petersburg, Richmond would inevitably fall, Grant ordered an attack on June 18. After four days of repeated assaults against the town's entrenched defenses, he decided to rest his exhausted troops, dig in, and lay siege to the beleaguered community. After seven weeks of fighting at a level of intensity never seen before, the Union and Confederate armies had become stalemated in trench warfare around Petersburg. Both sides were hurting. Indeed, the Army of the Potomac's 65,000 casualties exceeded the size of Lee's entire army at the outset of the campaign. Lee's casualty rates were equally grim. Between May and mid-June, he had lost at least 35,000 men, more than half of his army swept away. The psychological effects of such massive bloodletting got the best of even the more hardened soldiers. "For thirty days it has been one funeral procession past me," one of them cried, "and it has been too much!"

The Fall of Atlanta. While thousands of Union and Confederate soldiers were meeting their deaths in Virginia during the spring of 1864, General Sherman marched south from Chattanooga to capture Atlanta. His opponent, General Joseph E. Johnston, Braxton Bragg's successor, was a defensive specialist. His 60,000 men skillfully used the rugged Appalachian mountain terrain to oppose the advance of Sherman's larger 100,000-man army at Dalton, Resaca, Allatoona Pass, and New Hope Church, Georgia. Rather than confront Johnston's formidable defenses head-on, Sherman used his numerical superiority to outflank the Confederate army and repeatedly force it to fall back to new defensive positions. The one time Sherman attempted a frontal attack, at Kennesaw Mountain on June 27, his forces were thrown back with heavy losses (2,000 dead and wounded). From then on, he returned to the flanking maneuvers that had served him so well to force the Confederates off Kennesaw Mountain and push them southeast through Marietta, Smyrna, and across the Chattahoochee River to Atlanta.

Jefferson Davis, fearing that Johnston would abandon Atlanta without a fight, replaced him with the offensive-minded General John Bell Hood on July 17. Hood was not content to retreat while keeping his army intact. A grizzled veteran of Gettysburg as well as other battles, he immediately threw the Army of the Tennessee against Sherman's invading forces at the Battles of Peachtree Creek (July 20), Atlanta (July 22), and Ezra Church (July 28). The cost was high: devastating de-

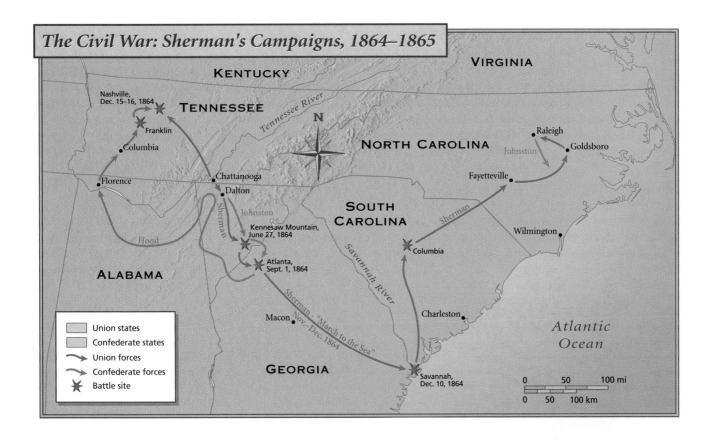

The Civil War: Sherman's Campaigns, 1864–1865

feats reduced his army by 15,000. Hood retreated within the formidable trenchworks that ringed Atlanta and waited for Sherman's next move. For a time, it appeared that Sherman, like Grant before Petersburg, would be forced into a lengthy siege. But after a month of cat-and-mouse tactics, Sherman captured the last remaining railroad that supplied Atlanta and forced Hood to evacuate the city on September 1. The next day, the Union general telegraphed Washington that "Atlanta is ours, and fairly won."

The Election of 1864. No Union victory came at a more opportune time: 1864 was a presidential election year, and Lincoln faced the greatest challenge of his political career. Public frustration had mounted during the summer when great expectations for decisive victories in Virginia and Georgia failed to materialize. As Union casualty lists skyrocketed, Democratic politicians accused Grant of butchery and insensitivity and Lincoln of sending white men to their deaths in order "to allay" his "negro mania." Democratic newspaper editors taunted "Abe the Widowmaker" who "loves his country less,

and the negroe more." "STOP THE WAR," they insisted, "all are tired of this damnable tragedy." Meeting in Chicago at the end of August, the Democratic Party nominated George B. McClellan for president on a platform that declared the war a failure and demanded "that immediate efforts be made for a cessation of hostilities." In Lincoln's words, they had nominated "a War Democrat on a peace platform." By then, some of the president's closest advisers had become convinced that "the people are wild for peace" and that his reelection was "an impossibility." With the election shaping up as a referendum on the war, even Lincoln admitted that "I am going to be beaten . . . and unless some great change takes place *badly* beaten."

The "great change" was the fall of Atlanta, the Confederacy's second-largest city and the symbolic center of the Confederate heartland. Three days after McClellan's nomination, the "glorious news" arrived. "The disaster at Atlanta," the Richmond *Examiner* observed, not only came "in the nick of time" to "save the party of Lincoln from irretrievable ruin," but also "diffuse[d] gloom over the South." Despair deepened

519

during September and October as a Union army under the command of General Philip Sheridan laid waste to Virginia's beautiful Shenandoah Valley, the breadbasket of Lee's army, and in three successive battles virtually destroyed the Confederate opposition. With his army pinned down between Petersburg and Richmond, Lee realized that Grant was slowly closing the circle around him. If Davis could not provide more troops, he warned, "a great calamity will befall us."

Boosted by good news from the battlefields, Lincoln handily won the election with 55 percent of the popular vote and a 212-to-21 margin over McClellan in the electoral college. Nearly 74 percent of eligible males voted, many of them soldiers who either cast absentee ballots or returned home to vote. Of the 154,000 soldiers who voted, more than three-fourths favored Lincoln. The president won every state except Kentucky, Delaware, and New Jersey, and except for those three states, Republicans captured every governorship and state legislature in the North, including three-fourths of the U.S. Congress. Political observers rightly interpreted the election as a triumph for Lincoln's war policy of abolition and unconditional surrender. "I am astonished," one of them wrote, at "the extent and depth of [the North's] determination to fight to the last." Jefferson Davis, however, remained as defiant as ever. "Nothing has changed," he told the Confederate Congress after the November elections. "We are fighting for existence; and by fighting alone can independence be gained."

Sherman's "March to the Sea." With the Confederacy down but not out, General Sherman proposed a bold plan. Instead of holding Atlanta and trying to maintain a vulnerable railway connection to Cincinnati through Chattanooga and Nashville as originally contemplated, he would cut his supply lines and strike out for Savannah and the Atlantic coast while living off the land and destroying everything that lay in his path. He understood that in order to win the war, he had to break the will of the civilian population as well as crush the armies they supported. "We cannot change the hearts of those people of the South," he argued, "but we can make war so terrible and make them so sick of war that generations would pass away before they would again appeal to it." "I can make the march," he assured his superiors, "and make Georgia howl." Although Grant and Lincoln considered the proposal risky, they approved it.

On November 16, Sherman began his fabled "March to the Sea." Before leaving Atlanta, he sent 60,000 men under General George H. Thomas to pursue Hood's battered Confederate army into Tennessee while taking the remaining 62,000 on his advance through the Confederacy's heartland. Within two weeks, Thomas reported that his troops had beaten back a suicidal attack at Franklin, Tennessee. Two weeks later, on December 15–16, Thomas's forces attacked and virtually destroyed Hood's army at Nashville. Hood had evacuated Atlanta seven weeks earlier. After the Battle of Nashville, he was left with barely half his force, many of them barefoot and poorly armed. In the meantime, Sherman's army roared unopposed through Georgia and stood at the gates of Savannah on December 10. In a festive mood, the general telegraphed Lincoln: "I beg to present you, as a Christmas gift, the city of Savannah, with 150 heavy guns and

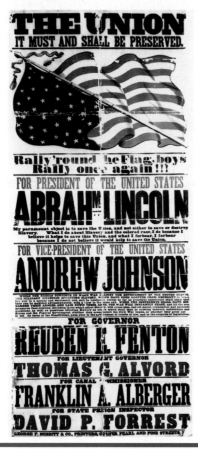

A Republican Party campaign poster urging the reelection of Abraham Lincoln, his vice-presidential running mate, Andrew Johnson of Tennessee, and Reuben Fenton, who subsequently became the Republican governor of New York.

about 25,000 bales of cotton." The same news sent a wave of despondency throughout the South. "One of the gloomiest [days] in our struggle," Confederate general Josiah Gorgas noted in his diary on December 19.

Lee's Surrender at Appomattox (April 1865). By January 1865, Lee's Army of Northern Virginia was the only major military force remaining in the Confederacy. With desertions mounting, supplies growing short, and Sherman's army moving rapidly through the Carolinas to join Grant at Petersburg, Lee's situation grew more desperate with each passing day. He hoped that a 20,000-man force consisting mainly of remnants of Hood's once-powerful army and Georgia and Carolina militia groups might join up with him to halt Sherman's advance and then turn on Grant and the Army of the Potomac.

Much of Atlanta lay in ruins after Sherman's departure from the city in November 1864, as this photo of the Atlantic and Western Railroad shops indicates.

But with Confederate strongholds falling from South Carolina to southern Virginia, the prospects looked grim. At one point in February, Lee even recommended arming slaves to fight in his army, a measure that ended up being defeated by one vote in the Confederate Senate. Nearly surrounded and outnumbered by more than two to one, with all avenues of escape cut off save one railroad, Lee knew that it was only a matter of time before he would have to abandon Petersburg and, with it, the cherished Confederate capital at Richmond. That day came on April 2, when Grant mounted a full-scale attack on Lee's thin gray line and forced it to retreat. The following day, Grant and Lincoln entered Petersburg, and the next day Lincoln, escorted by only ten sailors, walked the burned-out streets of Richmond and sat at Jefferson Davis's desk, less than forty hours after the Confederate president hastily left it.

A week later, on April 9, after several futile attempts to break through the Union lines and escape, Lee surrendered his starving army to Grant at Appomattox Court House. For all intents and purposes, the war was over. On April 11, a tired but greatly relieved Lincoln delivered a public address from the White House balcony calling for peace and national reconciliation. Among the throng of listeners was an actor

and Confederate sympathizer named John Wilkes Booth. Upon hearing the president's remarks, Booth remarked angrily to a friend, "That means nigger citizenship. Now, by God, I'll put him through. That is the last speech he will ever make." True to his word, Booth shot Lincoln three days later as he and his wife, Mary, were attending a play at Ford's Theater in Washington. The following morning, the president was dead. The great American tragedy thus ended in yet another tragedy, with more to come.

The Deadliest War

The Civil War was the deadliest war in American history. A total of 620,000 soldiers—360,000 Federals, 260,000 Confederates—lost their lives; another 500,000 were wounded, and some 75,000 of them later died of their wounds. Indeed, more Americans died in one day at Antietam (4,800) than during the entire Revolutionary War (4,000). The three-day Battle of Gettysburg, in fact, claimed more lives than did the American Revolution and the War of 1812 put together. Adding some 50,000 southern civilians who died as a direct result of the conflict, the loss of human life comes close to 750,000. The combined total of American deaths from all the other wars fought by the United States from 1776 to 1990 does not equal the carnage produced by the Civil War.

For every soldier who died of battle wounds, two died of disease. The absence of scientific knowledge about disease-causing bacteria was coupled with lax sanitary practices. Epidemics broke out, ranging from measles and mumps to the greater dangers of smallpox and erysipelas. Often deadly bacterial infections like dysentery, typhoid, and pneumonia reduced 1,000-man regiments by half before they actually marched into battle. General Sherman contracted malaria in Mississippi yet continued to lead his troops; Lee suffered from a heart condition throughout the war; and Hood lost the use of his left arm at Gettysburg and had his right leg amputated at Chickamauga, yet carried on. One of Lee's brigade commanders could hardly walk yet mounted his steed to participate in Pickett's Charge at Gettysburg.

"The combined total of American deaths from all the other wars fought by the United States from 1776 to 1990 does not equal the carnage produced by the Civil War."

Nothing was more horrifying to soldiers than to see comrades lying on the ground either dead or crying out in pain. A Union cavalry officer who looked over the battlefield at Malvern Hill, Virginia, on the morning of July 2, 1862, recalled some twenty years later, "Our ears had been filled with agonizing cries from thousands before the fog was lifted. But now our eyes saw an appalling spectacle upon the slopes down to the woodlands half a mile away. Over five thousand dead and wounded men were on the ground . . . enough were alive and moving to give the field a singular crawling effect." Soldiers assigned to burial details wrote of the sickening "sights and smells that assailed us" as they encountered "corpses swollen to twice their size, some of them actually burst asunder with the pressure of foul gases." Others, working in field surgery units, described how hogs from local farms ate amputated arms and legs, that accumulated in piles outside surgeons' tents.

THE NEW RIFLED FIREARMS

The chief cause of such suffering was the introduction of a new, more lethal technology. The Civil War was the first conflict to be fought largely with rifled firearms. The standard infantry weapon of all nations up to then was the smoothbore musket, a muzzle-loading gun that fired a .69-inch (or cal-iber) single lead ball or, more often, a multiple load called "buck and ball" that consisted of one large ball accompanied by three or four smaller balls. In the hands of common troops, a musket could rarely hit its target more than fifty or sixty yards away. Given their limited range, smoothbores proved most effective when equipped with bayonets and used in frontal assaults; a charging soldier might get off two or three shots before closing in hand-to-hand combat.

The new rifled firearms changed all that. The spiral grooves cut into the barrels of these rifled weapons imparted a spinning motion to the bullets they fired, making them more accurate at longer distances. Standard single-shot rifle-muskets and breech-loading carbines were complemented by rapid-firing repeating rifles using self-contained paper and brass cartridges. These new guns fired hollowed-out, conically shaped bullets that had an effective killing range of over 100 yards—more than double that of the traditional smoothbore musket. This change made attacking more difficult and defense more effective. It took military officials some time to figure out what was going on and to change their tactical manuals accordingly. In the meantime, defenders, dug in behind stone walls or other entrenchments, could mow down those who attempted to take their positions by frontal assault. The Army of the Potomac's disaster at Fredericksburg, Pickett's Charge at Gettysburg, and Grant's casualties at Spotsylvania, Cold Harbor, and Petersburg testified to the deadly fire of defenders wielding rifled firearms.

Amputations accounted for 75 percent of the surgical procedures performed on soldiers. Since the large, hollowed-out, .58-caliber "Minie" bullets fired from rifles had a low muzzle velocity compared with modern rifles, they tended to flatten out when they hit human flesh and rarely exited the body. The resulting wounds destroyed vital organs, shattered and splintered bones, and chewed up the tissue surrounding them. If wounded soldiers were not treated on the spot, they could bleed to death or die of shock. Physicians could do very little for stomach and chest wounds other than probe for the bullet with forceps or their fingers, remove it, and hope for the best. Mortality rates for such wounds approached 100 percent. Wounds to the arms or legs presented greater hope. But lacking the facilities and knowledge to repair such wounds, surgeons more often than not resorted to amputation.

TREATING THE WOUNDED

Most operations took place at temporary field hospitals hastily set up in houses or barns within a mile or two of the battlefront. There, bare-armed doctors assisted by orderlies worked frantically to save the lives of the wounded. The implements they used bore a striking resemblance to those used in butcher shops, and, not surprisingly, they were often unfairly accused of butchery and even resisted by patients at gunpoint. Chloroform and ether were commonly used to put patients under. When supplies of these anesthetics ran out, as they often did in the Confederate army, orderlies gave men whiskey to help dull the pain and prevent shock. Unaware of the need for antiseptic conditions, surgeons used the same unsterilized knives and saws on different patients, frequently wiping them as well as their bloody hands on their aprons or whatever cloth was available. Although such surgeries generally succeeded from a technical standpoint, many patients subsequently died of gangrene, pyemia (blood poisoning), osteomyelitis, and other bacterial infections.

Once wounded soldiers received emergency treatment at field hospitals, they were taken by wagon to regimental hospitals and, from there, on to general hospitals to undergo further treatment and recuperate. Since few officials had anticipated a long war, neither side was prepared either to move the wounded from one hospital to another or properly house them once they had arrived. Although a small ambulance service had been organized before the war by the U.S. Army Medical Department, it quickly disintegrated at First Manassas and other early battles. Thanks largely to the lobbying efforts of a civilian volunteer organization known as the U.S. Sanitary Commission, established by Lincoln's executive order in June 1861, the surgeon general set up an ambulance corps staffed by specially uniformed and unarmed soldiers who entered battle areas and removed the wounded. These "medics" proved so proficient that they served as a model for other nations as late as World War I.

In addition to supplying bandages, medicine, and volunteer nurses to army camps and hospitals, the U.S. Sanitary Commission instructed soldiers about proper cooking methods, the placement of drainage ditches and latrines, and personal hygiene. The commission's growing popularity with

> *"The surgeon general set up an ambulance corps staffed by specially uniformed and unarmed soldiers who entered battle areas and removed the wounded. These 'medics' proved so proficient that they served as a model for other nations as late as World War I."*

soldiers led Congress in April 1862 to give it the power to reform outdated army medical procedures. The result was such important innovations as the outfitting of hospital ships and specially designed railway cars, staffed by volunteer nurses, for transporting the wounded to **army hospitals.** These innovations help to explain why 4 percent fewer Union soldiers died of their wounds than did Confederates.

During the first two years of the war, everything from government buildings to factories and prisons were converted into hospital wards. The filthy conditions of these overcrowded hospitals were evidenced by sickening odors, unemptied bedpans, used dressings strewn about, clogged toilets and latrines, and contaminated water supplies. Gradually, such appalling conditions improved. The Confederate government led the way in 1862 with the Chimborazo complex in Richmond, an enormous facility consisting of five separate hospitals with 8,000 beds in 150 newly constructed buildings. The North, for its part, built a hospital system that by the summer of 1863 consisted of 182 newly built hospitals with 84,000 beds; by the end of the war, the number had expanded to 204 hospitals with 136,894 beds. In both the North and the South, the new army hospitals were built in a "pavilion" style, with well-ventilated one- or two-story wings projecting out from a central area. Different wings housed soldiers with different sorts of ailments, a pattern that reflected a desire for administrative efficiency as well as growing specializations in medicine.

By war's end, the United States had some of the best hospitals in the world. What's more, the war had served as a training ground for surgeons, anesthetists, epidemiologists, and general practitioners. One former Confederate medical officer observed that "the whole country is now furnished with a medical corps which the war has thoroughly educated and reliably trained." "I have lost much," another wrote, "but I have gained much, especially as a medical man. I return home a better surgeon, a better doctor." Yet much remained to be learned, especially in the operating room, where surgeons continued to probe for bullets with their bare fingers and used unsterilized bandages. Although a few practitioners were beginning to experiment with carbolic acid, iodine, chlorine, and other chemical agents in treating gangrenous wounds, the widespread adoption of antiseptic methods lay far in the future. Thousands who survived surgical procedures consequently died of bacterial infections.

WOMEN AT WAR

Thousands of women, black and white, participated in the Civil War. Indeed, hundreds disguised themselves as men and served as soldiers in both armies, often seeing combat. Others engaged in espionage by gathering and transmitting information about troop movements and enemy fortifications to military officials. In July 1861, for example, a Washington, D.C., resident named Rose Greenhow rode ahead to alert General Pierre Beauregard about an impending Union army attack on Manassas, thus giving the Confederate army a significant advantage in the battle that followed. Greenhow, like many other female agents, was arrested, imprisoned, and eventually released, only to continue her surreptitious activities. Still, over the course of the war, not a single woman was executed for treasonous activities by either government.

Hundreds of women accompanied the Union and Confederate armies as laundresses, cooks, nurses, provisioners (also called "sutlers"), and "camp followers" (another name for prostitutes). Regardless of their primary calling, these army women tended to diversify their work as the war wore on.

A Union nurse tending her patients.

A Union "daughter of the regiment" poses with her husband and three children in the camp of the Thirty-first Pennsylvania Infantry Regiment, Washington, D.C., 1862.

This was especially true of those who accompanied their husbands to the front lines and subsequently became known as "daughters of the regiment."

When James Etheridge enlisted in the Second Michigan Infantry Regiment at the outset of the war, his wife, Annie, not only followed him for four years but became a veteran of some of the bloodiest engagements of the Civil War. At Chancellorsville in May 1863, a soldier from the Seventeenth Maine wrote to his mother that he saw Annie Etheridge "in the very front of the battle dressing wounds and aiding the suffering where few Surgeons dared show themselves." Other soldiers also documented Annie's heroics, noting that from Bull Run in July 1861 to Spotsylvania in May 1864, "Gentle Annie" had served as a nurse, cook, seamstress, letter writer, and general morale booster for her husband's battered regiment. When she died in 1913, she was accorded the unprecedented honor of being buried in Arlington National Cemetery.

Most army women served as nurses in Union and Confederate hospitals. As one writer observed, "Hospital nurses were of all sorts, and came from various sources of supply; volunteers paid or unpaid; soldiers' wives and sisters who had come to see their friends and remained without any clear commission or duties; women sent by State agencies and aid societies; women assigned by the General Superintendent of Nurses." In a preprofessional era, none were professionally trained. Even in the hurricane of war, they frequently encountered opposition from army surgeons, who felt that the dreadful sights, coarse language, and exposure to male body parts made army hospitals "no place for a woman." The general superintendent of army nurses, Dorothea Dix, moved to disarm such criticisms and protect her nurses from charges of unwomanly behavior. Dix, already well known for her pre-war reform work in insane asylums, emphasized "good conduct," "good character," and plain dress "without ornaments of any sort" for her nurses. "Habits of neatness, order, sobriety, and industry are pre-requisites," her instructions intoned, adding that "obedience to the rules of the service . . . will be required and enforced."

Not surprisingly, some young women chafed under such factory-like rules and flaunted them. At the same time, they worked hard to see to their patients' comfort and considered their labor as much an act of Christian benevolence as patriotism. "I am here to do my Master's work," one wrote. "I never wash [the soldiers'] hard, worn, and sore feet without a sweet memory of Him who gave us the example." Another wrote to her mother in May 1862, "We are changed by all this contact with terror." By war's end, they went home satisfied that they had helped to bring a "moral atmosphere" to the institutions they served while garnering respect in a world that had been an exclusive preserve of men. Thanks largely to their perseverance and good works, nursing and, to a lesser extent, medicine became increasingly professionalized and open to women after the Civil War.

THE HOME FRONT

One of the great achievements of wartime productivity on both sides occurred in agriculture. The American population was still overwhelmingly rural in 1861; over 75 percent either farmed or lived in small towns with populations under 2,500. Yet although hundreds of thousands (680,000 from the Midwest alone) of men left their farms to join the Union army, agricultural output expanded dramatically. Northern farms raised more wheat in 1862 and again in 1863 than the entire country had before the war. Indeed, the fall harvests of the early 1860s were so bountiful that the United States actually doubled its exports of wheat, corn, pork, and beef to famine-plagued Europe. No one doubted that the Union army was the best fed in the world.

Here, women played another key role in the war. With so many menfolk away, farm women had no choice but to add men's work—plowing, planting, and harvesting—to the cooking, washing, milking, butter making, cleaning, sewing, and rearing of children and livestock that they had always done. Women who could not cope with these added tasks ei-

Envelopes depicting patriotic themes like this one, with the woman sewing representing the home front, were commonly used during and after the Civil War to send letters or as souvenirs.

ther sold out, went bankrupt, or abandoned farming until their husbands returned home. Those who stayed on, and could afford it, turned to new types of farm machinery.

The New Farm Machinery. To be sure, plenty of machinery existed. In the 1840s and 1850s, the agricultural machinery industry had emerged, led by the McCormick Harvester Company in Chicago and John Deere's plow works in Moline, Illinois. Now farm women equipped themselves with horse- or mule-drawn mowing machines and self-raking reapers. "Farming is comparatively child's play to what it was twenty years ago," the editor of the *Scientific American* noted in mid-1863. "So perfect is machinery," wrote another observer, "that men seem to be of less necessity. . . . We have seen, within the past few weeks, a stout matron whose sons are in the army, with her team cutting hay. . . . She cut seven acres with ease in a day, riding leisurely upon her cutter."

But while northern farmers hailed the new technology, few southerners did. Hampered by the lack of foundries and machine shops and constrained by mounting pressures for arms, wagons, and munitions, the South had scant resources to devote to manufacturing agricultural machinery. Even though southern farmers converted thousands of acres from cotton to food crops, food shortages arose as early as 1862. A key factor was the loss of Tennessee—a major food-producing state—to Union forces early in the war. Then a lack of salt to preserve meat and a serious drought during the summer of

525

Although both sides engaged in the practice, this photo shows Union soldiers with Sherman's army destroying railroad tracks in Atlanta in 1864. After being removed from their beds, rails were piled on bonfires made from the wooden ties, brought to a red heat, then bent around trees, forming what became known as "Sherman neckties."

Financing the War

THE CONFEDERACY AND ILLICIT TRADING

A particular hardship for southerners was the failure of the Confederate government to pay its debts and guard against inflation. Strapped for hard money from the start, the Davis administration sought to pay for the war by selling interest-paying bonds. Subscribers eagerly bought up the first $15 million issued in April 1861, but subsequent efforts raised little money. Unwilling to levy taxes, short of cash, and its debts rapidly escalating, the Confederate Congress in 1861 issued $119 million in unbacked paper currency. A year later, a second printing mounted to $400 million, with nowhere near enough gold or silver in the vaults to back their worth. The best the government could do was to promise that these "treasury notes" would be redeemed in specie two years after the war ended. The only thing backing such "fiat money" was the faith of holders that the Confederacy would ultimately win the war.

Their faith was soon shaken by the effectiveness of the Union blockade, the deteriorating condition of southern railroads, and the ups and downs of the land war. An inflationary spiral began. Millions in unbacked paper bills followed millions, and prices soared accordingly. The downward spiral accelerated after the double shock of Lee's defeat at Gettysburg and the fall of Vicksburg in July 1863. Within three months, prices skyrocketed 58 percent, and they continued to rise. In October 1863, a barrel of flour cost $70 in Richmond; four months later, it cost $250. Consequently, desertions from Confederate armies swelled as the war wore on. "Poor men have been compelled to leave the army to come home to provide for their families," a soldier absent without leave protested to the governor of Mississippi in December 1862. "We . . . are willing to defend our country but our families [come] first."

By the time the Confederate Congress realized it had no choice but to impose taxes on the citizenry, the southern economy was already out of hand. Faced with excise, property, and income taxes, people either evaded them or paid them in worthless Confederate currency. As prices shot up and scarcities mounted, people began to trade with the enemy even though both governments officially forbade it. The smuggling and black-market trading that had existed in border states since the beginning of the war swelled from

1862 drastically reduced the fall harvest. Equally serious, southern railroads carried less and less from food-producing areas to troops in the field and cities that lay in harm's way. By the summer of 1862, railroads within Confederate war zones began to show significant wear and tear as armies crossed their paths, fought for their control, ripped up their rails, and destroyed their locomotives.

By March 1863, conditions had grown so bad in Richmond that a Confederate War Department clerk recorded in his diary that "my wife and children are emaciated," and "the shadow of the gaunt of famine is upon us." Several weeks later, wives of workers in the Confederacy's largest cannon foundry and armory in Richmond marched on the governor's mansion, demanding that the government release emergency food stocks being held in its warehouses. When the governor refused, a riot broke out as the mob, chanting "Bread or blood!," proceeded to smash windows and loot stores. Only after President Jefferson Davis appeared on the scene and threatened to order the local militia to fire on the crowd did it disperse.

A Confederate $100 bill issued in December 1862. Note the portrait of John C. Calhoun in the lower left corner.

1862 as Union armies penetrated into Confederate territory. Southerners were desperately in need of salt, medicine, shoes, and clothing, and northern merchants were equally desirous of acquiring raw cotton for textile manufacturing. To a certain extent, the U.S. government encouraged such trade by issuing special permits to southern merchants and planters in occupied areas who took an oath of allegiance to the Union. In July 1863, the editor of the Richmond *Examiner* condemned the "shameless moral turpitude" of "those rampant cotton and sugar planters, who were so early and furiously in the field of secession" yet, "having taken the oath of allegiance to the Yankees, are now raising cotton in partnership with their Yankee *protectors*, and shipping it to Yankee markets." While he viewed illicit trade as sapping the morale of southerners, even Jefferson Davis had to concede that trading with the enemy "might be justified" in dire circumstances and "as a last resort." In doing so, he came close to the viewpoint of Abraham Lincoln.

Not so Ulysses Grant or William Tecumseh Sherman. Both generals roundly condemned such activity, asserting that "we cannot carry on war and trade with a people at the same time." They issued a series of regulations tightening trade permits to southerners and requiring all northern payments for cotton to be made in U.S. Treasury notes rather than gold (thus preventing hard money from finding its way into Confederate coffers for the purchase of arms in Europe). Even so, a War Department official who visited Memphis in 1863 reported that "every colonel, captain, or quartermaster is in secret partnership with some operator in cotton," and "every soldier dreams of adding a bale of cotton to his monthly pay." Such "mania for sudden fortunes in cotton," he concluded, "has to an alarming extent corrupted and demoralized the army." The problem was particularly evident in New Orleans, where the brother of the occupying Union army commander, General Benjamin Butler, and some unscrupulous agents of the northern textile industry illegally exchanged gold and salt for cotton and sugar owned by planters who sympathized with the Confederacy. Although Lincoln later transferred Butler, a "War Democrat," to an important command in Virginia, political imperatives often forced him to look the other way in the face of such dealings.

UNION EFFORTS IN FINANCE

In contrast with those of the increasingly desperate Confederacy, Union efforts to finance the war proved both innovative and successful. Like the South, the Union had three ways to pay for the war: making loans in the form of bond sales, levying taxes, and issuing paper currency called treasury notes. While the Confederate government opted primarily for the third way and experienced runaway inflation that by war's end exceeded 9,000 percent, the Lincoln administration tried a combination of all three measures and held inflation to 80 percent.

Such a remarkable performance owed much to the fiscal leadership of the Secretary of Treasury Salmon Chase of Ohio,

This cartoon from the British humor magazine *Punch* points to the serious fiscal and manpower problems that confronted the North in 1862. The South's problems were even greater.

527

who, with the assistance of a Philadelphia banker named Jay Cooke, conducted a massive advertising campaign aimed at selling war bonds throughout the North. Altogether, Cooke's firm marketed over $2.5 billion in bonds, financing two-thirds of the Union's war costs. Another 21 percent came from revenues realized from higher tariffs on imports, excise taxes, and the first federal income tax in American history. The remaining 12 percent came from $750 million in non-interest-bearing treasury notes sanctioned by four Legal Tender Acts passed by Congress in 1862 and 1863. Issued in denominations from $1 to $1,000 and popularly known as "greenbacks" because their reverse sides were printed in green ink, they proved extremely popular even though they had no backing other than public faith in the federal government's promise to redeem them in the future. Their success, moreover, paved the way for the National Banking Act in 1863, which sought to create a uniform national currency by allowing banks to issue currency equal to 90 percent of their holdings in government war bonds. As its title suggests, the National Banking Act signaled the establishment of a national bank system and, eventually, the demise of state-chartered banks, whose erratic behavior had caused financial panics and seriously disrupted the American economy.

THE REPUBLICAN BLUEPRINT

With Republicans dominating Congress, they were now in a position to enact a series of laws described by one historian as a "blueprint for modern America." That blueprint provided the legal framework for the emergence of the United States in the 1880s as the world's leading industrial power.

The first corner of the blueprint was the Homestead Act of May 20, 1862, which granted any citizen over twenty-one 160 acres of free survey land if the settler lived on the land for five years and made improvements on it. Next came the Pacific Railroad Act, passed on July 1, 1862, authorizing the construction of a transcontinental railroad from Omaha, Nebraska, to San Francisco Bay and resolving disputes that went back to the Mexican War. The cost was colossal, and only the U.S. government could finance it. In addition to lending the two companies (the Union Pacific and Central Pacific) that built the railroad $16,000 per mile on prairie land and $48,000 per mile for mountainous areas, the bill also made the generous provision of 6,400 acres of public land to the railroads for each mile completed. Even so, the railroads were

desperate for money. Subsequent legislation, passed in 1864, doubled the land grants to 12,800 acres per mile and extended them to the construction of other transcontinental railroads. Altogether the federal government doled out 120 million acres to the transcontinentals during and after the Civil War, making them among the richest corporations in America.

The blueprint included bold designs for education. On July 2, 1862, the day after the Battle of Malvern Hill and the end of McClellan's fruitless Peninsula Campaign, Lincoln signed the Morrill Act into law. Named after the Republican senator from Vermont who sponsored the legislation, the bill

Poster announcing the opening of the nation's first transcontinental railroad in 1869.

provided each state loyal to the Union with 30,000 acres of public land for each senator and representative then sitting in Congress. Each state could then sell the land to provide an endowment for at least one public college devoted to training in "agriculture and the mechanical arts." The long-term result was the establishment of sixty-nine "land-grant" institutions—from the University of Massachusetts (1862) and the University of Maine (1865) in the Northeast to the University of Illinois (1867) and Ohio State University (1870) in the Midwest, to the University of California at Berkeley (1868) in the West. These schools, owing their origins to the Morrill Act, form the backbone of America's public system of higher education today.

The impact of the Homestead, Pacific Railroad, and Morrill Acts was enormous. Beginning with the junction of the Union Pacific and Central Pacific Railroads and the driving of the famed "golden spike" at Promontory Point, Utah, in 1869, the transcontinental railroads carried hundreds of thousands of settlers across the Great Plains to the Pacific. By free grant and by sale, the Homestead Act and railroads provided many of these settlers with land on which to seek a fresh start. Not least of all, the Morrill Act established institutions of higher education that helped to populate the Midwest and West with professional engineers, agriculturalists, doctors, lawyers, and schoolteachers. The only people who did not profit from these developments were those already on the land—Native Americans and people of Hispanic ancestry, who found themselves pushed aside by the "march of the white man's civilization" and condemned to second-class status in the aftermath of what some historians refer to as the "Second American Revolution."

MARSHALING MANPOWER

As casualties and losses from disease mounted during the winter and spring of 1862, the enthusiasm that had initially greeted the war quickly subsided. Having been overwhelmed by too many volunteers (and not enough weapons) early in the conflict, both sides now faced serious manpower shortages. The Confederacy acted first. At the urging of Robert E. Lee, Jefferson Davis asked his Congress to enact a conscription law that would require current enlistees to serve an addi-

> *"The Morrill Act established institutions of higher education that helped to populate the Midwest and West with professional engineers, agriculturalists, doctors, lawyers, and schoolteachers."*

tional two years while subjecting all other able-bodied white males between eighteen and thirty-five to a draft of three years' service. The bill—the first of its kind in American history—passed in April 1862, shortly after the bloody Battle of Shiloh, but not without bitter debate. In addition to exempting a broad range of workers (from teachers and civil servants to telegraphers and miners), the law also allowed draftees to buy their way out of the army by hiring substitutes. Most controversial of all, owners and overseers of plantations with twenty or more slaves received automatic exemptions, thus giving rise to the phrase "A rich man's war but a poor man's fight."

Although the Confederate draft served its purpose in getting more men into the army (which increased by some 200,000 men in 1862), countless draftees evaded service by leaving their communities and moving to other areas. Others sold themselves as substitutes for as much as $300 in gold, only to desert from their units and sell themselves again to the highest bidder. Such practices became so prevalent that the Confederate Congress abolished substitutes in December 1863.

Although Lincoln had no direct statutory power to institute a draft, he cited the authorization granted him under the Militia Act of July 1862 "to provide for enrolling the militia" and ordered various state governors to supply 300,000 men between eighteen and forty-five for nine months' service. When some governors protested the order as an unconstitutional usurpation of states' rights and riots broke out in Pennsylvania and several midwestern states, Lincoln quietly rescinded the call. But not before federal troops had been sent to the trouble spots and several hundred draft resisters had been imprisoned without trial. On September 24, citing his executive war powers under the Constitution, Lincoln issued a proclamation suspending writs of habeas corpus (court orders that protected people against illegal imprisonment) throughout the country and ordering the arrest of anyone "guilty of any disloyal practice, affording aid and comfort to Rebels." This order, together with the release of the Emancipation Proclamation only two days earlier, elicited bitter denunciations on the part of Democrats opposed to the war. Delaware senator James A. Bayard asserted that Lincoln was "declaring himself a Dictator." To be sure, the suspension of habeas corpus and the effective declaration of martial law had a chilling effect on the administration's enemies. Fearful of arrest, Democratic editors began to tone down what they printed. Even private letter writers became careful about what they said.

The Enrollment Act. In the spring of 1863, at the height of Confederate military success and the depth of Union despair, Lincoln got what he wanted: a draft law called the Enrollment Act. While the new legislation did not allow occupational exemptions, it did permit the hiring of substitutes. What's more, the law allowed draftees to avoid service by paying a $300 "commutation fee" each time their names were drawn. Thaddeus Stevens, a radical Republican congressman from southeastern Pennsylvania, denounced the Enrollment Act as "a rich man's bill." Even more outspoken was Clement L. Vallandigham, a former congressman and Peace Democrat from Dayton, Ohio. Accusing Lincoln of abolitionist fanaticism and betraying the Union, Vallandigham made speeches pillorying the administration for "defeat, debt, taxation . . . the suspension of *habeas corpus* . . . of freedom of the press and of speech" and calling on his countrymen to "stop fighting. Make an armistice. . . . Withdraw your army from the seceded States."

With Vallandigham stumping around the country and Peace Democrats from Ohio to New York urging him on, it was only a matter of time before a reaction occurred. That moment arrived on May 5, 1863, when General Ambrose Burnside—the disgraced Union commander at Fredericksburg, now in charge of the military district bordering the Ohio River—had Vallandigham arrested at his Dayton home in the middle of the night and hauled off in chains to army headquarters in Cincinnati. Charged with making treasonous remarks, Vallandigham was quickly tried and convicted by a military court in Cincinnati and sentenced to two years in military prison. When the Ohioan sued for a writ of habeas corpus under civil law, a federal judge informed him that no such writ could be issued because the president had declared a military emergency.

When news of Vallandigham's trial and conviction became public, Lincoln faced a firestorm of criticism from outraged Democrats and anxious Republicans. Fearful that Vallandig-

> *"'Must I shoot a simple-minded soldier boy who deserts, while I must not touch a hair of a wily agitator who induces him to desert?' Lincoln asked. 'In such a case to silence the agitator, and save the boy is not only constitutional, but withal a great mercy.'"*

ham would become a political martyr for the cause of Peace Democrats and damage his chances for reelection in 1864, Lincoln commuted Vallandigham's sentence and banished him to the Confederacy. At the same time, he prepared a lengthy response to Democratic critics who accused him of ordering "arbitrary arrests" and abrogating civil liberties. In it, he pointed out that the Constitution provided for the suspension of these liberties "in cases of Rebellion or Invasion" and claimed that he had been "slow to adopt . . . strong measures" and did so only because the actions of Vallandigham and other protesters were "damaging the army, upon the existence . . . of which, the life of the nation depends." As for Vallandigham, the president took the moral high ground. "Must I shoot a simple-minded soldier boy who deserts, while I must not touch a hair of a wily agitator who induces him to desert?" he asked. "In such a case to silence the agitator, and save the boy is not only constitutional, but withal a great mercy."

Initially published in the *New York Tribune* and subsequently reprinted in pamphlet form, Lincoln's public letter was read by 10 million people. In addition to stigmatizing Vallandigham as a "wily agitator," the president's justification of his actions did much to quiet criticism within the Republican Party and disarm his Democratic critics. But not completely. Army provost marshals had already begun enrolling draftees under the new conscription law and using warrantless searches to track down evaders. Riled by the law as well as the army's strong-arm tactics, antidraft riots broke out in parts of the North, culminating in a week-long display of violence in New York City.

New York, with its large Irish Catholic population and powerful Democratic base, had never been Lincoln country. As much anti-Protestant as antiblack, Catholic leaders now hammered away at the rich man/poor man theme, warning also that the draft would force white workers to fight for black freedom only to see their jobs taken by blacks once the war had ended. Consequently, when New York officials began drawing names of draftees on July 11, 1863, hundreds of angry Irishmen gathered at local pubs and churches, vowing that they would be damned before they would "go and carry on a war for the nigger." The next day the rioting began, with mobs setting fires to draft offices and singling out blacks for beatings and lynchings. As the violence escalated during the next four days, the rioters—two-thirds of whom were thought to be Irish—burned a black orphanage and, with chants of "Down with the rich," turned their wrath on the homes and businesses of leading Republicans and abolitionists. Police tried to quell the uprising, but only after July 16, when Lincoln's secretary of war dispatched federal troops fresh from the Battle of Gettysburg, did the violence end. In the weeks that followed, 20,000 soldiers occupied New York as the draft process proceeded. Overall, the results of the July draft proved meager. Only 35,883 men throughout the North were actually inducted from the 292,441 names drawn, while another 52,288 paid commutation fees.

Lincoln would issue three more draft calls in 1863 and 1864. Although he did away with commutation fees in July 1864, the practice of hiring substitutes remained. In an effort to avoid the despised draft system, many northern districts filled their quotas by offering monetary bonuses to men who volunteered for duty. As a result, only 6 percent of the more than 2.5 million men who served the Union during the war were draftees. Nonetheless, the Enrollment Act set an important precedent. In an age when the raising of armies had rested primarily with state governments, the new draft law fundamentally shifted the process of mobilization. In doing so, the federal government established the principle that it could call citizens to military service—something that would be repeated on a much larger scale and to greater effect by the selective service drafts of World Wars I and II.

Why the South Lost

No sooner had the war ended than participants as well as observers began to hypothesize about why the North won and the South lost. Some paraphrased Napoleon, arguing, in effect, that "God was on the side of the heaviest battalions." Indeed, Robert E. Lee admitted as much in his famous farewell to his troops at Appomattox, when he noted that "after four years of arduous service . . . the Army of Northern Virginia has been compelled to yield to overwhelming numbers and resources." In 1872, on the second anniversary of Lee's death, former Confederate corps commander Jubal A. Early asserted in a speech that "General Lee had not been conquered in battle, but surrendered because he had no

An arm and hammer symbolize labor in early American iconography. In this instance, "The Strong Arm of the North" stands not only for labor but also for the Union's industrial might.

longer an army with which to give battle. What he surrendered was the skeleton, the mere ghost of the Army of Northern Virginia, which had been gradually worn down by the combined agencies of numbers, steam-power, railroads, mechanism, and all the resources of physical science." In the end, superior technology coupled with unlimited manpower forced Lee's submission, Early went on. Fearful that the North's "spirit of progress" would overwhelm the South's "cherished traditions," he urged his audience to hold tenaciously to the spirit of the "Lost Cause." "We lost nearly everything but honor," he had earlier written to Lee, "and that should be religiously guarded."

Not everyone agreed with Early. Former Confederate generals Pierre Beauregard and Joseph E. Johnston castigated Jefferson Davis for his defensiveness, limited vision, and general failure of leadership, while others pointed to his disastrous financial policies as "the greatest single weakness of the Confederacy." Generals James Longstreet and Edward Porter Alexander, on the other hand, criticized Davis and Lee for limiting their strategic vision to the Virginia theater and refusing to send troops to relieve Vicksburg during the critical summer of 1863. Davis was no match for Lincoln, later critics concluded, and only Lee rivaled Grant and Sherman as a great field commander.

Even so, historians characterized Grant and Sherman as being more "modern-minded" than Lee. Recognizing the inherent relationship between politics and war, Grant and Sherman developed the practice of total war and used it to great advantage during the last year of the conflict. Lee, by contrast, remained wedded to an older style of warfare that emphasized offensive strategy and tactics while neglecting to take into account the lethal effect that recently developed rifled firearms had brought to the battlefield. Although he achieved dazzling victories at Second Manassas, Fredericksburg, and Chancellorsville, his tendency to take the offensive whenever possible yielded casualty rates that the Army of Northern Virginia could not absorb. As a result, critics charged that Lee bled his army to death. A force of more than 70,000 at Gettysburg had been reduced to less than 30,000 by Appomattox. At the same time, Virginia's proud Stonewall Brigade, once consisting of five full regiments numbering 5,000 men, was left with only 210 "ragged survivors."

Other students of the Civil War maintain that the Confederacy's defeat owed less to failures of leadership than to tensions within southern society. Citing the ongoing conflict over states' rights between certain governors and the Davis administration, resentments over a rich man's war and a poor man's fight, pockets of Unionist sympathy throughout the South, libertarian protests over increasingly centralized state policies, and the defection of tens of thousands of slaves to the Union cause (many of whom joined the army and navy), these analysts contend that loss of will rather than the lack of means led to the Confederacy's demise. Nevertheless, the most persuasive accounts of the war hold that the ultimate determinant of the Confederacy's collapse rested with events on the battlefield. Lincoln put it best in his second inaugural address when he referred to "the progress of our arms, upon which all else chiefly depends." Military events, not disillusionment at home, decided the outcome of the war.

Since the contest came down to military dominance, it is important to recall that the South was fighting for its independence, while the North was fighting to prevent it. In order to achieve its goal, the Confederacy did not necessarily have to invade and conquer the North or destroy its armies. The North, on the other hand, had to subjugate the South, which meant invading its territory and destroying its capacity to make war. Of the two, the Confederacy's task seemed more manageable. It needed to convince the North that a complete military victory was either unlikely or too costly in human and financial terms to be worth the price. The key to victory for both sides rested with breaking the other's will to fight, and that could only be accomplished through a string of military victories. In the end, the Confederacy failed to hold its territory against the Union juggernaut. By calling upon its vast human and material resources and bringing relentless military pressure on the South, the North eventually won the war.

A GREAT DIVIDE

The Civil War marks a great divide in American history. Before the war, most Americans lived in rural areas and followed agricultural pursuits. During the war, people learned how to mobilize and equip armies on a massive scale, lessons that would be applied often in the postwar period with the expansion of the factory system, the rise of big business, and the spread of mass transportation and communication networks.

These were the ingredients of a new era, the beginning of the "modern age." They took root before the war, matured during the war, and predominated afterward. In the process, the United States was reconfigured, indeed reinvented.

Equally important, Americans emerged from the war with an altered idea of what their country and government meant. The United States had survived as a nation. Instead of speaking of the United States as a pluralist "union" of states (as they had since the Revolution), people began to refer to it as a singular nation—"the United States is" rather than "the United States are." What's more, the locus of governmental power shifted from states' rights and local rule to a greater emphasis on central state authority. Through military drafts, wartime taxes, emergency confiscations, and pieces of legislation like the Homestead Act and National Banking Act, people experienced a more direct relationship with the federal government. This, too, demarcated the "old" America from the "new."

Above all, the war advanced democracy. In Lincoln's words, the country experienced "a new birth of freedom" so

> *"Instead of speaking of the United States as a pluralist 'union' of states (as they had since the Revolution), people began to refer to it as a singular nation—'the United States is' rather than 'the United States are.'"*

that "government of the people, by the people, for the people shall not perish from the earth." Nowhere was this more evident than in the liberation of some 4 million slaves with the passage of the Thirteenth Amendment in 1865. Three years later, the Fourteenth Amendment would extend the boundary of freedom by guaranteeing citizenship and civil rights to "all persons born or naturalized in the United States." Finally, the Fifteenth Amendment (1870) granted the right to vote to all adult males regardless of "race, color, or previous condition of servitude." These legal guarantees marked great advances, to be sure, but would they be enforced? Would racism decline and justice prevail? Such questions remained unanswered as the new America faced the future.

Suggested Reading

Carl L. Davis, *Arming the Union* (1973)

Robert E. Denney, *Civil War Medicine* (1994)

Edward Hagerman, *The American Civil War and the Origins of Modern Warfare* (1988)

Herman Hattaway, *Shades of Blue and Gray: An Introductory Military History of the Civil War* (1997)

Gerald E. Linderman, *Embattled Courage: The Experience of Combat in the American Civil War* (1987)

David A. Mindell, *War, Technology, and Experience Aboard the USS "Monitor"* (2000)

James M. McPherson, *Battle Cry of Freedom* (1988)

Philip Paul Paludan, *A People's Contest* (1988)

Charles Royster, *The Destructive War* (1991)

Emory M. Thomas, *The Confederate Nation: 1861–1865* (1979)

Stephen R. Wise, *Lifeline of the Confederacy: Blockade Running During the Civil War* (1988)

Chronology

Date	Event
February 1861	The Confederate States of America established.
April 14, 1861	Fort Sumter falls to the Confederates.
July 21, 1861	First Battle of Manassas.
March 9, 1862	*Monitor* vs. *Virginia*.
May 20, 1862	The Homestead Act.
July 2, 1862	The Morrill (land-grant) Act.
August 29–30, 1862	Second Battle of Manassas.
September 17, 1862	Battle of Antietam.
January 1, 1863	Emancipation Proclamation takes effect.
July 3, 1863	Battle of Gettysburg.
September 1, 1864	Fall of Atlanta.
April 9, 1865	Lee surrenders at Appomattox.

Focus
QUESTIONS

■ **What were the major issues at stake in the political Reconstruction of the United States?**

■ **How did blacks and whites piece together their lives in the postwar South?**

■ **Why did Reconstruction come to an end in the South?**

■ **What national issues were resolved during Reconstruction, and what issues remained unresolved?**

"The trail of war," noted an English traveler to the Tennessee Valley in the late 1860s, "is visible throughout the valley in burnt up gin-houses, ruined bridges, mills, and factories . . . and in large tracts of once cultivated land stripped of every vestige of fencing." The city of Charleston, South Carolina, was "ruined"; "many fine mansions, long deserted, were fast mouldering into decay." Carl Schurz, a leading Republican and a general in the Union army, wrote that it was "difficult to imagine circumstances more unfavorable for the development of a calm and unprejudiced public opinion than those under which the southern people are at present laboring. . . . When the rebellion was put down they found themselves not only conquered in a political and military sense, but economically ruined."

The North's military victory had settled two critical issues: the **states of the Confederacy** would remain part of the Union, and slavery would be abolished everywhere in the United States. But the end of military hostilities did not mean that the problems that had spawned the war had all been solved, and the conquest of one region by another brought new issues to the fore. When would the rebellious states again participate in the national government? On what terms would these states be readmitted to the Union? How severely would the rebel leaders be punished? Most important, what would become of the South's black population, the ex-slaves—and, with them, of southern society as a whole? What should southern society look like after the war and after slavery?

The nation wrestled with these questions for more than a decade after the Civil War. Most white southerners hoped to restore as much of the antebellum order as they could; the 4 million freed slaves, not surprisingly, had very different visions of the future. Northerners were divided over how harsh or magnanimous a peace to impose on the conquered South; they also disagreed about the degree to which southern society would have to be transformed for the states of the Confederacy to regain power in the national government. The era of Reconstruction was tumultuous, filled with sharp partisan and regional conflict, bitter contests between Congress and the president, and recurrent outbreaks of violence in the South.

The changes wrought during this period, moreover, were not confined to the South. Reconstruction was national in scope, characterized everywhere by the growing economic prominence of industry and the political ascendancy of industrialists and financiers. Between 1865 and 1873, the nation's industrial output rose by nearly 75 percent, while more new miles of railroad track were laid than had existed before the Civil War. Manufacturing towns boomed throughout the Northeast. Chicago tripled its 1860 population and became a center of iron and steel production, meat packing, and the manufacture of agricultural machinery. Even more striking was the opening of the trans-Mississippi West through formal and informal—and sometimes downright shady—partnerships of government with railroad corporations and mining, lumber, and agricultural interests. Largely unsettled by Europeans in 1860, the West became the scene of rapid, helter-skelter development encouraged by the pro-business Republican Party.

The Fate of the Union

RECONSTRUCTION IN WARTIME

Even before the war ended, officials in Washington were taking steps to shape the contours of the postwar South and chart a course for its reintegration into the Union. The most fundamental issue on the agenda was slavery. Lincoln's 1863 Emancipation Proclamation clearly signaled the North's intention to bring an end to the peculiar institution. That intention was translated into law by the **Thirteenth Amendment to the Constitution,** approved by the Senate in 1864 and the House of Representatives in 1865: once ratified by the states, later in 1865, it permanently abolished slavery throughout the nation.

Lincoln, in 1863, also issued a Proclamation of Amnesty and Reconstruction, which spelled out the terms on which rebellious states could rejoin the Union. His action was based on the belief that Reconstruction was primarily an executive, rather than congressional, responsibility. The proclamation, commonly called the Ten-Percent Plan, reflected both his personal impulse to be magnanimous in victory and the hope that a generous Reconstruction policy might speed the end of the war. The plan offered a full pardon and the restoration of all property, except slaves, to all "persons" who took a loyalty oath and vowed to accept the abolition of slavery. Only a small number of high-ranking Confederate officials were deemed ineligible. When, in any state, such pledges numbered 10 percent of the number of votes cast in 1860, those who had vowed their loyalty could form a new state government. Once that government had determined to abolish slavery and provide for the education of black children, the state could be represented in Congress.

The Ten-Percent Plan was sketchy in its details and lenient in thrust: it did not address the political or civil rights of freedmen, and it put few obstacles in the way of ex-rebels who might seek to regain control of their state governments. The plan, consequently, drew criticism from congressional Republicans who believed that Reconstruction ought to include active support for the freedmen as well as a transformation of social and political life in the South.

The Republican alternative, sponsored by Senator Benjamin Wade of Ohio and Representative Henry Davis of Maryland, offered a more punitive approach. The Wade-Davis Bill, which Congress approved in July 1864, permitted

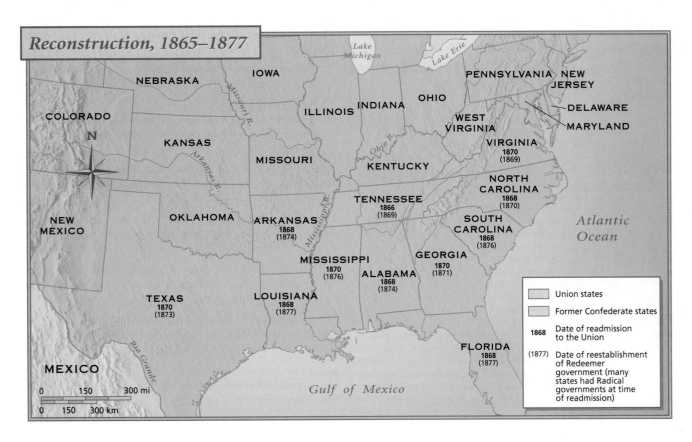

Reconstruction, 1865–1877

537

the states of the Confederacy to hold constitutional conventions and form new governments only after a majority of their voters had taken an "ironclad" loyalty oath. Officials of the Confederacy and those who had borne arms "voluntarily" would not be permitted to vote for, or participate in, these conventions. The state constitutions themselves had to ban slavery and repudiate all Confederate debts. Lincoln pocket-vetoed the Wade-Davis Bill (by not signing it), which angered his congressional critics and left the Ten-Percent Plan as the official, if vague, blueprint for Reconstruction.

Federal officials also found themselves confronted with another issue: once freed, how would ex-slaves support themselves? Should the government help them to become economically independent of their former masters? Lincoln, intent on restoring the southern states to the Union with maximum speed, believed that federal intervention in the affairs of the South ought to be held to a minimum. (His deepest hope, in fact, was that the "problem" of the ex-slaves would be solved by their emigration—a notion that was neither practical nor statesmanlike.) But many Radical Republicans, including Congressmen George Julian and Thaddeus Stevens, were convinced that the liberty of the

"Nearly everywhere, the freedmen displayed a preference for becoming self-supporting, for dividing the land into plots on which they could grow foodstuffs rather than cotton."

freedmen would be illusory unless they owned property, landed property in particular. Four million landless, impoverished black laborers would, according to Julian, quickly be reduced to "a system of wages slavery . . . more galling than slavery itself."

Julian and other Radicals proposed to address the problem by confiscating Confederate lands and redistributing them to the freedmen. This idea came to the fore as early as 1862, when Congress passed the second Confiscation Act, which made all rebel property liable to confiscation. (A previous act applied only to property used in support of the rebellion.) At Lincoln's insistence, however, the second Confiscation Act limited any seizure of land to the lifetime of the owner, which effectively prohibited its permanent redistribution to freedmen. Moreover, the Ten-Percent Plan, by guaranteeing to return all property to rebels who took a loyalty oath, seemed to preclude the mass redistribution of land. Nonetheless, in 1864 and 1865, proconfiscation sentiment mounted in Congress, and both houses repealed the limiting clauses of the 1862 resolution: there was significant sentiment in favor of a program that would substantially alter the distribution of land, and economic power, in the South.

Meanwhile, in parts of the South that had been captured by northern armies, military commanders found themselves dealing concretely, and urgently, with the same issues. On the South Carolina Sea Islands, in southern Louisiana, and eventually throughout the Mississippi Valley south of Vicksburg, victorious northern armies ended up in possession of fertile lands temporarily abandoned by their owners; at the same time, they became responsible for the welfare of tens of thousands of impoverished freedmen, many of them refugees. What ensued was a series of experiments in land and labor policy. Nearly everywhere, the freedmen displayed a preference for becoming self-supporting, for dividing the land into plots on which they could grow foodstuffs rather than cotton. In Davis Bend, Mississippi, a large group of slaves demonstrated they could also organize cotton production by themselves, as they took over and profitably ran plantations owned by Jefferson Davis and his brother. In most locales, however, northern officials adopted more traditional arrangements: they leased the lands to white owners and mobilized the freedmen to work as agricultural laborers, for low wages and on year-long contracts enforced by the army. By the war's

A depiction from *Harper's Weekly* of a freedmen's village, established under the auspices of the Freedmen's Bureau at Trent River, North Carolina, 1866.

end, hundreds of thousands of ex-slaves were working on plantations that were directly or indirectly superintended by the government.

It was against this backdrop that Congress, just before adjourning in March 1865, created the Bureau of Refugees, Freedmen, and Abandoned Lands, commonly called the Freedmen's Bureau. The bureau was charged with monitoring the condition of ex-slaves and delivering fuel, food, and clothing to the destitute, white and black alike. It also had the power to divide confiscated and abandoned lands into forty-acre parcels that could be rented, and eventually sold, to the freedmen. Although the bureau's powers were extraordinary—and set a precedent for public activism and intervention—Congress did not appropriate any funds for the bureau and anticipated that it would exist for only a year.

ANDREW JOHNSON AND PRESIDENTIAL RECONSTRUCTION

Six weeks after the Freedmen's Bureau was created, Abraham Lincoln was dead, and Andrew Johnson had become the fifteenth president of the United States. Johnson, a pro-Union Democrat from Tennessee, had been nominated for the vice-presidency by the Republicans in 1864 to broaden their appeal in the border states. He seemed eminently qualified for the job. Born in humble circumstances in North Carolina, Johnson had served an apprenticeship as a tailor and then moved to the mountains of eastern Tennessee, where he married, learned to read and write, acquired a farm, and began a long career in politics. Elected first to the state legislature, he then served as governor, U.S. congressman, and U.S. senator. Johnson courageously stuck by his Unionist principles when Tennessee seceded, presenting himself as a champion of the yeoman farmer and antagonist of the southern plantation elite. "I will show the stuck-up aristocrats who is running the country, " he once declared. "A cheap, purse-proud set they are, not half as good as the man who earns his bread by the sweat of his brow."

Experienced as he was, Johnson possessed personal traits that were not well suited to politics and that served him ill in the presidency. He was stubborn, intolerant of those who disagreed with him, reluctant to negotiate or compromise. "A slave to his passions and prejudices," as one contemporary noted, he was given to "unreasoning pugnacity." Indecisive and tactless, he lacked both close confidants and the suppleness of mind and vision so characteristic of his predecessor. A

Andrew Johnson, seventeenth president of the United States (1865–69), shortly before his inauguration.

deeply insecure man, he also seemed to crave approval from the very aristocrats he claimed to despise.

Johnson's political beliefs, moreover, differed in key respects from those of Lincoln and other Republicans. A Democrat and not a Whig, as Lincoln had been, Johnson's vision of the good society was Jacksonian and agrarian, rather than industrial or urban; he was wary of northern commercial interests and hostile to government intervention in the name of economic progress. Of equal importance, his racial views were conservative even by mid-nineteenth-century standards. Although Johnson fought the political dominance of aristocratic planters, he was not, until late in his career, an opponent of slavery. Indeed, he had bought some slaves himself, and he once voiced the peculiar wish "that every head of a family in the United States had one slave to take the drudgery and menial service off his family." In 1866, after a meeting with Frederick Douglass, Johnson commented that Douglass was "just like any nigger . . . he would sooner cut a white man's throat than not."

Nonetheless, Johnson's accession to the presidency was initially welcomed by the Radical Republicans, who believed that the Tennesseean's vision of Reconstruction was closer to their own than Lincoln's had been. Senator Zechariah Chan-

539

dler of Michigan even proclaimed that "the Almighty continued Mr. Lincoln in office as long as he was useful, and then substituted a better man to finish the work." In the wake of Lincoln's assassination, a punitive mood swept the North, and Johnson's public utterances lent support to the notion that he would not be lenient in his treatment of the rebels. "Treason is a crime and must be made odious," he declared. "Traitors must be impoverished. . . . They must not only be punished, but their social power must be destroyed."

Johnson's first acts as president suggested that he would depart little from the course charted by his predecessor. Although Congress had adjourned in March 1865 and was not scheduled to meet again until December, Johnson declined to call a special session because he, like Lincoln, believed that Reconstruction was primarily an executive responsibility. In May and June, he issued a series of proclamations that replaced the Ten-Percent Plan. The first was a proclamation of amnesty and restitution that granted pardons and the restoration of all property rights (except slave ownership) to everyone who took an oath avowing loyalty to the Union and support for emancipation. Confederate officials, as well as owners of taxable property valued at more than $20,000, were ineligible, although they could apply for amnesty individually to the president. (Johnson, true to his rhetoric, was taking aim at the rich as well as at political and military leaders.) Johnson then issued orders appointing provisional governors and instructing them to call state constitutional conventions; only white men who had received amnesty would be eligible to vote for delegates to the conventions. In order to rejoin the Union, these conventions were expected to abolish slavery, nullify their acts of secession, and repudiate all Confederate debts.

Although most Radical Republicans were critical of Johnson's willingness to exclude blacks, including ex-soldiers, from the suffrage, his plan seemed, for a time, to be working. The provisional governors were generally pro-Union Democrats, and most delegates to the constitutional conventions were either Unionists or reluctant Confederates. Ex-rebels took the loyalty oath en masse, while 15,000 members of the elite applied to Johnson personally for pardons.

But the white South—perhaps sensing the president's personal sympathies as a southerner as well as his hopes of rebuilding a national Democratic Party that could carry him to reelection—grew defiant of its northern conquerors. The elected governor of Louisiana began to fire Unionist officeholders, replacing them with ex-Confederates. Mississippi and South Carolina refused to repudiate their Confederate debt; Texas and Mississippi chose not to ratify the Thirteenth Amendment; several states repealed without repudiating their secession ordinances. In the fall elections of 1865, large numbers of ex-Confederates were elected to office, particularly in the lower South: among them were twenty-five ex-Confederate leaders (including Alexander Stephens, the former vice-president of the Confederacy) who were elected to the U.S. Congress. Meanwhile, rebels whose lands had been seized were demanding their return, a demand that Johnson often bent over backward to satisfy.

Led by Mississippi and South Carolina, the new state governments also passed elaborate laws to govern the civil, social, and economic behavior of the freedmen. Some of this legislation, such as prohibitions on intermarriage or black jury service, also existed in the North. But the Black Codes, as these laws came to be called, went a great deal further, severely restricting the economic rights of the freedmen. In Mississippi, freedmen were required to sign year-long labor contracts that they could not break without forfeiting their wages and being subject to arrest; prospective employers could not offer a higher wage to a laborer already under contract; freedmen were prohibited from renting land in urban areas and could be arrested for vagrancy if they could not provide evidence of

Under the Black Code of Florida, any man fined for vagrancy and unable to pay the fine could have his services sold to the highest bidder. This engraving depicts a freedman's services sold at auction, 1867.

being employed. In South Carolina, African Americans had to obtain a license and pay a tax to perform any work other than farm work or domestic service, while Louisiana and Texas tried to force black women to work by specifying that labor contracts had to include "all the members of the family able to work." Young blacks deemed to lack "adequate" parental support could be forcibly bound out as apprentices to their former masters. The Black Codes made clear that ex-slaves would be second-class economic citizens, at best.

By the time the Thirty-ninth Congress finally convened in December 1865, all of the Confederate states had formed new governments and elected representatives to Congress. President Johnson, acknowledging that Congress had the constitutional right to judge the qualifications of its own members, urged that these representatives be seated—which would, in effect, have brought an end to Reconstruction. Congress, however, declined to do so. Instead, expressing deep concern about reports emanating from the South, it formed a Joint Committee on Reconstruction to investigate the impact of Johnson's policies.

Despite this rebuff, the president was well positioned to carry out his Reconstruction policy or something close to it. Although Republicans dominated Congress by three to one, there were serious divisions within the party. Roughly half of all congressional Republicans (and more in the Senate) belonged to a loose coalition of moderates and conservatives. They sought more ample guarantees of black rights as well as legislation to protect freedmen and Unionists from violence, but they were not altogether dissatisfied with Johnson's approach, and they shared his desire to readmit the rebel states as expeditiously as possible. Standing in opposition to this coalition was the strong and ideologically coherent Radical wing of the party. Drawn primarily from New England and the northern states west of New England, the Radicals were moralists whose political views were forged by the struggle against slavery and by the successes of small-scale, competitive capitalism in the North. They sought to remake the South in the image of the North, a goal that demanded an active federal government, black suffrage, and land distribution. Committed and passionate as they were, most Radicals were nonetheless aware that they were out ahead of northern public opinion (three northern states had rejected black suffrage in 1865), and that they themselves were outnumbered in Congress.

Soon after Congress convened, the Joint Committee on Reconstruction, chaired by "moderate" senator William Fessenden of Maine, began extensive hearings, at which witnesses testified to the upsurge of violence, discrimination, and Confederate sentiment in the South. "It is of weekly, if not of daily, occurrence that freedmen are murdered" in Texas, reported General George Custer. In rural Alabama, "gangs of ruffians, mostly operating at night, hold individuals under a reign of terror," another general observed. A Confederate colonel was quoted as saying, "You have not subdued us; we will try you again." In response to such testimony, Republican moderates, led by the influential senator Lyman Trumbull of Illinois, drafted two pieces of legislation to protect the freedmen. The first extended the powers and life of the Freedmen's Bureau: the bill called for direct funding of the bureau, empowered it to build and support schools, and authorized bureau agents to assume legal jurisdiction over crimes involving blacks and over state officials who denied blacks their civil rights. The second measure, the Civil Rights Bill, defined blacks (indeed all native-born persons except Indians) as U.S. citizens; it also specified the rights inherent in citizenship, including the right to make contracts, own or rent property, and have access to the courts. No state could deprive any citizen of those rights; cases involving such violations would be heard in federal rather than state courts; and individuals who deprived a citizen of his rights would be subject to fine or imprisonment. Sweeping as the Civil Rights Bill was, it did not enfranchise blacks, permit them to sit on juries, or desegregate public accommodations.

To the shock of many, especially in moderate Republican circles, President Johnson vetoed both the Freedmen's Bureau and Civil Rights Bills in February and March of 1866. In his veto messages, he insisted that the bills were illegal because they had been passed while the states of the South were unrepresented in Congress, a claim that completely denied Congress the right to formulate Reconstruction policy, or any policy, for that matter. Johnson attacked the Freedmen's Bureau as a fiscally unsound and constitutionally dubious agency, while maintaining that the Civil Rights Bill was an unconstitutional intrusion of the federal government into the

> *"The Radicals were moralists whose political views were forged by the struggle against slavery and by the successes of small-scale, competitive capitalism in the North. They sought to remake the South in the image of the North."*

541

affairs of states. His quarrel was not with the details of the bills but with the principles that lay behind them.

The president's vetoes were grounded in both conviction and political strategy. As a lifelong Democrat, Johnson believed in strong state governments and limited national power; he was also convinced that blacks were not the equals of whites and that government policies designed to promote equality could only have undesirable consequences. (He raised the specter of interracial marriage in one of his veto messages.) Yet Johnson's actions were also aimed at dividing the Republican Party and isolating the Radicals. Doing so would leave a coalition of Democrats and moderate-to-conservative Republicans in control of Congress and boost his chances of being elected president in 1868.

Here, Johnson miscalculated badly. Instead of dividing the Republican Party, his vetoes pushed the moderates toward more radical positions. While Democrats, North and South, celebrated Johnson's actions, moderate and even conservative Republicans found themselves with a choice between allying with the Radicals or abandoning goals for which the war had been fought in the first place. In fact, they had no real choice, unless they were prepared to leave the freedmen at the mercy of the same southerners who had enslaved them. Moderate and conservative Republicans broke with the president and sharply attacked his policies. "Those who formerly defended [Johnson] are now readiest in his condemnation," observed one Republican leader.

THE FOURTEENTH AMENDMENT

The Republicans seized the initiative in the spring of 1866. In April, Congress overrode Johnson's veto of the Civil Rights Bill (marking the first time that a significant piece of legislation was passed over a presidential veto), and it then revised the Freedmen's Bureau Bill so that it, too, could be passed over a veto. In addition, the Joint Committee on Reconstruction worked throughout the spring to draft a constitutional amendment that would secure key objectives in a form that could not easily be reversed by presidential action or shifting legislative majorities. By the middle of June, the **Fourteenth Amendment** had received the necessary two-thirds majority from both houses of Congress and was sent to the states for ratification.

The Fourteenth Amendment contained three clauses that dealt with specific post–Civil War issues. One clause upheld the validity of the national (Union) debt while declaring that neither the United States nor any individual state would repay any debts incurred by the Confederacy during the rebellion. A second barred from public office anyone who, as an office-holder, had taken an oath to support the Constitution and then violated that oath by engaging in insurrection. A third mandated that a state that kept any adult male citizens from voting would have its representation in Congress reduced proportionately. This last section was designed to prevent southern states from increasing their representation as a result of the demise of slavery (a slave, in the original Constitution, had counted as only three-fifths of a person for the purpose of representation) while still denying freedmen the right to vote. It implicitly recognized that states had the right to deny men the franchise because of their race, but it reduced their power in the national government if they did so. To the chagrin of women's suffrage advocates, the amendment, by using the word "male," also implicitly recognized the right of states to deny women the vote without incurring any penalty.

Section 1 of the Fourteenth Amendment also addressed immediate issues but in language that was deliberately general and that would long reverberate across the constitutional landscape. This section nullified the *Dred Scott* decision (which had denied the citizenship of blacks) by declaring all native-born and naturalized persons to be citizens; at the same time, it prohibited the states from abridging the "privileges or immunities" of citizens. Section 1 also declared that no state could "deprive any person of life, liberty, or property, without due process of law"; nor could a state deny to any person "the equal protection of the laws." Although the precise meaning of these phrases would be debated by lawyers and judges for more than a century, their core intent was clear. The Fourteenth Amendment enshrined the principle of "equality before the law" in the Constitution; it also authorized the federal government to actively defend equal rights when they were threatened by state governments. Written to protect African Americans in the post–Civil War South, the amendment articulated principles so significant and far-reaching that they would, over time, be applied to people and circumstances well removed from Reconstruction.

The Fourteenth Amendment became the platform of the Republican Party in the congressional elections of 1866, which were widely regarded as a referendum on Reconstruction. Opposing the Republicans was a new political grouping, the National Union Movement, organized by President Johnson as a coalition of conservatives from both parties. Johnson hoped that the movement could mobilize support for ending

Reconstruction and readmitting the southern states while avoiding the taint of treason that still clung to the Democrats.

Yet the National Union was destined to defeat: the northern electorate remained suspicious of Democrats, whatever they called themselves, and incidents of mob violence against blacks in Memphis and New Orleans graphically underscored the need for the continued protection of black rights. Johnson himself antagonized voters with an ill-tempered campaign tour around the nation. "Why not hang Thad Stevens and Wendell Phillips?" he shouted to an audience in Cleveland. The Republicans won a far more lopsided victory than anyone had predicted, gaining ground in every northern state and retaining large majorities in both houses of Congress.

RADICAL RECONSTRUCTION AND THE IMPEACHMENT OF ANDREW JOHNSON

Despite the election results, neither Johnson nor the political leaders of the South seemed ready to capitulate, or even conciliate. Johnson defiantly predicted that his allies would win the next round of elections, while the southern legislatures, with Johnson's backing, emphatically rejected the Fourteenth Amendment. This intransigence tipped the balance for many moderate Republicans, leading them to embrace black suffrage as a central element in reordering the South. Without the franchise, blacks would be powerless to protect themselves against whites who would not accept them as equal citizens.

Working together, the moderates and the Radicals devised a Reconstruction Act that was passed in March 1867 over Johnson's veto. The act declared existing state governments to be merely provisional and reinstituted military authority everywhere in the ex-Confederacy except Tennessee, which had ratified the Fourteenth Amendment and been readmitted to the Union. The bill also outlined the steps that states would have to follow to regain full membership in the national government: holding new constitutional conventions (elected by adult males), ratifying the Fourteenth Amendment, and adopting constitutions that permitted blacks to vote. In the first months of 1867, Congress passed measures to limit the president's ability to obstruct Reconstruction. Among them was the Tenure of Office Act, which required the president to obtain the consent of the Senate before dismissing any official whose appointment required senatorial confirmation.

The Republicans were right to anticipate that Johnson would attempt to obstruct their program. Throughout 1867

A contemporary engraving showing Andrew Johnson's attempt to undermine Radical Republican candidates during his midwestern "swing around the circle" in late 1866.

and early 1868, he interfered in every way he could, appointing military commanders unsympathetic to the Republicans' goals, removing officials who seemed too sympathetic, insisting on interpretations of the Reconstruction Act that weakened its thrust, and encouraging the South to defy federal law. The skirmishing came to a head early in 1868 when Johnson removed Secretary of War Edwin Stanton, a Lincoln appointee and the one member of Johnson's cabinet who favored Radical Reconstruction. As secretary of war, Stanton occupied a critical place in the chain of command between Washington and the Union armies occupying the South. His removal, according to the Republicans, constituted a violation of the Tenure of Office Act.

Johnson's attempt to remove Stanton (who refused to turn in the keys to his office) prompted the House of Representatives to take the unprecedented step of impeaching the president. According to the Constitution, federal officials could be impeached for "treason, bribery, or other high crimes and misdemeanors," and many Radicals had talked of impeachment for more than a year, but it was the removal of Stanton that prompted some moderates to join their ranks. After two-thirds of the House had voted to impeach, the process moved to the Senate, where a two-thirds vote was necessary to convict the president and remove him from office.

The trial of Andrew Johnson in the Senate lasted from March 13 to May 26, 1868. Johnson's defenders maintained that what he had done was not an impeachable offense, that the president was merely testing the constitutionality of the Tenure of Office Act, and that the act didn't actually apply to

543

A cartoon implying that President Johnson lacked the capacity to grasp the U.S. Constitution and was subsequently flattened by it.

the Radicals in the House, and his counterpart in the Senate, Charles Sumner of Massachusetts. Stevens, the Republican floor leader of the House and the senior member of the Joint Committee on Reconstruction, was widely respected for his honesty and idealism while feared for his sharp tongue and mastery of parliamentary tactics. Although frequently outvoted, Stevens saw himself as the leader of a righteous vanguard that would press forward the cause of social and racial justice against all opposition; even in death, he made a statement for racial equality by asking to be buried in a black cemetery. Sumner similarly was a man of principle, devoted to the notion that all individuals had to be equal before the law. An eloquent, charismatic figure, he had little patience for day-to-day politics, but he wielded enormous popular influence and was regarded by many African Americans as their most devoted champion in government.

The obstinacy of the white South lent support to the land-reform arguments of Stevens, Sumner, and others. Confiscation and redistribution, as Stevens pointed out, would simultaneously destroy the power of the plantation aristocracy and provide an economic foundation for black political and civil rights. "Strip a proud nobility of their bloated states; reduce them to a level with plain republicans; send them forth to labor and teach their children to enter the workshops or handle the plow, and you will thus humble the proud traitors." Appealing as this vision may have been, however, the confiscation of land conflicted with basic Republican values: private property was to be protected, not seized, and free labor was to be rewarded with wages, not with gifts of land from the government. *The Nation*, a respected Republican magazine, voiced the fear that the government giving freedmen land would imply "that there are other ways of securing comfort or riches than honest work." The *New York Tribune* proclaimed that "people who want farms work for them. The

Thaddeus Stevens.

only class we know that takes other people's property because they want it is largely represented in Sing Sing." The Radical argument that blacks had already worked hard for this land, for two centuries, fell on few receptive ears.

Stanton anyway (because he had been appointed by Lincoln). Yet the legal arguments never did more than cloak the real issue: did Johnson's unceasing opposition to congressional Reconstruction, coupled with his apparent intention of restoring ex-Confederates to power and to the Union, constitute sufficient grounds to remove him from office? Most senators thought that they did. But a sizable minority did not—in part for legal reasons, in part because they feared setting a destabilizing precedent, and in part because they did not want Benjamin Wade, the Radical leader of the Senate, to ascend to the presidency. Johnson, who behaved with uncharacteristic decorum during the Senate proceedings, was acquitted by a margin of 1 vote. The final tally was 35 to 19 in favor of conviction, with 7 Republicans voting for acquittal.

Johnson's acquittal was not the only defeat suffered by the Radical Republicans in 1867 and 1868. In the state elections of 1867, black suffrage was rejected in Ohio, Minnesota, and Kansas, while the Democrats, who openly paraded their hostility to black rights, registered electoral gains in many northern states.

THE DEFEAT OF LAND REFORM

The Radical idea of confiscating Confederate lands and distributing them to the freedmen was never widely embraced in the Republican Party, but it had powerful supporters. Among them were Thaddeus Stevens of Pennsylvania, the leader of

This ideological resistance thwarted efforts at land redistribution in the mid-1860s. The issue came to a head in the spring and summer of 1867 when Stevens—gravely ill but fiercely committed to the cause—introduced a bill to give forty acres of confiscated land to each freedman. Stevens hoped that continued southern defiance would finally prod exasperated moderates to accept confiscation, just as they had come to endorse civil rights and black suffrage. But his hopes were not fulfilled. Although the possibility of land reform captured the imagination of both the freedmen and poor whites in the South, northern Republicans were simply not prepared to go that far. Investment in the southern economy was rumored to be frozen because of fears of confiscation, and moderate Republicans began to worry that confiscation would both hinder the growth of the party in the South and harm relations between labor and capital in the North. By the end of the summer of 1867, a congressional committee of Republicans issued a declaration that Reconstruction would not infringe property rights in the South. Land redistribution—the most radical approach to reconstructing the South—was a dead letter.

While these momentous events, and nonevents, were transpiring in Washington, the program of congressional Reconstruction was proceeding in the South. Under the supervision of the army, whites and blacks were registered to vote, and in the fall of 1867 elections were held for new constitutional conventions. Many whites boycotted the elections, so a large majority of the elected delegates were Republicans, roughly a third of whom were black, with another quarter consisting of recent migrants from the North.

These delegates, derided by southern conservatives as "ignorant Negroes cooperating with a gang of white adventurers," drew up impressively progressive constitutions. Not only did they institute male suffrage (often expressly repudiating financial and literacy requirements for voting), they also created statewide public school systems for both whites and blacks and set up progressive tax systems that lightened the tax burden of small landowners. The constitutions were ratified, beginning in the spring of 1868, and Republican state governments began to be elected soon thereafter, thanks in good part to black voters. The Republican governments quickly approved the Fourteenth Amendment, which made their states eligible to be readmitted to full membership in the Union. In the summer of 1868, the representatives of seven states were seated in Congress (joining Tennessee); by 1870, Virginia, Mississippi, and Texas were also readmitted. In formal terms, at least, the Union was restored.

THE ELECTION OF 1868

Although the Republicans had failed to remove Andrew Johnson from office, they had high hopes of electing a new president in 1868. To carry the party's banner, they nominated sixty-six-year-old Ulysses Grant, a West Point gradu-

Lithograph showing a parade held in Baltimore in May 1870 to celebrate ratification of the Fifteenth Amendment, which prohibited states from denying men the vote because of their race, color, or previous condition of servitude. President Grant is at the upper left, Vice-President Colfax at the upper right; also pictured are Abraham Lincoln (lower left), John Brown (lower right), and, in the threesome at top, Frederick Douglass (middle) and Hiram Revels (right).

An engraving of the First African Church at Richmond, Virginia, 1874. Churches were among the most important institutions in the lives of freedmen in the years after the war.

they had not been permitted to move as slaves. As Richard Edwards, a black preacher in Florida, observed in 1865: "So long ez de shadder ob de gret house falls acrost you, you ain't gwine ter feel lake no free man, an' you ain't gwiner ter feel lak no free 'oman. You mus' all move—you mus' move clar away from de ole places what you knows, ter de new places what you don't know, whey you kin raise yore head douten no fear Marse Dis ur Marse Tudder."

Yet moving did not mean going far. Although there was a visible migration from the countryside to the city and, over time, a significant postwar migration southward (to the belt of states stretching from Florida to Texas), most freedmen chose to remain in nearby rural areas. Their first postemancipation homes were different spots in a familiar world.

They also began rebuilding that world, starting with their families. One of the most compelling goals of the freedmen was to reunite families that had been torn apart by slave sales: "in their eyes, the work of emancipation was incomplete until the families dispersed by slavery were reunited," observed a Freedmen's Bureau agent in South Carolina. "They had a passion for getting together. Every mother's son among them seemed to be in search of his mother; every mother in search of her children." Freedmen and women placed ads in newspapers in search of their loved ones and walked hundreds of miles to find them. Men and women also formalized relationships they had not been permitted to solemnize under slavery: mass weddings, with dozens of couples at a time, were

frequent occurrences in the early months of emancipation. Family identities were further reinforced as the freedmen began to take last names, often selecting the name of someone known to them. "Precious few of 'em ever took that of their old masters," noted an overseer in Louisiana.

In addition to their families, the freedmen sought to build or rebuild two other institutions: churches and schools. Denied equal footing in the biracial, yet white-dominated, churches that the South inherited from the antebellum era, African Americans withdrew from those congregations and created their own religious communities. In Charleston, the first new building erected after the war was a black church, and ten more had been constructed by 1866. Churches—sometimes makeshift, sometimes not—sprouted up across the countryside, serving both as places of worship and as centers for community social life.

Schools were built with even greater ardor. Since schooling had been denied to most slaves (90 percent of whom were illiterate in 1860), the freedmen greeted their emancipation as an opportunity to learn to read and write and to obtain education for their children. Helped by funding from the Freedmen's Bureau, northern benevolent societies, and, later, the Republican state governments, the freedmen began operating schools everywhere—sometimes committing large portions of their own meager funds to keep schools running. Schools held sessions in churches, warehouses, storerooms, and stables; the Bryant Slave Mart was transformed into a school in Savannah, and in New Orleans a former slave pen was reborn

A congregation of African Americans in Washington, D.C., 1876.

548

A racially integrated jury in a southern courtroom, 1867.

as the Frederick Douglass School. In rural areas, freedmen negotiated labor contracts that included educational provisions for children; field hands in Selma, Alabama, demanded that their employer provide the materials to build a school, which they would construct and operate by themselves. Education was a source of independence and autonomy, second in importance only to the ownership of land.

Although ex-slaves tacitly accepted racially separate churches and schools, they pressed for changes in the rules and conventions governing social interactions between blacks and whites. Particularly in urban areas, freedmen did not always stand when spoken to by whites or touch their hats or cede sidewalks to their "betters." They also began to question rules that either banned blacks or gave them inferior accommodations on railroads, streetcars, steamboats, or other public facilities. Grounded as much in custom as in law, these rules were sometimes challenged by freedmen through civil disobedience, litigation, and appeals to Union army commanders; occasionally the freedmen even won. A newspaper article in 1867 reported that in Charleston, "another streetcar difficulty occurred today. Two negroes got inside a streetcar, and, refusing to leave, were ejected by the police." In some states, the Republican governments of the late 1860s and early 1870s passed legislation outlawing discrimination in public facilities. Although rarely enforced, these civil rights laws did, at least briefly, help to diminish the strength of the color line.

To most whites, in contrast, the end of slavery only heightened the need for racial separation: "if we have social equality, we shall have intermarriage, and if we have intermarriage we shall degenerate," warned one anxious survivor of the war. Indeed, whites, too, were rebuilding their world during Reconstruction, socially as well as physically. In the sugar- and rice-growing regions of the coastal Carolinas, Georgia, and Louisiana, patterns of land ownership, wealth, and power changed substantially in the wake of the war—although that was not true where the economy was based on tobacco or cotton. Yet even where the social structure changed little, whites had to adjust to a postemancipation social order that was unsettling. Ex-slaves could not be counted on to be deferential, to remain apart, to take orders, to stay in their "place." Whites often described the freedmen as "insolent" or "saucy."

White southerners also found that they could not count on the coercive powers of the state to compel the freedmen to act "properly." In contrast to the antebellum world, state power, particularly after 1866, was wielded by Union army commanders and elected officials who were no longer committed to maintaining white control over blacks. In part for this reason, whites frequently began to take the law into their own hands, making this one of the most violent—if not *the* most violent—periods in the nation's history. Acts of violence against blacks, provoked by black "impudence" or "disrespect," were commonplace. In Greenville, South Carolina, a group of young white men stabbed a black man who had refused to step off a sidewalk when their paths crossed. Race riots, in which blacks were attacked and beaten by whites, erupted in Memphis, Charleston, New Orleans, Atlanta, Richmond, and Norfolk (Virginia): during the Memphis riot in 1866, white mobs killed forty-six African Americans.

This engraving depicts an incident that occurred in early May 1866, when whites assaulted blacks in Memphis, killing forty-six.

"Worse Than Slavery," an 1874 cartoon by Thomas Nast, depicts the plight of African Americans in the post–Civil War South.

Antiblack violence was also expressed in a more organized fashion, through groups such as the Ku Klux Klan. The Klan was founded in Tennessee in 1866 as a social club, but it rapidly became a terrorist organization, dedicated to restoring full-blown white supremacy throughout the South. Klansmen—who came from all walks of life, including the landed elite—roamed the countryside dressed in white sheets and assaulting, beating, and sometimes murdering freedmen, northerners, Republicans, and wartime Unionists. They attacked black churches and schools as well as interracial couples, individuals who had been "impudent" or had financial disputes with whites, and freedmen who were outspoken politically or successful economically. Intent on destroying the Republican Party and preventing blacks from wielding political power, the Klan particularly targeted political leaders: at least 10 percent of the black members of the constitutional conventions of the late 1860s became victims of violence. And over time, the Klan's violence succeeded in silencing opposition.

LAND AND LABOR

Agriculture remained the heart of the southern economy, but just how it would be organized was sharply contested. Most freedmen wanted to own their own land, but within a year after the end of the war, almost all the land that had been dis-tributed to blacks had been returned to its white owners, and the possibility of any significant governmental distribution of land soon became remote. It was, moreover, exceedingly difficult for ex-slaves to buy land even if they had the means to do so: most whites would not, or were afraid to, sell land to freedmen. Consequently, the great majority of ex-slaves remained landless tillers of the soil; as late as 1880, only 20 percent of all black farm operatives owned land.

Whites, on the other hand, owned land, but needed labor to make their property productive. In pursuit of inexpensive, hardworking labor, southern whites tried to attract immigrants or to import gangs of Chinese workers, but had limited success. The agricultural labor force would have to be black, and in the eyes of many whites, it would therefore have to be coerced and closely supervised. "The nigger," commented one Alabama farmer, "*never* works except when he is compelled to." Becoming a cheap, disciplined plantation labor force was not, however, what the freedmen envisioned as their postemancipation future, even if they failed to own land. They preferred to farm small plots of land as families rather than to work in closely overseen gangs, reminiscent of slavery; they also wanted the freedom to move, change employers, and bargain over terms.

This clash of interests was played out in annual, sometimes daily, skirmishes between employers and employees: over the payment of wages, the terms of credit, the timing of pay-

This **1886** engraving shows a field hand in the South harvesting cotton with an early mechanical harvesting machine.

ments, the rental of land, the selection of crops, the payment of debts. It was also expressed legally and politically. Landowners, often with the support of the Freedmen's Bureau and the Union army, tried to impose annual contracts on the freedmen, which were particularly stifling when the freedmen were paid only at year's end and were penalized for leaving early. The Black Codes passed by the Johnson governments sought to limit the physical mobility of blacks (as did vagrancy laws aimed at discouraging urban migration) and restrict their job options. Landowners also sought to pass laws that would prevent employers from hiring someone else's employees—laws that would, in effect, prohibit the labor market from functioning as a market. When the Republican governments were in power, the tables were turned: laws restricting labor's rights were repealed, new measures helped to guarantee that workers would be paid when employers sold their property (including crops), and taxes on land were increased to encourage large landholders to sell portions of their property.

From this skirmishing and experimentation emerged the system of sharecropping that would dominate southern agriculture for decades. Sharecropping was a fairly simple mode of organizing agriculture: the landowner provided land and tools, the sharecropper performed all the labor, and they split the crop (often fifty-fifty, but the terms varied widely). Or, stated differently, land was rented to tenants, with the rental payment being a share of the crop. This system appeared to have advantages for both blacks and whites. Blacks were able to work in individual household units, with some autonomy and independence; whites were assured that blacks had an incentive to work hard and produce a good crop. By 1880, more than half of all rural blacks worked on shares.

Alongside sharecropping, there developed another institution that proved to be just as durable but far more pernicious in its consequences: the crop-lien system. Farmers always needed credit—to purchase seed, supplies, fertilizer—and before the war, they had borrowed annually from "factors," or banks, pledging their land as collateral for loans that would be repaid once their crops were sold. After the war, however, the banking system was shattered, and the breakup of plantations into small farms operated by tenants (whether sharecroppers or cash tenants) meant that there were many more farmers who needed to borrow, most of whom did not own land that could serve as collateral.

Into this vacuum in the credit system stepped country merchants, many of whom were also landowners. These mer-

chants advanced supplies to farmers, who secured the loans by giving the merchants a "lien" on their crops, which meant, in effect, that the merchant owned, or had the right to sell, the crop. The merchant, in addition, charged the farmer interest on the supplies advanced (often at exorbitant rates) and sometimes was able to set the price at which the crop would be sold. In theory, this was a mutually beneficial set of transactions: a farmer who worked hard, had good weather, and sold his crop at a good price would pay off his debt to the merchant at the end of the year and pocket the difference.

But things rarely worked that simply. Most merchants had monopolies in their local areas and thus had the power to dictate the terms of the transaction, limiting the chances of a farmer actually profiting from his labors. Moreover, bad weather or declining prices would often leave the farmer in debt to the merchant at the end of the year; this generally obliged him to borrow from the merchant (and perhaps rent the merchant's land) again the following year. Most important, perhaps, merchants decided what crops the farmers

Upland Cotton, a painting by Winslow Homer of sharecroppers at work, 1879.

The Way They Live, a painting by Thomas Anshuntz depicting sharecroppers, 1879.

would grow, and they commonly demanded that farmers grow *the* cash crop: cotton. Consequently, farmers grew more cotton and less food, which obliged them to buy foodstuffs from the merchants and increase their indebtedness. Even worse, this practice led to a sharp increase in cotton production, which lowered cotton prices (and thus incomes) through much of the 1870s. In this way, small farmers became trapped in a system of "debt peonage," while the South's economy became excessively dependent on cotton.

Thanks in part to declining cotton prices, southern agriculture had difficulty recovering from the war. The region's per capita agricultural output remained below prewar levels for the remainder of the nineteenth century, while the per capita income of whites in the cotton states declined by one-third between the late 1850s and 1879. The income of blacks, of course, increased sharply in the first years after emancipation, but that trend was not sustained, and blacks continued to earn only half as much as whites.

Of equal importance, the stagnation of southern agriculture was accompanied by the region's failure to generate much industrial growth. In the eyes of many Republicans, North and South, such growth was essential: railroad construction and industrial development, they believed, would stimulate urban growth and immigration, thereby enriching the region and reducing the power of landowning planters. State and local governments, particularly those dominated by the Republicans in the late 1860s, sought to encourage railroad construction and industrial growth. They offered railroad corporations financial inducements, including outright monetary grants, to get them to rebuild old lines and build new ones. To lure private enterprise, state legislatures passed laws to protect the property rights of corporations, to provide cheap labor in the form of leased convicts, and to exempt many enterprises (including railroads, banks, and factories) from taxation.

These efforts failed. Although the railroad system was rebuilt and even extended to many interior towns, the overall growth was modest: 7,000 miles of new track were laid in the South between 1865 and 1879, compared with 45,000 miles in the North. The state governments had difficulty paying for the ambitious railroad projects they had launched, and they ended up both raising taxes and, later, cutting back on their commitments. The flow of funds between the public and private sectors, moreover, created fertile soil for corruption: bribery became commonplace in some states, and the Republican Party was tainted by publicly visible corruption. Despite the incentives offered to private enterprise, the politically unstable southern states had difficulty attracting northern and European investment, a problem that was compounded after 1873 by the economic depression that gripped the nation. The fruits of the Republican dedication to the "gospel of prosperity" were limited, and the planting of new industries proceeded far too slowly to alter the overwhelmingly agricultural character of the region.

The Road to Redemption

While the South was rebuilding, the North was booming. The economy grew rapidly, if unevenly, during the war, and, after a brief pause, the growth resumed after Appomattox. Between 1865 and 1873, industrial output soared, while 3 million immigrants poured into the country, most of them headed for the cities of the North and West. The North's victory was, in a sense, a victory of industrial capitalism over a more agrarian, paternalist social order, and the postwar years were a celebration of that triumph. Not only was the Republican Party (which was closely linked to the interests and personnel of industrial capitalism) in power in Washington, but the first transcontinental railroad was completed, George Westinghouse invented air brakes for trains, and the Bessemer process for making steel (by blowing air through molten iron) was introduced into the United States. With fitting symbolism, the stock ticker was invented in 1872 by Thomas Alva Edison.

"Throughout the South, ex-slaves became active participants not only in politics but in governance."

This unleashing of productive, and speculative, energies was felt throughout the North and in the West, which, with the issue of slavery resolved, was thrown wide open to new settlement. Businesses were built, fortunes were made, and new territories were inhabited. Yet the very ebullience of the economy, followed later by the shock of economic depression, had the effect of drawing attention away from Reconstruction, the South, and the issues that had led to war. By the mid 1870s, the eyes of the nation were more focused on the stock ticker than on the still-incomplete process of reconstructing the South.

THE REPUBLICAN PARTY IN THE SOUTH

By the late 1860s, the fate of Reconstruction was closely tied to the fate of the Republican Party in the South. Yet despite their electoral victories in 1868, the Republicans' hold on power was tenuous. Support for the party came from up-country whites (small farmers, many of whom had been Unionists), from low-country entrepreneurs who sympathized with the economic policies of the Republicans, and from northern immigrants. The great majority of Republican voters, however, were black, and the Republican leadership was convinced that the party's fortunes, North and South, would be imperiled if it failed to attract more white support and became identified as the "black" party.

Despite these concerns, the Republican Party made it possible for sizable numbers of African Americans to participate in electoral politics for the first time. Not only did freedmen vote, they were also elected to office. Fourteen blacks, including some who were self-educated and others who were lawyers, were elected to Congress. Two went to the Senate from Missis-

sippi; one of these, Hiram Revels, was a Methodist minister who had organized black regiments at the outset of the war. Several held statewide office, many were elected to state legislatures, and hundreds of black men held local positions. Only in South Carolina did the freedmen hold office in numbers proportionate to their share of the electorate, but throughout the South ex-slaves became active participants not only in politics but in governance.

The policies implemented by the Republican state governments were aimed at protecting the freedmen, modernizing Southern society, and constructing a more active state. They created public schools for both whites and blacks, revamped the judicial system, and built hospitals, penitentiaries, and asylums. In addition to rebuilding the infrastructure that had been destroyed during the war (roads, bridges, public buildings), the governments actively sought private investment in railroads and industry. Yet these projects cost money—which meant raising taxes and increasing the public debt by issuing bonds. Although not high by northern standards, tax rates by 1870 were often triple or quadruple the rates that had prevailed in 1860. Not surprisingly, such sharp increases in an era of economic stress spawned vehement opposition: in nearly every state, white landowners, who resented not only paying taxes but paying taxes that benefited both freedmen and allegedly corrupt Republican officials, formed taxpayers' associations to demand reductions in state budgets.

LEFT: Joseph Rainey, U.S. representative from South Carolina, First District (1870–79).

RIGHT: Hiram Revels, U.S. senator from Mississippi (1870–71).

High taxes and charges of corruption certainly fueled op-position to the Reconstruction governments, but the heart of that opposition remained what it always had been: the desire to restore white supremacy and to restrict the civil and eco-nomic rights of blacks. Although there briefly emerged a group of "New Departure" Democrats who spoke of accept-ing Reconstruction, putting the Civil War behind them, and coexisting with Republicans, most southern Democrats re-mained devoted to the goal of "Redemption": driving the Re-publicans out of power and restoring the South's traditional leadership. Democratic Redeemers began to win elections as early as 1869, and their electoral strength mounted in the early 1870s; so, too, did antiblack and anti-Republican vio-lence, led by the Klan.

THE GRANT ADMINISTRATION

Reconstruction was only occasionally on Washington's front burner after Ulysses Grant assumed the presidency in 1869. With Republican governments elected in the South and southern congressional representation restored, both Con-gress and the new president—who tended to follow the lead of Congress—turned their attention to other matters.

One such matter was civil service reform. The 1860s witnessed an eruption of criticism of the spoils system so prevalent in American politics: victorious politicians gave government jobs to the party faithful, who, in turn, con-tributed a percentage of their salaries to the party treasuries. Reformers, most of whom were well-educated Republicans from the Northeast, regarded such patronage practices as corrupt and inefficient, and they demanded that appoint-ments be based on merit, certified by competitive examina-tions. President Grant endorsed these views but did not act on them very energetically. After a presidential commission recommended both competitive exams and the prohibition of salary assessments, Grant did attempt to implement re-forms through an executive order. But Congress, which was even more reluctant than Grant to abandon patronage, re-fused to appropriate sufficient funds to enforce the regula-tions, and the spoils system lived on.

Much of the passion generated by this issue stemmed from a widespread concern about corruption in public life, an ap-prehension that public positions and institutions were being used to serve private ends. That the state, at all levels, was be-coming larger only heightened these apprehensions. The Grant administration itself was subject to charges of nepo-tism and cronyism thanks to the large number of appointees who were either former army officers or relatives of the presi-dent's wife. Early in his administration, the president had to intervene to quash a scheme in which speculators were using inside government information to corner the gold market, a scheme from which Grant's sister and perhaps his wife stood to profit. In addition, several high officials in the administra-tion, including the secretary of war, ended up leaving office in disgrace after being charged with accepting bribes. Although personally honest, Grant was both politically naive and alto-gether too trusting of his friends.

The most celebrated scandal of the era, however, the Credit Mobilier affair, involved congressmen. Credit Mobilier, a company created by the directors of the Union Pacific Rail-road (who were also the directors of Credit Mobilier), was constructing major new rail lines with financial assistance from the federal government. To keep Congress from taking any steps that might limit the profitability of the venture or peering too closely at the use of federal loans, shares in Credit Mobilier were given to a number of prominent congressmen in 1867 and 1868. Remarkably, when these transactions were finally exposed in 1872, only one member of Congress was formally censured, although the taint of involvement fol-lowed others.

Reconstruction moved back to center stage during the Grant administration only in 1870–71. In an attempt to un-

Ulysses S. Grant, eighteenth president of the United States (1869–77).

dermine the Republican state governments, the Ku Klux Klan and other organizations ratcheted up the level of violence in 1870, killing hundreds of freedmen and causing local Republicans to plead for federal assistance. Congress responded with a series of Enforcement Acts making it a federal crime for state officials to discriminate against voters because of their race or to deprive any individual of his civil and political rights. The third such act, the Ku Klux Klan Act of April 1871, made it a federal crime for individuals to conspire to deprive others of their rights and authorized the president to use the army to enforce these laws and to suspend the writ of habeas corpus, if necessary.

The Enforcement Acts were significant in two respects. First, they enlarged federal power: they gave the national government jurisdiction not only over state actions but also over certain categories of crimes committed by individuals. (The Democrats were so incensed over this expansion of the central government that twenty years later they repealed most provisions of these acts.) Second, the Enforcement Acts worked. The Justice Department, led by Attorney General Amos Akerman, born in New Hampshire but a longtime resident of Georgia, vigorously used its new powers to prosecute the Klan, while president Grant sent troops to, and suspended habeas corpus in, parts of South Carolina. Although the president, sensitive to charges of "military despotism," used his powers sparingly, the government's actions were energetic enough to cripple the Klan and dramatically lower the incidence of violence, thereby bolstering the morale of both the freedmen and southern Republicans.

THE ELECTION OF 1872

Despite the success of some of Grant's policies, many Republicans lost faith in the president personally and in the party that he nominally headed but which seemed to hold him captive; in 1872, these disaffected Republicans joined some Democrats to form the Liberal Republican Party. Most Liberal Republicans were middle-class reformers who supported civil service reform, opposed high tariffs, and favored amnesty for ex-Confederates as well as the end of "bayonet rule" in the South. They were also convinced that the Republican Party, which some of them had helped to found, had lost its moral bearings and been taken over by unsavory professional politicians.

The Liberal Republicans met in convention in the spring of 1872 and, to the surprise of many, nominated journalist

A campaign poster for the Republican ticket in the 1872 election, emphasizing both Grant's and Wilson's backgrounds as workingmen.

Horace Greeley as their presidential candidate. Greeley was a well-known figure with a track record of embracing quixotic, and sometimes contradictory, views; he was also not particularly interested either in civil service reform or lower tariffs. The centerpiece of his campaign quickly became sectional reconciliation and "home rule" by "the best people" of the South. Sensing the chance to beat Grant and to get a president sympathetic to their views, the Democrats also nominated Greeley, despite his having spent much of his career attacking the Democratic Party. But this fusion strategy backfired. Many Democrats could not bring themselves to support an old antagonist, and most Republicans feared that Greeley would deliver the South back to the Klan and ex-Confederates. Grant, despite a lackluster public image, was reelected with 56 percent of the popular vote, winning every state north of the Mason-Dixon line.

RECONSTRUCTION IN RETREAT

Although Grant's reelection seemed to affirm the nation's commitment to Reconstruction, that commitment eroded rapidly, for several reasons. The most important was the absence of any sign that things in the South were improving, that a stable political order was being established. In closely watched Louisiana, for example, disputes about the results of the 1872 elections led to the convening of two legislatures, the inauguration of two governors, and the arrival of federal troops. These episodes were followed, in 1873, by a clash between armed whites and black militiamen known as the Colfax massacre, which left roughly seventy blacks and two whites dead. Violence also enveloped the 1874 elections in Louisiana, setting off a train of events that culminated in federal troops entering the state capitol building and evicting five Democrats before the Democrats could deny key legislative seats to Republicans.

Similar conflicts raged throughout the South, as splits emerged within the Republican Party and the Democrats grew emboldened by success. Redeemers, committed to white supremacy, low taxes, and home rule (which meant the removal of federal troops), captured the state governments in Arkansas, Alabama, and Texas, while making inroads in most other states. In 1875, Redeemers in Mississippi—a state with a black majority—put into action what became known as the "Mississippi Plan": a coordinated effort to force whites to abandon the Republican Party and then, through violence and intimidation, to prevent blacks from voting. "Carry the election peacefully if we can, forcibly if we must," declared Democratic newspapers. The plan worked, in part because the Grant administration declined to send troops to protect blacks and Republicans. Democrats in Mississippi gained power in an election in which extraordinarily tiny Republican tallies (for example, 0, 2, and 4) were somehow recorded in counties with large black majorities.

> *"The North's weariness with Reconstruction was also shaped by the severe economic depression that began in 1873."*

Once in office, the Redeemers were not bashful about dismantling Reconstruction. They cut taxes, education spending (especially for blacks), and state funds for internal improvements. They altered the structure of local government by making key offices appointive rather than elected, and they excluded blacks altogether from law enforcement. The Redeemers also passed new vagrancy laws (designed to inhibit the movement of rural blacks and compel them to work) and lien laws that gave landlords the first claim on crops.

The successes of Redemption made clear that Reconstruction could be continued only with the prolonged, active, and military involvement of the federal government, a prospect that grew increasingly unpalatable in the North. As one northern Republican acknowledged, "The truth is our people are tired out with this worn out cry of 'Southern outrages.'" Republican disillusion with Reconstruction was only deepened by the 1874 elections, in which Democrats scored major gains in all regions and won control of the House of Representatives for the first time in eighteen years.

An 1868 cartoon by Thomas Nast criticizing the Democratic Party's opposition to Reconstruction. The three men standing represent the urban Irish of the North, unreconstructed southern Confederates, and northern capitalists.

The North's weariness with Reconstruction was also shaped by the severe economic depression that began in 1873. Precipitated by the collapse of the financial and railroad empire of Jay Cooke, the Panic of 1873 marked the end of the post–Civil War economic boom and the beginning of the longest uninterrupted business-cycle downturn of the nineteenth century. (See Chapter 18.) In the short run, the stock market closed, banks failed, and commercial houses and railroads went under; as the panic dragged on, farm prices declined, wages were sharply cut, and unemployment reached unprecedented levels. The Grant administration did little in response to the crisis, but this was not a failing peculiar to the president: the common wisdom throughout the late nineteenth century was that there was nothing much the federal government could do to alleviate a panic.

One critical upshot of the economic downturn was that the buoyant optimism of the late 1860s vanished. People worried about how to pay their rent, feed their families, pay their debts, and find work. In the South, the economic condition of the freedmen worsened because of falling cotton prices; in the Northeast, Midwest, and West, people were preoccupied with their own problems rather than those of African American freedmen in faraway states. Under the best of circumstances, distant political and social upheavals can hold the attention of a people only so long before being overridden by private concerns; and the mid-1870s were not the best of circumstances.

While the North's resolve was weakened by both politics and economics, the ability of the federal government to promote civil and political equality was diminished by the Supreme Court. In what are known as the *Slaughterhouse Cases*, decided in 1873, the Court delivered a highly restrictive interpretation of the Fourteenth Amendment. The cases emerged in 1869 when the state of Louisiana granted one company a monopoly on slaughtering livestock in New Orleans. Other butchers in the city sued, asserting that the state had violated the clause of the Fourteenth Amendment mandating that "no state shall make or enforce any law which shall abridge the privileges or immunities of citizens of the United States." The Court disagreed, arguing that the Fourteenth Amendment protected only the "privileges and immunities" of "national citizenship" (rather than "state citizenship"), and that these privileges and immunities were of a very narrow sort—such as the right to use the nation's navigable waters. This narrow definition clearly limited the reach of the Fourteenth Amendment as a weapon against discriminatory state laws; so, too, did the Court's insistence that the Fourteenth Amendment did not significantly alter the relationship between the states and the federal government and that the Court itself ought not to act as a "permanent censor" of state legislation.

Three years later, in *U.S. v. Cruikshank*, a case that arose out of the Louisiana Colfax massacre, the Court undercut the enforcement clause of the Fourteenth Amendment. Overturning the conviction of three men who had been charged with violating the civil rights of their victims, the Court argued that the postwar amendments only gave the federal government power to prohibit rights violations by states, *not by individuals*. In the same year, in *U.S. v. Reese*, the Court ruled

This Thomas Nast cartoon, published at the beginning of the Panic of 1873, suggests that the "bust up" on Wall Street was well deserved.

that the Fifteenth Amendment did not guarantee anyone the right to vote; it simply specified that certain reasons for denying someone the vote were unacceptable. In practice, *Cruikshank* meant that the enforcement of black rights depended almost entirely on local officials, while the *Reese* decision set the stage for legally disfranchising blacks for ostensibly nonracial reasons.

THE ELECTION OF 1876 AND THE COMPROMISE OF 1877

With the country in depression, Reconstruction faltering, and the Republican Party stained by corruption scandals, the Democrats were well positioned for the 1876 elections. They chose for their standard-bearer the prominent reform governor of New York, Samuel J. Tilden, who was nationally known for having overthrown the Tweed ring (see Chapter 20). Tilden and the Democrats ran in opposition to the "corrupt centralism" of a Republican government, "which, after inflicting upon ten States the rapacities of carpet-bag tyrannies, has honeycombed . . . the Federal Government . . . with incapacity, waste, and fraud." To run against Tilden, the Republicans nominated Rutherford B. Hayes, an ex–Civil War general and

Reconstruction had political effects as well, some local, some national. The rout of the Republican Party in the South opened the way for the one-party system that came to dominate southern political life for nearly a century, stifling dissent and depressing political participation. The existence of a conservative, one-party region in which most working people were excluded from politics pushed the national political spectrum rightward, complicating or preventing reforms. The wording of the Fourteenth and Fifteenth Amendments, moreover, formalized the exclusion of women from electoral politics.

The era of Reconstruction came to an end without having set the nation on a course that could heal the wounds of slavery and promote greater racial harmony and social justice. Whether any other outcome was possible is difficult to judge; but the shortcomings of Reconstruction set the stage for the troubling history of race in modern America.

Suggested Reading

R. H. Abbott, *The Republican Party and the South, 1855–1877: The First Southern Strategy* (1986)

Michael Les Benedict, *A Compromise of Principle: Congressional Republicans and Reconstruction, 1863–1869* (1974)

Walter L. Fleming, *Documentary History of Reconstruction* (1906)

Eric Foner, *Reconstruction: America's Unfinished Revolution* (1989)

Leon Litwack, *Been in the Storm So Long: The Aftermath of Slavery* (1980)

Geoffrey Perret, *Ulysses S. Grant, Soldier and President* (1999)

Michael Perman, *Reunion Without Compromise* (1973)

THE DECLARATION OF INDEPENDENCE

When in the course of human events, it becomes necessary for one people to dissolve the political bands which have connected them with another, and to assume among the Powers of the earth, the separate and equal station to which the Laws of Nature and of Nature's God entitle them, a decent respect to the opinions of mankind requires that they should declare the causes which impel them to the separation.

We hold these truths to be self-evident, that all men are created equal, that they are endowed by their Creator with certain unalienable rights, that among these are Life, Liberty, and the pursuit of Happiness. That to secure these rights, Governments are instituted among Men, deriving their just powers from the consent of the governed. That whenever any Form of Government becomes destructive of these ends, it is the Right of the People to alter or to abolish it, and to institute new Government, laying its foundation on such principles and organizing its powers in such form, as to them shall seem most likely to effect their Safety and Happiness. Prudence, indeed, will dictate that Governments long established should not be changed for light and transient causes; and accordingly all experience hath shown, that mankind are more disposed to suffer, while evils are sufferable, than to right themselves by abolishing the forms to which they are accustomed. But when a long train of abuses and usurpations, pursuing invariably the same Object evinces a design to reduce them under absolute Despotism, it is their right, it is their duty, to throw off such Government, and to provide new Guards for their future security.—Such has been the patient sufferance of these Colonies; and such is now the necessity which constrains them to alter their former Systems of Government. The history of the present King of Great Britain is a history of repeated injuries and usurpations, all having in direct object the establishment of an absolute Tyranny over these States. To prove this, let Facts be submitted to a candid world.

He has refused his Assent to Laws, the most wholesome and necessary for the public good.

He has forbidden his Governors to pass Laws of immediate and pressing importance, unless suspended in their operation till his Assent should be obtained; and when so suspended, he has utterly neglected to attend to them.

He has refused to pass other Laws for the accommodation of large districts of people, unless those people would relinquish the right of Representation in the Legislature, a right inestimable to them and formidable to tyrants only.

He has called together legislative bodies at places unusual, uncomfortable, and distant from the depository of their public Records, for the sole purpose of fatiguing them into compliance with his measures.

He has dissolved Representative Houses repeatedly, for opposing with manly firmness his invasions on the rights of the people.

He has refused for a long time, after such dissolutions, to cause others to be elected; whereby the Legislative powers, incapable of Annihilation, have returned to the People at large for their exercise; the State remaining in the mean time exposed to all dangers of invasion from without, and convulsions within.

He has endeavoured to prevent the population of these States; for that purpose obstructing the Laws of Naturalization of Foreigners; refusing to pass others to encourage their migrations hither, and raising the conditions of new Appropriations of Lands.

He has obstructed the Administration of Justice, by refusing his Assent to Laws for establishing Judiciary powers.

He has made Judges dependent on his Will alone, for the tenure of their offices, and the amount and payment of their salaries.

He has erected a multitude of New Offices, and sent hither swarms of Officers to harass our People, and eat out their substance.

He has kept among us, in times of peace, Standing Armies without the Consent of our legislatures.

He has affected to render the Military independent of and superior to the Civil Power.

He has combined with others to subject us to a jurisdiction foreign to our constitution, and unacknowledged by our laws; giving his Assent to their Acts of pretended Legislation:

For quartering large bodies of armed troops among us:

For protecting them, by a mock Trial, from Punishment for any Murders which they should commit on the Inhabitants of these States:

For cutting off our Trade with all parts of the world:

For imposing taxes on us without our Consent:

For depriving us of many cases, of the benefits of Trial by jury:

For transporting us beyond Seas to be tried for pretended offences:

For abolishing the free System of English Laws in a neighbouring Province, establishing therein an Arbitrary government, and enlarging its Boundaries so as to render it at once an example and fit instrument for introducing the same absolute rule into these Colonies:

For taking away our Charters, abolishing our most valuable Laws, and altering fundamentally the Forms of our Governments:

For suspending our own Legislatures, and declaring themselves invested with Power to legislate for us in all cases whatsoever.

He has abdicated Government here, by declaring us out of his Protection and waging War against us.

He has plundered our seas, ravaged our Coasts, burnt our towns, and destroyed the lives of our people.

He is at this time transporting large armies of foreign mercenaries to compleat the works of death, desolation, and tyranny, already begun with circumstances of Cruelty & perfidy scarcely paralleled in the most barbarous ages, and totally unworthy the Head of a civilized nation.

He has constrained our fellow Citizens taken Captive on the high Seas to bear Arms against their Country, to become the executioners of their friends and Brethren, or to fall themselves by their Hands.

He has excited domestic insurrections amongst us, and has endeavoured to bring on the inhabitants of our frontiers, the merciless Indian Savages, whose known rule of warfare, is an undistinguished destruction of all ages, sexes, and conditions.

In every stage of these Oppressions We have Petitioned for Redress in the most humble terms: Our repeated Petitions have been answered only by repeated injury. A Prince, whose character is thus marked by every act which may define a Tyrant, is unfit to be the ruler of a free people.

Nor have We been wanting in attention to our British brethren. We have warned them from time to time of attempts by their legislature to extend an unwarrantable jurisdiction over us. We have reminded them of the circumstances of our emigration and settlement here. We have appealed to their native justice and magnanimity, and we have conjured them by the ties of our common kindred to disavow these usurpations, which, would inevitably interrupt our connections and correspondence. They too must have been deaf to the voice of justice and of consanguinity. We must, therefore, acquiesce in the necessity, which denounces our Separation, and hold them, as we hold the rest of mankind, Enemies in War, in Peace Friends.

WE, THEREFORE, the Representatives of the UNITED STATES OF AMERICA, in General Congress, Assembled, appealing to the Supreme Judge of the world for the rectitude of our intentions, do, in the Name, and by Authority of the good People of these Colonies, solemnly publish and declare, That these United Colonies are, and of Right ought to be FREE AND INDEPENDENT STATES; that they are Absolved from all Allegiance to the British Crown, and that all political connection between them and the State of Great Britain, is and ought to be totally dissolved; and that as Free and Independent States, they have full Power to levy War, conclude Peace, contract Alliances, establish Commerce, and to do all other Acts and Things which Independent States may of right do. And for the support of this Declaration, with a firm reliance on the Protection of Divine Providence, we mutually pledge to each other our Lives, our Fortunes, and our sacred Honor.

The foregoing Declaration was, by order of Congress, engrossed, and signed by the following members:

John Hancock

NEW HAMPSHIRE
Josiah Bartlett
William Whipple
Matthew Thornton

MASSACHUSETTS BAY
Samuel Adams
John Adams
Robert Treat Paine
Elbridge Gerry

RHODE ISLAND
Stephen Hopkins
William Ellery

CONNECTICUT
Roger Sherman
Samuel Huntington
William Williams
Oliver Wolcott

NEW YORK
William Floyd
Philip Livingston
Francis Lewis
Lewis Morris

NEW JERSEY
Richard Stockton
John Witherspoon
Francis Hopkinson
John Hart
Abraham Clark

PENNSYLVANIA
Robert Morris
Benjamin Rush
Benjamin Franklin
John Morton
George Clymer
James Smith
George Taylor
James Wilson
George Ross

DELAWARE
Caesar Rodney
George Read
Thomas M'Kean

MARYLAND
Samuel Chase
William Paca
Thomas Stone
Charles Carroll,
 of Carrollton

VIRGINIA
George Wythe
Richard Henry Lee
Thomas Jefferson
Benjamin Harrison
Thomas Nelson, Jr.
Francis Lightfoot Lee
Carter Braxton

NORTH CAROLINA
William Hooper
Joseph Hewes
John Penn

SOUTH CAROLINA
Edward Rutledge
Thomas Heyward, Jr.
Thomas Lynch, Jr.
Arthur Middleton

GEORGIA
Button Gwinnett
Lyman Hall
George Walton

Resolved, That copies of the Declaration be sent to the several assemblies, conventions, and committees, or councils of safety, and to the several commanding officers of the continental troops; that it be proclaimed in each of the United States, at the head of the army.

ARTICLES OF CONFEDERATION

To all to whom these Presents shall come, we the undersigned Delegates of the States affixed to our Names send greeting.

Whereas the Delegates of the United States of America in Congress assembled did on the fifteenth day of November in the Year of our Lord One Thousand Seven Hundred and Seventy-seven, and in the Second Year of the Independence of America agree to certain articles of Confederation and perpetual Union between the States of Newhampshire, Massachusetts-bay, Rhodeisland and Providence Plantations, Connecticut, New York, New Jersey, Pennsylvania, Delaware, Maryland, Virginia, North-Carolina, South-Carolina and Georgia in the Words following, viz.

Articles of Confederation and perpetual Union between the States of Newhampshire, Massachusetts-bay, Rhodeisland and Providence Plantations, Connecticut, New-York, New-Jersey, Pennsylvania, Delaware, Maryland, Virginia, North-Carolina, South-Carolina and Georgia.

ARTICLE I. The stile of this confederacy shall be "The United States of America."

ARTICLE II. Each State retains its sovereignty, freedom and independence, and every power, jurisdiction and right, which is not by this confederation expressly delegated to the United States, in Congress assembled.

ARTICLE III. The said States hereby severally enter into a firm league of friendship with each other, for their common defence, the security of their liberties, and their mutual and general welfare, binding themselves to assist each other, against all force offered to, or attacks made upon them, or any of them, on account of religion, sovereignty, trade or any other pretence whatever.

ARTICLE IV. The better to secure and perpetuate mutual friendship and intercourse among the people of the different States in this Union, the free inhabitants of each of these States, paupers, vagabonds and fugitives from justice excepted, shall be entitled to all privileges and immunities of free citizens in the several States; and the people of each State shall have free ingress and regress to and from any other State, and shall enjoy therein all the privileges of trade and commerce, subject to the same duties, impositions and restrictions as the inhabitants thereof respectively, provided that such restrictions shall not extend so far as to prevent the removal of property imported into any State, to any other State of which the owner is an inhabitant; provided also that no imposition, duties or restriction shall be laid by any State, on the property of the United States, or either of them.

If any person guilty of, or charged with treason, felony, or other high misdemeanor in any State, shall flee from justice, and be found in any of the United States, he shall upon demand of the Governor or Executive power, of the State from which he fled, be delivered up and removed to the State having jurisdiction of his offence.

Full faith and credit shall be given in each of these States to the records, acts and judicial proceedings of the courts and magistrates of every other State.

ARTICLE V. For the more convenient management of the general interests of the United States, delegates shall be annually appointed in such manner as the legislature of each State shall direct, to meet in Congress on the first Monday in November, in every year, with a power reserved to each State, to recall its delegates, or any of them, at any time within the year, and to send others in their stead, for the remainder of the year.

No State shall be represented in Congress by less than two, nor by more than seven members; and no person shall be capable of being a delegate for more than three years in any term of six years; nor shall any person, being a delegate, be capable of holding any office under the United States, for which he, or another for his benefit receives any salary, fees or emolument of any kind.

Each State shall maintain its own delegates in a meeting of the States, and while they act as members of the committee of the States.

In determining questions in the United States, in Congress assembled, each State shall have one vote.

Freedom of speech and debate in Congress shall not be impeached or questioned in any court, or place out of Congress, and the members of Congress shall be protected in their persons from arrests and imprisonments, during the time of their going to and from, and attendance on Congress, except for treason, felony, or breach of the peace.

ARTICLE VI. No State without the consent of the United States in Congress assembled, shall send any embassy to, or receive any embassy from, or enter into any conference, agreement, alliance or treaty with any king, prince or state; nor shall any person holding any office of profit or trust under the United States, or any of them, accept of any present, emolument, office or title of any kind whatever from any king, prince or foreign state; nor shall the United States in Congress assembled, or any of them, grant any title of nobility.

No two or more States shall enter into any treaty, confederation or alliance whatever between them, without the consent of the

United States in Congress assembled, specifying accurately the purposes for which the same is to be entered into, and how long it shall continue.

No State shall lay any imposts or duties, which may interfere with any stipulations in treaties, entered into by the United States in Congress assembled, with any king, prince or state, in pursuance of any treaties already proposed by Congress, to the courts of France and Spain.

No vessels of war shall be kept up in time of peace by any State, except such number only, as shall be deemed necessary by the United States in Congress assembled, for the defence of such State, or its trade; nor shall any body of forces be kept up by any State, in time of peace, except such number only, as in the judgment of the United States, in Congress assembled, shall be deemed requisite to garrison the forts necessary for the defence of such State; but every State shall always keep up a well regulated and disciplined militia, sufficiently armed and accoutred, and shall provide and constantly have ready for use, in public stores, a due number of field pieces and tents, and a proper quantity of arms, ammunition and camp equipage.

No State shall engage in any war without the consent of the United States in Congress assembled, unless such State be actually invaded by enemies, or shall have received certain advice of a resolution being formed by some nation of Indians to invade such State, and the danger is so imminent as not to admit of a delay, till the United States in Congress assembled can be consulted: nor shall any State grant commissions to any ships or vessels of war, nor letters of marque or reprisal, except it be after a declaration of war by the United States in Congress assembled, and then only against the kingdom or state and the subjects thereof, against which war has been so declared, and under such regulations as shall be established by the United States in Congress assembled, unless such State be infested by pirates, in which case vessels of war may be fitted out for that occasion, and kept so long as the danger shall continue, or until the United States in Congress assembled shall determine otherwise.

ARTICLE VII. When land-forces are raised by any State of the common defence, all officers of or under the rank of colonel, shall be appointed by the Legislature of each State respectively by whom such forces shall be raised, or in such manner as such State shall direct, and all vacancies shall be filled up by the State which first made the appointment.

ARTICLE VIII. All charges of war, and all other expenses that shall be incurred for the common defence or general welfare, and allowed by the United States in Congress assembled, shall be defrayed out of a common treasury, which shall be supplied by the several States, in proportion to the value of all land within each State, granted to or surveyed for any person, as such land and the buildings and improvements thereon shall be estimated according to such mode as the United States in Congress assembled, shall from time to time direct and appoint.

The taxes for paying that proportion shall be laid and levied by the authority and direction of the Legislatures of the several States within the time agreed upon by the United States in Congress assembled.

ARTICLE IX. The United States in Congress assembled, shall have the sole and exclusive right and power of determining on peace and war, except in the cases mentioned in the sixth article—of sending and receiving ambassadors—entering into treaties and alliances, provided that no treaty of commerce shall be made whereby the legislative power of the respective States shall be restrained from imposing such imposts and duties on foreigners, as their own people are subjected to, or from prohibiting the exportation or importation of and species of goods or commodities whatsoever—of establishing rules for deciding in all cases, what captures on land or water shall be legal, and in what manner prizes taken by land or naval forces in the service of the United States shall be divided or appropriated—of granting letters of marque and reprisal in times of peace—appointing courts for the trial of piracies and felonies committed on the high seas and establishing courts for receiving and determining finally appeals in all cases of captures, provided that no member of Congress shall be appointed a judge of any of the said courts.

The United States in Congress assembled shall also be the last resort on appeal in all disputes and differences now subsisting or that hereafter may arise between two or more States concerning boundary, jurisdiction or any other cause whatever; which authority shall always be exercised in the manner following. Whenever the legislative or executive authority or lawful agent of any State in controversy with another shall present a petition to Congress, stating the matter in question and praying for a hearing, notice thereof shall be given by order of Congress to the legislative or executive authority of the other State in controversy, and a day assigned for the appearance of the parties by their lawful agents, who shall then be directed to appoint by joint consent, commissioners or judges to constitute a court for hearing and determining the matter in question: but if they cannot agree, Congress shall name three persons out of each of the United States, and from the list of such persons each party shall alternately strike out one, the petitioners beginning, until the number shall be reduced to thirteen; and from that number not less than seven, nor more than nine names as Congress shall direct, shall in the presence of Congress be drawn out by lot, and the persons whose names shall be so drawn or any five of them, shall be commissioners or judges, to hear and finally determine the controversy, so always as a major part of the judges who shall hear the cause shall agree in the determination: and if either party shall neglect to attend at the day appointed, without reasons, which Congress shall judge sufficient, or being present shall refuse to strike, the Congress shall proceed to nominate three persons out of each State, and the Secretary of Congress shall strike in behalf of such party absent or refusing; and the judgment and sentence of the court to be appointed, in the manner before prescribed, shall be final and conclusive; and if any of the parties shall refuse to submit to the authority of such court, or to appear or defend their claim or cause, the court shall nevertheless proceed to pronounce sentence, or judgment, which shall in like manner be final and decisive, the judgment or sentence and other proceedings being in either case transmitted to Congress, and lodged among the acts of Congress for the security of the parties concerned: provided that every commissioner, before he sits in judgment, shall take an oath to be administered by one of the judges of the supreme or superior court of the State where the case shall be tried, "well and truly to hear and determine the matter in question, according to the best of his judgment, without favour, affection or hope of reward:" provided also that no State shall be deprived of territory for the benefit of the United States.

All controversies concerning the private right of soil claimed under different grants of two or more States, whose jurisdiction as they may respect such lands, and the states which passed such grants are adjusted, the said grants or either of them being at the same time claimed to have originated antecedent to such settlement of jurisdiction, shall on the petition of either party to the Congress of the United States, be finally determined as near as may be in the same manner as is before prescribed for deciding disputes respecting territorial jurisdiction between different States.

The United States in Congress assembled shall also have the sole and exclusive right and power of regulating the alloy and value of coin struck by their own authority, or by that of the respective States—fixing the standard of weights and measures throughout the United States—regulating the trade and managing all affairs with the Indians, not members of any of the States, provided that the legislative right of any State within its own limits be not infringed or violated—establishing and regulating post-offices from one State to another, throughout all of the United States, and exacting such postage on the papers passing thro' the same as may be requisite to defray the expenses of the said office—appointing all officers of the land forces, in the service of the United States, excepting regimental officers—appointing all the officers of the naval forces, and commissioning all officers whatever in the service of the United States—making rules for the government and regulation of the said land and naval forces, and directing their operations.

The United States in Congress assembled shall have authority to appoint a committee, to sit in the recess of Congress, to be denominated "a Committee of the States," and to consist of one delegate from each State; and to appoint such other committees and civil officers as may be necessary for managing the general affairs of the United States under their direction—to appoint one of their number to preside, provided that no person be allowed to serve in the office of president more than one year in any term of three years; to

ascertain the necessary sums of money to be raised for the service of the United States, and to appropriate and apply the same for defraying the public expenses—to borrow money, or emit bills on the credit of the United States, transmitting every half year to the respective States an account of the sums of money so borrowed or emitted,—to build and equip a navy—to agree upon the number of land forces, and to make requisitions from each State for its quota, in proportion to the number of white inhabitants in such State; which requisition shall be binding, and thereupon the Legislature of each State shall appoint the regimental officers, raise the men and cloath, arm and equip them in a soldier like manner, at the expense of the United States; and the officers and men so cloathed, armed and equipped shall march to the place appointed, and within the time agreed on by the United States in Congress assembled: but if the United States in Congress assembled shall, on consideration of circumstances judge proper that any State should not raise men, or should raise a smaller number of men than the quota thereof, such extra number shall be raised, officered, cloathed, armed and equipped in the same manner as the quota of such State, unless the legislature of such State shall judge that such extra number cannot be safely spared out of the same, in which case they shall raise officer, cloath, arm and equip as many of such extra number as they judge can be safely spared. And the officers and men so cloathed, armed and equipped, shall march to the place appointed, and within the time agreed on by the United States in Congress assembled.

The United States in Congress assembled shall never engage in a war, nor grant letters of marque and reprisal in time of peace, nor enter into any treaties or alliances, nor coin money, nor regulate the value thereof, nor ascertain the sums and expenses necessary for the defence and welfare of the United States, or any of them, nor emit bills, nor borrow money on the credit of the United States, nor appropriate money, nor agree upon the number of vessels to be built or purchased, or the number of land or sea forces to be raised, nor appoint a commander in chief of the army or navy, unless nine States assent to the same: nor shall a question on any other point, except for adjourning from day to day be determined, unless by the votes of a majority of the United States in Congress assembled.

The Congress of the United States shall have power to adjourn to any time within the year, and to any place within the United States, so that no period of adjournment be for a longer duration than the space of six months, and shall publish the journal of their proceedings monthly, except such parts thereof relating to treaties, alliances or military operations, as in their judgment require secrecy; and the yeas and nays of the delegates of each State on any question shall be entered on the Journal, when it is desired by any delegate; and the delegates of a State, or any of them, at his or their request shall be furnished with a transcript of the said journal, except such parts as are above excepted, to lay before the Legislatures of the several States.

ARTICLE X. The committee of the States, or any nine of them, shall be authorized to execute, in the recess of Congress, such of the powers of Congress as the United States in Congress assembled, by the consent of nine States, shall from time to time think expedient to vest them with; provided that no power be delegated to the said committee, for the exercise of which, by the articles of confederation, the voice of nine States in the Congress of the United States assembled is requisite.

ARTICLE XI. Canada acceding to this confederation, and joining in the measures of the United States, shall be admitted into, and entitled to all the advantages of this Union: but no other colony shall be admitted into the same, unless such admission be agreed to by nine States.

ARTICLE XII. All bills of credit emitted, monies borrowed and debts contracted by, or under the authority of Congress, before the assembling of the United States, in pursuance of the present confederation, shall be deemed and considered as a charge against the United States, for payment and satisfaction whereof the said United States, and the public faith are hereby solemnly pledged.

ARTICLE XIII. Every State shall abide by the determinations of the United States in Congress assembled, on all questions which by this confederation are submitted to them. And the articles of this con-federation shall be inviolably observed by every State, and the Union shall be perpetual; nor shall any alteration at any time hereafter be made in any of them; unless such alteration be agreed to in a Congress of the United States, and be afterwards confirmed by the Legislatures of every State.

And whereas it has pleased the Great Governor of the world to incline the hearts of the Legislatures we respectively represent in Congress, to approve of, and to authorize us to ratify the said articles of confederation and perpetual union. Know ye that we the undersigned delegates, by virtue of the power and authority to us given for that purpose, do by these presents, in the name and in behalf of our respective constituents, fully and entirely ratify and confirm each and every of the said articles of confederation and perpetual union, and all and singular the matters and things therein contained: and we do further solemnly plight and engage the faith of our respective constituents, that they shall abide by the determinations of the United States in Congress assembled, on all questions, which by the said confederation are submitted to them. And that the articles thereof shall be inviolably observed by the States we respectively represent, and that the Union shall be perpetual.

In witness thereof we have hereunto set our hands in Congress. Done at Philadelphia in the State of Pennsylvania the ninth day of July in the year of our Lord one thousand seven hundred and seventy-eight, and in the third year of the independence of America.

THE CONSTITUTION OF THE UNITED STATES

We the People of the United States, in order to form a more perfect Union, establish Justice, insure domestic Tranquility, provide for the common defence, promote the general Welfare, and secure the Blessings of Liberty to ourselves and our Posterity, do ordain and establish this Constitution for the United States of America.

ARTICLE. I.

Section. 1. All legislative Powers herein granted shall be vested in a Congress of the United States, which shall consist of a Senate and House of Representatives.

Section. 2. The House of Representatives shall be composed of Members chosen every second Year by the People of the several States, and the Electors in each State shall have the Qualifications requisite for Electors of the most numerous Branch of the State Legislature.

No Person shall be a Representative who shall not have attained to the Age of twenty five Years, and been seven Years a Citizen of the United States, and who shall not, when elected, be an Inhabitant of that State in which he shall be chosen.

Representatives and direct Taxes shall be apportioned among the several States which may be included within this Union, according to their respective Numbers, which shall be determined by adding to the whole Number of free Persons, including those bound to Service for a Term of Years, and excluding Indians not taxed, three fifths of all other Persons. The actual Enumeration shall be made within three Years after the first Meeting of the Congress of the United States, and within every subsequent Term of ten Years, in such Manner as they shall by Law direct. The Number of Representatives shall not exceed one for every thirty Thousand, but each State shall have at Least one Representative; and until such enumeration shall be made, the State of New Hampshire shall be entitled to chuse three, Massachusetts eight, Rhode-Island and Providence Plantations one, Connecticut five, New York six, New Jersey four, Pennsylvania eight, Delaware one, Maryland six, Virginia ten, North Carolina five, South Carolina five, and Georgia three.

When vacancies happen in the Representation from any state, the Executive Authority thereof shall issue Writs of Election to fill such Vacancies.

The House of Representatives shall chuse their Speaker and other Officers; and shall have the sole Power of Impeachment.

Section. 3. The Senate of the United States shall be composed of two Senators from each State, chosen by the legislature thereof, for six Years; and each Senator shall have one Vote.

Immediately after they shall be assembled in Consequence of the first Election, they shall be divided as equally as may be into three Classes. The Seats of the Senators of the first Class shall be vacated at the Expiration of the second Year, of the second Class at the Expiration of the fourth Year, and of the third Class at the Expiration of the sixth Year, so that one third maybe chosen every second Year; and if Vacancies happen by Resignation, or otherwise, during the Recess of the Legislature of any State, the Executive thereof may make temporary Appointments until the next Meeting of the Legislature, which shall then fill such Vacancies.

No Person shall be a Senator who shall not have attained to the Age of thirty Years, and been nine Years a Citizen of the United States, and who shall not, when elected, be an Inhabitant of that State for which he shall be chosen.

The Vice President of the United States shall be President of the Senate, but shall have no Vote, unless they be equally divided.

The Senate shall chuse their other Officers, and also a President pro tempore, in the Absence of the Vice President, or when he shall exercise the Office of President of the United States.

The Senate shall have the sole Power to try all Impeachments. When sitting for that Purpose, they shall be on Oath or Affirmation. When the President of the United States is tried, the Chief Justice shall preside: And no Person shall be convicted without the Concurrence of two thirds of the Members present.

Judgment in Cases of Impeachment shall not extend further than to removal from Office, and disqualification to hold and enjoy any Office of honor, Trust or Profit under the United States: but the Party convicted shall nevertheless be liable and subject to Indictment, Trial, Judgment and Punishment, according to Law.

Section. 4. The Times, Places and Manner of holding Elections for Senators and Representatives, shall be prescribed in each State by the Legislature thereof; but the Congress may at any time by Law make or alter such Regulations, except as to the Places of chusing Senators.

The Congress shall assemble at least once in every Year, and such Meeting shall be on the first Monday in December, unless they shall by Law appoint a different Day.

Section. 5. Each House shall be the Judge of the Elections, Returns and Qualifications of its own Members, and a Majority of each shall constitute a Quorum to do Business; but a smaller Number may adjourn from day to day, and may be authorized to compel the Attendance of absent Members, in such Manner, and under such Penalties as each House may provide.

Each House may determine the Rules of its Proceedings, punish its Members for disorderly Behaviour, and, with the Concurrence of two thirds, expel a Member.

Each House shall keep a Journal of its Proceedings, and from time to time publish the same, excepting such Parts as may in their

Judgment require Secrecy; and the Yeas and Nays of the Members of either House on any question shall, at the Desire of one fifth of those Present, be entered on the Journal.

Neither House, during the Session of Congress, shall, without the Consent of the other, adjourn for more than three days, not to any other Place than that in which the two Houses shall be sitting.

Section. 6. The Senators and Representatives shall receive a Compensation for their Services, to be ascertained by Law, and paid out of the Treasury of the United States. They shall in all Cases, except Treason, Felony and Breach of the Peace, be privileged from Arrest during their Attendance at the Session of their respective Houses, and in going to and returning from the same; and for any Speech or Debate in either House, they shall not be questioned in any other Place.

No Senator or Representative shall, during the Time for which he was elected, be appointed to any civil Office under the Authority of the United States, which shall have been created, or the Emoluments whereof shall have been encreased during such time; and no Person holding any Office under the United States, shall be a Member of either House during his Continuance in Office.

Section. 7. All Bills for raising Revenue shall originate in the House of Representatives; but the Senate may propose or concur with Amendments as on other Bills.

Every Bill which shall have passed the House of Representatives and the Senate shall, before it become a Law, be presented to the President of the United States; If he approve he shall sign it, but if not he shall return it, with his Objections to that House in which it shall have originated, who shall enter the Objections at large on their Journal, and proceed to reconsider it. If after such Reconsideration two thirds of that House shall agree to pass the Bill, it shall be sent, together with the Objections, to the other House, by which it shall likewise be reconsidered, and if approved by two thirds of that House, it shall become a Law. But in all such Cases the Votes of both Houses shall be determined by Yeas and Nays, and the Names of the Persons voting for and against the Bill shall be entered on the Journal of each House respectively. If any Bill shall not be returned by the President within ten Days (Sundays excepted) after it shall have been presented to him, the Same shall be a Law, in like Manner as if he had signed it, unless the Congress by their Adjournment prevent its Return, in which Case it shall not be a Law.

Every Order, Resolution, or Vote to which the Concurrence of the Senate and House of Representatives may be necessary (except on a question of Adjournment) shall be presented to the President of the United States; and before the Same shall take Effect, shall be approved by him, or being disapproved by him, shall be repassed by two thirds of the Senate and House of Representatives, according to the Rules and Limitations prescribed in the Case of a Bill.

Section. 8. The Congress shall have Power To lay and collect Taxes, Duties, Imposts and Excises, to pay the Debts and provide for the common Defence and general Welfare of the United States; but all Duties, Imposts and Excises shall be uniform throughout the United States;

To borrow Money on the credit of the United States;

To regulate Commerce with foreign Nations, and among the several States, and with the Indian Tribes;

To establish an uniform Rule of Naturalization, and uniform Laws on the subject of Bankruptcies throughout the United States;

To coin Money, regulate the Value thereof, and of foreign Coin, and fix the Standard of Weights and Measures;

To provide for the Punishment of counterfeiting the Securities and current Coin of the United States;

To establish Post Offices and Post Roads;

To promote the Progress of Science and useful Arts, by securing for limited Times to Authors and Inventors the exclusive Right to their respective Writings and Discoveries;

To constitute Tribunals inferior to the supreme Court;

To define and punish Piracies and Felonies committed on the high Seas, and Offences against the Law of Nations;

To declare War, grant Letters of Marque and Reprisal, and make Rules concerning Captures on Land and Water;

To raise and support Armies, but no Appropriation of Money to that Use shall be for a longer Term than two Years;

To provide and maintain a Navy;

To make Rules for the Government and Regulation of the land and naval Forces;

To provide for calling forth the Militia to execute the Laws of the Union, suppress Insurrections and repel Invasions;

To provide for organizing, arming, and disciplining, the Militia, and for governing such Part of them as may be employed in the Service of the United States, reserving to the States respectively, the Appointment of the Officers, and the Authority of training the Militia according to the discipline prescribed by Congress;

To exercise exclusive Legislation in all Cases whatsoever, over such District (not exceeding ten Miles square) as may, by Cession of Particular States, and the Acceptance of Congress, become the Seat of the Government of the United States, and to exercise like Authority over all Places purchased by the Consent of the Legislature of the State in which the Same shall be, for the Erection of Forts, Magazines, Arsenals, dock-Yards, and other needful Buildings;— And

To make all Laws which shall be necessary and proper for carrying into Execution the foregoing Powers, and all other Powers vested by this Constitution in the Government of the United States, or in any Department or Officer thereof.

Section. 9. The Migration or Importation of such Persons as any of the States now existing shall think proper to admit, shall not be prohibited by the Congress prior to the Year one thousand eight hundred and eight, but a Tax or duty may be imposed on such Importation, not exceeding ten dollars for each Person.

The Privilege of the Writ of Habeas Corpus shall not be suspended, unless when in Cases of Rebellion or Invasion the public Safety may require it.

No Bill of Attainder or ex post facto Law shall be passed.

No Capitation, or other direct, Tax shall be laid, unless in Proportion to the Census or Enumeration herein before directed to be taken.

No Tax or Duty shall be laid on Articles exported from any State.

No Preference shall be given by any Regulation of Commerce or Revenue to the Ports of one State over those of another: nor shall Vessels bound to, or from, one State, be obliged to enter, clear, or pay Duties in another.

No Money shall be drawn from the Treasury, but in Consequence of Appropriations made by Law; and a regular Statement and Account of the Receipts and Expenditures of all public Money shall be published from time to time.

No Title of Nobility shall be granted by the United States: And no Person holding any Office of Profit or Trust under them, shall, without the Consent of the Congress, accept of any present, Emolument, Office, or Title, of any kind whatever, from any King, Prince, or foreign State.

Section. 10. No State shall enter into any Treaty, Alliance, or Confederation; grant Letters of Marque and Reprisal; coin Money; emit Bills of Credit; make any Thing but gold and silver Coin a Tender in Payment of Debts; pass any Bill of Attainder, ex post facto Law, or Law impairing the Obligation of Contracts, or grant any Title of Nobility.

No State shall, without the Consent of the Congress, lay any Imposts or Duties on Imports or Exports, except what may be absolutely necessary for executing its inspection Laws: and the net Produce of all Duties and Imposts, laid by any State on Imports or Exports, shall be for the Use of the Treasury of the United States; and all such Laws shall be subject to the Revision and Controul of the Congress.

No State shall, without the Consent of Congress, lay any Duty of Tonnage, keep Troops, or Ships of War in time of Peace, enter into any Agreement or Compact with another State, or with a foreign Power, or engage in War, unless actually invaded, or in such imminent Danger as will not admit of delay.

ARTICLE. II.

Section. 1. The executive Power shall be vested in a President of the United States of America. He shall hold his Office during the term of four Years, and, together with the Vice President, chosen for the same Term, be elected, as follows:

Each State shall appoint, in such Manner as the Legislature thereof may direct, a Number of Electors, equal to the whole Number of Senators and Representatives to which the State may be entitled in the Congress: but no Senator or Representative, or Person holding an Office of Trust or Profit under the United States, shall be appointed an Elector.

The Electors shall meet in their respective States, and vote by Ballot for two Persons, of whom one at least shall not be an Inhabitant of the same State with themselves. And they shall make a List of all the Persons voted for, and of the Number of Votes for each; which List they shall sign and certify, and transmit sealed to the Seat of the Government of the United States, directed to the President of the Senate. The President of the Senate shall, in the Presence of the Senate and House of Representatives, open all the Certificates, and the Votes shall then be counted. The Person having the greatest Number of Votes shall be the President, if such Number be a Majority of the whole Number of Electors appointed; and if there be more than one who have such Majority, and have an equal Number of Votes, then the House of Representatives shall immediately chuse by Ballot one of them for President; and if no Person have a Majority, then from the five highest on the List the said House shall in like Manner chuse the President. But in chusing the President, the Votes shall be taken by States, the Representation from each State having one Vote; A quorum for this Purpose shall consist of a Member or Members from two thirds of the States, and a Majority of all the States shall be necessary to a Choice. In every Case, after the Choice of the President, the Person having the greatest Number of Votes of the Electors shall be the Vice President. But if there should remain two or more who have equal Votes, the Senate shall chuse from them by Ballot the Vice President.

The Congress may determine the Time of chusing the Electors, and the Day on which they shall give their Votes; which Day shall be the same throughout the United States.

No Person except a natural born Citizen, or a Citizen of the United States, at the time of the Adoption of this Constitution, shall be eligible to the Office of President; neither shall any Person be eligible to that Office who shall not have attained to the Age of thirty five Years, and been fourteen Years a Resident within the United States.

In Case of the Removal of the President from Office, or of his Death, Resignation, or Inability to discharge the Powers and Duties of the said Office, the Same shall devolve on the Vice President, and the Congress may by Law provide for the Case of Removal, Death, Resignation or Inability, both of the President and Vice President, declaring what Officer shall then act as President, and such Officer shall act accordingly, until the Disability be removed, or a President shall be elected.

The President shall, at stated Times, receive for his Services, a Compensation, which shall neither be encreased or diminished during the Period for which he shall have been elected, and he shall not receive within that Period any other Emolument from the United States, or any of them.

Before he enters on the Execution of his Office, he shall take the following Oath or Affirmation:—"I do solemnly swear (or affirm) that I will faithfully execute the Office of President of the United States, and will to the best of my Ability, preserve, protect and defend the Constitution of the United States."

Section. 2. The President shall be Commander in Chief of the Army and Navy of the United States, and of the Militia of the several States, when called into the actual Service of the United States; he may require the Opinion, in writing, of the principal Officer in each of the executive Departments, upon any Subject relating to the Duties of their respective Offices, and he shall have Power to grant Reprieves and Pardons for Offences against the United States, except in Cases of Impeachment.

He shall have Power, by and with the Advice and Consent of the Senate, to make Treaties, provided two thirds of the Senators present concur; and he shall nominate, and by and with the Advice and Consent of the Senate, shall appoint Ambassadors, other public Ministers and Consuls, Judges of the supreme Court, and all other Officers of the United States, whose Appointments are not herein otherwise provided for, and which shall be established by Law; but the Congress may by Law vest the Appointment of such inferior Officers, as they think proper, in the President alone, in the Courts of Law, or in the Heads of Departments.

The President shall have Power to fill up all Vacancies that may happen during the Recess of the Senate, by granting Commissions which shall expire at the End of their next Session.

Section. 3. He shall from time to time give to the Congress Information of the State of the Union, and recommend to their Consideration such Measures as he shall judge necessary and expedient; he may, on extraordinary Occasions, convene both Houses, or either of them, and in Case of Disagreement between them, with Respect to the Time of Adjournment, he may adjourn them to such Time as he shall think proper; he shall receive Ambassadors and other public Ministers; he shall take Care that the Laws be faithfully executed, and shall Commission all the Officers of the United States.

Section. 4. The President, Vice President and all civil Officers of the United States, shall be removed from Office on Impeachment for, and Conviction of, Treason, Bribery, or other high Crimes and Misdemeanors.

ARTICLE. III.

Section. 1. The judicial Power of the United States, shall be vested in one supreme Court, and in such inferior Courts as the Congress may from time to time ordain and establish. The Judges, both of the supreme and inferior Courts, shall hold their Offices during good Behavior, and shall, at stated Times, receive for their Services, a Compensation, which shall not be diminished during their Continuance in Office.

Section. 2. The judicial Power shall extend to all Cases, in Law and Equity, arising under this Constitution, the Laws of the United States, and Treaties made, or which shall be made, under their Authority;—to all Cases affecting Ambassadors, other public Ministers and Consuls;—to all Cases of admiralty and maritime Jurisdiction;—the Controversies to which the United States shall be a Party;—to Controversies between two or more States;—between a State and Citizens of another State;—between Citizens of different States;—between Citizens of the same State claiming Lands under Grants of different States, and between a State, or the Citizens thereof, and foreign States, Citizens or Subjects.

In all cases affecting Ambassadors, other public Ministers and Consuls, and those in which a State shall be Party, the supreme Court shall have original Jurisdiction. In all the other Cases before mentioned, the supreme Court shall have appellate Jurisdiction, both as to Law and Fact, with such Exceptions, and under such Regulations as the Congress shall make.

The Trial of all Crimes, except in Cases of Impeachment, shall be by Jury; and such Trial shall be held in the State where the said Crimes shall have been committed; but when not committed within any State, the Trial shall be at such Place or Places as the Congress may by Law have directed.

Section. 3. Treason against the United States, shall consist only in levying War against them, or in adhering to their Enemies, giving them Aid and Comfort. No Person shall be convicted of Treason unless on the Testimony of two Witnesses to the same overt Act, or on Confession in open Court.

The Congress shall have Power to declare the Punishment of Treason, but no Attainder of Treason shall work Corruption of Blood, or Forfeiture except during the Life of the Person attainted.

ARTICLE. IV.

Section. 1. Full Faith and Credit shall be given in each State to the public Acts, Records, and judicial Proceedings of every other State. And the Congress may by general Laws prescribe the Manner in which such Acts, Records and Proceedings shall be proved, and the Effect thereof.

Section. 2. The Citizens of each State shall be entitled to all Privileges and Immunities of Citizens in the several States.

A Person charged in any State with Treason, Felony, or other Crime, who shall flee from Justice, and be found in another State, shall on Demand of the executive Authority of the State from which he fled, be delivered up, to be removed to the State having Jurisdiction of the Crime.

No Person held to Service or Labour in one State, under the Laws thereof, escaping into another, shall, in Consequence of any Law or Regulation therein, be discharged from such Service or Labour, but shall be delivered up on Claim of the Party to whom such Service or Labour may be due.

Section. 3. New States may be admitted by the Congress into this Union; but no new State shall be formed or erected within the Jurisdiction of any other State; nor any State be formed by the Junction of two or more States, or Parts of States, without the consent of the Legislatures of the States concerned as well as of the Congress.

The Congress shall have Power to dispose of and make all needful Rules and Regulations respecting the Territory or other Property belonging to the United States; and nothing in this Constitution shall be so construed as to Prejudice any Claims of the United States, or of any particular States.

Section. 4. The United States shall guarantee to every State in this Union a Republican Form of Government, and shall protect each of them against Invasion; and on Application of the Legislature, or of the Executive (when the Legislature cannot be convened) against domestic Violence.

ARTICLE. V.

The Congress, whenever two thirds of both Houses shall deem it necessary, shall propose Amendments to this Constitution, or, on the Application of the Legislatures of two thirds of the several States, shall call a Convention for proposing Amendments, which, in either Case, shall be valid to all Intents and Purposes, as Part of this Constitution, when ratified by the Legislatures of three fourths of the several States, or by Conventions in three fourths thereof, as the one or the other Mode of Ratification may be proposed by the Congress; Provided that no Amendment which may be made prior to the Year One thousand eight hundred and eight shall in any Manner affect the first and fourth Clauses in the Ninth Section of the first Article; and that no State, without its Consent, shall be deprived of its equal Suffrage in the Senate.

ARTICLE. VI.

All Debts contracted and Engagements entered into, before the Adoption of this Constitution, shall be as valid against the United States under this Constitution, as under the Confederation.

This Constitution, and the Laws of the United States which shall be made in Pursuance thereof; and all Treaties made, or which shall be made, under the Authority of the United States, shall be the supreme Law of the Land; and the Judges in every State shall be bound thereby, any Thing in the Constitution or Laws of any State to the Contrary notwithstanding.

The Senators and Representatives before mentioned, and the Members of the several State Legislatures, and all executive and judicial Officers, both of the United States and of the several States, shall be bound by Oath or Affirmation, to support this Constitution; but no religious Test shall ever be required as a Qualification to any Office or public Trust under the United States.

ARTICLE. VII.

The Ratification of the Conventions of nine States, shall be sufficient for the Establishment of this Constitution between the States so ratifying the Same.

Done in Convention by the Unanimous Consent of the States present the Seventeenth Day of September in the Year of our Lord one thousand seven hundred and Eighty seven and of the Independence of the United States of America the Twelfth. In witness thereof We have hereunto subscribed our Names,

G°. WASHINGTON—Presd[t].
and deputy from Virginia.

NEW HAMPSHIRE
John Langdon
Nicholas Gilman

MASSACHUSETTS
Nathaniel Gorham
Rufus King

CONNECTICUT
W[m] Sam[l] Johnson
Roger Sherman

NEW YORK
Alexander Hamilton

NEW JERSEY
Wil: Livingston
David A. Brearley
W[m] Paterson
Jona: Dayton

PENNSYLVANIA
B Franklin
Thomas Mifflin
Rob[t] Morris
Geo. Clymer
Tho[s] FitzSimons
Jared Ingersoll
James Wilson
Gouv Morris

DELAWARE
Geo: Read
Gunning Bedford jun
John Dickinson
Richard Bassett
Jaco: Broom

MARYLAND
James M[c]Henry
Dan of S[t] Tho[s] Jenifer
Dan[l] Carroll

VIRGINIA
John Blair—
James Madison Jr.

NORTH CAROLINA
W[m] Blount
Rich[d] Dobbs Spaight
Hu Williamson

SOUTH CAROLINA
J. Rutledge
Charles Cotesworth
  Pinckney
Charles Pinckney
Pierce Butler

GEORGIA
William Few
Abr Baldwin

Amendments to the Constitution

Articles in addition to, and Amendment of the Constitution of the United States of America, proposed by Congress, and ratified by the Legislatures of the several States, pursuant to the fifth Article of the original Constitution.

AMENDMENT I.

Congress shall make no law respecting an establishment of religion, or prohibiting the free exercise thereof; or abridging the freedom of speech, or of the press; or the right of the people peaceably to assemble, and to petition the Government for a redress of grievances.

AMENDMENT II.

A well regulated Militia, being necessary to the security of a free State, the right of the people to keep and bear Arms, shall not be infringed.

AMENDMENT III.

No Soldier shall, in time of peace be quartered in any house, without the consent of the Owner, nor in time of war, but in a manner to be prescribed by law.

AMENDMENT IV.

The right of the people to be secure in their persons, houses, papers, and effects, against unreasonable searches and seizures, shall not be violated, and no Warrants shall issue, but upon probable cause, supported by Oath or affirmation, and particularly describing the place to be searched, and the persons or things to be seized.

AMENDMENT V.

No person shall be held to answer for a capital, or otherwise infamous crime, unless on a presentment or indictment of a Grand Jury, except in cases arising in the land or naval forces, or in the Militia, when in actual service in time of War or public danger; nor shall any person be subject for the same offence to be twice put in jeopardy of life or limb; nor shall be compelled in any criminal case to be a witness against himself, nor be deprived of life, liberty, or property, without due process of law; nor shall private property be taken for public use, without just compensation.

AMENDMENT VI.

In all criminal prosecutions, the accused shall enjoy the right to a speedy and public trial, by an impartial jury of the State and district wherein the crime shall have been committed, which district shall have been previously ascertained by law, and to be informed of the nature and cause of the accusation; to be confronted with the witnesses against him; to have compulsory process for obtaining witnesses in his favor, and to have the Assistance of Counsel for his defence.

AMENDMENT VII.

In Suits at common law, where the value in controversy shall exceed twenty dollars, the right of trial by jury shall be preserved, and no fact tried by a jury, shall be otherwise re-examined in any Court of the United States, than according to the rules of the common law.

AMENDMENT VIII.

Excessive bail shall not be required, nor excessive fines imposed, nor cruel and unusual punishments inflicted.

AMENDMENT IX.

The enumeration in the Constitution, of certain rights, shall not be construed to deny or disparage others retained by the people.

AMENDMENT X.

The powers not delegated to the United States by the Constitution, nor prohibited by it to the States, are reserved to the States respectively, or to the people. [The first ten amendments went into effect December 15, 1791.]

AMENDMENT XI.

The Judicial power of the United States shall not be construed to extend to any suit in law or equity, commenced or prosecuted against one of the United States by Citizens of another State, or by Citizens or Subjects of any Foreign State. [January 8, 1798]

AMENDMENT XII.

The Electors shall meet in their respective states, and vote by ballot for President and Vice-President, one of whom, at least, shall not be an inhabitant of the same state with themselves; they shall name in their ballots the person voted for as President, and in distinct ballots the person voted for as Vice-President, and they shall make distinct lists of all persons voted for as President, and of all persons voted for as Vice President, and of the number of votes for each, which lists they shall sign and certify, and transmit sealed to the seat of the government of the United States, directed to the President of the Senate;—The President of the Senate shall, in the presence of the Senate and House of Representatives, open all the certificates and the votes shall then be counted;—The person having the greatest number of votes for President, shall be the President, if such number be a majority of the whole number of Electors appointed; and if no person have such majority, then from the persons having the highest numbers not exceeding three on the list of those voted for as President, the House of Representatives shall choose immediately, by ballot, the President. But in choosing the President, the votes shall be taken by states, the representation from each state having one vote; a quorum for this purpose shall consist of a member or members from two-thirds of the states, and a majority of all the states shall be necessary to a choice. And if the House of Representatives shall not choose a President whenever the right of choice shall devolve upon them, before the fourth day of March next following, then the Vice-President shall act as President, as in the case of the death or other constitutional disability of the President.—The person having the greatest number of votes as Vice-President, shall be the Vice-President, if such number be a majority of the whole number of Electors appointed, and if no person have a majority, then from the two highest numbers on the list, the Senate shall choose the Vice-President; a quorum for the purpose shall consist of two-thirds of the whole number of Senators, and a majority of the whole number shall be necessary to a choice. But no person constitutionally ineligible to the office of President shall be eligible to that of Vice-President of the United States. [September 25, 1804]

AMENDMENT XIII.

Section 1. Neither slavery nor involuntary servitude, except as a punishment for crime whereof the party shall have been duly convicted, shall exist within the United States, or any place subject to their jurisdiction.

Section 2. Congress shall have power to enforce this article by appropriate legislation. [December 18, 1865]

AMENDMENT XIV.

Section 1. All persons born or naturalized in the United States, and subject to the jurisdiction thereof, are citizens of the United States and of the State wherein they reside. No State shall make or enforce any law which shall abridge the privileges or immunities of citizens of the United States; nor shall any State deprive any person of life, liberty, or property, without due process of law; nor deny to any person within its jurisdiction the equal protection of the laws.

Section 2. Representatives shall be apportioned among the several States according to their respective numbers, counting the whole number of persons in each State, excluding Indians not taxed. But when the right to vote at any election for the choice of electors for President and Vice President of the United States, Representatives in Congress, the Executive and Judicial officers of a State, or the members of the Legislature thereof, is denied to any of the male inhabitants of such State, being twenty-one years of age, and citizens of the United States, or in any way abridged, except for participation in rebellion, or other crime, the basis of representation therein shall be reduced in the proportion which the number of such male citizens shall bear to the whole number of male citizens twenty-one years of age in such State.

Section 3. No person shall be a Senator or Representative in Congress, or elector of President and Vice President, or hold any office, civil or military, under the United States, or under any State, who, having previously taken an oath, as a member of Congress, or as an officer of the United States, or as a member of any State legislature, or as an executive or judicial officer of any State, to support the Constitution of the United States, shall have engaged in insurrection or rebellion against the same, or given aid or comfort to the enemies thereof. But Congress may by a vote of two-thirds of each House, remove such disability.

Section 4. The validity of the public debt of the United States, authorized by law, including debts incurred for payment of pensions and bounties for services in suppressing insurrection or rebellion, shall not be questioned. But neither the United States nor any State shall assume or pay any debt or obligation incurred in aid of insurrection or rebellion against the United States, or any claim for the loss or emancipation of any slave; but all such debts, obligations and claims shall be held illegal and void.

Section 5. The Congress shall have power to enforce, by appropriate legislation, the provisions of this article. [July 28, 1868]

AMENDMENT XV.

Section 1. The right of citizens of the United States to vote shall not be denied or abridged by the United States or by any State on account of race, color, or previous condition of servitude—

Section 2. The Congress shall have power to enforce this article by appropriate legislation. [March 30, 1870]

AMENDMENT XVI.

The Congress shall have power to lay and collect taxes on incomes, from whatever source derived, without apportionment among the several States, and without regard to any census or enumeration. [February 25, 1913]

AMENDMENT XVII.

The Senate of the United States shall be composed of two senators from each State, elected by the people thereof, for six years; and each Senator shall have one vote. The electors in each State shall have the qualifications requisite for electors of the most numerous branch of the State legislatures.

When vacancies happen in the representation of any State in the Senate, the executive authority of such State shall issue writs of election to fill such vacancies: *Provided,* That the legislature of any State may empower the executive thereof to make temporary appointments until the people fill the vacancies by election as the legislature may direct.

This amendment shall not be so construed as to affect the election or term of any senator chosen before it becomes valid as part of the Constitution. [May 31, 1913]

AMENDMENT XVIII.

After one year from the ratification of this article, the manufacture, sale, or transportation of intoxicating liquors within, the importation thereof into, or the exportation thereof from the United States and all territory subject to the jurisdiction thereof for beverage purposes is hereby prohibited.

The Congress and the several States shall have concurrent power to enforce this article by appropriate legislation.

This article shall be inoperative unless it shall have been ratified as an amendment to the Constitution by the legislatures of the several States, as provided in the Constitution, within seven years from the date of the submission thereof to the States by Congress. [January 29, 1919]

AMENDMENT XIX.

The right of citizens of the United States to vote shall not be denied or abridged by the United States or by any State on account of sex.

The Congress shall have power by appropriate legislation to enforce the provisions of this article. [August 26, 1920]

AMENDMENT XX.

Section 1. The terms of the President and Vice-President shall end at noon on the twentieth day of January, and the terms of Senators and Representatives at noon on the third day of January, of the years in which such terms would have ended if this article had not been ratified; and the terms of their successors shall then begin.

Section 2. The Congress shall assemble at least once in every year, and such meeting shall begin at noon on the third day of January, unless they shall by law appoint a different day.

Section 3. If, at the time fixed for the beginning of the term of the President, the President-elect shall have died, the Vice-President-elect shall become President. If a President shall not have been chosen before the time fixed for the beginning of his term, or if the President-elect shall have failed to qualify, then the Vice-President-elect shall act as President until a President shall have qualified; and the Congress may by law provide for the case wherein neither a President-elect nor a Vice-President-elect shall have qualified, declaring who shall then act as President, or the manner in which one who is to act shall be selected, and such person shall act accordingly until a President or Vice-President shall have qualified.

Section 4. The Congress may by law provide for the case of the death of any of the persons from whom the House of Representatives may choose a President whenever the right of choice shall have devolved upon them, and for the case of the death of any of the persons from whom the Senate may choose a Vice-President whenever the right of choice shall have devolved upon them.

Section 5. Sections 1 and 2 shall take effect on the 15th day of October following the ratification of this article.

Section 6. This article shall be inoperative unless it shall have been ratified as an amendment to the Constitution by the legislatures of three-fourths of the several States within seven years from the date of its submission. [February 6, 1933]

AMENDMENT XXI.

Section 1. The eighteenth article of amendment to the Constitution of the United States is hereby repealed.

Section 2. The transportation or importation into any State, Territory or possession of the United States for delivery or use therein of intoxicating liquors, in violation of the laws thereof, is hereby prohibited.

Section 3. This article shall be inoperative unless it shall have been ratified as an amendment to the Constitution by convention in the several States, as provided in the Constitution, within seven years from the date of the submission thereof to the States by the Congress. [December 5, 1933]

AMENDMENT XXII.

Section 1. No person shall be elected to the office of the President more than twice, and no person who has held the office of President, or acted as President, for more than two years of a term to which some other person was elected President shall be elected to the office of the President more than once. But this Article shall not apply to any person holding the office of President when this Article was proposed by the Congress, and shall not prevent any person who may be holding the office of President, or acting as President, during the term within which this Article becomes operative from holding the office of President or acting as President during the remainder of such term.

Section 2. This article shall be inoperative unless it shall have been ratified as an amendment to the Constitution by the legislatures of three-fourths of the several states within seven years from the date of its submission to the States by the Congress. [February 27, 1951]

AMENDMENT XXIII.

Section 1. The District constituting the seat of government of the United States shall appoint in such manner as the Congress may direct:

A number of electors of President and Vice-President equal to the whole number of Senators and Representatives in Congress to which the District would be entitled if it were a State, but in no event more than the least populous State; they shall be in addition to those appointed by the States, but they shall be considered, for the purposes of the election of President and Vice-President, to be electors appointed by a State; and they shall meet in the District and perform such duties as provided by the twelfth article of amendment.

Section 2. The Congress shall have the power to enforce this article by appropriate legislation. [March 29, 1961]

AMENDMENT XXIV.

Section 1. The right of citizens of the United States to vote in any primary or other election for President or Vice President, for electors for President or Vice President, or for Senator or Representative in Congress, shall not be denied or abridged by the United States or any State by reason of failure to pay any poll tax or other tax.

Section 2. The Congress shall have power to enforce this article by appropriate legislation. [January 23, 1964]

AMENDMENT XXV.

Section 1. In case of the removal of the President from office or of his death or resignation, the Vice President shall become President.

Section 2. Whenever there is a vacancy in the office of Vice President, the President shall nominate a Vice President who shall take office upon confirmation by a majority vote of both Houses of Congress.

Section 3. Whenever the President transmits to the President pro tempore of the Senate and the Speaker of the House of Representatives his written declaration that he is unable to discharge the powers and duties of his office, and until he transmits to them a written declaration to the contrary, such powers and duties shall be discharged by the Vice President as Acting President.

Section 4. Whenever the Vice President and a majority of either the principal officers of the executive departments or of such other body as Congress may by law provide, transmit to the President pro tempore of the Senate and the Speaker of the House of Representatives their written declaration that the President is unable to discharge the powers and duties of his office, the Vice President shall immediately assume the powers and duties of the office as Acting President.

Thereafter, when the President transmits to the President pro tempore of the Senate and the Speaker of the House of Representatives his written declaration that no inability exists, he shall resume the powers and duties of his office unless the Vice President and a majority of either the principal officers of the executive departments or of such other body as Congress may by law provide, transmit within four days to the President pro tempore of the Senate and the Speaker of the House of Representatives their written declaration that the President is unable to discharge the powers and duties of his office. Thereupon Congress shall decide the issue, assembling within forty-eight hours for that purpose if not in session. If the Congress, within twenty-one days after receipt of the latter written declaration, or, if Congress is not in session, within twenty-one days after Congress is required to assemble, determines by two-thirds vote of both Houses that the President is unable to discharge the powers and duties of his office, the Vice President shall continue to discharge the same as Acting President; otherwise, the President shall resume the powers and duties of his office. [February 10, 1967]

AMENDMENT XXVI.

Section 1. The right of citizens of the United States, who are eighteen years of age or older, to vote shall not be denied or abridged by the United States or by any State on account of age.

Section 2. The Congress shall have power to enforce this article by appropriate legislation. [June 30, 1971]

AMENDMENT XXVII.

No law, varying the compensation for the services of the Senators and Representatives shall take effect, until an election of Representatives shall have intervened. [May 8, 1992]

PRESIDENTIAL ELECTIONS

Year	Number of States	Candidates	Parties	Popular Vote	% of Popular Vote	Electoral Vote	% Voter Participation
1789	11	**GEORGE WASHINGTON**	NO PARTY DESIGNATIONS			69	
		John Adams				34	
		Other candidates				35	
1792	15	**GEORGE WASHINGTON**	NO PARTY DESIGNATIONS			132	
		John Adams				77	
		George Clinton				50	
		Other candidates				5	
1796	16	**JOHN ADAMS**	FEDERALIST			71	
		Thomas Jefferson	Democratic-Republican			68	
		Thomas Pinckney	Federalist			59	
		Aaron Burr	Democratic-Republican			30	
		Other candidates				48	
1800	16	**THOMAS JEFFERSON**	DEMOCRATIC-REPUBLICAN			73	
		Aaron Burr	Democratic-Republican			73	
		John Adams	Federalist			65	
		Charles C. Pinckney	Federalist			64	
		John Jay	Federalist			1	
1804	17	**THOMAS JEFFERSON**	DEMOCRATIC-REPUBLICAN			162	
		Charles C. Pinckney	Federalist			14	
1808	17	**JAMES MADISON**	DEMOCRATIC-REPUBLICAN			122	
		Charles C. Pinckney	Federalist			47	
		George Clinton	Democratic-Republican			6	
1812	18	**JAMES MADISON**	DEMOCRATIC-REPUBLICAN			128	
		DeWitt Clinton	Federalist			89	
1816	19	**JAMES MONROE**	DEMOCRATIC-REPUBLICAN			183	
		Rufus King	Federalist			34	
1820	24	**JAMES MONROE**	DEMOCRATIC-REPUBLICAN			231	
		John Quincy Adams	Independent			1	
1824	24	**JOHN QUINCY ADAMS**	DEMOCRATIC-REPUBLICAN	108,740	30.5	84	26.9
		Andrew Jackson	Democratic-Republican	153,544	43.1	99	
		Henry Clay	Democratic-Republican	47,136	13.2	37	
		William H. Crawford	Democratic-Republican	46,618	13.1	41	
1828	24	**ANDREW JACKSON**	DEMOCRATIC	647,286	56.0	178	57.6
		John Quincy Adams	National Republican	508,064	44.0	83	
1832	24	**ANDREW JACKSON**	DEMOCRATIC	688,242	54.5	219	55.4
		Henry Clay	National Republican	473,462	37.5	49	
		William Wirt	Anti-Masonic	101,051	8.0	7	
		John Floyd	Democratic			11	

Year	Number of States	Candidates	Parties	Popular Vote	% of Popular Vote	Electoral Vote	% Voter Participation
1836	26	**MARTIN VAN BUREN**	DEMOCRATIC	765,483	50.9	170	57.8
		William H. Harrison	Whig			73	
		Hugh L. White	Whig	739,795	49.1	26	
		Daniel Webster	Whig			14	
		W. P. Mangum	Whig			11	
1840	26	**WILLIAM H. HARRISON**	WHIG	1,274,624	53.1	234	80.2
		Martin Van Buren	Democratic	1,127,781	46.9	60	
1844	26	**JAMES K. POLK**	DEMOCRATIC	1,338,464	49.6	170	78.9
		Henry Clay	Whig	1,300,097	48.1	105	
		James G. Birney	Liberty	62,300	2.3		
1848	30	**ZACHARY TAYLOR**	WHIG	1,360,967	47.4	163	72.7
		Lewis Cass	Democratic	1,222,342	42.5	127	
		Martin Van Buren	Free Soil	291,263	10.1		
1852	31	**FRANKLIN PIERCE**	DEMOCRATIC	1,601,117	50.9	254	69.6
		Winfield Scott	Whig	1,385,453	44.1	42	
		John P. Hale	Free Soil	155,825	5.0		
1856	31	**JAMES BUCHANAN**	DEMOCRATIC	1,832,955	45.3	174	78.9
		John C. Frémont	Republican	1,339,932	33.1	114	
		Millard Fillmore	American	871,731	21.6	8	
1860	33	**ABRAHAM LINCOLN**	REPUBLICAN	1,865,593	39.8	180	81.2
		Stephen A. Douglas	Democratic	1,382,713	29.5	12	
		John C. Breckinridge	Democratic	848,356	18.1	72	
		John Bell	Constitutional Union	592,906	12.6	39	
1864	36	**ABRAHAM LINCOLN**	REPUBLICAN	2,206,938	55.0	212	73.8
		George B. McClellan	Democratic	1,803,787	45.0	21	
1868	37	**ULYSSES S. GRANT**	REPUBLICAN	3,013,421	52.7	214	78.1
		Horatio Seymour	Democratic	2,706,829	47.3	80	
1872	37	**ULYSSES S. GRANT**	REPUBLICAN	3,596,745	55.6	286	71.3
		Horace Greeley	Democratic	2,843,446	43.9	66	
1876	38	**RUTHERFORD B. HAYES**	REPUBLICAN	4,036,572	48.0	185	81.8
		Samuel J. Tilden	Democratic	4,284,020	51.0	184	
1880	38	**JAMES A. GARFIELD**	REPUBLICAN	4,453,295	48.5	214	79.4
		Winfield S. Hancock	Democratic	4,414,082	48.1	155	
		James B. Weaver	Greenback-Labor	308,578	3.4		
1884	38	**GROVER CLEVELAND**	DEMOCRATIC	4,879,507	48.5	219	77.5
		James G. Blaine	Republican	4,850,293	48.2	182	
		Benjamin F. Butler	Greenback-Labor	175,370	1.8		
		John P. St. John	Prohibition	150,369	1.5		
1888	38	**BENJAMIN HARRISON**	REPUBLICAN	5,477,129	47.9	233	79.3
		Grover Cleveland	Democratic	5,537,857	48.6	168	
		Clinton B. Fisk	Prohibition	249,506	2.2		
		Anson J. Streeter	Union Labor	146,935	1.3		

Year	Number of States	Candidates	Parties	Popular Vote	% of Popular Vote	Electoral Vote	% Voter Participation
1892	44	**GROVER CLEVELAND**	DEMOCRATIC	5,555,426	46.1	277	74.7
		Benjamin Harrison	Republican	5,182,690	43.0	145	
		James B. Weaver	People's	1,029,846	8.5	22	
		John Bidwell	Prohibition	264,133	2.2		
1896	45	**WILLIAM McKINLEY**	REPUBLICAN	7,102,246	51.1	271	79.3
		William J. Bryan	Democratic	6,492,559	47.7	176	
1900	45	**WILLIAM McKINLEY**	REPUBLICAN	7,218,491	51.7	292	73.2
		William J. Bryan	Democratic; Populist	6,356,734	45.5	155	
		John C. Wooley	Prohibition	208,914	1.5		
1904	45	**THEODORE ROOSEVELT**	REPUBLICAN	7,628,461	57.4	336	65.2
		Alton B. Parker	Democratic	5,084,223	37.6	140	
		Eugene V. Debs	Socialist	402,283	3.0		
		Silas C. Swallow	Prohibition	258,536	1.9		
1908	46	**WILLIAM H. TAFT**	REPUBLICAN	7,675,320	51.6	321	65.4
		William J. Bryan	Democratic	6,412,294	43.1	162	
		Eugene V. Debs	Socialist	420,793	2.8		
		Eugene W. Chafin	Prohibition	253,840	1.7		
1912	48	**WOODROW WILSON**	DEMOCRATIC	6,296,547	41.9	435	58.8
		Theodore Roosevelt	Progressive	4,118,571	27.4	88	
		William H. Taft	Republican	3,486,720	23.2	8	
		Eugene V. Debs	Socialist	900,672	6.0		
		Eugene W. Chafin	Prohibition	206,275	1.4		
1916	48	**WOODROW WILSON**	DEMOCRATIC	9,127,695	49.4	277	61.6
		Charles E. Hughes	Republican	8,533,507	46.2	254	
		A. L. Benson	Socialist	585,113	3.2		
		J. Frank Hanly	Prohibition	220,506	1.2		
1920	48	**WARREN G. HARDING**	REPUBLICAN	16,143,407	60.4	404	49.2
		James M. Cox	Democratic	9,130,328	34.2	127	
		Eugene V. Debs	Socialist	919,799	3.4		
		P. P. Christensen	Farmer-Labor	265,411	1.0		
1924	48	**CALVIN COOLIDGE**	REPUBLICAN	15,718,211	54.0	382	48.9
		John W. Davis	Democratic	8,385,283	28.8	136	
		Robert M. La Follette	Progressive	4,831,289	16.6	13	
1928	48	**HERBERT C. HOOVER**	REPUBLICAN	21,391,993	58.2	444	56.9
		Alfred E. Smith	Democratic	15,016,169	40.9	87	
1932	48	**FRANKLIN D. ROOSEVELT**	DEMOCRATIC	22,809,638	57.4	472	56.9
		Herbert C. Hoover	Republican	15,758,901	39.7	59	
		Norman Thomas	Socialist	881,951	2.2		
1936	48	**FRANKLIN D. ROOSEVELT**	DEMOCRATIC	27,752,869	60.8	523	61.0
		Alfred M. Landon	Republican	16,674,665	36.5	8	
		William Lemke	Union	882,479	1.9		
1940	48	**FRANKLIN D. ROOSEVELT**	DEMOCRATIC	27,307,819	54.8	449	62.5
		Wendell L. Willkie	Republican	22,321,018	44.8	82	

Year	Number of States	Candidates	Parties	Popular Vote	% of Popular Vote	Electoral Vote	% Voter Participation
1944	48	FRANKLIN D. ROOSEVELT	DEMOCRATIC	25,606,585	53.5	432	55.9
		Thomas E. Dewey	Republican	22,014,745	46.0	99	
1948	48	HARRY S. TRUMAN	DEMOCRATIC	24,179,345	49.6	303	53.0
		Thomas E. Dewey	Republican	21,991,291	45.1	189	
		J. Strom Thurmond	States' Rights	1,176,125	2.4	39	
		Henry A. Wallace	Progressive	1,157,326	2.4		
1952	48	DWIGHT D. EISENHOWER	REPUBLICAN	33,936,234	55.1	442	63.3
		Adlai E. Stevenson	Democratic	27,314,992	44.4	89	
1956	48	DWIGHT D. EISENHOWER	REPUBLICAN	35,590,472	57.6	457	60.6
		Adlai E. Stevenson	Democratic	26,022,752	42.1	73	
1960	50	JOHN F. KENNEDY	DEMOCRATIC	34,226,731	49.7	303	62.8
		Richard M. Nixon	Republican	34,108,157	49.5	219	
1964	50	LYNDON B. JOHNSON	DEMOCRATIC	43,129,566	61.1	486	61.9
		Barry M. Goldwater	Republican	27,178,188	38.5	52	
1968	50	RICHARD M. NIXON	REPUBLICAN	31,785,480	43.4	301	60.9
		Hubert H. Humphrey	Democratic	31,275,166	42.7	191	
		George C. Wallace	American Independent	9,906,473	13.5	46	
1972	50	RICHARD M. NIXON	REPUBLICAN	47,169,911	60.7	520	55.2
		George S. McGovern	Democratic	29,170,383	37.5	17	
		John G. Schmitz	American	1,099,482	1.4		
1976	50	JIMMY CARTER	DEMOCRATIC	40,830,763	50.1	297	53.5
		Gerald R. Ford	Republican	39,147,793	48.0	240	
1980	50	RONALD REAGAN	REPUBLICAN	43,901,812	50.7	489	52.6
		Jimmy Carter	Democratic	35,483,820	41.0	49	
		John B. Anderson	Independent	5,719,437	6.6		
		Ed Clark	Libertarian	921,188	1.1		
1984	50	RONALD REAGAN	REPUBLICAN	54,451,521	58.8	525	53.1
		Walter F. Mondale	Democratic	37,565,334	40.6	13	
1988	50	GEORGE H. BUSH	REPUBLICAN	47,917,341	53.4	426	50.1
		Michael Dukakis	Democratic	41,013,030	45.6	111	
1992	50	BILL CLINTON	DEMOCRATIC	44,908,254	43.0	370	55.0
		George H. Bush	Republican	39,102,343	37.4	168	
		H. Ross Perot	Independent	19,741,065	18.9	0	
1996	50	BILL CLINTON	DEMOCRATIC	47,401,185	49.0	379	49.0
		Bob Dole	Republican	39,197,469	41.0	159	
		H. Ross Perot	Independent	8,085,295	8.0	0	
2000	50	GEORGE W. BUSH	REPUBLICAN	50,455,156	47.9	271	50.4
		Albert Gore	Democratic	50,997,335	48.4	266	
		Ralph Nader	Green Party	2,882,897	2.7	0	

Candidates receiving less than 1 percent of the popular vote have been omitted. Thus, the percentage of popular vote given for any election year may not total 100 percent. Before the passage of the Twelfth Amendment in 1804, the electoral college voted for two presidential candidates; the runner-up became vice-president.

A-19

ADMISSION OF STATES

Order of Admission	State	Date of Admission	Order of Admission	State	Date of Admission
1	Delaware	December 7, 1787	26	Michigan	January 26, 1837
2	Pennsylvania	December 12, 1787	27	Florida	March 3, 1845
3	New Jersey	December 18, 1787	28	Texas	December 29, 1845
4	Georgia	January 2, 1788	29	Iowa	December 28, 1846
5	Connecticut	January 9, 1788	30	Wisconsin	May 29, 1848
6	Massachusetts	February 7, 1788	31	California	September 9, 1850
7	Maryland	April 28, 1788	32	Minnesota	May 11, 1858
8	South Carolina	May 23, 1788	33	Oregon	February 14, 1859
9	New Hampshire	June 21, 1788	34	Kansas	January 29, 1861
10	Virginia	June 25, 1788	35	West Virginia	June 30, 1863
11	New York	July 26, 1788	36	Nevada	October 31, 1864
12	North Carolina	November 21, 1789	37	Nebraska	March 1, 1867
13	Rhode Island	May 29, 1790	38	Colorado	August 1, 1876
14	Vermont	March 4, 1791	39	North Dakota	November 2, 1889
15	Kentucky	June 1, 1792	40	South Dakota	November 2, 1889
16	Tennessee	June 1, 1796	41	Montana	November 8, 1889
17	Ohio	March 1, 1803	42	Washington	November 11, 1889
18	Louisiana	April 30, 1812	43	Idaho	July 3, 1890
19	Indiana	December 11, 1816	44	Wyoming	July 10, 1890
20	Mississippi	December 10, 1817	45	Utah	January 4, 1896
21	Illinois	December 3, 1818	46	Oklahoma	November 16, 1907
22	Alabama	December 14, 1819	47	New Mexico	January 6, 1912
23	Maine	March 15, 1820	48	Arizona	February 14, 1912
24	Missouri	August 10, 1821	49	Alaska	January 3, 1959
25	Arkansas	June 15, 1836	50	Hawaii	August 21, 1959

POPULATION OF THE UNITED STATES

Year	Number of States	Population	% Increase	Population per Square Mile
1790	13	3,929,214		4.5
1800	16	5,308,483	35.1	6.1
1810	17	7,239,881	36.4	4.3
1820	23	9,638,453	33.1	5.5
1830	24	12,866,020	33.5	7.4
1840	26	17,069,453	32.7	9.8
1850	31	23,191,876	35.9	7.9
1860	33	31,443,321	35.6	10.6
1870	37	39,818,449	26.6	13.4
1880	38	50,155,783	26.0	16.9
1890	44	62,947,714	25.5	21.1
1900	45	75,994,575	20.7	25.6
1910	46	91,972,266	21.0	31.0
1920	48	105,710,620	14.9	35.6
1930	48	122,775,046	16.1	41.2
1940	48	131,669,275	7.2	44.2
1950	48	150,697,361	14.5	50.7
1960	50	179,323,175	19.0	50.6
1970	50	203,235,298	13.3	57.5
1980	50	226,504,825	11.4	64.0
1985	50	237,839,000	5.0	67.2
1990	50	250,122,000	5.2	70.6
1995	50	263,411,707	5.3	74.4
2000	50	281,421,906	6.8	77.0

IMMIGRATION TO THE UNITED STATES (1820–1998)

Year	Number	Year	Number	Year	Number	Year	Number
1820–1998	**64,599,082**						
1820	8,385						
1821–30	**143,439**	**1871–80**	**2,812,191**	**1921–30**	**4,107,209**	**1971–80**	**4,493,314**
1821	9,127	1871	321,350	1921	805,228	1971	370,478
1822	6,911	1872	404,806	1922	309,556	1972	384,685
1823	6,354	1873	459,803	1923	522,919	1973	400,063
1824	7,912	1874	313,339	1924	706,896	1974	394,861
1825	10,199	1875	227,498	1925	294,314	1975	386,194
1826	10,837	1876	169,986	1926	304,488	1976	398,613
1827	18,875	1877	141,857	1927	335,175	1976, TQ[1]	103,676
1828	27,382	1878	138,469	1928	307,255	1977	462,315
1829	22,520	1879	177,826	1929	279,678	1978	601,442
1830	23,322	1880	457,257	1930	241,700	1979	460,348
						1980	530,639
1831–40	**599,125**	**1881–90**	**5,246,613**	**1931–40**	**528,431**		
1831	22,633	1881	669,431	1931	97,139	**1981–90**	**7,338,062**
1832	60,482	1822	788,992	1932	35,576	1981	596,600
1833	58,640	1883	603,322	1933	23,068	1982	594,131
1834	65,365	1884	518,592	1934	29,470	1983	559,763
1835	45,374	1885	395,346	1935	34,956	1984	543,903
1836	76,242	1886	334,203	1936	36,329	1985	570,009
1837	79,340	1887	490,109	1937	50,244	1986	601,708
1838	38,914	1888	546,889	1938	67,895	1987	601,516
1839	68,069	1889	444,427	1939	82,998	1988	643,025
1840	84,066	1890	455,302	1940	70,756	1989	1,090,924
						1990	1,536,483
1841–50	**1,713,251**	**1891–1900**	**3,687,564**	**1941–50**	**1,035,039**		
1841	80,289	1891	560,319	1941	51,776	**1991–98**	**7,605,068**
1842	104,565	1892	579,663	1942	28,781	1991	1,827,167
1843	52,496	1893	439,730	1943	23,725	1992	973,977
1844	78,615	1894	285,631	1944	28,551	1993	904,292
1845	114,371	1895	258,536	1945	38,119	1994	804,416
1846	154,416	1896	343,267	1946	108,721	1995	720,461
1847	234,968	1897	230,832	1947	147,292	1996	915,900
1848	226,527	1898	229,299	1948	170,570	1997	798,378
1849	297,024	1899	311,715	1949	188,317	1998	660,477
1850	369,980	1900	448,572	1950	249,187		
1851–60	**2,598,214**	**1901–10**	**8,795,386**	**1951–60**	**2,515,479**		
1851	379,466	1901	487,918	1951	205,717		
1852	371,603	1902	648,743	1952	265,520		
1853	368,645	1903	857,046	1953	170,434		
1854	427,833	1904	812,870	1954	208,177		
1855	200,877	1905	1,026,499	1955	237,790		
1856	200,436	1906	1,100,735	1956	321,625		
1857	251,306	1907	1,285,349	1957	326,867		
1858	123,126	1908	782,870	1958	253,265		
1859	121,282	1909	751,786	1959	260,686		
1860	153,640	1910	1,041,570	1960	265,398		
1861–70	**2,314,824**	**1911–20**	**5,735,811**	**1961–70**	**3,321,677**		
1861	91,918	1911	878,587	1961	271,344		
1862	91,985	1912	838,172	1962	283,763		
1863	176,282	1913	1,197,892	1963	306,260		
1864	193,418	1914	1,218,480	1964	292,248		
1865	248,120	1915	326,700	1965	296,697		
1866	318,568	1916	298,826	1966	323,040		
1867	315,722	1917	295,403	1967	361,972		
1868	138,840	1918	110,618	1968	454,448		
1869	352,768	1919	141,132	1969	358,579		
1870	387,203	1920	430,001	1970	373,326		

[1] Transition quarter, July 1 through September 30, 1976.

NOTE: The numbers shown are as follows: from 1820 to 1867, figures represent alien passengers arrived at seaports; from 1868 to 1892 and 1895 to 1897, immigrant aliens arrived; from 1892 to 1894 and 1898 to 1998, immigrant aliens admitted for permanent residence. From 1892 to 1903, aliens entering by cabin class were not counted as immigrants. Land arrivals were not completely enumerated until 1908.

PRESIDENTS, VICE-PRESIDENTS, AND SECRETARIES OF STATE

President	Vice-President	Secretary of State
1. George Washington, Federalist 1789	John Adams, Federalist 1789	Thomas Jefferson 1789 Edmund Randolph 1794 Timothy Pickering 1795
2. John Adams, Federalist 1797	Thomas Jefferson, Democratic-Republican 1797	Timothy Pickering 1797 John Marshall 1800
3. Thomas Jefferson, Democratic-Republican 1801	Aaron Burr, Democratic-Republican 1801 George Clinton, Democratic-Republican 1805	James Madison 1801
4. James Madison, Democratic-Republican 1809	George Clinton, Democratic-Republican 1809 Elbridge Gerry, Democratic-Republican 1813	Robert Smith 1809 James Monroe 1811
5. James Monroe, Democratic-Republican 1817	Daniel D. Tompkins, Democratic-Republican 1817	John Q. Adams 1817
6. John Quincy Adams, Democratic-Republican 1825	John C. Calhoun, Democratic-Republican 1825	Henry Clay 1825
7. Andrew Jackson, Democratic 1829	John C. Calhoun, Democratic 1829 Martin Van Buren, Democratic 1833	Martin Van Buren 1829 Edward Livingston 1831 Louis McLane 1833 John Forsyth 1834
8. Martin Van Buren, Democratic 1837	Richard M. Johnson, Democratic 1837	John Forsyth 1837
9. William H. Harrison, Whig 1841	John Tyler, Whig 1841	Daniel Webster 1841
10. John Tyler, Whig and Democratic 1841	None	Daniel Webster 1841 Hugh S. Legaré 1843 Abel P. Upshur 1843 John C. Calhoun 1844
11. James K. Polk, Democratic 1845	George M. Dallas, Democratic 1845	James Buchanan 1845
12. Zachary Taylor, Whig 1849	Millard Fillmore, Whig 1849	John M. Clayton 1849
13. Millard Fillmore, Whig 1850	None	Daniel Webster 1850 Edward Everett 1852
14. Franklin Pierce, Democratic 1853	William R. King, Democratic 1853	William L. Marcy 1853
15. James Buchanan, Democratic 1857	John C. Breckinridge, Democratic 1857	Lewis Cass 1857 Jeremiah S. Black 1860
16. Abraham Lincoln, Republican 1861	Hannibal Hamlin, Republican 1861 Andrew Johnson, Unionist 1865	William H. Seward 1861
17. Andrew Johnson, Unionist 1865	None	William H. Seward 1865

President	Vice-President	Secretary of State
18. Ulysses S. Grant, Republican 1869	Schuyler Colfax, Republican 1869 Henry Wilson, Republican 1873	Elihu B. Washburne 1869 Hamilton Fish 1869
19. Rutherford B. Hayes, Republican 1877	William A. Wheeler, Republican 1877	William M. Evarts 1877
20. James A. Garfield, Republican 1881	Chester A. Arthur, Republican 1881	James G. Blaine 1881
21. Chester A. Arthur, Republican 1881	None	Frederick T. Frelinghuysen 1881
22. Grover Cleveland, Democratic 1885	Thomas A. Hendricks, Democratic 1885	Thomas F. Bayard 1885
23. Benjamin Harrison, Republican 1889	Levi P. Morton, Republican 1889	James G. Blaine 1889 John W. Foster 1892
24. Grover Cleveland, Democratic 1893	Adlai E. Stevenson, Democratic 1893	Walter Q. Gresham 1893 Richard Olney 1895
25. William McKinley, Republican 1897	Garret A. Hobart, Republican 1897 Theodore Roosevelt, Republican 1901	John Sherman 1897 William R. Day 1898 John Hay, 1898
26. Theodore Roosevelt, Republican 1901	Charles Fairbanks, Republican 1905	John Hay 1901 Elihu Root 1905 Robert Bacon 1909
27. William H. Taft, Republican 1909	James S. Sherman, Republican 1909	Philander C. Knox 1909
28. Woodrow Wilson, Democratic 1913	Thomas R. Marshall, Democratic 1913	William J. Bryan 1913 Robert Lansing 1915 Bainbridge Colby 1920
29. Warren G. Harding, Republican 1921	Calvin Coolidge, Republican 1921	Charles E. Hughes 1921
30. Calvin Coolidge, Republican 1923	Charles G. Dawes, Republican 1925	Charles E. Hughes 1923 Frank B. Kellogg 1925
31. Herbert Hoover, Republican 1929	Charles Curtis, Republican 1929	Henry L. Stimson 1929
32. Franklin D. Roosevelt, Democratic 1933	John Nance Garner, Democratic 1933 Henry A. Wallace, Democratic 1941 Harry S. Truman, Democratic 1945	Cordell Hull 1933 Edward R. Stettinius Jr. 1944
33. Harry S. Truman, Democratic 1945	Alben W. Barkley, Democratic 1949	Edward R. Stettinius Jr. 1945 James F. Byrnes 1945 George C. Marshall 1947 Dean G. Acheson 1949
34. Dwight D. Eisenhower, Republican 1953	Richard M. Nixon, Republican 1953	John F. Dulles 1953 Christian A. Herter 1959

President	Vice-President	Secretary of State
35. John F. Kennedy, Democratic 1961	Lyndon B. Johnson, Democratic 1961	Dean Rusk 1961
36. Lyndon B. Johnson, Democratic 1963	Hubert H. Humphrey, Democratic 1965	Dean Rusk 1963
37. Richard M. Nixon, Republican 1969	Spiro T. Agnew, Republican 1969 Gerald R. Ford, Republican 1973	William P. Rogers 1969 Henry Kissinger 1973
38. Gerald R. Ford, Republican 1974	Nelson Rockefeller, Republican 1974	Henry Kissinger 1974
39. Jimmy Carter, Democratic 1977	Walter Mondale, Democratic 1977	Cyrus Vance 1977 Edmund Muskie 1980
40. Ronald Reagan, Republican 1981	George Bush, Republican 1981	Alexander Haig 1981 George Shultz 1982
41. George Bush, Republican 1989	J. Danforth Quayle, Republican 1989	James A. Baker 1989 Lawrence Eagleburger 1992
42. William J. Clinton, Democratic 1993	Albert Gore Jr., Democratic 1993	Warren Christopher 1993 Madeleine Albright 1997
43. George W. Bush, Republican 2001	Richard B. Cheney, Republican 2001	Colin L. Powell 2001

tional Portrait Gallery, London; **147:** Jonathan Edwards College, Yale University; **148:** (*left*) Courtesy of the National Portrait Gallery, London; (*right*) The Historical Society of Pennsylvania; **149:** New Brunswick Museum, Saint John, N.B.; **150:** Washington and Lee University, Lexington, Va.; **152:** National Gallery of Canada, Ottawa; **153:** Library of Congress; **156:** The Granger Collection, New York; **160:** Leeds Museums and Galleries (City Art Gallery) U.K./Bridgeman Art Library; **161:** The Granger Collection, New York; **162:** The New York Public Library: Astor, Lenox, and Tilden Foundations; **163:** The Granger Collection, New York; **164:** Library of Congress; **165:** Courtesy, Museum of Fine Arts, Boston. Deposited by the City of Boston; **166:** The Library Company of Philadelphia; **167:** Bettmann/Corbis; **168:** Library of Congress; **169:** The Warder Collection; **170:** The British Museum; **171:** The Granger Collection, New York; **172:** Courtesy, Museum of Fine Arts, Boston. Gift of Joseph W., William B., and Edward H. R. Revere; **173:** (*left*) Bridgeman Art Library; (*right*) The Putnam Foundation, Timken Museum of Art, San Diego; **174:** *Attack on Bunker's Hill, with the Burning of Charles Town,* National Gallery of Art, Washington, D.C. Gift of Edgar Williams and Bernice Chrysler Garbisch. Photograph © 2001 Board of Trustees; **176:** Courtesy of the National Portrait Gallery, London; **178:** The British Museum; **179:** Yale University Art Gallery, Trumbull Collection; **183:** Chicago Historical Society; **184:** Anne S. K. Brown Military Collection, Brown University Library; **185:** The Frick Collection, New York; **187:** The Maryland Historical Society, Baltimore, Md.; **189:** The Henry Francis Dupont Winterthur Museum; **194:** Courtesy of the Massachusetts Historical Society; **198:** (*left*) Chicago Historical Society; (*right*) Corbis; **200:** (*left*) Courtesy of the Massachusetts Historical Society; (*right*) Independence National Historical Park; **202:** Library of Congress; **204:** Bettmann/Corbis; **205:** Virginia Museum of Fine Arts, Richmond. Gift of David K. E. Bruce; **206:** Virginia Historical Society; **209:** *The Cheney Family,* National Gallery of Art, Washington, D.C. Gift of Edgar William and Bernice Chrysler Garbisch. Photograph © 2001 Board of Trustees; **210:** The Library Company of Philadelphia; **211:** Virginia Museum of Fine Arts, Richmond. Gift of Miss Dorothy Payne; **213:** The Granger Collection, New York; **214:** Courtesy of the Chapin Library of Rare Books, Williams College; **215:** (*foreground*) The Metropolitan Museum of Art, Bequest of William Nelson, 1905; (*background*) Courtesy of the Chapin Library of Rare Books, Williams College; **216:** Courtesy of the Massachusetts Historical Society; **217:** (*left*) Yale University Art Gallery, Trumbull Collection; (*right*) Colonial Williamsburg Foundation; **218:** Courtesy Peabody Essex Museum; **219:** The Granger Collection, New York; **220:** (*left*) Courtesy of the Rhode Island Historical Society; (*right*) Copyright National Portrait Gallery, Smithsonian Institution/Art Resource, N.Y.; **221:** The New York Public Library: Astor, Lenox, and Tilden Foundations; **222:** Collection of the New-York Historical Society; **226:** Collection of the New-York Historical Society; **229:** Chicago Historical Society; **230:** The Granger Collection, New York; **233:** (*left*) Copyright National Portrait Gallery, Smithsonian Institution/Art Resource, N.Y.; (*right*) Courtesy of Credit Suisse First Boston; **234:** Library of Congress; **235:** Copyright National Portrait Gallery, Smithsonian Institution/Art Resource, N.Y.; **237:** The New York Public Library: Astor, Lenox, and Tilden Foundations, I. N. Phelps Stokes Collection; **238:** The Library of Virginia; **240:** The Gilder Lehrman Collection on Deposit at the Pierpont Morgan Library, New York. GLC 819.01; **243:** Bettmann/Corbis; **244:** Library of Congress; **245:** Collection of the New-York Historical Society; **246:** (*left*) Copyright National Portrait Gallery, Smithsonian Institution/Art Resource, N.Y.; (*right*) The Granger Collection, New York; **248:** Museum of the City of New York, Bequest of Mrs. J. Insley Blair in memory of Mr. and Mrs. J. Insley Blair, 52.100.1; **250:** The New York Public Library: Astor, Lenox, and Tilden Foundations, I. N. Phelps Stokes Collection; **251:** Collection of the New-York Historical Society; **253:** Chicago Historical Society; **254:** The Granger Collection, New York; **256:** Library of Congress; **258:** The Granger Collection, New York; **259:** Library of Congress; **260:** Corbis; **262:** Courtesy, Museum of Fine Arts, Boston. Gift of Maxim Karolik; **264:** Courtesy Peabody Essex Museum; **265:** Courtesy Peabody Essex Museum; **267:** The Granger Collection, New York; **269:** The Metropolitan Museum of Art. Gift of Edgar and Bernice Chrysler Garbisch, 1963 (63.201.2). Photograph © 1983 the Metropolitan Museum of Art; **270:** Collection of the New-York Historical Society; **271:** Albany Institute of History & Art, Bequest of George Clinton Genet, son of the subject; **272:** Courtesy of the Burton Historical Collection, Detroit Public Library; **274:** Copyright National Portrait Gallery, Smithsonian Institution/Art Resource, N.Y.; **275:** (*left*) The Granger Collection, New York; (*right*) Yale University Art Gallery, Mabel Brady Garvan Collection; **276:** The Mariner's Museum/Corbis; **277:** Bettmann/Corbis; **280:** The Granger Collection, New York; **282:** Chicago Historical Society; **285:** (*left*) The New York Public Library: Astor, Lenox, and Tilden Foundations, I. N. Phelps Stokes Collection; (*right*) White House Collection, Courtesy White House Historical Association; **286:** Courtesy of the Society for the Preservation of New England Antiquities; **287:** Copyright National Portrait Gallery, Smithsonian Institution/Art Resource, N.Y.; **288:** Copyright National Portrait Gallery, Smithsonian Institution/Art Resource, N.Y.; **291:** Collection of the New-York Historical Society; **292:** Yale Collection of Western Americana, Beinecke Rare Book and Manuscript Library; **296:** Library of